Publisher's Letter

Graham & Casey Jones

Promoting a Better Boating Experience

Congratulations! You've made a great decision in trusting the Waterway Guide team to help organize and lead your next adventure on the water. Our goal is to keep you informed on all there is to see because we know everyone on a boat appreciates an informed and confident captain. We're here to help.

In this edition of *Waterway Guide*, you'll find the latest on marinas and anchorages, great navigation advice, and the best towns and cities to visit by water. There's also a "Skipper's Handbook" in the front with details regarding on-the-water safety and etiquette, from properly using a VHF radio to procedures for transiting bridges and locks, proper anchoring, "reading" the weather and much more.

Whether you just bought your first boat or have been out on the water for decades, you may have noticed there are a lot of positive changes in boating today. Driving these exciting trends are marinas and the other companies that service the boating lifestyle. They are investing heavily, consolidating where it makes the most sense and looking to improve areas that really need it. This includes the U.S. government, which is providing infrastructure grants to keep boaters safe and facilities in good shape. We work with many of these companies and the trend to improve infrastructure is a common goal. Whether it's a management company, laser-focused on the customer experience or a private equity firm looking to finally move ahead with new docks or a big renovation at a marina, there is one thing for sure…it will result in a better experience for you. Your satisfaction is paramount. Many marinas offer exceptional loyalty programs to keep you as a happy customer, and it is a great benefit to both the facility and the boater.

One way we are focused on making the boating lifestyle easier is through investments in technology. At Waterway Guide our media platforms are always evolving, and most recently we introduced several new ways to access our guidebooks and content. For example, we launched the Waterway Guide mobile app (available on iOS and Android) that includes all our guidebooks and map-planning data (i.e., points of interest) in one tool. This technology allows us to expand our partnerships with leading content providers to include their regional titles so you can access a wider range of regional boating advice and navigational knowledge in one place.

The point is, it's a great time to be a boat owner or captain. Today's technologies, along with the exciting trends we're seeing, are making the boating lifestyle easier and more satisfying. At Waterway Guide Media, we will continue to work every day to improve safe boating, travel and adventure on the waterways.

Thank you for bringing Waterway Guide along on your adventure. Just don't forget to look up and enjoy the ride!

See you on the water!

Graham Jones, President

WATERWAY GUIDE MEDIA, LLC

P.O. Box 419, Midlothian, VA 23113

Phone: 800-233-3359
Fax: 888-951-7890
www.waterwayguide.com

BOOK SALES
waterwayguide.com/shipstore
Phone: 800-233-3359
Support@waterwayguide.com

Waterway Guide is published in the following editions—Bahamas, Southern, Florida Keys, Gulf Coast, Mid-Atlantic, Chesapeake Bay, Northern, Great Lakes Vol. 1, Great Lakes Vol. 2 and Cuba—by Waterway Guide Media, LLC © 2023. All rights reserved. Reproduction in whole or part or use of any data compilation without written permission from the publisher is prohibited. The title Waterway Guide is a registered trademark. ISBN Number: 979-8-9866525-5-9 for the Southern 2024 Edition. Purchase and use of Waterway Guide constitutes acceptance of the restrictions set forth herein.

Waterway Guide Media, LLC, the publisher of Waterway Guide (Guide), makes reasonable efforts to ensure the accuracy of the information in this Guide. However, Waterway Guide must rely on others over which it has no control for certain information. In addition, no book or guide is a substitute for good judgment, experience and firsthand knowledge. Therefore, Waterway Guide hereby gives notice that the charts, descriptions, and illustrations in this Guide are not to be used for navigation. The use of any navigational reference or description contained in the Guide is at the user's own risk. Inclusion in the Waterway Guide of marine facilities, services, restaurants and other information is for informational purposes only; no guarantee is provided as to the accuracy or current status of this information, nor does Waterway Guide Media, LLC endorse any of the facilities or services described herein.

Because Waterway Guide Media, LLC cannot and does not guarantee or warrant that the information in the Guide is complete or current, Waterway Guide Media, LLC disclaims all warranties, express or implied, relating to the information in any manner, including, without limitation, implied warranties of merchantability and fitness for a particular purpose.

Waterway Guide Media, LLC shall not be liable to the purchaser or any third party for any loss or injury allegedly caused, in whole or in part, by Waterway Guide Media, LLC and/or Waterway Guide (or the information contained therein) or for consequential, exemplary, incidental or special damages. Furthermore, in any event, Waterway Guide Media, LLC's liability, if any, shall never exceed the amount paid by the original purchaser for the directory.

To provide the most complete and accurate information, all facilities have been contacted within the past year. Although facility operators supplied this data, we cannot guarantee accuracy or assume responsibility for errors. Entrance and dockside soundings tend to fluctuate. Always approach marinas carefully. Reference numbers on spotting charts indicate marina locations. Aerial photos are for general overview only and are not to be used for navigation.

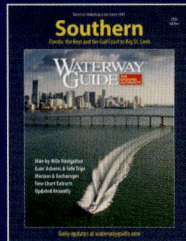

On the cover:
Biscayne Bay and Miami Skyline.
©Onne van der Wal

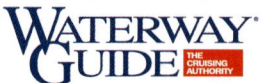

FOUNDED IN 1947

Publisher	**JEFF JONES** jjones@waterwayguide.com
President	**GRAHAM JONES** graham@waterwayguide.com
Editor-in-Chief	**ED TILLETT** etillett@waterwayguide.com
Operations Manager	**HEATHER SADEG** heather@waterwayguide.com
Managing Editor	**JANI PARKER** jparker@waterwayguide.com
Art Director/ Production Manager	**SCOTT MCCONNELL** scott@waterwayguide.com
Customer Success Manager	**ETHAN JETT** ethan@waterwayguide.com
Marketing/News Editor	**WHITNEY LAW** whitney@waterwayguide.com
Customer Support Specialists	**LINDA JERNIGAN** linda@waterwayguide.com
	ANNE EMERSON anne@waterwayguide.com
Data Support Specialist	**RILEY VAUGHN** riley@waterwayguide.com
Senior Advisor/ Skipper Bob Editor	**TED STEHLE** tstehle@waterwayguide.com
Software Engineer	**MIKE SCHWEFLER**
National Sales	**GRAHAM JONES** graham@waterwayguide.com
Sales & Marketing Manager	**KELLY CROCKETT** kelly@waterwayguide.com
Regional Account Executives	**RAY CLARK** ray@waterwayguide.com
	MARLÈNE CROCKETT marlene@waterwayguide.com
	BOB BOWER bobby@waterwayguide.com

REGIONAL CRUISING EDITORS

SCOTT RICHARD BERG
MATT & LUCY CLAIBORNE
GINA L. CICOTELLO
CAPT. GEORGE & PAT HOSPODAR
MICHAEL O'REILLY & ANN PHILLIPS
MALCOLM RUBEL & DEBORAH BOSWELL
BOB SHERER (CONTRIBUTING EDITOR)
ONNE VAN DER WAL (CONTRIBUTING EDITOR)

CUBA CRUISING EDITORS

ADDISON CHAN
NIGEL CALDER (CONTRIBUTING EDITOR)

@Waterway Guide

@waterway_guide

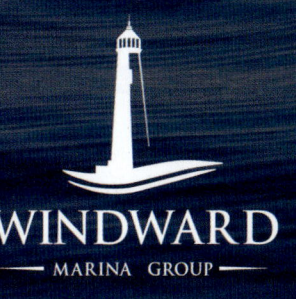

WINDWARD
MARINA GROUP

DISCOVER MORE WITH *WINDWARD*

Conveniently Located Across The Eastern Seaboard And Gulf Coast, Windward Marina Group Is Creating A Lifestyle Of Sustainable Waterfront Experiences. With Premier Amenities And An Elite Team, We Provide The Best In Class Marine Services To All Boaters. From Dry, Wet, And Lift Storage To Restaurants And Fun On The Water, Windward Has It All.

Scan QR code with mobile camera

Visit us online at

www.MYWINDWARD.com

MAIN HEADQUARTERS: | 3070 Harbor Drive St. Augustine, FL 32084

Southern Chapter Guide

Note that the direction of travel for the Waterway Guide content is from south to north along the west coast of Florida and east to west along the northern Gulf Coast as you transit the Gulf Intracoastal Waterway (GIWW). Some sections of the coasts do not have recognized or charted GIWW waterways.

Table of Contents 2024 Southern Edition

Introduction
- Publisher's Letter 1
- Southern Chapter Guide 4
- Meet Our Cruising Editors 12

Preferred Destinations 17
- Onancock, VA 18
- Deltaville, VA 20
- Hampton, VA 22
- Beaufort & Port Royal, SC 24
- Franklin County, FL 26

Skipper's Handbook 29
- Port Security 30
- Customs Reporting Procedures 32
- Float Plan 33
- VHF Communications 34
- Rules of the Road 36
- Coast Guard Requirements 38
- Reference Materials 39
- About the Weather 40
- Tropical Weather & Hurricanes 42
- Picking an Anchorage (excerpt) 44
- Florida Anchoring Restrictions 45
- Dealing with Onboard Waste 46
- Distance Tables 48
- Ditch Bag Checklist 51
- GPS Waypoints 52
- Bridge Basics 54
- Locks & Locking Through 56
- Bridge & Lock Schedules 58

Inlets: St. Johns River Entrance to Mobile Bay

Introduction	67
Inside vs. Outside Mileage	70
East Coast Inlets	72
Gulf Coast Inlets	97

Section 1: Florida's Upper East Coast — 117

Chapter 1 Fernandina Beach to St. Johns River 118
Chapter 2 Side Trip on the St. Johns River 131
Chapter 3 St. Johns River to New Smyrna Beach 159
Chapter 4 Space Coast Area 189
Chapter 5 St. Lucie River Area 223
Chapter 6 Side Trip on the Okeechobee Waterway 249

Cruising south on the ICW, mariners enter Florida at Mile 714. As you cross Cumberland Sound and the St. Marys River, the broad expanses of the marsh-bordered Georgia ICW give way to the narrower, more protected and more populated Florida route. Below St. Lucie Inlet, the coastline becomes truly tropical, with a profusion of palm trees and exotic flowers. The Florida ICW is well marked and easy to follow.

Section 2: Florida's Lower East Coast & the Keys — 275

Chapter 7 St. Lucie to Pompano Beach 276
Chapter 8 Fort Lauderdale to Hollywood 305
Chapter 9 Miami & Biscayne Bay 331
Chapter 10 The Florida Keys 364

More than 300 miles of mostly navigable inland waterways carve through the Fort Lauderdale area, making it the "Venice of America." It is well known as a yachting center and boating amenities and services are readily available. Fort Lauderdale to Miami is known as "Florida's Gold Coast," and it glimmers with glamour and charm. Extending in a sweeping southwesterly curve from Miami and the mainland, the Florida Keys offer the cruising boater an environment unlike other waterway areas. In many ways, the Keys resemble the islands of the Bahamas. However, a main highway and a total of 18.94 miles of bridges tie them together.

Table of Contents 2024 Southern Edition

Section 3: Florida's West Coast 431
Chapter 11 Florida Keys to Fort Myers Beach 432
Chapter 12 Sanibel Island to Sarasota Bay 456
Chapter 13 Tampa Bay to Tarpon Springs 489

Zoologically and geographically, Florida's lower west coast differs substantially from the east. The cruising, too, is entirely different. The sophistication, glamour and luxury so prevalent on the east coast comes in more measured doses here. The pace is slower, the atmosphere more relaxed and the amenities somewhat more limited and spaced farther apart, but the cruising is superb.

Section 4: Upper Gulf Coast 520
Chapter 14 The Big Bend: Anclote Key to Carrabelle 522
Chapter 15 The Florida Panhandle 543
Chapter 16 Mobile Bay, AL to Bay St. Louis, MS 573

Florida's Panhandle, stretching from Carrabelle or Apalachicola on the eastern end to Pensacola and Perdido Bay on the west, is sometimes called the Forgotten Coast. It can be reached in one of three ways: From the east, either directly across the Gulf of Mexico or by skirting the Big Bend area just offshore; or from the west, where the inland rivers of the midwest merge into Mobile Bay.

Indexes
Marina/Sponsor Index* 601
Subject Index 609
Goin' Ashore & Inlets Index 612

*Sponsors are listed in **BOLD** and are highlighted in yellow in marina tables.

HILTON HEAD ISLAND
Shelter Cove Marina

Dock. Shop. Dine. Play.

Located in the middle of Hilton Head Island across from Palmetto Dunes Oceanfront Resort and just off the Intracoastal Waterway, Shelter Cove Harbour & Marina offers easy access to great shopping & restaurants plus bikes, watersports, golf, tennis & pickleball. The Ship's Store offers a large selection of apparel, accessories, convenience items & fishing tackle.

- **Floating docks / vessels up to 150'** • **Electrical: 30, 50, 100 amp** • **9' MLW, well marked channel**
- **Pump-out boat** • **Monitor channel 16/71** • **Restrooms, showers, laundry** • **Grocery store nearby**
- **Full service yacht maintenance** • **Wi-Fi internet access & cable available** • **Seasonal resort shuttle**
- **Private 70' transient dock with in-slip fueling & pump-out services**

BEST HARBOR IN THE US — SOUTHEAST REGION WINNER 2022 — USHARBORS.COM

MARINALIFE Best Large Marina 2022 Winner

1 SHELTER COVE LN, HILTON HEAD ISLAND, SC 29928
877-567-6517 • SHELTERCOVEHILTONHEAD.COM

Shelter Cove Marina
32° 10' 52" N   80° 43' 56" W
HILTON HEAD ISLAND, SC

GET ON BOARD

Cruise your way around The Bahamas and 100,000 sq miles of the world's most stunning waters. Start island-hopping to discover 16 major islands and countless cays, each with a vibe all its own.

Cast off at Bahamas.com/boating

THE ISLANDS OF THE
bahamas

The adventure of a lifetime
America's Great Loop

2+ Countries • 14+ States and Provinces • 100+ Locks • 5,250+ Miles...
... all aboard your own boat!

Are you ready for a journey that is both high-adventure and low-risk?

Join our group of likeminded boaters exploring the 6,000-mile waterway known as the Great Loop. There's no better way to travel extensively while remaining socially distant than aboard your own vessel! Whether you're brand new to the idea of the Great Loop, actively planning your trip, or ready to drop the dock lines and head out, we offer something for you!

Visit us at www.greatloop.org or call 877-GR8-LOOP

Membership in America's Great Loop Cruisers' Association includes:

- Access to hundreds of harbor hosts to assist you with local knowledge around the route
- Participation in our discussion forum that offers a deep-dive into Great Loop-related questions and topics
- Webinars exclusively for members
- Discounts on dockage, fuel, equipment, and more
- Monthly digital magazines and newsletters
- Access to our distinctive AGLCA burgee
- Members-only events

and so much more!

Scan the QR code to start your adventure

Meet Our Cruising Editors

Waterway Guide's on-the-water Cruising Editors bring us firsthand information about the navigation, news and trends along the waterways we cover. In addition to contributing to the annual guide, they provide daily updates on the Waterway Explorer at www.waterwayguide.com. We are pleased to introduce you to our crew.

Scott Richard Berg has been sailing, racing and cruising for the past 50 years and has experience on a range of power and sailing vessels from an El Toro Pram to a 135' Baltic Trader. Scott is an experienced delivery and commercial captain and the owner of Chardonnay Boatworks, a full service marine repair and consulting company focusing on the repair and re-engineering of sail and motor yachts. He frequently lectures on marine electrical systems, communication, electronics, and yacht systems for off shore cruising. Scott holds multiple certifications from the ABYC and NMEA. He is the co-founder of the SSCA HF Radio Network (KPK), holds both commercial and amateur radio licenses, and represents recreational boaters as member of the USCG's Global Maritime Distress & Safety System(GMDSS) Task Force. Scott is a member of the Capital Yacht Club, the Ocean Cruising Club and the Seven Seas Cruising Association (Past President). He holds a USCG 100T Masters license and currently lives on his 60-foot Seaton Ketch, CHARDONNAY.

Addison Chan is an experienced software entrepreneur, a world traveler and a committed sailing cruiser. He is the founder of Land and Sea Software Corp., which has engineered a revolutionary platform to produce mobile friendly, piracy-resistant, interactive content for traditional publishers. Waterwayguide Media is using the platform to provide its users with an enhanced digital experience that always delivers the most currently available information to mobile devices. Addison and his wife, Pat, have traveled extensively through Cuba, Mexico and the Bahamas on their 42-foot Catalina sailboat, acquiring deep local knowledge over the years. The depth of his local knowledge and understanding of local culture is evident in his work as the coauthor of *Waterway Guide Cuba*, which is the gold standard of cruising guides for Cuba. His latest project has the working title of "A Handbook for Comfortable Cruising in The Bahamas" which will be representative of a new breed of interactive cruising guides. He is active within the cruising community and maintains the popular Cuba, Land and Sea and Bahamas Land and Sea groups on Facebook.

Capts. Matt & Lucy Claiborne are full-time cruising sailors and storytellers. After college, Matt and Lucy lived on a 32-foot sailboat in the Florida Keys. Even while working in the "real-world" as professors at a university, they continued cruising and camping with a trailerable 21-foot cuddy cabin. In 2014, they cast off on a full-time sailing adventure on a 38-foot Lagoon catamaran. Both Matt and Lucy have USCG Master and FAA pilot licenses. They are full-time digital nomads who work from their boat. Their favorite offices are quiet anchorages; their favorite coworkers are dolphins and pelicans. Matt and Lucy are passionate about education and helping new boaters fulfill their cruising dreams. In 2019, they purchased their "forever dream boat"—a Cabo Rico 38 named *Dulcinea*. After a year outfitting for off-the-grid living and long-distance cruising, you'll now find them cruising Chesapeake Bay, the ICW, Bahamas and beyond with their adventure dog, Chelsea.

Gina L. Cicotello & Peter Henry share an irrational love of old wooden boats. Together they became caretakers of a 1958 Laurent Giles Vertue. *Ariel* didn't need a full restoration, but her new owners find endless opportunities to practice their skills in woodworking, old school rigging, and proper techniques for varnishing. Once they had a boat, Gina's next challenge was learning to sail. She started with classes sailing Flying Scots around the Anacostia River, and they've been cruising around the Chesapeake Bay ever since. Someday *Ariel* and her crew will broaden their adventures beyond the estuary. Gina lives in Arlington, VA. She's had a long career working for various publishers, which culminated in a dream job with National Geographic that lasted 14 years. She managed technology systems while collaborating with the cartographers, explorers and storytellers. After easing out of the corporate world she started freelancing and became her own boss, which means spending more time on the boat.

America's Waterway Guide Since 1947

Capt. George & Patricia Hospodar have been boaters for over 45 years and have cruised more than 50,000 miles together aboard two sailboats and their 48-foot Symbol motor yacht, *Reflection*. George has been a 100-ton licensed U.S. Coast Guard Captain for 30 years. He and Pat are proud Platinum Loopers, lifetime members of the America's Great Loop Cruisers' Association and New Jersey Harbor Hosts. Together they have authored two popular boating books: *Reflection on America's Great Loop* and *The Great Loop Experience from Concept to Completion*. They have also been featured speakers at many boat shows, TrawlerFests and other nautical events.

Michael O'Reilly & Ann Phillips came to sailing by first messing about with canoes and kayaks while living on the Canadian shore of Lake Superior. Sailing replaced the smaller boats and over the last 15-plus years they have enjoyed many extended summer cruises. After completing a cruise through four of the five Great Lakes, they spent a few years exploring Lake Ontario and the Thousand Islands. One season was spent traveling the St. Lawrence River all the way to Newfoundland, which is the current "home" for their boat. Mike is a long-time freelance journalist, writing mostly about the sciences. With the transition to this new watery life, Mike now spends most of his work time writing about traveling, destinations and cruising. Ann is an accomplished photographer. Together they are chronicling their life afloat.

Malcolm & Deb Rubel: For the past four years, Deb and Mac have been cruising on their DeFever 48 Europa, *Janthina*, from Houston to Florida to Maine. They crossed their wake in January 2022 to complete the Great Loop. They have covered 15,000 miles so far and are looking forward to many more years on their boat along with Ceili the Wonder Beagle. This fall and winter they plan to cruise from the Chesapeake to Florida and back to their "dirt home" in North Carolina in the spring. Deb navigates and is responsible for keeping the boat from falling apart. She is also the resident naturalist and photographer. Mac is a retired Master Maine Fishing Guide and a USCG Master. He drives the boat most of the time and takes care of the mechanical stuff.

Bob & Ann Sherer started sailing in 1985 with charters in Maine, Florida and the Caribbean followed by their first sailboat in 1986, which then lead to a 38-foot Ericson, followed by their present boat, a 42-foot Beneteau 423 in 2004. They started their yearly cruises on the ICW from New York to Key West in 2010 and Bob became known as Bob423, the person to follow for advice navigating through the many shoals of the ICW. He published his first *ICW Cruising Guide* in 2015 and has published an updated edition every year. The guide not only includes charts to avoid groundings but also tips learned from years of boating and a review of basic and advanced topics covering the ICW. In 2018, Bob started the ICW Cruising Guide Facebook page, which has grown to 13,500 members. His most recent efforts include the publishing of Bob423 Tracks in GPX format for free downloading, which follow the deep-water path around the shoals of the ICW to enable a less stressful cruise in staying out of the mud. He is routinely consulted by NOAA, the USACE, and the Coast Guard on matters affecting the boating public. Bob and Ann reside 9 months of the year aboard their latest boat, a 42-foot Beneteau 423 sailboat, with their fearless dog, Hoolie, a Brittany.

Onne van der Wal is one of the most prolific and talented marine photographers in the world of sailing. Before he learned to walk, he learned to sail aboard his grandfather's boat, and after progressing through youth sailing training programs he discovered his passion for ocean racing. As the bowman and engineer aboard the Dutch maxi-boat *Flyer II*, Onne won all four legs of the 1981-82 Whitbread Round the World Race. Along the way, he took his camera everywhere to document the experience, even to the top of the mast and the end of the spinnaker pole. Many admirers of Onne's work believe that his background as a world-class sailor informed the artistic choices he made as a world-class artist. In addition to editorial work, Onne has shot for blue chip commercial clients, including the likes of Hinckley Yachts, J Boats, Sperry, Patagonia, North Sails, and Harken. Despite all of the accolades and accomplishments over a career that has covered more than three decades and all seven seas, Onne is always looking forward to the next assignment.

Other Contributors: Waterway Guide gathers information and photos from a variety of sources, including boaters, marinas, communities and tourism divisions. We would like to thank everyone who contributed to this edition.

About Our NOAA Chart Extracts

The U.S. Department of Commerce National Oceanic and Atmospheric Administration (NOAA) has advanced its plan of phasing out the updating and printing of nautical charts, which went into effect in February 2021. Under the new practice NOAA will revise and refresh vector data that will be available to Electronic Navigational Charts (ENC) platforms only. The standardized data can be used by chart plotters and other map applications for creating visual displays of depths, aids to navigation (ATONS), points of interest and extensive details related to navigation, tides, shorelines, hazards and more. Updating of paper charts by NOAA will conclude in 2025, as will chart number references. For those who want printed outputs of nautical charts at various scales for specific geographical areas, the charts may still be obtained using several methods and suppliers. Visit www.noaa.gov for details.

Waterway Guide's objective is to offer the most up-to-date information available through use of NOAA's data superimposed on appropriate base maps. Because the printed charts from NOAA that have served us over the years are no longer supported and have been supplanted by a new method of management and distribution of information, the chart extracts in this publication have been designed to address our distinctive editorial objectives.

Waterway Guide participated in workshops and seminars to develop a working relationship with NOAA and arrived at solutions for displaying acceptable levels of navigation and situational awareness in our various media platforms. Using NOAA-supplied vector data superimposed on geographically accurate base maps that were generated and supplied by Aqua Map, our publications now contain uncomplicated extracts of the geographical areas described in the accompanying text and tables throughout our guidebooks. The chartlets, as we identify them, contain shorelines, ATONS, water depths (in feet), landmarks, street and city names when available, and locations of marinas, all at sufficient levels of detail and scale for ease of interpretation. The chartlets are provided for reference only and not to be used for navigation.

Scan the QR code included with every marina table to see the interactive Aqua Map charts for the surrounding area.

America's Waterway Guide Since 1947

Abaco Beach Resort
AND BOAT HARBOUR MARINA
EST. 1955

ABACO'S PREMIER RESORT & MARINA

Experience the aquatic & mystical charm of our boating, fishing & beaching paradise

- 200 slips & yachts up to 200ft
- 9ft MLW entrance
- 11ft maximum dockside
- 120/240/480V, single & 3-phase
- Customs & Immigration
- Gas & Diesel
- 95 Oceanfront Rooms & Suites
- 2 Tropical Pools one heated
- 2 Restaurants & Bars
- Water Toys & Fitness Center
- Marina Concierge Services
- 24 Hour Security

Call: 877-533-4799 or 242-367-2158 E-mail: reservations@abacobeachresort.com
www.abacobeachresort.com

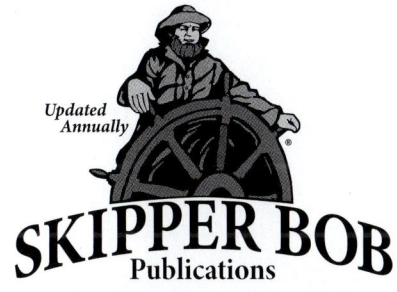

Updated Annually

SKIPPER BOB Publications

ATLANTIC AND GULF ICW GUIDES
- Anchorages Along The Intracoastal Waterway
- Marinas Along The Intracoastal Waterway
- Cruising the Gulf Coast

CANAL AND INLAND RIVER GUIDES
- Cruising the New York Canal System
- Cruising the Rideau and Richelieu Canals
- Cruising the Trent-Severn Waterway, Georgian Bay and North Channel
- Cruising From Chicago to Mobile

PLANNING GUIDES
- Cruising America's Great Loop
- Bahamas Bound

Published by
WATERWAY GUIDE MEDIA
WaterwayGuide.com

Available in Print and the Waterway Guide App

804-776-8999 • skipperbob.net

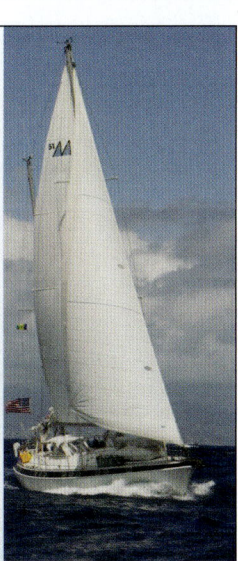

LIVE THE DREAM

Join Seven Seas Cruising Association and turn your cruising dreams into reality.

Benefits include:
- Connection, Advocacy and Much More
- Seven Seas U Webinars & Member Discounts
- Cruisers' Bulletin & Destination Information
- Cruising Stations Worldwide —instant help and local knowledge around the globe
- Member Locator
- Online Discussion Forum

Check out our website
www.ssca.org

SEVEN SEAS CRUISING ASSOCIATION
Est. 1952

www.SSCA.org
(754) 702-5068

SOUTHERN EDITION

America's Waterway Guide Since 1947

Preferred Destinations from Waterway Guide Media

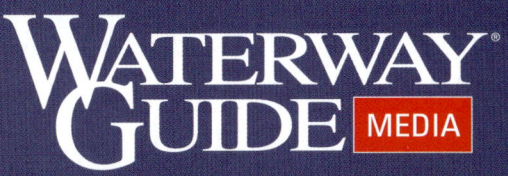

Preferred Destinations

SOUTHERN EDITION

Preferred Destinations from **WATERWAY GUIDE MEDIA**®

Onancock, VA
A Little Slice of Nowhere Else

Onancock, located between the bay and the sea, has a fascinating history that connects the past and present through its people, places, food, and art. This hidden treasure on Virginia's Eastern Shore impressed Captain John Smith over four centuries ago, and it's likely to leave a lasting impression on you too.

Chartered in 1680, Onancock has a history spanning over 300 years as a deep-water port with a safe harbor, catering to pleasure boats cruising the Chesapeake and offering convenient access for kayakers and day sailors.

It takes a full day's sail at an average speed of 6 knots to reach Onancock from most bayfront points on Virginia's western shores. However, keep in mind that the weather on Chesapeake Bay can be unpredictable, so it's crucial to consider this when planning a boat trip. Once you arrive, the six-mile journey up Onancock Creek by boat provides a pleasant respite from the open waters of the Chesapeake, giving you ample time to contemplate the area's rich history. The town offers a charming marina with floating docks, and you can make reservations online at Onancock.com/Wharf.

Where To Dine

Onancock, Virginia, boasts a diverse dining scene that captures the coastal charm of the town. From fresh seafood to farm-to-table options, there are various restaurants catering to different tastes. Whether it's cozy cafes or family-owned eateries, locals and visitors have plenty of choices. The town's proximity to the Chesapeake Bay ensures that you can savor the freshest seafood, making dining in Onancock a truly enjoyable experience that reflects the region's heritage.

If you're looking for a great waterfront dining experience in Onancock, we highly recommend Mallards at the Wharf. Located in the historic Hopkins and Brothers Store dating back to 1842 and positioned at the head of Onancock Creek, this restaurant offers a friendly and relaxed atmosphere. Johnny Mo and his team provide excellent service, ensuring you have a memorable time.

Things To Do Ashore

The town's wharf serves as a central hub for marine activities, offering kayak tours and boat excursions.

Taking a stroll east on Market Street, you'll encounter a cluster of well-preserved 19th-century homes and churches. On College Avenue lies the Historic Onancock School, a 13-acre oasis within the town, offering recreational activities and a Nature Trail alongside Onancock Creek. Inside, you'll encounter many artisans working in their studios (often by appointment), and the Eastern Shore Watermen's Museum & Research Center, which delves into the rich history and culture of those making their livelihood from the surrounding waters.

When the sun sets, Onancock comes alive with a surprisingly sophisticated selection of evening entertainment. Catch first-run films at the Roseland Theater, which also hosts monthly international films. For live performances, head to the North Street Playhouse, featuring a range of plays and other productions throughout the year. Several eateries in town offer live music, spanning from soothing jazz to soulful Celtic ballads.

This hidden gem on Virginia's Eastern Shore has a charm that has withstood the test of time, leaving a lasting impression on all who visit. Onancock offers a fulfilling experience for every traveler. Whether you're drawn to its coastal allure, its welcoming community, or its deep-rooted heritage, Onancock is a place that will captivate your heart and beckon you to return for more unforgettable memories.

Deltaville, VA

A Place With More Boats Than People

Deltaville, Virginia, known as the Boating Capital of the Chesapeake Bay, is a hidden gem that offers a peaceful escape from the hustle and bustle of everyday life. With over 35 marinas and service facilities, it's easy to see why this charming waterfront town has become a haven for boaters.

Deltaville's quiet and relaxed atmosphere with just the right amount of small town fun and charm makes it a perfect destination for boaters. Whether you're headed north or south, be sure to add Deltaville as a stop to your journey, but be warned, you may not want to leave.

America's Waterway Guide Since 1947

A Quiet Place To Tuck In

Whether you are stopping by on your northbound or southbound journey, or you are making Deltaville your final destination, it's not difficult to find a quiet marina with amenities to call "home" during your stay. Some of the more popular marinas in the area include Fishing Bay Marina, Deltaville Yachting Center, Nomad Marinas at Norview Marina, Regatta Point Yachting Center, Jackson Creek Marina and Safe Harbor Stingray Point Marina.

Waterfront Dining

While there are numerous delicious dining choices inland, Deltaville and its surroundings also offer a range of waterfront restaurants. Among them, Deltaville Tap & Raw Bar is a popular spot for both locals and visitors. It provides stunning views of Jackson Creek, delectable seafood, local oysters, and an impressive selection of Virginia craft beers on tap. If you're seeking a river excursion, neighboring towns along the Rappahannock River offer more options.

Provisioning & Local Purveyors

Whether you seek gear or gourmet provisions in Deltaville, the local shops have it all. The West Marine storefront offers a wide range of marine essentials, while Nauti Nell's is perfect for unique finds. Discover more than hardware at Hurd's, Ace Hardware as they cater to boaters with a curated marine selection. For freshest seafood, J&W Seafood is a must, boasting delightful options like crabmeat, oysters and gourmet ingredients. Deltaville Market covers essentials like groceries and toiletries.

Local History & Charm

Explore maritime history at Deltaville Maritime Museum, with exhibits spanning from the Delmarva meteorite's impact to wooden boatbuilding since the late 1800s. The museum hosts concerts, markets, and Family Boatbuilding Week in summer. Nearby, Historic Deltaville Ballpark, Virginia's oldest all-wooden baseball stadium, hosts lively games during summer. Watch the Deltaville Deltas play at this historic venue – check their schedule for upcoming matches.

SOUTHERN EDITION

Preferred Destinations from Waterway Guide Media

Visit a Place Where Adventures are as Vast as the Sea

Hampton, VA.

America's Waterway Guide Since 1947

There's more than meets the eye in this charming Coastal Virginia community, which has welcomed travelers to explore its shores for centuries thanks to its magical mix of awe and wonder, and intrigue and inspiration.

As the home to the world's greatest natural harbor, the water is a way of life in Hampton, Virginia. You can feel its spirit with all five senses, and see it in the faces of the people who call our community home. After all, it's hard not to smile when the breathtaking Chesapeake Bay is right in your own backyard.

We're home to a vibrant boating, fishing and ocean-faring culture that dates back centuries, with unforgettable experiences as vast as the sea. Tour the Chesapeake Bay and cast your line for an incredible time on the James T. Wilson Fishing Pier. Soak up the sun and the fun at Buckroe beach where you can fulfill your thrill with watersports, jet skiing, kayaking and paddle-boarding. Savor the moment, and the flavors, with waterfront dining and fresh, delicious seafood.

Looking for something more personal? Charter a boat for a private tour or climb aboard the all-new Hampton Queen and cruise through four centuries, from the 1607 founding of Jamestown, to the state-of-the-art submarines and aircraft carriers stationed at Norfolk Naval Base. Grab a front row seat to highlights, including Fort Wool and Old Point Comfort Lighthouse.

Need an adventure outside the water? Experience our attractions, history and culture. Hampton's numerous world-class attractions, including Fort Monroe National Monument, the Virginia Air & Space Science Center, and the Hampton University Museum, have been inspiring visitors for decades. See history and adventure come alive in Hampton.

Virginia is a place for lovers — Hampton is a place for lovers of life. So if you love the scent of salt in the air, the sounds of the open ocean, and life on the water, go beyond familiar and plan your trip at VisitHampton.com

Get Inspired at VisitHampton.com

VISIT HAMPTON VIRGINIA

SOUTHERN EDITION

Preferred Destinations from Waterway Guide Media

Discovering Timeless Treasures In
Beaufort & Port Royal
South Carolina

Welcome to the picturesque haven of Beaufort and Port Royal, South Carolina, where a delightful blend of southern hospitality, rich culture, and tantalizing cuisine awaits your discovery. Nestled between the Beaufort River and Battery Creek, these enchanting twin cities are loved by history enthusiasts, nature lovers, and those yearning for a peaceful escape.

Founded in 1562, Port Royal Island has been a beacon of attraction for explorers throughout its rich history. Upon your arrival, you'll be transported to a bygone era, where exquisitely preserved pre-Civil War architecture graces every corner. Wander through the historic downtown, a designated district that offers a glimpse into the past, and lose yourself in the splendor of the south's most extraordinary bed and breakfasts, restaurants, and hotels.

Where To Dine

This area boasts a wide array of restaurants, catering to every preference, from laid-back coastal cuisine to elegant fine dining.

When it comes to seafood, the Beaufort & Port Royal area is a reigning champion, and your visit here would be incomplete without savoring the culinary delights offered by its many local eateries, where seafood dishes take center stage on the menus. Witness the docks of Battery Creek bustling with activity as a vibrant fleet of trawlers sets sail daily, ensuring a continuous supply of the freshest catches. Prepare to revel in a delightful assortment of oysters, shrimp, crab, and freshly caught fish, all sourced from the local waters.

For an authentic taste of Lowcountry living, head over to Fishcamp on 11th Street – a beloved spot cherished by locals and visitors alike. The menu here is a true treasure trove, featuring mouthwatering seafood delicacies alongside succulent steaks, catering to the diverse preferences of every palate.

If you're looking for a fine dining experience, head to the Ribaut Social Club, a fine dining and social space for Beaufort locals and visitors to mingle over cocktails and impeccable regional cuisine. This culinary haven showcases the remarkable cuisine of executive chef Daniel Salazar. The concise menu presents imaginative interpretations of meats, seafood, and fresh vegetables. Be sure to secure reservations ahead of time, as this culinary haven is in high demand and promises an unforgettable dining experience.

Local Events & Festivals

Throughout the year, Beaufort, South Carolina, is a bustling hub of annual festivals and events, ensuring there is never a dull moment for both locals and visitors. Mark your calendars and embrace the opportunity to partake in these local events.

Take a Journey into Gullah Culture

Delve into the rich heritage of the Gullah people, African Americans who have made their home in the Lowcountry region of South Carolina and Georgia, including the coastal plains and Beaufort Sea Islands. Immerse yourself in the culture and history of the Gullah community with a guided tour by native experts from St. Helena, courtesy of Gullah-N-Geechie Mahn Tours. The Gullah culture is a source of immense pride and has inspired documentary films, children's books, and popular novels that celebrate its unique traditions and contributions.

Travel Back in Time

Exploring the local history of Beaufort and Port Royal is like stepping into a living time capsule, where every street corner and historic landmark reveals fascinating stories from the past. Beaufort and Port Royal, both deeply intertwined with the nation's history, boast an exquisitely preserved charm that takes visitors on a captivating journey through time.

Founded in 1711, Beaufort holds a significant place in history as the second oldest city in South Carolina, only trailing behind Charleston. With its roots intertwined with early European explorations, this charming city thrived as one of the economic hubs of the Lowcountry throughout the 1800s.

To truly immerse oneself in the past, a visit to the numerous cultural sites scattered across historic Beaufort is a must. Step back in time and witness the echoes of bygone eras as you explore the rich heritage that has shaped this captivating city.

Discover a haven that effortlessly transforms overnight anchorages into week-long retreats, and visitors into locals captivated by the enchanting allure of this coastal gem. Learn more about the Beaufort and Port Royal area at https://www.beaufortsc.org/

Preferred Destinations from WATERWAY GUIDE MEDIA

Florida's Forgotten Coast

is a Boater's Paradise

Florida's Forgotten Coast, along the North Florida Gulf Coast, is a boater's paradise with hundreds of miles of freshwater creeks, sloughs and rivers that empty into nutrient-rich bays and out to the Gulf of Mexico.

Getting out on the water is easy here. The area features more than 40 boat ramps stretching from Alligator Point to Apalachicola. Bring your boat and tie up at one of the area's 10 commercial marinas.

America's Waterway Guide Since 1947

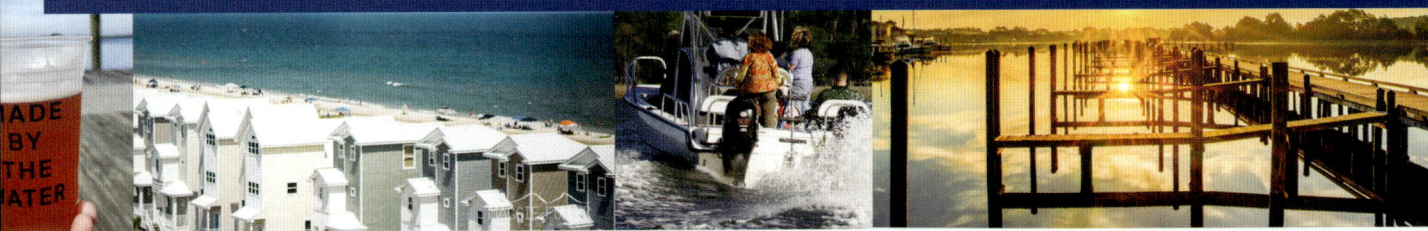

APALACHICOLA

The downtown historic district of Apalachicola stretches three blocks deep from where the historic Apalachicola River meets the oyster-famous Apalachicola Bay. Everything is walkable here - stroll along the wide tree-lined streets with historic homes or hole up along the waterfront and enjoy the music scene in pubs and local eateries just blocks from the waterfront. Apalachicola's commercial marina facilities include the Scipio Creek, Water Street and Apalachicola Marina with services and available at Scipio Creek.

EASTPOINT

Across the bay from Apalachicola, Eastpoint features rustic seafood houses, weather-worn docks and fresh seafood markets run by families four generations deep. There are RV parks here, two boat ramps, a full-service bait and tackle shop, fresh seafood restaurants, causal fare and even a waterfront brewery!

ST. GEORGE ISLAND

Just offshore, St. George Island is a 22- mile barrier island that hosts some of Florida's most beautiful and serene beaches. There is a protected anchorage spot on the bayside of St. George Island. Don't expect to walk to amenities from this anchorage but it's not far from the Julian G. Bruce St. George Island State Park which boasts some of the best camping facilities in the region. Elsewhere on the island, accommodations range from quaint beach cottages to luxurious beach homes and can be reserved with any of the island's vacation rental companies. The historic St. George Island Lighthouse is located at the St. George Island public beach park.

CARRABELLE

Carrabelle is about 30 nautical miles from Apalachicola and it's a must stop spot for boaters and fishermen. Carrabelle features three public commercial marinas along the Carrabelle River and all are located within walking distance of restaurants, a grocery and all three offers either fuel or service facilities. There is public dockage along the river and a private boat club nearby on Timber Island.

Carrabelle is considered ground zero for fishing enthusiasts because of its easy access to offshore fishing and boating. The town features a natural deep-water harbor plus a nearby renowned golf resort. The nearby Crooked River Lighthouse reminds you of the town's maritime importance and features monthly full moon climbs.

To learn more about Franklin County boating, fishing charters, restaurants, and accomodations, visit Floridasforgottencoast.com/waterways

SOUTHERN EDITION   27

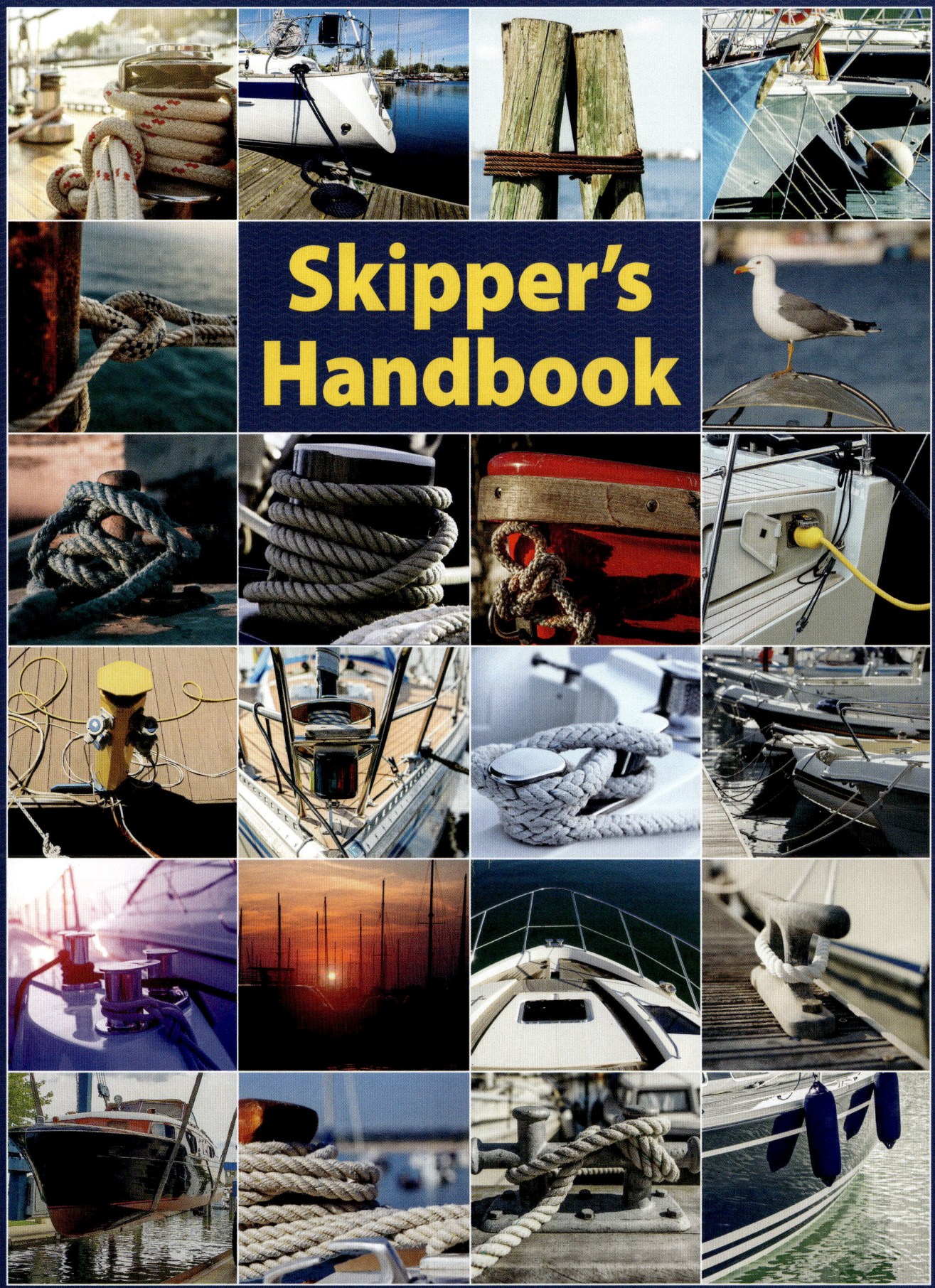

Skipper's Handbook

SOUTHERN EDITION

Skipper's Handbook

Port Security

The U.S. Coast Guard and Customs and Border Patrol–both components of the Department of Homeland Security–handle port security in the United States. Local law enforcement agencies and the FBI also have a role in port security at the local and regional level. Each year more than 11 million maritime containers arrive at our seaports. At land borders, another 11 million arrive by truck and 2.7 million by rail. Homeland Security is responsible for knowing what is inside those containers, whether it poses a risk to the American people and ensuring that all proper revenues are collected.

As an example, one in five food items is now imported. American consumers demand fresh limes and blueberries all year round and, as a result, during the winter months in the U.S. nearly 80 percent of the fresh fruits and vegetables on our tables come from other countries. With the ever-increasing amount of trade, the agricultural risks to the United States grow. The threat to crops and livestock is real.

In response to this threat and others, the U.S. Coast Guard has established "protection zones" around all U.S. Navy vessels, tank vessels and large-capacity cruise vessels, even when underway. U.S. Navy bases, U.S. Coast Guard bases and some shoreside facilities such as nuclear power plants are also in protection zones. Non-military vessels (this means YOU) are not allowed within 100 yards of these protection zones. To do so can rack up serious civil penalties and even imprisonment. These protection zones vary from port to port and from facility to facility but ignorance of the protection zones is not a viable excuse. Having said that, law-abiding boaters sometimes find themselves unable to comply with the letter of the law without hitting a jetty, for example. In such cases, common sense and good communication should prevail.

America's Waterway Watch Program

Government officials view the recreational boating community as an ally. We can do our part (and perhaps stave off more stringent regulations and surveillance measures) by becoming familiar with the Coast Guard's America's Waterway Watch program. Think of it as a neighborhood watch program for the waterways.

It is not the intent of America's Waterway Watch to spread paranoia or to encourage spying on one another and it is not a surveillance program; it is instead a simple deterrent to potential terrorist activity. The purpose of the program is to allow boaters and others who spend time along the water to help the authorities counter crime and terrorism. To report suspicious behavior, call the National Response Center at 877-249-2824 (877-24WATCH). For immediate danger to life or property, call 911 or contact the U.S. Coast Guard on Marine VHF Channel 16.

Staying safe and responsible requires a little forethought and vigilance on your part. Following the steps outlined below will help ensure a trouble-free journey and keep you and your crew out of the headlines.

Be Prepared

- Before you leave, check the current charts for the area in which you will be traveling and identify any security areas. Security zones are highlighted and outlined in magenta with special notes regarding the specific regulations pertaining to that area.

- Check the latest *Local Notice to Mariners* (available online at www.navcen.uscg and posted at some marinas) and identify any potential security areas that may not be shown on the chart.

- Prior to your departure, listen to VHF Channel 16 for any Sécurité alerts from the Coast Guard (departing cruise ships, U.S. Navy vessels, fuel tankers, etc.) for the area you will be cruising.

- Talk to other boaters in your anchorage or marina about the areas where you will be traveling. They may have tips and suggestions on potential security zones or special areas they may have encountered along the way.

Stay Alert While Underway

- Mind the outlined magenta security areas noted on your charts.

- Look for vessels with blue or red warning lights in port areas and, if approached, listen carefully and strictly obey all instructions given to you.

- Keep your VHF radio switched to VHF Channel 16 and keep your ears tuned for bulletins, updates and possible requests for communication.

- Avoid commercial port operation areas, especially those that involve military, cruise line or petroleum facilities. Observe and avoid other restricted areas near power plants, national monuments, etc.

- If you need to pass within 100 yards of a U.S. Navy vessel for safe passage, you must contact the U.S. Navy vessel or the Coast Guard escort vessel on VHF Channel 16 to let them know your intentions.

- We advise that if government security or the U.S. Coast Guard hails you, do exactly what they say, regardless of whether or not you feel their instructions have merit.

Additional Resources

Atlantic Intracoastal Waterway Association:
www.atlanticintracoastal.org.

America's Waterway Watch:
www.americaswaterwaywatch.org

Department of Homeland Security:
www.dhs.gov

U.S. Customs and Border Protection:
www.cbp.gov

Skipper's Handbook

Customs Reporting Procedures

Operators of small pleasure vessels, arriving in the U.S. from a foreign port are required to report their arrival to Customs and Border Patrol (CBP) immediately. The master of the vessel reports their arrival at the nearest Customs facility or other designated location. These reports are tracked in the Pleasure Boat Reporting System. An application to lawfully enter the U.S. must be made in person to a CBP officer at a U.S. port-of-entry when the port is open for inspection.

CBP has designated specific reporting locations within the Field Offices that are staffed during boating season for pleasure boats to report their arrival and be inspected by CBP. The master of the boat must report to CBP telephonically and be directed to the nearest Port of Entry to satisfy the face-to-face requirement, or report to the nearest designated reporting location, along with the boat's passengers for inspection.

You may be required to rent a car or take a cab to the nearest airport or federal office several miles away for the inspection. These offices are often closed on weekends. If your arrival is after working hours, you are required to stay on board and clear in the next morning. You must, however, clear in within 24 hours of your arrival. Everyone on board, regardless of nationality, has to report in person. U.S. nationals must take their passports or passport cards. All non-U.S. Nationals should take their passports with valid visas and a Green Card, if held. Take your boat papers, either U.S. documentation or state registration with state decal number. You should also present a list of firearms and ammunition on board.

Clearing In with the ROAM App

Travelers arriving by boat into many popular U.S. ports can check into the country on their phones or tablets. The Reporting Offsite Arrival–Mobile (ROAM) app is the official replacement for the Local Boater Option (LBO) and Small Vessel Reporting System (SVRS) programs that have been used over the years. These programs required an initial interview to get in but usually resulted in a quick phone call instead of a face-to-face meeting to re-enter the U.S.

If you have a www.Login.gov account, you can log into the app immediately. If you need a password, the app directs you to the website. Then it walks you through the steps, including entering the specifics for each person on board and for your vessel. Once you've entered all of the details and submitted it for a review, an officer may initiate a video call to discuss the trip or to ask any necessary questions. All of this happens directly inside the app. Of course, there are still instances where in-person reporting is required. If you require an I-94, need to pay customs fees or duties, or need to obtain a cruising permit, you will still need to check in in-person. Boaters are still required to have a current fee decal onboard.

Now that the app has been implemented on a larger scale, travelers entering by boat in the Great Lakes; most of the East Coast (Delaware to Florida); Texas and San Diego, CA; and the U.S. territories in the Caribbean can use the app. New locations are continually being added, and because the program is new, it's probably a good idea to call your port of arrival to ensure they are using the ROAM app.

To download the ROAM app, just search the Apple App Store or the Google Play Store on your device. For more information, visit the CBP website or contact the CBP office at your port of arrival.

Additional Resources

U.S. Customs and Border Control:
www.cbp.gov/travel/pleasure-boats-private-flyers

Designated Port of Entry (Key West):
301 Simonton St., Ste. 20, 305-296-5411

America's Waterway Guide Since 1947

Float Plan   BoatU.S.

1. Phone Numbers

Coast Guard: _____

Marine Police: _____

Local TowBoatU.S. Company: _____

2. Description of the Boat

Boat Name: _____ Hailing Port: _____

Type: _____ Model Year: _____

Make: _____ Length: _____ Beam: _____ Draft: _____

Color, Hull: _____ Cabin: _____ Deck: _____ Trim: _____ Dodger: _____

Other Colors: _____ # of Masts: _____

Distinguishing Features: _____

Registration No: _____ Sail No: _____

Engine(s) Type: _____ Horsepower: _____ Cruising Speed: _____

Fuel Capacity, Gallons: _____ Cruising Range: _____

Electronics/Safety Equipment Aboard

VHF Radio: _____ Cell Phone: _____ CB: _____ SSB: _____

Frequency Monitored: _____ Loran: _____ SatNav: _____

Depth Sounder: _____ Radar: _____ GPS: _____

Raft: _____ Dinghy: _____ EPIRB: _____ A/B/C/406M
                                    (Indicate Type)

3. Trip Details

Owner/Skipper (Filing Report): _____

Phone: _____ Age: _____

Address: _____

Additional Persons Aboard, Total: _____

Name: _____ Age: _____
Address: _____ Phone: _____
Boating Experience: _____

Name: _____ Age: _____
Address: _____ Phone: _____
Boating Experience: _____

Name: _____ Age: _____
Address: _____ Phone: _____
Boating Experience: _____

Name: _____ Age: _____
Address: _____ Phone: _____
Boating Experience: _____

Name: _____ Age: _____
Address: _____ Phone: _____
Boating Experience: _____

Departure Date/Time: _____ Return No Later Than: _____

Depart From: _____

Marina (Home Port): _____ Phone: _____

Auto Parked At: _____

Model/color: _____ Lic. # _____

Destination Port: _____

_____ ETA: _____ No Later Than: _____

Phone: _____

Anticipated Stopover Ports: _____

_____ ETA: _____ No Later Than: _____
Phone: _____

_____ ETA: _____ No Later Than: _____
Phone: _____

_____ ETA: _____ No Later Than: _____
Phone: _____

_____ ETA: _____ No Later Than: _____
Phone: _____

_____ ETA: _____ No Later Than: _____
Phone: _____

Plan Filed With: _____

Name: _____ Phone: _____

Get in the habit of filing a Float Plan. It can assure quicker rescue in the event of a breakdown, stranding or weather delay. Fill out the permanent data in Sections 1 and 2. Then, make enough copies to last for the season. If you file a Float Plan with someone not at your home, such as a harbormaster or boating friend, be sure to notify them as soon as you return. Don't burden friends or authorities with unnecessary worry and responsibility if you are safe.

Check your *BoatU.S. Towing Guide*. Some listed companies will accept a verbal Float Plan via telephone or VHF.

SOUTHERN EDITION

Skipper's Handbook

VHF Communications

Skippers traveling the U.S. inland waterways use their VHF radios almost every day to contact other vessels and bridgetenders, make reservations at marinas, arrange to pass other vessels safely and conduct other business. Waterway Guide has put together the following information to help remove any confusion as to what frequency should be dialed in to call bridges, marinas, commercial ships or your friend anchored down the creek.

Remember to use low power (1 watt) for your radio transmission whenever possible. If you are within a couple of miles of the responding station (bridge, marina or other craft), there is no need to broadcast at 25 watts and disturb the transmissions of others 25 miles away.

Channel Usage Tips

- VHF Channel 16 (156.8 MHz) is by far the most important frequency on the VHF-FM band. VHF Channel 16 is the international distress, safety and calling frequency.

- If you have a VHF radio on your boat, Federal Communications Commission (FCC) regulations require that you maintain a watch on either VHF Channel 09 or 16 whenever you are underway and the radio is not being used to communicate on another channel. Since the Coast Guard does not have the capability of announcing an urgent marine information broadcast or weather warning on VHF Channel 09, it recommends that boaters remain tuned to and use VHF Channel 16.

- Recreational craft typically communicate on VHF Channels 68, 69, 71, 72 or 78A. Whenever possible, avoid calling on VHF Channel 16 altogether by prearranging initial contact directly on one of these channels. No transmissions should last longer than 3 minutes.

- The Coast Guard's main working VHF Channel is 22A and both emergency and non-emergency calls generally are switched there to keep VHF Channel 16 clear. Calling the Coast Guard for a radio check on VHF Channel 16 is prohibited.

- Radio-equipped bridges on the Atlantic ICW use VHF Channel 09 with a few exceptions.

- The Bridge-to-Bridge Radio Telephone Act requires many commercial vessels, including dredges and tugboats, to monitor VHF Channel 13. VHF Channel 13 is also the frequency used by bridges in several states.

Distress Calls

MAYDAY: The distress signal "MAYDAY" is used to indicate that a vessel is threatened by grave and imminent danger and requests immediate assistance.

PAN PAN: The urgency signal "PAN PAN" is used when the safety of the ship or person is in jeopardy.

SÉCURITÉ: The safety signal "SÉCURITÉ" is used for messages about the safety of navigation or important weather warnings.

VHF Channel 16 is the distress call frequency. The codeword "MAYDAY" is the international alert signal of a life-threatening situation at sea. After a MAYDAY message is broadcast, VHF Channel 16 must be kept free of all traffic, other than those directly involved in the rescue situation, until the rescue has been completed.

If you hear a MAYDAY message and no one else is responding, it is your duty to step in to answer the call, relay it to the nearest rescue organization and get to the scene to help. Remember, a MAYDAY distress call can only be used when life is threatened. For example, if you have run on the rocks but no one is going to lose their life, that is NOT a MAYDAY situation.

> Note: The Coast Guard has asked the FCC to eliminate provisions for using VHF Channel 09 as an alternative calling frequency to VHF Channel 16 when it eliminates watch-keeping on VHF Channel 16 by compulsory-equipped vessels. Stay tuned for updates.

America's Waterway Guide Since 1947

How to Make a Distress Call

MAYDAY! MAYDAY! MAYDAY!

This is: Give your vessel name and call sign.

Our position is: Read it off the GPS or give it as something like "2 miles southwest of Royal Island." (Your rescuers must be able to find you!)

We are: Describe what's happening (e.g., on fire/hit a reef/sinking).

We have: Report how many people are on board.

At this time we are: Say what you're doing about the crisis (e.g., standing by/abandoning ship).

For identification we are: Describe your boat type, length, color, etc. (so your rescuers can more readily identify you).

We have: List safety equipment you have (e.g., flares/smoke/ocean dye markers/EPIRB).

We will keep watch on Channel 16 as long as we can.

VHF Channels	
09	Used for radio checks and hailing other stations (boats, shoreside operations). Also used to communicate with drawbridges in Florida.
13	Used to contact and communicate with commercial vessels, military ships and drawbridges. Bridges in several states monitor VHF Channel 13.
16	**Emergency use only.** May be used to hail other vessels, but once contact is made, conversation should be immediately switched to a working (68, 69, 71, 72, 78A) VHF channel.
22	Used for U.S. Coast Guard safety, navigation and Sécurité communications.
68 69 71 72 78A	Used primarily for recreational ship-to-ship and ship-to-shore communications.

SOUTHERN EDITION

Skipper's Handbook

Rules of the Road

Anyone planning to cruise U.S. waterways should be familiar with the rules of the road. *Chapman Piloting: Seamanship and Small Boat Handling* and *The Annapolis Book of Seamanship* are both excellent on-the-water references with plentiful information on navigation rules. For those with a penchant for the exact regulatory language, the U.S. Coast Guard publication *Navigation Rules: International–Inland* covers both international and U.S. inland rules. (Boats over 39.4 feet are required to carry a copy of the U.S. Inland Rules at all times.)

Following is a list of common situations you may likely encounter on the waterways. Make yourself familiar with them, and if there is ever a question as to which of you has the right-of-way, let the other vessel go first.

Sailors need to remember that a boat under sail with its engine running is considered a motorboat.

Passing or Being Passed:

- If you intend to pass a slower vessel, try to hail them on your VHF radio to let them know you are coming.

- In close quarters, BOTH vessels should slow down, which normally allows the faster vessel to pass quickly without throwing a large wake onto the slower boat.

- A boat passing another is the "give-way" vessel and is required to keep clear of the slower "stand-on" vessel until past and well clear of it.

- Sound signals when overtaking (both vessels heading the same way):
  "See you on the one (whistle)" = overtake on his starboard (your port)
  "See you on the two (whistle)" = overtake on his port (your starboard)

- Sound signals when passing (vessels going in opposite directions):
  "See you on the one (whistle)" = pass port to port
  "See you on the two (whistle)" = pass starboard to starboard

- As you pass a slower boat, take a look back to see how they were affected by your wake. Remember: YOU are responsible for your wake. It is the law to slow down and it is common courtesy.

At Opening Bridges:

- During an opening, boats traveling with the current go first and generally have the right-of-way.

- Boats constrained by their draft, size or maneuverability (e.g., dredges, tugs and barges) take priority.

- Standard rules of the road apply while circling or waiting for a bridge opening.

Tugs, Freighters, Dredges & Naval Vessels:

- These vessels are usually constrained by draft or their inability to easily maneuver. For this reason, you will almost always need to give them the right-of-way and keep out of their path.

- You must keep at least 100 yards away from any Navy vessel. If you cannot safely navigate without coming closer than this, you must notify the ship of your intentions over VHF Channel 16.

- Keep a close watch for freighters, tugs with tows and other large vessels while offshore or in crowded ports. They often come up very quickly, despite their large size.

- It is always a good practice to radio larger vessels (VHF Channel 13 or 16) to notify them of your location and your intentions. The skippers of these boats are generally appreciative of efforts to communicate with them. This is especially true with dredge boats on all the waterways.

Additional Resources

U.S. Coast Guard Boating Safety Division:
www.uscgboating.org

U.S. Coast Guard Navigation Center:
www.navcen.uscg.gov

America's Waterway Guide Since 1947

In a Crossing Situation:

- When two vessels under power are crossing and a risk of collision exists, the vessel that has the other on her starboard side must keep clear and avoid crossing ahead of the other vessel.

- When a vessel under sail and a vessel under power are crossing, the boat under power is usually burdened and must keep clear. The same exceptions apply as per head-on meetings.

- On the Great Lakes and western rivers (e.g., the Mississippi River system), a power-driven vessel crossing a river shall keep clear of a power-driven vessel ascending or descending the river.

Power Vessels Meeting Any Other Vessel:

- When two vessels under power (either sailboats or powerboats) meet "head-to-head," both are obliged to alter course to starboard.

- Generally, when a vessel under power meets a vessel under sail (i.e., not using any mechanical power), the powered vessel must alter course accordingly.

- Exceptions are vessels not under command, vessels restricted in ability to maneuver, vessels engaged in commercial fishing or those under International Rules such as a vessel constrained by draft.

Two sailboats meeting under sail:

- When each has the wind on a different side, the boat with the wind on the port side must keep clear of the boat with the wind on the starboard side.

- When both have the wind on the same side, the vessel closest to the wind (windward) will keep clear of the leeward boat.

- A vessel with wind to port that sees a vessel to windward but cannot determine whether the windward vessel has wind to port or starboard will assume that windward vessel is on starboard tack and keep clear.

Keep Watch for Crab Pots!

While crab pots with marker buoys are not intentionally placed inside navigational channels, they sometimes break loose and find their way there. The terms "pot" refers to the enclosed traps (usually a framework of wire) used to catch crabs in shallow waters. The attached retrieval markers can range from colorful buoys to empty milk jugs (or anything else that floats). Most buoys are painted in a color that contrasts the water surface but some are black or even dark blue, which are especially difficult to see in the best of conditions. You do NOT want to get a line wrapped around your prop so it is advisable to have a spotter on the foredeck when traversing fields of pots.

Skipper's Handbook

Coast Guard Requirements

The U.S. Coast Guard stands watch at all times to aid vessels of all sizes and the persons on board. In some areas, you can quickly reach the Coast Guard by dialing *CG on a cellular phone. If you have a question of a non-emergency nature, the Coast Guard prefers that you telephone the nearest station. As always, if there is an emergency, initiate a "MAYDAY" call on VHF Channel 16.

In addition to aiding boaters in distress, the Coast Guard also enforces maritime law and conducts safety inspections. While a Coast Guard boarding can be unnerving, if you are responsible and prepared, it will only take 15 to 30 minutes and will be a non-event. First, have your boat in order. This includes having your vessel documentation, registration and insurance documents on hand, as well as your passport. Organize this in a binder and keep it in the nav station so you don't have to fumble around looking for documents and paperwork. You will need to acknowledge the location of any weapons on board and show a permit (when required by state law). The officers will likely focus on areas with the largest safety concerns including the following.

Note that state and local requirements are also considered. If there is a minor violation, they may give you a written warning explaining what needs to be fixed to be in compliance. If you are found with a small violation and correct it quickly, then this will merely be a chance to interact with those whose goal is to keep you as safe as possible on the water.

Life Jackets: One Type I, II, II or V per person plus one Type IV throwable device is required. PFDs must be U.S. Coast Guard-approved, wearable by the intended user and readily accessible. The Type IV throwable device must be located so that it is immediately available.

Visual Distress Signals: All vessels 16 feet and over must be equipped with minimum of 3 day-use and 3 night-use or 3 day/night combination pyrotechnic devices. Non-pyrotechnic substitutes are orange flag (for day use) and electric S-O-S signal light (for night use). Flares must be up to date (e.g., not expired).

Sound Producing Devices: A whistle, horn, siren, etc. capable of a 4-second blast audible for 0.5 mile must be on board for use during periods of reduced visibility. Boats 65 feet and over must have a bell and one whistle or horn required to signal intentions.

Navigation Lights: All powered vessels under 12 meters (39.4 feet) must have working navigational lights and an independent all-around anchor light. Sailboats under power are considered powerboats and must follow "power" rules.

Fire Extinguisher: U.S. Coast Guard-approved, marine-type fire extinguishers are required on any boat with enclosed fuel or engine spaces, enclosed living spaces or permanent (not movable by one person) fuel tanks. They must be in good working condition and readily accessible. (Number of units required depends on vessel length.)

Ventilation: Boats built after August 1, 1980, with enclosed gasoline engines must have a powered ventilation system with one or more exhaust blowers.

Backfire Flame Arrester: All gasoline-powered inboard/outboard or inboard motor boats must be equipped with an approved backfire flame arrester.

Pollution Placard: It is illegal to discharge oil or oily waste into any navigable waters of the U.S. Boats over 26 feet must display a durable oily waste pollution placard of at least 5 by 8 inches in a prominent location.

MARPOL Trash Placard: It is illegal to dump plastic trash anywhere in the ocean or navigable waters of the U.S. Boats over 26 feet must display a durable trash placard at least 4 by 9 inches in a prominent location.

Navigation Rules: Boats 39.4 feet and over must have a copy of current Navigation Rules on board. You can download a copy at www.uscgboating.org.

Marine Sanitation Devices: The discharge of treated sewage is allowed within 3 nm of shore except in designated "No Discharge Zone" areas. The Coast Guard will check that overboard discharge outlets can be sealed (and remain sealed if within 3 nm of shore).

America's Waterway Guide Since 1947

Reference Materials

U.S. Coast Guard Local Notice to Mariners

The U.S. Coast Guard provides timely marine safety information for the correction of all U.S. Government navigation charts and publications from a wide variety of sources, both foreign and domestic via the *Local Notice to Mariners*. These are divided by district, updated weekly and available as a PDF at www.navcen.uscg.gov. (Select LNMs tab at top of page.)

Cruising Guides

- *ICW Cruising Guide (by Bob423)*, Robert A. Sherer
- *Skipper Bob Cruising Guides*, Ted Stehle (editor)

Navigation

- *A Boater's Guide to Federal Requirements for Recreational Boaters.* Covers equipment requirements, navigation rules and aids to navigation, a sample float plan and safety and survival tips. Can be downloaded as a PDF at www.uscgboating.org/images/420.PDF.
- *NAVIGATION RULES, INTERNATIONAL—INLAND*, U.S. Dept. of Homeland Security. The U.S. Coast Guard requires all vessels over 39 feet carry this book of the national and international rules of the road. Can be downloaded as a PDF at www.navcen.uscg.gov.
- *U.S. Coast Pilot (1-5)*, NOAA. Includes piloting information for coasts, bays, creeks and harbors. Also includes tide tables and highlights restricted areas. Updated weekly and can be downloaded as a PDF at www.nauticalcharts.noaa.gov/publications/coast-pilot/index.html.
- *U.S. Chart No 1. (Chart Symbols).* Describes the symbols, abbreviations and terms used on NOAA nautical charts. Available online at www.nauticalcharts.noaa.gov/publications/us-chart-1.html.
- *U.S. Aids to Navigation System* is a downloadable guide from the U.S. Coast Guard with basic information on the recognition of U.S. Aids to Navigation System (ATONS). Find it at www.uscgboating.org/images/486.PDF.

Maintenance

- *Boatowner's Mechanical & Electrical Manual* (4th Edition), Nigel Calder
- *Boatowner's Illustrated Electrical Handbook*, Charlie Wing
- *Boat Mechanical Systems Handbook*, David Gerr

Seamanship

- *Anchoring: A Ground Tackler's Apprentice*, Rudy and Jill Sechez
- *Boater's Pocket Reference*, Thomas McEwen
- *Chapman Piloting & Seamanship* (68th Edition), Charles B. Husick
- *Eldridge Tide and Pilot Book* (Annual), Robert E. and Linda White
- *Heavy Weather Sailing* (7th Edition), Peter Bruce
- *Nigel Calder's Cruising Handbook*, Nigel Calder
- *Offshore Cruising Encyclopedia*, Steve & Linda Dashew
- *The Annapolis Book of Seamanship* (4th Edition), John Rousmaniere
- *The Art of Seamanship*, Ralph Naranjo
- *World Cruising Essentials*, Jimmy Cornell

First Aid & Medical

- *Advanced First Aid Afloat* (5th Edition), Dr. Peter F. Eastman
- *DAN Pocket Guide to First Aid for Scuba Diving*, Dan Orr & Bill Clendenden
- *First Aid at Sea*, Douglas Justin and Colin Berry
- *Marine Medicine: A Comprehensive Guide* (2nd Edition), Eric Weiss and Michael Jacobs
- *On-Board Medical Emergency Handbook: First Aid at Sea*, Spike Briggs and Campbell Mackenzie

Skipper's Handbook

About the Weather

Every day on the water can't have balmy breezes, abundant sunshine and consistently warm weather; however, staying out of bad weather is relatively easy if you plan ahead. The National Weather Service (NWS) provides mariners with continuous broadcasts of weather warnings, forecasts, radar reports and buoy reports over VHF-FM and Single Side Band (SSB) radio. There are almost no areas on the Atlantic ICW where a good quality, fixed-mount VHF cannot pick up one or more coastal VHF broadcasts. Also, there is no substitute for simply looking at the sky, and either stay put or seek shelter if you don't like what you see.

Reading the Skies

Water and metal are excellent conductors of electricity, making boating in a thunderstorm a risky prospect. While the odds of a given boat being hit are small, the consequences are severe and deadly. Do not try and play the odds! The best advice if you are out on the water and skies are threatening is get back to land and seek safe shelter, but that's not always practical for cruisers who live aboard or are not near land.

Thunderstorms occur when air masses of different temperatures meet over inland or coastal waters. An example of this would be when air with a high humidity that is warm near the ground rises and meets cooler air, which condenses and creates water droplets. This releases energy, which charges the atmosphere and creates lightning. This is why thunderstorms are a daily occurrence between March and October near southern waterways.

A tell-tale sign of a thunderstorm is cumulonimbus clouds: those tall clouds with an anvil-shaped (flat) top. Thunderstorms can also precede even a minor cold front. Keep in mind that thunderstorms generally move in an easterly direction so if you see a storm to the south or southwest of you, start preparing.

Don't Wait Until It's Too Late!

Almost all lightning will occur within 10 miles of its parent thunderstorm, but it can strike much farther than that. Also, the current from a single flash will easily travel for long distances. Because of this, if you see lightning or hear thunder, you CAN get struck!

Weather Apps (Free)
Boat Weather
Buoycast: NOAA Marine Forecast
National Hurricane Center Tracker
NOAA Marine Weather Radar
NOAA Weather
PredictWind
Wind Alert
Windfinder
Windy
Weather Online
Accuweather (www.accuweather.com)
BoatUS Hurricane Tracking & Resource Center (www.boatus.com/hurricanes/tracking)
Buoy Weather (www.buoyweather.com)
Coastal Marine Forecast (www.weather.gov/marine)
National Hurricane Center (www.nhc.noaa.gov)
National Weather Service (www.weather.gov)
Passage Weather (www.passageweather.com)
Predict Wind (www.predictwind.com)
Sailflow (www.sailflow.com)
The Weather Channel (www.weather.com)
Windfinder (www.windfinder.com)

The ability to see lightning will depend on the time of day, weather conditions and obstructions, but on a clear night it is possible to see a strike more than 10 miles away. Thunder can also be heard for about 10 miles, provided there is no background noise such as traffic, wind or rain.

If you see lightning, you can determine the distance by timing how long it takes before you hear thunder. The old rule that every 5 seconds of time equals 1 mile of distance works well. So if it takes 20 seconds to hear thunder after you see lighting, then the storm is 4 miles away. Time to drop anchor and "hunker down"!

Lightning Safety Tips

Lightning tends to strike the tallest object and boats on the open water fit this profile. The lightning will try to take the most direct path to the water, which is usually down the mast on a sailboat or the VHF antenna on a powerboat. However, both sailboats and powerboats with cabins—especially those with lightning protection systems properly installed—are relatively safe, provided you keep a few things in mind:

- Before the storm strikes, lower, remove or tie down all antennas, fishing rods and flag poles.

- Stay down below and in the center of the cabin. Avoid keel-stepped masts and chain plates (on sailboats) and large metal appliances such as microwaves or TVs. Remove any metal jewelry.

- Disconnect the power and antenna leads to all electronics including radios. Do not use the VHF radio unless absolutely necessary.

- If you are stuck on deck, stay away from metal railings, the wheel, the mast and stays (on sailboats) or other metal fittings. Do not stand between the mast and stays as lightning can "side-flash" from one to the other.

- Stay out of the water and don't fish or dangle your feet overboard. Salt water conducts electricity, which means that it can easily travel through the water toward you.

- Don't think rubber-soled deck shoes will save you; while rubber is an electric insulator, it's only effective to a certain point. The average lightning bolt carries about 30,000 amps of charge, has 100 million volts of electric potential and is about 50,000°F.

If You Are Struck:

1. **Check people first.** Many individuals struck by lightning or exposed to excessive electrical current can be saved with prompt and proper cardiopulmonary resuscitation (CPR). Contrary to popular belief, there is no danger in touching persons after they have been struck by lightning.

2. **Check the bilge** as strikes can rupture through-hull fittings and punch holes in hulls. Props and rudders are natural exit points on boats.

3. **Check electronics and the compasses.** Typically everything in the path of the lightning is destroyed on the way down to the water including instruments, computers and stereos.

4. **Consider a short haul** to check the bottom thoroughly. Lightning strikes sometimes leave traces of damage that may only be seen when the boat is out of the water.

Don't Rush Back Out

Because electrical charges can linger in clouds after a thunderstorm has passed, experts agree that you should wait at least 30 minutes after a storm before resuming activities. And remember: If you can hear thunder, you can still be struck by lightning!

Natural Seasickness Remedies

- *Take slow, deep breaths.* This helps soothe upset stomach and dizziness.

- *Focus on the horizon.* Keep your body still and head facing forward and watch a stationary object. Taking the helm always helps.

- *Ginger can help.* Eat ginger snaps, drink ginger tea or ginger ale or digest in capsule form ahead of time.

- *Peppermint works too.* Sucking on a peppermint candy, drinking peppermint tea or breathing in peppermint oil dabbed on a cloth can help with stomach issues.

- *Try acupuncture wristbands.* Apply pressure to specific points on your wrist to reduce nausea.

Skipper's Handbook

Tropical Weather & Hurricanes

While all coastal areas of the country are vulnerable to the effects of a hurricane (especially from June through November), the Gulf Coast, Southern and Mid-Atlantic states typically have been the hardest hit. But northern locales aren't immune; several destructive hurricanes have dealt a blow to areas in New England over the last 100 years including Hurricane Sandy in 2012 and Matthew in 2016. While hurricanes can create vast swaths of devastation, ample preparation can help increase your boat's chances of surviving the storm.

According to the National Weather Service, a mature hurricane may be 10 miles high with a great spiral several hundred miles in diameter. Winds are often well above the 74 mph required to classify as hurricane strength, especially during gusts. Hurricane damage is produced by four elements: tidal surge, wind, wave action and rain.

Distance from Eye	Force Level	Wind Speed
150 miles	Force 8	34–40 knots
100 miles	Force 11	56–63 knots
75 miles	Force 12	over 64 knots

- Tidal surge is an increase in ocean depth prior to the storm. This effect, amplified in coastal areas, may cause tidal heights in excess of 15 to 20 feet above normal. Additionally, hurricanes can produce a significant negative tidal effect as water rushes out of the waterways after a storm.

- Wind gusts can exceed reported sustained winds by 25 to 50 percent. For example, a storm with winds of 150 mph might have gusts of more than 200 mph, according to the National Weather Service.

- Wave action is usually the most damaging element of a hurricane for boaters. The wind speed, water depth and the amount of open water determine the amount of wave action created. Storm surges can transform narrow bodies of water into larger, deeper waters capable of generating extreme wave action.

- Rainfall varies but hurricanes can generate anywhere from 5 to 20 inches or more of rain.

Hurricane Categorization

CATEGORY	PRESSURE	WIND SPEED	SURGE
1	Above 980 mb (Above 28.91 in.)	64–82 knots (74–95 mph)	4–5 ft. (1–1.5 m)
	Visibility much reduced. Maneuvering under engines just possible. Open anchorages untenable. Danger of poorly secured boats torn loose in protected anchorages.		
2	965-979 mb (28.50-28.91 in.)	83-95 knots (96-110 mph)	6–8 ft. (1.5-2.5 m)
	Visibility close to zero. Boats in protected anchorages at risk, particularly from boats torn loose. Severe damage to unprotected boats and boats poorly secured and prepared.		
3	945-964 mb (27.91-28.50 in.)	96-113 knots (111-130 mph)	9–12 ft. (2.5-3.5 m)
	Deck fittings at risk and may tear loose, anchor links can fail and unprotected lines will chafe through. Extensive severe damage.		
4	920-944 mb (27.17-27.91 in.)	114-135 knots (131-155 mph)	13-18 ft. (3.5-5.4 m)
	Very severe damage and loss of life.		
5	Below 920 mb (Below 27.17 in.)	Above 135 knots (131-155 mph)	Above 18 ft. (Above 5.4 m)
	Catastrophic conditions with catastrophic damage.		

If your boat is in a slip, you have three options: Leave it where it is (if it is in a safe place); move it to a refuge area; or haul it and put it on a trailer or cradle. Some marinas require mandatory evacuations during hurricane alerts. Check your lease agreement and talk to your dockmaster before a hurricane if you are uncertain. Keep in mind that many municipalities close public mooring fields in advance of the storm. In some localities, boaters may be held liable for any damage that their boat inflicts to marina piers or property; check locally for details. Because of this, rivers, canals, coves and other areas away from large stretches of open water are best selected as refuges.

Consult your insurance agent if you have questions about coverage. Many insurance agencies have restricted or canceled policies for boats that travel or are berthed in certain hurricane-prone areas. Review your policy and check your coverage as many insurance companies will not cover boats in hurricane-prone areas during the June through November hurricane season. Riders for this type of coverage are notoriously expensive.

Preparing Your Boat

- Have a hurricane plan made up ahead of time to maximize what you can get done in the amount of time you will have to prepare (no more than 12 hours in some cases). Plan how to tie up the boat or where to anchor before a hurricane is barreling down on you. Make these decisions in advance!

- Buy hurricane gear well in advance. When word of a hurricane spreads, local ship stores run out of storm supplies (anchors and line, especially) very quickly.

- Strip everything that isn't bolted down off the deck of the boat (e.g., canvas, sails, antennas, bimini tops, dodgers, dinghies, dinghy motors, cushions, unneeded control lines on sailboats) as this will help reduce windage and damage to your boat. Remove electronics and valuables and move them ashore.

- Any potentially leaky ports or hatches should be taped up. Dorades (cowls) should be removed and sealed with deck caps.

- Make sure all systems on board are in tip-top shape in case you have to move quickly. Fuel and water tanks should be filled, bilge pumps should be in top operating condition and batteries should be fully charged.

- You will need many lengths of line to secure the boat; make certain it is good stretchy nylon (not Dacron). It is not unusual to string 600 to 800 feet of dock line on a 40-foot-long boat in preparation for a hurricane. If you can, double up your lines (two for each cleat) as lines can break during a strong storm. Have fenders and fender boards out and make sure all of your lines are protected from chafing.

- If you are anchored out, use multiple large anchors; there is no such thing as an anchor that is too large. If you can, tie to trees with a good root system such as mangroves or live oaks. Mangroves are particularly good because their canopy can have a cushioning effect. Be sure mooring lines include ample scope to compensate for tides 10 to 20 feet above normal.

- Lastly, do not stay aboard to weather out the storm. Many people have been seriously injured (or worse) trying to save their boats during a hurricane. Take photos of the condition in which you left your boat and take your insurance papers with you.

Returning Safely After the Storm

- Before hitting the road, make sure the roads back to your boat are open and safe for travel. Beware of dangling wires, weakened docks, bulkheads, bridges and other structures.

- Check your boat thoroughly before attempting to move it. If returning to your home slip, watch the waters for debris and obstructions. Navigate carefully as markers may be misplaced or missing.

- If your boat should sink, arrange for engine repairs before floating it but only if it is not impeding traffic. Otherwise, you will need to remove it immediately. Contact your insurance company right away to make a claim.

Additional Resources

National Hurricane Center: www.nhc.noaa.gov

BoatUS Hurricane Tracking & Resource Center: www.boatus.com/hurricanes

Skipper's Handbook

Picking an Anchorage (excerpt)

We all know that unless it is an emergency, in addition to being verboten, it's just plain common sense and courteous to avoid encroaching on or anchoring in a marked channel, or in a location that inhibits a boat's access to or from a slip, mooring, boatyard, or marina, or that interferes with another anchored vessel.

Otherwise, just about any other location is fair game, but there are a few prerequisites that should be met in order to qualify it as an acceptable anchorage.

First, there's a minimum acceptable depth of water, which is determined by your boat's draft, plus any additional distance the tide will drop, plus another foot or two–just in case. In dam controlled waterways, the height of the water level above normal pool should also be considered, as the elevated pool level can be lowered back to normal pool without notice, often quickly–think hours.

Also, the wind, depending on its direction can blow water out, anywhere from a few feet in gale force conditions, to ten feet or more in storms or hurricane force winds. Water levels can also become lower than normal when: the moon is in perigee, or during seiches, spring tides, and winter solstice. Neglecting these influences could leave the boat bottoming out, aground, or with too little water to get over a bar.

The amount of rode that you can deploy establishes the maximum depth in which you can anchor. If you're anchoring to 5:1 scope, then one fifth the length of your rode is the maximum depth where you can set your anchor; however, in demanding conditions you may need to use 10:1 scope; if so, one tenth the length of your rode would be the maximum depth where you'd want to set your anchor.

Fetch–the distance that the wind can blow over the water without obstruction–can also be a factor when choosing an anchorage, as it can affect comfort. The greater the fetch, the bigger the seas or waves, the more uncomfortable the boat's motion. Our goal is to try to anchor where the fetch is less than a few hundred yards, as beyond this, wave action becomes livelier.

It's prudent to enter unfamiliar anchorages slowly, remaining alert to potential hazards, not just below the surface, but overhead, too–you want enough clearance to prevent snagging bridges, tree limbs, or other dangers, and with power lines, to prevent arcing.

If obstructions are a concern or soundings reveal questionable depths, not only where the boat will initially be anchored, but later where the boat might swing if wind or current shifts direction or strength, then relocate the anchor, or set out an additional anchor or two in a manner that would keep the boat away from any danger.

And keep in mind that your anchor must be compatible with the type of seabed in which you will be anchoring, as well as sized for the wind speed and seas that you will encounter.

Cruising guides are a great resource for identifying anchorages, but if you keep the above guidelines in mind, you just might discover many others, perhaps some that are picturesque, others offering solitude… maybe both.

Rudy and Jill Sechez are the authors of "ANCHORING—A Ground Tackler's Apprentice." To read more, order a copy at the Waterway Guide Ship Store or call 800-233-3359. Rudy and Jill are Trawler Training and Anchoring Consultants, providing one-on-one onboard sessions, consultations, and group seminars. They are also available to talk to groups and clubs. To arrange to have them speak to your organization, contact them at rudyandjill@yahoo.com.

Florida Anchoring Restrictions

For over a decade, Florida legislators have grappled with the rules of anchoring. Following the completion of an 8-year pilot program conducted by the U.S. Fish & Wildlife Service that provided insight into the multitude of issues associated with vessels anchoring in the state's waterways, the Florida legislature approved House Bill 7043 that codified anchoring regulations in the state. The regulations, which offer clear guidance and specific requirements for boaters, localities, public safety agencies and law enforcement, went into effect July 1, 2017.

The following densely populated urban areas, which have narrow state waterways, residential docking facilities and significant recreational boating traffic, are designated as anchoring limitation areas, within which a person may not anchor a vessel at any time during the period between one-half hour after sunset and one-half hour before sunrise

- The section of Middle River lying between Northeast 21st Court and the ICW in Broward County.
- Sunset Lake in Miami-Dade County.
- The sections of Biscayne Bay in Miami-Dade County lying between: Rivo Alto Island and Di Lido Island; San Marino Island and San Marco Island; and San Marco Island and Biscayne Island

Exceptions

- If the vessel suffers a mechanical failure that poses an unreasonable risk of harm to the vessel or the persons onboard unless the vessel anchors. The vessel may anchor for three business days or until the vessel is repaired, whichever occurs first.

- If imminent or existing weather conditions in the vicinity of the vessel pose an unreasonable risk of harm to the vessel or the persons onboard unless the vessel anchors. The vessel may anchor until weather conditions no longer pose such risk. During a hurricane or tropical storm, weather conditions are deemed to no longer pose an unreasonable risk of harm when the hurricane or tropical storm warning affecting the area has expired.

- During special events, including public music performances, local government waterfront activities or fireworks displays. A vessel may anchor for the lesser of the duration of the special event or three days.

- Vessels engaged in commercial fishing or recreational fishing if the persons onboard are actively tending hook and line fishing gear or nets.

The bill provides that citations will result in a mandatory court appearance and a $50 civil penalty. Those failing to show up for court may be found guilty of a misdemeanor of the second degree, with more severe penalties (including impoundment).

The Bottom Line

As of July 2021, the State of Florida enacted a law that allows municipal governments and counties to manage anchorages. These new measures also provide guidance on the definitions of derelict vessels, use of unpermitted moorings and proof of pump-out when anchored for 10 days or longer in permitted mooring fields or No-Discharge Zones. These new measures also provide guidance on the definitions of derelict vessels, use of unpermitted moorings and proof of pump-out when anchored for 10 days or longer in permitted mooring fields or No-Discharge Zones.

Be advised that regulations and laws will change for many designated and favorite anchorages in the state. Boaters should be aware of local ordinances before choosing an anchorage. Law enforcement will most likely be polite and understanding if you don't know the rules, but pulling up anchor and moving is not an activity you want to engage in after settling in following a day underway.

Dinghy Restriction in Miami Beach

It is also important to note that in the City of Miami Beach it is unlawful to tie a dinghy to a canal wall to visit the city. The city is also strictly enforcing the 20-minute limit for the dinghy dock at the end of 17th St. These restrictions carry stiff civil fines.

Skipper's Handbook

Dealing With Onboard Waste

Up until the late 1980s, many boaters simply discharged their untreated sewage overboard into the water. After a revision to the Clean Water Act was passed in 1987, the discharge of untreated sewage into U.S. waters within the 3-mile limit was prohibited. Shortly thereafter, pump-out stations became a regular feature at marinas and fuel docks throughout the U.S. waterways.

Simply stated, if you have a marine head installed on your vessel and are operating in coastal waters within the U.S. 3-mile limit (basically all of the waters covered in the guide you are now holding), you need to have a holding tank and you will obviously need to arrange to have that tank pumped out from time to time.

Government regulation aside, properly disposing of your waste is good environmental stewardship. While your overboard contribution to the waterways may seem small in the grand scheme of things, similar attitudes among fellow boaters can quickly produce unsavory conditions in anchorages and small creeks. The widespread availability of holding tank gear and shoreside pump-out facilities leaves few excuses for not doing the right thing.

No-Discharge Zones

- No-Discharge means exactly what the name suggests: No waste, even waste treated by an onboard Type I marine sanitation device (MSD), may be discharged overboard. All waste must be collected in a holding tank and pumped out at an appropriate facility.

- Keep in mind that there are some areas that forbid overboard discharge of any waste including gray water from showers or sinks. Familiarize yourself with local regulations before entering new areas to ensure you don't get hit with a fine.

The Law

- If you have a marine head onboard and are operating on coastal waters within the U.S. 3-mile limit (basically all of the waters covered in this guide), you need to have an approved holding tank or Type I MSD. In a No-Discharge area even a Type I MSD system must have a holding tank.

- All valves connected to your holding tank or marine head that lead to the outside (both Y-valves AND seacocks) must be wire-tied, padlocked or absent of the valve handle and in the closed position. Simply having them closed without the (non-releasable) wire ties will not save you from a fine if you are boarded.

- You may discharge waste overboard from a Type I MSD in all areas except those designated as No-Discharge Zones. A Type I MSD treats waste by reducing bacteria and visible solids to an acceptable level before discharge overboard.

- While small and inconvenient for most cruisers, "Port-A-Potties" meet all the requirements for a Type III MSD as the holding tank is incorporated into the toilet itself.

Pump-Out and Holding Tank Basics

- Some marinas are equipped with pump-out facilities, normally located at the marina's fuel dock. Note that some marinas charge a fee for the service.

- Several municipalities and local governments have purchased and staffed pump-out boats that are equipped to visit boats on request, especially those at anchor. Radio the local harbormaster to see if this service is available in the area you are visiting. There is normally a small fee involved.

- You will want to keep an eye out on your holding tank level while you are cruising, especially if you are getting ready to enter an area where you many not have access to proper pump-out services for a few days. Plan a fuel stop or marina stay to top off the fuel and water tanks and empty the other tank before you set out into the wild.

NEW: Pump-Out App

Pumpout Nav, a free iOS and Android app, uses a boater's location information to suggest the nearest public pump-out station on a map or list. The app helps boaters find the amenities they need and helps marinas promote their services. The app catalogs more than 250 pump-out stations along the coast and in some inland waterways and provides the cost, hours and detailed location for each facility.

Marine Sanitation Devices

- Type I MSD: Treats sewage before discharging it into the water using maceration. The treated discharge must not show any visible floating solids and must meet specified standards for bacteria content. Raritan's Electro Scan and Groco's Thermopure systems are examples of Type I MSDs. Not permitted in No-Discharge Zones.

- Type II MSD: Type II MSDs provide a higher level of waste treatment than Type I units and are larger as a result. They employ biological treatment and disinfection. These units are usually found on larger vessels due to their higher power requirements. These may not be discharged in No-Discharge Zones.

- Type III MSD: Regular holding tanks store sewage until the holding tank can either be pumped out to an onshore facility or at sea beyond the U.S. boundary waters (i.e., 3 miles offshore).

Composting Heads

Composting heads are essentially Type III MSDs but rather than simply storing sewage, composters separate liquid and solid waste, which speeds up decomposition and reduces odors. This "dry" system promotes decomposition through controlled composting in which the solid portion is converted into an easy-to-handle, safe, non-odorous humus. There is no need for plumbing, valves, pump or thru-hull and no components to break down, clog up or leak. Other advantages include no pump-outs, uses no water, reduces onboard weight and opens up storage space.

Penalties and Fines

- Misuse or failure to equip a vessel with a Marine Sanitation Device may result in a non-criminal infraction with a $56 penalty.

- Illegal dumping/discharge of a Marine Sanitation Device may result in a non-criminal infraction with a $250 penalty.

Additional Resources

BoatU.S. Guide to Overboard Discharge:
www.boatus.com/foundation/guide/environment_7.html

EPA Listing of No-Discharge Zones:
www.epa.gov/vessels-marinas-and-ports/no-discharge-zones-ndzs-state

Distances: Fernandina Beach to Key West, FL

Inside Route Distances - Fernandina Beach, Florida to Key West, Florida
(nautical and statute miles)

	Key West	Flamingo	Marathon	Matecumbe Harbor	Tavernier	Miami	Port Everglades	Fort Lauderdale	Port of Palm Beach	Jupiter	Fort Myers	Moore Haven	Clewiston	Port Mayaca	Stuart	Salerno	Fort Pierce	Vero Beach	Melbourne	Eau Gallie	Cocoa	Titusville	New Smyrna Beach	Daytona Beach	Marineland	St. Augustine	Jacksonville	Fernandina Beach	Norfolk, VA
Norfolk, VA	1061	1050	1045	1017	999	947	927	925	885	873	975	926	915	892	865	860	839	827	798	795	780	764	735	722	692	676	659	623	•
Fernandina Beach	458	427	422	394	378	324	304	303	262	251	353	303	292	269	242	237	216	204	175	172	157	141	113	99	69	53	36	•	717
Jacksonville	454	423	418	390	374	320	300	299	258	247	349	299	288	265	238	233	212	200	171	168	153	137	108	95	65	49	•	41	758
St. Augustine	405	374	369	341	324	271	251	249	209	197	299	250	239	216	189	184	163	151	122	119	104	88	59	46	16	•	56	60	778
Marineland	389	358	353	325	309	255	235	234	193	182	284	235	223	200	173	169	148	136	106	103	89	72	44	30	•	18	75	79	796
Daytona Beach	359	328	323	295	279	225	205	204	163	152	254	204	193	170	143	138	117	105	76	73	58	42	14	•	35	53	109	114	831
New Smyrna Beach	345	315	309	282	265	211	191	190	150	18	240	191	180	157	130	125	104	92	63	59	45	28	•	16	51	68	124	130	846
Titusville	317	286	281	253	237	183	163	162	121	110	212	163	151	128	101	97	76	64	34	31	17	•	32	48	83	101	158	162	879
Cocoa	301	270	264	237	220	166	146	145	105	93	195	146	135	112	85	80	59	47	18	14	•	20	52	67	102	120	176	181	898
Eau Gallie	286	255	250	223	206	152	132	131	90	79	181	132	120	97	70	66	45	33	3	•	16	36	68	84	119	137	193	198	915
Melbourne	283	252	247	219	203	149	129	128	87	76	178	128	117	94	67	62	41	29	•	14	21	39	72	87	122	140	197	201	918
Vero Beach	254	223	217	190	173	119	99	98	58	46	148	99	88	65	38	33	12	•	34	38	54	74	106	121	157	174	230	235	952
Fort Pierce	242	211	205	178	161	107	87	86	46	34	136	87	76	53	26	21	•	14	47	52	68	87	120	135	170	188	244	249	966
Salerno	224	193	188	161	144	90	70	69	28	17	119	70	58	35	8	•	24	38	71	76	92	112	144	159	194	212	268	273	990
Stuart	229	198	193	165	149	95	75	74	33	22	111	61	50	27	•	9	30	44	77	81	98	116	150	165	199	217	274	278	995
Port Mayaca	256	225	220	192	176	122	102	101	60	49	83	34	23	•	31	40	61	75	108	112	129	147	181	196	230	248	305	310	1026
Clewiston	279	248	243	215	199	145	125	124	83	72	61	11	•	26	58	67	87	101	135	138	155	174	207	222	257	275	331	336	1053
Moore Haven	290	259	254	227	210	156	136	135	94	83	49	•	13	40	70	81	100	114	148	152	168	188	220	235	270	288	344	349	1066
Fort Myers	339	309	303	276	259	205	185	184	144	132	•	56	70	96	128	137	157	170	205	208	224	244	276	292	327	344	402	406	1122
Jupiter	207	177	171	144	127	73	53	52	12	•	152	96	83	56	25	20	39	53	87	91	107	127	159	175	209	227	284	289	1005
Port of Palm Beach	196	165	160	132	116	62	42	41	•	14	166	108	96	69	38	32	53	67	100	104	121	139	173	188	222	241	297	302	1018
Fort Lauderdale	155	125	119	92	75	21	1	•	47	60	212	155	143	116	85	79	99	113	147	151	167	186	219	235	269	287	344	348	1064
Port Everglades	154	123	118	91	74	20	•	1	48	61	213	156	144	117	86	80	100	114	148	152	168	188	220	236	270	289	345	350	1067
Miami	134	104	98	71	54	•	23	24	71	84	236	180	167	141	109	104	123	137	171	175	191	211	243	259	293	312	368	373	1090
Tavernier	83	52	47	19	•	62	85	86	133	146	298	242	229	203	171	166	185	199	234	237	253	273	305	321	356	373	430	435	1150
Matecumbe Harbor	65	35	29	•	22	82	105	106	152	166	318	261	247	221	190	185	205	219	252	257	273	291	323	339	374	392	449	453	1170
Marathon	42	34	•	33	54	113	136	137	184	197	349	292	280	253	222	216	236	250	284	288	304	323	356	372	407	425	481	486	1203
Flamingo	73	•	39	40	60	120	142	144	190	204	356	296	285	259	228	222	243	257	290	293	311	329	362	377	412	430	486	491	1208
Key West	•	84	48	75	96	154	177	178	226	239	390	334	321	295	264	258	278	292	326	329	346	365	397	413	448	466	522	527	1244

Distances: St. Johns River, FL

Distances on St. Johns River, Florida
(nautical and statute miles)

	Lake Harney	Sanford	Astor-Volusia	Georgetown	Leesburg	Moss Bluff Lock	Silver Springs	Welaka	Crescent City	Palatka	Doctors Lake Inlet	Jacksonville	Broward River (mouth)	Intracoastal Waterway	Mayport	St. Johns River (mouth)
St. Johns River (mouth)	161	143	109	95	162	145	136	86	89	68	32	20	12	4	2	•
Mayport	159	141	107	93	160	143	134	84	87	66	30	18	10	2	•	2
Intracoastal Waterway	157	139	105	91	158	141	132	82	85	64	28	16	8	•	2	5
Broward River (mouth)	149	131	97	83	150	133	124	74	77	56	20	8	•	9	12	14
Jacksonville	141	123	89	75	142	125	116	66	69	48	12	•	9	18	21	23
Doctors Lake Inlet	129	111	77	62	129	112	104	54	56	36	•	14	23	32	35	37
Palatka	93	75	41	26	94	76	68	18	20	•	41	55	64	74	76	78
Crescent City	101	83	49	35	102	85	76	26	•	23	64	79	89	98	100	102
Welaka	75	57	23	8	75	58	50	•	30	21	62	76	85	94	97	99
Silver Springs	123	105	71	56	31	14	•	58	87	78	120	134	143	152	154	157
Moss Bluff Lock	131	113	79	65	17	•	16	67	98	87	129	144	153	162	165	167
Leesburg	148	131	96	82	•	20	36	86	117	108	148	163	173	182	184	186
Georgetown	66	49	14	•	94	75	64	9	40	30	71	86	96	105	107	109
Astor-Volusia	52	34	•	16	110	91	82	26	56	47	89	102	112	121	123	125
Sanford	18	•	39	56	151	130	121	66	96	86	128	142	151	160	162	165
Lake Harney	•	21	60	76	170	151	142	86	116	107	148	162	171	181	183	185

Skipper's Handbook

Distances: Key West to Apalachicola, FL

Coastwise and Inside Route Distances – Key West, FL to Apalachicola, FL
(nautical miles)

	Apalachicola, FL	Carrabelle, FL	St. Marks, FL	Cedar Key, FL	Tarpon Springs, FL	Clearwater, FL	Tampa, FL	St. Petersburg, FL	Bradenton, FL	Sarasota, FL	Venice, FL	Port Boca Grande, FL	Fort Myers, FL	Naples, FL	Everglades, FL	Cape Sable, FL	Flamingo, FL	Matecumbe Harbor, FL	Marathon, FL	Key West, FL
Key West, FL	406	389	367	310	250	234	232	218	210	186	172	144	134	96	88	57	70	65	42	-
Marathon, FL	408	391	389	313	253	237	235	221	213	189	174	146	136	100	80	31	37	29	-	
Matecumbe Harbor, FL	411	394	392	316	255	240	237	224	215	191	177	149	139	103	81	32	35	-		
Flamingo, FL	396	379	377	301	240	225	222	209	200	176	162	134	124	88	66	17	-			
Cape Sable, FL	379	362	360	284	223	208	205	192	183	159	145	117	107	71	49	-				
Everglades, FL	350	334	332	255	195	179	177	163	155	131	116	88	79	38	-					
Naples, FL	316	299	297	221	160	145	143	129	120	96	82	54	44	-						
Fort Myers, FL	297	280	278	202	142	126	124	110	102	78	63	35	-							
Port Boca Grande, FL	262	245	244	167	107	91	89	75	67	43	28	-								
Venice, FL	234	218	216	139	79	63	61	47	39	15	-									
Sarasota, FL	221	204	202	125	65	49	42	33	25	-										
Bradenton, FL	209	193	191	114	54	38	36	22	-											
St. Petersburg, FL	202	186	184	107	47	31	18	-												
Tampa, FL	218	202	200	123	63	47	-													
Clearwater, FL	174	157	155	79	18	-														
Tarpon Springs, FL	164	147	145	68	-															
Cedar Key, FL	118	101	91	-																
St. Marks, FL	69	52	-																	
Carrabelle, FL	25	-																		
Apalachicola, FL	-																			

Routes used in table:
- Hawk Channel – between Marathon and Key West
- Northwest Channel (Key West) and outside to places between Cape Sable and San Carlos Bay, thence inside to Anclote Keys, thence outside to St. George Sound.

Distances from Everglades northward are inside via Big Marco River and Gordon Pass.

Ditch Bag Checklist

Rescue Items

- ☐ Functioning, registered EPIRB
- ☐ Handheld VHF radio (waterproof or in sealed pouch with extra batteries)
- ☐ Sea anchor, drogue and line
- ☐ Manual inflation pump
- ☐ Selection of flares (parachute and handheld) and smoke signals
- ☐ Strobe light (may be present in inflatable PFD)
- ☐ Flashlight & batteries (headlamp is ideal)
- ☐ Whistle (may be present in inflatable PFD)
- ☐ Signal mirror
- ☐ Handheld GPS or compass (for position)
- ☐ Small pair of binoculars (to confirm a boat or plane spotting before using flares)

Survival Items

- ☐ Sponges and bailer (with handle)
- ☐ Patch kit for inflatable dinghy or life raft (or emergency clamps)
- ☐ Water (individually sealed or in collapsible containers)–at least 2 gallons per person
- ☐ Emergency food rations and can opener (if needed)
- ☐ Power Bars
- ☐ Prescription medications
- ☐ Seasickness medications/remedies
- ☐ First aid kit
- ☐ Multipurpose tool or sailor's knife
- ☐ Waterproof matches

Other Items

- ☐ Solar blanket
- ☐ Heavy-duty coated gloves
- ☐ Duct tape
- ☐ Sewing kit
- ☐ Simple fishing gear (line, jigs, hooks, etc.)
- ☐ Polypropylene line
- ☐ Waterproof sunscreen and zinc oxide
- ☐ Bug repellent
- ☐ Ziploc bags (gallon size)
- ☐ Paper and pen in Ziploc bag
- ☐ Spare prescription glasses and sunglasses (polarized to reduce glare)
- ☐ Laminated copies of passports or license
- ☐ Cash ($50 in small bills)
- ☐ Copy of the yacht's papers (including insurance)

Skipper's Handbook

GPS Waypoints

The following list provides selected waypoints for the waters covered in this book. The latitude/longitude readings are taken from government light lists and must be checked against the appropriate chart and light list for accuracy. Some waypoints listed here are lighthouses and should not be approached too closely as they may be on land, in shallow water or on top of a reef. Many buoys must be approached with caution, as they are often located near shallows or obstructions. The positions of every aid to navigation should be updated using the Coast Guard's *Local Notice to Mariners* (www.navcen.uscg.gov/lnm).

The U.S. Coast Guard will continue to provide Differential GPS (DGPS) correction signals for those who need accuracy of 10 meters or less, even though most GPS receivers now come with an internal capability for receiving differential signals.

Prudent mariners will not rely solely on these waypoints to navigate. Every available navigational tool should be used at all times to determine your vessel's position.

Florida East Coast

LOCATION	LATITUDE	LONGITUDE
St. Marys Entrance Lighted Buoy STM	N 30° 42.900'	W 081° 14.650'
St. Johns Lighted Buoy STJ	N 30° 23.583'	W 081° 19.133'
St. Augustine Lighted Whistle Buoy STA	N 29° 54.917'	W 081° 15.283'
Ponce de Leon Inlet Lighted Bell Buoy 2	N 29° 04.767'	W 080° 53.483'
Cape Canaveral App. Chnl. Lig. Buoy 8	N 28° 23.867'	W 080° 33.433'
Fort Pierce Inlet Lighted Buoy 2	N 27° 28.650'	W 080° 15.417'
St. Lucie Entrance Lighted Buoy 2	N 27° 10.017'	W 080° 08.383'
Lake Worth Inlet Lighted Buoy LW	N 26° 46.367'	W 080° 00.600'
Boca Raton Inlet North Jetty Light 2	N 26° 20.167'	W 080° 04.183'
Hillsboro Inlet Entrance Lighted Buoy HI	N 26° 15.133'	W 080° 04.467'
Port Everglades Lighted Buoy PE	N 26° 05.500'	W 080° 04.767'
Bakers Haulover Inlet Jetty Light	N 25° 53.933'	W 080° 07.183'
Miami Lighted Buoy M	N 25° 46.100'	W 080° 05.000'

Florida Keys

LOCATION	LATITUDE	LONGITUDE
Biscayne National Park N. Lig. Buoy N	N 25° 38.733'	W 080° 05.367'
Fowey Rocks Light	N 25° 35.433'	W 080° 05.800'
Triumph Reef Light 2TR	N 25° 28.267'	W 080° 06.917'
Pacific Reef Light	N 25° 22.267'	W 080° 08.517'
Carysfort Reef Light	N 25° 13.317'	W 080° 12.683'
Elbow Reef Light 6	N 25° 08.667'	W 080° 15.500'
Molasses Reef Light 10	N 25° 00.717'	W 080° 22.583'
Davis Reef Light 14	N 24° 55.550'	W 080° 30.167'
Alligator Reef Light	N 24° 51.100'	W 080° 37.133'
Tennessee Reef Light	N 24° 44.767'	W 080° 46.933'
Coffins Patch Light 20	N 24° 40.550'	W 080° 57.500'
Sombrero Key Light	N 24° 37.667'	W 081° 06.650'
Big Pine Shoal Light 22	N 24° 34.117'	W 081° 19.550'
Looe Key Light 24	N 24° 32.800'	W 081° 24.150'
American Shoal Light	N 24° 31.500'	W 081° 31.167'
Pelican Shoal Light 26	N 24° 30.367'	W 081° 35.983'
Stock Island Approach Channel Light 32	N 24° 28.483'	W 081° 44.533'
Key West Ent. Lighted Whistle Buoy KW	N 24° 27.683'	W 081° 48.033'
Key West NW Chan. Ent. Lig. Bell Buoy 1	N 24° 38.867'	W 081° 53.967'
Sand Key Light	N 24° 27.233'	W 081° 52.650'
Cosgrove Shoal Light	N 24° 27.467'	W 082° 11.100'
Twenty-Eight Foot Shoal Light	N 24° 25.800'	W 082° 25.533'
Halfmoon Shoal Light WR2	N 24° 33.500'	W 082° 28.433'
Rebecca Shoal Light	N 24° 34.733'	W 082° 35.117'

America's Waterway Guide Since 1947

Location	Latitude	Longitude
Dry Tortugas Light	N 24° 38.000'	W 082° 55.233'
New Ground Rocks Light	N 24° 40.000'	W 082° 26.650'
Ellis Rock Light	N 24° 38.950'	W 082° 11.033'
Smith Shoal Light	N 24° 43.100'	W 082° 55.300'

Florida Bay and West Coast

LOCATION	LATITUDE	LONGITUDE
Bullfrog Banks Light BB	N 24° 50.733'	W 081° 20.567'
Arsenic Bank Light 1	N 24° 52.250'	W 080° 53.017'
East Cape Light 2	N 25° 05.000'	W 081° 04.967'
Northwest Cape Light 4	N 25° 12.833'	W 081° 11.750'
Little Shark River Entrance Light 1	N 25° 19.350'	W 081° 09.233'
Broad Creek Light 6	N 25° 26.317'	W 081° 12.200'
Lostmans River Light 8	N 25° 32.567'	W 081° 14.983'
Pavilion Key Light 10	N 25° 40.917'	W 081° 21.400'
Cape Romano Shoals Light	N 25° 41.300'	W 081° 38.783'
Indian Key Pass Light 1	N 25° 47.983'	W 081° 28.067'
Coon Key Light	N 25° 52.900'	W 081° 37.933'
Capri Pass Light 2	N 25° 58.500'	W 081° 46.267'
Gordon Pass Shoal Light	N 26° 05.483'	W 081° 48.683'
San Carlos Bay Light SC	N 26° 25.133'	W 081° 57.550'
Sanibel Island Light	N 26° 27.183'	W 082° 00.850'
Charlotte Harbor Ent. Lig. Bell Buoy 2	N 26° 39.850'	W 082° 19.567'
Venice Inlet Light 1	N 27° 06.767'	W 082° 28.217'
Big Sarasota Pass Light 1	N 27° 15.567'	W 082° 33.767'
New Pass Entrance Light NP	N 27° 18.917'	W 082° 35.883'
Longboat Pass Approach Light LP	N 27° 25.850'	W 082° 41.850'
Southwest Channel Ent. Lig. Bell Buoy 1	N 27° 32.333'	W 082° 48.600'
Tampa Bay Lighted Buoy T	N 27° 35.317'	W 083° 00.717'
Pass-A-Grille Entrance Light PG	N 27° 40.583'	W 082° 46.017'
Johns Pass Light JP	N 27° 46.500'	W 082° 48.033'
Clearwater Pass Channel Light 1	N 27° 58.267'	W 082° 50.850'
Anclote Anchorage South Ent. Light 1	N 28° 08.283'	W 082° 51.950'
Anclote River Entrance Light 1	N 28° 10.383'	W 082° 49.533'
Anclote Anchorage North Ent. Light 2	N 28° 15.050'	W 082° 52.900'
Homosassa Bay Entrance Light 2	N 28° 41.433'	W 082° 48.650'
Crystal River Lighted Buoy 2	N 28° 47.517'	W 082° 58.583'
Withlacoochee River Entrance Light 1	N 28° 58.133'	W 082° 49.717'
Cedar Keys Main Channel Light 1	N 29° 04.000'	W 083° 04.550'
Cedar Keys NW Channel App. Light 2	N 29° 08.483'	W 083° 07.850'
Suwannee River, Alligator Pass Light 2	N 29° 14.583'	W 083° 11.783'
Suwannee R., McGriff Pass Daybeacon 1	N 29° 18.583'	W 083° 12.017'
Steinhatchee River Light 1	N 29° 39.383'	W 083° 27.433'
St. Marks River Lighted Buoy SM	N 30° 04.300'	W 084° 10.800'
Carrabelle Channel Lighted Bell Buoy 2	N 29° 44.550'	W 084° 39.200'
St. George Island W Jetty Lig. Buoy 1	N 29° 36.167'	W 084° 57.217'
St. Joseph Bay Lig. & Ent. Rg. A Rear Lig.	N 29° 55.100'	W 085° 22.833'
St. Andrew Bay Ent. Lig. Whistle Buoy SA	N 30° 05.500'	W 085° 46.433'
Choctawhatchee Bay Ent. Lig. Whi. By CB	N 30° 22.250'	W 086° 30.900'
Pensacola Bay Ent. Lig. Gong Buoy 1	N 30° 16.267'	W 087° 17.550'

Alabama

LOCATION	LATITUDE	LONGITUDE
Perdido Pass Ent. Lig. Whistle Buoy PP	N 30° 15.517'	W 087° 33.400'
Mobile Entrance Lighted Horn Buoy M	N 30° 07.517'	W 088° 04.117'

SOUTHERN EDITION

Skipper's Handbook

Bridge Basics

Bridges have to be factored in when planning a trip. Depending on where you cruise, you may be dependent on bridge openings; a particular bridge's schedule can often decide where you tie up for the evening or when you wake up and get underway the next day. While many are high (over 65 feet) and some usually remain open (such as railroad bridges), others are restricted for different hours in specific months, closed during rush hours and/or open on the quarter-hour, half-hour or even at 20 minutes and 40 minutes past the hour.

To add to the confusion, the restrictions are constantly changing. Just because a bridge opened on a certain schedule last season does not mean it is still on that same schedule. Changes are posted in the Coast Guard's *Local Notice to Mariners* reports, which can be found online at www.navcen.uscg.gov/lnm. It is also a good idea to check locally to verify bridge schedules before your transit.

Measuring Vertical Clearance

Most bridges carry a tide board to register vertical clearance at "low steel" or the lowest point on the bridge. (Note that in the State of Florida waters the tide board figure–and the one noted on the chart–is generally for a point that is 5 feet toward the channel from the bridge fender.) In the case of arched bridges, center channel clearance is frequently higher than the tide gauge registers. Some bridges bear signs noting extra height at center in feet.

Calling a Bridge

Most bridges monitor VHF Channel 13, designated by the Federal Communications Commission as the "bridgetender channel" until you get to South Carolina (southbound), where it changes to VHF Channel 09. (The exception is the locks on the Okeechobee Waterway, which respond to VHF Channel 13).

In any waters, it is a good idea to monitor both the bridge channel and VHF Channel 16–one on your ship's radio and one on a handheld radio, if your main set doesn't have a dual-watch capability–to monitor oncoming commercial traffic and communications with the bridgetender.

Swing bridges have an opening section that pivots horizontally on a central hub, allowing boats to pass on one side or the other when it is open.

Lift bridges normally have two towers on each end of the opening section that are equipped with cables that lift the road or railway vertically into the air.

When using VHF, always call bridges by name and identify your vessel by name and type (such as sailing vessel or trawler) and whether you are traveling north or south. If you are unable to raise the bridge using VHF radio, use a horn signal.

Note that some bridges are not required to open in high winds. If you encounter a bridge that won't open (for whatever reason), it is prudent to drop the hook in a safe spot until the situation is resolved.

Pontoon bridges consists of an opening section that must be floated out of the way with a cable to allow boats to pass. Do not proceed until the cables have had time to sink to the bottom.

Bascule bridges are the most common type of opening bridge you will encounter. The opening section has one or two leaves that tilt vertically on a hinge like doors being opened skyward.

Bridge Procedures:

■ First, decide if it is necessary to have the drawbridge opened. You will need to know your boat's clearance height above the waterline before you start. Drawbridges have "clearance gauges" that show the closed vertical clearance with changing water level but a bascule bridge typically has 3 to 5 feet more clearance than what is indicated on the gauge at the center of its arch at mean low tide. Bridge clearances are also shown on NOAA charts.

■ Contact the bridgetender well in advance (even if you can't see the bridge around the bend) by VHF radio or phone. Alternatively, the proper horn signal for a bridge opening is one prolonged blast (four to six seconds) and one short blast (approximately one second). Bridge operators sound this signal when ready to open the bridge, and then usually the danger signal–five short blasts–when they are closing the bridge. The operator of each vessel is required by law to signal the bridgetender for an opening, even if another vessel has already signaled. Tugs with tows and U.S. government vessels may go through bridges at any time, usually signaling with five short blasts. A restricted bridge may open in an emergency with the same signal. Keep in mind bridgetenders will not know your intentions unless you tell them.

■ If two or more vessels are in sight of one another, the bridgetender may elect to delay opening the bridge until all boats can go through together.

■ Approach at slow speed and be prepared to wait as the bridge cannot open until the traffic gates are closed. Many ICW bridges, for example, are more than 40 years old and the aged machinery functions slowly.

■ Once the bridge is open, proceed at no-wake speed. Keep a safe distance between you and other craft as currents and turbulence around bridge supports can be tricky.

■ There is technically no legal right-of-way (except on the Mississippi and some other inland rivers) but boats running with the current should always be given the right-of-way out of courtesy. As always, if you are not sure, let the other boat go first.

■ When making the same opening as a commercial craft, it is a good idea to contact the vessel's captain (usually on VHF Channel 13), ascertain his intentions and state yours to avoid any misunderstanding in tight quarters.

■ After passing through the bridge, maintain a no-wake speed until you are well clear and then resume normal speed.

Skipper's Handbook

Locks & Locking Through

Many rivers in North America are a series of pools created by dams. When the dams also include locks, navigation is possible beyond the dam. Locks are watertight chambers with gates at each end. They raise and lower boats from one water level to the next. Many cruisers find locking through a pleasant experience and part of the adventure of boating.

Lock Types

- Conventional lift locks are single chambers that raise and lower boats.

- Flight locks are a series of conventional lift locks.

- Hydraulic lift locks have water-filled chambers supported by rams or pistons that move in opposite directions. The movement of one chamber forces the movement of the other via a connected valve. The chamber in the upper position adds sufficient water to cause it to drop, forcing the lower chamber to rise. The chambers have hinged gates fore and aft that contain the water and allow boats to enter or leave.

- Marine railways convey boats over obstacles, usually a landmass, by containing boats in a gantry crane that moves over the land and deposits the boat on the other side of the obstruction.

River locks are usually conventional lift locks. The dam deepens water around shoals and the lock allows vessels to bypass the dam. Conventional lift locks work by gravity alone. Water passively flows into or out of the lock. When the lock is filling, the valve at the upper end of the lock is opened and water flows in. The downstream lock gate is closed, preventing the escape of the water. This is the time of greatest turbulence in the locks and the time of greatest vigilance for boaters. When the upper water level is reached, the upper lock gate opens to allow boats to exit or enter.

When the lock empties, both lock doors are closed, a valve on the lower end of the lock is opened and water exits. This creates a surge of water outside the lock but inside the lock, the water recedes like water in a tub. When the water level in the lock is the same as the lower river level, the lower lock gate opens and vessels leave.

Locking Protocol

Call ahead on VHF Channel 13 (or sound three blasts) for permission to lock through. Indicate whether you are northbound (upbound) or southbound (downbound). Your presence and communication indicate to the locktender your desire to lock through.

Wait a safe distance from the lock or find an anchorage nearby and within sight of the lock.

Prepare for locking by placing large fenders fore and aft and having lines ready. Fender boards are useful because they protect your fenders and provide a skid plate against the dirt and algae on the lock wall.

When approaching the lock, stay back to allow outbound vessels to clear the lock. Do not enter until signaled to do so. Signals vary. Look for a telephone/pull rope at the lock wall; listen for a whistle blast–one long and one short blast or three blasts; look for a "traffic" light–green, yellow or red. Follow directions given by the locktender. The order of priority is:

1. U.S. Military
2. Mail boats
3. Commercial passenger boats
4. Commercial tows
5. Commercial fishermen
6. Pleasure Craft

When the locktender turns on the green light or calls for you to enter, enter in the order that boats arrived at the lock. The longest waiting boat goes first, unless directed by the locktender, who may call boats in according to size and the configuration of the lock. Do not jump the line, do not scoot in front of others and defer to faster boats so you do not have them behind you after you leave the lock.

When entering the lock, leave no wake, heed instruction and respect other boaters. If they are having trouble and appear unsettled, stand by until they are secure. Listen to the directives of the locktenders. Some lock systems require all line handlers to wear personal flotation devices (PFDs). Crew members on the bow should wear PFDs.

You will be directed by the locktender to a place along the lock wall. You will find an inset mooring pin (floating bollard), vertical cable or a rope.

If there is a floating bollard, secure the boat to the pin via a center cleat by wrapping the line around the pin then back to the boat cleat.

If there is a vertical cable, wrap the line around the cable and bring it back to the boat; the loop will ride up or down the cable.

If there is a drop-down line, bring the line around a cleat and hold it. DO NOT TIE THE LINES!

If you are asked to provide a line, throw it to the locktender. After the locktender has secured it, take the bitter end and wrap–but do not tie–around a cleat. Attend the bow and the stern, and adjust the line(s) as the boat rises or falls in the lock chamber.

In crowded locks, move forward as far as you can to make room for others coming in behind you. Small boats may raft to bigger boats. Set adequate fenders for fending off another vessel.

Inside the lock chamber, turn off engines when secure. Exhaust fumes contained in the lock chamber are an irritant to people in small, open boats. Attend the lines at all times. Be prepared for turbulence when the lock fills. Never use hands or feet to fend a boat off a lock wall. Stay alert to other boats. Be prepared to quickly cut a line if needed.

When the lock reaches its determined depth/height, the locktender will loosen the line and drop it to you if you are using a line attached at the top of the lock. After receiving a whistle blast by the locktender, recover any lines used, and prepare to exit. Leave the lock in the same order as entering. Do not rush ahead of those in front of you.

Skipper's Handbook

Bridge & Lock Schedules

KEY:

Statute Miles from ICW Mile 0
Vertical Clearance

Drawbridge clearances are vertical, in feet, when closed and at Mean High Water in tidal areas. Bridge schedules are subject to schedule changes due to repairs, maintenance, events, etc. Check Waterway Explorer at waterwayguide.com for the latest schedules or call ahead.

FLORIDA BRIDGES MONITOR VHF CHANNEL 09

Florida's East Coast ICW

720.7 — 5'
Kingsley Creek Railroad Bridge: Usually open

720.8 — 65'
Thomas J. Shave, Jr. Twin Bridges: (Also known as Kingsley Creek Hwy. Bridges.) Fixed.

739.2 — 65'
SR 105 (Sisters Creek) Bridge: Fixed

St. Johns River

13.1 — 169'
Napoleon Bonaparte Broward Bridge: (Also known as Dames Point Bridge.) Fixed.

21.8 — 86'
John E. Mathews Bridge: Fixed

22.8 — 135'
Isaiah D. Hart Bridge: (Also known as Hart-Commodore Point Bridge.) Fixed.

24.7 — 40'
Main Street Bridge: Opens on signal except from 7:00 a.m. to 8:30 a.m. and from 4:30 p.m. to 6:00 p.m., Mon. through Sat. (except federal holidays), when the draw need not open.

24.8 — 75'
Acosta Bridge: Fixed

24.9 — 5'
Florida East Coast Railroad Bridge: Usually open, displaying flashing green lights to indicate that vessels may pass. When a train approaches, large signs on both the upstream and downstream sides of the bridge flash "Bridge Coming Down," the lights go to flashing red, and siren signals sound. After an 8-minute delay, the draw lowers and locks if there are no vessels under the draw. The draw remains down for a period of 8 min. or while the approach track circuit is occupied. After the train has cleared, the draw opens and the lights return to flashing green.

25.5 — 75'
Fuller Warren Bridge: Fixed

35.1 — 65'
Henry H. Buckman, Sr (I-295) Bridge: (Also known as Three-Mile Bridge.) Fixed.

52.4 — 45'
Shands Bridge: Fixed. (Note: A new fixed 65-foot vertical clearance bridge has been in the planning stages for several years.)

81.5 — 65'
Memorial Bridge: Fixed

91.8 — 7'
Buffalo Bluff Railroad Bridge: Usually open. Remotely operated.

119.9 — 20'
Astor Bridge: Opens on signal. (Note: Open bascule overhangs channel at a height of 72 feet.)

136.1 — 15'
SR 44 (Whitehair) Bridge: Opens on signal

155.7 — 7'
CFRC (SunRail) Railroad Bridge: Usually open

155.8 — 45'
US 17/US 92 Bridge: Fixed

156.6 — 45'
I-4 (St. Johns River Veterans Memorial) Bridges: Fixed

Florida's East Coast ICW (cont.)

742.1 — 65'
Wonderwood Dr. (SR 116) Bridges: Fixed

744.7 — 65'
Atlantic Twin Bridges: Fixed

747.5 — 65'
B.B. McCormick (U. 90) Bridge: (Also known as Jacksonville Beach Bridge.) Fixed.

749.5 — 65'
Butler Boulevard (SR 202) Bridge: (Also known as Pablo Creek Bridge.) Fixed.

758.8 — 65'
Palm Valley (SR 210) Bridge: Fixed

775.8 — 65'
Francis and Mary Usina (SR A1A/Vilano) Bridge: Fixed

777.9 — 18'
Bridge of Lions (SR A1A): Opens on signal, except from 7:00 a.m. to 6:00 p.m., when the draw need only open on the hour and half-hour; however, the draw need not open at 8:00 a.m., 12 noon and 5:00 p.m. Mon. through Fri. (except federal holidays). In addition, from 7:00 a.m. to 6:00 p.m. on Sat., Sun. and federal holidays, the draw need only open only on the hour and half-hour (904-824-7372). (Note: Additional 4 feet of vertical clearance observed at center of bridge.)

FLORIDA BRIDGES MONITOR VHF CHANNEL 09

780.3 / 65' — **SR 312 Bridges:** Fixed

788.6 / 25' — **Crescent Beach (SR 206) Bridge:** Opens on signal (904-461-4094)

803.0 / 65' — **Hammock Dunes Bridge:** (Also known as Palm Coast Hwy. Bridge.) Fixed.

810.6 / 65' — **SR 100 (Moody Blvd./Flagler) Bridge:** Fixed

816.0 / 15' — **L.B. Knox Bridge:** (Also known as Bulow Bridge.) Opens on signal (386-441-0777)

824.9 / 65' — **SR 40 Bridge:** (Also known as Ormond Beach Bridge.) Fixed.

829.1 / 65' — **Seabreeze Bridges:** Fixed

829.7 / 22' — **Main Street Bridge:** Opens on signal (386-441-0777)

830.1 / 65' — **International Speedway Blvd. Bridge:** Fixed

830.6 / 65' — **Memorial Bridge:** Fixed

835.5 / 65' — **A1A Port Orange Relief Bridge:** (Also known as Dunlawton Ave. Bridge.) Fixed.

845.0 / 24' — **George E. Musson/Coronado Beach (SR 44) Bridge:** Opens on signal, except from 7:00 a.m. until 7:00 p.m. daily, when the draw opens only on the hour and half hour. 386-424-2024. (Note: This is a hydraulic bridge and may be slow in opening.)

846.5 / 65' — **Harris Saxon (South Causeway) Bridge:** (Also known as New Smyrna Bridge.) Fixed.

869.2 / 27' — **Allenhurst (Haulover Canal) Bridge:** Opens on signal (321-867-4859). (Note: This is a manatee feeding area. Proceed slowly.)

876.6 / 7' — **NASA (Jay-Jay) Railroad Bridge:** Usually open and displaying flashing green lights to indicate that vessels may pass. When a train approaches, the lights go to flashing red, and the draw lowers and locks if there are no vessels under the draw. The draw remains down for a period of 5 min. or while the approach track circuit is occupied. After the train has cleared, the draw opens and the lights return to flashing green.

878.9 / 65' — **A. Max Brewer (SR 406) Bridge:** Fixed

885.0 / 66' — **NASA Causeway (SR 405) Bridge:** (Also known as Indian River or Addison Point Bridge.) Fixed.

894.0 / 65' — **Bennett Causeway Bridges:** Fixed

897.4 / 65' — **Hubert Humphrey (FL 520) Bridges:** (Also known as Merritt Island or Cocoa Twin Bridges.) Fixed.

909.0 / 65' — **Pineda Causeway Bridge:** Fixed

914.4 / 65' — **Eau Gallie Causeway (SR 518) Bridge:** Fixed

918.2 / 65' — **Melbourne Causeway (SR 192) Bridges:** Fixed

943.3 / 65' — **Wabasso Bridge:** Fixed

951.9 / 66' — **Merrill P. Barber (SR 60) Bridge:** (Also known as Vero Beach Bridge.) Fixed.

953.2 / 65' — **Alma Lee Loy (SR 656/17th St.) Bridge:** Fixed

964.8 / 26' — **SR A1A North Causeway (Banty Saunders) Bridge:** Opens on hour and half-hour (772-468-3993).

965.8 / 65' — **Peter B. Cobb Memorial (SR A1A) Bridge:** (Also known as Fort Pierce Bridge.) Fixed.

981.4 / 65' — **Jensen Beach Causeway (Frank A. Wacha/SR 707A) Bridge:** Fixed

984.9 / 65' — **Ernest Lyons (SR A1A) Bridge:** Fixed

Skipper's Handbook

OKEECHOBEE LOCKS MONITOR — CHANNEL 13

Okeechobee Waterway (East to West)

3.4 / 65' — **Evans Crary (SR A1A) Bridge:** Fixed

7.3 / 65' — **Roosevelt (US 1) Bridge:** Fixed

7.4 / 7' — **Florida East Coast Railroad Bridge:** Usually in the fully open position, displaying flashing green lights to indicate that vessels may pass. When a train approaches, the navigation lights go to flashing red and a horn sounds four blasts, pauses, and then repeats four blasts. After an 8-min. delay, the draw lowers and locks, if there are no vessels under the draw. The draw remains down for a period of 8 min. or while the approach track circuit is occupied. After the train has cleared, the draw opens and the lights return to flashing green. Note: Only 50 feet of charted horizontal clearance.

7.4 / 14' — **Old Roosevelt (Dixie Highway) Bridge:** Opens on signal. The draw opens on signal, except from 7:00 a.m. to 6:00 p.m., Mon. through Fri. (except federal holidays), when the draw need open only on the hour and half hour. However, the draw need not open between 7:30 a.m. and 9:00 a.m. and 4:00 p.m. and 5:30 p.m. except at 8:15 a.m. and 4:45 p.m. On Saturdays, Sundays, and federal holidays from 8:00 a.m. to 6:00 p.m. the draw need open only on the hour, 20 minutes after the hour, and 40 minutes after the hour. When the adjacent railway bridge is in the closed position at the time of a scheduled opening the draw need not open, but it must then open immediately upon opening of the railroad bridge to pass all accumulated vessels. 772-692-0321

9.5 / 54' — **Palm City (SR 714) Bridge:** Fixed

10.9 / 55' — **Southwest Martin Highway Bridge:** Fixed

14.0 / 56' — **I-95 Twin Bridges:** Fixed

14.5 / 55' — **Florida Turnpike Bridges:** Fixed

15.1 — **St. Lucie Lock:** Opens on signal, 7:00 a.m. to 5:00 p.m. Last lockage at 4:30 p.m. Normally make fast on south wall. 772-287-2665

17.1 / 56' — **SR 76A Bridge:** Fixed

28.1 / 55' — **Indiantown (SR 710) Bridge:** Fixed

28.2 / 7' — **Seaboard System Railroad Bridge:** (Also known as Indiantown Railroad Bridge.) Remains in open to navigation position from 7:00 a.m. to 7:00 p.m. unless a train is coming. At all other times, swing bridge will only open with 3-hour advance notice. Remotely operated. 772-597-3822

38.0 / 7' — **Florida East Coast Railroad Bridge:** Usually in the fully open position, displaying flashing green lights to indicate that vessels may pass. When a train approaches, it will stop and a crewmember will observe the waterway for approaching vessels, which will be allowed to pass. Upon manual signal, the bridge lights will go to flashing red, and the horn will sound four blasts, pause then repeat four blasts. The draw will lower and lock, if there are no vessels under the draw. After the train has cleared, the draw will open, and the lights will return to flashing green. (Note: Vertical clearance when open is 49 feet, setting the overhead clearance for the OCWW.) Remotely operated.

38.8 / 55' — **US 98/441 Bridge:** Fixed

39.1 — **Port Mayaca Lock:** Opens on signal, 7:00 a.m. to 5:00 p.m. Last lockage at 4:30 p.m. Normally make fast on south wall. 561-924-2858

60.7 / 11' — **Torry Island (CR 717) Bridge:** Opens on signal from 7:00 a.m. to 6:00 p.m., Mon. through Thurs., and from 7:00 a.m. to 7:00 p.m., Fri. through Sun. At all other times, the draw need not open for the passage of vessels. Manual operation. (May not open in winds in excess of 20 mph.) 561-996-3844

75.5 — **Clewiston Lock:** Normally open. If the lock is closed due to high lake levels, an operator will be on site.

78.0 — **Julian Keen Jr. (Moore Haven) Lock:** Opens on signal, 7:00 a.m. to 5:00 p.m. Last lockage at 4:30 p.m. Normally make fast on south wall. 863-946-0414

78.3 / 5' — **Seaboard System Railroad Bridge:** Opens on signal, except from 10:00 p.m. to 6:00 a.m., when the draw need not open. (Note: Normally open. Manual operation.)

78.4 / 55' — **Moore Haven (US 27) Bridges:** Fixed

93.5 — **Ortona Lock:** Opens on signal, 7:00 a.m. to 5:00 p.m. Last lockage at 4:30 p.m. Normally make fast on south wall. 863-946-0414

FLORIDA BRIDGES MONITOR VHF CHANNEL 09

103.0 / 28' — **La Belle (SR 29) Bridge:** Opens on signal, except from 7:00 a.m. to 9:00 a.m. and from 4:00 p.m. to 6:00 p.m., Mon. through Fri. (except federal holidays), when the bridge need not open. From 10:00 p.m. to 6:00 a.m. the bridge will open on signal only if at least 3-hour notice is given. 863-674-4663

108.2 / 9' — **Fort Denaud Bridge:** Opens on signal, except from 10:00 p.m. to 6:00 a.m., when the bridge will open on signal only if at least 3-hour notice is given. 863-675-2055

116.0 / 23' — **Alva Drawbridge:** Opens on signal, except from 10:00 p.m. to 6:00 a.m., when the bridge will open on signal only if at least 3-hour notice is given. 239-278-2704

121.4 — **W.P. Franklin Lock:** Opens on signal from 7:00 a.m. to 5:00 p.m. Last lockage at 4:30 p.m. Normally make fast on south wall. 239-694-5451

126.3 / 27' — **Wilson Pigott Drawbridge:** Opens on signal, except from 10:00 p.m. to 6:00 a.m., when the bridge will open on signal only if at least 3-hour notice is given.

128.9 / 55' — **I-75 Bridges:** Fixed

129.9 / 5' — **SCL Railroad Bridge:** Usually open. (Note: Span overhangs channel when open, resulting in a vertical clearance of 55 feet.)

134.6 / 56' — **Edison Bridges:** Fixed

135 / 55' — **US 41/Caloosahatchee River Bridge:** Fixed

138.6 / 55' — **Midpoint Memorial Bridge:** Fixed

142 / 55' — **Cape Coral Bridge:** Fixed

Florida's East Coast ICW (cont.)

995.9 / 21' — **Hobe Sound (SR 708) Bridge:** Opens on signal (772-546-5234).

1004.1 / 25' — **Jupiter Island (CR 707) Bridge:** Opens on signal (561-746-4261). (Hail as "707 Bridge.")

1004.8 / 26' — **US 1 (Jupiter) Bridge:** Opens on signal (561-746-4907).

1006.2 / 35' — **Indiantown (SR 706) Bridge:** Opens on the hour and half-hour.

1009.3 / 35' — **Donald Ross Bridge:** Opens on the hour and half-hour (561-626-3030).

1012.6 / 24' — **PGA Boulevard Bridge:** Opens on the hour and half-hour (561-626-3030).

1013.7 / 25' — **Parker (US 1) Bridge:** Opens on the quarter and three-quarter hour (561-626-5445).

1017.2 / 65' — **Blue Heron (SR A1A) Bridge:** Fixed

1021.8 / 21' — **Flagler Memorial (SR A1A) Bridge:** Opens on the quarter hour and three-quarter hour. When the security zone is enforced, the draw will remain closed to navigation from 2:15 p.m. to 5:30 p.m. with the exception of a once an hour opening at 2:15 p.m., 3:15 p.m., 4:15 p.m. and 5:15 p.m. (weekdays only) if vessels request an opening (561-833-7339).

1022.6 / 21' — **Royal Park (SR 704) Bridge:** Opens on the hour and half-hour. When the security zone is enforced, the draw will remain closed to navigation from 2:15 p.m. to 5:30 p.m. with the exception of a once an hour opening at 2:15 p.m., 3:15 p.m., 4:15 p.m. and 5:15 p.m. (weekdays only) if vessels request an opening (561-655-5617).

1024.7 / 25' — **Southern Boulevard (SR 700/80) Bridge:** Opens on the quarter hour and three-quarter hour (863-224-5706). When the security zone is enforced, the draw may be closed without advance notice.

1028.8 / 35' — **Lake Ave. (SR 802) Bridge:** Opens on signal (561-540-2516).

1031.0 / 21' — **E. Ocean Ave. (Lantana) Bridge:** Opens on the hour and half-hour (561-582-2320).

1035.0 / 21' — **E. Ocean Ave. (Boynton Beach) Bridge:** Opens on the hour and half-hour (561-733-0214).

1035.8 / 25' — **E. Woolbright Rd. (SE 15th St.) Bridge:** Opens on signal (561-732-6461).

1038.7 / 9' — **George Bush Boulevard Bridge:** Opens on signal (561-276-5948).

1039.6 / 12' — **Atlantic Ave. (SR 806) Bridge:** Opens on the quarter hour and three-quarter hour (561-276-5435).

1041.0 / 30' — **Linton Boulevard Bridge:** Opens on the hour and half-hour (561-278-1980). (Note: Clearance is at center. Low vertical clearance is 26 feet.)

SOUTHERN EDITION

Skipper's Handbook

FLORIDA BRIDGES MONITOR VHF CHANNEL 09

1044.9 / 25' — **Spanish River Boulevard Bridge:** Opens on the hour and half-hour (561-395-5417).

1047.5 / 19' — **Palmetto Park Bridge:** Opens on the hour and half-hour (561-392-5903).

23' — **Boca Inlet (Haven Ashe) Bridge (to ocean):** (Also known as Boca Raton Inlet Bridge.) Opens on signal.

1048.2 / 9' — **Camino Real Bridge:** Opens on the hour, 20 min. past the hour and 40 min. past the hour (561-395-7132).

1050.0 / 21' — **Hillsboro Boulevard (SR 810) Bridge:** Opens on the hour and half-hour (954-428-1090).

13' — **SR A1A (Hillsboro Inlet) Bridge (to ocean):** Opens on signal, except from 7:00 a.m. to 6:00 p.m., when the draw need only open on the hour, quarter hour, half-hour, and three-quarter hour.

1055.0 / 15' — **NE 14th Street Bridge:** Opens on the quarter hour and three-quarter hour (954-942-6909).

1056.0 / 15' — **Atlantic Boulevard (SR 814) Bridge:** Opens on the hour and half-hour (954-941-7119).

1059.0 / 15' — **Commercial Boulevard (SR 870) Bridge:** Opens on the hour and half-hour (954-772-3987).

1060.5 / 22' — **Oakland Park Boulevard Bridge:** Opens on the quarter hour and three-quarter hour (954-566-3711).

1062.6 / 25' — **East Sunrise Boulevard (SR 838) Bridge:** Opens on the hour and half hour (954-564-6986). On the first Sat. in May, the draw need not open from 9:45 p.m. to 10:45 p.m. The draw also need not open from 4:00 p.m. to 6:00 p.m. on both Sat. and Sun. of that weekend.

1064.0 / 24' — **East Las Olas Boulevard Bridge:** Opens on the quarter hour and three-quarter hour (954-463-0842).

New River (North Fork)

1.4 / 16' — **SE 3rd Avenue Bridge:** The draw opens on signal, except from 7:30 a.m. to 9:00 a.m. and 4:30 p.m. to 6:00 p.m., Mon. through Fri. (except federal holidays), when the draw need not open.

2.3 / 21' — **Andrews Avenue Bridge:** The draw opens on signal, except from 7:30 a.m. to 9:00 a.m. and 4:30 p.m. to 6:00 p.m., Mon. through Fri. (except federal holidays), when the draw need not open. The draw need not open for inbound vessels when the draw of the Florida East Coast Railroad Bridge is in the closed position for the passage of a train.

2.5 / 4' — **Florida East Coast Railroad Bridge:** Usually in the fully open position, displaying flashing green lights to indicate that vessels may pass. When a train approaches, the navigation lights go to flashing red and a horn sounds four blasts, pauses, and then repeats four blasts then the draw lowers and locks. After the train has cleared, the draw opens and the lights return to flashing green. The bridge shall not be closed more than 60 minutes combined for any 120-minute time period beginning at 12:01 a.m.

2.7 / 20' — **William H. Marshall (7th Avenue) Bridge:** The draw opens on signal, except from 7:30 a.m. to 9:00 a.m. and 4:30 p.m. to 6:00 p.m., Mon. through Fri. (except federal holidays), when the draw need not open.

New River (South Fork)

0.9 / 21' — **Davie Boulevard Bridge:** The draw opens on signal, except from 7:30 a.m. to 9:00 a.m. and 4:30 p.m. to 6:00 p.m., Mon. through Fri. (except federal holidays), when the draw need not open.

2.0 / 55' — **I-95 Twin Bridges:** Fixed

2.1 / 2' — **SCL Railroad Bridge:** Opens on signal. Usually open if no train is approaching.

4.4 / 21' — **SR 84 Bridge:** Opens on signal if at least a 24 hour notice is given. Call 954-776-4300 (no VHF).

4.5 / 40' — **I-595 Bridge:** Fixed

America's Waterway Guide Since 1947

FLORIDA BRIDGES MONITOR VHF CHANNEL 09

Florida's East Coast ICW (cont.)

1065.9 / 55' — **SE 17th Street (Brooks Memorial) Bridge:** Opens on the hour and half-hour (954-524-7783).

1069.4 / 22' — **Dania Beach Boulevard (SR A1A) Bridge:** Opens on the hour and half-hour (954-922-7833).

1070.5 / 21' — **Sheridan Street Bridge:** Opens on the quarter hour and three-quarter hour (954-922-7833).

1072.2 / 25' — **Hollywood Beach Boulevard (SR 820) Bridge:** Opens on the hour and half-hour (954-922-3366).

1074.0 / 26' — **Hallandale Beach Boulevard (SR 858) Bridge:** Opens on the quarter hour and three-quarter hour (954-456-6630).

1076.3 / 65' — **William Lehman Causeway (SR 856) Bridge:** Fixed

1078.0 / 30' — **NE 163rd Street (SR 826) Bridge:** (Also known as Sunny Isles Bridge.) Opens on signal, except from 7:00 a.m. to 6:00 p.m., Mon. through Fri. (except federal holidays) and from 10:00 a.m. to 6:00 p.m. on Sat., Sun., and federal holidays, when the draw need open only on the quarter hour and three-quarter hour.

32' — **Bakers Haulover Inlet Bridge (to ocean):** Fixed

1081.4 / 16' — **Broad Causeway Bridge:** Opens on signal, except from 8:00 a.m. to 6:00 p.m., when the draw need open only on the quarter hour and three-quarter hour (305-891-2221).

1084.6 / 25' — **West 79th Street Bridge:** Opens on signal, except from 7:00 a.m. to 7:00 p.m., Mon. through Fri. (except federal holidays), when the draw need only open on the hour and half hour (305-758-1834).

1087.2 / 56' — **Julia Tuttle Causeway Bridge:** Fixed (Note: Bridge is less than standard ICW vertical clearance of 64 feet and sets the controlling vertical clearance for the ICW.)

1088.6 / 12' — **Venetian Causeway Bridge (West):** Opens on signal, except from 7:00 a.m. to 7:00 p.m., Mon. through Fri. (except federal holidays), when the bridge need only open on the hour and half-hour (305-358-6258).

1088.8 / 65' — **MacArthur Causeway Bridges:** Fixed

1089.3 / 65' — **Dodge Island Bridges:** Fixed

1089.4 / 22' — **Dodge Island Railroad Bridge:** Usually open (unless train is approaching).

Miami River

23' / 0.1 — **Brickell Avenue Bridge:** Opens on signal, except from 7:00 a.m. to 7:00 p.m., Mon. through Fri. (except federal holidays), when the draw need only open on the hour and half-hour; however, from 7:35 a.m. to 8:59 a.m., 12:05 p.m. to 12:59 p.m. and 4:35 p.m. to 5:59 p.m., the draw need not open.

75' / 0.2 — **Metro Train Bridge:** Fixed

21' / 0.3 — **South Miami Avenue Bridge:** Opens on signal, except from 7:35 a.m. to 8:59 a.m., 12:05 p.m. to 12:59 p.m. and 4:35 p.m. to 5:59 p.m., Mon. through Fri. (except federal holidays), when the draw need not open.

75' / 0.4 — **Retro Rail/M Path Bridge:** Fixed

11' / 0.5 — **SW Second Avenue Bridge:** Opens on signal, except from 7:35 a.m. to 8:59 a.m., 12:05 p.m. to 12:59 p.m. and 4:35 p.m. to 5:59 p.m., Mon. through Fri. (except federal holidays), when the draw need not open.

75' / 0.6 — **I-95 Twin Bridges:** Fixed

18' / 0.9 — **SW 1st Street Bridge:** Opens on signal, except from 7:35 a.m. to 8:59 a.m. and 4:35 p.m. to 5:59 p.m., Mon. through Fri. (except federal holidays), when the draw need not open.

35' / 1.0 — **West Flagler Street Bridge:** Opens on signal, except from 7:35 a.m. to 8:59 a.m. and 4:35 p.m. to 5:59 p.m., Mon. through Fri. (except federal holidays), when the draw need not open.

12' / 0.5 — **NW 5th Street Bridge:** Opens on signal, except from 7:35 a.m. to 8:59 a.m. and 4:35 p.m. to 5:59 p.m., Mon. through Fri. (except federal holidays), when the draw need not open.

22' / 2.0 — **NW 12th Avenue Bridge:** Opens on signal, except from 7:35 a.m. to 8:59 a.m. and 4:35 p.m. to 5:59 p.m., Mon. through Fri. (except federal holidays), when the draw need not open.

75' / 2.2 — **Dolphin Expressway Bridge:** Fixed

17' / 2.6 — **NW 17th Avenue Bridge:** Opens on signal, except from 7:35 a.m. to 8:59 a.m. and 4:35 p.m. to 5:59 p.m., Mon. through Fri. (except federal holidays), when the draw need not open.

25' / 3.2 — **NW 22nd Avenue Bridge:** Opens on signal, except from 7:35 a.m. to 8:59 a.m. and 4:35 p.m. to 5:59 p.m., Mon. through Fri. (except federal holidays), when the draw need not open.

21' / 3.5 — **NW 27th Avenue Bridge:** Opens on signal, except from 7:35 a.m. to 8:59 a.m. and 4:35 p.m. to 5:59 p.m., Mon. through Fri. (except federal holidays), when the draw need not open.

SOUTHERN EDITION

Skipper's Handbook

FLORIDA BRIDGES MONITOR CHANNEL 09

Florida Keys

1091.6 / 76' — **Rickenbacker Causeway Bridge:** Fixed

1126.9 / 65' — **Card Sound Road Bridge:** Fixed

1134.1 / 65' — **Jewfish Creek (US 1) Bridge:** Fixed

1152.0 / 15' — **Tavernier Creek Bridge:** Fixed

1156.0 / 27' — **Snake Creek Bridge:** Opens on signal, except from 8:00 a.m. to 6:00 p.m., when the draw need open only on the hour.

1157.0 / 10' — **Whale Harbor Channel Bridge:** Fixed

1162.0 / 7' — **Teatable Key Relief Bridge:** Fixed

1162.1 / 10' — **Teatable Key Channel Bridge:** Fixed

1163.0 / 27' — **Indian Key Channel Bridge:** Fixed

1164.5 / 10' — **Lignumvitae Channel Bridge:** Fixed

1168.5 / 10' — **Channel Two Bridge:** Fixed

1170.0 / 65' — **Channel Five Bridge:** Fixed

1176.0 / 23' — **Long Key Viaduct Bridge:** Fixed

1179.0 / 8' — **Toms Harbor Cut Bridge:** Fixed

1180.0 / 7' — **Toms Harbor Channel Bridge:** Fixed

1188.0 / 13' — **Vaca Cut Bridge:** Fixed

1194.0 / 19' — **Knight Key Channel Bridge:** Fixed

1197.0 / 65' — **Seven Mile Bridge:** (Also known as Moser Channel Bridge.) Fixed.

1205.0 / 20' — **Bahia Honda Bridges:** Fixed

1209.0 / 11' — **Spanish Harbor Channel Bridge:** Fixed

1215.0 / 15' — **Pine Channel Bridge:** (Also known as Little Torch Key Bridge.) Fixed.

1215.0 / 40' — **Niles Channel Bridge:** Fixed

1217.5 / 15' — **Kemp Channel Bridge:** Fixed

Florida's Gulf ICW (GIWW)

34.3 / 22' — **Boca Grande Swing Bridge:** Opens on signal, except from 7:00 a.m. to 6:00 p.m., Mon. through Fri., when the draw opens on the hour and half-hour. On Sat., Sun. and federal holidays, the draw opens every 15 min. (Note: Vessels must request an opening.)

43.5 / 26' — **Tom Adams Bridge:** (Also known as Manasota Key Bridge.) Opens on signal.

49.9 / 26' — **Manasota Bridge:** Opens on signal.

54.9 / 25' — **Tamiami Trail (Circus) Bridges:** Opens on signal.

56.6 / 30' — **Venice Avenue Bridge:** Opens on signal, except from 7:00 a.m. to 4:30 p.m., Mon. through Fri. (except holidays), when the draw opens only at 10 min. after the hour, 30 min. after the hour and 50 min. after the hour. Between 4:35 p.m. and 5:35 p.m., the draw need not open.

56.9 / 30' — **Hatchett Creek (US 41) Bridge:** Opens on signal, except from 7:00 a.m. to 4:20 p.m., Mon. through Fri. (except federal holidays), when the draw opens only on the hour, 20 min. after the hour and 40 min. after the hour. Between 4:25 p.m. and 5:25 p.m., the draw need not open. On Sat., Sun. and federal holidays from 7:30 a.m. to 6:00 p.m., the draw will open only on the hour and every 15 min. thereafter.

59.3 / 14' — **Albee Road Bridge:** (Also known as Casey Key Bridge.) Opens on signal.

63.0 / 9' — **Blackburn Point Swing Bridge:** Opens on signal.

68.6 / 18' — **Stickney Point (SR 72) Bridge:** Opens on signal, except from 6:00 a.m. to 7:00 p.m. daily, when the draw need open only on the hour and half hour.

71.6 / 25' — **Siesta Drive Bridge:** Opens on signal, except from 6:00 a.m. to 7:00 p.m. daily, when the draw need open only on the hour and half hour.

73.6 / 65' — **Ringling Causeway (SR 789) Bridge:** Fixed

23' — **New Pass (SR 789) Bridge (to Gulf):** The draw need only open on the hour, 20 min. past the hour, and 40 min. past the hour from 7:00 a.m. to 6:00 p.m. From 6:00 p.m. to 7:00 a.m., the bridge will open on signal only if at least 3-hour notice is given.

17' — **Longboat Pass (SR 789) Bridge (to Gulf):** Opens on signal.

FLORIDA BRIDGES MONITOR VHF CHANNEL 09

Mile	Vert. Clear.	Bridge
87.4	22'	**Cortez (SR 684) Bridge:** Opens on signal, except from 6:00 a.m. to 7:00 p.m. daily, when the draw need open only on the quarter hour and three-quarter hour.
89.2	24'	**Anna Maria (SR 64/Manatee Ave. West) Bridge:** Opens on signal, except from 6:00 a.m. to 7:00 p.m. daily, when the draw need open only on the quarter hour and three-quarter hour.
98.8	180'	**Bob Graham Sunshine Skyway Bridge (to Tampa Bay):** Fixed
110.5	65'	**Maximo Bridge:** Fixed
113.0	65'	**Pinellas Bayway Structure 'E' Bridge:** Fixed
114.0	65'	**Pinellas Bayway Structure 'C' Bridge:** Fixed (Note: May be less than charted clearance.)
114.0	11'	**Pinellas Bayway Structure 'B' Bridge:** Fixed
114.0	18'	**Pinellas Bayway Structure 'A' Bridge:** Fixed
117.7	23'	**Corey Causeway (SR 693) Bridge:** Opens on signal, except from 8:00 a.m. to 7:00 p.m., Mon. through Fri., and from 10:00 a.m. to 7:00 p.m., Sat., Sun. and federal holidays, when the draw need only open only on the hour, 20 min. after the hour and 40 min. after the hour.
118.9	21'	**Treasure Island Causeway Bridge:** Opens on signal, except from 7:00 a.m. to 7:00 p.m., Mon. through Fri., when the draw will open on the hour, 20 min. after the hour and 40 min. after the hour and on the quarter hour and three-quarter hour on Sat., Sun. and federal holidays.
	27'	**Johns Pass Drawbridge (to Gulf):** Opens on signal.
122.8	25'	**Welch Causeway (SR 699) Bridge:** Opens on signal, except from 7:00 a.m. to 7:00 p.m. on Sat., Sun. and federal holidays, when the draw opens only on the hour, 20 min. after the hour and 40 min. after the hour.
126.6	20'	**Park Boulevard North Bridge:** Opens on signal.
129.3	25'	**Indian Rocks Beach Bridge:** Opens on signal.
131.8	75'	**Belleair Causeway Bridge:** Fixed
	74'	**Sand Key Pass Bridge (to Gulf):** (Also known as Clearwater Pass Bridge.) Fixed.
136.0	74'	**Clearwater Memorial Causeway Bridge:** Fixed
141.9	24'	**Dunedin Causeway Drawbridge:** Opens on signal. (Note: May be closer to 18 feet than charted clearance.)

GIWW, East of Harvey Lock (EHL)

Mile	Vert. Clear.	Bridge
361.4	65'	**Bryant Patton (SR 300) Bridge:** (Also known as Apalachicola–St. George Island Bridge.) Fixed.
351.4	65'	**John Gorrie Memorial (US 98) Bridge:** Fixed
347.0	11'	**Apalachicola Northern Railroad Bridge:** Swing bridge maintained in the fully open-to-navigation position and untended.
329.3	65'	**Elgin Bayless (SR 71) Bridge:** (Also known as White City Bridge.) Fixed.
	75'	**US 98/SR 30 Bridge (to Gulf):** (Also known as Port St. Joe Bridge.) Fixed.
315.4	65'	**Overstreet (SR 386) Bridge:** Fixed
295.4	50'	**Dupont (US 98) Bridge:** Fixed
284.6	65'	**Hathaway (US 98) Bridge:** Fixed
271.8	65'	**West Bay Creek (SR 79) Bridge:** Fixed
250.3	65'	**Clyde B. Wells & Choctawhatchee Bay (US 331/SR 83) Bridge:** Fixed
234.3	64'	**Mid-Bay (SR 293) Bridge:** Fixed
	49'	**William T. Marler (US 98/SR 30) Bridge (to Gulf):** (Also known as Destin Bridge.) Fixed.
223.1	50'	**Brooks Memorial Bridge:** Fixed
206.7	50'	**Navarre Beach Causeway (CR 399) Bridge:** Fixed
189.1	65'	**Bob Sikes (Pensacola Beach/SR 399) Bridge:** Fixed
171.8	73'	**Gulf Beach Highway (SR 292) Bridge:** Fixed

ALABAMA BRIDGES MONITOR VHF CHANNEL 13

Mile	Vert. Clear.	Bridge
	54'	**Perdido Pass (SR 182) Channel Bridge (to Gulf):** Fixed
158.7	73'	**Foley Beach Expressway Bridge:** Fixed
154.9	73'	**Gulf Shores Parkway (SR 59) Bridges:** Fixed
127.8	83'	**Dauphin Island Causeway Bridges:** Fixed

SOUTHERN EDITION

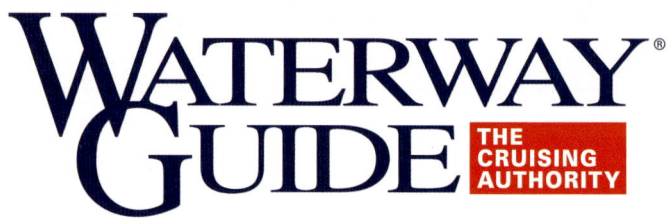

Scan to subscribe now at
www.waterwayguide.com

Navigate with the Cruising Authority

Inlets: St. Johns River Entrance to Mobile Bay

Introduction

Intracoastal Waterway (ICW): Cruising the "inside waterway" (the ICW) is a bit like driving down I-95. There are areas where every amenity and convenience you need is but an exit away (especially in FL), and then there are stretches with only marsh and woods as far as the eye can see (mostly in SC and GA). And like I-95 there is constant construction, varying speed-restricted areas, and many bridges to pass under or through. The main difference between the highway and the waterway is the "road maintenance." With federal funding for dredging being scarce, shoaling has been more commonplace on the ICW and the "projected depths" on the NOAA charts can no longer be considered valid. This, alone, will drive (pun intended) some vessels to take the offshore (Atlantic Ocean) route.

Gulf Intracoastal Waterway (GIWW): The GIWW is the inland route that runs from Cape Coral FL, to Brownsville, TX, with an open-water gap between Tarpon Springs and Carrabelle, FL. As on the ICW, distances are measured in statute miles. The GIWW is either a dredged channel behind barrier islands or a passage through one of Florida's large Gulf Coast bays. Much of the waterway is constrained to a narrow marked channel with shoals lurking just outside the buoys. While the option of an "inside route" is reassuring, many cruisers make the trip northward on the Gulf as a series of open water hops. Seas are generally manageable in the shallow off-shore waters and refuge can be sought at regular intervals.

Offshore Runs: Some boaters choose the offshore run to save time or to get a break from the bridge openings and speed restrictions. Many sailboats will take this option to turn off the engine and unfurl the sails. You may be forced to take the offshore route due to vessel draft or vertical clearance. Regardless of your reasons for exiting the inland waterways, there are numerous inlets along both Atlantic Ocean and Gulf coasts that will allow you to duck in or back out should the weather turn.

Cautions & Warnings: Keep in mind that not all inlets are navigable and some are treacherous under certain conditions. This section will assist you in recognizing those but it is still important to study the charts, pay attention to the weather and seek current local knowledge before proceeding on an offshore run. Be sure to check for a suitable weather window and plan your passage based on inlets with sufficient depth.

Before you begin an offshore passage, take an honest accounting of your vessel, your crew and yourself. Is each of you up to the task? Is the vessel properly outfitted? Do you have the necessary safety equipment, charts, long distance communications gear such as single sideband radio (SSB), an Emergency Position Indicating Radio Beacon (EPIRB) and life raft? Do you

SOUTHERN EDITION

Inlets: St. Johns River Entrance to Mobile Bay

and your crew have adequate experience in boating and navigation to attempt an offshore coastal passage?

Check the weather using as many sources as possible. If you have access to weather routing services, they are a good option, particularly for longer offshore passages. You are seeking a weather window with enough space on each side to get you safely out and back in, with room for unexpected contingencies.

Of course, always file a float plan with a reliable person. A sample float plan is provided in the Skippers Handbook of this guide. You might also look into the free app BoatSafe Free, which allows you to create a float plan and email it to participants or emergency contacts.

Entering & Exiting: Plan your trip so that you enter in daylight, with the tide, particularly if your boat is slow or underpowered. Remember that wind against tide can create short, steep waves in an inlet that can quickly make even a ship channel impassable for slower boats. If conditions are bad when you reach the sea buoy for an inlet, you may find yourself being driven ashore by wind or waves and unable to find the inlet buoys. It may be better to remain well offshore in rough conditions, possibly continuing to a better inlet.

Be advised that the markers at some inlets are moved on a regular basis and the buoys should be honored. Should you find yourself at an inlet and needing direction, a call on VHF Channel 16 for local knowledge is likely to bring you a response. Sea Tow and TowBoatU.S. are two other knowledgeable sources. The Coast Guard may also be able to assist you, but only if it is indeed an emergency.

Overall Mileage: Heading north or south, many skippers mistakenly assume that they will shorten their trips by going out to sea and running down the coast. The distances shown here–both inside and outside (from inlet to inlet)–demonstrate that this is not necessarily true. Keep in mind that even if outside distances from sea buoy to sea buoy are virtually the same as the inside distances, the mileage in and out to the buoys adds to the total coastwise figure.

Resources: Prior to your voyage, there are a number of online sources that can familiarize you with the inlets, including the following:

- **Waterway Explorer** (www.waterwayguide.com): Provides chart and satellite views of the inlets plus cruising details from local boaters.

- **United States Coast Pilot** (www.nauticalcharts.noaa.gov): Nine-volume annual publication distributed by the Office of Coast Survey (NOAA) to supplement nautical charts.

- **Local Notice to Mariners** (www.navcen.uscg.gov, then select the LNMs tab): Weekly updates provided by the U.S. Coast Guard to provide corrections to navigational publications and nautical charts.

- **Tide Tables** (www.tidesandcurrents.noaa.gov): Provided by NOAA to provide tidal predictions (highs and lows) for specific areas.

East Coast

- St. Johns River Entrance 72
- St. Augustine Inlet 74
- Ponce de Leon (New Smyrna) Inlet 76
- Port Canaveral Inlet 78
- Fort Pierce Inlet 80
- St. Lucie Inlet ("The Crossroads") 82
- Jupiter Inlet 84
- Lake Worth (Palm Beach) Inlet 86
- Boca Raton Inlet 88
- Hillsboro Inlet 89
- Port Everglades (Fort Lauderdale) Inlet 90
  - Bakers Haulover (North Miami Beach) Inlet ... 92
- Government Cut (Miami) Inlet 94
  - Cape Florida (Biscayne Bay) Inlet 96

Gulf Coast

- Indian Key Pass 97
- Capri Pass (Marco Island) 98
- Gordon Pass (Naples Bay) 100
- San Carlos Bay Entrance/Matanzas Pass 101
- Boca Grande Pass (Charlotte Harbor) 102
- Venice Inlet 104
- New Pass (Sarasota Bay South) 106
- Longboat Pass (Sarasota Bay North) 107
- Egmont Channel Inlet (Tampa Bay) 108
- Saint Andrew Bay Entrance (Panama City) ... 110
- Pensacola Bay Entrance 112
- Mobile Bay Entrance 114

These inlets can accommodate vessels that draw 10 feet or greater and offer amenities and facilities for pleasure vessels.

Fort Pierce Inlet

SOUTHERN EDITION

Inside vs Outside Mileage

Inlet Distances

East Coast

St. Johns River Entrance to Port Canaveral Inlet:
150 nm (outside)/173 sm (ICW)

Port Canaveral Inlet to Fort Pierce Inlet:
65 nm (outside)/75 sm (ICW)

Fort Pierce Inlet to Lake Worth Inlet:
45 nm (outside)/52 sm (ICW)

Lake Worth Inlet to Port Everglades Inlet:
40 nm (outside)/46 sm (ICW)

Port Everglades Inlet to Government Cut:
20 nm (outside)/23 sm (ICW)

Gulf Coast

Boca Grande Pass to Egmont Channel Inlet (Tampa Bay):
113 nm (outside)/89 sm (GIWW)

Egmont Channel Inlet (Tampa Bay) to Saint Andrew Bay Entrance:
265 nm (outside)/(no direct inside route)

Saint Andrew Bay Entrance to Pensacola Bay Entrance:
139 nm (outside)/114 sm (GIWW)

Pensacola Bay Entrance to Mobile Bay Entrance:
89 nm (outside)/84 sm (GIWW)

Note: In keeping with standard NOAA conventions, outside (ocean and Gulf) distances are measured in nautical miles (nm), while ICW and GIWW distances are measured in statute miles (sm):

1 nm = 1.15 sm

America's Waterway Guide Since 1947

FLORIDA

Atlantic Ocean

- St. Johns River Entrance — ICW MILE 738
- St. Augustine Inlet
- 150 nm
- Ponce de Leon Inlet
- Port Canaveral Inlet — ICW MILE 894
- 65 nm
- Fort Pierce Inlet — ICW MILE 965
- St. Lucie Inlet
- 45 nm
- Jupiter Inlet
- Lake Worth Inlet — ICW MILE 1027
- 40 nm
- Boca Raton Inlet
- Hillsboro Inlet
- Port Everglades Inlet — ICW MILE 1066
- 20 nm
- Bakers Haulover Inlet
- Government Cut — ICW MILE 1089
- Cape Florida

Lake Okeechobee

- Egmont Channel — Tampa Bay — GIWW MILE 95
- Longboat Pass
- New Pass
- 113 nm
- Venice Inlet
- Boca Grande Pass — Charlotte Harbor — GIWW MILE 26.1
- San Carlos Bay/Matanzas Pass
- Gordon Pass
- Capri Pass
- Indian Key Pass

SOUTHERN EDITION 71

East Coast: St. Johns River Entrance

Overview: This is one of the safest and easiest gateways from the Atlantic Ocean. This entrance is used by ocean freighters, military vessels and recreational craft. Cruisers use this inlet as an entry and departure point for passages along the coast. Significant local traffic comes from the busy marinas at Mayport (2 miles upriver) and on the ICW (5 miles upriver). Operators should stay alert, especially when rounding curves and in poor visibility situations. It is 150 nm south from St. Johns River Entrance to the next big ship entrance at Port Canaveral Inlet.

Approach: St. Johns Approach Lighted Buoy "2SJA" is located at N 30° 22.043'/W 081° 12.292'.

Navigation: Use NOAA Chart 11490. Approach from the east. Ocean approach landmark is St. Johns Light, which stands 83 feet above the shore and 1 nm south of the St. Johns north jetty. Use waypoint N 30° 23.860'/W 81° 22.000', which is located about halfway between flashing red buoy "4" and flashing red buoy "6" and over 0.25 nm from the jetties. Follow buoys in. Landmarks include a tower at Jacksonville Beach and a water tank (painted in a red and white checkerboard design) at the naval station. Inside the jetties the St. Johns River runs unobstructed and naturally deep past the Mayport Basin, which is usually occupied by enormous naval craft. The basin

Source: Aqua Map and NOAA data

America's Waterway Guide Since 1947

is off-limits to recreational craft except in extreme emergencies.

Cautions & Hazards: None, other than the large-vessel traffic, which can be heavy at times. Slower boats are well advised to pick their tide coming in here or prepare to settle down for a very long transit; the tide can run up to 3 to 4 knots.

ICW Connection: The jetties of the St. Johns River Entrance are 5 nm from Mile 738 of the ICW. If headed south, it is important to know that the entrance to the ICW is farther west than the original channel.

Make sure that you continue in the main channel until you see green daybeacon "1" and red daybeacon "2" marking the beginning of a new chain heading south on the ICW. On a full outgoing tide expect to see currents in excess of 3 knots for the first 10 miles of your trip. If heading north into Sisters Creek, favor red daybeacon "88" as you enter so as not to attract the attention of the security boats guarding the restricted area on the eastern shore of the entrance.

SOUTHERN EDITION 73

East Coast: St. Augustine Inlet

Overview: Inlet opens to the east splitting Vilano Beach from Conch Island. The dead-end Salt Run is to the south between Conch Island and Anastasia Island.

Approach: St. Augustine Lighted Whistle Buoy "STA" is at N 29° 54.910'/W 081° 15.272'.

Navigation: Use NOAA Chart 11485. From the sea buoy, proceed slightly south of east towards the inlet, paying close attention to the markers. A prominent landmark is a tall cross on shore providing an approximate range to the inlet. Once past Cape Francis on the south, bear to the middle and south side of the channel. There is a large shoal at marker "2A." Stay on the south side of the inlet. While markers positions cannot be anticipated, typically the north edge of the channel is marked by a series of red buoys and the south side is unmarked. Vessels headed in both directions tend to keep close to (and south of) the red markers.

If heading north, it is important to run a sufficient distance past the tip of the beach to the north of the inlet channel before turning north into the ICW channel. Keep flashing green buoy "59" (an ICW marker) to starboard turning. the approach is roughly southwest toward the "Castillo," a large stone fort south the cross on the mainland. To add to the confusion, the numbering of ICW markers restarts where the Tolomato and Matanzas Rivers meet at the inshore-end of the inlet. Passing south of flashing green ICW marker "59" and keeping north of the entrance to the dead-end Salt Run, continue southwest splitting flashing green "1" and red nun "2" to enter the ICW then round the prominent thumb of Anastasia Island towards the Bridge of Lions.

Cautions & Hazards: It is highly recommended that you only attempt passage through this inlet with good visibility and in light wind conditions. Avoid this channel when the substantial tidal flow (particularly on ebb) is opposed by medium to strong winds. Breakers can often be seen in the shallow waters bordering the channel even in calm conditions. Charts do not show depth details nor the position of navigational aids as this inlet is prone to frequent change. This is considered a "fair weather" inlet and local knowledge is recommended.

ICW Connection: Connects just inside the inlet at ICW Mile 776.

America's Waterway Guide Since 1947

East Coast: Ponce de Leon (New Smyrna) Inlet

Overview: Used extensively by locals and sportfishing vessels and is a convenient point to enter or leave the ICW between Daytona and Cape Canaveral. This is a fair weather inlet only. The next opportunity going south to leave the ICW and go offshore is the Canaveral Barge Canal at Mile 894 then east to Port Canaveral Inlet.

Approach: Ponce De Leon Inlet Lighted Bell Buoy "2" is located at N 29° 04.700'/W 80° 53.700'.

Navigation: Use NOAA Chart 11485. Note that it is safer to access the inlet from the south, which is used extensively by locals and sportfishing boats and is a convenient point to enter or leave the ICW between Daytona and Cape Canaveral. The north approach channel to the inlet branches eastward from flashing green "1." To access the marine facilities on the east bank of the north approach channel to the Ponce de Leon Inlet enter the channel from the ICW at the north end of the Ponce de Leon Cut at Mile 839.6 near green can buoy "3." When approaching the inlet from the ocean, aids to navigation may not match what is charted but the channel should be well marked. The inlet is considered a fair weather route; shoaling is continuous and dredging is frequent here. The shoaling is particularly bad extending from the beach along the inlet's south shore. Deeper water is generally found closer the inlet's north jetty, which was extended in 2021. The USCG station is located on the south channel of the inlet and will respond to calls for inlet conditions, and the local TowBoat US is always up-to-date on local conditions. Both can be hailed on VHF Channel 16.

Webcam: For a live view of the inlet visit www.livebeachcam.net/ponce-inlet-florida-webcam.

Cautions & Hazards: Seemingly constant reclamation, dredging and seawall construction is ongoing, yet shoaling has been reported in the approaches both north and south of the inlet coming from the ICW. Inlet markers are continually moved by the USCG to reflect deep water. Expect substantial traffic at all hours. This is a fair weather inlet only, particularly for weather out of the south and east, which creates large swells into the inlet. Local knowledge is strongly advised before using this inlet.

ICW Connection: The inlet is 2.5 miles from ICW Mile 840 with one channel leading north, another south. The north channel is not as well marked as the south channel until well inside and shows charted depths of just 7 feet MLW.

America's Waterway Guide Since 1947

Source: Aqua Map and NOAA data

SOUTHERN EDITION 77

East Coast: Port Canaveral Inlet

America's Waterway Guide Since 1947

Overview: Well-marked, deep ship inlet protected from the north by the long and shallow Southeast Shoal off Cape Canaveral. The lock inside the inlet eliminates current, making this one of the easier to use inlets on the Florida coast.

Approach: Canaveral Harbor Approach Channel Lighted Buoy "4" (2.5 sec) is located at N 28° 22.618/W 080° 31.720'.

Navigation: Use NOAA Chart 114780. Southbound cruisers can make for N 28° 23.490'/W 80° 33.000' after rounding red buoy "4," while northbound craft could go in much closer, at N 28° 24.570'/W 80° 34.480'. The channel is well marked; simply run down the channel, turning due west at Middle Reach. Cape Canaveral Lock (321-783-5421) operates from 6:00 a.m. to 9:30 p.m. year-round.

Webcam: For a live view of the inlet visit www.portcanaveralwebcam.com.

Cautions & Hazards: Coming from the north, the Southeast Shoal off Cape Canaveral keeps boaters several miles offshore. Stay east of W 80° 27.000' before turning in to the sea buoy after rounding red buoy "4" at N 28° 23.470'/W 80° 29.100' marking the southern edge of the shoal. Note that this cuts off the offshore waypoint. From the south, cruisers can approach from within 0.5 nm of the shore in depths greater than 20 feet MLW.

ICW Connection: Inlet is 7.5 nm from ICW Mile 894 (across the Banana River and through the Barge Canal).

Source: Aqua Map and NOAA data

SOUTHERN EDITION

East Coast: Fort Pierce Inlet

Overview: Many cruisers make Fort Pierce Inlet their exit or entry point for an outside run. It's a 65-nm north run to Cape Canaveral Inlet and 45-nm south run to Lake Worth Inlet. The proximity of the Gulf Stream to this safe, deep inlet makes it an attractive area for deep-sea fishing. Fort Pierce is also a popular Inlet when making landfall returning from West End Point on Grand Bahama Island. (The Gulf Stream gives a boost to cruisers heading north.) The inlet is wide and deep with two stone jetties, an inner channel (30-foot MLW depths) and a turning basin (28-foot MLW depths). The 22-mile long Hutchinson Island lies to the south and 28-mile long Orchid Island (also known as North Hutchinson Island) lies to the north.

Approach: Fort Pierce Inlet Lighted Buoy "2" is located at N 27° 28.653'/W 080° 15.411' (1.5 nm seaward of the channel).

Navigation: Use NOAA Chart 11475. Above waypoint takes you 1.5 nm from the channel in deep water. Smaller craft can approach in over 20 feet MLW to green buoy "5" and red buoy "6" at N 27° 28.160'/W 80° 16.900', which is just 0.2 nm from the jetties. The channel is marked with ranges and buoys (both lighted and unlighted). Tidal currents in the inlet are strong averaging 3 to 4 knots.

Webcam: For live view of the inlet visit www.visitstlucie.com/fort-pierce-inlet-waterway.

Cautions & Hazards: It is best to pass through with the tide or at slack tide as standing waves are possible. An area of shallow shoals along the north jetty near flashing red buoy "8" are a popular weekend hangout for local boaters and fishermen. Be aware of traffic in this area. Where the inlet channel crosses the ICW down to the Peter B. Cobb Memorial (SR A1A) Bridge (Mile 965.8), strong crosscurrents exist with a set to the south on the flood and to the north on the ebb. Currents are strongest through the narrow neck of the channel inside the barrier islands near flashing green buoy "9." In strong east winds swells can create rough conditions inside the jetties (especially on ebb tides).

ICW Connection: Connects directly to the ICW at Mile 965.

East Coast: St. Lucie Inlet ("The Crossroads")

Overview: This marks the intersection of the Indian River, Saint Lucie, Okeechobee Waterway and ICW (hence "The Crossroads") and is used by sport fishermen, megayachts and offshore sailors.

Approach: St. Lucie Inlet Lighted Buoy "2" (4 sec) is located at N 27° 10.018'/W 080° 08.370'.

Navigation: Use NOAA Chart 11472. Zoning laws restrict most buildings to a maximum of four stories so local captains returning from the Bahamas are said to locate St. Lucie Inlet by merely aiming for the "valley" midway between the high rise buildings of St. Lucie County to the north and Palm Beach County to the south. Jetty to the north and small breakwater to the south mark the entrance.

Webcam: For a live view of the inlet visit www.stlucieinlet.com.

Cautions & Hazards: The 2-mile run from the ICW to the ocean is subject to continuous shoaling, currents may be strong and markers may be off station. Temporary buoys have been placed between the inlet and the ICW. Most markers are unlit; therefore, nighttime navigation is not recommended.

Frequently dredged occurs but this inlet requires caution due to problematic shoaling. Jetty to the north and breakwater to the south offer protection once inside, although protection from the south is marginal in east to southeast winds. The USCG has placed temporary markers denoting best water. Local knowledge should be obtained before using this inlet.

The current can be strong. Avoid this inlet in an east wind (over 15 knots) on an outgoing tide.

ICW Connection: ICW is approximately 1 nm away at Mile 988.

America's Waterway Guide Since 1947

Source: Aqua Map and NOAA data

SOUTHERN EDITION 83

East Coast: Jupiter Inlet

Overview: Fair weather inlet only. With any swell, mariners should divert to another inlet. The inlet is considered impassable in a northeast swell of any size and is cited by the USCG as "not navigable without local knowledge."

Approach: Jupiter Inlet Jetty Light "1" is at N 26° 56.612'/W 080° 04.240'.

Navigation: Use NOAA Chart 11472. If you must enter, proceed in a westerly direction from the waypoint to the markers on the jetties. A short jetty protects the inlet entrance to the north and a steel barricade extends halfway into the inlet from the south bank.

Webcam: For a live view of the inlet visit www.evsjupiter.com.

Cautions & Hazards: This inlet channel is unsafe for all but small boats with local knowledge and very shallow draft. The mouth of the inlet has strong currents, eddies, turbulence and breaking seas over sandbars that extend from the south side of the inlet offshore towards the northeast. The average tidal range is 2.5 feet.

Shoals also flank the east edge of the channel south from green daybeacon "57" to the Jupiter Island (CR 707) Bridge (hail as the "707 Bridge") at Mile 1004.1. The bridge has a 25-foot closed vertical clearance and opens on signal. If your vessel is lightly powered, mind the swift current here while waiting for the bridge. Contact the bridgetender prior to your arrival and allow for the set of the current passing through.

ICW Connection: Connects directly to the ICW at Mile 1005.

East Coast: Lake Worth (Palm Beach) Inlet

Overview: Wide, well-marked and protected by jetties, Lake Worth (Palm Beach) Inlet boasts a deep straightforward big ship channel that is one of the easiest to enter on the Atlantic coast. The meandering Gulf Stream is closer here than at any point in the U.S. (sometimes as close as 1 mile offshore but usually out about 8 to 12 miles) and both commercial and recreational craft give the Lake Worth (Palm Beach) Inlet heavy use. It is located approximately midway between Fort Pierce Inlet (53 miles north) and Port Everglades (40 miles south), making it popular with boaters who prefer to travel offshore. Vessels returning from the Bahamas can clear Customs and Immigration here.

Approach: Lake Worth Lighted Buoy "LW" is located at N 26° 46.355'/W 080° 00.602" (1.1 nm east of the jetties).

Navigation: Use NOAA Chart 11459. To access the ocean continue on the ICW around the west side of Peanut Island to the Turning Basin and then pick up the main Lake Worth (Palm Beach) Inlet channel and follow it to the ocean. It is deep and well marked.

America's Waterway Guide Since 1947

Webcam: For a live view of the inlet visit www.pbcgov.com/webcams/lwi.

Cautions & Hazards: The Coast Guard establishes fixed and moving security zones at the Port of Palm Beach for the protection of passenger vessels (cruise ships), vessels carrying cargoes of a particular hazard and vessels carrying hazardous gases. A moving security zone activates when such a vessel passes red and white buoy "LW" when entering the port and becomes a fixed zone when the ship is docked. These zones cover the waters within 100 yards all around the subject vessels and no craft can enter without prior permission. Patrol craft may be contacted on VHF Channel 16 for the status of these security zones.

ICW Connection: Connects directly to the ICW at Mile 1027.

SOUTHERN EDITION   87

East Coast: Boca Raton Inlet

Overview: Narrow, dredged cut located 5 nm northward of Hillsboro Inlet Light. Mariners are advised to use extreme caution when transiting the area. The Boca Raton Inlet is not recommended for passage without local knowledge due to shoaling to 4 feet MLW. Continue to Hillsboro Inlet if possible.

Approach: Boca Raton Inlet Jetty Light "1" is at N 26° 20.111'/W 080° 04.183'.

Navigation: Use NOAA Chart 11467. Tall, pink Boca Raton Resort & Club is a landmark visible from many miles offshore. Quick flashing green buoy "1" marks the south jetty and quick flashing red buoy "2" is on the north jetty. It is strongly recommended to head south of green buoy "1" (south jetty) and approach the inlet from the south.

The Boca Inlet (Haven Ashe) Bridge crosses the inlet with 23-foot closed vertical clearance. It opens on signal. Be sure to request a bridge opening upon arrival in the inlet to avoid circling in the strong current.

Webcam: For a live view of the inlet visit www.video-monitoring.com/beachcams/bocainlet.

Cautions & Hazards: Local knowledge is required, as shoaling outside the inlet can limit access at low tide. Depths change frequently due to shoaling and shifting sandbars, and swift-moving currents cause swells where the outflow meets the ocean. The inlet channel and markers are not charted and transit is considered dangerous. Be aware that the current usually reverses in the ICW as it passes the Boca Raton Inlet.

ICW Connection: Connects directly to the ICW at Mile 1048.

Source: Aqua Map and NOAA data

East Coast: Hillsboro Inlet

Overview: Although shoals at Hillsboro Inlet shift rapidly, dredging is frequent and local boats and the large fleet of charter fishing and head boats heavily travel the passage here.

Approach: Hillsboro Entrance Lighted Buoy "HI" is located at N 26° 15.125'/W 080° 04.462' (approximately 0.4 nm from the inlet). A course to the northwest (paying close attention to the green day marks and lighted buoys) will bring you past the jetty.

Navigation: Use NOAA Chart 11467. Easily identified by 136-foot high Hillsboro Lighthouse (visible from 28 miles at sea). Proceed all the way to the red-and-white sea buoy "HI" before turning south to avoid shoals. A rock jetty extends southeast from the north side of the inlet and is submerged at the outer end. It is wise to seek local knowledge before running this inlet.

Hillsboro Inlet Bascule Bridge (13-foot closed vertical clearance) inside the inlet opens on signal, except from 7:00 a.m. to 6:00 p.m., the drawspans need only open only on the hour, quarter-hour, half-hour and three-quarter hour. Due to the very strong currents in this inlet, vessels should contact the bridgetender before entering the inlet. Wait for the bridge to open completely before approaching.

Webcam: For a live view of the inlet visit www.hillsborolighthouse.org/inlet-cam.

Cautions & Hazards: A southeast wind against a tide situation can kick up a short, vicious chop that can set an unwary boater onto the shoals to the south of the inlet. Currents to 6 knots have been reported.

ICW Connection: Connects directly to the ICW at Mile 1053.

SOUTHERN EDITION

East Coast: Port Everglades (Fort Lauderdale) Inlet

Overview: This big ship inlet, located 9 nm south of Hillsboro Inlet, is also known as Fort Lauderdale Inlet. This modern, deep water harbor hosts an endless stream of cruise ships, recreational craft, tankers, freighters and warships. The port is primarily used as a commercial harbor and may be crowded with both commercial and recreational traffic. This is a popular take-off point for cruisers heading to and from the Bahamas, fishermen heading out to the nearby Gulf Stream and skippers cruising north and south along the coast to escape the bridges and speed restrictions.

NOTE: Vessels with mast heights over 56 feet that are headed south of Miami's Julia Tuttle Causeway Bridge at Mile 1087.2 have no choice but to go outside at Port Everglades. These vessels can then rejoin the ICW via Miami's Government Cut at Dodge Island.

Approach: Port Everglades Lighted Buoy "PE" is located at N 26° 05.500'/ W 80° 04.790'. From the sea buoy, head due west into the cut.

Navigation: Use NOAA Chart 11470. This inlet is well marked with flashing buoys along the entrance

America's Waterway Guide Since 1947

channel. Currents average 0.7 knots with a tidal range of 3.1 feet in the Turning Basin. Note that the channel markers are spaced at approximately 0.5 nm apart and the jetty ends are not marked. Be sure to maintain a compass course line and maintain alignment on exit or entry.

Webcam: For a live view of the inlet visit www.portevergladeswebcam.com.

Cautions & Hazards: Frequent large ship traffic in and out of this inlet necessitate a careful watch, particularly at night and in poor weather. When military vessels are in port a security cordon is set up for which entry by private craft is prohibited. Occasionally all traffic is temporarily halted while ships are docking or leaving. Patrol craft may be contacted on VHF Channel 16 for the status of these security zones.

ICW Connection: Connects directly to the ICW at Mile 1066.

SOUTHERN EDITION   91

East Coast: Bakers Haulover (North Miami Beach) Inlet

Overview: Strictly a fair-weather inlet for cruising vessels due to problems with continual ICW shoaling. Mariners are advised to exercise extreme caution while transiting the area. Popular and busy with local recreational fishing boats.

Approach: Bakers Haulover Inlet Jetty Light (on south jetty) is at N 25° 53.950'/W 080° 07.231'.

Navigation: Use NOAA Chart 11467. There are no markers, other than a light on the south side of the inlet and once you have turned north, deep water is close to the shore on your port side. Inlet is spanned by the Bakers Haulover Inlet Bridge with 32-foot fixed vertical clearance.

Cautions & Hazards: Jetties are short here and currents are strong (2.0 to 3.0 knots). The inlet can become especially nasty when wind and current oppose. Cruisers would be wise to forgo this inlet in favor of Miami's Government Cut (8 nm to the south) or Port Everglades Inlet (11.5 nm to the north).

ICW Connection: Proceed due east into the inlet, turning south once inside to head for the ICW Mile 1080.

America's Waterway Guide Since 1947

WATERWAY GUIDE
THE CRUISING AUTHORITY

Navigate with the Cruising Authority

Subscribe today for the full package
(Guidebook of your choice, mobile app & online subscription)

Scan to shop now at
www.waterwayguide.com

SOUTHERN EDITION 93

East Coast: Government Cut (Miami) Inlet

Source: Aqua Map and NOAA data

Overview: This inlet is wide, deep and free of hazards. It runs between Miami Beach (to the north) and Fisher Island (to the south). The Main Ship Channel extends past the end of the Government Cut between Dodge Island and Watson Island to the Turning Basin.

Approach: Miami Main Channel Lighted Buoy "M" is located at N 25° 46.088'/W 80° 04.998'.

Navigation: Use NOAA Chart 11467. In settled conditions, use the waypoint N 25° 45.400'/ W 80° 06.880', which brings you in to just over 0.5 nm from the jetties; otherwise, use sea buoy waypoint is preferable. Follow a course of 253° magnetic inside the channel, then 299° magnetic from green buoy "7" through the jetties. Closures are announced on VHF Channel 16. During closures, Fisherman's Channel south of Dodge Island is the alternate inlet. It is similarly free of hazards, although when entering from the ICW heading south, leave buoys "53A" and "55" well to port before turning in to the channel due to shoaling extending into the channel.

Webcam: For a live view of the inlet visit www.portmiamiwebcam.com.

Cautions & Hazards: The Main Ship Channel (where cruise ships dock) is often closed for security reasons including when cruise ships are at the Main Ship Channel docks. Closures are announced on VHF Channel 16. Cruisers then must use a route combining Fishermans Channel and the Dodge Channel Cut to skirt the south shore of Dodge Island as an alternative. A short connector channel runs from the west terminus of the Dodge Island Cut to the ICW. The controlling depth is about 12 feet MLW but make sure you identify the markers carefully. Watch for frequent dredging operations in this area and for the numerous ferries headed to and from Fisher Island.

Commercial traffic is generally busy here as well and there is a car ferry that runs between Dodge Island and Fisher Island with frequent crossings. You must pay attention in this area and always give the ferry the right of way.

ICW Connection: Connects directly to the ICW at Mile 1089.

SOUTHERN EDITION

East Coast: Cape Florida (Biscayne Bay) Inlet

Overview: This inlet is primarily used by cruisers heading to the islands. Located 6 nm south of Miami.

Approach: Biscayne Channel Light "6M" is located at N 25º 38.742'/W 80º 05.373'.

Navigation: Use NOAA Chart 11465. Pass Biscayne Channel Light to port, then continue to Biscayne Bay entrance buoy green "1" and follow the marked channel.

Cautions & Hazards: Local knowledge should be obtained before entering this inlet for the first time. It is a well-marked channel, but attention is required in some shallow areas (7 to 9 feet).

ICW Connection: Connects to ICW (0.5 nm) at Mile 1094.

Source: Aqua Map and NOAA data

Gulf Coast: Indian Key Pass

Overview: Entrance is about 3.5 nm offshore of flashing green "1" at Indian Key. Twisty dredged channel leads through Indian Key Pass, across Chokoloskee Bay and up the Barron River to a turning basin at Everglades City about 1.3 miles above the mouth of the river.

Approach: Indian Key Pass Channel Light "IK" is located at N 25° 47.997' /W 081° 28.076'.

Navigation: Use NOAA Chart 11430. Well-marked Indian Key Pass starts as a natural channel but quickly narrows into a dredged channel. Maintains 6-foot MLW depths but be careful to maintain alignment as the channel is flanked by shoals on both sides. Some markers are lighted but entry in darkness is not recommended.

Cautions & Hazards: Tidal range is approximately 3 feet and "wind tide" can be a factor here in a strong northeast blow. Between the flashing red "22" and the red "30" daybeacon where the channel crosses the Chokoloskee Bay, there is a strong lateral current from the south during the ebb and to the south during the flood. The channel is deep but narrow, and you need to watch the marks ahead and behind as it is easy to drift into 2 to 3 feet of water. Some channel markers may be missing.

Source: Aqua Map and NOAA data

SOUTHERN EDITION

Gulf Coast: Capri Pass (Marco Island)

Overview: Channel leads south to Marco Island and the village of Goodland, while Big Marco-Gordon Pass channel splits off to the north to Naples. Capri Pass should be used in place of Big Marco Pass due to shoaling. Local knowledge is advised.

Approach: Capri Pass Light "2" is at N 25° 58.321'/W 081° 46.243'.

Navigation: Use NOAA Chart 11430. When approaching Capri Pass from the south, pass west of 16-foot-high flashing red buoy "2" before turning for entry to stay clear of the shoaling near Big Marco Pass. Coconut Island, once located in Capri Pass, just south of the green-over-red daybeacon is now submerged and has been removed from recent charts; however, it lies just under the surface.

Follow the markers carefully through Capri Pass. Head from flashing red "6" to the split marked by quick flashing green "9" and red daybeacon "8" while favoring the green side. There is plenty of room but traffic can be heavy on weekends and the markers are confusing where the inside channel to Naples splits off northward at the green-over-red daybeacon.

If headed north, proceed from red daybeacon "6" to green daybacon "7," where the Big Marco-Gordon Pass channel starts with green daybeacon "1" and continues to green daybeacon "3." (Be sure to observe green daybeacon "1A" and green nun "3A.") At this point, the channel splits for a second time. Follow the channel between green nun "3A" and red daybeacon "2A" to green daybeacon "5." (There is no red "4.")

Cautions & Hazards: Shoaling from the north side of the inlet has been reported in Capri Pass. Stay closer to red daybeacons "4" and "6" when traversing this channel. Shoaling has been observed at the south end of Big Marco-Gordon Pass in the vicinity of green nun "3A." The daybeacon marks active shoaling on the west side of the channel. Note that some markers to the north on the channel may be missing.

America's Waterway Guide Since 1947

SOUTHERN EDITION 99

Gulf Coast: Gordon Pass (Naples Bay)

Overview: Entrance to Naples Bay and the numerous passages that traverse the Ten Thousand Islands. Well marked and should present no problems except for heavy boat traffic, particularly on winter weekends.

Approach: Gordon Pass Channel Light "1" is at N 26° 05.290"/W 081° 48.410'.

Navigation: Use NOAA Chart 11430. The channel is marked by lights and daybeacons. A microwave tower, several water tanks and numerous hotels are visible from offshore. Follow the well-marked Gordon Pass Channel from green daybeacon "1" to the Naples area. Interesects Big Marco Pass-Gordon Pass Channel from south at red daybeacon "20."

Cautions & Hazards: Some markers to the north on the channel may be missing.

Gulf Coast: San Carlos Bay Entrance/Matanzas Pass

Overview: The entrance to San Carlos Bay is wide and mostly deep except for shoals to the west. Matanzas Pass is located to the east before passing under the high-rise Sanibel Causeway Bridge across the bay and provides access to the back bay of Fort Myers Beach.

Approach: San Carlos Bay Light "SC" is located 2.8 nm south-southeast of the entrance and 3.6 nm southeast of Pt. Ybel at N 26° 25.080"/W 81° 57.330'.

Navigation: Use NOAA Chart 11427. Sanibel Island Light (N 26° 27.110'/W 082° 00.510') at the east end of Sanibel Island is 98 feet above the water and is a good landmark. From San Carlos Bay Channel green "1" proceed to red daybeacon "4." If headed to Fort Myers Beach, pick up Matanzas Pass Channel "1."

The dredged channel, marked by lights and daybeacons, leads through Matanzas Pass to a turning basin off the shrimp terminals on San Carlos Island. Otherwise, continue to the Sanibel Causeway "A" Span with fixed 70-foot vertical clearance.

Cautions & Hazards: None. Last dredged July 2023.

GIWW Connection: The main entrance channel intersects the GIWW and the Okeechobee Waterway approximately 1.8 nm above the Sanibel Causeway "A" Span Bridge. It then turns more easterly leading to Cape Coral and Fort Myers. You can also elect to continue on eastbound on the Okeechobee Waterway until reaching the East Coast of Florida or continue northbound on the GIWW.

Source: Aqua Map and NOAA data

SOUTHERN EDITION 101

Gulf Coast: Boca Grande Pass (Charlotte Harbor)

Overview: Deepest natural inlet on the Gulf of Mexico, reaching depths to approximately 80 feet. Located 26.5 nm south-southeast of Venice Inlet and leads to Charlotte Harbor. Main inlet for accessing Boca Grande, Punta Gorda, Port Charlotte and the Peace River.

Approach: Charlotte Harbor Channel Lighted Buoy "1" is located at N 26° 40.314'/W 082° 18.903'.

Navigation: Use NOAA Chart 114260. Well-marked channel separating Gasparilla Island to the north and Cayo Costa to the south. Once inside, a natural channel leads from Port Boca Grande to the GIWW in Charlotte Harbor.

Cautions & Hazards: Shoals with depths of 2 to 5 feet MLW border the approach channel. If entering Boca Grande Channel from the north, take care to come all of the way to green buoy "3" and red nun buoy "4" before turning in to avoid the shoal entirely.

GIWW Connection: Intersects GIWW 0.9 nm above the entrance at approximately Mile 26.1, north of GIWW flashing red "76."

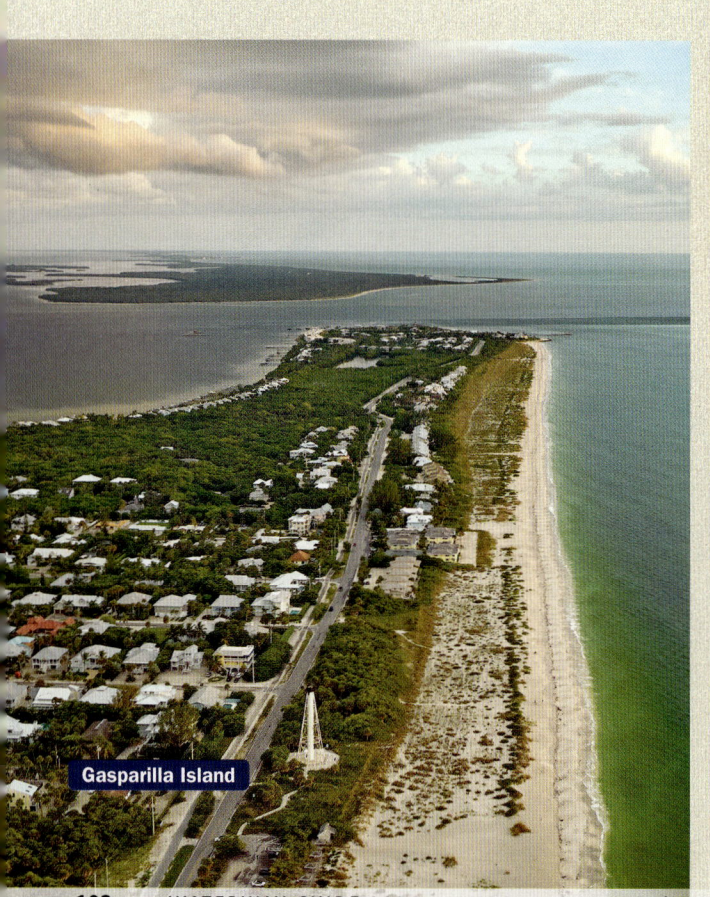
Gasparilla Island

America's Waterway Guide Since 1947

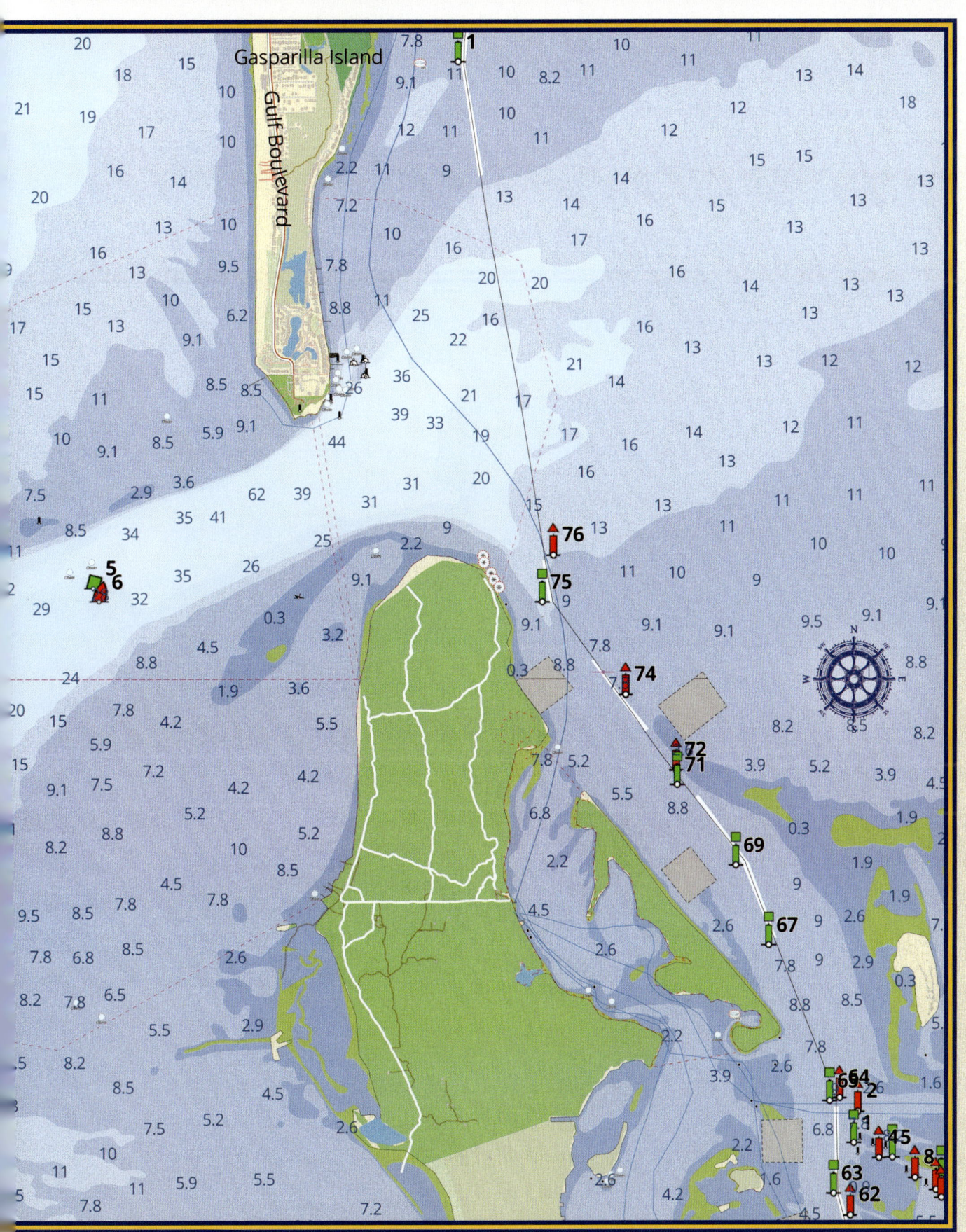

SOUTHERN EDITION 103

Gulf Coast: Venice Inlet

Overview: Well-jettied inlet that carries mid-line depths of at least 7 feet MLW all the way to the GIWW at Bird Island.

Approach: Venice Inlet Light "1" is at N 27° 06.760'/ W 082° 28.216' (north jetty).

Navigation: Use NOAA Chart 11424. Inside the inlet jetties past flashing green "1" and flashing red "2," you will next pick up green daybeacon "3" and red daybeacon "4," at which point you will continue farther east to intercept green daybeacons "5" and "7" before intersecting the GIWW.

Cautions & Hazards: None. Regularly dredged.

GIWW Connection: Interesects GIWW at Mile 58 at Bird Island and GIWW flashing red "16."

Source: Aqua Map and NOAA data

SOUTHERN EDITION **105**

Gulf Coast: New Pass (Sarasota Bay South)

Overview: Located 17 miles north of Venice Inlet and allows access to Sarasota Bay via a 4- to 7-foot MLW channel that, while constantly shifting, is fairly reliable and safe in most conditions.

Approach: New Pass Shoal Light is at N 27° 18.912' /W 082° 35.888'. Proceed to Interior New Pass Shoal Light.

Navigation: Use NOAA Chart 114250. Once inside the inlet, proceed to green daybeacon "9." The 23-foot closed vertical clearance New Pass (SR 789) Bridge crosses the pass. The draw need only open on the hour, 20 minutes past the hour, and 40 minutes past the hour from 7:00 a.m. to 6:00 p.m. From 6:00 p.m. to 7:00 a.m., the draw will open on signal if at least a 3-hour notice is given to the drawtender.

Cautions & Hazards: If you have to wait for an opening at the bridge, time your approach to avoid waiting in the channel when the current is running, especially on an incoming tide.

GIWW Connection: Intersects GIWW at Mile 74.5 east of New Pass Daybeacons "16" and "17."

Source: Aqua Map and NOAA data

Gulf Coast: Longboat Pass (Sarasota Bay North)

Overview: Longboat Key shields Sarasota Bay from the Gulf of Mexico and opens wide with central controlling depths of 7 to 12 feet MLW.

Approach: Longboat Pass Channel Lighted Buoy "LP" is at N 27° 26.102'/W 082° 42.166'. From there, set a course of approximately 008° magnetic until you reach green daybeacon "1," which marks a 5-foot MLW shoal just west of the inlet.

Navigation: Use NOAA Chart 11425. At green daybeacon "1," set another course, this time approximately 041° magnetic for 0.4 mile, which will bring you to red daybeacon "2" and green daybeacon "3." From here head into Longboat Pass. The 17-foot closed vertical clearance Longboat Pass (SR 789) Bridge crosses the pass. (Opens on request.)

Cautions & Hazards: If you have to wait for an opening at the bridge, time your approach to avoid waiting in the channel when the current is running, especially on an incoming tide. Watch for strong crosscurrents to and from Longboat Pass. A call to a towboat captain for local knowledge is recommended. Last dredged in 2023.

GIWW Connection: Intersects GIWW at Mile 86 at Longboat Pass Daybeacon "9" (GIWW green daybeacon "47").

SOUTHERN EDITION

Gulf Coast: Egmont Channel Inlet (Tampa Bay)

Overview: This is the largest ship port on Florida's West Coast and is wide, deep and well-buoyed. The channel extends between Mullet Key and Egmont Key and is used by deep-draft vessels entering Tampa Bay.

Approach: Tampa Bay Lighted Buoy "T" is at N 27° 35.296'/W 083° 00.698'. Proceed to Egmont Channel Lighted Buoy "2" and follow channel into Tampa Bay.

Navigation: Use NOAA Chart 11412. The channel is dredged to 45 feet MLW and includes a natural 90-foot-deep hole off the Egmont Key lighthouse. Main ship channel traverses through Mullet Key Channel and dredged cuts leading up Tampa Bay. Other options for small boats are Southwest Channel, running just south of Egmont Key and Passage Key Inlet, the southernmost

America's Waterway Guide Since 1947

route, which is deep but more narrow than Southwest Channel.

Cautions & Hazards: None. Last dredged in 2023.

GIWW Connection: Intersects the GIWW north near Mile 95 at GIWW flashing red "70." When crossing the main shipping channel remember that commercial shipping traffic has the right-of-way and stay alert. With its long fetch this stretch can kick up an uncomfortable chop.

SOUTHERN EDITION 109

Gulf Coast: Saint Andrew Bay Entrance (Panama City)

Overview: This manmade pass joins Saint Andrew Bay with the Gulf and accommodates big ships carrying a variety of products from nearby Panama City.

Approach: Saint Andrew Bay Entrance Lighted Whistle Buoy "SA" is located N 30° 05.466'/W 085° 46.416' about 2.2 miles southwest of the entrance to the dredged channel.

Navigation: Use NOAA Chart 11391. Saint Andrew Bay Entrance Lighted Buoys "1" and 2" mark the well-marked dredged channel.

Cautions & Hazards: Winds greatly affect the tide. South winds of long duration will raise the water level in the bay, while north winds will lower it. The strong ebb current sets outward through the dredged cut and causes heavy tide rips if the wind is south and of moderate strength. With a south or west breeze, small vessels should traverse the entrance during flood current.

GIWW Connection: Intersects GIWW at Mile 290 north of Saint Andrew Bay Entrance Lighted "15A."

America's Waterway Guide Since 1947

SOUTHERN EDITION

Gulf Coast: Pensacola Bay Entrance

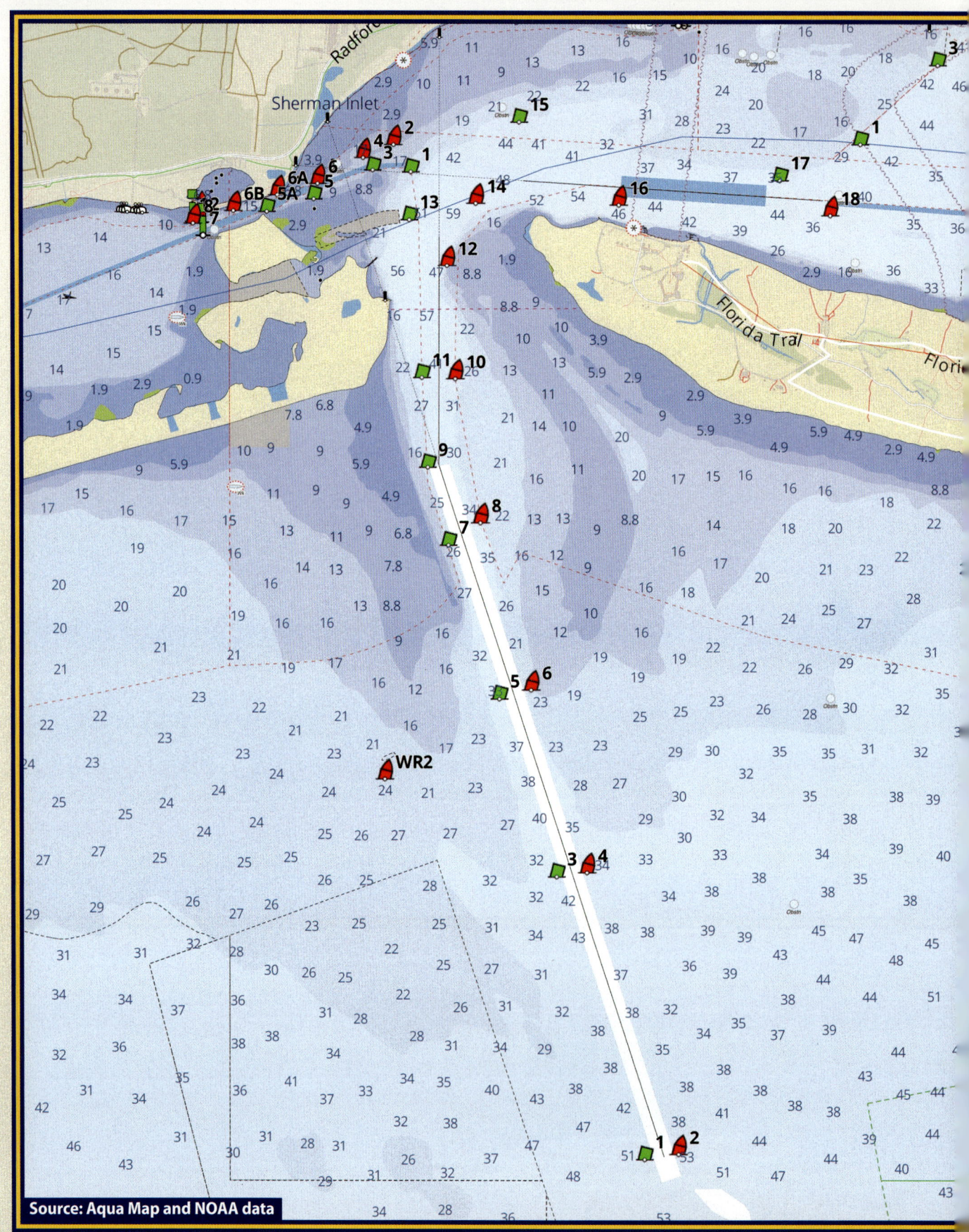

Source: Aqua Map and NOAA data

America's Waterway Guide Since 1947

Overview: Access to Pensacola Bay is through a dredged channel that extends 1.5 miles seaward from the entrance. Home to U.S. Navy carrier ships used to train pilots. As expected, the channel is wide and deep and serves a very busy port.

Approach: Pensacola Bay Entrance Lighted Buoy "1" is located at N 30° 16.264' /W 087° 17.556'.

Navigation: Use NOAA Chart 11383. A prominent landmark is Pensacola Light (N 30° 20.460'/W 87° 18.290'), which is 191 feet above the water on the shore (next to the Naval Station) north of the entrance. Follow well-marked channel passing between Perdido Key and Santa Rosa Island into Pensacola Bay.

Cautions & Hazards: None.

GIWW Connection: Intersects GIWW at Mile 179 just north of Pensacola Bay Entrance Lighted Buoy "13."

SOUTHERN EDITION   113

Gulf Coast: Mobile Bay Entrance

Overview: Mobile Bay is the approach to the city of Mobile and to the Alabama and Tombigbee Rivers.

Approach: Mobile Entrance Lighted Buoy "M" is at waypoint N 30° 07.465'/W 088° 04.124'.

Navigation: Use NOAA Chart 11376. Mobile Bar Lighted Buoys "1" and 2" mark the well-marked dredged channel. The bay has depths of 7 to 12 feet MLW outside the dredged channels.

Cautions & Hazards: The entrance is 3 miles wide between Mobile Point ton the east and Pelican Point to the west, but vessels should follow the dredged channel to avoid shoals that extend 4 miles south on both sides. The Coast Guard advises vessels to exercise particular caution where the channel intersects the GIWW. Collisions, groundings and close quarters passing have been reported. Because of this, the Coast Guard has requested vessels make a Sécurité call on VHF Channel 13 prior to crossing the GIWW, particularly during periods of restricted visibility.

GIWW Connection: Intersects the GIWW about 3 miles above Mobile Point at Mobile Bay Entrance Channel Lighted Buoys "25" and "26."

America's Waterway Guide Since 1947

Source: Aqua Map and NOAA data

SOUTHERN EDITION 115

&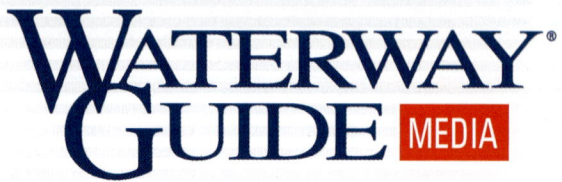

iNavX.com • WaterwayGuide.com

The Number One Handheld Chartplotter Just Got Better

Navigate Confidently

Award Winning Technology and Data Delivery from iNavX and Waterway Guide

Section 1: Florida's Upper East Coast

Chapter 1: Fernandina Beach to St. Johns River
Chapter 2: Side Trip on the St. Johns River
Chapter 3: St. Johns River to New Smyrna Beach
Chapter 4: Space Coast Area
Chapter 5: St. Lucie River Area
Chapter 6: Side Trip on the Okeechobee Waterway

SOUTHERN EDITION

Chapter 1: Fernandina Beach to St. Johns River

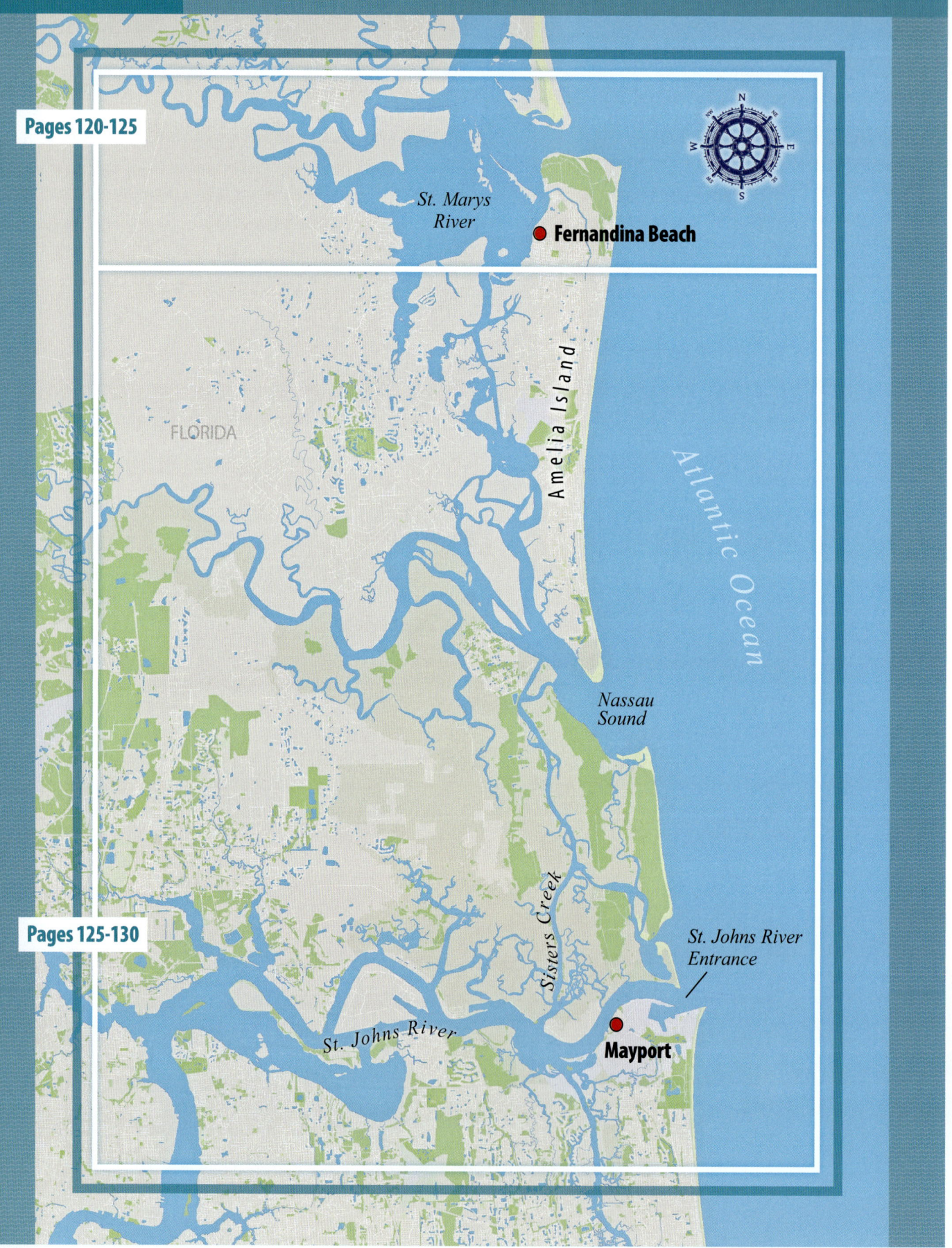

America's Waterway Guide Since 1947   Chapter 1

 Mile 716-Mile 740

■ NAVIGATION NOTES

Cruising south on the Intracoastal Waterway (ICW) boaters enter the mouth of the Amelia River and the State of Florida at Mile 714. As you cross the St. Marys River and enter the State of Florida you will notice a change in the characteristics of the ICW.

Georgia's long, open sounds and wide rivers gradually transform into a series of creeks and rivers connected by narrow land cuts, and you will see much more development and boat traffic will increase. For the 370 or so miles to Miami navigational aids are plentiful and marinas and urban centers intensify as you travel south.

The Upper Florida ICW is well marked and easy to follow. Track of your position by checking off markers on the chart as you pass. Take extra care where inlet, river and ICW channels meet; a few moments' study of the chart ahead of time will prevent confusion in those areas where a buoy system changes direction or marker numbering resets. Be prepared as these areas are also prone to shoaling and markers may be repositioned.

> **Reminder:** All mileage on the ICW is measured in statute rather than nautical miles (1 nm = 1.15 mile).

With a few exceptions, the ICW here is protected from strong winds and is usually free of rough water. Tidal range is more than 7 feet at Fernandina and currents up to 4 knots may be encountered between Fernandina and Haulover Canal, especially at inlets and narrows. Tidal

variances and currents decrease as you head south to Miami.

Manatee zones also have speed restrictions that are strictly enforced. Many are seasonal and the posted signs may be difficult to read so keep an eye out for them. Speed restrictions are subject to change. Always obey speeds as posted.

NO WAKE ZONE

No Wake Zones, Idle Speed Zones and various Speed Limit restrictions are in effect throughout the waterways included in this chapter. Exercise diligence in knowing the regulations by observing signs and other markers. Enforcement is always present. As always, be courteous to other vessels and avoid manatees and other marine life.

Crab Pot & Trap Markers

The terms "pot" and "trap" are somewhat interchangeable when referring to the enclosed traps (usually a framework of wire) used to catch crabs in shallow waters. The attached retrieval markers or "pots" can range from colorful buoys to empty milk jugs (or anything else that floats). They are so ubiquitous that some creeks and rivers along the ICW are clogged with pots making navigation tricky. Dark-colored markers are especially difficult to see in the best of conditions.

You do NOT want to get a line wrapped around your prop so it is advisable to have a spotter on the foredeck when traversing fields of pots. While it is against the law to place crab pots with marker buoys inside navigational channels, they

SOUTHERN EDITION

Chapter 1: Fernandina Beach to St. Johns River

Amelia Island Marina on Kingsleys Creek

sometimes break loose and find their way there. Crab pots can, however, assist with navigation. On many stretches of the ICW they delimit the channel and can often warn operators when they stray to the edge of the channel.

Docking & Anchoring

Much of Florida's eastern ICW channel is narrow with shallow edges and anchorages are sometimes widely spaced. As the population continues to increase, favorite anchorages become more crowded or re-designated. Good anchorages are still available if you plan ahead but not all allow shore access. Holding is generally good but keep in mind that the strong currents in the ICW may require extra scope and swing room. Also remember that most currents in the ICW run with the tides and ebb and flood currents might differ significantly. If possible pick a protected spot where tidal effects are minimal such as behind a causeway.

Use of an anchor light is important and required by law and, in some places, you will be ticketed for not having one on at night. Florida restrictions on anchoring are changing on a regular basis. Plan your stops in advance and be sure to check that anchoring is allowed at your chosen stop.

The same space shortage applies to marina dockage so you should reserve ahead or plan to arrive early at your chosen marina during the winter cruising season. Most dockmasters make every effort to find room for one more and the friendliness of the boating community more than makes up for the crowded conditions.

■ AMELIA ISLAND

Amelia Island–ICW Mile 716 to Mile 721

Tracing the ICW route south you can trace timelines in history as well. Amelia Island has enjoyed a colorful history. In its earlier years pirates and smugglers used it as their stronghold and rum runners continued the tradition during Prohibition. Eight different flags have flown over Amelia Island, among them the standard of the Conquistadors and the French Huguenots, the British Union Jack and the Stars and Bars of the Confederacy. The island's historic past can be explored at Fort Clinch State Park at the northern tip. The park has an impressive Civil War era fort and several walking trails but boats are not permitted to beach along the park's shoreline. Contact the park if planning a visit.

America's Waterway Guide Since 1947 — Chapter 1

Amelia River, FL

FERNANDINA BEACH AREA		Largest Vessel	VHF	Total Slips	Approach/ Dockside Depth	Floating Docks	Gas/ Diesel	Repairs/ Haulout	Min/Max Amps	Pump-Out Station
1. Tiger Point Marina WiFi MM 715.3	(904) 277-2720	55	16	50	7.0 / 8.0	F		RH	30 / 50	
2. Port Consolidated - Fernandina Beach MM 716.5	(904) 753-4258	285	16	13	50.0 / 30.0		D			
3. Oasis Marinas at Fernandina Harbor WiFi MM 716.7	(904) 310-3300	250	16		18.0 / 8.0	F	GD		30 / 100	P
4. Windward at Amelia Island Marina WiFi 720.6	(904) 277-4615	110	16	147	7.0 / 7.0	F	GD	RH	30 / 50	P

WiFi Wireless Internet Access
Visit www.waterwayguide.com for current rates, fuel prices, website addresses and other up-to-the-minute information. (Information in the table is provided by the facilities.)

Scan here for more details:

Source: Aqua Map and NOAA data

Today Amelia Island is a popular destination known for luxury resorts, golf courses and sandy beaches. Florida's northernmost city, Fernandina Beach, is on Amelia Island. The historic downtown district is located next to the waterfront and has several restaurants, taverns and gift shops.

NAVIGATION: Use NOAA Chart 11489.

> NOTE: Markers are constantly being moved along the channel inside Amelia Island and we recommend you have the latest chart editions. Consult the Waterway Explorer (www.waterwayguide.com) for updated location of the buoys and the most current information on how to navigate this section. Most of all, be mindful of the buoys and, if possible, favor the side of the channel away from where the shoaling is taking place. When in doubt, take it slow and schedule your passage on a rising tide near high water.

The Amelia River breaks off to the west from Mile 719.8 just southwest of the mouth of Jackson Creek. The ICW turns south here and enters Kingsley Creek. Two bridges span the ICW at Mile 720.7–**Kingsley Creek Railroad Bridge** and the high-rise **Thomas J. Shave, Jr. Twin Bridges** (also known as the **Kingsley Creek Twin Bridges**). Some charts may be off here. Maintain the visual center for 20 feet MLW approaching the bridges.

> CAUTION: The high-level bridges along this stretch are unofficially considered to be among the "lowest" of the 65-foot bridges on the ICW; expect no more than 64 feet at high tide. If in doubt check the clearance boards and go through at half tide. With the wide tidal range (7 feet) currents can be unexpectedly strong.

Although the Kingsley Creek Railroad Bridge (5-foot closed vertical clearance) is usually open, trains hauling

SOUTHERN EDITION

Chapter 1: Fernandina Beach to St. Johns River

Goin' Ashore

FERNANDINA BEACH, FL

ATTRACTIONS

1. **Amelia Island Lighthouse**
   Florida's oldest lighthouse was built in 1838 and is located on Egans Creek. Tours are available for a fee and pre-registration is required (904-310-3350).

2. **Amelia Island Museum of History**
   Located in an old jail at 233 S. 3rd St. (904-261-7378) with docent-led tours of homes, pubs and even ghost hangouts (for a fee).

3. **Blue Door Artists**
   Collective of 13 working artists showcasing a variety of fine art and crafts including jewelry, photography, sculpture, weaving, art objects, watercolors, oils, acrylics, mixed media and local inspired art. Open daily from 11:00 a.m. to 5:00 p.m. except Tuesday and until 7:00 p.m. the second Saturday of each month at 205 Centre St. (904-491-7733).

4. **Fernandina Beach Market Place**
   Outdoor Farmers' Market featuring local vendors selling produce, crafts and handmade goods. Open Saturdays from 9:00 a.m. to 1:00 p.m. at N. 7th St.

5. **Fort Clinch State Park**
   Historic fort features guided tours, reenactments and beautiful views of the beach and surrounding landscape. Open daily from 8:00 a.m. to 8:00 p.m. at 2601 Atlantic Ave. (904-277-7274).

6. **Maritime Museum of Amelia Island**
   Maritime history, pirate lore and marine artifacts are showcased at 115 S. 2nd St. (904-432-7086). Open Tuesday through Saturday; call for hours and admission fee.

7. **Marlin & Barrel Distillery**
   Stop in for a sampling and stay to hear about the distilling process at 232 S. 8th St. (904-556-3837).

SERVICES

8. **Amelia Island Welcome Center**
   102 Centre St. (904-277-0717)

9. **Fernandina Post Office**
   401 Centre St. (800-275-8777)

10. **Nassau County Public Library - Fernandina**
    25 N. 4th St. (904-530-6500)

MARINAS

11. **Oasis Marinas at Fernandina Harbor**
    3 S. Front St. (904-310-3300)

Fernandina Beach

America's Waterway Guide Since 1947

Chapter 1

The downtown historic district of Fernandina Beach, a 50-block section surrounding Centre St., is an attractive and popular gingerbread seaport dating from the 1850s, when Florida's first cross-state railroad ran from Fernandina to Cedar Key. The area is listed on the National Historic Register and the historic district features beautiful architecture, boutique shops and a variety of dining options, making this a wonderful cruising stopover. Provisions and supplies within an easy walk of the marina area and waterfront including Amelia Island Paint, Hardware & Marine Supply, which offers a good selection of hardware and boating staples at 516 Ash St. (904-261-6604).

SOUTHERN EDITION 123

Chapter 1: Fernandina Beach to St. Johns River

logs to the area's paper mills can delay your journey. The bridge gives no warning when it is going to close and it does not have a VHF radio. If you are in this area and you hear train whistles be aware that the bridge could close as you approach it.

After passing beneath the bridges you could see either a wide expanse of water or mud flats on either side of the channel depending on the state of the tide. Keep in the center of the dredged channel (20-foot MLW depths) as it shoals quickly on both sides.

Dockage/Moorings: At Mile 715.3 is the entrance to Egans Creek (east of the ICW), which leads to Tiger Point Marina, the first marina you will encounter as you enter Florida from the north. This is a full-service boat yard with limited transient slips to 55 feet.

Boats with large tankage can find great prices for diesel and gas at Port Consolidated (Mile 716.5). There is a 200-gallon minimum. It is best to approach their fixed commercial dock at higher tides. Many commercial vessels fuel here so even though the pumps are super fast, there may be a wait. Transient dockage is not available.

Oasis Marinas at Fernandina Harbor is at Mile 716.7 with 5,875 linear feet of dockage providing 60 lineal side-tie slips and 20 moorings. Deep water (8 foot MLW) dockside depths allows yachts up to 250 feet to take advantage of this modern marina and all the amenities the community offers. Advance reservations are recommended for this popular facility.

Windward at Amelia Island Marina is on the east side just north of the bridges at Mile 720.6. This well-protected marina offers 132 wet slips for long and short-term stays and accommodates boats up to 110 feet. It is a full-service facility personalized boat service. They also have a courtesy car and an on-site boat club for rentals. The narrow channel leading to the marina should be traversed with a mid-tide or higher. There is good protection here in strong winds when other marinas may be too exposed but the transient slips fill quickly in bad weather so call ahead to check availability.

Anchorage: A convenient place to drop the hook is across from downtown in the entrance to the Amelia River. The current is very strong and switches directions so be sure to use lots of scope. Take care that

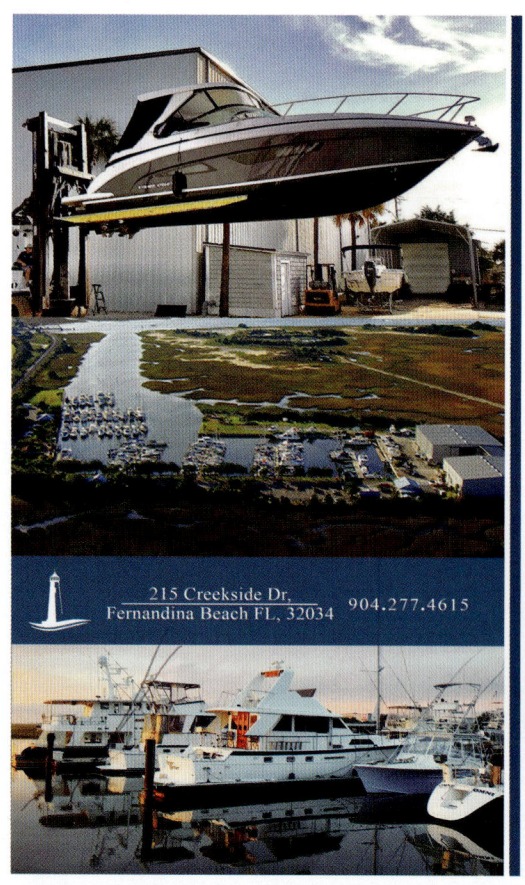

215 Creekside Dr, Fernandina Beach FL, 32034   904.277.4615

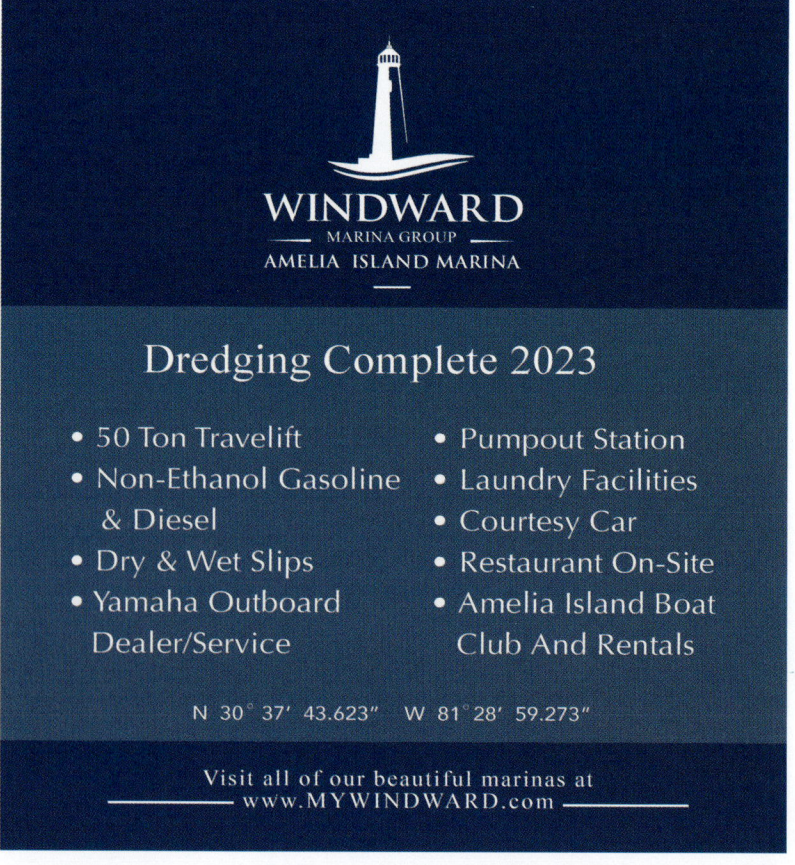

WINDWARD
MARINA GROUP
AMELIA ISLAND MARINA

Dredging Complete 2023

- 50 Ton Travelift
- Non-Ethanol Gasoline & Diesel
- Dry & Wet Slips
- Yamaha Outboard Dealer/Service
- Pumpout Station
- Laundry Facilities
- Courtesy Car
- Restaurant On-Site
- Amelia Island Boat Club And Rentals

N 30° 37' 43.623"   W 81° 28' 59.273"

Visit all of our beautiful marinas at
www.MYWINDWARD.com

your swing circle does not extend into the channel or the mooring area. Expect some small boat traffic during the day but at night its nice and calm. There is a very deep area of almost 50 feet just past this anchorage so when you drop the hook try and not get too close to this steep slope.

Anchored boats may use the dinghy dock and showers at Oasis Marinas at Fernandina Harbor for a modest fee. Although it is a relatively short dinghy ride to the marina dinghy dock, the anchorage and mooring areas are open to winds, wakes and considerable tidal current.

Another anchorage option is at Fernandina Beach, just north of the factory/paper mill on the ICW channel between red daybeacons "14" and "16." Watch for two shallow spots. There is good holding and wind protection from the south but no wake protection. Expect a strong current.

The Amelia River breaks off to the west of the ICW at Mile 719.8 at Piney Island with 6-to 7-foot MLW depths. Although it is preferred over Jackson Creek to the north, it is also quite narrow. Enter slowly with the depth sounder on. Be sure to lay out plenty of scope due to the swift currents but also be aware of your swing room.

If you get to the bridge only to find that you can't make it under due to tide or traffic, there is a spot to anchor just before the bridge in Kingsley Creek. The tide is very strong going each direction. This should be used while waiting for a bridge opening.

■ TO ST. JOHNS RIVER ENTRANCE

Fernandina Beach to Nassau Sound– ICW Mile 721 to Mile 731

The ICW follows a chain of rivers, creeks and cuts south from Amelia Island. With a tidal range of 6 feet or more this stretch is known for strong currents and changing shoals. This area has only light development but don't be distracted by the natural beauty and keep a watch on your course and depth sounder.

NAVIGATION: Use NOAA Chart 11489. Just past flashing red "28" (about Mile 724) you will pass Amelia City, tucked into a bend on the east side of the river. You will see bulkheads, some private docks and a few houses.

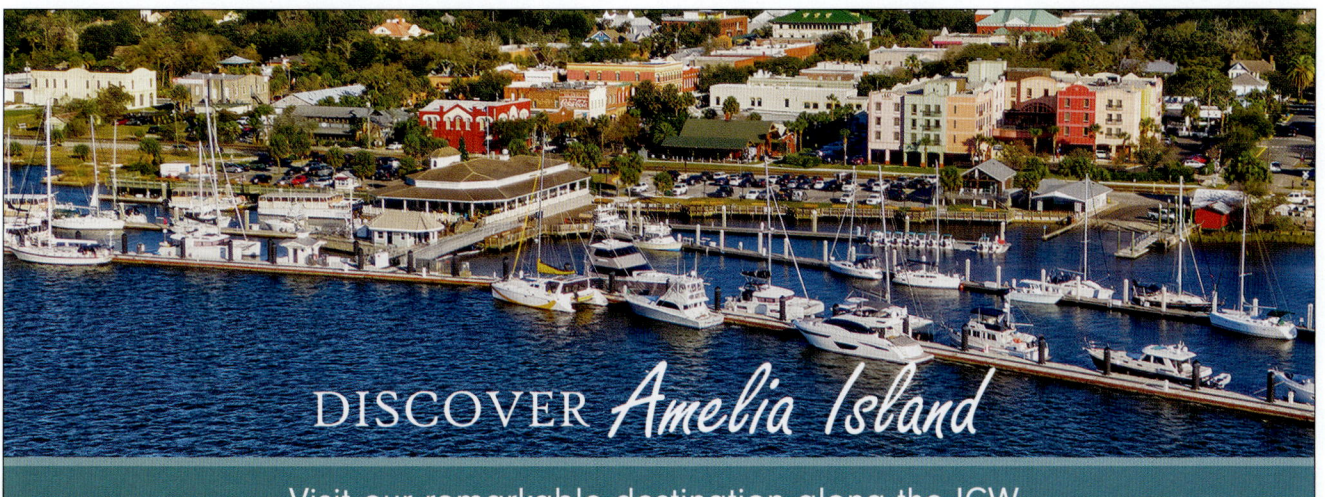

DISCOVER *Amelia Island*

Visit our remarkable destination along the ICW and explore the enchantment of Amelia Island, Florida!

For more information and to book your slip, visit fernandinaharbormarina.com or call 904-310-3300

Chapter 1: Fernandina Beach to St. Johns River

The current across Nassau Sound's ocean inlet at the southern end of Amelia Island may be very strong so watch your set and drift. Slow boats may have to crab across. The deepest water is closer to the inlet.

CAUTION: Because this is such a changeable area remember to be on the alert for shoaling and the possibility that there may be additional aids in place when you make passage here. This stretch is dredged frequently but shoaling is a continual problem.

The **George Crady Bridge** (15-foot fixed vertical clearance) and the **SR A1A Bridge** (21-foot fixed vertical clearance) block access to Nassau Sound Inlet for most boats. North of the bridges quick-flashing red "46" stands on a 16-foot mast and marks the turn to the entrance to the ICW cut leading southward.

NOTE: The lower portion of Amelia Island is home to a large and lovely resort community of Amelia Island Plantation. Dockage is not available on the premises.

Between ICW Miles 730 and 735 the shorelines close in somewhat as the channel runs through narrow land cuts and two natural creeks. Follow the aids to navigation as positioned and note that temporary markers may be present. Sawpit Creek and Gunnison Cut lead to Sisters Creek and the St. Johns River crossing.

Anchorage: The ICW channel hugs the Amelia Island shore south of Amelia City. To the west another deep channel meets the entrance to Alligator Creek. It is safer to enter this channel from the south of the ICW by turning to the northwest from flashing green "37." Be careful here; the entrance is shallow, carrying only 6-foot MLW depths, increasing to 8-foot MLW depths

Amelia Island Lighthouse

off Alligator Creek. Be aware that tugboats have been observed taking a shortcut through this anchorage area at high tide.

Just to the south it is also possible to anchor at the mouth of Harrison Creek inside green daybeacon "39" in 9 feet MLW with excellent holding in mud. Stay close to shore to avoid shoaling.

There is an excellent anchorage just east of red daybeacon "48" at Mile 731 in Nassau Sound. Enter Nassau Sound Island channel by hugging the southern shore as you enter for a minimum depth of 7 feet MLW deepening to 10 to 12 feet MLW to just short of the boat launch. There is good holding in sand but you must account for the tide when you let out scope to deal with the string reversing tidal current. Shore access (and trash disposal) is available at the boat launch.

Side Trip: Fort George River–ICW Mile 735

Fort George Island Cultural State Park makes an attractive side trip. The park features Indian mounds, the Kingsley Plantation, wildlife sanctuary and lush jungle growth.

NAVIGATION: Use NOAA Chart 11489. At Mile 735 the ICW meets the Fort George River. One mile east of the ICW channel, the Fort George Island Cultural State Park can be accessed from the river. The ICW channel is quite narrow here and some shoaling has been reported so it's best to slow down and closely monitor depths.

Anchorage: Enter the Fort George River just to the north for green daybeacon "73" and hug the southern shore for deeper water. There has been significant shoaling reaching out from the north shore so go slow and move farther to the south side if depths get uncomfortably shallow. Deep-draft vessels might consider other anchorages. Once past the shoal there is excellent anchoring in 6 to 15 feet MLW at Fort George Island. There is a good tidal current running through the anchorage so you will swing with the tide. Take the 6 foot tidal range into consideration as you let out scope. Shore access is available at the Kingsley Plantation.

Sisters Creek–ICW Mile 735 to Mile 740

NAVIGATION: Use NOAA Chart 11489. South of the ICW junction with the Fort George River the ICW route runs a straightforward path through Sisters Creek to the St. Johns River. (The ICW picks up on the other side at Pablo Creek.) As you travel along some sections of Sisters Creek you may see the superstructures of large ships headed up or down the St. Johns River. The **Napoleon Bonaparte Broward Bridge** (locally known as **Dames Point Bridge**) at the western end of Blount Island can be used as a landmark when you are headed south.

CAUTION: Watch for shoaling on both sides near Mile 735 where the Fort George River enters into Sisters Creek. The ICW channel is quite narrow here so it's best to slow down and monitor depths closely.

The **SR 105 (Sisters Creek) Bridge** at Mile 739.2 has 65-foot fixed vertical clearance. Expect heavy currents when passing under the bridge and approaching the St. Johns River.

> **NOTE:** Stay alert for large ships traversing the St. Johns River. Shipping traffic may be heavy. Keep in mind that large, oceangoing vessels have the right of way.

The pilots and captains of large vessels in this area always announce their approach and intentions at the Sisters Creek and St. Johns River intersection via Sécurité warnings. Listen on VHF Channel 16. Smaller vessels in the area should stay clear of these large vessels.

Crossing the St. Johns River where the river meets the ICW can present problems to lightly powered vessels due to the strong currents (2 to 3 knots on the ebb), obstructed visibility and continuous commercial traffic. Observe markers closely until you are safely into the ICW land cut (Pablo Creek) across the St. Johns River. This area has a clearly marked channel that should be very carefully followed. Note that the shipyard on the east side where Sisters Creek meets the St. Johns River creates a blind spot for small boats heading into the river.

The land cut from this point southward through the Jacksonville Beach area is well marked. The entrance from the St. Johns River into Pablo Creek has been dredged and the course of the ICW has been moved westward towards a large spoil island. Buoys have been repositioned to show the way through but they are small and often hard to see in hazy conditions and you must pass them by at least 50 feet off.

SOUTHERN EDITION 127

Chapter 1: Fernandina Beach to St. Johns River

Follow the markers carefully to stay on the channel's centerline and be prepared to squeeze over for tugs with barges. Note that you cannot proceed directly from flashing green "5" to green daybeacon "7" and must bend around the turn.

Dockage: Just above SR 105 (Sisters Creek) Bridge at Mile 739 is Jim King Park and Boat Ramp, which is for day dockage only. (No overnight dockage.) Dockside water, restrooms and pump-out service are available. This is a large boat ramp area that is usually congested, particularly on weekends. Don't even consider it during the Greater Jacksonville Kingfish Tournament in July.

For an overnight stay, try the free Jim King Park at Sisters Creek Marina located in a park up a small creek just west of Sisters Creek and across from Sisters Island. A concrete floating dock is designated as available for transient boaters for up to 72 hours. This dock is very stable with strong cleats and rubber edging. There is considerable current (up to 2 knots) that flows parallel to the dock when at other than slack tide so plan accordingly.

Anchorage: It is possible to anchor north of the bridge at Mile 739 in Sisters Creek with 8 to 11 feet MLW and good holding in mud. Nose in as draft/tide dictates to anchor. The strong current will be evident but there is surprisingly good protection from southeast wind-driven waves. Exposed to north winds and ICW wakes.

St. Johns River Entrance

The jetties of the St. Johns River Entrance are 5 nm from Mile 738 of the ICW. This is one of the safest and easiest gateways from the Atlantic Ocean. This entrance is used by ocean freighters, military vessels and recreational craft. Cruisers use this inlet as an entry and departure point for passages along the coast.

Significant local traffic comes from the busy marinas at Mayport (2 miles upriver) and on the ICW (5 miles upriver). Operators should stay alert, especially when rounding curves and in poor visibility situations. It is 150 nm south from St. Johns River Entrance to the next big ship entrance at Port Canaveral Inlet.

America's Waterway Guide Since 1947 — Chapter 1

St. Johns River Entrance, FL

ST. JOHNS RIVER		Largest Vessel	VHF	Total Slips	Approach/ Dockside Depth	Floating Docks	Gas/ Diesel	Repairs/ Haulout	Min/Max Amps	Pump-Out Station
1. Morningstar Marinas Mayport WiFi	(904) 246-8929	160	16	10	40.0 / 20.0	F	GD		30 / 50	
2. Fort George Island Marina	(904) 251-0050	80	16	13	40.0 / 25.0	F	GD	H	30 / 50	

WiFi Wireless Internet Access
Visit www.waterwayguide.com for current rates, fuel prices, website addresses and other up-to-the-minute information. (Information in the table is provided by the facilities.)

Scan here for more details:

OASIS MARINAS at FORT GEORGE ISLAND

Located on the beautiful St. John's River in Jacksonville!

INDOOR DRY STORAGE FACILITY

FUEL DOCK | PUMPOUT | BOATER'S LOUNGE

- 904-251-0050
- 9954 Heckscher Drive, Jacksonville, FL 32226
- fortgeorgeislandmarina.com
- 30° 24' 6.984" N / 81° 25' 54.192" W

BOOK NOW WITH SNAG A SLIP

SOUTHERN EDITION 129

Chapter 1 — Fernandina Beach to St. Johns River

NAVIGATION: Use NOAA Charts 11489, 11490 and 11491. The ocean approach landmark is St. Johns Light, which stands 83 feet above the shore 1 mile south of the St. Johns River north jetty. The light shines from a square white tower and is easy to spot from the ocean. The St. Johns River red and white sea buoy, flashing Morse (A) "STJ," is located 3 miles east of the jetties and guides boaters into the marked inlet channel. Other landmarks include a tower at Jacksonville Beach and a water tank (painted in a red and white checkerboard design) at the Mayport Naval Air Station. Other water tanks line the beaches to the south.

Inside the jetties the St. Johns River runs unobstructed and naturally deep past the Mayport Basin, which is usually occupied by enormous naval craft. The basin is off-limits to recreational craft except in extreme emergencies.

Tidal range on the St. Johns River varies from 5 feet at its mouth to 1 foot just south of Jacksonville. While the natural current of the St. Johns River is extremely slow, tidal currents range up to 3 knots with the 5-foot tide at Mayport and are strongest on ebb.

The town of Mayport, located 3 miles inside the entrance jetties on the south side of the river, is an important commercial and sportfishing center that provides dockage for cruising boats. Mayport is a good place to lay over before you start your cruise up the St. Johns River as supplies are readily available here. A Coast Guard station is located at the south end of the Mayport waterfront as well as a private luxury residential and marina project (Fort George Harbour).

> NOTE: A ferry runs across the St. Johns River from Mayport Village to Fort George Island weekdays on the hour and half-hour between 6:00 a.m. and 7:00 p.m. On weekends it runs from 7:00 a.m. to 8:30 p.m. The ferry operates every day (including holidays).

Dockage: On the south side of the river Morningstar Marinas Mayport provides transient dockage and services that include a courtesy car, a full-service laundry facility, a fully-stocked Ship Store and concierge services. They also have a full-service mechanic on site. This is a great place to wait for a weather window with easy access to the ICW and the Atlantic.

On the north side of the river is Fort George Island Marina, which is mostly a storage facility but they do maintain a few transient slips. The marina is rooted in maritime history and surrounded by historic landmarks that can be easily be explored on foot or by bicycle.

St. Johns Boat Company is a full-service boatyard that can handle all manner of services and repairs. They also offer bulk diesel fueling (with 24-hour notice) and emergency towing and welcome participation from subcontractors and boat crews (DIY).

■ NEXT STOP

The splendid St. Johns River, which winds its way from Mayport to Sanford, is described in the following chapter. Cruisers continuing south on the ICW will find the route resuming in Chapter 3: "St. Johns River to New Smyrna Beach."

ST. JOHNS BOAT COMPANY

With over 100 years in the marine industry, we seek to provide a facility that offers accessibility, versatility, and flexibility. We are conveniently located on the St. Johns River between the Atlantic Ocean & the Intracoastal Waterway with no approach restrictions.

- Emergency Towing
- 150 Metric Ton Travelift (up to 24'6" beam)
- 400' + Commercial Dock Space
- Blasting and Painting
- Fiberglass Detailing
- Prop and Shaft Repair
- Decking and Flooring
- Upholstery
- Carpentry, Sheet Metal and Insulation
- Steel and Aluminum Welding
- Shipfitting
- Pipefitting and Outside Machining
- Electrical
- Tank Cleaning
- Gas Free Services
- Potable Water
- Diesel Fuel and Lubricants

9852 Heckscher Drive • Jacksonville, FL 32226
904-251-3707
frontdesk@stjmarinegroup.com
stjmarinegroup.com

Side Trip on the St. Johns River

Chapter 2

SOUTHERN EDITION

Chapter 2: Side Trip on the St. Johns River

NAVIGATION NOTES

The St. Johns River is one of the few north-flowing rivers in the U.S. and travels 248 miles from the heart of central Florida to Mayport. The St. Johns River is a cruising ground with reliably mild winter weather and interesting towns, villages and secluded anchorages that should not be missed. The beauty is astounding and the cruising is wonderful. This is the route to the City of Jacksonville and is well worth the effort.

Residential areas with private piers line the shores south of Jacksonville to the Green Cove Springs area but the trees have been carefully preserved making it difficult to see some of the houses. The river is less developed and more scenic farther south. Part of the river is a wildlife sanctuary and many skippers make this beautiful trip an annual cruise. Shoreside development includes state parks, fish camps (both primitive and luxurious) and a few proper marinas, some large and some small.

In its narrow, winding sections, subtropical vegetation and heavy stands of trees grow right down to the water's edge. Its sloughs, creeks, oxbows and backwaters are often choked with water hyacinths but restraining fences and bulkheads help keep most of this floating vegetation out of the channel.

No Wake Zones, Idle Speed Zones and various Speed Limit restrictions are in effect throughout the waterways included in this chapter. Exercise diligence in knowing the regulations by observing signs and other markers. Enforcement is always present. As always, be courteous to other vessels and avoid manatees and other marine life.

Cruising Conditions

From the intersection of the St. Johns River and the ICW at ICW Mile 739.5, you are likely to meet several types of commercial vessels, from freighters, tankers and container ships to tugs towing large barges and even cruise ships. Upriver from Jacksonville commercial traffic consists mostly of the occasional tug and barge.

Overhead clearance is set by a series of fixed bridges. Upstream from Jacksonville the Henry H. Buckman Sr. (I-295) Bridge at Mile 35.1 has a clearance of 65 feet, but the most significant is the Shands Bridge at Mile 51.4 (opposite Red Bay Point), which carries a 45-foot vertical clearance.

Snags are seldom a problem in main channels of the St. Johns River, but approach side streams and sloughs carefully. Keep a sharp eye out for the ubiquitous crab trap markers, which vary from commercially produced floats to plastic bottles, and may drift into the channels. They can be tough to spot. Some are painted black, some are heavily fouled with dark vegetation and some are even pulled under water by the current.

A good outboard-powered dinghy will enhance your pleasure in discovering the varied scenery along the St. Johns River's upper reaches. (Note, however, that alligators are common enough to warrant wariness in letting your pets roam.) If you plan to gunkhole, it would be advisable to carry a lead line or long boat pole to supplement your depth sounder. We find the crowd-sourced Navionics Sonar Charts useful along the St. Johns River, as fishermen have explored most of the creeks and uploaded their soundings.

It is important to recognize that Central Florida has two unique, seasonal, non-biting flying hazards–blind mosquitoes and lovebugs. The first is neither blind nor a mosquito but actually a freshwater midge that swarms in late spring and summer and is attracted to lights at night. Lovebugs also swarm in great numbers as they mate into bizarre "push me-pull you" flying unions for a short period in April/May and August/September but are active only in daytime. Either species can cover your boat with their fiberglass-staining carcasses. Inquire before you get here to learn if a hatch of these pests is underway.

Recreational craft use the river year-round. On weekends and holidays, especially when the weather is good, parts of the river carry heavy traffic. You will see everything from mid-sized cruisers and small runabouts to bass boats and personal watercraft, all in a great hurry to reach their destinations. Fishing is good but remember that you need a Florida fishing license if you are 16 or older. Florida residents who are 65+ get a break.

River Currents, Tides & Depths

Skippers of sailboats with auxiliary power or low-powered motor cruisers should check their tidal current tables before starting upriver to Jacksonville from the ICW or Atlantic Ocean entrance. River currents meeting strong

America's Waterway Guide Since 1947 **Chapter 2**

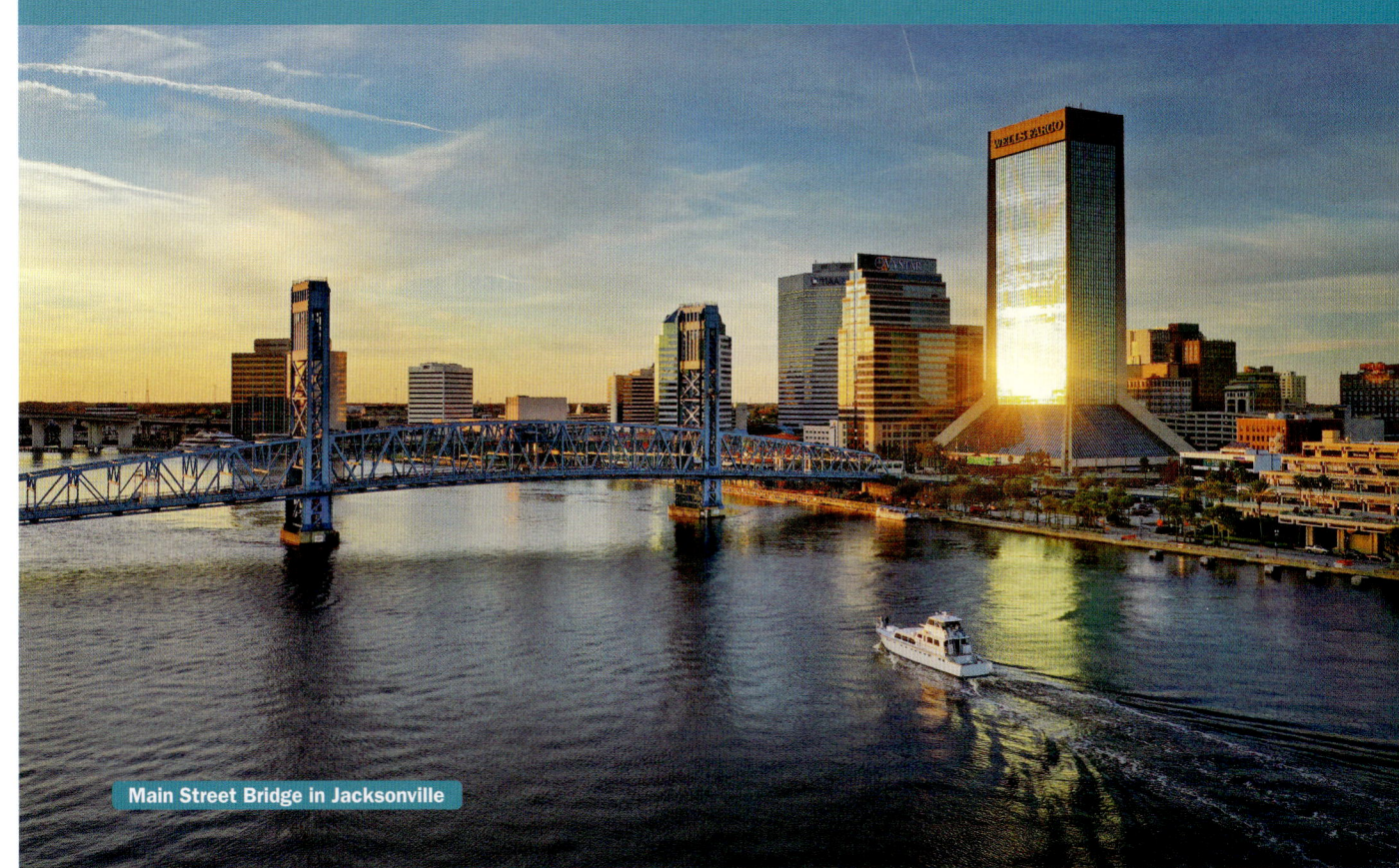
Main Street Bridge in Jacksonville

ocean tides can create tricky conditions, especially near Jacksonville's cluster of downtown bridges.

Currents are more important than tidal range as the ebb in the river can run 2 to 3 knots making for a slow passage for underpowered boats. Up-to-date NOAA Tide Tables (www.tidesandcurrents.noaa.gov) give corrections to the Shands Bridge at Red Bay Point near Green Cove Springs. The average maximum flood given is 0.9 knots and the average maximum ebb is 0.6 knots.

The next noteworthy location is Tocoi, approximately 15 miles upriver. Current past Tocoi can be strongly influenced by the water level in the upper (southern) part of the river, which varies with seasonal rainfall. Summer is wet while winter is dry. Crosscurrents can be strong enough to make docking difficult for the unwary.

The spring range (full and new moon) at Mayport can exceed 5 feet and at Palatka, around 1.5 feet. Wind and rainfall affect depths dramatically in the upper reaches. Lake Monroe (Mile 164) may be 5 feet deeper after summer rains and storms than at the end of a dry winter in March. The river currents are strongest when the water is high and draining rapidly into the ocean. Usually a current sets with the tide as far as Lake George. South of the lake the weak current sets downstream (northward).

There's another variable: the St. Johns River Authority operates a system of dams and canals that control the water in connected lakes so cruisers may encounter unexpected water level changes in the entire network. One useful indicator is the depth of Lake Monroe at the navigable headwaters of the river.

JACKSONVILLE AREA

Southbound on the ICW the waterway crosses the St. Johns River just west of Mile Point about 5 miles from the St. Johns River Entrance and a little over 1 mile west of Mayport. At that point the ICW leaves Sisters Creek and enters Pablo Creek at red nun "2" (Mile 740) for the run south. In this chapter, however, we are going to make a turn to starboard and then travel south "up" the St. Johns River (red markers to starboard), which flows from the heart of central Florida northward for 248 miles to the Atlantic Ocean at Mayport.

The route to Jacksonville is a big ship channel that generally follows the wide, natural course of the river and is simple to run. The main precaution is to avoid commercial traffic. The channel is well marked and many markers are lighted for nighttime passage. There

Chapter 2 — Side Trip on the St. Johns River

are no intricate ranges and the next light or marker is always within sight. For the most part deep water prevails alongside the marked channel, although there are some partially submerged wrecks and shoals near the edge so it is best to stay within the marked channel. Our mileage guide starts with Mile 0 at the mouth of Sisters Creek.

St. Johns River to Dames Point

NAVIGATION: Use NOAA Chart 11491. (NOAA Chart 11491 covers the mouth of the St. Johns River from the Atlantic Ocean to the Ortega River just past downtown Jacksonville.)

While currents gradually decrease upriver on the St. Johns River, the flow runs up to 3 knots at first and can be a major factor near the downtown Jacksonville bridges where the river narrows. If you require an opening contact the operator of the **Main Street Bridge–St. Johns River** on VHF Channel 09 well before approach (Mile 24.7). Plan your trip for a fair current by calculating slack before flood and maximum flood at Mile Point (at flashing red buoy "22") on the St. Johns River to get an interval of time to arrive at the ICW crossing.

The *United States Coast Pilot (Volume 4)* points out four critical traffic areas on the St. Johns:

1. Junction of the St. Johns River and the ICW
2. Dames Point Turn
3. Trout River Cut
4. Commodore Point

Commercial vessels must give a Sécurité call on VHF Channel 13 to avoid meeting one another at these points. Recreational boats do not need to do so (as you will have enough maneuvering room to stay out of the way) but you should monitor VHF Channel 13 so you will know whether you will be meeting a big ship or a tug with tow.

West of Sisters Creek and the ICW the channel enters wide and straight Dames Point–Fulton Cutoff, which is frequently dredged to eliminate a bend in the St. Johns River's natural course. The impressive high-level **Napoleon Bonaparte Broward Bridge** (locally known as **Dames Point Bridge**) across the St. Johns River and Mill Cove is locally known as Dames Point Bridge.

Mainly a complex of wharves, warehouses and a container terminal, Blount Island (created by dredge spoil) is on the north side of the Dames Point–Fulton

Dames Point Bridge

Cutoff channel. Although the loop behind the island is deep, three low bridges (with 5-, 8- and 10-foot fixed vertical clearances) prevent a complete circuit. Blount Island Marine Terminal Entrance Channel (Back River) pierces Blount Island from the Dames Point–Fulton Cutoff Channel; it is entirely commercial. Recreational craft should not attempt to anchor or fish in the channel.

Dockage: Palms Fish Camp Restaurant east of Blount Island offers free dockage for diners. Located on Clapboard Creek, this Old Florida "Cracker" style fish camp features amazing views of the Timucuan Ecological and Historic Preserve from the large rear deck, especially at sunset. Boaters are welcome to tie up to the floating dock to visit the restaurant.

Anchorage: You may anchor off Little Marsh Island east of Blount Island but be sure to stay clear of the channel. Watch for pot markers and do not interfere with the private docks along Little Marsh Island. There is no place to go ashore here and it is very busy with commercial traffic.

A better anchorage is at Reed Island (across from Blount Island) in at least 10 feet at MLW with good holding in mud. It is, however, open to north and south wind and wakes from river traffic. Depths may be less than charted.

Dames Point to Trout River

NAVIGATION: Use NOAA Chart 11491. The unmarked Broward River requires local knowledge and is blocked off by a wharf extending 500 yards from shore as well as the SR 105 Bridge (20-foot fixed vertical clearance) crossing the entrance. Many shallow-draft local boats use the Trout River just 2 miles to the south. (Note that the dinghy dock at the Jacksonville Zoo on the Trout River was destroyed by Hurricane Irma and there are plans to rebuild but no estimated timeframe.)

To access the Trout River turn off the main St. Johns River channel between flashing red buoys "64" and "66" into the Trout River and then pick up red daybeacon "2" and green daybeacon "3," which mark the Trout River Channel. Enter close to green daybeacon "43" to miss the shallow water surrounding green "45."

The fixed 29-foot fixed vertical clearance **Trout River (US 17) Bridge** and **CSX Transportation Railroad Bridge** cross the river a short distance upstream. The 2-foot closed vertical clearance railroad swing bridge is not tended and is usually open. The lights change to flashing red and a horn continuously sounds while the draw closes when a train approaches.

Dockage: Twin daybeacons red "2" and green "3" mark the entrance to the family-friendly Seafarer's Marina on the Trout River, which has some transient space and dockside and approach depths of 10 feet MLW. The owners are boaters and there is a fair representation of sailboats here. Groceries and restaurants are nearby.

City of Jacksonville

Following the Civil War Jacksonville became a popular winter resort due to its mild climate, low labor costs and easy rail access. Jacksonville International Airport, 10 miles north of the city, has commercial air service to all major cities.

NAVIGATION: Use NOAA Chart 11491. From the ICW crossing the river generally winds in an east-west direction until it broadens at Hendricks Point in South Jacksonville and turns south. Most of the development is on the western shore, south of the Ortega River, ranging from summer cabins and elegant homes to large commercial complexes. The heavily industrialized riverfront (with the largest deep water harbor on the southern Atlantic coast) begins just off the Trout River near flashing red "64."

The St. Johns River runs wide and deep past the yards and wharves. About 12 miles past the high-level Napoleon Bonaparte Broward Bridge at Mile 13.1. At Mile 21.8 is the red **John E. Mathews Bridge** (86-foot fixed vertical clearance) followed by the green high-level **Isaiah D. Hart Bridge** (locally known as the **Hart-Commodore Bridge**) at Mile 22.8.

> NOTE: Tugs and barges cross the river channel at all hours of the day and night so be cautious in this area.

The four remaining Jacksonville bridges are less than 1 mile apart. Starting from the east is the unmistakable blue **Main Street Bridge** (Mile 24.7), followed by the high-level **Acosta Bridge** (Mile 24.8), the **Florida East Coast Railroad Bridge** (Mile 24.9) and the high-level **Fuller Warren Bridge** (Mile 25.5).

The 40-foot closed vertical clearance Main Street Bridge opens on signal except from 7:00 a.m. to 8:30 a.m. and from 4:30 p.m. to 6:00 p.m., Monday through Saturday (except federal holidays), when the draw need not open for the passage of vessels. The 5-foot closed

Chapter 2: Side Trip on the St. Johns River

GOIN' ASHORE
JACKSONVILLE, FL

ATTRACTIONS

1. **Cummer Museum of Art & Gardens**
   Museum showcases 5,000 works of art from all eras in a riverfront site surrounded by gardens at 829 Riverside Ave. (904-356-6857).

2. **Museum of Contemporary Art**
   Changing exhibits and permanent works of art can be viewed at 333 N. Laura St. (904-366-6911).

3. **Museum of Science & History (MOSH)**
   Features interactive exhibits of native wildlife and home to the Bryan-Gooding Planetarium (1025 Museum Cir., 904-396-6674).

4. **Riverside Arts Market**
   Lively market held Saturdays under the bridge featuring local artists, food vendors and entertainment (904-389-2449).

SERVICES

5. **Baptist Medical Center Jacksonville**
   4050 Town Center Pkwy. (904-202-6800)

6. **Jacksonville Public Library**
   303 N. Laura St. (904-630-2665)

7. **Visit Jacksonville**
   208 N. Laura St. #102 (904-798-9111)

Chapter 2
America's Waterway Guide Since 1947

Beyond the busy commercial area, the Jacksonville waterfront is delightful. Tranquil riverside parks and open space line both banks of the river. A variety of dining options and shops are only a block away from the 2-mile-long Northbank Riverwalk. Across the river is the 1.25-mile wooden zigzag boardwalk known as Southbank Riverwalk. A highlight is the Friendship Fountain, a huge, circular fountain with jets of water that shoot as high as 120 feet into the air.

The 110-acre Jacksonville Zoo and Gardens is home to over 2,000 animals as well as botanical gardens and a train ride through the park (904-757-4463). Transportation required.

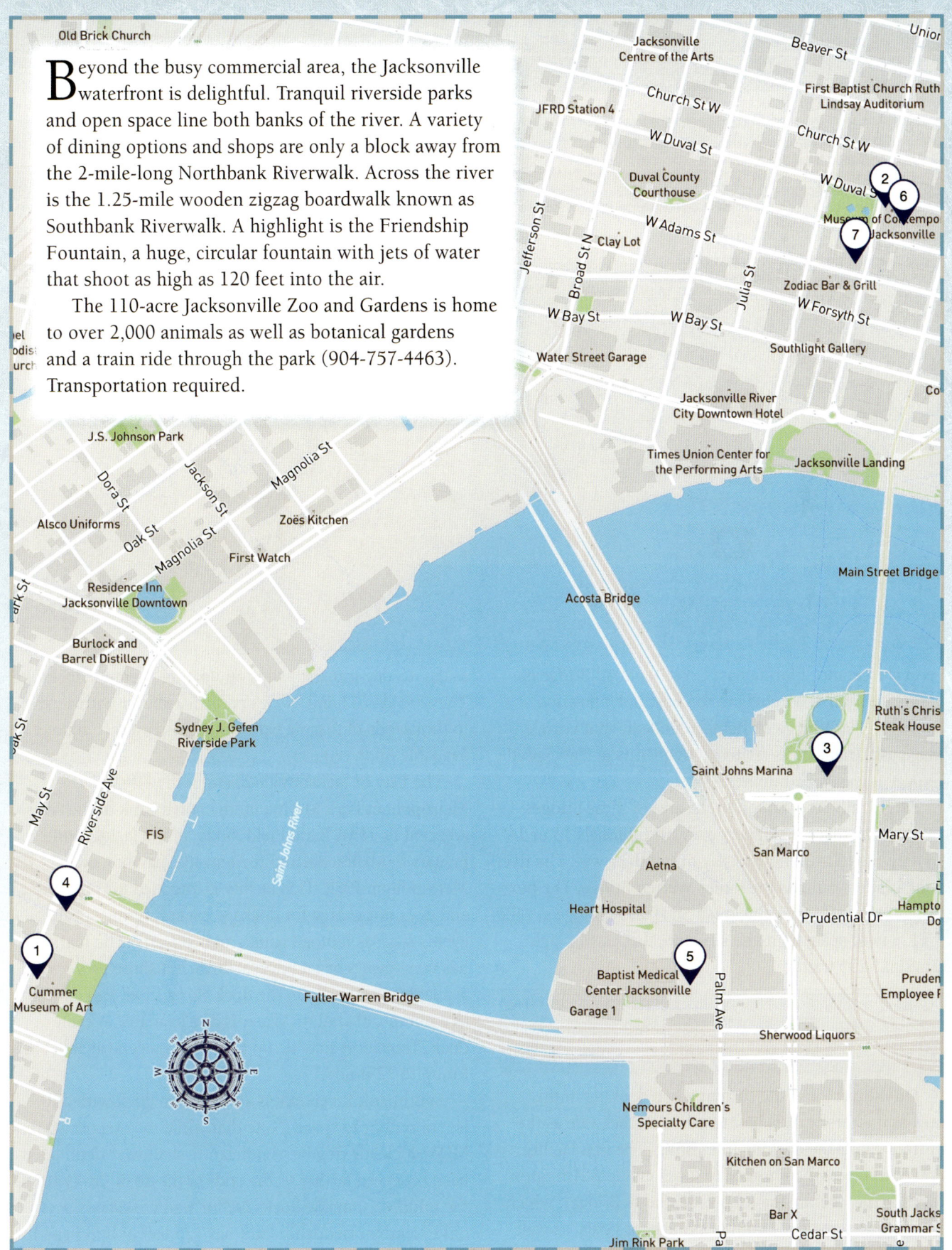

SOUTHERN EDITION 137

Chapter 2: Side Trip on the St. Johns River

St. Johns River, FL

TROUT RIVER		Largest Vessel	VHF	Total Slips	Approach/ Dockside Depth	Floating Docks	Gas/ Diesel	Repairs/ Haulout	Min/Max Amps	Pump-Out Station
1. Seafarer's Marina WiFi	(904) 765-8152	80	16	75	10.0 / 10.0				30 / 50	P
ARLINGTON										
2. Arlington Marina, Inc. WiFi	(904) 743-2628	60	16	30	16.0 / 5.0	F	GD	H	30 / 50	

WiFi Wireless Internet Access
Visit www.waterwayguide.com for current rates, fuel prices, website addresses and other up-to-the-minute information. (Information in the table is provided by the facilities.)

Scan here for more details:

Source: Aqua Map and NOAA data

vertical clearance Florida East Coast Railroad Bridge is automated and is normally in the fully open position displaying flashing green lights to indicate that vessels may pass. Trains cross relatively frequently at slow speed. Expect at least a 20-minute delay.

Barge traffic is common in the area of these bridges. Contact the tugboat skippers on VHF Channels 13 or 16 so they can tell you how to stay out of their way. The river widens after you pass the Fuller Warren Bridge. The next bridge is the Henry H. Buckman Sr. (I-295) Bridge at Mile 35.1, a twin-span, high-rise structure that carries eight lanes of I-295 traffic.

> NOTE: Rather than calling the Coast Guard directly for navigation information, listen to the *Local Notice to Mariners* broadcast on VHF Channel 22A at 8:15 a.m. and 6:15 p.m. daily.

Dockage: Mind the current when docking in this area as it is strong. It is best to arrive at slack tide as the current can make docking interesting. The first facility you encounter when headed to Jacksonville is Arlington Marina, Inc. (before the John E. Mathews Bridge), which has both wet and dry monthly storage for boats, as well as day-to-day transient slips on floating concrete docks. They are also a Land 'N' Sea parts distributor with access to thousands of marine parts and accessories. (Catalogs available upon request.)

The City of Jacksonville operates the 78-slip Metropolitan Park Marina on the north bank of the river adjacent to TIAA Bank Field, home of the Jacksonville Jaguars football team and the tent-like pavilion of Metropolitan Park. This facility is intended for public use and does not charge for dockage except during special events such as football games and concerts. The marina has no showers or laundry facilities but shore power is available via a kiosk on the dock (for a small fee) as well as a pump-out station. Water is also available at each dock. Transients may tie up here on a space-available basis for up to 72 hours.

Southbank Riverwalk is another free dock with 120 feet of bulkhead space. Note that while they report 10-foot MLW dockside depths, significantly shallower depths have been observed farther to the ends of the dock (away from the middle). Outside docks are for water taxi/contracts only. Nearby Friendship Park has 125 feet of bulkhead for boats to 65 feet. Use caution and check depths carefully. Public washroom about 400 feet east at turn in Riverwalk in small building. Short walking distance to the Museum of Science History (MOSH). This area offers a nice view of city at night. Posted signs at both facilities state that stays are limited to 72 hours in any month.

Directly across the river is Jacksonville Landing - Northbank Riverwalk with 250 feet of bulkhead. Part of the dock is painted yellow with signage for the water taxi so do not dock there. Overnight dockage rules appear to change frequently so consult current signage. A short walk downriver is the Navy Ship *USS Orleck*, which is temporarily moored on the wall until it is moved to old shipyard slip about another 0.3 miles downriver, where it will function as a museum.

About 1 mile west is Northbank Riverwalk with new (in March 2022) solid docks with two slips and a 66-foot T-head. Signage indicates 72 hours of free dockage is allowed. As noted above, consult current signage for rules. It is a short walk for groceries or restaurants.

Anchorage: You can anchor near the John E. Mathews Bridge between Exchange Island and the Arlington waterfront. Holding ground is best north of the bridge in 9- to 11-foot MLW depths. With the wind is out of the north you might elect to anchor in 8 to 20 feet MLW on the southern side of the bridge. (Expect some bridge traffic noise here in a north wind.) Traffic in the main channel might jostle you on either side of the bridge. Just north of the anchorage is a dock for tugs. Note that local folks may party late on the island during weekends. You may also see college rowing teams honing their skills against the swift current.

▌ TO PALATKA

Through the 1920s-vintage classic Ortega River Bridge lies a busy series of marinas and yards aptly named "Jacksonville Marina Mile." Because of its low clearance in an area of high marine traffic, this is the most frequently opened drawbridge in Florida (about 15,000 openings per year).

The northwest bank of the Ortega River is almost a solid wall of yards, marinas and boatbuilders. The southwest shore is entirely residential with private docks and wooded plots. The only problem in finding a berth here may be choosing among the yards and marinas, many of which welcome transients.

OUR LOCATION IS EASY TO FIND, BUT THE SERVICE IS OFF THE CHARTS.

HUCKINS FULL-SERVICE BOATYARD OFFERS:

- Certified mechanics, electricians, painters and carpenters
- 40-ton and 77-ton travel lifts
- 36' high dust free paint booth
- 11 service bays for restoration and repairs
- Boat transport service (to-and-from yard)
- Complimentary boat wash
- Authorized parts available

AMENITIES:

- Dockage up to 60'
- 20 Wet Slips
- 30/50 AMP Electric
- Night Security
- Complimentary Wi-Fi
- Parts & Supplies Available
- Walking distance to West Marine, Publix, restaurants and shops
- 25 minutes from Jacksonville International Airport (JAX)

HUCKINS YACHT

3482 Lakeshore Boulevard · Jacksonville, Florida 32210 ·
(904) 389-1125 · huckinsyacht.com · service@huckinsyacht.com

— SERVICES —

Hauling & Launching · Fiberglass & Composites ·
Restoration · Carpentry · Paint & Varnish · Design & Engineering · Diesel Conversions · Engine Repair ·
Repowering · Remodeling or Upgrading · Rewiring · Generator Work · Mechanical & Electronics · Warranty Work ·
Prop Work · Bottom Work ·
Canvas & Upholstery · Refrigeration & A/C

Chapter 2: Side Trip on the St. Johns River

All of the marinas are close to Roosevelt Square, which is only five blocks from the waterfront. It has a large variety of shore amenities (restaurants and shops, a pharmacy, a West Marine and a large grocery store). There is also convenient city bus service here that runs to downtown Jacksonville.

CAUTION: Note that depending on your draft and clearance, fuel may not be available between Ortega River and Monroe Harbor (where diesel can be delivered as needed by truck with a two-day advance notice).

If you are planning on continuing south on the St. Johns River, this is the last place to conveniently provision and fuel the boat. There are stores along the St. Johns but you will need ground transportation to get to most of them, which could be a problem in some of the small, out-of-the-way places you'll encounter.

NAVIGATION: Use NOAA Chart 11491. While heading due south from the Fuller Warren Bridge, delay your westward turn to the Ortega River until you pass flashing red "2" in the St. Johns River and the orange-white daybeacon marking the shoal extending south off Winter Point. A series of private buoys mark a channel from the mouth of the Ortega River to the marinas beyond the bridge. Be sure your charts are up-to-date. If in doubt, follow a local boat in and mind the charted obstructions and pilings north of Sadler Point.

Large local yachts use the entrance regularly. Depths here are 5 to 8 feet MLW in the river (with shallower spots) so watch the depth sounder and proceed slowly, especially if you have a draft of 5 feet or more. The tidal range is about 1 foot.

For the deepest water give a wide berth to the shoal off Sadler Point and line up for the **Ortega River Bridge** after you are clear of the shallow water. The bridge has 9-foot closed vertical clearance and opens on signal. Depths are relatively consistent at 5 to 8 feet MLW beyond the fixed **Roosevelt Blvd. Bridge** (45-foot vertical clearance). The busy **CSX Transportation Railroad Bridge** crosses the Ortega River just past the Roosevelt Blvd. Bridge.

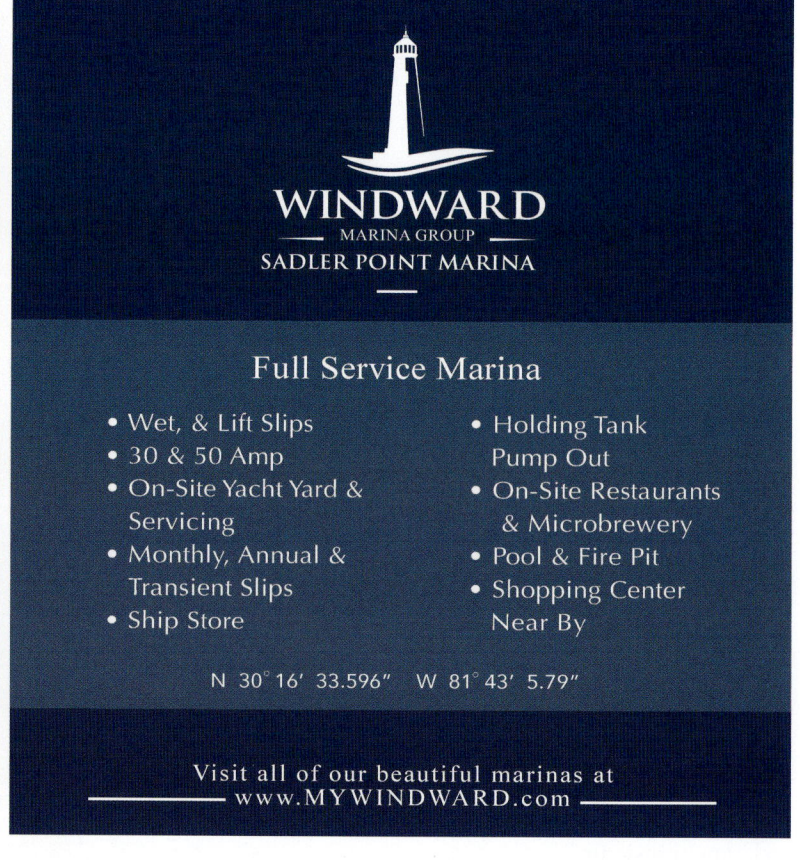

America's Waterway Guide Since 1947   **Chapter 2**

Ortega River, FL

ORTEGA RIVER		Largest Vessel	VHF	Total Slips	Approach/ Dockside Depth	Floating Docks	Gas/ Diesel	Repairs/ Haulout	Min/Max Amps	Pump-Out Station
1. PORT 32 Jacksonville WiFi	(904) 387-5538	130	16	192	6.0 / 6.0	F			30 / 100	P
2. Windward at Sadler Point Marina WiFi	(904) 384-1383	60	16	99	7.0 / 6.0			RH	30 / 50	P
3. Cedar Point Marina	(904) 384-5577	60		23	12.0 / 5.0	F			30 / 50	P
4. Lamb's Yacht Center WiFi	(904) 384-5577	120	16	240	8.0 / 7.0		GD	RH	30 / 100	P
5. Florida Yacht Club-PRIVATE	(904) 387-1653	70	16	73	8.0 / 6.0	F			30 / 50	

WiFi Wireless Internet Access
Visit www.waterwayguide.com for current rates, fuel prices, website addresses and other up-to-the-minute information.
(Information in the table is provided by the facilities.)

Scan here for more details:

Source: Aqua Map and NOAA data

Dockage: In the basin beyond the Ortega River Bridge) the well-maintained PORT 32 Jacksonville is the first marina to on the northwest shore. This popular marina has full cruiser amenities including a heated pool and hot tub, loaner bikes and a free laundry.

Windward at Sadler Point Marina, the last facility before the Roosevelt Blvd. Bridge, is a full-service boatyard and Yamaha Service Center with some transient space and full amenities including use of beach cruisers (bicycles) for exploring the area.

Several marinas are beyond the 45-foot fixed vertical clearance Roosevelt Blvd. Bridge and the CSX Transportation Railroad Bridge (usually open). Immediately to starboard past the railroad bridge is Huckins Yacht Corp., known for its beautiful custom yachts. Frank Pembroke Huckins was instrumental in designing the famous PT boats of World War II. They offer major restorations and large repairs and are well known for excellent workmanship but do not have reserved transient slips. Call ahead.

Nearby Cedar Point Marina has dockage to 60 feet and some reserved transient space. Their sister facility to the south is the large full-service Lamb's Yacht Center, a working boat yard with transient slips to 120 feet. They have extensive repair capabilities and haul-out equipment includes two 30-ton hoists, one 40-ton hoist and a 100-ton hoist. They also offer storage and sell marine parts.

About 2 miles past the entrance to the Ortega River at Pirates Cove on the western shore is the private Florida Yacht Club. First organized in 1876, it is one of the country's oldest yacht clubs. It is open only to members of clubs that belong to the Florida Council of Yacht Clubs or by advanced approval from the Board of Directors.

SOUTHERN EDITION

Chapter 2 — Side Trip on the St. Johns River

St. Johns River, FL

DOCTORS LAKE		Largest Vessel	VHF	Total Slips	Approach/ Dockside Depth	Floating Docks	Gas/ Diesel	Repairs/ Haulout	Min/Max Amps	Pump-Out Station
1. Doctors Lake Marina WiFi	(904) 264-0505	65		100	7.0 / 6.0		GD	R	30 / 50	P
JULINGTON CREEK										
2. Mandarin Holiday Marina	(904) 268-1036	50	16	150	6.0 / 6.0		GD	RH	30	P
3. Julington Creek Pier 3 Marina	(904) 337-6924	40	16	326	6.0 / 5.0		G	H	30	P

WiFi Wireless Internet Access
Visit www.waterwayguide.com for current rates, fuel prices, website addresses and other up-to-the-minute information. (Information in the table is provided by the facilities.)

Scan here for more details:

Anchorage: A few boats can anchor on the south shore between the Ortega River Bridge and the Roosevelt Blvd. Bridge in 6- to 7-foot MLW depths with good holding in mud. At publication time anchoring here is still unrestricted, despite some local attempts to prohibit it. Be a considerate cruising neighbor.

There is an excellent anchorage in Pirates Cove near the Florida Yacht Club with at least 6 feet MLW all the way in. It is well protected from wind and wake from all directions with good holding. This is located in a residential area.

Beyond Goodbys Creek on the eastern side of the river you can anchor in Plummers Cove between Beauclerc Bluff and the Buckman Bridge. The entrance is straightforward. Just avoid the shoal off Beauclerc Bluff, which is marked by green daybeacon "9." Go in at the approximate middle of the bight while being careful to dodge the pot markers that sometimes pepper both the entrance and interior. Choose your weather carefully as this anchorage has no protection from the west. Anchor in depths of 6 to 8 feet MLW. The holding is good in mud. Expect to hear some noise from the naval air station across the river at Piney Point and from I-295.

To Doctors Lake

The St. Johns River seems to transform itself into a lake immediately beyond the Ortega River with widths averaging a couple of miles or more for most of the 54 miles to Palatka. This section is great for sailing although strong winds out of the north or south can kick up quite a chop. Deep water stretches from shore to shore, providing plenty of room for sailboats to make long, pleasant tacks. Be aware that there are also some submerged hazards, particularly as you near Green Cove Springs. A well-marked channel indicates the safest route.

NAVIGATION: Use NOAA Chart 11492. The **Henry H. Buckman Sr. (I-295) Bridge** at Mile 35.1 has 65-foot fixed vertical clearance. About 2 miles south of the bridge on the west side of the St. Johns River is Doctors Lake. The lake is 4 miles long with 7- to 10-foot MLW depths extending almost to its banks; however, the **Park Ave. (U.S. 17) Bridge** with 37-foot fixed vertical clearance spans the entrance making this unaccessible to most sailboats. The lake is beautiful and well protected and its wooded shores are dotted with homes, many with their own docks. Eight miles of paths for walking and bicycling provide access from the marina to restaurants, laundry, pharmacies and a grocery.

Even when the going is tranquil it is wise to run compass courses for each lengthy reach between the daybeacons and lights so you always have a good idea of your position. Note that green daybeacon "15" shown on older charts at Mile 37.5 has been removed. This country is great for fishing and crabbing but the bobbing floats of the commercial crabber's pots–some of which are dark and difficult to see–are numerous enough to warrant close attention.

> NOTE: Watch for the remnants of old docks (possibly submerged) and other hazardous debris along the St. Johns River shoreline.

When headed to Doctors Lake, swing wide around Orange Point keeping well off red daybeacon "2," which has been repositioned farther away from shore. Stay clear of the shoaling on both sides of Doctors Inlet and steer toward the middle of the entrance. To enter Doctors Lake you must be able to pass under the 37-foot fixed vertical clearance Park Ave. (U.S. 17) Bridge.

Dockage: One long transient dock (with free pump-out service) is available at Doctors Lake Marina just inside the Park Ave. Bridge on the south shore of Doctors Inlet. They may rent out other slips as available. A tiki bar with entertainment and a food truck on weekends keeps this place hopping.

Proceed southwest to Swimming Pen Creek near the CR 220 Bridge to reach Whiteys Fish Camp Restaurant, which has free slips for diners. This family-owned establishment has been around since 1963 and includes a seafood restaurant, campground, bait and tackle shop and boat and kayak rentals (904-269-4198).

Anchorage: If you can clear the 37-foot fixed vertical clearance Park Ave. (U.S. 17) Bridge and wish to anchor in Doctors Lake do so with care because the holding in some places is poor with very fine, soft silt. Be certain to power down on your hook and check it frequently. Choose your location according to wind protection. Mill Cove, Sugarhouse Cove and Macks Point are all good choices.

Julington Creek

NAVIGATION: Use NOAA Chart 11492. Almost directly across the St. Johns River from Doctors Lake is Julington Creek, crossed by the fixed **Julington Creek Bridge** with 15-foot vertical clearance. Depths are shallow beyond the bridge so sound your way in. Inside the opening the creek shoals quickly to 4-foot MLW depths or less, especially on the north side.

Dockage: Mandarin Holiday Marina is located before the fixed Julington Creek Bridge. The marina has both a restaurant and snack shop on site. Additional restaurants, bars, shopping and groceries are nearby. In addition to transient slips to 50 feet and top-notch amenities, they can accommodate boat service and repair needs. Julington Creek Pier 3 Marina is after the 15-foot fixed vertical clearance bridge with over 70 slips with availability on a first-come, first-served basis. They also provide boat storage services.

Anchorage: Julington Creek is shoaling so sound your way in and check the depth of your full swing circle if you choose to anchor here. For larger boats the more exposed Old Bull Bay at Julington Creek's mouth is a good anchorage with shelter from north through southeast winds. You will find 7- to 8-foot MLW depths on a line between the points of land and 4 to 6 feet MLW closer to the Julington Creek Bridge. This attractive area is especially good for dinghy exploration.

To Green Cove Springs

The town of Green Cove Springs is on a very shallow, pretty cove off the St. Johns River at Mile 50. Here the long piers of a World War II Navy facility jut out into the river. These piers clearly show up on the chart for the area.

Green Cove Springs took its name from the sulfur mineral spring found here. The waters here have long reputed to have medicinal qualities and attracted many famous visitors in the late 1800s and early 1900s. Today visitors will find the spring in the midst of a city park fringed with fine old homes. St. Mary's Episcopal Church, built in the late 19th century, is an elegant riverfront structure.

Chapter 2: Side Trip on the St. Johns River

St. Johns River, FL

GREEN COVE SPRINGS AREA		Largest Vessel	VHF	Total Slips	Approach/Dockside Depth	Floating Docks	Gas/Diesel	Repairs/Haulout	Min/Max Amps	Pump-Out Station
1. Green Cove Springs City Pier 49.8	(904) 297-7060	50		12	8.0 / 8.0	F			30 / 50	
2. Reynolds Park Yacht Center WIFI 51.0	(904) 284-4667	400	16	70	12.0 / 6.0	F		RH	30 / 200+	P
3. Green Cove Springs Marina WIFI 51.1	(904) 284-1811	100	16	21	14.0 / 11.0	F		RH	30	P
4. Trout Creek Marina	(904) 342-2471			13	7.0 /	F	GD		30	

WIFI Wireless Internet Access
Visit www.waterwayguide.com for current rates, fuel prices, website addresses and other up-to-the-minute information. (Information in the table is provided by the facilities.)

Scan here for more details:

Source: Aqua Map and NOAA data

NOTE: Green Cove Springs is home to St. Brendan's Isle (www.sbimailservice.com), a well-known mail forwarding service used by many cruisers.

NAVIGATION: Use NOAA Charts 11487 and 11492. Just north of Green Cove Springs at Mile 47 Black Creek empties into the west side of the St. Johns River just north of Green Cove Springs on the western bank of the St. Johns River at Wilkies Point. The creek is deep, placid, unspoiled and offers a microcosm of the world's subtropical rivers. If you make the trip in late spring or summer don't be surprised if you disturb a slumbering alligator along the banks.

The **US 17 (SR 15) Bridge** at the entrance has a fixed vertical clearance of 30 feet and upstream are two additional bridges, each with a fixed vertical clearance of 20 feet. An overhead cable with an authorized vertical clearance of 47 feet also crosses the creek about 2 miles above the first bridge. If you can get under all of these (or have your mast unstepped at a nearby marina), you can cruise upriver to the headwaters and the town of Middleburg, which was founded in the early 19th century but with possible genealogical roots to the original St. Augustine settlement. A grocery store is a pleasant walk from the Middleburg waterfront but there are no transient docks.

When transiting the Green Cove Springs area stick to the marked channel to avoid both charted shoals and possible submerged obstructions.

CAUTION: Your journey of the St. Johns River ends at Mile 52.4 if you cannot pass under the 45-foot fixed vertical clearance Shands Bridge. (Construction on replacement of 65-foot bridge is scheduled for completion in 2023.)

Dockage/Moorings: Green Cove Springs City Pier allows visitors to dock and explore the amenities of the city. The long pier with the octagonal pavilion has 8- to 9-foot MLW depths. Twelve slips are available on a first-come, first-served basis and an envelope will be available for leaving the payment in the drop box at the pier. There is a 72 hour limit within a 30-day period.

To the south is Reynolds Park Yacht Center, a unique post-WWII Navy pier built for destroyers with a 49,000 linear feet fixed concrete pier and bulkhead. Tying off to huge bollards and climbing up the attached metal ladder to disembark could be a challenge for the mobility impaired. This is a large facility and bathrooms and lounge area can be a bit of a hike. They also offer full yacht maintenance and services. It is an easy dinghy ride around the corner to the downtown area where there are city docks for tying up the dinghy. There is a private airstrip nearby.

Green Cove Springs Marina has slips but is best known as a long-term storage and DIY yard. If the marina does not have space available at the dock, a mooring may be available. Call ahead for details.

Trout Creek Marina across the river and south of Green Cove Springs may have space for you on their floating docks. Note that the marina is located beyond a fixed bridge with vertical clearance of 17 feet.

Anchorage: Boats that clear the 30-foot vertical clearance US 17 (SR15) Bridge can anchor in Black Creek in at least 15 feet MLW with excellent all-around protection. Most of the bottom here is sticky black mud offering good holding for a well-set hook. Taller air-draft boats can anchor outside the first bridge in all but east winds.

At Green Cove Springs you can anchor just north of the town in the mouth of Governors Creek in 8 feet MLW with fair holding in mud. There is a boat ramp and a dinghy dock here. The anchorage is open to north through east winds and has quite a bit of highway noise but provisions are available within an easy walk. Should you choose to head upstream watch for the charted overhead power lines (30-foot vertical clearances) and fixed bridges (8- and 11-foot vertical clearances, respectively).

Across the river between Popo Point and the Shands Bridge at Orangedale is another anchorage. Note the shoal water south of Hallowes Cove, as well as the 3-foot MLW spot northeast of flashing red "20." Enter well southeast of flashing red "20" avoiding the charted cable area. Holding is excellent in 7 to 10 feet MLW but protection is good only from the northeast.

To the southeast of the Shands Bridge, Trout Creek enters the St. Johns River on the north side of Palmo Cove around the east end of Jack Wright Island. This is a popular anchorage but note that there is a fixed bridge about 0.5 miles up the creek. The official listed vertical clearance is 14 feet at high water but locals report a few feet more. Trout Creek is a deep and picturesque stream. For boats that cannot clear the bridge, Palmo Cove is an alternative anchorage with protection from all but west winds.

You can also drop the hook at the mouth of Six Mile Creek with good protection and depths. Minimal tide/current with a mud/muck bottom that holds well. This is a quiet anchorage away from residential areas and out of boat traffic.

Palatka

Palatka retains the ambiance of an old river town. A city park along the riverfront has picnic shelters, boat ramps and restrooms, as well as brick-paved residential streets that run beneath grand old oaks hung with Spanish moss. A 1-mile walk from the marinas south of the high-rise Memorial Bridge will bring you to Ravine Gardens State Park. The 59-acre state park was built in 1933 around natural ravines. Nature trails wander among thousands of azaleas and other ornamental plants growing near streams and ravines. The park is open daily from 8:00 a.m.

NAVIGATION: Use NOAA Charts 11487 and 11492. It is a 28-mile journey along the river's wooded and narrow banks from Green Cove Springs to Palatka. Fish weirs (stakes) and numerous pot markers populate the river hereabouts. When transiting the Green Cove Springs area stick to the marked channel to avoid both charted shoals and possible submerged obstructions. Beam winds, particularly from the west, can be very strong here so mind the chart plotter or remain lined up on the visual ranges if you have a deeper draft.

Most recreational boats will have enough depth anywhere in the center of the river here. Palatka's high and low tides happen about 7.25 and 8.5 hours, respectively, after Mayport's tides. The water depth in the channel ranges from 8 to 12 feet at MLW. The tidal range is about 1 foot.

Chapter 2 — Side Trip on the St. Johns River

Heading south from Green Cove Springs the St. Johns River is wide and relatively deep all the way to Palatka. There are shoals near the shorelines (some marked) but keeping to the visual center of the river should suffice. Midline depths decrease from about 20 feet MLW at the **Shands Bridge** to 8 feet MLW just north of Palatka.

An exception is a series of charted but unmarked shoals starting south of green daybeacon "27" at Mile 60 and ending at Mile 62. These begin off Willis Point and end off Tocoi Creek and carry a minimum depth of 5 feet MLW. The safer water is closer to the east side of the river for this stretch. Only one range remains in this section of the river. If you need the deepest water, align the 6-second flashing green on Racy Point with the quick-flashing green to its south as a back range past Ninemile Point. For most vessels there is enough water outside this channel.

A well-marked channel begins at flashing red "42" approaching Forrester Point at Mile 72. This channel takes a wide turn around Forrester Point and aligns with a final range for the commercial channel to Hog Eye Point near Palatka. The main hazard on this turn is just west of flashing red "42A" off Rice Creek.

Dockage: Close to Palataka, Crystal Cove Marina & RV Resort is a nice small marina with a friendly atmosphere and very accommodating staff. All slips are open to the public on a first-come, first-served basis. The 21-slip Quality Inn & Suites Riverfront just north of Memorial Bridge may have space for you and hotel amenities but call ahead for availability.

The free Palatka Town Dock south of the bridge is an option for smaller boats but may be busy on weekends. No electric and no water. The dock is exposed to current and to wind from the north through east to southeast and can be bouncy with a good wind. However, it is located 200 yards downstream from the downtown landing providing easy access to local park, shops, Post Office and restaurants.

Family-owned and -operated Boathouse Marina is south of the

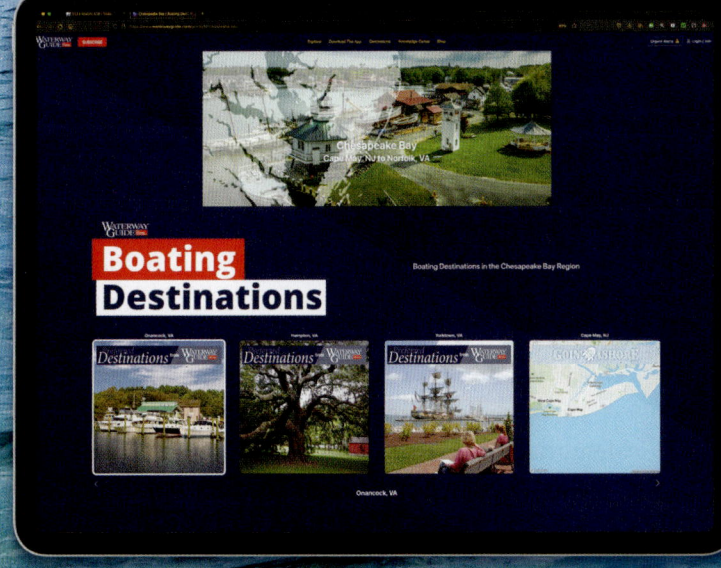

Chapter 2: Side Trip on the St. Johns River

St. Johns River, FL

PALATKA		Largest Vessel	VHF	Total Slips	Approach/ Dockside Depth	Floating Docks	Gas/ Diesel	Repairs/ Haulout	Min/Max Amps	Pump-Out Station
1. Crystal Cove Marina & RV Resort 79.0	(386) 328-4000	70		45	5.0 / 5.0		GD	R	30 / 50	
2. Quality Inn & Suites Riverfront WIFI 81.3	(386) 328-3481	100		21	25.0 / 8.0				30	
3. Boathouse Marina WIFI 81.9	(386) 328-2944	60	16	40	8.0 / 8.0				30 / 50	P

WIFI Wireless Internet Access
Visit www.waterwayguide.com for current rates, fuel prices, website addresses and other up-to-the-minute information. (Information in the table is provided by the facilities.)

Scan here for more details:

Source: Aqua Map and NOAA data

town dock with slips with full amenities. This marina has an Old Florida vibe and solid facilities. Head for the dock approximately midway between flashing green "1" and flashing red "2." Approach and dockside depths of 8 feet MLW are reported. The town is just 3 blocks away. Contact the marina in advance for reservations.

Corky Bell's Seafood and Steak at Gator Landing (386-325-1094) is at Devils Elbow in East Palatka (across from flashing red "6"). They have a dock and will let you do some nearby shopping if you eat a meal there. Nearby are a large hardware store, a drugstore and an independent grocery store.

Anchorage: About 4 miles upriver (south) from the Shands Bridge there is a scenic cove on the west side of the river south of Bayard Point and north of an unmarked shoal northeast of Clark Creek. Depths are 9 to 10 feet MLW in Bayard Point Cove, which is protected from the northwest and offers good holding in sandy mud. Sound your way in while dodging the pot markers that are often set here.

Farther south and on the east side of the St. Johns River is Solano Cove with 6- to 7-foot MLW depths and good holding. It is open to the northwest through south. To the south is a remote, quiet anchorage at Deep Creek with all-around protection and good holding in mud. It has a tricky entrance, however, that is best navigated with up-to-date charts.

Cow Creek is directly across from Crystal Cove Marina & RV Resort with good holding in 9 to 11 feet MLW. On the same side of the river to the south is Carman Cove at Maritoni Point with 5 to 7 feet MLW. This is open northwest through southeast.

There is some anchoring room south of the Memorial Bridge at Palatka on the west side of the river near the Palatka Town Dock. There is good depth here (12 to 15 feet MLW) with good holding in mud and silt. Sound your way in and use an anchor light at night making sure to stop well off the channel to clear tug and barge traffic. Stay to the north to avoid shoal areas.

Avoid Wilson Cove, which is situated south of Memorial Bridge on the west side of the river. An old sawmill here was removed years ago but abandoned wrecks, stumps and sunken logs make passage treacherous.

The south end of Porters Cove, approximately 3.3 miles upriver from Memorial Bridge at Mile 81.5, offers good protection from the west and fair protection from the northwest and southwest. The cove has wooded banks and is between the overhead power cables at River Crest and flashing red "12" on the west side of the river. Sound your way in to anchor in 8- to 10-foot MLW depths.

> NOTE:,Keep an eye out for the plentiful osprey nests here, which have Spanish moss woven in with the usual twigs and sticks. All the way to Lake Monroe osprey architecture (nest building) on the daybeacons grows more profuse so pay attention when reading the markers.

All types of wildlife call this home including playful otters, lazily swimming manatees and sleepy alligators sunning along the shore.

■ TO LAKE MONROE

To Welaka

From Palatka upriver to Welaka (about 20 miles away) the relatively narrow St. Johns River has navigational aids and adequate depths for barge traffic. Many of the boats you will encounter here are fishing skiffs and rented pontoon boats. Use caution around the rental boats as their skippers may not be highly skilled in the art of boat handling. Fish traps, stakes and submerged pilings are sometimes along the edge of the marked channel and require your attention at all times so follow the markers carefully, cruise slowly and take no shortcuts.

At the foot of Murphy Island is winding Dunns Creek, a wilderness stream with a bridge with fixed vertical clearance of 45 feet near its entrance and a controlling depth of 5 feet. It leads through 8 miles of untamed country to Crescent Lake (about 10 miles long with depths of 7 to 13 feet MLW). The creek itself has several very sharp turns but both Dunns Creek and the Murphy Creek side channel make for lovely gunkholing.

Now a sleepy hamlet with friendly residents Welaka was once a bustling steamboat depot for the transportation of wood, produce and tourists. Nowadays elegant antique steamboats rendezvous up the Ocklawaha River to its headwaters at Silver Springs, one of Florida's early tourist attractions. Welaka is a good stopover area about halfway up the river. You might want to visit the Welaka National Fish Hatchery and Aquarium (386-467-2374) where striped bass are hatched and grown for reintroduction to other rivers.

NAVIGATION: Use NOAA Charts 11487 and 11495. Once past the common mouths of Murphy and Dunns Creeks proceed marker to marker. Two hard sand shoals extend from Murphy Island almost into the south side of the channel. Favor the north side of the river just before and at flashing green "23" to avoid shoaling and submerged pilings.

Near green daybeacon "27" at Mile 91.8 the **Buffalo Bluff Railroad Bridge** (7-foot closed vertical clearance) is normally open but closes 20 to 30 minutes before trains arrive usually several times a day. The bridgetender responds on VHF Channel 09 and is usually on duty during the day. You will not see the bridge until you approach green daybeacon "27." You have to get closer still before you will spot the draw on the southeast (port) side close to shore. The Coast Guard has proposed modifications to the operating schedule to be remotely monitored and operated so check ahead.

This section of the river has several dangerous shoals. Show particular care as you approach Welaka in either direction from red daybeacon "42A" to flashing red "52." Check your chart and watch the depth sounder carefully for mid-river shoals; some are marked but many are not.

Between the Buffalo Bluff Railroad Bridge and flashing red "52" the early morning sun and ground fog might make it difficult to see the markers. Also the bird nests built on the pilings obscure some marker numbers along the way and can change the shapes of triangles into squares. Close attention to your plotter is recommended.

Also note that in this section of the St. Johns River crabbers are about as likely to set their traps (also called "pots") in the channel as out of it.

Chapter 2: Side Trip on the St. Johns River

St. Johns River, FL

LAKE GEORGE

		Largest Vessel	VHF	Total Slips	Approach/Dockside Depth	Floating Docks	Gas/Diesel	Repairs/Haulout	Min/Max Amps	Pump-Out Station
1. Georgetown Marina, Lodge & RV Park WiFi 111.0	(386) 467-2002	70	16	7	12.0 / 5.5		G		30 / 50	P

WiFi Wireless Internet Access
Visit www.waterwayguide.com for current rates, fuel prices, website addresses and other up-to-the-minute information.
(Information in the table is provided by the facilities.)

Scan here for more details:

Source: Aqua Map and NOAA data

Dockage: The free Murphy Island Dock has 20 feet MLW and no amenities. It is somewhat exposed to the southwest and southeast and wakes. Small vessels can also try the free Welaka City Dock–Bryant's Wharf, which has good water depths and short finger piers but no services. Larger boats might be able to dock alongside the end. Note that Acosta Creek Marina near red daybeacon "42A" is currently closed for renovations.

Anchorage: A snug anchorage is in Murphy Creek. Enter in the middle of the Dunns Creek mouth at Rat Island between pilings and pot markers. Watch the depth sounder and proceed slowly; you should find at least 5- to 7-foot MLW depths in the channel but depths are far less outside. Murphy Creek is to the east about 0.5-mile ahead and has pilings on both sides. Anchor anywhere past the pilings in 7- to 20-foot MLW depths. Crab pots are the only signs of civilization here among the pristine wooded banks.

Browns Landing across from Murphy Island has a good anchorage. Leave the channel between flashing red "16" and red daybeacon "18" and head north. Holding is good in 10- to 14-foot MLW depths. Watch for the shoal marked by red daybeacon "18." The Murphy Island Dock offers shore access for your four-legged crewmembers.

About 1.5 miles south of Dunns Creek a good spot lies in the first bend of the S-turn leading to the Buffalo Bluff Railroad Bridge (7-foot closed vertical clearance). When headed south, the 0.5-mile sign (small, white and illegible) for Buffalo Bluff anchorage is between green daybeacon "25" and flashing red "26." You will find 14 to 17 feet MLW and plenty of swing room in the space between the daybeacon and the southeast shore. Keep clear of the shoals marked "Emergent Vegetation" on the chart and the fish traps just inshore to the south and set an anchor light.

There is a comfortable anchorage near Seven Sisters Island; however, shore access for pets may be difficult to find. Behind Stokes Island you will be well protected in 8- to 9-foot MLW depths.

Several places around Turkey Island have good holding and 8- to 17-foot MLW depths but watch for shoals near green daybeacon "43" and flashing green daybeacon "45" and around the islets at the entrance. Anchor inside past the islets. Up-to-date charts are useful here.

Anchor just south of red daybeacon "46" at Stephens Point for a nice overnight spot on the river in 7 to 15 feet MLW. Great spot to dinghy ashore to the Welaka City Dock–Bryant's Wharf.

The Oklawhaha River South is a spring-fed river with a 1 mph current. It offers good holding and is very protected from wind and wakes from all sides. Serene and quiet with a wooded shore.

Side Trip: Cross-Florida Canal

A couple of miles beyond the Buffalo Bluff Railroad Bridge the entrance to the Cross-Florida Greenway (officially named the Marjorie Harris Carr Cross Florida Greenway) is to starboard at Mile 95 and is marked by red-green "C" opposite Trout Island. A series of historic events transformed this corridor from one of the nation's largest uncompleted public works project to a 110-mile greenway.

The Cross-Florida Greenway offers hiking, biking, equestrian and paddling trails, boat ramps, fishing spots and campgrounds. If you fancy an exploration of Old Florida and have a fast dinghy it can make a fine side trip. The section to Rodman Reservoir and a 9-mile canal on the west coast at Yankeetown were the only two portions of the canal completed before public opposition–caused by environmental concerns and right-of-way problems– halted the project in 1971. Every few years (in winter) the water is drawn down to a much lower level. Contact the Office of Greenways and Trails at 352-236-7143 for the latest canal conditions and clearances.

To Lake George

The second largest lake in the State of Florida (with the first being Lake Okeechobee) is Lake George, located 75 miles south of Jacksonville. This 11-mile-long lake is 5 miles wide and can be rough when winds are strong up or down its length.

CAUTION: Lake George is the site of a Navy bombing range. As the NOAA charts show the bombing range runs parallel to the channel along three sets of pilings and encompasses much of the eastern half of the lake. The rim is marked by tall pilings while shorter pilings mark the target area. Avoid it!

Two beautiful springs in the Ocala National Forest on the west shore of Lake George draw many visitors by boat and by road: Salt Springs and Silver Glen Springs. In settled weather you can anchor a short distance offshore and dinghy into the shallow creeks that lead to the springs. These two springs feature crystal-clear water at a constant 72 degrees year-round. Bring a mask and snorkel and enjoy watching the underwater wildlife. Go on a weekday to avoid crowds.

NAVIGATION: Use NOAA Chart 11495. South of Welaka to Lake George a good part of the channel is dredged. Pay attention to markers, watch for lateral drift and keep the depth sounder on because it is easy to get out of the channel. In some spots depths are only 2 to 3 feet MLW on both sides. Follow the channel carefully from red daybeacon "54" to flashing red daybeacon "58" and again between red daybeacon "60" and flashing green daybeacon "65" as it is narrow with shoaling on both sides.

CAUTION: Two antique ferries cross the channel in this area that deserve your attention. Fort Gates Ferry landing is about 4 miles south of Welaka at Mile 105. The ferry crossed just south of the overhead power cable between Buzzards Point and Mount Royal at flashing green "61A." It is the oldest operating ferry in Florida. A second ferry is 8 miles south at Georgetown south of flashing red "70." It provides the only vehicular connection between the mainland and Drayton Island.

Markers for the channel across Lake George are easy to see and 9- to 11-foot MLW depths prevail elsewhere. A hyacinth fence at the south end of the lake looks like a long set of bridge fenders. The channel across the Volusia Bar is between the fenders while outside it are rocks and declining depths. There are no range markers on Lake George.

Salt Springs is at the head of a long, winding creek west of green daybeacon "3" just after you enter the lake from the north. Silver Glen Springs (a state park) is farther south, west of green daybeacon "9." Both have marked entrances but not much water depth unless the river is high after rainfall.

Dockage: On the north side of Lake George, Georgetown Marina, Lodge & RV Park has a few reserved transient slips to 70 feet and reports 5.5-foot dockside depths. They sell bait and tackle and some marine supplies plus have cabins for rent, should you wish to entertain or get off the boat.

Anchorage: A good secluded anchorage is in the curve east and behind Buzzards Point in 13 feet MLW. Entering from the west turn off the channel halfway between flashing green "59" and red "60" avoiding the charted 6-foot MLW shoal. Leaving the anchorage follow

Chapter 2: Side Trip on the St. Johns River

Astor Bridge

the water's edge in 13 feet MLW until a course due south brings you to flashing green "61A" avoiding the 3-foot MLW shoal to starboard. The anchorage is protected in northerly and easterly winds but is also prone to wakes from local fishing boats.

Another pretty spot to drop the hook is 1.5 miles south of Little Lake George in Fruitland Cove on the eastern shore of the river. You will find good shelter here from north through east winds and the many houses along the shore prevent feelings of isolation. Watch the depth sounder and you can anchor out of the channel by flashing green "63A" in 8 to 11 feet MLW. Avoid the cable area shown on the chart.

Crossing Lake George to Hontoon Landing

The river deepens towards Astor about 4 miles south of Lake George. Fishing camps and waterside restaurants surround the Astor Bridge. Waterfront homeowners with docks and boat slips in the Astor area have rigged various devices–PVC pipes, float lines, fences, etc.–to keep water hyacinths from building up and choking access to the river. Without such devices the docks become surrounded by plant life and look as if they were constructed inland.

> **NOTE:** From here to Lake Monroe you may be joined by bald eagles, anhingas, ibises, herons and egrets. In the cool months alligators migrate south beyond Sanford to Lake Harney but if the winter is warm chances are you will find many of them in the river. Manatee regulations upriver from Astor are strictly enforced.

NAVIGATION: Use NOAA Chart 11495.

> ⚠ *CAUTION:* St. Johns River to Lake George is tidal. South of Lake George a north setting river current dominates that is mild during dry periods but somewhat stronger during rainy periods.

St. Johns River, FL

ASTOR

		Largest Vessel	VHF	Total Slips	Approach/Dockside Depth	Floating Docks	Gas/Diesel	Repairs/Haulout	Min/Max Amps	Pump-Out Station
1. Big River Marina and Lodge WiFi 120.0	(386) 749-4407	70		60	8.0 /		G		30 / 50	P

WiFi Wireless Internet Access
Visit www.waterwayguide.com for current rates, fuel prices, website addresses and other up-to-the-minute information.
(Information in the table is provided by the facilities.)

Scan here for more details:

SOUTHERN EDITION   153

Chapter 2 — Side Trip on the St. Johns River

The **Astor Bridge** at Mile 119.9 monitors VHF Channels 09 and 16 and opens on signal. Note that the 20-foot closed vertical clearance bridge span hangs over the channel when open at a height of 72 feet and the overhead power cable here is at 70 feet. Two other cables (Internet and phone) are a few feet lower but none should be a problem for boats that can clear the other fixed bridges on the river.

Dredged cuts have eliminated many turns in the St. Johns River channel. Bars block entrance to many of the oxbows that show deep water inside. Overhanging foliage sometimes obscures daybeacons adding confusion to some of the cuts where the natural course of the river makes abrupt turns off the channel (with some turns actually wider than the channel itself). The markers are there, however, so go slow, pay attention and enjoy the beauty of this special place.

Lake Dexter is 4.5 miles south of Astor as the crow flies and less than 20 miles from Lake Monroe. On the river, however, it is more like 30 miles through a wilderness broken only by a few marinas. The route is well marked but if you lose your concentration you will quickly find yourself aground. The **Rt. 44 (Whitehair) Bridge** at Mile 136.1 has 15-foot closed vertical clearance and opens on signal.

NO WAKE ZONE
There are No-Wake Zones on both sides of the Rt. 44 (Whitehair) Bridge.

Dockage: Big River Marina and Lodge has transient slips to 70 feet and rooms for rent should you want to get off the boat for a night or two.

Flanking the Rt. 44 (Whitehair) Bridge are St. Johns Marina North and South. The 20-acre St. Johns Marina North encompasses 150 wet slips, a 106-site campground, kayak and canoe rentals, a restaurant, a recreation room and laundry facilities. St. Johns Marina South is a full-service marina with wet slips, a service and parts department and motor and boat sales. These are both easy stops right on the river. Note that these facilities do not monitor VHF (nor the phone).

Anchorage: More than halfway down and on the western side of the lake is Silver Glen Springs, a popular gathering place to enjoy the clear water spring. Shallow draft vessels only.

On the south side of Lake George near flashing green daybeacon "19" you will find all-around protection in 5 to 10 feet MLW at Zinder Point. Just beyond that is Hitchens Creek. Pull into the creek past the fish camp for 5.5 feet MLW of water and all-around protected. A nice spot is 2 miles south by Morrison Island with excellent holding in mud in 5 to 6 feet MLW.

Still farther south is Alexander Spring Run, a spring-fed waterway about 60 feet wide with a sand and mud bottom. This is quiet with little boat traffic and waterfowl and alligators abound. Great place for smaller vessels to get off the river for a night or day cruise.

Beyond Saint Francis there are two unnamed loops with anchoring options. The first is between red buoys "30" and "32" and has good holding in mud and 8 to 10 feet MLW. The second, known locally as Catfish Bend, is located between red daybeacons "36" and "38" and just north of Crows Bluff. This has good holding and protection in at least 6 feet MLW. Sound your way in. If you do not have time for the entire trip to Sanford, Crows Bluff is a good place to turn around and start back downriver (i.e., north).

An anchorage at Drigger Island (Mile 139.1) at flashing green "41" is shallow (5 to 7 feet MLW) but has excellent holding in mud and all-around protection.

Hontoon Landing to Lake Monroe

Blue Springs State Park is just south of flashing green "71." The springs are worth exploring. Hontoon Island Park and Blue Springs State Park are independent of each other but share a common manatee area that is carefully monitored by the marine patrol. If you are moving too fast (and even auxiliary sailboats sometimes do) expect to get a ticket or at least a warning.

Evidence of Native American habitation over thousands of years can be witnessed as visitors hike through Hontoon Island Park. (Note that the park has a leash law to prevent your pet from falling prey to an alligator.) Take a walk through the Visitor Center to learn more about the many inhabitants and uses of Hontoon Island over the years. The island is accessible only by private boat or park ferry. Fishermen, campers and picnickers frequently use the free pedestrian ferry, which crosses the river between the island and the mainland. The ferry operates daily from 8:00 a.m. to one hour before sunset.

St. Johns River, FL

HONTOON LANDING AREA		Largest Vessel	VHF	Total Slips	Approach/ Dockside Depth	Floating Docks	Gas/ Diesel	Repairs/ Haulout	Min/Max Amps	Pump-Out Station
1. St. Johns Marina North WiFi	(386) 736-6601	70		170	12.0 / 10.0				30 / 50	P
2. St. Johns Marina South 138.3	(352) 589-8370	50		53	/		GD	R	30	
3. Hontoon Landing Resort & Marina WiFi 141.5	(386) 734-2474	60		50	12.0 / 6.0		G		30 / 50	
4. Hontoon Island State Park 141.6	(386) 736-5309	50		40	17.0 / 6.0	F			30 / 50	

WiFi Wireless Internet Access
Visit www.waterwayguide.com for current rates, fuel prices, website addresses and other up-to-the-minute information.
(Information in the table is provided by the facilities.)

Scan here for more details:

Source: Aqua Map and NOAA data

Chapter 2: Side Trip on the St. Johns River

NAVIGATION: Use Chart 11498. The winding river from Hontoon Landing (Mile 141.2) to Lake Monroe (Mile 156.1) has narrow channels, land cuts, water hyacinths and snags, but there are good navigational aids. This waterway is extremely beautiful with an abundance of birds, turtles and manatees.

At flashing red "96" the narrow entrance to the Wekiva Reach is almost totally obscured by water hyacinths. Although a boat with a 5-foot draft can be taken several miles up the Wekiva River's entrance is tricky. Explore this river only with local knowledge.

Dockage: Hontoon Landing Resort & Marina has slips to 60 feet with resort amenities including a pool, manicured lawn and grounds, a hummingbird garden, a boardwalk and a deli. Rooms and suites are available as well.

Hontoon Island State Park offers dockage along the St. Johns' western shore opposite green daybeacon "55." The dock must be approached from the south; head for the face dock. The water is reported to be 6 feet MLW on the approach. (Larger boats will have to dock on the dock T ends.) There is water and shore power at the docks for a nominal fee and a small store on site. Canoe, kayak and bicycle rentals are also available.

Anchorage: Real wilderness lies on the Hontoon Dead River at Hontoon Landing. Leave the St. Johns at red daybeacon "50" and proceed as far into the river as you like. Anchor in 10- to 15-foot MLW depths with mud, silt and good holding. The protection is very good from all directions with almost no current. Be sure to bring along a camera and fishing gear because you may not find a prettier place and the fishing is fantastic. This is a busy area on weekends when the state park is most popular.

Starks Landing Loop at Mile 144.3 near red daybeacon "70" is a little-used river loop behind the island off the western bank. Enter at the north end by flashing green "69" and proceed slowly as this is a manatee refuge and depths are less than charted with shoaling to less than 5 feet MLW. The bottom is soft mud. Be sure to show an anchor light. You can dinghy to the beach just past the entrance to Blue Springs.

Emanuel Bend, a favorite anchorage for locals, is at Mile 150.4 across from the Wekiva River between green daybeacons "95" and "97." Both ends are navigable but the south end should be avoided as it is very narrow and may be full of hyacinths and overhanging trees plus other debris on the bottom. There may be campers on the island. Depths are less than the NOAA chart indicates.

Enter Butchers Bend at Mile 152.9 at either end. Expect 7.5-foot MLW depths at the north entrance at flashing green daybeacon "109" and 6-foot MLW depths at the south at green daybeacon "111." This pretty spot is popular with locals and fishermen. Eagles, manatees and turtles like it too.

Hontoon Island State Park

Lake Monroe, FL

SANFORD AREA		Largest Vessel	VHF	Total Slips	Approach/ Dockside Depth	Floating Docks	Gas/ Diesel	Repairs/ Haulout	Min/Max Amps	Pump-Out Station
1. Downtown Sanford Marina WiFi 159.7	(407) 322-2910	80		236	6.0 / 5.5	F	G	RH	20 / 50	P
2. Sanford Boat Works & Marina, Inc. 163.0	(407) 322-6613	67	16	140	8.0 / 5.0	F	GD	H	30 / 50	P

WiFi Wireless Internet Access
Visit www.waterwayguide.com for current rates, fuel prices, website addresses and other up-to-the-minute information.
(Information in the table is provided by the facilities.)

Scan here for more details: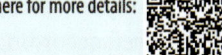

Source: Aqua Map and NOAA data

Lake Monroe (Sanford)

Sanford, located at the southeast side of Lake Monroe (Mile 155), was at one time an important river port and the largest celery-producing area in the nation but it is now a pleasure boat center. Here you enter civilization again with businesses, stores, motels and accommodations for cruising boats. Sanford is home to Riverwalk, a 2-mile paved walking and bike path that meanders along Lake Monroe. It is a great way to spend a day.

Historic Sanford (1st Street) has a number of good restaurants that sponsor street parties and other public social events most weekends. The historic Sanford Welcome Center) at 230 E. 1st St. is behind the public library. A Post Office is nearby and a grocery store is about 1.5 miles south of the waterfront. Connections from here are good including Orlando-Sanford (SFB) and Orlando International (MCO) airports. Stations with the Auto Train and commuter trains to Orlando are only a few miles from the marina.

Lake Monroe is broad and shallow and can vary greatly in depth with summer rainfall or winter drought. The charted values are correct for a low-water season but upstream runoff from a wet summer or a hurricane may raise the water level more than 5 feet.

Beyond Sanford Boat Works & Marina, Inc., the St. Johns River system is wild, natural and unimproved and cruising is restricted to small skiffs with shallow drafts and airboats. Numerous cattle ranches are here and the area is excellent for bird watching.

NOTE: The municipal Downtown Sanford Marina can provide details on Lake Monroe water depths and conditions.

Chapter 2: Side Trip on the St. Johns River

NAVIGATION: Use NOAA Chart 11498. The St. Johns River continues to meander 6 miles from the Wekiva River to the three bridges before Lake Monroe. Just before the bridges is a power plant with multiple overhead cables crossing the river. The last two cable crossings are significantly lower than the others with vertical clearances of 48.9 feet, according to the latest NOAA Chart.

The first bridge before the lake is **Port of Sanford Railroad Bridge** at Mile 155.7, which will open promptly unless a train is coming. On weekends, it remains open except for twice daily closures for Amtrak service. Adjacent to that is the fixed **US 17/US 92 Bridge** with 45-foot fixed vertical clearance. The boat ramp on the south shore is very active and can generate significant congestion in the river channel. The 45-foot fixed vertical clearance **I-4 (St Johns River Veterans Memorial) Bridges** at Mile 155.8 are the last bridges before the lake. Be sure to use the latest charts for Lake Monroe buoyage. From the I-4 (St Johns River Veterans Memorial) Bridges follow the markers carefully to the channel junction at flashing red daybeacon "8." An unmarked old charted channel leads toward the north. Stay out of the area to the northeast between that channel and the main channel; the spar buoys mark where sunken trees were placed to attract fish. Follow red daybeacon "10" to "12" to flashing green "13" and red daybeacon "14" at the Sanford turning basin.

A straight line at the Sanford waterfront from red daybeacon "6" to flashing red "2" at what locals call the "Government Cut" south of Mothers Arms will keep you in the deepest water to Indian Mound Slough. Stay close to flashing red "2" and to red daybeacon "4" and head straight for green daybeacon "5."

To continue up to the headwaters of the St. Johns River go from the unnumbered red daybeacon directly to flashing red daybeacon "2" south of Grassy Point. Depths of at least 5 feet MLW hold to Sanford Boat Works & Marina, Inc. if you stay quite close to the west shore once you have passed through the cut.

Dockage: To reach the east entrance to the municipal Downtown Sanford Marina, turn to port to red daybeacon "4" and red daybeacon "6." The marina welcomes transients in either the east or west basin with full amenities. You will not see the entrance to the west basin until you are almost on it. This is just two blocks from downtown.

Sanford Boat Works & Marina, Inc. in Indian River Slough has some transient dockage to 64 feet. Operated by the Smith family since 1924, the marina has continually provided boat storage with a natural harbor and a friendly atmosphere.

Gator's Riverside Grille (407-688-9700) may be able to accommodate you if you dine with them. Note that pets are not allowed due to Seminole County code. Call ahead to be sure there is space for you.

Lake Monroe carries 7-foot MLW depths outside the channel and there is no wind or wake protection. We recommend taking a slip.

■ NEXT STOP

Our coverage continues southbound on the ICW in the next chapter, where we pick up Pablo Creek (Mile 741) to St. Augustine and beyond.

St. Johns River to New Smyrna Beach

Chapter 3

Chapter 3: St. Johns River to New Smyrna Beach

 ICW Mile 740-Mile 847

■ TO ST. AUGUSTINE

The beach regions running south from Jacksonville are collectively referred to as the "First Coast" because this is the location of Florida's first European settlements. It vigorously competes with the Gold Coast, the Sun Coast and the Treasure Coast for developer and tourist dollars. The area begins a parade of shoreside communities such as Atlantic Beach, Neptune Beach, Jacksonville Beach and Ponte Vedra Beach.

No Wake Zones, Idle Speed Zones and various Speed Limit restrictions are in effect throughout the waterways included in this chapter. Exercise diligence in knowing the regulations by observing signs and other markers. Enforcement is always present. As always, be courteous to other vessels and avoid manatees and other marine life.

Pablo Creek to Jacksonville Beach–ICW Mile 741 to Mile 748

Ponce de Leon landed in Jacksonville Beach in the 1500s in his search for the Fountain of Youth and it has been a lively community ever since. This popular stopover has beautiful beaches and offers a full range of services, stores and restaurants. It is also a convenient central base for road trips to Fernandina Beach, Fort Clinch, Fort Caroline, the Kingsley Plantation and the City of Jacksonville. Many mariners cruise south to this point in the fall, leave their boats and fly home from Jacksonville or Daytona Beach.

NAVIGATION: Use NOAA Chart 11489. After crossing the St. Johns River at Mile 740 the ICW enters Pablo Creek and continues south toward Jacksonville Beach. Keep red markers to starboard heading south. Follow the markers carefully to stay on the dredged channel's centerline and be prepared to squeeze over for tugs with barges. The strong currents make "going slow" difficult here so be sure to occasionally look behind for markers to verify that you are staying in the narrow channel.

Eddies between red nun buoy "2" and flashing green buoy "1" at the entrance to Pablo Creek require close attention to the helm. Passing close to flashing green buoy "1" take a heading for green daybeacon "5." Persistent shoaling at the entrance to Pablo Creek near Mile Point at Mile 740 has resulted in a realignment of the ICW by the Coast Guard. Honor the buoys.

Follow the markers closely as positioned noting that the new buoys are small and hard to see but must pass them by at least 50 feet off. The dredged channel follows the concrete bulkheads along the spoil islands west of the ICW. For safe passage cruisers can split the distance between the green markers and the bulkheads. However, it is generally deeper closer to the bulkheads.

The channel widens from red daybeacon "8" to flashing red "10" past the high-rise **Wonderwood Drive (SR 116) Bridges** (65-foot fixed vertical clearance) at Mile 742.1. Note that NOAA Chart 11489 shows few soundings here. It's best to stay in the center of the marked channel.

The fixed **Atlantic Blvd. Twin Bridges** (Mile 744.7) mark the gateway to the Jacksonville Beach region. The bridges have a charted 65-foot vertical clearance but expect slightly less on higher tides.

CAUTION: The islands and partial causeway under the Atlantic Blvd. Twin Bridges help create strong currents here and eddies form above, under and below the bridges. It is easy to lose control here and there is not much horizontal clearance. Also watch for fishermen who work this area in small boats.

Near the high-rise **B. B. McCormick (U.S. 90) Bridge** at Mile 747.5 watch for strong currents, especially on the ebb (although they are not as strong as the currents through the Atlantic Blvd. Twin Bridges).

Dockage: North of the B. B. McCormick (U.S. 90) Bridge flashing red "32" marks the entrance to a small creek leading to Lake Cusic (unnamed on the chart) to the west. Stay to the middle of the privately marked channel (with 6 feet at MLW) into the lake to access Palm Cove Marina. This marina offers wet and dry storage as well as transient dockage for boats up to 90 feet. There are nine other businesses on site ranging from boat sales and service to Marker 32 Restaurant (904-223-1534), which provides great views and first class dining.

America's Waterway Guide Since 1947 — Chapter 3

Jacksonville Beach, FL

JACKSONVILLE BEACH AREA		Largest Vessel	VHF	Total Slips	Approach/ Dockside Depth	Floating Docks	Gas/ Diesel	Repairs/ Haulout	Min/Max Amps	Pump-Out Station
1. Palm Cove Marina (WiFi) MM 747.4	(904) 223-4757	90	16	221	6.0 / 6.0	F	GD	RH	30 / 50	P
2. Windward Jax Beach Marine (WiFi) MM 747.6	(904) 249-8200	125	16	350	6.0 / 6.0	F	GD		30 / 100	P

(WiFi) Wireless Internet Access
Visit www.waterwayguide.com for current rates, fuel prices, website addresses and other up-to-the-minute information.
(Information in the table is provided by the facilities.)

Scan here for more details:

Source: Aqua Map and NOAA data

Across the waterway is the well-regarded Windward Jax Beach Marine with transient slips with amenities, a repair yard and a on-site restaurant. This large, enclosed basin is also home to a very busy Freedom Boat Club.

Anchorage: To the east of the ICW at Mile 744.2 and south of flashing green "17" at Pablo Creek lies a wide and surprisingly deep channel. If you choose to anchor behind the island in Pablo Creek, enter only from the north with an eye out for shoaling to the south. Leftover mooring anchors may still be on the bottom so be wary of snags and set the hook well against the swift current. The current should keep you away from the shore unless there is a strong crosswind at slack tide. This is not a great anchorage but will do in a pinch. The next anchorage is over 20 miles away on the Tolomato River.

Palm Valley Cut to St. Augustine Inlet– ICW Mile 749 to Mile 776

NAVIGATION: Use NOAA Charts 11489 and 11485. South from the B. B. McCormick (U.S. 90) Bridge the channel is well marked and the tidal range is about 4 feet. Passing under the high-rise **Butler Blvd. (SR 202) Bridge** at Mile 749.5 the ICW enters a narrow dredged channel. Just south of Mile 750 at the intersection of Pablo and Cabbage Creeks, strong cross-currents are possible depending of tidal phase and recent rainfall. Watch for shoals encroaching from the west side here. Immediately south of this intersection the route enters 10-mile-long Palm Valley Cut with a charted depth of 10 feet MLW.

There are numerous pot markers along the cut that appear to be near the centerline. The deeper water is to the east of these floats. The only marker in Palm Valley

SOUTHERN EDITION 161

Chapter 3: St. Johns River to New Smyrna Beach

Cut–red daybeacon "2"–marks shoaling on the west side along the 0.5-mile approach to the **Palm Valley (SR 210) Bridge** at Mile 758.8. Stay in the middle of the channel or favor the east side if depths start to decrease suddenly. Also watch for small craft entering from the paddling launch and launch ramp north of the bridge.

> NOTE: As always, skippers are responsible for their own wakes. The east side of Palm Valley Cut is residential. Watch for debris, manatees and alligators through this popular fishing area and mind the depth sounder.

At Mile 760, the ICW enters the headwaters of the Tolomato River, which flows south to meet the Matanzas River at the St. Augustine Inlet. The dredged channel between Mile 760 and Mile 765 provides a deep water route through the marshes and side waters but there are shoals near the channel edge on both sides. Avoid corner cutting through this stretch. Watch in particular between red daybeacons "16" and "18" for shoaling created by a small creek to the west.

The natural river channel begins to deepen below green daybeacon "19" at Mile 763.5 north of the cut across the Pine Island Loop (Mile 765). Note that the north arm of Pine Island Loop has filled in and is no longer navigable. The ICW follows this natural deep channel all the way to St. Augustine. Despite this depth there are several dangerous shoals along the upper stretch of the Tolomato River from Mile 765 to Mile 770. Pay close attention to the chart and your depth and observe navigation aids.

Center up south of red daybeacon "44A" (Mile 770) to avoid the shoal to the north of the Guana River mouth, which extends south from flashing green "45" into the river opening. Be alert for strong cross-currents at the junction of the Guana River and the ICW, which also may drag pot markers underwater. You will see an airport about 1 mile south of the Guana River to the west.

Heading south the river deepens considerably. Keep a sharp eye out for markers through this stretch as they tend to blend in with the buildings and docks along the shoreline.

America's Waterway Guide Since 1947 — Chapter 3

It is safe to follow the river's mid-line approaching the high-rise **Francis and Mary Usina (SR A1A/Vilano) Bridge** at Mile 775.8 (locally known as the **Usina Bridge**). There may be strong currents at an angle at the bridge and some cruisers report that the clearance may be less than the posted 65 feet at high tide. (Tidal range is about 4 feet here.) A dredged private basin at a condominium development south of flashing red "54" on the Tolomato River has two entrances on the east side of the river adding to boat traffic.

Dockage: Several restaurants with dockage for patrons are north of the Usina Bridge on the east side of the ICW. Tying up at Cap's on the Water, a popular restaurant in the vicinity of flashing green "51," can be very rough, especially on busy summer weekends. Call ahead (904-824-8794) to check on the approach and dockside depths as well as dockage availability. Pass this area with no wake as there are usually boats at the dock sometimes rafted several deep.

Anchorage: At Mile 765 is the entrance to the Pine Island Loop, which is a fine place to drop the hook and enjoy a pleasant evening or two. Enter south of green daybeacon "25" giving it some berth then favor the north bank where it is deeper as there is a shoal extending out from the south bank of the loop. A line of crab pot markers indicates the shoal line on the southern edge of the anchorage. Mind the depth and allow for the full range of tide through your entire swing circle. The current is minimal but will affect your set. Holding and protection are excellent; however, it can be very buggy when there is no wind. Shoals and submerged obstructions make the entrance to the loop north of the island between green daybeacon "21" and flashing green "23" impassable.

Another anchorage is in the Tolomata River. When abeam of red daybeacon "42" turn northeast toward shore. Be sure to avoid the southern tip of the charted shoal. Go about halfway between mid-channel and shore and turn northwest into the pocket behind the charted shoal until roughly abeam of green daybeacon "41." You should have 10 feet MLW. The farther you anchor from the ICW the less you will be affected by wakes of passing boats. This is a beautiful natural area to explore with your dinghy

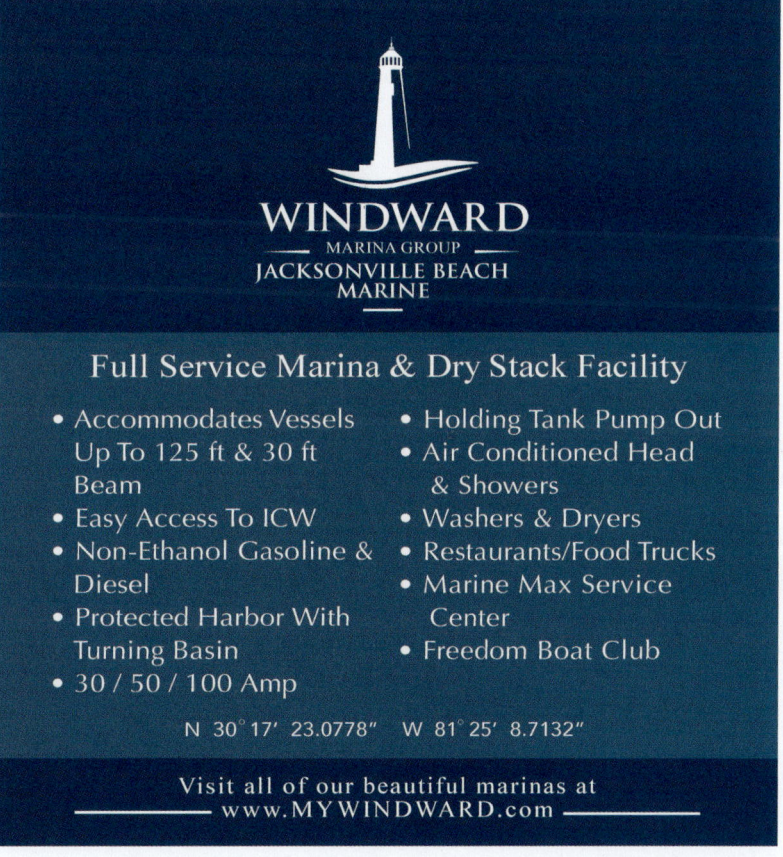

WINDWARD MARINA GROUP — JACKSONVILLE BEACH MARINE

Full Service Marina & Dry Stack Facility

- Accommodates Vessels Up To 125 ft & 30 ft Beam
- Easy Access To ICW
- Non-Ethanol Gasoline & Diesel
- Protected Harbor With Turning Basin
- 30 / 50 / 100 Amp
- Holding Tank Pump Out
- Air Conditioned Head & Showers
- Washers & Dryers
- Restaurants/Food Trucks
- Marine Max Service Center
- Freedom Boat Club

N 30° 17' 23.0778"   W 81° 25' 8.7132"

2315 Beach Blvd, Jacksonville FL, 32350   904.249.8200

Visit all of our beautiful marinas at www.MYWINDWARD.com

SOUTHERN EDITION

Chapter 3: St. Johns River to New Smyrna Beach

before the waterway becomes more developed to the south. You can see alligators, dolphins and a huge variety of birds and other wildlife.

> NOTE: St. Augustine Inlet can be confusing; this is good time to review charts and to prepare yourself for the transit of this busy inlet.

St. Augustine Inlet

The St. Augustine Inlet opens to the east splitting Vilano Beach from Conch Island. The dead-end Salt Run is to the south between Conch Island and Anastasia Island.

NAVIGATION: Use NOAA Chart 11485. St. Augustine Inlet is frequently dredged and is well marked and wide. It is highly recommended that you only attempt passage with good visibility and in light wind conditions. Avoid this channel when the substantial tidal flow (particularly on ebb) is opposed by medium to strong winds. Breakers can often be seen in the shallow waters bordering the channel even in calm conditions. Charts do not show depth details nor the position of navigational aids as this inlet is prone to frequent change. This is considered a "fair weather" inlet and local knowledge is recommended.

When preparing to enter the inlet orient yourself as you approach the red and white sea buoy offshore. The large cross near the "Castillo" can serve as a shore reference. The inlet is frequently dredged and surveyed with typical depths of 12 to 15 feet MLW at the outside bar; however, remember that a single storm can affect depths at any time. Shoaling is continual and the markers are frequently moved and have no set position.

While markers positions cannot be anticipated, typically the north edge of the channel is marked by a series of red buoys and the south side is unmarked. Vessels headed in both directions tend to keep close to (and south of) the red markers. On flood and ebb in particular currents can run up to 3 knots or more; these currents often run cross-channel presenting additional challenges at the helm.

If intending to head northbound on the ICW from St. Augustine Inlet, it is important to run a sufficient distance past the tip of the beach to the north of the inlet channel before turning north into the ICW channel. Keep flashing green buoy "59" (an ICW marker) to starboard turning.

Bridge of Lions

If heading southbound on the ICW from St. Augustine Inlet, the approach is roughly southwest toward the "Castillo," a large stone fort south the cross on the mainland. To add to the confusion, the numbering of ICW markers restarts where the Tolomato and Matanzas Rivers meet at the inshore-end of the inlet. Passing south of flashing green ICW marker "59" and keeping north of the entrance to the dead-end Salt Run, continue southwest splitting flashing green "1" and red nun "2" to enter the ICW then round the prominent thumb of Anastasia Island towards the Bridge of Lions (SR A1A).

> NOTE: Windward at Camachee Cove Yacht Harbor and the local towing services (SeaTow and TowBoat U.S.) have updated information on possible shoaling and will be very accommodating if called on for "local knowledge."

St. Augustine–ICW Mile 776 to 779

St. Augustine ranks as one of America's finest visitor destinations. One draw is the battlements and dungeons of Castillo de San Marcos National Monument built in 1672. This is a place to relax, explore and enjoy.

NAVIGATION: Use NOAA Chart 11485. The ICW traverses the inner reach of St. Augustine Inlet, exposing this area to surge in harsh weather conditions. There is also continual shoaling between Mile 776 and Mile 780, near constant dredging and frequent repositioning of aids to navigation making passage of the ICW through St. Augustine complex. Study the chart before arrival but realize that even the most recent charts may not be up to date and you may have to adapt.

In addition, there are numerous marked channels, significant marine traffic (both recreational and commercial), strong currents and a strict schedule for the **Bridge of Lions (SR A1A)**. All of these factors suggest you should slow down and navigate this area with extreme care.

The ICW channel south of the Usina Bridge tracks deceptively close to the beach to the east approaching the St. Augustine Inlet. Honor all markers in place south of the bridge at the time of your arrival. A pair of markers define the ICW channel heading south from the bridge: flashing green daybeacon "57A" and red nun buoy "58." Once centered between this pair head for flashing green buoy "59" (an east-side ICW marker), which is just off the southern tip of Vilano Beach. Depths are more reliable on the green side along Vilano Beach.

St. Augustine

Take a minute to orient yourself here. Looking southwest towards the mainland you should see a tall white cross and then the fort Castillo de San Marcos (both charted) on the shore of St Augustine. Farther south is the ornate bascule Bridge of Lions. The St. Augustine Inlet opens to the east splitting Vilano Beach from Conch Island. The dead-ended Salt Run is straight ahead lying between Conch Island and Anastasia Island. At flashing green buoy "59" the ICW turns southwest towards the Castillo.

Leaving flashing green buoy "59" to port and flashing red buoy "60" to starboard the ICW channel turns sharply southwest into the Matanzas River. The first set of Matanzas River markers are flashing green "1" located just off the northwest tip of Conch Island and red nun buoy "2," which should be lined up with the Castillo. The ICW markers can get lost in the jumble of markers here. Use flashing red "2A" if red nun "2" is not visible.

| Chapter 3 | St. Johns River to New Smyrna Beach |

Goin' Ashore
ST. AUGUSTINE, FL

Matanzas River

Castillo de San Marcos

ATTRACTIONS

1. Castillo de San Marcos
Remarkable feat of engineering built in 1672 is the oldest and largest masonry fort in the continental U.S. Features daily guided tours and historical reenactments. Call 904-829-6506 for hours and admission fee.

2. Colonial Quarter
Living history museum with demonstrations of old-world skills and reenactments of colonial life in a Spanish village (14 S. Castillo Dr., 904-342-2857).

3. Flagler College/Old Ponce de Leon Hotel
Tours of the beautifully restored building at 74 King St. are scheduled at 10:00 a.m. and 2:00 p.m. (for a fee). The old hotel now serves as the Flagler College offices and main dormitory but it maintains the original Tiffany stained glass windows, fountains, mosaics and sculpture (904-829-6481).

4. Lightner Museum
Built by Henry Flagler in 1887, museum of art and artifacts from the Gilded Age including Tiffany glass, furniture and other decorative arts housed within historic Hotel Alcazar at 75 King St. (904-824-2874).

5. Ponce de Leon's Fountain of Youth Archaeological Park
Historic 16th-century Spanish settlement on 15 acres that features exhibits and artifacts on the local history and culture as well as reenactments and demonstrations. The largest draw is the site of the original Fountain of Youth discovered by Ponce De Leon in 1513 at 11 Magnolia Ave. (904-829-3168).

6. St. Augustine Pirate & Treasure Museum
Transports you back in time over 300 years to Port Royal, Jamaica, at the height of the Golden Age of Piracy at 12 S. Castillo Dr. Open daily from 10:00 a.m. to 7:00 p.m. (877-467-5863).

7. Villa Zorayda Museum
Displays an eclectic collection of artifacts from the near and far east in a circa 1883 building based on a Moorish palace in Spain (83 King St., 904-829-9887).

MARINAS

8. St. Augustine Municipal Marina
111-E Avenida Menendez (904-825-1026)

SERVICES

9. St. Augustine Post Office
99 King St. (800-275-8777)

10. Visitor Information Center
10 San Marco Ave. (904-825-1000)

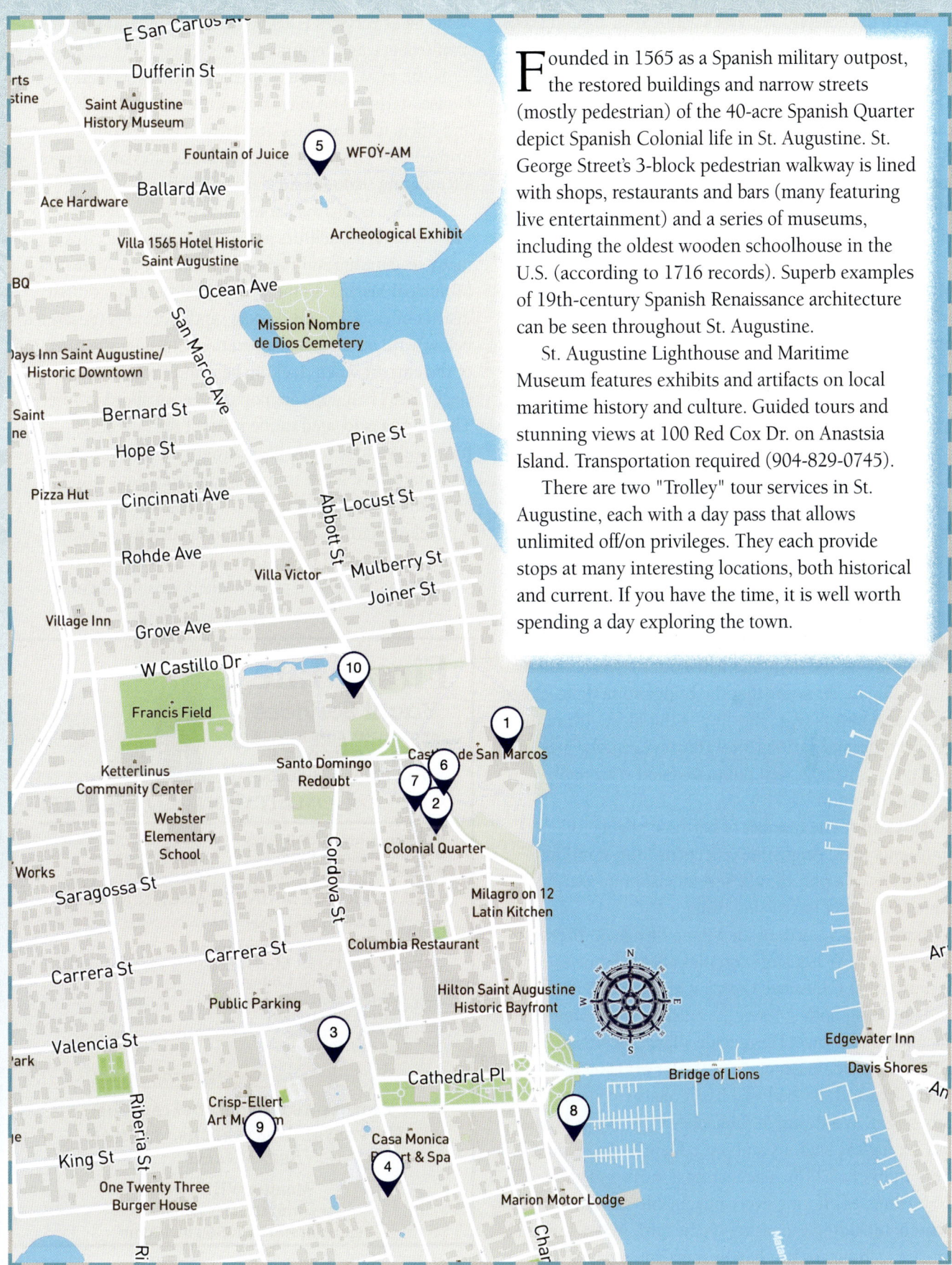

Founded in 1565 as a Spanish military outpost, the restored buildings and narrow streets (mostly pedestrian) of the 40-acre Spanish Quarter depict Spanish Colonial life in St. Augustine. St. George Street's 3-block pedestrian walkway is lined with shops, restaurants and bars (many featuring live entertainment) and a series of museums, including the oldest wooden schoolhouse in the U.S. (according to 1716 records). Superb examples of 19th-century Spanish Renaissance architecture can be seen throughout St. Augustine.

St. Augustine Lighthouse and Maritime Museum features exhibits and artifacts on local maritime history and culture. Guided tours and stunning views at 100 Red Cox Dr. on Anastsia Island. Transportation required (904-829-0745).

There are two "Trolley" tour services in St. Augustine, each with a day pass that allows unlimited off/on privileges. They each provide stops at many interesting locations, both historical and current. If you have the time, it is well worth spending a day exploring the town.

Chapter 3: St. Johns River to New Smyrna Beach

Green daybeacon "5" starts a gentle turn around Davis Shores thumb-like point (Anastasia Island's northern tip). Upon reaching green daybeacon "7," Bridge of Lions is due south. Observe the ICW markers around the turn keeping about 100 yards off Davis Shores. This is a high traffic area. Call one of the local towing services for advice if you are unable to sort out the numerous markers. Always remember that the ICW markers have either a yellow square or a yellow triangle.

Check your speed approaching Bridge of Lions at Mile 777.9. Vertical clearance is 18 feet at the center when closed and you will likely need to wait for an opening. This bridge, one of the most attractive on the ICW, was originally completed in 1927. The bridge has been rebuilt in recent years with the goal to improve the bridge's safety while preserving its historic value.

Normal flood currents of 1 knot and ebb currents of 1.5 knots may be expected under the Bridge of Lions so exercise caution when approaching the bridge. The bridge opens on signal except between 7:00 a.m. and 6:00 p.m., when the draw only opens on the hour and half-hour; however, the draw need not open at 8:00 a.m., 12:00 p.m. or 5:00 p.m., Monday through Friday (except federal holidays). On weekends and holidays it opens only on the hour and half-hour between 7:00 a.m. and 6:00 p.m. Be aware that the bridge sometimes closes for special events (e.g., Blessing of the Fleet, 4th of July celebrations and various 5K walk/run events). These closures are usually well publicized and reasonably short in duration.

Dockage: The number of berths available to transients in St. Augustine reflects its long-standing popularity as a port of call. Several elaborate marine complexes cater to cruising boats.

Immediately north of the Vilano Bridge on the west side of the ICW is a large complex that is home to Windward at Camachee Cove Yacht Harbor. Bulkheads and jetties on both sides of the entrance help prevent shoaling and protect the outside slips. The entrance channel provides adequate depths for cruising boats of all sizes and the enclosed basin offers excellent protection. Windward at Camachee Cove Yacht Harbor has six fueling stations and some fueling can be done from individual slips. The marina is surrounded by 20 businesses offering every imaginable service for boaters including Camachee Yacht Yard, where trained on-site technicians can handle most any repair. First Mate Yacht Services is also on site offering full-service maintenance and repairs.

South of St. Augustine Inlet on Salt Run is Conch House Marina. The 200-slip marina has a tropical motif and offers full amenities. It is easy to get to from the inlet or the ICW. The popular Conch House Restaurant is on site offering seafood and Caribbean fare.

Dockage is also available south of the Bridge of Lions and these facilities are convenient to the city's many restaurants and historic attractions. St. Augustine Municipal Marina on the west side close to the tourist district offers transient dockage and moorings (described below) with all the usual amenities. Consider the direction of the current when docking here and time arrival for slack tide. Their slips are popular so call ahead to reserve. The marina is located in the heart of the downtown historical/tourist area with many attractions, shops, and restaurants just a few minutes walk from your slip.

Across the river on the east shore is the 24-slip Marker 8 Hotel & Marina. There is a strong current so docking and leaving should be at slack tide. There is usually staff around to help. The hotel offers a complimentary

---

First Mate Yacht Services
AT CAMACHEE COVE HARBOR
(904) 829-0184
Fax (904) 824-5605

COMMITMENT TO QUALITY

- Marine Fasteners - All Types
- Marine Pumps & Parts
- Paint & Varnish Supplies
- Marine Electrical Gear
- Cleaning Supplies

FULL SERVICE MAINTENANCE & REPAIRS
We Come to Your Boat!

Fuel Filtration & Treatment
Gas and Diesel Mechanics
Diving & Prop Changes
Refrigeration and A/C
Marine Electrician
Bottom Cleaning
General Repairs

Factory Authorized Dealers For:
Universal Westerbeke, Yanmar, BetaMarine

Monitor VHF 16
www.firstmateys.com
email: firstmate235@gmail.com

Chapter 3

St. Augustine Inlet, FL

		Largest Vessel	VHF	Total Slips	Approach/Dockside Depth	Floating Docks	Gas/Diesel	Repairs/Haulout	Min/Max Amps	Pump-Out Station
TOLOMATO RIVER										
1. Windward at Camachee Cove Yacht Harbor WiFi MM 775.7	(904) 829-5676	135	16	260	6.0 / 7.0	F	GD	RH	30 / 100	P
MATANZAS RIVER										
2. Conch House Marina 0.65 mi. W of MM 776.8	(904) 824-4347	200	16	200	8.5 / 8.5	F	GD	R	20 / 100	
3. St. Augustine Municipal Marina WiFi MM 778.3	(904) 825-1026	280	16	100	20.0 / 15.0	F	GD		30 / 100	P
4. Marker 8 Hotel & Marina WiFi MM 777.7	(904) 829-9042	103	16	24	9.0 / 7.0	F			30 / 100	

WiFi Wireless Internet Access
Visit www.waterwayguide.com for current rates, fuel prices, website addresses and other up-to-the-minute information.
(Information in the table is provided by the facilities.)

Scan here for more details:

Source: Aqua Map and NOAA data

SOUTHERN EDITION 169

Chapter 3: St. Johns River to New Smyrna Beach

San Sebastian River, FL

SAN SEBASTIAN RIVER		Largest Vessel	VHF	Total Slips	Approach/ Dockside Depth	Floating Docks	Gas/ Diesel	Repairs/ Haulout	Min/Max Amps	Pump-Out Station
1. Oasis Boatyard & Marina WiFi 1.2 mi. NW of MM 780	(904) 824-2520	65		45	16.0 / 16.0	F		RH	30 / 50	
2. Windward at St. Augustine Shipyard	(904) 342-5159	120		293	/ 10.0	F	G			
3. English Landing Marina WiFi	(904) 669-7363	55		44	20.0 / 15.0	F			30	
4. Rivers Edge Marina WiFi 1.7 mi. NW of MM 780.0	(904) 827-0520	120	16	100	10.0 / 10.0	F	GD	R	30 / 100	P

WiFi Wireless Internet Access
Visit www.waterwayguide.com for current rates, fuel prices, website addresses and other up-to-the-minute information.
(Information in the table is provided by the facilities.)

Scan here for more details:

Source: Aqua Map and NOAA data

America's Waterway Guide Since 1947 — Chapter 3

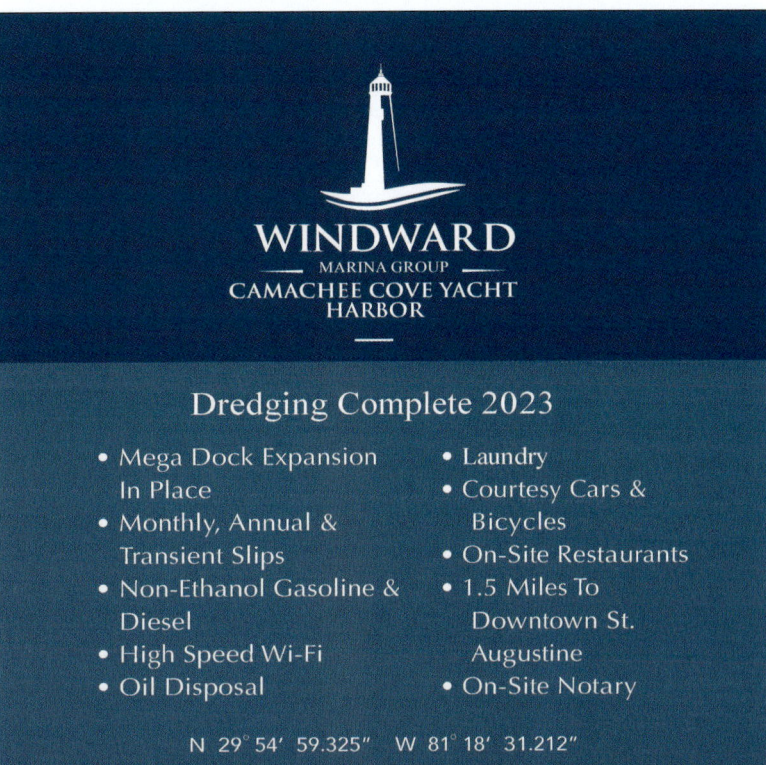

WINDWARD
MARINA GROUP
CAMACHEE COVE YACHT HARBOR

Dredging Complete 2023

- Mega Dock Expansion In Place
- Monthly, Annual & Transient Slips
- Non-Ethanol Gasoline & Diesel
- High Speed Wi-Fi
- Oil Disposal
- Laundry
- Courtesy Cars & Bicycles
- On-Site Restaurants
- 1.5 Miles To Downtown St. Augustine
- On-Site Notary

N 29° 54' 59.325" W 81° 18' 31.212"

Visit all of our beautiful marinas at
www.MYWINDWARD.com

3070 Harbor Dr, St. Augustine FL, 32084
904.829.5676

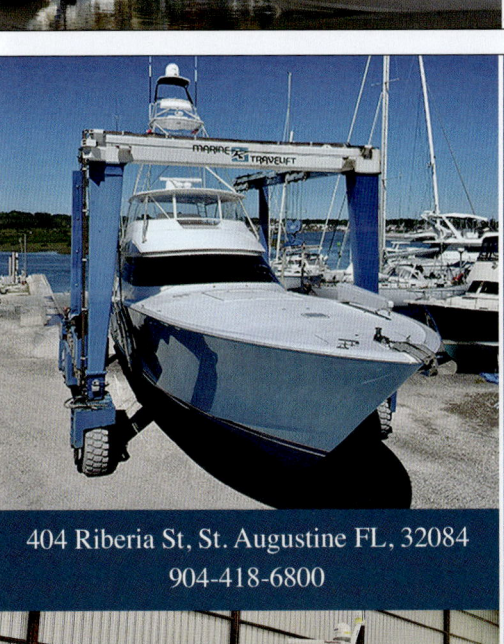

404 Riberia St, St. Augustine FL, 32084
904-418-6800

ST. AUGUSTINE MARINE CENTER
SINCE 1992

Full Service & Storage Facility

- 110 Ton Travel Lift To 23' 6" Beam
- 30 Ton Hydraulic Catamaran Trailer
- Fully Enclosed Paint Bays Accommodating Vessels Up To 100'
- Engine, Saildrive And Mechanical Services
- On-Site Prop Shop
- U/W Gear Service & Prep
- Standing & Running Rigging Service
- Sandblast Bottom Job Services
- Composite Repair
- Deep Water- Certified Clean Boatyard

N 29° 52' 44.273" W 81° 18' 48.117"

For more information visit us at
https://www.staugustinemarine.com/

SOUTHERN EDITION

Chapter 3: St. Johns River to New Smyrna Beach

breakfast and an afternoon social hour. They do not monitor the VHF radio so you will need to contact them by phone (904-829-9042).

The San Sebastian River, which branches off the Matanzas River at Mile 780, is a better spot for provisioning and has a number of marine businesses and associated docks but not many transient slips. Most, however, will not turn you away if they have an empty slip. You should exercise caution when docking anywhere on this river as the current can be swift.

Facilities with transient dockage include Oasis Boatyard & Marina, which has 45 slips and offers haul-out service (including catamarans). Call ahead for slip availability.

English Landing Marina has slips to 55 feet and is a 5-minute walk to grocery stores and fresh produce markets, marine supply stores as well as wonderful local and chain restaurants.

Pet-friendly Rivers Edge Marina at green daybeacon "33" has slips and the usual cruiser amenities plus an on-site restaurant, Hurricane Patty's (904-342-7338). It is a short walk from here to Sailor's Exchange (222 W. King St.), which buys-sells-trades new and used boating equipment.

There are numerous boat yards and repair businesses here including Windward Service Center St. Augustine, Windward at St. Augustine Shipyard, Cat's Paw Marina and Xynides Boat Yard. The Marine Supply & Oil Company is here as well for your fueling needs. Must have current vessel documentation or boat registration. (No exceptions.)

Moorings: The municipal mooring field consists of approximately 175 moorings, which are managed by St. Augustine Municipal Marina. There are four different mooring fields: Salt Run Mooring Field has two fields (north and south with a total of 80 moorings), while the downtown area has two additional fields–St. Augustine South (Menendez) Mooring Field with 70 moorings and St. Augustine North (San Marcos) Mooring Field with 28 moorings. There is a dinghy dock at the municipal marina.

St. Augustine

The Salt Run Mooring Field can be reached by following the private channel markers of the Conch House Marina. Once past the marina you will see the mooring fields (north and south). Both mooring areas have access to a pump-out boat and dinghy dock; however, if you want to be close to the City of St. Augustine, Salt Run Mooring Field is a poor choice. It would be a very long dinghy ride and a very long walk just to get there. This area is used primarily for long-term mooring.

The St. Augustine South (Menendez) Mooring Field is south of the Bridge of Lions and the St. Augustine North (San Marcos) Mooring Field is north of the Bridge of Lions. Both moorings fields have access to a free pump-out boat that operates daily between the hours of 9:00 a.m. and 12:00 p.m., a dinghy dock, a launch service (no need to "launch" your dinghy) and use of all of the facilities at the municipal marina. The moorings can accommodate vessels to 120 feet.

Enter the St. Augustine South (Menendez) Mooring Field just west of red daybeacon "8" on the ICW. Do not enter the field between red daybeacons "8" and "10A" as it has shoaled and has less than 4 feet MLW. Shoaling to 3 feet MLW has also been observed near and below some of the moorings. Ask the marina when you call for a mooring and get advice on where to enter the mooring field. This can be a little lumpy during the day on a weekend as it is not in a designated "no wake/minimum wake" zone and traffic on the Matanzas River can get heavy.

Anchorage: Anchoring is permitted but not within 100 feet of the mooring field boundaries and not within 50 feet of any other marine structure (such as private docks along the waterway). You can actually anchor in St. Augustine just outside the channel south of green daybeacon "7" in a pinch but expect to be waked, sometimes badly. Holding is good. You can dinghy to the city marina for shore access (for a reasonable fee).

Vilano Beach Pier is a public dock with a 4-hour limit located just south of the Usina Bridge. This is an easy dinghy ride across from Saint Augustine. There is a Publix less than 0.5 mile from the dock for easy provisioning.

An anchorage west of the ICW protected by a shoal can be found at Mile 781.2 on the Matanzas River. Enter from the north keeping flashing red "18" to the east. This anchorage offers deep water (at least 7 feet MLW). Tide can be up to 5 feet. There are several derelict and semi-submerged boats here so exercise caution.

Chapter 3: St. Johns River to New Smyrna Beach

■ TO DAYTONA BEACH

Matanzas River to Palm Coast– ICW Mile 780 to Mile 803

Marshland alternates with forests along the banks of the Matanzas River as you pass through a part of the Guana-Tolomato-Matanzas National Estuarine Research Reserve south of Marineland Marina on the east side of the ICW. You will likely encounter kayak tour groups here during warmer weather. Give them a slow, no-wake pass out of courtesy. This cut seems eerie and almost desolate in places so it comes as a surprise when farther down several wide, rip-rapped channels appear on the west side. This is part of the community of Palm Coast, which is accessible via three canals.

NAVIGATION: Use NOAA Chart 11485. The Matanzas River channel is deep but narrow so follow markers carefully until the dredged cut takes over south of Matanzas Inlet (closed to navigation). Shoals are encroaching on the channel from both sides through this stretch so holding the magenta line is advised. Expect heavy small-craft traffic on this stretch, especially on weekends. Also watch for wake-wash in the narrow channel.

The river narrows south of St. Augustine at Mile 780.3 at the high-rise **SR 312 Bridges** and the current is swift here. This area is dredged regularly but shoals are constantly forming on the east side of the channel south of the bridge. The navigable channel narrows considerably at flashing red "50" at Mile 787. Stay close to the magenta line all the way south to the Matanzas Inlet (closed to navigation).

At Crescent Beach you will encounter the **Crescent Beach (SR 206) Bridge** (Mile 788.6) with 25-foot closed vertical clearance. The bridge opens on signal and the bridgetender is particularly helpful and accommodating. On both sides of the bridge for approximately 200 feet is an enforced No-Wake Zone. Traffic starts to increase again along this stretch due to numerous boat ramps along the east shore.

Just south of Mile 792 the waters from the Matanzas Inlet (closed to navigation) meet the ICW resulting in constant shoaling. This is one of the shallowest sections of the ICW in eastern Florida. To make matters worse the beach here is a popular swimming spot with locals and boat traffic is often quite busy. Slow down and exercise extreme caution.

Buoys here are constantly being moved, added or removed. Follow the channel "as marked" during passage. The deepest water is surprisingly close to the beach around the outside of the curve on the west. The newly added bulkheads on the west bank seem to be improving depths. The channel holds a measured depth of 7 feet MLW. Honor the buoys. This area is always evolving and filling in. Check Waterway Explorer (www.waterwayguide.com) before transiting the area.

The current between the ICW crossing of Matanzas River (Mile 792) and Marineland Marina (Mile 796) can be strong enough to pull pot markers underwater but it decreases as you proceed toward Palm Coast. The fixed, high-level **Hammock Dunes Bridge** is at Mile 803.0 just south of the entrance to Palm Coast Marina.

At the north end of Rattlesnake Island (Mile 792) you will see the stark remains of Fort Matanzas, once a Spanish outpost and now a national monument. Like its larger cousin, Castillo de San Marcos in St. Augustine, this fort was built of coquina, a rock made of fused tiny shells. A small National Park Service Center, located on Anastasia Island on the north shore of the inlet, runs a ferry service to Fort Matanzas, located on Rattlesnake Island. Its terminal is just north of the Matanzas Inlet (closed to navigation). Dinghy tie up is forbidden at either dock but there is plenty of shore.

> **CAUTION:** Shoaling has been observed in the ICW channel by Fort Matanzas. Nun buoys are moved to mark shoaling encroaching from the east.

Dockage: If you are looking to stop for the night, Marineland Marina at Mile 796 can accommodate boats up to 100 feet in one of their 20 transient slips. They also accept catamarans on bulkhead tie-ups. After an extensive renovation the marina has new restrooms, showers and laundry facilities and offers pump-out service at each slip. Marineland Dolphin Adventure is directly across the street with hands-on exhibits and educational programs with Atlantic bottlenose dolphins (for a fee). Call 407-563-4701 for details.

At the corner of the ICW and the main canal at Mile 803 is the well-kept Palm Coast Marina. Once inside the canal, favor the south side of the channel. The marina welcomes transients and is known

Palm Coast, FL

PALM COAST AREA		Largest Vessel	VHF	Total Slips	Approach/ Dockside Depth	Floating Docks	Gas/ Diesel	Repairs/ Haulout	Min/Max Amps	Pump-Out Station
1. Marineland Marina WiFi MM 796.0	(904) 814-9886	100	16	41	6.5 / 6.0	F			30 / 100	P
2. Palm Coast Marina WiFi MM 803.2	(386) 446-6370	165	16	80	8.0 / 8.0		GD		30 / 50	P
3. Hammock Beach Marina WiFi MM 803.0	(386) 348-3114	180	16	213	10.0 / 8.0	F			30 / 100	P

WiFi Wireless Internet Access
Visit www.waterwayguide.com for current rates, fuel prices, website addresses and other up-to-the-minute information. (Information in the table is provided by the facilities.)

Scan here for more details:

for its friendly and attentive service. The facility has walking trails along the ICW and kayak rentals. Within walking distance from the marina (approximately 0.5 mile) is European Village, a one-stop destination for dining, lounging, shopping and entertainment in the heart of Palm Coast.

Hammock Beach Marina at Mile 803 in Palm Coast offers accommodations and amenities in a unique private club setting. On-site facilities include two golf courses and a putting course, tennis courts, a multi-level fantasy pool complex and a spa. At the entrance markers, contact the marina office on VHF Channel 16 for docking assignment, instructions and assistance.

Anchorage: South at Butler Beach at Mile 786.2 there is good holding in 6 to 7 feet MLW south of flashing green "43" behind the spoil area. There are boat ramps nearby so this may get busy during the day.

Enter the Fort Matanzas anchorage by turning east between red can "80A" and "80B" and strongly favor the north shore as you enter. Anchor between the ICW and just north of the ferry landing on Rattlesnake Island in 10 to 12 feet MLW. Holding is good but make sure you allow for the 4 foot plus tide and a current that will reach 3 knots at full ebb or flood. Good ground tackle is a must. Smaller boats can continue pass the Visitors Center, still favoring the north shore and anchor below in 10 to 12 feet of water near the beach on Rattlesnake Island. This is a great stop.

To Ormond Beach–ICW Mile 804 to Mile 825

If you leave the Palm Coast area marinas on a slower boat (less than 10-knot speed) at the start of the ebb tide you can ride the current all the way south to Ponce De Leon (New Smyrna) Inlet. For several miles south of Palm Coast Marina condominiums with community docks and boat lifts, golf courses and private homes line both sides of the ICW.

Chapter 3: St. Johns River to New Smyrna Beach

As a point of interest, a narrow interconnecting canal intersects the east side of the ICW at Mile 804. This was part of the original ICW and gives an idea of the size of some earlier sections. A low clearance fixed bridge prevents passage through the older channel.

> **NOTE:** You will pass Tomoka State Park at Mile 819, which was once home to the Timucua Indians. Today you can walk beneath the same ancient oaks that shaded their villages nearly 400 years ago or explore the marshes and tidal creeks by dinghy.

NAVIGATION: Use NOAA Chart 11485. Stay in the center of the channel, especially south of the high-rise **SR 100 (Moody Blvd., Flagler Beach) Bridge** near the long series of docks on the west side. Be aware that the presence of residential docks is not an indication of deep water and should keep some distance off shore. If you see boats in the water at these docks, slow down out of courtesy and give them a "no-wake" pass. This area of the waterway is locally known as Smiths Creek.

From Mile 805 exposed rocks line both sides of Fox Cut from green daybeacon "1" to green daybeacon "5." Red daybeacons "2" and "4" and flashing green "3" mark rocks that extend to the edge of the channel. A ramp, dock and launch facility have been dug out of the west side of the ICW opposite flashing green "3."

The high-rise Flagler Beach Bridge crosses the ICW at Mile 810.6. Watch for shoals near the bridge along the edges of the channel. A dock development on the east side of the ICW just north of the bridge has been empty of boats since being built and the entrance is roped off. This marina has been abandoned for a number of years and there are prominent signs indicating "NO TRESPASSING/PRIVATE DOCKS." (This means you!)

There is a busy ramp south of the bridge; pass at idle speed. For the 5 miles between the Flagler Beach Bridge and the **Bulow (L.B. Knox) Bridge**, the channel is lined with pot markers on both sides; expect some markers in the channel itself.

At Mile 812.4 red daybeacon "20" marks the start of an eastward bend in Smith Creek and red daybeacon "20A" provides a reference to align cruisers in the narrow, dredged channel. At Mile 814 a small, marked side channel leads to a state park and a ramp. This is the beginning of a Manatee Zone with a 30-mph speed limit in the channel (25 mph at night) and slow speed required outside the ICW channel.

At Mile 816 expect congestion at the boat ramp next to the L.B. Knox Bridge. Vertical clearance is only 15 feet but the bridge opens on signal. South of the bridge shoals encroach the channel from both sides through to red daybeacon "30," particularly where small creeks enter the ICW. Mind your depth through this section and center yourself between the crab pots.

The ICW enters the headwaters of the Halifax River at Mile 816 and gradually widens on its run to Daytona Beach. The channel is straight and well marked and follows closely along the eastern bank as it passes a series of attractive homes. There is a negligible tidal range here.

For deeper-draft boats the 5-mile-long passage hugging the east shore of the Halifax River from the Tomoka Basin at ICW Mile 819 to the high-rise **SR 40 (Ormond Beach) Bridge** at Mile 824.9 calls for close attention. Stick to the middle on the marked channel along this stretch because both edges shoal quickly and it is very shallow outside. Markers are well spaced along this stretch but it can be difficult to maintain the channel close to the edge of

L.B. Knox Bridge

what sometimes appears to be a wide basin particularly in strong crosswinds. Check behind occasionally to check your alignment. Depths are generally 8 feet MLW at mid-channel in this area. Just north of the Ormond Beach Bridge the channel gradually angles toward the middle of the river.

> NOTE: The open water of the Halifax River here is a popular windsurfing area. On a blustery day expect to see several windsurfers crisscrossing the channel.

The Ormond Beach Bridge at Mile 824.9 has 65-foot fixed vertical clearance. Heading south to Daytona Beach the ICW follows a narrow, dredged channel that runs roughly down the center of the Halifax River. Markers are spaced approximately 0.50 miles apart; take care to observe them carefully as depths shallow quickly at the channel edges.

Dockage: There are 14 complimentary floating slips and a restroom at Cassen Park City Docks at the foot of the Ormond Beach Bridge but no other amenities. Note that two busy boat launches are nearby so stay alert.

Anchorage: The Cement Plant basin at Mile 809 appears to be open for anchoring with 6 feet MLW, despite ongoing land-based construction.

Daytona Beach–ICW Mile 830

The official tourist season for this northern Florida "summer resort" runs from Memorial Day to Labor Day but Daytona Beach is a popular destination year round. In spring and fall boats on the north–south run stop here and skippers often come to have work done at one of the area's excellent repair yards.

NAVIGATION: Use NOAA Chart 11485. It's a straight 5-mile shot from Ormond Beach to the series of closely packed bridges that welcome you to Daytona Beach. The ICW channel opens up slightly as you reach these bridges:

- **Seabreeze Bridges** (65-foot fixed vertical clearance)
- **Main Street Bridge** (22-foot closed vertical clearance). Opens on signal. (Also known as **Daytona Beach Bridge**.)
- **International Speedway Blvd. Bridge** (65-foot fixed vertical clearance)
- **Memorial Bridge** (65-foot vertical clearance)

Take care to follow the "hockey stick" alignment of the ICW channel between the Main Street Bridge and International Speedway Blvd. Bridge to avoid the dangerous shoal areas noted on the charts. If you take a direct line between bridge openings you will run aground!

Dockage: Marinas and boatyards line the shore on the west side of the ICW from north of the city all the way to Ponce De Leon (New Smyrna) Inlet. Just south of the Seabreeze Bridges at Mile 829 is the 62-slip Coquina Marina, which offers transient dockage for vessels to 120 feet in a manicured resort setting with amenities such as a fitness facility, a large pool and jacuzzi and a tennis court. Groceries are available within 1 mile.

Just to the south, Loggerhead Marina–Daytona Beach Marina offers transient dockage to 75 feet with first-class amenities. The on-site Caribbean Jack's (386-523-3000) is open daily. (We recommend snagging a swinging glider table on the waterfront deck.)

Private Halifax River Yacht Club is located at Mile 830.7 in a basin just south of Memorial Bridge. They recognize reciprocity with many clubs. Call ahead for slip availability.

The municipal Halifax Harbor Marina is in a separate enclosed basin just to the south. Enter the marina through the marked entrance channel just west of ICW green daybeacon "39A." This large facility has 550 slips on a 60-acre property with excellent amenities and a well-stocked marine store. The marina is convenient to downtown Daytona and the city bus stop is an easy walk away.

In the next basin of the channel is the full-service Daytona Marina & Boat Works, open 24/7 for fuel (both gas and diesel) and offering dockage and repairs. They can accommodate boats up to 200 feet in length. The gold dome you see is the on-site Chart House Restaurant (386-255-9022).

Anchorage: There are anchorages both above and below the Seabreeze Bridges. The anchorage south of the bridge is deeper but there is scattered debris on the bottom. The north anchorage shallows up quickly and is in an area with submerged cables. Signs on each shore mark the location of the cables but the signs are difficult to pick out from the water. The sign on the western shore is just south of the twin condos. This entire anchorage area seems to be generally shoaling but it is still handy when you arrive late in the day from St. Augustine.

Chapter 3: St. Johns River to New Smyrna Beach

Goin' Ashore

DAYTONA BEACH, FL

ATTRACTIONS

1. **Cici & Hyatt Brown Museum of Art**
   Airy museum featuring large collection of Florida-themed paintings plus a gift shop and cafe at 352 S. Nova Rd. (386-255-0285).

2. **Halifax Historical Museum**
   Experience Daytona Beach from a historical perspective at 252 S. Beach St. (386-255-6976).

3. **Jackie Robinson Memorial Baseball Park**
   Fans can take in some minor league baseball at this historic ballpark (105 E. Orange Ave., 386-257-3172).

4. **Museum of Arts and Sciences**
   Long-standing venue located on nature preserve with global art, Florida history exhibits and a planetarium (352 S. Nova Rd., 386-255-0285).

SERVICES

5. **Daytona Beach Area Convention & Visitor Bureau**
   126 Orange Ave. (386-255-0415)

6. **Daytona Beach Post Office**
   220 N. Beach St. (386-258-9352)

7. **Daytona Beach Regional Library (City Island)**
   105 E. Magnolia Ave. (386-257-6036)

8. **Rawls Veterinary Hospital**
   127 Mason Ave. (386-253-2525)

MARINAS

9. **Coquina Marina**
   841 Ballough Rd. (386-317-0555)

10. **Daytona Marina & Boat Works**
    645 S. Beach St. (386-252-6421)

11. **Halifax River Yacht Club**
    331 S. Beach St. (386-255-7459)

12. **Halifax Harbor Marina**
    450 Basin St. (386-671-3601)

13. **Loggerhead (Daytona Beach) Marina**
    721 Ballough Rd. (386-523-3100)

America's Waterway Guide Since 1947 — Chapter 3

Riverfront Park is bordered by shops and eateries on one side and Halifax River on the other. The park's 0.5-mile walkway starts just north of the main yacht basins and is a great place for water-weary boaters to stretch their legs. A moving stop in the park is the gravesite of Brownie the Town Dog who was "owned by no one but loved by all." Should you need more exercise, 23 miles of wide sand beaches are nearby, as well as the iconic boardwalk and pier, a bandstand and a splash park, playground and picnic areas. The large Daytona Flea & Farmers Market is open weekends 9:00 a.m. to 5:00 p.m. with fruit and vegetables, clothing and jewelry plus a monthly classic car show (1425 Tomoka Farms Rd., 386-253-3330).

If you have transportation, tours are available of the famous Daytona International Speedway, which hosts events like the Daytona 500. This is also home to the Motorsports Hall of Fame of America (800-748-7467).

SOUTHERN EDITION

Chapter 3: St. Johns River to New Smyrna Beach

Daytona Beach, FL

DAYTONA BEACH		Largest Vessel	VHF	Total Slips	Approach/ Dockside Depth	Floating Docks	Gas/ Diesel	Repairs/ Haulout	Min/Max Amps	Pump-Out Station
1. Coquina Marina WiFi MM 829.4	(386) 317-0555	120	16	62	9.0 / 9.0	F			30 / 200+	
2. Loggerhead Marina - Daytona Beach Marina WiFi MM 829.6	(386) 523-3100	75	16	85	6.0 / 6.0		G		30 / 100	P
3. Halifax River Yacht Club-PRIVATE WiFi MM 830.7	(386) 290-9454	75	16	39	7.0 / 7.0				30 / 50	
4. Halifax Harbor Marina WiFi MM 830.7	(386) 671-3601	100	16	550	8.0 / 8.0	F	GD		30 / 100	P
5. Daytona Marina & Boat Works WiFi MM 831.0	(386) 252-6421	200	16	159	8.0 / 8.0		GD	RH	30 / 100	P

WiFi Wireless Internet Access
Visit www.waterwayguide.com for current rates, fuel prices, website addresses and other up-to-the-minute information.
(Information in the table is provided by the facilities.)

Scan here for more details:

Source: Aqua Map and NOAA data

America's Waterway Guide Since 1947 — Chapter 3

There is a cozy anchorage east of the ICW in the vicinity of the charted 11-foot depths at Mile 830.7 southeast of Memorial Bridge. To reach this anchorage turn east off the ICW immediately south of the bridge. Using the yacht club's green daybeacons "3" and "5" as a back range, proceed east to within 100 to 150 feet of shore. If you stay on the range you should find at least 6 feet of water over the bar. At this point, turn south along the shore to find a slot of water 9 to 13 feet deep about 100 feet from shore. The shoal between the ICW and the anchorage is less than 3 feet MLW.

The Bethune Park anchorage at Mile 831 has lots of room and near-shore access for dog relief at a sandy beach. You must approach the anchorage from red daybeacon "44" to the south for at least 7 feet MLW. (Do not try to approach from red daybeacon "40.")

■ TO NEW SMYRNA BEACH

Daytona Beach to Ponce De Leon Cut– ICW Mile 831 to Mile 840

NAVIGATION: Use NOAA Chart 11485. South of Daytona Beach the ICW channel briefly opens up but narrows again at Mile 833.5 (near red daybeacon "50") and numerous shoals flank the channel to Mile 838.5. Channel markers are closely spaced through this section and must be closely observed.

The **A1A Port Orange Relief Bridge** at Mile 835.5 is charted with a 65-foot fixed vertical clearance but tide boards at a full-moon high tide sometimes show a center span clearance of 63 feet. The channel under the bridge is constrained by a causeway and some small islands causing swift currents here. Avoid the shoals outside the narrow channel and watch for heavy boat traffic, especially on weekends. Watch your wake.

> **NOTE:** Just below the A1A Port Orange Relief Bridge, a small mangrove island on the west side of the ICW channel is a nesting ground for pelicans, egrets and cormorants during the spring. Confine your activity to watching only and do not disturb the nests.

The entrance channel for the private Harbour Village Marina between green daybeacon "71" and red daybeacon "72" is marked with a rather large red nun buoy and green can buoy on the east side of the ICW south of Daggett island. Do not confuse these for the floating ICW markers marking the beginning of the Ponce de Leon Cut just to the south of flashing green "1."

New Smyrna Beach

SOUTHERN EDITION

Chapter 3: St. Johns River to New Smyrna Beach

Ponce de Leon Inlet Area, FL

PORT ORANGE		Largest Vessel	VHF	Total Slips	Approach/Dockside Depth	Floating Docks	Gas/Diesel	Repairs/Haulout	Min/Max Amps	Pump-Out Station
1. Seven Seas Marina & Boatyard MM 835.2	(386) 761-3221	44	16	30	6.0 / 9.0		GD	RH	30 / 50	
2. Windward at Adventure Yacht Harbor WiFi MM 836.8	(386) 756-2180	65	16	137	4.5 / 7.0		GD		30 / 50	P
PONCE DE LEON INLET										
3. Loggerhead Marina - Inlet Harbor Marina 0.8 mi. SE of MM 839.5	(386) 767-3266	180	6	84	9.0 / 15.0	F	GD		30 / 100	P
4. Sea Love Boat Works Inc. WiFi 1.3 mi. SE of MM 839.5	(386) 761-5434	90	16	10	12.0 / 12.0	F	GD	RH	30 / 100	

WiFi Wireless Internet Access
Visit www.waterwayguide.com for current rates, fuel prices, website addresses and other up-to-the-minute information.
(Information in the table is provided by the facilities.)

Scan here for more details:

Source: Aqua Map and NOAA data

Dockage: Seven Seas Marina & Boatyard is located above the A1A Port Orange Relief Bridge on the east side at Mile 835.2. They have transient slips (to 44 feet) and a DIY boatyard. Pat's Riverfront Café (386-756-8070) is on the premises with breakfast all day (plus other options).

A short distance below the A1A Port Orange Relief Bridge on the east side of the ICW south of flashing green "59" is Windward Adventure Yacht Harbor with slips to 65 feet. Look for the marked entry channel. Note that there is a tidal range here of 2.5 feet and the channel can be as low as 5 feet MLW. Call ahead for more exact depths. This facility mostly caters to sportfishing boats and is close to amenities and provisioning supplies.

Ponce de Leon Cut–ICW Mile 840 to Mile 843.5

At about Mile 840, the ICW leaves the Halifax River and enters the Ponce de Leon Cut, bypassing the Ponce De Leon (New Smyrna) Inlet. The main ICW channel passes 2 miles west of the inlet through the Ponce de Leon Cut. The cut is protected from ocean surge but subject to extreme shoaling, especially at its north and south ends. The Cut ends at Mile 843.5 where it meets the Indian River North.

NAVIGATION: Use NOAA Chart 11485.

CAUTION: This is a traditional shoaling area that is frequently dredged. Depths may be more shallow than shown on charts and aids to navigation are moved on a regular basis. The depth and alignment of all the channels in this area change constantly and even the most recent charts are often outdated so up-to-date soundings are essential. See up-to-date tracks and navigation alerts at Waterway Explorer (www.waterwayguide.com).

When heading northbound on the ICW from New Smyrna, watch carefully for the turn into the Ponce de Leon Cut at Mile 843.5. The cut's opening is marked by a green-over-red buoy "C" to the north and red nun "18A" to the south. These markers are less obvious than the larger set marking the Ponce De Leon (New Smyrna) Inlet and can be missed.

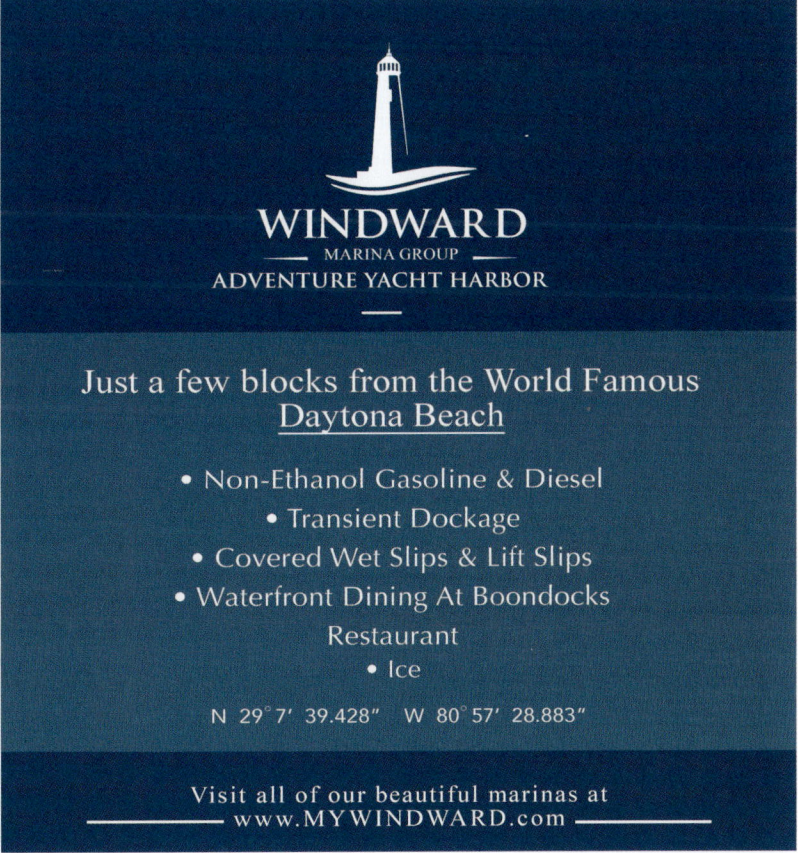

Chapter 3: St. Johns River to New Smyrna Beach

Anchorage: Note that all the side creeks in this area have approximately 7 to 9 feet MLW but are not included in the periodic dredging because they are not authorized federal channels. Rockhouse Creek at Mile 842.2 is a popular weekend anchorage and a congested small boat passage. Enter along the centerline of the cut from the ICW as shoals are building from both the north and south shores. Once inside 8- to 10-foot MLW depths are easy to find and holding is good. Provisioning opportunities are nearby.

Ponce de Leon (New Smyrna) Inlet

The historic Ponce de Leon Lighthouse located north of the Ponce De Leon (New Smyrna) Inlet is open to the public (daily except Thanksgiving and Christmas) and provides a stunning panoramic view of the area.

NAVIGATION: Use NOAA Chart 11485. Note that it is safer to access the inlet from the south, which is used extensively by locals and sportfishing boats and is a convenient point to enter or leave the ICW between Daytona and Cape Canaveral. This is a fair weather inlet only. The next opportunity going south to leave the ICW and go offshore is the Canaveral Barge Canal at Mile 894 then east to Port Canaveral Inlet.

The north approach channel to Ponce De Leon Inlet branches eastward from flashing green "1." To access the marine facilities on the east bank of the north approach channel to the Ponce de Leon Inlet enter the channel from the ICW at the north end of the Ponce de Leon Cut at Mile 839.6 near green can buoy "3."

Initially the Halifax River channel is well marked with good water on the eastern shore but it shallows radically before the inlet, and south of red nun buoy "4" the channel is unmarked. The deeper water is close to the beach on the west side. Skippers of deeper draft boats should avoid this route unless they have local knowledge.

When approaching the inlet from the ocean, aids to navigation may not match what is charted but the channel should be well marked. The inlet is considered a fair weather route; shoaling is continuous and dredging is frequent here. The shoaling is particularly bad extending from the beach along the inlet's south shore. Deeper water is generally found closer the inlet's north jetty, which was extended in 2021.

A U.S. Coast Guard station is located on the south channel of the inlet and will respond to calls for inlet conditions and the local TowBoat U.S. is up to date on local conditions. Both can be hailed on VHF Channel 16.

Dockage: The first facility on the Halifax River approaching Ponce De Leon Inlet is the full-service Loggerhead Marina–Inlet Harbor Marina, where a helpful staff will assist you into a transient space. The on-site restaurant, Off the Hook (386-202-4490), offers good food, live music and brilliant sunsets. Opposite red nun buoy "4" to the south is the locally-owned and -operated Sea Love Boat Works Inc. with transient berths and full repair and maintenance services.

Anchorage: Anchorage space may be available along the shores of the North Approach Channel. This is a restricted manatee zone. Nevertheless, you may experience wakes and expect some strong currents. Piddler Island north of Sea Love Boat Works Inc. has depths to 9 feet MLW and good holding in sand. There are several restaurants where you can dock or dinghy up to. This is a protected and quiet location.

To New Smyrna Beach–ICW Mile 844 to Mile 847

New Smyrna Beach is known for its beaches including nearby Canaveral National Seashore and Smyrna Dunes Park, which has incredible views of the inlet and its lighthouse. All manner of attractions and shopping can be found along the downtown's palm-lined Canal Street Historic District.

NAVIGATION: Use NOAA Chart 11485. The South Channel from Ponce De Leon (New Smyrna) Inlet is well marked with floating markers and the channel is always active with mostly recreational boat traffic. The inlet markers are repositioned occasionally and it is best to use up-to-date charts.

The **George E. Musson/Coronado Beach (SR 44) Bridge** at Mile 845.0 has 24-foot closed vertical clearance and its hydraulic mechanism is relatively slow in opening; expect a swift-moving current that can complicate the approach to the bridge. The bridge opens on signal except from 7:00 a.m. to 7:00 p.m. daily, when the draw opens only on the hour and half-hour.

South of the bridge continue to favor the eastern shore until the channel begins to swing west at flashing red "30." The area around red daybeacon "34" (Mile 845.5) always seems to be shoaling (currently at 10.9 feet MLW) even when recently dredged. It may be less stressful to use the Sheephead Cut for 11.9 MLW, which runs south

New Smyrna Beach, FL

NEW SMYRNA BEACH AREA		Largest Vessel	VHF	Total Slips	Approach/Dockside Depth	Floating Docks	Gas/Diesel	Repairs/Haulout	Min/Max Amps	Pump-Out Station
1. New Smyrna Marina dba The Fishing Store WiFi MM 846.0	(386) 427-4514	125	16	31	12.0 / 10.0	F	GD		30 / 100	
2. North Causeway Marine MM 846.0	(386) 427-5267	60	16	35	8.0 / 10.0		G	RH	30 / 50	
3. New Smyrna Beach City Marina WiFi MM 846.5	(386) 409-2042	65	16	43	8.0 / 10.0	F			30 / 100	P
4. Night Swan Bed & Breakfast MM 847.0	(386) 423-4940	40		6	12.0 / 9.0	F			30 / 50	
5. Smyrna Yacht Club-PRIVATE WiFi MM 847.0	(386) 427-4040	65	16	77	/ 4.0	F			30 / 50	P

WiFi Wireless Internet Access
Visit www.waterwayguide.com for current rates, fuel prices, website addresses and other up-to-the-minute information.
(Information in the table is provided by the facilities.)

Scan here for more details:

of Chicken Island. The entrance is indicated by a green-over-red daybeacon at the island's eastern tip. The channel carries 9 to 12-foot MLW depths and re-joins the ICW at another green-over-red daybeacon at the western end of Chicken Island. Stay centered in the marked channel to avoid shoals and watch for anchor lines as the cut is a popular anchorage.

New Smyrna Beach's harbor comes up suddenly beyond flashing red "38," which marks the turn toward the high-rise **Harris Saxon (South Causeway) Bridge** at Mile 846.6. Note that south of the bridge the ICW channel has charted 10-foot MLW depths just off the Smyrna Yacht Club close to flashing green "45." As a courtesy, slow down and give the Yacht Club a "no-wake" pass.

The City of New Smyrna's attractive Riverside Park runs north of the bridge along the west bank of the Indian River North. The park has a boardwalk, fishing pier and three small docking areas The free dock in New Smyrna Beach no longer allows overnight stays. There is a 5-hour limit and it is enforced. There is room for two 40-foot boats and easy access to downtown should you need to go ashore. This can be a great stop for provisions.

NOTE: New Smyrna Beach's FLEX is a "call first" curb-to-curb, flexible transportation service that can ferry cruisers from the downtown district to the beach or larger grocery stores further inland for a nominal fee. To use this service call 386-424-6810 at least 2 hours before you wish to travel.

Dockage: Located just 2.5 miles from Ponce De Leon Inlet, New Smyrna Marina dba The Fishing Store is a deep water, full-service marina with 31 slips offering upscale amenities including a heated swimming pool. A fleet of offshore and inshore fishing charters and daily pontoon boat rentals are based here. The on-site Outriggers Tiki Bar & Grille (386-428-6888) offers lunch, dinner and Sunday brunch. Family-owned North

Source: Aqua Map and NOAA data

Chapter 3: St. Johns River to New Smyrna Beach

Goin' Ashore: NEW SMYRNA BEACH, FL

Old Fort Park

ATTRACTIONS

1. **Marine Discovery Center**
   This nonprofit educational center focuses on the Indian River Lagoon and coastal waters through live aquariums, interactive exhibits and a gift shop at 520 Barracuda Blvd. (386-428-4828).

2. **New Symrna Beach Brewing Company**
   Taproom specializing in ales with live music most weekends at 143 Canal St. (386-957-3802).

3. **New Smyrna Beach Farmers Market**
   Weekly market with fresh produce, artisanal goods and live music at 210 Sams Ave. Saturdays from 7:00 a.m. to 12:30 p.m. (386-314-1224).

4. **New Smyrna Museum of History**
   Interpretive exhibits of local culture and history, including Native American artifacts, railroad memorabilia and Civil War displays (120 Sams Ave., 386-478-0052).

5. **New Smyrna Outfitters**
   Brand name clothing is sold alongside fishing tackle and gear at 223A Canal St. (386-402-8853).

6. **Old Fort Park**
   Home of the historic Turnbull Ruins and site of summer concerts and the annual Art Fiesta in February (115 Julia St., 386-424-2175).

SERVICES

7. **AdventHealth New Smyrna Beach**
   401 Palmetto St. (386-424-5000)

8. **Beachwood Animal Clinic**
   508 E. 3rd Ave. (386-426-0075)

9. **New Smyrna Beach Regional Library**
   1001 S. Dixie Fwy. (386-424-2910)

MARINAS

10. **New Smyrna Marina**
    200 Boatyard St. (386-427-4514)

11. **New Smyrna Beach City Marina**
    201 N. Riverside Dr. (386-409-2042)

12. **Night Swan Bed & Breakfast**
    512 S. Riverside Dr. (386-423-4940)

13. **North Causeway Marina**
    4 N. Causeway (386-427-5267)

14. **Smyrna Yacht Club**
    1201 S. Riverside Dr. (386-427-4040)

America's Waterway Guide Since 1947

Chapter 3

The downtown area of New Smyrna Beach begins only 1 block away from the municipal marina where a variety of restaurants and shops line the streets for local shoppers and visitors.

The fort-like coquina ruins in Old Fort Park lead some historians to believe New Smyrna was originally the site of St. Augustine and that it could be even 500 years older. Across the Musson Bridge and 2 miles to the east is an extraordinarily wide, sandy ocean beach that extends 13 miles.

SOUTHERN EDITION

Chapter 3: St. Johns River to New Smyrna Beach

Causeway Marine to the south has limited space (two slips) reserved for transients and offers routine maintenance and repairs to re-power, rigging, electronics, detailing and much more.

The municipal New Smyrna Beach City Marina at Mile 846.5 offers slips with a full suite of amenities. This is a well-run establishment that goes out of their way to accommodate visitors. Boat slips are available to the public on a first-come, first-served basis. Minimum allowed vessel length is 28 feet. It is close to the Canal Street Historic District, where you can find arts, history, shopping and dining. It is also across the street from the Old Fort Park historical site, which hosts a weekly Farmers' Market every Saturday.

Want to get off the boat? Night Swan Bed & Breakfast just south of the Harris Saxon (South Causeway) Bridge sometimes has tie-ups in this very walkable and bikeable areas. The dock has Adirondack chairs for a comfortable relaxing space off the boat. Call ahead for slip availability. (Usually full on the weekends.)

Farther south on an island west of the ICW, the private Smyrna Yacht Club welcomes guests of members and members of certain clubs on their docks. (Call ahead.) The docks are relatively easy to access since they are parallel to the current and, consequently, should be approached against the tide. They can accommodate boats up to 45 feet with amenities that include tennis and pickleball courts, a pool, dining and a tiki bar. Bring your blue blazer. There is a dress code.

Anchorage: There are numerous good spots for anchoring between Ponce Inlet and New Smyrna Beach. Anchor south of the cable area south of the George E. Musson/Coronado Beach (SR 44) Bridge at Buena Vista Park. Anchor in 9 feet north west of red daybeacon "30" north of the bend. There is enough room for 4 to 5 boats here. Holding was good and the bit of current will keep you in line with the river.

There is space in Sheephead Cut for three or four boats to anchor on the south side of the channel between green daybeacon "1" and just beyond green daybeacon "3" (between the markers and the condominium docks on Bouchelle Island). Show an anchor light and make sure that you will not swing into the channel or the docks at the tidal change; this is a very small, tight anchorage. The depths are 8 to 10 feet MLW and the holding is good but local boats use the channel at all hours.

It is possible to anchor south of the Harris Saxon (South Causeway) Bridge at Mile 846.5 in 12 feet MLW with good holding in mud. (Best water is found about 500 feet north of Harris Saxon Bridge G45). This anchorage provides easy access to the Riverside Park dinghy dock and the town; however, it is exposed to the south and passing boat wakes. There is a lot of debris on the bottom so a trip line on your anchor is recommended in case of snags.

■ NEXT STOP

South of New Smyrna Beach the ICW joins the Indian River North, which leads to the "Space Coast." This is a delightful stop worthy of a few days off the boat.

Space Coast Area — Chapter 4

SOUTHERN EDITION

Chapter 4: Space Coast Area

 ICW Mile 847-Mile 952

■ TO TITUSVILLE

In what has come to be known as the Space Coast Area the coastal topography changes from a slender barrier strip to a broad stretch of land forming Cape Canaveral. Inside the Cape area, the waters divide around Merritt Island separating Indian River on the mainland side from Banana River to the east.

NO WAKE ZONE

No Wake Zones, Idle Speed Zones and various Speed Limit restrictions are in effect throughout the waterways included in this chapter. Exercise diligence in knowing the regulations by observing signs and other markers. Enforcement is always present. As always, be courteous to other vessels and avoid manatees and other marine life.

Indian River: Cruising Conditions

The Indian River starts at the Haulover Canal as a wide and shallow basin and the ICW follows a narrow dredged channel. Boaters in this basin are vulnerable to chop in any strong wind conditions. Note also that the nearest ocean inlets are some distance in either direction and rainfall or wind conditions can affect water levels by as much as 2 feet here.

Boaters headed south should take note as elevated water levels will reduce bridge clearances from their charted minimums. While most of the bridges that cross the Indian River are fixed, high-rise bridges with a charted 65-foot clearance elevated water levels can still be an important factor if your air-draft is near the limit.

South of Titusville the shorelines close in and the river deepens creating a wider navigable channel. This section of the Indian River is a pleasure to navigate, although strong winds can still kick up an uncomfortable chop in either north or south winds. Sailors often unfurl their sails along here if winds allow.

Currents are typically modest in the upper stretches of the river and strengthen as you head south but consider that elevated water levels can affect currents as well. Wider channels also provide extra maneuvering space should you have to wait for a bridge opening. Extra space also allows you to drop anchor either to wait for an opening or overnight in the deeper waters outside the marked channel. Anchoring is preferable to navigating into a strange harbor at night.

Mosquito Lagoon to Haulover Canal–ICW Mile 847 to Mile 869

Heading south from New Smyrna the waterway follows the Indian River North and traverses Mosquito Lagoon to the Haulover Canal. For the most part this is a beautiful journey through the wild Canaveral National Seashore, which is managed by the National Park Service. Note that access to and use of some areas within the park are restricted.

The river is rich in seafood so watch for crab pots and fish traps along this route as commercial fishermen work the area north of the park boundary at Mile 961. Numerous fishing camps also dot the shores north of the park.

The Indian River North is initially flanked to the east by a jumble of small islets but in truth the river is bound on both sides by the mainland. Were it not for the man-made Haulover Canal the narrow strip of land that forms a barrier to the Atlantic Ocean to the east (and Cape Canaveral itself) would still be a natural peninsula.

Mosquito Lagoon is an open, shallow expanse of water that can only be explored by dinghy or shallow-draft boat. The same conditions that make this water popular for mosquitoes and deer flies also create an ideal feeding and breeding ground for sport and commercial fish including redfish, sea trout and mullet. Flocks of white pelicans and the small fishing boats that fill Mosquito Lagoon attest to the abundance of fresh seafood.

The man-made Haulover Canal is a 1-mile-long rocky cut allowing passage from the Indian River North (Mosquito Lagoon) into the Indian River. Though the canal connects the headwaters of two distinct river systems the ICW's approach appears near identical at both ends–a narrow dredged channel through wide basins. The canal also marks the western extent of the Canaveral National Seashore. Look for increased activity by both commercial and recreational fishermen to the south.

NAVIGATION: Use NOAA Chart 11485. For about the next 10 miles the ICW runs down a straight, dredged channel between the mainland and a group of small islets. Staying in the center of the channel you will see 11- to 14-foot MLW depths and markers are closely placed. It shoals very quickly on the edges of the channel so extra care is required especially in a strong crosswind.

Markers are closely spaced in Mosquito Lagoon and boaters can see spots with 8-foot MLW depths in the marked channel but expect depths to decrease suddenly outside the marked channel, particularly to the west. Uncharted spoil banks flank the dredged Mosquito Lagoon channel and deeper draft boats should monitor the depth. Favor the green side but don't hug the markers too closely as the channel shallows near the edges.

Maintaining channel alignment can be difficult, especially in a strong crosswind. Strong winds can also cause an uncomfortable chop on the lagoon. Several fishing camps and the usual Florida waterfront housing run along on the west side above the park boundary at green daybeacon "19" (Mile 861). Keep an eye out for kayaks and small fishing boats here. They frequently anchor in the channel or too close to the edge. Reduce your wake as you pass.

> NOTE: As you reach the middle of Mosquito Lagoon you may be able to see a large building in the distance to the south. This is NASA's Vehicle Assembly Building (VAB) at Kennedy Space Center. In clear weather the giant VAB is visible for distances of 20 miles or more. In the past, the southern end of Mosquito Lagoon (from Haulover Canal east to 3 miles out in the Atlantic Ocean, excluding the ICW) was off limits to all watercraft 72 hours before any launches. Pay attention and ask local marinas for updates.

The sharp approach corner at Mile 869.2 should be taken wide. If you attempt to hug the red markers on the inside of the curve you will find shallow water. Follow the magenta line and give the red markers considerable berth.

Passing through the Haulover Canal the ICW enters the upper stretch of the Indian River and exits the Canaveral National Seashore. Watch for an increase in both recreational and commercial fishermen here. Initially the route traverses a broad, shallow basin before the river narrows and the Indian River becomes better defined. Beyond the marked channel edges the basin is extremely shallow with visible and submerged spoil islands. Deeper draft boats should carefully maintain channel alignment and proceed through this section with caution.

The **Allenhurst (Haulover Canal) Bridge** (27-foot closed vertical clearance) crosses the canal at Mile 869.2 and opens promptly on signal. If the bridgetender

Haulover Canal Bridge

does not respond on VHF Channel 09 use a horn signal (one long, one short) to request an opening or call 321-867-4859.

The ramp in the small basin off the middle of the canal southeast of the bridge is always busy (particularly on weekends) and the Haulover Canal is often congested with small boats of every type and description. These small boats may have as many as three people standing up to cast at the edge of the channel or under the bridge.

> NOTE: This is one of the best spots to observe manatees (often visible) on the ICW. Wildlife also abounds on shore, which is overgrown with vegetation. Heed the slow speed signs and keep a lookout for herons, egrets, alligators, stingrays and manatees.

Anchorage: If you are transiting the Mosquito Lagoon, there are few good anchorages off the ICW in good water between Haulover Canal and New Smyrna. Mosquito Lagoon does offer some deeper sections but wind protection is minimal. Be sure to exit the channel at minimum speed so that release from a possible grounding

Chapter 4: Space Coast Area

will be easier. Expect a mud bottom and beware that snags are possible so use of a trip line is advised.

The area east of Mosquito Lagoon G19 at Mile 861.3 has 6- to 7-foot MLW depths. Enter south of the maker. This has good holding in sand but can be bumpy if the winds are up from almost any direction due to the long fetch. There is good fishing on the bar to the northeast. With a dinghy you can explore many of the islands in the lagoon from here.

A small area just outside the channel southeast of Mosquito Lagoon R24 (Mile 862.8) has charted 10-foot MLW depths. Exit the channel at the marker. There is deeper water to the south. As with other anchorages in Mosquito Lagoon, chop forms quickly in all but west winds due to the fetch between the ICW and land.

Indian River to Titusville–ICW Mile 869 to Mile 878

Titusville is an important agricultural center for the Florida citrus industry. It is also good port from which to visit Disney World and the Orlando area theme parks. It is also conveniently located for a visit Kennedy Space Center (an excursion not to be missed).

> NOTE: Check the Kennedy Space Center launch schedule if you're passing through and you may be rewarded; the small deck at the center of the high-rise A. Max Brewer (SR 406) Bridge provides an excellent view.

For most of the next 120 miles southward to the St. Lucie River, the Indian River is wide and deep. In many places the navigable channel is much wider than the marked channel. Several stretches allow sailboats to hoist their canvas and all boaters to temporarily relax at the helm. Beware though that much of the ICW to Cocoa is a dredged channel, there are numerous shoal areas and depths outside the marked may be less than charted.

NAVIGATION: Use NOAA Chart 11485. After exiting the Haulover Canal the ICW enters the upper stretch of the Indian River and exits the Canaveral National Seashore. Watch for an increase in both recreational and commercial fishermen here. Initially the route traverses a broad, shallow basin before the river narrows and the Indian River becomes better defined.

Beyond the marked channel edges the basin is extremely shallow, with visible and submerged spoil islands. Deeper draft boats should carefully maintain channel alignment and proceed through this section with caution. This is one of the best spots to observe manatees (often visible) on the ICW. Wildlife abounds on shore, which is overgrown with vegetation.

Note that depths are shallower in the Indian River immediately past the Haulover Canal. Entrance jetties at both ends reduce chop and control shoaling in the canal but watch for shoaling outside the jetty at the south exit. Be advised the current in the canal can be swift. The tidal range is minimal but heavy rainfall or strong winds may raise or lower water levels here by as much as 2 feet.

Flashing green "1" and red daybeacon "2" are the first two markers you will encounter as you head southwest out of the Haulover Canal. After reaching these markers two huge white tanks on the Indian River's west bank line up with the less visible red markers lining the channel's northern edge and may be used as a forward navigation target. These tanks are charted as "TANK (NW OF TWO)." When steering for the tanks keep an eye on the markers ahead and astern watching for leeway. You do not want to stray out of the channel in this area as it shoals quickly.

A straight, dredged channel extends from Haulover Canal's western mouth across the flats of the upper Indian River. This channel tends to shoal along both sides, although depths are usually well maintained in the center and in the 10-foot MLW range (remembering water levels fluctuate under certain conditions here). Navigate cautiously and avoid being pushed out of the channel by beam winds.

After the turn south at green daybeacon "11" the channel begins to widen and the riverbed deepens. To avoid shoaling just outside the channel stay within the markers until reaching the **NASA (Jay-Jay) Railroad Bridge** (7-foot closed vertical clearance) at Mile 876.6. The bridge is normally left in the open position unless a train is approaching, which is infrequent. The bridge will close as a train approaches. The bridge control lights will flash red and an automatic check will make sure that the span is clear before this happens. After passage the bridge will open either when empty for five minutes or on operator command. Once opened the control lights will return to flashing green.

South of the NASA (Jay-Jay) Railroad Bridge the navigable channel in the Indian River widens significantly. Continue to observe channel markers in this area as many indicate shoal positions. Just south of Titusville's municipal marina, the high-rise **A. Max Brewer (SR 406) Bridge** crosses the ICW at Mile 878.9.

Stay well inside the marked channel from the A. Max Brewer Bridge to the **NASA Causeway (SR 405) Bridge**. There is shoaling to depths as shallow as 7.5 feet MLW at the edge of the channel, especially from green daybeacon "33" to south of red daybeacon "34" where the channel narrows. If you leave the marked channel proceed carefully and monitor your depth sounder.

Dockage/Moorings: The protected harbor at Titusville (north of the A. Max Brewer (SR 406) Bridge) has a well-marked entry channel that normally carries 7-foot MLW depths. Depths increase as soon as you enter the harbor. Two marinas and a mooring field are located in the basin. The first is the well-regarded municipal Titusville Marina, which welcomes transients on both fixed and floating docks and can accommodate boats up to 130 feet. Security gates are on the entrance to each dock with a badge lock so no sharing of combinations. They also have a mooring field (normally tranquil but can be bouncy in a north wind) for vessels up to 50 feet. The mooring fee includes the use of the marina facilities along with a pump-out boat that will come out to you.

The second facility in the Titusville basin is Westland Marina with an over 6-acre yard and all types of services and repairs. This facility is also popular with DIY boaters. Groceries, a pharmacy and other amenities are a short walking distance from the basin.

Anchorage: Anchoring is restricted north of the A. Max Brewer (SR 406) Bridge due to the proliferation of moorings. Be aware that your swing arc must maintain at least 150 feet from the mooring field.

There is some space to anchor west of Titusville R30 in 8 feet MLW but it can get bouncy here. Note that some spoil areas and shoals shown on the chart seem to be expanding in this area and mind the charted "Cable Area" under the bridge. It is a short dinghy ride from here to the Titusville Marina, where boaters may tie up at the dinghy dock and use showers for a nominal fee.

To Canaveral Barge Canal

About 6 miles below Titusville at Addison Point (Mile 885.0), the new **NASA Causeway (SR 405) Bridge** (66-foot fixed vertical clearance) crosses the channel. There's room to anchor if you have an extended wait here due to construction. (See navigation alert.)

Chapter 4: Space Coast Area

Goin' Ashore
TITUSVILLE, FL

Apollo Monument

ATTRACTIONS

1. American Space Museum & Walk of Fame
Working consoles from Launch Pad 36A and a Model 4 Sequencer from Launch Pad 16 are among the attractions. Open Monday through Saturday from 10:00 a.m. to 5:00 p.m. at 308 Pine St. (321-264-0434.)

2. Pritchard House
Tours available of this restored circa-1891 Queen Anne mansion with period furnishings at 424 S. Washington Ave. (321-607-0203).

3. The Downtown Art Gallery
Five showrooms feature local art and photography of the Indian River Lagoon area (335 S. Washington Ave., 321-268-0122).

4. North Brevard Historical Museum
Features exhibits and artifacts on local history and culture including Native American artifacts and other historical items at 301 S. Washington Ave. (321-269-3658).

SERVICES

5. Parrish Medical Center
951 N. Washington Ave. (321-268-6111)

6. Titusville Welcome Center
419 S. Hopkins Ave. (321-607-6216)

MARINAS

7. Titusville Marina
451 Marina Rd. (321-383-5600)

8. Westland Boatyard & Marina
419 N. Washington Ave. (321-267-1667)

America's Waterway Guide Since 1947 — Chapter 4

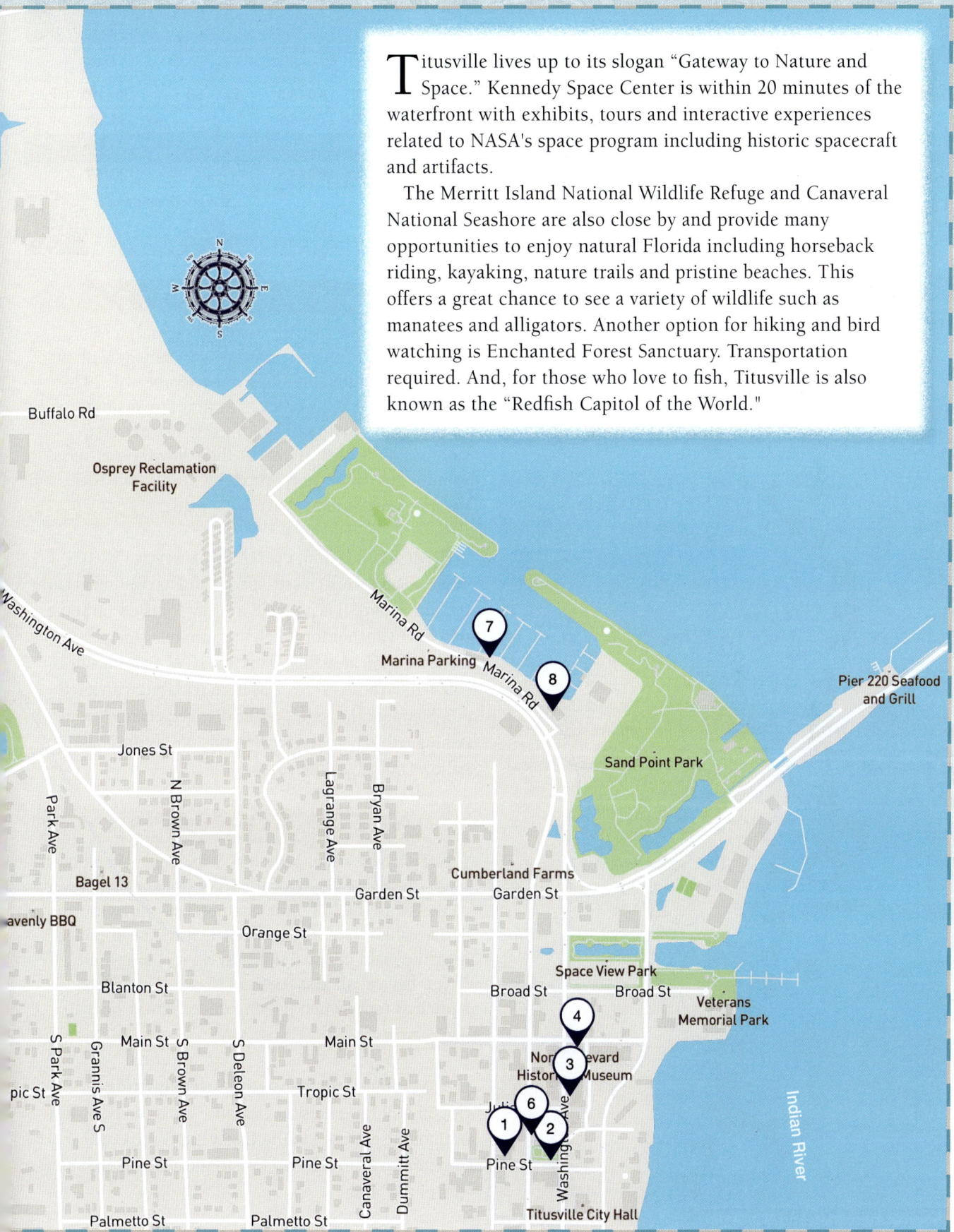

Titusville lives up to its slogan "Gateway to Nature and Space." Kennedy Space Center is within 20 minutes of the waterfront with exhibits, tours and interactive experiences related to NASA's space program including historic spacecraft and artifacts.

The Merritt Island National Wildlife Refuge and Canaveral National Seashore are also close by and provide many opportunities to enjoy natural Florida including horseback riding, kayaking, nature trails and pristine beaches. This offers a great chance to see a variety of wildlife such as manatees and alligators. Another option for hiking and bird watching is Enchanted Forest Sanctuary. Transportation required. And, for those who love to fish, Titusville is also known as the "Redfish Capitol of the World."

Chapter 4: Space Coast Area

Indian River, FL

TITUSVILLE		Largest Vessel	VHF	Total Slips	Approach/ Dockside Depth	Floating Docks	Gas/ Diesel	Repairs/ Haulout	Min/Max Amps	Pump-Out Station
1. Titusville Marina WiFi MM 878.1	(321) 383-5600	130	16	197	8.0 / 8.0	F	GD		30 / 100	P
2. Westland Marina WiFi MM 878.3	(321) 267-1667	55	16	70	7.0 / 8.0			RH	30 / 50	P
INDIAN RIVER CITY										
3. Kennedy Point Yacht Club & Marina WiFi MM 883.0	(321) 383-0280	70	16	80	6.0 / 4.5				30 / 50	P

WiFi Wireless Internet Access

Visit www.waterwayguide.com for current rates, fuel prices, website addresses and other up-to-the-minute information. (Information in the table is provided by the facilities.)

Scan here for more details:

Source: Aqua Map and NOAA data

> **CAUTION:** Note that removal and replacement of the old NASA Causeway Bridge is underway with an anticipated completion date of November 12, 2025. The channel may be blocked at times to facilitate construction. Mariners are urged to use extreme caution in the area, transit at their slowest safe speed to minimize wake, and proceed with caution after passing arrangements have been made.

Heading south from the NASA Causeway (SR 405) Bridge, markers are closely spaced and navigation is fairly straightforward. It is possible to stray "outside" in some stretches to anchor for lunch or for minor repairs but watch for spoil areas that flank the ICW on both sides. Note red daybeacon "52" has been replaced with a red nun. Maintain the center of the dredged channel from flashing red "64" to red daybeacon "66" as the channel shallows quickly at the edges.

> **CAUTION:** At about Mile 888.5 there is a large power plant on the west side of the ICW from which power cables cross the ICW in a northeasterly direction. These cables have an authorized clearance of 85 feet over the main channel but only 45 feet elsewhere. If you have a tall mast be sure that you will have sufficient room when passing under power lines to avoid arcing.

At Mile 894.0 the **Bennett Causeway Bridges** with 65-foot fixed vertical clearance cross the ICW. Just south of the entrance to the Canaveral Barge Canal. There are spoil areas here close to the channel on both sides of the bridge.

Dockage: A few miles south of Titusville off charted "Indian River City" a marked channel branches to the west at green daybeacon "39." This channel, with reported 6-foot MLW depths, leads to the newly refurbished and expanded Kennedy Point Yacht Club & Marina. This facility welcomes transients (yacht club affiliation is not required), has reasonable rates and offers long-term discounts. Some shopping and restaurants are within an easy walk. Call in advance for a reservation and to confirm dockside depths.

Anchorage: Just south of Titusville at about Mile 883 (opposite Indian River City on the mainland) you will see a large charted area of deeper water with depths of 7 to 8 feet MLW to the east of the ICW (another excellent spot to watch launches). The holding is good in from Indian River R38 to R40 but there is little protection from wind or chop. To avoid the charted spoil areas, enter at the mid-point between flashing greens "41" and "43." If you sound your way in far enough (a mile or more from the ICW) wakes from channel traffic are almost entirely eliminated, although boats moving around in the anchorage may cause some rolling.

The NASA Causeway (SR 405) Bridge at Addison Point at Mile 885.0 (and subsequent causeway bridges) provides the best overnight anchorages and wind protection along the Indian River. Holding is fair in mud. Simply choose the side that will be best sheltered from the wind at Addison Point, either north or south of the bridge. This may change with the ongoing construction at the bridge so have a back-up plan. Anytime you leave the channel to seek out protection behind a causeway, proceed slowly and keep an eye on your depth sounder.

Side Trip: Canaveral Barge Canal

The 8-mile journey on the Canaveral Barge Canal leads from the ICW to the Atlantic Ocean at the Port Canaveral Inlet, a well-marked, deep ship inlet. The route includes a 3-mile cut through Merritt Island. The cut is very scenic with beautiful natural flora and an abundance of marine and wildlife. If you have some time this interesting side trip leads right into the Canaveral launch facilities and is worth the effort.

NAVIGATION: Use NOAA Chart 11485 (Banana River) and NOAA Chart 11478 (Cape Canaveral Lock and Inlet).

Just north of the high-rise Bennett Causeway Bridges at ICW Mile 894, look for markers to the east indicating the entrance to the Canaveral Barge Canal, which cuts through Merritt Island to the Banana River.

Persistent northerly winds and low water levels in the Indian River Lagoon at the junction of the ICW and Canaveral Barge Canal have built up a sandbar from the western shore of the spoils island southward across the Canaveral Barge Canal between markers flashing red "12" and green daybeacon "11." Line up for the dredged canal well before entering and don't attempt to cut the corners.

CAUTION: If entering the canal from the south, give green daybeacons "13," "11A" and "11" a wide berth while turning to avoid severe shoaling.

Use caution transiting through here; it sets the minimum controlling depth for the route to the Atlantic. Note there is a slight jog in the course set by red flashing "10" and green daybeacon "9." These can be hard to pick out against the shoreline. The shallowest area observed was about 100 yards west of red flashing "10" at 7 to 8 feet

Chapter 4: Space Coast Area

Canaveral Barge Canal, FL

CANAVERAL BARGE CANAL		Largest Vessel	VHF	Total Slips	Approach/Dockside Depth	Floating Docks	Gas/Diesel	Repairs/Haulout	Min/Max Amps	Pump-Out Station
1. Cape Crossing Marina WiFi	(321) 576-4967	65	9	150	7.5 / 7.0				30 / 50	P
2. Harbortown Marina - Canaveral WiFi E of MM 893.6	(321) 453-0160	60	16	272	6.0 / 6.0		GD	H	30 / 50	P

WiFi Wireless Internet Access
Visit www.waterwayguide.com for current rates, fuel prices, website addresses and other up-to-the-minute information.
(Information in the table is provided by the facilities.)

Scan here for more details:

MLW (center channel with a typical river level). The canal cut itself is deeper at 9 to 13 feet MLW.

> **NOTE:** The spoils island north of the canal and closest to Merritt Island is a rookery for egrets, herons and roseate spoonbills. Please use binoculars and keep your distance from this active nesting site.

The **Christa McAuliffe Drawbridge** with 21.6-foot closed vertical clearance opens on the hour and half hour from 6:00 a.m. to 10:00 p.m. daily but is closed between 6:15 a.m. and 8:15 a.m. and from 3:10 p.m. to 6:00 p.m., Monday through Friday (except federal holidays). The bridge requires a 3-hour advance notice to open between 10:00 p.m. and 5:59 a.m. Call 321-452-5220 (daytime) or 321-213-2694 (after 10:00 p.m.).

Once you have transited Merritt Island via the Barge Canal, maintain the same course through the fairly narrow but well-marked channel across the Banana River carrying about 10-foot MLW depths. It is very shallow outside the channel to red daybeacon "6." Glance behind occasionally to check for lateral displacement by wind or current. The channel leading from red daybeacon "6" to the lock is wider.

A north-south channel intersects this route prior to the Cape Canaveral Lock. To the north green daybeacon "13" and red daybeacon "14" define the entrance to the Saturn Barge Channel (as noted on NOAA Chart 11481). These waters are the backyard of Kennedy Space Center and provide unique views of the spaceport, cruise ship terminals and Canaveral National Seashore.

> **CAUTION:** Vessels fitted with a propeller (even stowed) are not allowed into the Sanctuary.

The Bennett Memorial Causeway (SR A1A) Bridge to the south has a fixed vertical clearance of 36 feet. This is discussed in more detail in the "To Cocoa Beach" section below.

Dockage: The first facility you will encounter headed east in the Canaveral Barge Canal is Cape Crossing Marina, which is under new management and boasts newly renovated seawalls, docks, power pedestals and slip-side pump-outs. Plans include a complete Ship Store, laundry and community area.

Harbortown Marina–Canaveral is located farther east in the Canaveral Barge Canal and is considered a "hurricane hole" by the locals as the lock prevents any major tidal surge and has exceptionally good wind protection. The marina is located in a basin 1 mile west of the Banana River. The marina offers resort-style amenities along with a fenced-in dog play area.

Anchorage: It is possible to anchor south of the Bennett Causeway Bridges. Enter the anchorage on the southwest side and anchor behind the causeway in 7- to 8-foot MLW depths with good holding. The overhead cables make anchoring north of the bridges dangerous.

Cape Canaveral Lock

Continue easterly to the **Cape Canaveral Lock** (321-783-5421). Hours of operation are from 6:00 a.m. to 9:30 p.m. year-round. If locking through the lockmasters request arrival no later than 9:15 p.m. It is the largest lock in Florida and is designed to reduce tidal currents and prevent hurricane storm surge from entering the Banana River. The lift of the lock ranges from negligible to 3 to 4 feet depending on the ocean tide stage and Banana River water level.

Contact the Cape Canaveral lockmaster on VHF Channel 13 for instructions. Provide vessel name and direction of travel. Report that you will stand by until next green light. Set your fenders in place before entering the lock and fix your own lines to your boat fore and aft (lines are not provided in the lock). Line handlers (or anyone on deck) are required to wear a PFD while locking through. Be prepared. The lockmaster will typically remind you if you are not in compliance.

There are synthetic rub rails with cleats spaced every 10 feet making line control simple when locking through. Once in the Cape Canaveral Lock, loop (don't tie) to cleats as you will have to adjust these lines as the lock's water level changes. Passing through a lock is a two-person effort. Each line must be tended by a crew member. There is not much of a raise/drop but lines must be tended during the flood and drain, which is done by cracking open the doors.

Dolphins will occasionally share the lock chamber with you and you may see manatee so be ready to put your engine in neutral as you glide past them. Expect congestion around the two sets of boat ramps near the east exit of the lock.

East of the Cape Canaveral Lock, the **State Route 401 Drawbridge** with 25-foot closed vertical clearance has restricted openings. The bridge opens on signal, except from 6:30 a.m. to 8:00 a.m. and 3:30 p.m. to 5:15 p.m., Monday through Friday (except federal holidays) and from 11:00 a.m. to 2:00 p.m. on Saturdays and Sundays, when the draw need not open for the passage of vessels. From 10:00 p.m. to 6:00 a.m. the draws will open on signal only if at least a 3-hour notice is given.

Side Trip: Kennedy Space Center

You will need a full day to tour the Kennedy Space Center Visitor Complex. "Must sees" include the U.S. Astronaut Hall of Fame, Astronaut Encounter (have lunch with a real astronaut), Shuttle Launch Simulator and Control Center tour.

You will also want to visit the aptly named rocket garden as well as the final resting place of the Space Shuttle Atlantis. Complete your visit by visiting the inspiring tribute to America's fallen astronauts, The Astronaut Memorial. Admission includes a bus tour to the launch sites and two 3-D IMAX movies. For more information, contact the Visitors Center at 866-737-5235. Because the launch site itself is in a secured area, visitors must board buses for the 2-hour tour. The Visitor Complex opens daily at 9:00 a.m. daily except on Christmas Day (closed). For updated launch information, check the schedule at www.kennedyspacecenter.com.

Chapter 4 — Space Coast Area

Canaveral Barge Canal, FL

CAPE CANAVERAL LOCK		Largest Vessel	VHF	Total Slips	Approach/ Dockside Depth	Floating Docks	Gas/ Diesel	Repairs/ Haulout	Min/Max Amps	Pump-Out Station
1. Ocean Club Marina at Port Canaveral WiFi E of MM 893.6	(321) 783-9001	110	16	73	14.0 / 12.0	F	GD		30 / 100	P
2. Port Canaveral Yacht Club-PRIVATE WiFi 6.9 mi. E of MM 893.6	(321) 482-0167	60		50	40.0 / 10.0	F		H	30 / 50	P
3. Cape Marina, Port Canaveral WiFi 7.0 mi. E of MM 893.6	(321) 783-8410	130	16	115	12.0 / 12.0	F	GD	H	30 / 50	P
4. Sunrise Marina WiFi	(321) 783-9535	98	16	21	20.0 / 8.0	F	GD	H	30 / 50	

WiFi Wireless Internet Access
Visit www.waterwayguide.com for current rates, fuel prices, website addresses and other up-to-the-minute information. (Information in the table is provided by the facilities.)

Scan here for more details:

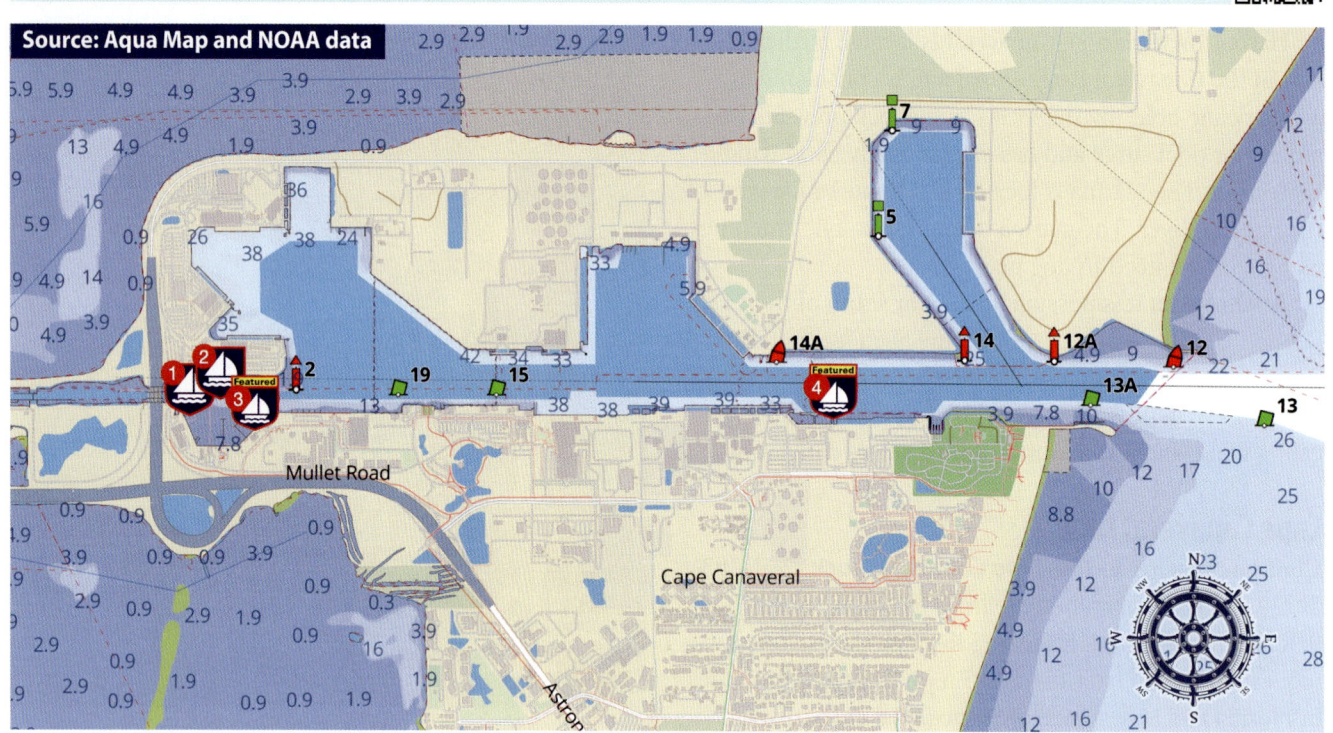

Dockage: On the east side of the Cape Canaveral Lock is a protected basin containing several marinas and boatyards. Ocean Club Marina at Port Canaveral can accommodate vessels ranging from 40 feet to 110 feet in length (including catamaran slips) with full services offered at each slip. The small and welcoming Port Canaveral Yacht Club is in the same basin. The member-owned facility accepts transient boaters as well as reciprocating yacht club vessels and offers a full range of amenities.

The family-owned Cape Marina, Port Canaveral is a full-service marina and boatyard with a DIY area. They have high-speed fuel pumps on a 150-foot dock and a complete Ship Store that carries everything from "bait to batteries." Relax in poolside lounge chairs or enjoy the on-site game room.

Sunrise Marina is closer to the inlet and provides easy ocean access. They cater to sport fisherman and welcome transients (with advance reservations). They also have an on-site waterfront restaurant (Grills Seafood & Tiki Bar, 321-868-2226) and a well-stocked tackle and gift shop.

Anchorage: A short run north in the Saturn Barge Channel offers access to anchorage possibilities near the spoil islands just off the eastern side with 6 to 7 foot MLW depths. If the winds are from the west or northwest this anchorage will be rocky. These islands are outside the "No-Motor Zone," which begins to their north and east.

West of the Canaveral Locks serves as an ideal spot while waiting for eastbound lockage or overnighting when you're headed west to pick up the ICW. The area is well protected from easterly and northern winds but open to south westerlies. Excellent holding in sand/mud in 6 to 8 feet MLW. To avoid shoaling, enter on the north side, parallel to the Canaveral Lock's fender wall.

Port Canaveral Inlet

The well-marked, deep ship Port Canaveral Inlet is protected from the north by the long and shallow Southeast Shoal off Cape Canaveral. The lock inside the inlet eliminates current, making this one of the easier to use inlets on the Florida coast.

NAVIGATION: Southbound cruisers can make for N 28° 23.490'/W 80° 33.000' after rounding red buoy "4," while northbound craft could go in much closer, at N 28° 24.570'/W 80° 34.480'. The channel is well marked; simply run down the channel, turning due west at Middle Reach.

Coming from the north, the Southeast Shoal off Cape Canaveral keeps boaters several miles offshore. Stay east of W 80° 27.000' before turning in to the sea buoy after rounding red buoy "4" at N 28° 23.470'/W 80° 29.100' marking the southern edge of the shoal. Note that this cuts off the offshore waypoint. From the south, cruisers can approach from within 0.5 nm of the shore in depths greater than 20 feet MLW.

Side Trip: To Cocoa Beach

Cocoa Beach is often associated with the Kennedy Space Center, thanks to the 1960s sitcom "I Dream of Jeannie," and it is still a great place to watch the rockets take off. It is also a quintessential beach town, known for its 6 miles of excellent beaches and home to the world's largest surf shop. Ron Jon Surf Shop's flagship facility is 52,000 square feet and is filled floor to ceiling with a wide selection of surf, skate, swim and beach essentials. They are one of the several surf shops here that offer lessons, if you are interested. Shopping, museums and historic sites and great restaurants round out the offerings.

NAVIGATION: Use NOAA Charts 11481 and 11476. While this route has reasonable depths at its north end, it shallows quickly. This is not a dredged channel and there are some challenges on this route. The air-draft restriction is 36 feet. Local knowledge is recommended.

If heading south on the Banana River is your intention approach flashing green "5" at the junction of the barge canals and then turn south for the center of the high span of the **Bennett Memorial Causeway (SR A1A) Bridge** with a fixed vertical clearance of 36 feet.

The first marker on the Banana River route south is red daybeacon "28," which is a straight shot 2.5 miles south of the Bennett Memorial Causeway Bridge and just north of

CAPE MARINA
321-783-8410

Marina/Boatyard
Do-It Yourself Yard
Long Term Inactive Storage

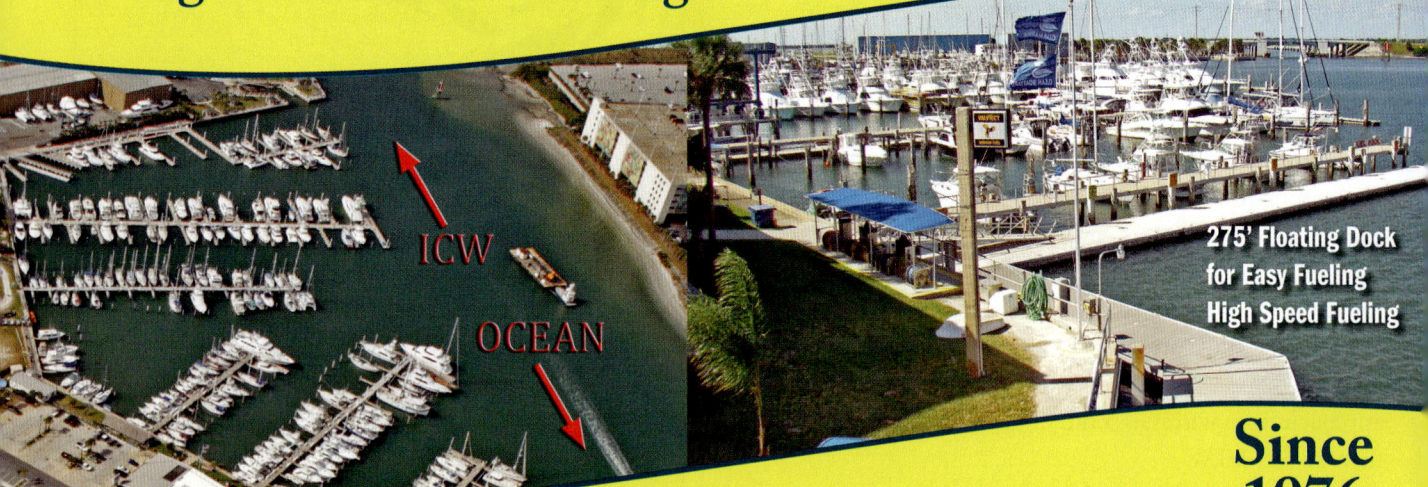

275' Floating Dock for Easy Fueling
High Speed Fueling

Since 1976

45 min to Orlando Int Airport, Disney, Sea World

Visit Kennedy Space Center & Cocoa Beach.

- Dockage (12'MLW)
- 110/208V Electric
- Haulouts to 75 Tons
- List of Authorized Vendors available for Hull, Engine & I/O Repairs
- Marine Hardware & Supplies
- Captain Lounge/Game Room/Exercise Room
- Heated Swimming Pool
- Pavilion with BBQ Grills
- Clean Bathroom/Showers
- Laundry Facilities
- Food & Beverages
- Bait, Tackle & Ice
- Beautiful Boutique, Fine & Fashion Jewelry, Nautical Gifts
- Pumpout-out Station
- ATM On-Site
- Wireless Internet

Easy Access from either ocean or ICW. Avoid Delays Due to ICW Bridge Schedules and No Wake Zones. Use Port Canaveral And "Go Outside".

Fax (321) 783-7839
www.capemarina.com

Visit us on Facebook.com/capemarina
800 Scallop Drive • Port Canaveral, Fl 32920

Open 7 days - Open Holidays except Thanksgiving, Christmas & New Years
Seasonal Hours - Please call, open later during Spring & Summer

VALVTECT MARINE FUEL
Gasoline & Diesel - 89 Octane
Ethanol Free - High-Speed Fueling
Cam-Lock System To Fit All Boats

Banana River, FL

BANANA RIVER		Largest Vessel	VHF	Total Slips	Approach/Dockside Depth	Floating Docks	Gas/Diesel	Repairs/Haulout	Min/Max Amps	Pump-Out Station
1. Island Time Marina WiFi	(321) 613-4852	42		30	6.0 / 6.0				30	P
2. Marker 24 Marina WiFi 24	(321) 453-7888	60	16	63	5.5 / 5.5		GD	RH	30 / 50	P

WiFi Wireless Internet Access
Visit www.waterwayguide.com for current rates, fuel prices, website addresses and other up-to-the-minute information.
(Information in the table is provided by the facilities.)

Scan here for more details:

Source: Aqua Map and NOAA data

the **Willard Peebles Bridge** (with fixed 36-foot vertical clearance). Expect depths as low as 5 to 6 feet MLW for this stretch to the bridge and depths to shallow further to the south of the bridge. Proceed with caution keeping an eye on your sounder and chartplotter.

NOTE: When proceeding southbound on the Banana River, keep red to port.

The channel begins some 18 miles south at green daybeacon "1" off Dragon Point (ICW Mile 914.5) where the Banana River drains into the Indian River near Melbourne. This is covered in "Side Trip: North on the Banana River" in the next section.

Dockage: Island Time Marina is on the east bank just south of the Willard Peebles Bridge and may have space for you. They have a happy hour and feature live music. It is a 15-minute walk to Cocoa Beach amenities. Across the river is the well-kept Marker 24 Marina with transient slips to 50 feet. They also have a full-service boatyard and riverfront grill. The entry to the marina is well marked and has 5.5-foot approach depths.

Anchorage: While there appears to be a pocket of deep water south of Cocoa Beach on the Banana River, you likely are not able to reach it. As previously stated, this route is reasonable deep at its north end, but shallows quickly and there is no dredged channel. Because of this, we cannot recommend anchoring here.

COCOA VILLAGE TO MELBOURNE

Cocoa Village–ICW Mile 897

Cocoa Village is on the western shore and Merritt Island is on the eastern shore of the Indian River. Both offer

Chapter 4 — Space Coast Area

Indian River, FL

COCOA VILLAGE		Largest Vessel	VHF	Total Slips	Approach/Dockside Depth	Floating Docks	Gas/Diesel	Repairs/Haulout	Min/Max Amps	Pump-Out Station
1. Cocoa Village Marina WiFi MM 897.3	(321) 632-5445	300	16	117	6.0 / 6.0				30 / 100	P

WiFi Wireless Internet Access

Visit www.waterwayguide.com for current rates, fuel prices, website addresses and other up-to-the-minute information. (Information in the table is provided by the facilities.)

Scan here for more details:

Source: Aqua Map and NOAA data

numerous cruiser amenities. Lee Wenner Park at Cocoa Village is a 12-acre community riverfront park featuring a pavilion, picnic tables, restrooms, playground and benches along a paved walkway. A boardwalk adjacent to the boat docks extends to Cocoa Riverfront Park and Historic Cocoa Village where you will find many restaurants and shopping opportunities.

NAVIGATION: Use NOAA Chart 11485. The high-rise Hubert Humphrey (FL 520) Bridge (which is also known as Merritt Island or Cocoa Bridges) crosses the ICW at Mile 897.4 at Cocoa. There is essentially zero lunar tide range in Cocoa since the ocean inlets are far distant. However, strong currents and some variation in level are possible as the river responds to wind load and other factors. Check tide boards for clearance if you are close to the limit.

CAUTION: While the high voltage overhead cables that cross the Indian River just south of the Hubert Humphrey Bridge are charted at 88 feet, they progressively descend towards shore and vertical clearance is substantially reduced (charted at 38 feet at landfall). This poses a serious risk for vessels operating or anchoring near the cables, not just from physical contact but open-air arcing from the power lines to a mast. We recommend a minimum mast-to-wire distance of 12 feet.

Dockage: The ever-popular Cocoa Village Marina is a fully modern, clean facility with an exceptionally friendly and helpful staff. This is a good place to stay or leave your boat. The well-marked approach channel is about a 0.25 mile north of the twin bridges. Enter north of the marina's wave attenuation fence. This marina is convenient to the attractions, shops and restaurants of Historic Cocoa Village.

The T-dock, day slips, boat ramp and dinghy landing for Cocoa Village at Lee Wenner Park have reopened after a complete renovation including dredging. Transient traffic is welcome to stay for free for 48 consecutive hours. No water or electricity is available but the park is just one block away from the vibrant downtown.

Anchorage: You can anchor west of the ICW and south of the bridges just off Cocoa Village in Cocoa Yacht Basin. Sound your way in to a suitable depth avoiding the charted cable and pipeline area south of the Hubert Humphrey Bridge and be sure to stay well clear of the low power lines (charted 38 feet). Lee Wenner Park has a dinghy dock.

The anchorage extends for 0.50 mile downriver on the western shore, along which you should find 6 to 9 feet MLW. Expect lots of crab pots. A particularly popular spot is west of the ICW at flashing green "77." Drop the hook in the lee of Rockledge in west wind.

The Merritt Island (east) side of the river offers the closest major provisioning. To anchor north of the Hubert Humphrey Bridge head easterly off the ICW paralleling the causeway and hold about 7-foot MLW depths all the way to the daybeacons "1" and "2" for the Griffis Park anchorage. Griffis Landing at Blue Crab Cove county park has six finger docks for small boats, a ramp and a pump-out station; however, the approach/dockside depth is only 2 to 3 feet MLW precluding use by most cruisers. This is a 10-minute walk to businesses along SR 520.

Should you choose to visit Cocoa Village on the mainland from here, you can walk across the bridge. Note that walkways are narrow and exposed; exercise caution. The south bridge walkway is wider. It is easier/safer to access Cocoa Village via dinghy.

Cocoa Village to Eau Gallie– ICW Mile 898 to Mile 914

NAVIGATION: Use NOAA Charts 11485 and 11472. The stretch from Cocoa to Palm Shores presents few problems but watch for the ever-present pot markers that sometimes stray into the channel. Most spoil areas are well outside the marked channel and to the east. The only craft that may have problems are sailboats attempting to tack back and forth across the river.

At Mile 909 the high-rise **Pineda Causeway Bridge** crosses the ICW. As with other bridges built on causeways, be aware of increased currents under the bridge. Although the charted fixed vertical clearance is 65 feet, clearances may be closer to 64 feet.

Dockage: The very popular Grills Riverside located at Mile 908.5 is a fun stop. Call ahead to check slip availability. Good Natured River Tours is based here offering relaxing wildlife and sight-seeing tours on the Indian River.

Anchorage: There are several good anchorages on the Indian River including Boy Scout Island. To reach the island, proceed east from just south of green daybeacon "83" then head toward the prominent house with a red roof until 200 to 300 feet from shore. Next, turn north and proceed to the anchorage east of the island, avoiding the shoal that extends south of the island to green daybeacon "83." Good protection from all except south winds. This is much less crowded than the anchorage off to the northwest. Land your dingy on the small beach on the north side of the island but be aware of a shoal extending to the northeast from the island for several hundred feet.

At Mile 904.5 on the east shore is The Point-Honeymoon Lake with good holding and plenty of room to swing. You can get far enough off of the ICW that wakes are not a problem.

> **NOTE:** Don't be alarmed if you hear the cry of peacocks on shore. (It can sound like someone yelling "help.")

At Palm Shores, anchor in protection of causeway either north or south of Pineda Causeway Bridge, depending on wind direction. Sound your way in to dinghy ashore on the east side of the bridge.

Eau Gallie–ICW Mile 914

On the mainland side of the ICW two once distinct towns, Eau Gallie and Melbourne, have merged under the name of Melbourne to form a "metropolis." Each town has its own harbor and facilities. To the east the Banana River meets the Indian River at Rocky Dragon Point where there are additional facilities. (Described below.) Many skippers leave their boats in this area for extended periods, catch a plane from Orlando Melbourne International Airport and then return later.

NAVIGATION: Use NOAA Chart 11472. Although the NOAA chart doesn't mention it by name, Eau

| Chapter 4 | Space Coast Area |

GOIN' ASHORE
COCOA VILLAGE, FL

ATTRACTIONS

1. Cocoa Village Farmers Market
Held every Wednesday from 9:00 a.m. to 4:00 p.m. in Myrt Tharpe Gazebo Square (Brevard Ave. and Stone St.).

2. Cocoa Village Playhouse
Historic theater in operation since 1924 that features a variety of performances and events throughout the year at 300 Brevard Ave. (321-636-5050).

3. Library of Florida History
Housed at the The Florida Historical Society (425 Brevard Ave., 321-690-1971).

4. S.F. Travis & Co. Hardware
Multi-building, old-style hardware store (circa 1885) with extensive inventory. Open weekdays only (300 Delannoy Ave., 321-636-1441).

SERVICES

5. Cocoa Post Office
600 Florida Ave. (321-632-6846)

6. Historic Cocoa Village Association
600 Florida Ave., Ste. 104 (321-631-9075)

7. Omni Healthcare
505 Delannoy Ave. (321-633-0988)

8. Village Cycle Shoppe
Bicycle services, rentals and new/used sales at 4 Harrison St. (321-806-3917).

MARINAS

9. Cocoa Village Marina
90 Delannoy Ave. (321-632-5445)

America's Waterway Guide Since 1947 — Chapter 4

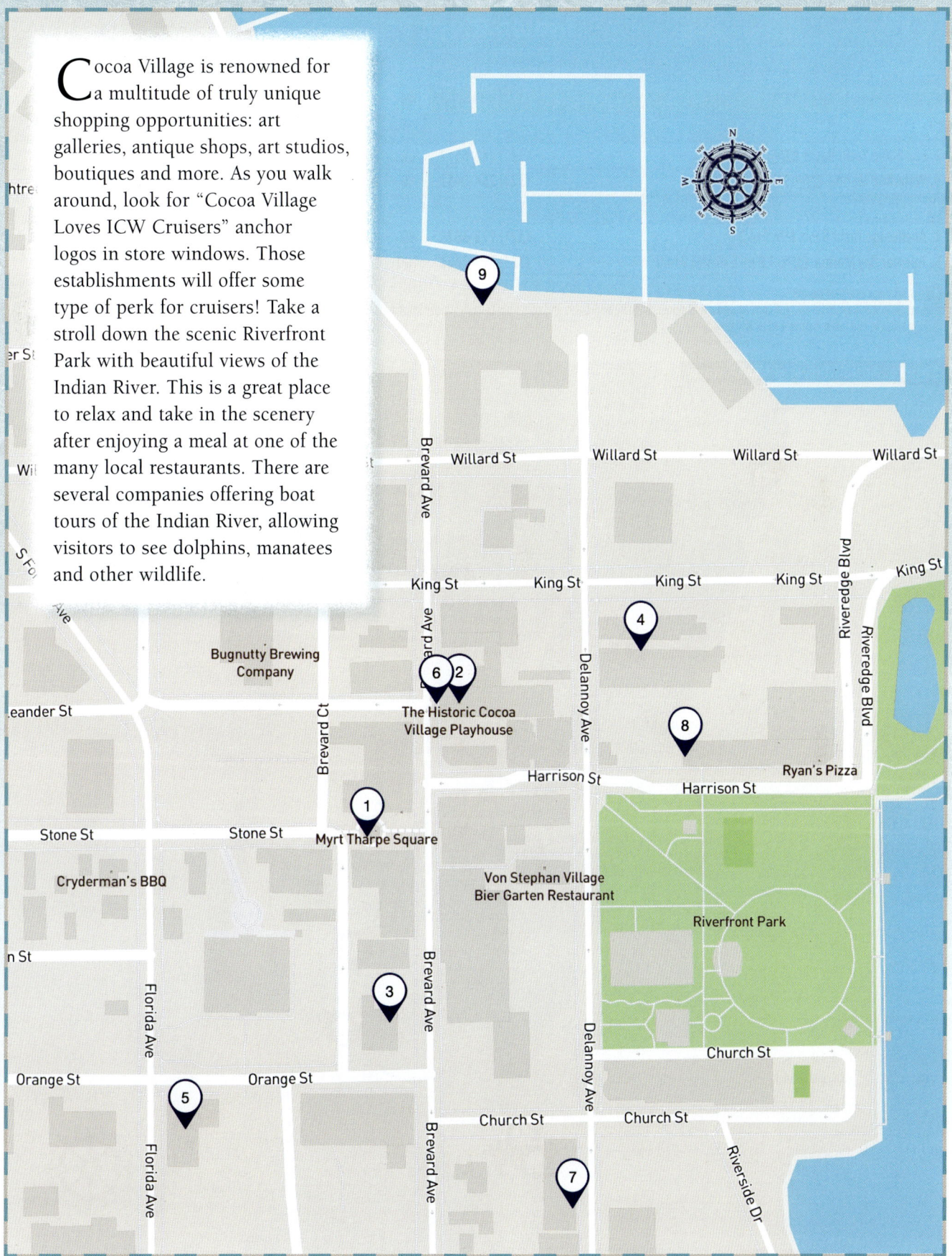

Cocoa Village is renowned for a multitude of truly unique shopping opportunities: art galleries, antique shops, art studios, boutiques and more. As you walk around, look for "Cocoa Village Loves ICW Cruisers" anchor logos in store windows. Those establishments will offer some type of perk for cruisers! Take a stroll down the scenic Riverfront Park with beautiful views of the Indian River. This is a great place to relax and take in the scenery after enjoying a meal at one of the many local restaurants. There are several companies offering boat tours of the Indian River, allowing visitors to see dolphins, manatees and other wildlife.

SOUTHERN EDITION

Chapter 4: Space Coast Area

Indian River, FL

		Largest Vessel	VHF	Total Slips	Approach/Dockside Depth	Floating Docks	Gas/Diesel	Repairs/Haulout	Min/Max Amps	Pump-Out Station
PALM SHORES										
1. Grills Riverside MM 908.5	(321) 242-8999	45		12	5.0 / 5.0		G		30	P
EAU GALLIE										
2. Eau Gallie Yacht Basin WiFi MM 914.7	(321) 242-6577	60	16	60	8.0 / 7.0				30 / 50	P
3. Waterline Marina WiFi 914.7	(321) 254-0452	80	16	92	8.0 / 8.0			R	30 / 50	P
INDIAN HARBOR										
4. Anchorage Yacht Basin MM 914.2	(321) 773-3620	60		80	6.0 / 10.0		GD	RH	30 / 50	
5. Telemar Bay Marina WiFi 1.8 mi E of MM 914.0	(321) 773-2468	100	16	205	9.0 / 7.0		GD		30 / 50	P

WiFi Wireless Internet Access
Visit www.waterwayguide.com for current rates, fuel prices, website addresses and other up-to-the-minute information.
(Information in the table is provided by the facilities.)

Scan here for more details:

208 WATERWAY GUIDE 2024 www.waterwayguide.com

Gallie at Mile 914 is on the west side of the Indian River. Just south of the high-rise **Eau Gallie Causeway (SR 518) Bridge** at Mile 914.4 the numbering sequence for ICW markers resets at Mile 915 with flashing red "2." (There is no green "1.") Avoid confusion at this point with the closely spaced markers for the channel to Eau Gallie's protected harbor to the west with a marker sequence in the same range. Just off the ICW are green daybeacons "1," "3" and "5" and then flashing red "6" closer to shore.

The controlling depth for Eau Gallie's entrance channel is reported as 6 feet MLW but deeper draft vessels use it. Beware of shoaling extending to the southeast of flashing red "6." Stay mid-channel or favor the green for the best water. Entering the narrows the channel bends to the northwest and continues into the harbor on the Eau Gallie River. Favor the seawalled north shoreline through this narrow passage and be alert to increased traffic from a launch ramp at Ballard Park to the south.

Dockage: Eau Gallie's harbor has good protection and an easy-to-enter, well-maintained entrance. Friendly and accommodating Eau Gallie Yacht Basin has 60 slips to 60 feet including transients slips and operates a DIY yard. Karen's Canvas is on site for all your marine canvas needs. Waterline Marina, part of a condominium development at the head of the harbor, has transient slips (including catamaran slips) with all the usual amenities and offers some repairs. It's a short walk from either of these facilities to the quaint streets of Eau Gallie's restored historic downtown.

Anchorage: Boats can anchor on either side of Eau Gallie Causeway (SR 518) Bridge depending on wind direction. (Avoid the charted cable areas and shoals.) Both north and south of Eau Gallie Bridge offers at least 9 feet MLW but both are exposed to wakes.

In Eau Gallie Basin you can drop the hook north of the channel past the park or beyond Waterline Marina and dinghy to the park docks (located both north and south of the channel) or use the marina dinghy dock (for a small daily fee).

Side Trip: North on the Banana River

The Banana River continues north up to Cape Canaveral and intersects the Canaveral Barge Canal near the Cape Canaveral Lock in about 18 miles. While this route has reasonable depths at its south end, it shallows quickly. This is not a dredged channel and there are some challenges on this route. The air-draft restriction is 36 feet. Local knowledge is desirable.

NAVIGATION: Use NOAA Chart 11472 (also NOAA 11476 and 11481). North of the Eau Gallie Causeway (SR 518) Bridge and across the Indian River to the east, the narrow mouth of the Banana River turns to the northeast around Dragon Point. To enter keep at least 100 feet south of green daybeacon "1" marking rocky shoals off Dragon Point. Continue to maintain 100 feet off of this daybeacon as you turn northward.

CAUTION: Stay in the channel to avoid Dragon Point's rocky rim. Reports are that the charted shoal extending up from the bridge causeway to the south ends well clear of green daybeacon "1." This is a sandy shoal and it would be better to ground there than on Dragon Point's rocks. If you do hit the rocks, edge off backwards; do not try to go over them!

One-half mile north of Dragon Point, **Mathers (SR A1A) Swing Bridge** has 7-foot vertical clearance and opens on signal except from 10:00 p.m. to 6:00 a.m., Sunday through Thursday (except federal holidays) when the draw opens on signal if at least a 2-hour notice is given. The bridge opens on demand 24 hours Friday, Saturday, and all federal holidays. Call ahead (321-265-5115) to verify schedule.

Four miles north of Dragon Point is the Banana River span of the fixed **Pineda Causeway (East) Bridge** with a fixed vertical clearance of 36 feet. (Note that the span of the same bridge has a vertical clearance of 65 feet where it crosses the Indian River.)

The route north from here can be tricky due to widely spaced markers and skinny water. The controlling depth is 5 to 6 feet MLW but it is typically deeper. Follow the channel up to red daybeacon "8A" and green daybeacon "9" and proceed west being careful to avoid the charted "Subm Piles" as shown. This cut-across provides about 7-foot MLW depths into the adjacent deeper water. (This deeper water is the result of dredging for fill to extend the landmass for the runways of adjacent Patrick Air Force Base.)

Once into the deep water and around the submerged pilings head north for 4.25 miles to pick up the marked channel at green daybeacon "11" and red daybeacon "12." (Note that there is no daybeacon "10.")

Willard Peebles Bridge is about 8 miles beyond that and Bennett Memorial Causeway (SR A1A) Bridge is

| Chapter 4 | Space Coast Area |

Goin' Ashore

EAU GALLIE, FL

Eau Gallie began as a small coastal town along the Indian River Lagoon in 1860 and quickly became a busy thoroughfare as steamers, riverboats and freighters transported residents, cargo and tourists. Now merged into the City of Melbourne, Eau Gallie retains a quaint, historical district that strives to retain its cultural heritage and distinct early Floridian flavor. Many historic buildings remain in and around the downtown area, some dating back to the early 1900s. The scenic river offers beautiful views of the natural landscape and is a great place to spot wildlife. Should you need them, Boasthouse Discount Marine has a large selection of boat parts and accessories at 557 N. Harbor City Blvd. (321-254-2535).

ATTRACTIONS

1. **Eau Gallie Arts District**
   Vibrant community located in the historic district that boasts a rich history, an eclectic mix of art galleries, restaurants and shops at Eau Gallie Square (1492 Highland Ave., 321-622-4223).

2. **Eau Gallie Farmers Market**
   Offers assortment of organic food, vegetables, crafts, fruits and local specialties at Eau Gallie Square Park (corner of Eau Gallie Blvd. and Highland Ave.). Open year round on Saturdays from 8:00 a.m. to 1:00 p.m.

3. **Intracoastal Brewing Company**
   This neighborhood taproom features a rotating menu of original brews. "Namaste for one more" yoga and beer Sundays at 11:30 a.m. (for a fee) at 652 W. Eau Gallie Blvd. (321-872-7395).

4. **Rossetter House Museum and Gardens**
   Restored home and garden offering a glimpse into the history of Eau Gallie and the Rossetter family (1320 Highland Ave., 321-254-9855).

SERVICES

5. **Gallie Medical Center**
   1403 Highland Ave. (321-751-1414)

6. **Eau Gallie Post Office**
   681 St. Clair St. (321-259-5574)

7. **Eau Gallie Public Library**
   1521 Pineapple Ave. (321-255-4304)

8. **Florida Aid to Animals (Vet)**
   741 Creel St. (321-242-9826)

MARINAS

9. **Eau Gallie Yacht Basin**
   587 Young St. (321-242-6577)

10. **Waterline Marina**
    911 N. Harbor City Blvd. (321 254-0452)

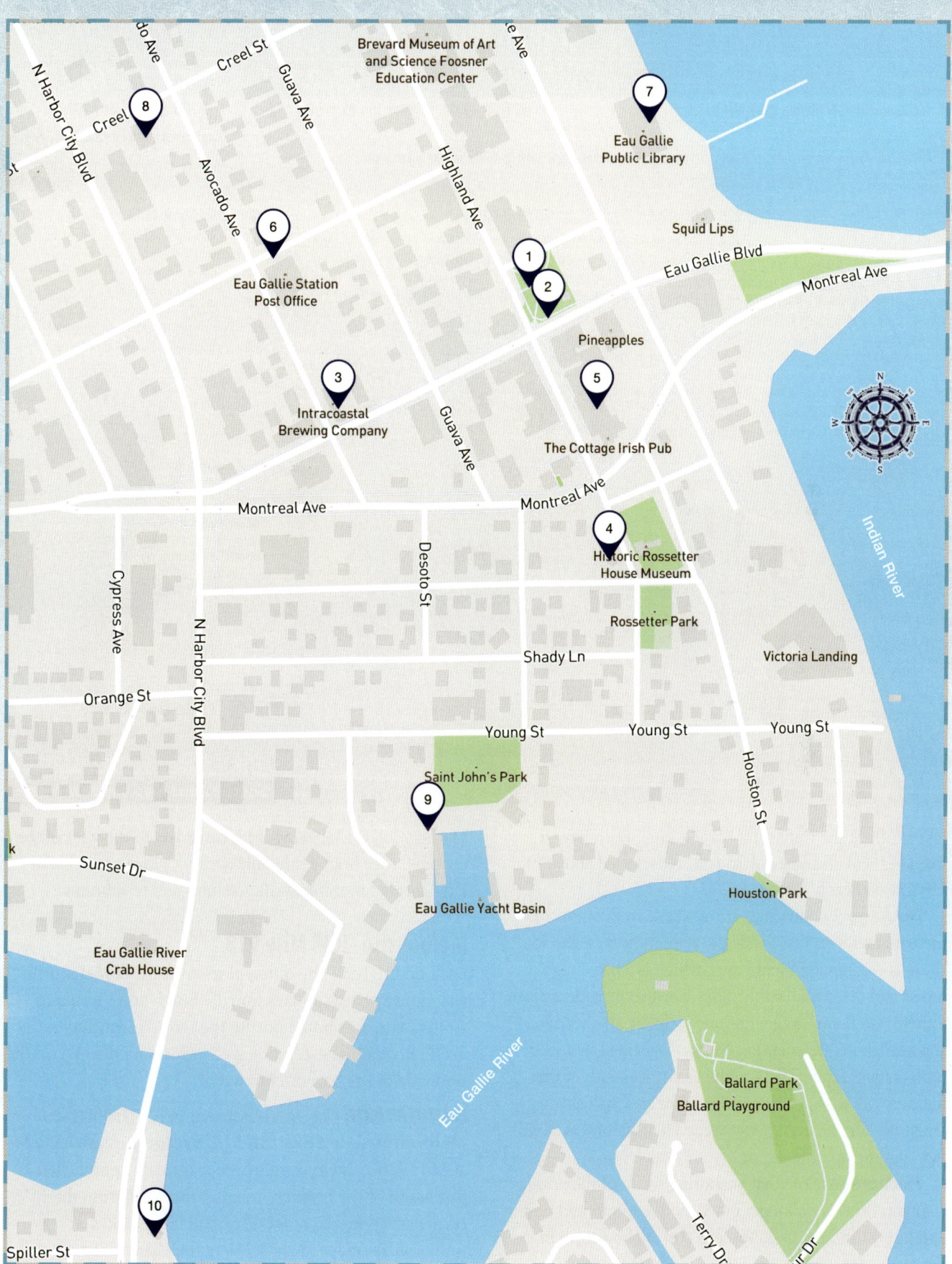

Chapter 4

SOUTHERN EDITION 211

Chapter 4: Space Coast Area

Indian River, FL

MELBOURNE		Largest Vessel	VHF	Total Slips	Approach/Dockside Depth	Floating Docks	Gas/Diesel	Repairs/Haulout	Min/Max Amps	Pump-Out Station
1. Melbourne Harbor Marina WiFi MM 918.5	(321) 725-9054	130	16	85	8.0 / 8.0		GD	R	30 / 100	

WiFi Wireless Internet Access

Visit www.waterwayguide.com for current rates, fuel prices, website addresses and other up-to-the-minute information. (Information in the table is provided by the facilities.)

Scan here for more details:

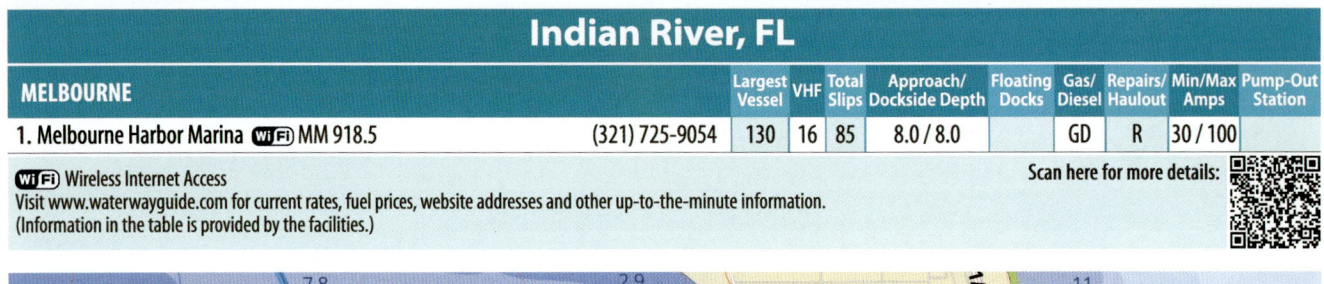

Source: Aqua Map and NOAA data

just south of the Canaveral Barge Canal. Both have a fixed vertical clearance of 36 feet. (Discussed above in "To Cocoa Beach.")

Dockage: Two marinas are available in the mouth of the Banana River. Just inside the river mouth on the south shore is Anchorage Yacht Basin, which is a brokerage, repair and dry stack facility. They can also provide a diver to help you if you snag while anchoring. Call ahead for slip availability. Telemar Bay Marina is located in a well-protected and quiet basin to the east (just south of the Mathers (SR A1A) Swing Bridge.) The marina has great amenities and an even better view. Their helpful staff will help you tie up or haul out.

Anchorage: Note that anchoring south of the bridge (Dragon Run) is no longer practical due to moored vessels and lack of shore access. You can still anchor north of

Mathers (SR A1A) Swing Bridge in 8 feet to the west of the channel. (See bridge schedule above.) Dinghy to Telemar Bay Marina for a short walk to shops and restaurants.

Melbourne–ICW Mile 918

Back on the ICW, the quiet, pleasant town of Melbourne sits midway between Jacksonville Beach and Florida's Gold Coast. It is home port to the Florida Institute of Technology's big research vessels, which are docked on the port side of the harbor entrance.

NAVIGATION: Use NOAA Chart 11472. The high-rise **Melbourne Causeway (SR 516) Bridge** crosses the ICW at Mile 918.2. Melbourne's harbor is easily approached just south of the bridges. To enter the basin from the ICW turn west at red daybeacon "6" and follow the markers until you are close to shore. Here the channel turns sharply to starboard and leads to the enclosed basin.

The harbor and channel are dredged to a controlling depth of 8 feet MLW, although the depth is reported to be closer to 6 or 7 feet MLW between red daybeacon "6" and flashing green "7." Local knowledge advises favoring the red side. The fixed 14-foot vertical clearance railroad bridge that follows the 65-foot vertical clearance highway bridge plus low water depths makes the northern reaches of Crane Creek inaccessible to most vessels.

Dockage: The well-regarded Melbourne Harbor Marina is to starboard at the head of the basin. The marina welcomes transients to 130 feet with full amenities. It has two restaurants on site–the fun Ichabods Bar & Grille-Dockside and the more upscale Chart House. It is a short walk to the quaint restored historical area with additional restaurants, shopping and art galleries.

To the south at Mile 921.2 is Palm Bay Marina located in a basin between two fixed bridges (15-foot and 10-foot vertical clearance, respectively) on Turkey Creek. This is a brokerage that may be able to fit you in and offers some repairs. Call ahead for approach directions and depths (reported as 3 feet).

Anchorage: Boats anchor on east of the channel both sides of the high-rise Melbourne Causeway Bridge. Pick a spot that offers the best wind protection but avoid the charted cable area. You can tie your dinghy up at a park to the east on the south side of the causeway and walk one-half mile to a beach. You will find restaurants but no groceries here.

■ TO VERO BEACH

Sebastian Area–Mile 937

The Sebastian area includes the town of Micco, north of the St. Sebastian River, and the City of Sebastian to the south as well as the Sebastian Inlet. The scenery becomes a bit more natural from here to Vero Beach making this stretch of the ICW very pleasant for cruisers.

There are also a few interesting stops along the way, which justify a slower passage. Ocean beaches are accessible by dinghy at the inlet near the state park and the Environmental Learning Center in Wabasso is worth a gander.

NAVIGATION: Use NOAA Chart 11472. While the Indian River appears to widen over this stretch, the ICW is confined to a narrow, dredged channel with shoaling just at the edges. Mariners must take precautions to stay inside the marked ICW channel, even in the open lagoons, where there is a string of shoals (many just below the surface) and spoil islands outside the channel to the west. Exercise particular care south of red daybeacon "8" where depths of 7 feet MLW have been observed. Boats with deeper draft may want to pass east of the marked channel to find deeper water.

Shoals border the western edge of the channel off Cape Malabar (western shore between green daybeacon "15" and red daybeacon "16"). The channel also shallows quickly off both sides through the small cut near red daybeacon "18." The spoils island between red daybeacons "18" and "20" (Mile 925) is now very small but has a long sandy spit extending to the west.

Just past ICW Mile 925 the channel slants a bit toward the west and narrows considerably. You will enter a dredged channel at red daybeacon "20" with less than 6 feet MLW on both sides and on the spoils islands that are close in so take care to maintain channel alignment. Note that the spoils islands in this area are spreading, mostly on their north and west sides.

With frequent bends the ICW channel passes west of Grant Farm Island at green daybeacon "39" (Mile 930), the only inhabited spoils island in the Indian River and accessible only by boat. The lower part of Grant Farm Island is a rookery used mainly by ibis and egrets.

From here on proceed cautiously and be careful not to stray outside the channel where the MLW may only be a few feet deep. You may have to strain to make out the markers, which seem to blend into the shoreline. Also be alert for uncharted oyster beds and pot markers on both sides of the ICW.

Sebastian Inlet is accessed from a marked channel that proceeds eastward from flashing green "63." This a local knowledge, fair-weather inlet used largely by smaller recreational fishing boats. The inlet is crossed by the fixed **A1A Bridge** (37-foot vertical clearance). Constant shoaling necessitates careful piloting and up-to-date local knowledge. Swift crosscurrents and the resulting shifting channel make navigation difficult in Sebastian Inlet, even with up-to-date local information.

Dockage: Several marinas welcome cruising boats in the small community of Micco, north of Sebastian. At Mile 934 is the well-regarded Sebastian River Marina &

Chapter 4 — Space Coast Area

Goin' Ashore
MELBOURNE, FL

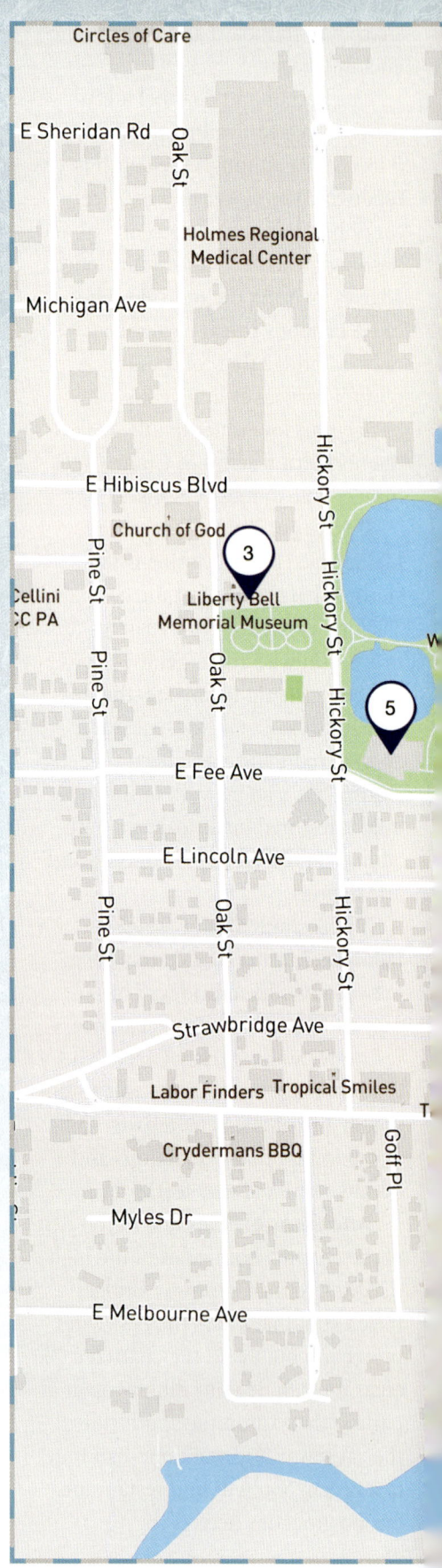

ATTRACTIONS

1. **Crane Creek Promenade**
Famous viewing point for observing manatees as well as site of interpretative mammal exhibits. Located at 990 E. Melbourne Ave.

2. **Green Gables**
Circa 1896 home showcases beautiful Queen Anne-style architecture located along the scenic Indian River at 1501 S. Harbor City Blvd. One of first houses in Melbourne to have electricity. Original site consisted of 150 acres that extended all the way to Wells Park and the Fee Avenue Library.

3. **Liberty Bell Memorial Museum**
Museum featuring a full-size replica of the Liberty Bell, plus American and military history exhibits at 1601 Oak St. (321-373-2311).

4. **Strawbridge Art League Gallery**
Interesting selection of artwork, each with a uniquely Floridian flavor at 819 E. Strawbridge Ave. (321-952-3070).

SERVICES

5. **Brevard County Public Library**
540 E. Fee Ave. (321-952-4514)

6. **Melbourne Post Office**
640 E New Haven Ave. (321-723-6164)

7. **Melbourne Chamber of Commerce**
1005 E. Strawbridge Ave. #4740 (321-724-5400)

MARINA

8. **Melbourne Harbor Marina**
2210 S. Front St. (321-725-9054)

America's Waterway Guide Since 1947 — Chapter 4

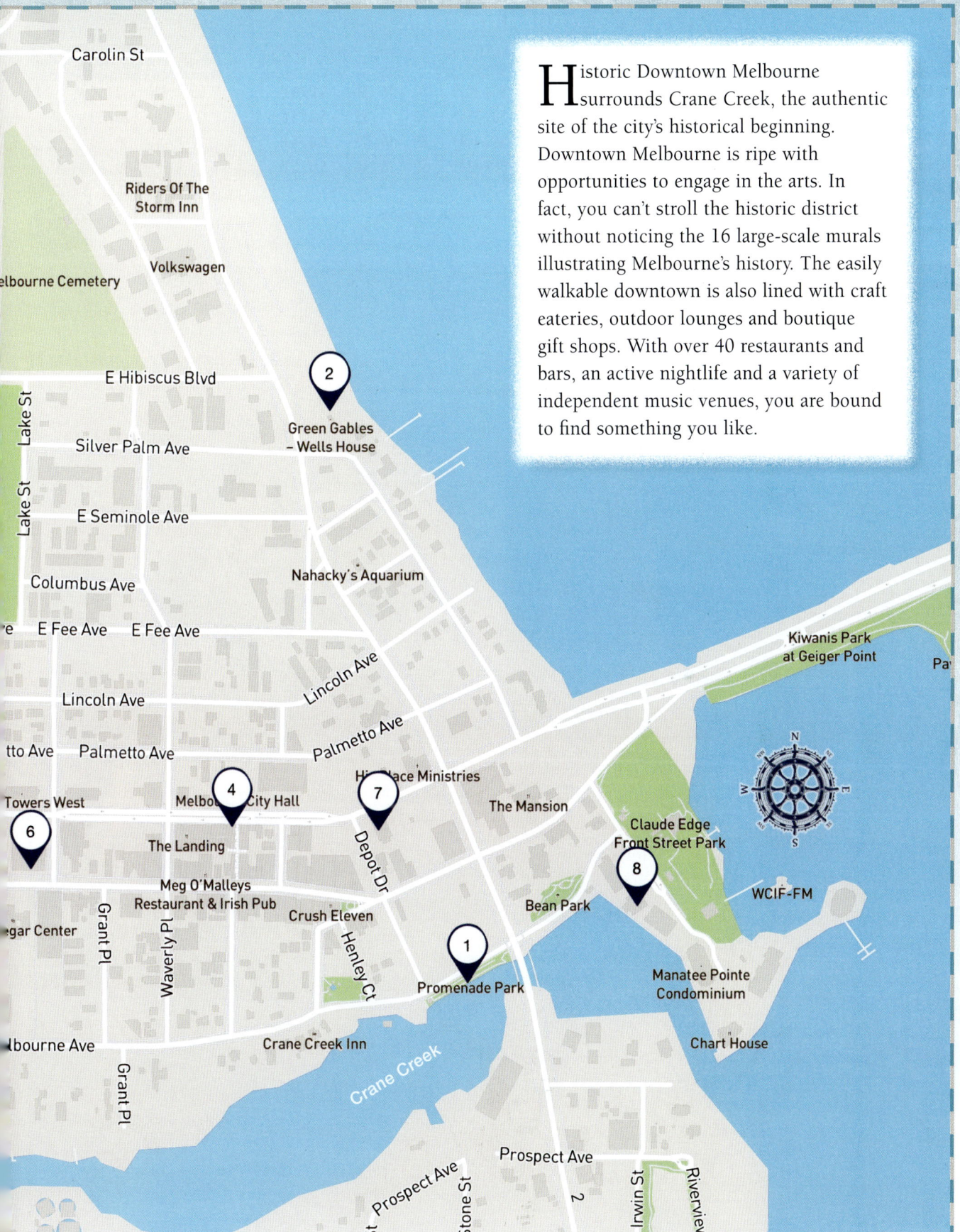

Historic Downtown Melbourne surrounds Crane Creek, the authentic site of the city's historical beginning. Downtown Melbourne is ripe with opportunities to engage in the arts. In fact, you can't stroll the historic district without noticing the 16 large-scale murals illustrating Melbourne's history. The easily walkable downtown is also lined with craft eateries, outdoor lounges and boutique gift shops. With over 40 restaurants and bars, an active nightlife and a variety of independent music venues, you are bound to find something you like.

SOUTHERN EDITION

Chapter 4: Space Coast Area

Indian River, FL

SEBASTIAN AREA		Largest Vessel	VHF	Total Slips	Approach/ Dockside Depth	Floating Docks	Gas/ Diesel	Repairs/ Haulout	Min/Max Amps	Pump-Out Station
1. Sebastian River Marina & Boatyard WiFi MM 934.0	(772) 664-3029	70	16	60	5.0 / 5.0		GD	RH	30 / 50	
2. Sebastian Saltwater Marina Restaurant WiFi MM 937.2	(772) 589-2552	50		25	5.0 / 5.0		GD		20 / 50	P
3. Fins Marina MM 937.5	(772) 589-4843	65	16	78	6.0 / 6.0				30 / 50	
4. Capt. Hiram's Sebastian Marina WiFi MM 937.7	(772) 589-4345	50	16	46	5.0 / 5.0				30 / 50	P

WiFi Wireless Internet Access
Visit www.waterwayguide.com for current rates, fuel prices, website addresses and other up-to-the-minute information.
(Information in the table is provided by the facilities.)

Scan here for more details:

Source: Aqua Map and NOAA data

Boatyard, a full-service facility offering slips, dry storage, maintenance and repairs. The facility is in a seawall-protected basin close to a grocery store and restaurants. They maintain a few transient slips to 70 feet.

At Mile 937.5 in Sebastian there are two entrance channels on the west side that give access to three facilities located in a small basin behind spoils islands. The northern channel (across from green daybeacon "65") has shoaled in and is reported to carry somewhat less than the charted 6-foot MLW depths from the ICW to the marinas; therefore, we recommend the southern entrance channel just north of red daybeacon "66" for approaching. Call ahead for depth information prior to arrival as this area is continually changing.

The northernmost facility is Sebastian Saltwater Marina Restaurant. This is a very good restaurant that can accommodate power boats to 50 feet. Stay in the channel when approaching for 5 foot MLW depths. Call ahead about slip availability. Next is Fins Marina, home to the popular Squid Lips Overwater Grill and welcoming transients to 80 feet.

The southernmost facility is Capt. Hiram's Sebastian Marina, which can be identified by its colorful rooftops. The resort features an inn, restaurant and popular Tiki-style bar where you can relax with your feet in the sand and a drink in your hand. They also have slips to 50 feet and mainly cater to sportfishing vessels.

Anchorage: Because of the beach on the west side, the spoil island accessed by heading west off the ICW just north of North Rocky Point R20 at Mile 925 has become a favorite local anchoring spot. On less crowded weekdays ICW travelers often use this area for overnight anchorage. (It will be too crowded and noisy during "peak" season.) Depths are slightly less than shown on the chart (5 to 8 feet MLW). Shoals extend westward from these islands and are usually marked with pipes or stakes. Passing boats on the ICW create wakes here.

In an eastern blow it may be more comfortable snugged in closer to the barrier island to the east or south at Coconut Point. Just follow one of the deeper lobes off the ICW between Mile 924 and Mile 925. Note there are few anchorage opportunities between here and

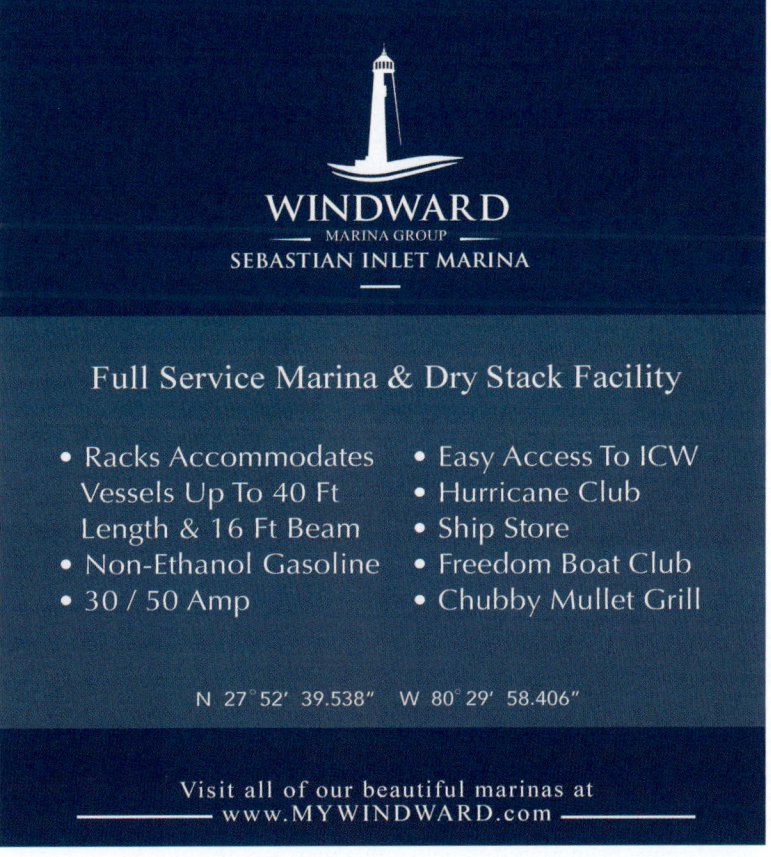

Chapter 4: Space Coast Area

Sebastian Inlet at Mile 936. (Running in the dark is not advised in this area.)

Vessels often anchor off Capt. Hiram's Sebastian Marina at Sebastian in approximately 5-foot MLW depths. There are a number of permanently moored vessels here. This is close to several active pubs and restaurants and can get crowded, even through the marked channel. This basin has minimal protection and is very congested.

> **NOTE:** You can take the dinghy to the basin to the north side of the inlet near the fixed bridge for snorkeling and swimming. Beach the dinghy on the sand beach prior to the "lagoon." Visibility for snorkeling is fair and the beach is perfect for a picnic or a dog run. You will be joined by a lot of fishermen and small boats.

To Vero Beach—ICW Mile 937 to Mile 952

The heavily congested areas are temporarily behind you as you enter one of the Indian River's most natural and attractive stretches. South from Wabasso small wooded islands suddenly crowd the narrowing river and create a maze through which the ICW channel twists and turns. This is a good place to spot manatees and other wildlife. Many islands here are bird rookeries. Vero Beach is a major boating center and stopover with all the amenities a cruiser would ever need.

On the way to Vero Beach, you will pass the Environmental Learning Center (772-589-5050) at Mile 943.4. This is a 64-acre habitat for birds, fish, crustaceans and mammals of many kinds. Museum exhibits include a 145-gallon touch tank, several aquariums and hands-on activities. They also have 2 miles of elevated boardwalk and nature trails. Note the campus is a "no pet zone."

NAVIGATION: Use NOAA Chart 11472. The dredged ICW channel runs straight for 6 miles to Wabasso. Be aware that numerous dangerous shoals flank the channel's edge. Observe the closely spaced markers through this section. At Mile 938 near red daybeacon "66A" be aware of shoaling into the east side of the ICW that extends out to mid-channel from a small spoils island. Depths as low as 4 feet MLW have been reported on the east side of the channel. Stay 100 feet west of green daybeacon "67."

Observe markers carefully and do not cut corners through this tight and winding stretch; dangerous shoals are immediately outside the marked channel. There is sporadic shoaling through this entire section. Additional markers have been placed to help guide mariners through this area; keep to the center.

>
> *CAUTION:* The high-rise **Wabasso Bridge** crosses the ICW at Mile 943.3. The bridge has a charted 65-foot fixed vertical clearance; however, actual clearance varies from 62 to 65 feet due to water level changes. The water level gauge reading can be accessed real time online at the USGS website.

After weaving past some sizable islands, Vero Beach finally appears at Mile 952. This is a boating center and favorite cruiser stopover with a variety of facilities lining both sides of the Indian River above and below the high-rise **Merrill P. Barber (SR 60) Bridge** (also known as the **Vero Beach Bridge**). (May have less than published 66-foot vertical clearance.) A little more than 1 mile south is another high rise bridge, the **Alma Lee Loy (SR-656/17th Street) Bridge** with a 65-foot fixed vertical clearance. The warm discharge of the power plant to the west along this segment attracts manatees and you must maintain a posted slow speed from November 15 through April 30.

This is the beginning of the more densely populated areas along Florida's East Coast and boat traffic increases accordingly. Keep well inside the marked channel when passing through the bridge and maintain a firm hand on the helm, as winds and current can be strong here.

Dockage/Moorings: At Mile 948.5 on the west side of the ICW and north of Vero Beach, a charted, marked channel with observed depths of 6 foot MLW at the centerline leads to the docks of Loggerhead Marina–Vero Beach Marina, located in a pretty planned community with condominiums, golf, tennis and handsome waterfront homes. The marina can accommodate transients (including catamarans) up to 120 feet with a 6.5-foot dockside depths. There is a shopping center about 1 mile away for provisioning and the marina has loaner bikes available.

The entrance channel to the popular Vero Beach City Marina exits the ICW just north of the Merrill P. Barber Bridge. Markers to the east lead up the old ICW route past a city park to the marina. Call ahead for approach directions and depths. The marina is situated in a park-like setting and is protected from ICW wakes with transient dockage and free pump-out boat service (twice weekly). Located just south of the marina is a large dog park where your pet can get ashore and stretch its legs. There is also a free shuttle to town and to the beach

Vero Beach Area, FL

		Largest Vessel	VHF	Total Slips	Approach/ Dockside Depth	Floating Docks	Gas/ Diesel	Repairs/ Haulout	Min/Max Amps	Pump-Out Station
WABASSO										
1. Loggerhead Marina - Vero Beach Marina WiFi MM 948.5	(772) 770-4470	120	16	161	6.0 / 6.5	F	GD		30 / 100	P
VERO BEACH										
2. Vero Beach City Marina WiFi MM 951.7	(772) 231-2819	160	16	88	8.0 / 10.0	F	GD		30 / 100	P

WiFi Wireless Internet Access
Visit www.waterwayguide.com for current rates, fuel prices, website addresses and other up-to-the-minute information.
(Information in the table is provided by the facilities.)

Scan here for more details:

Source: Aqua Map and NOAA data

SOUTHERN EDITION 219

| Chapter 4 | Space Coast Area |

Goin' Ashore
VERO BEACH, FL

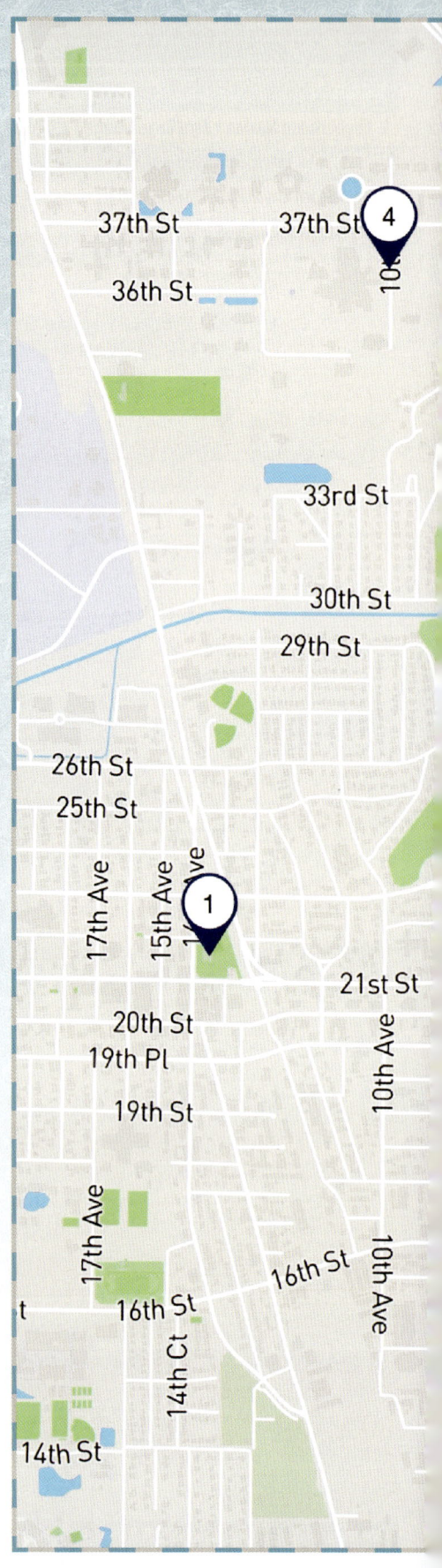

ATTRACTIONS

1. Indian River Citrus Museum
Small museum dedicated to citrus industry pioneers with a shop for citrus-themed art and gifts at 2140 14th Ave. (772-770-2263).

2. Riverside Theater
Performing arts campus with live theater, children's programs and lectures (3250 Riverside Park, 772-231-6990).

3. Vero Beach Museum of Art
American and international art collections and programs in art education (3001 Riverside Park Dr., 772-231-0707).

SERVICES

4. Cleveland Clinic Indian River Hospital
1000 36th St. (772-567-4311)

5. Divine Animal Hospital
654 21st St. (772-299-3665)

6. Vero Beach Post Office
3320 Cardinal Dr. (772-231-4070)

7. Vero Beach Veterinary Hospital
498 22nd Place (772-562-0200)

MARINA

8. Vero Beach City Marina
3611 Rio Vista Blvd. (772-231-2819)

America's Waterway Guide Since 1947   **Chapter 4**

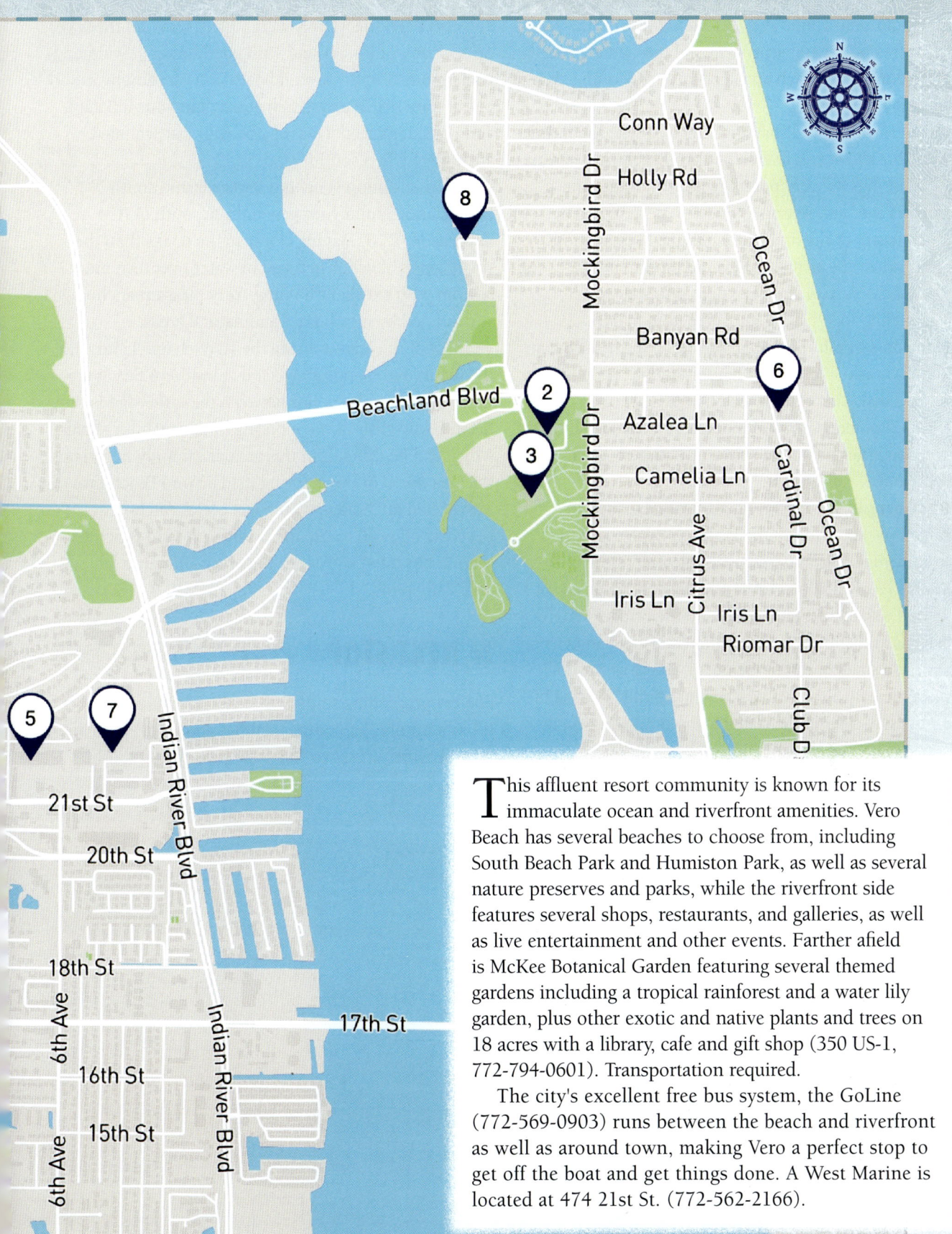

This affluent resort community is known for its immaculate ocean and riverfront amenities. Vero Beach has several beaches to choose from, including South Beach Park and Humiston Park, as well as several nature preserves and parks, while the riverfront side features several shops, restaurants, and galleries, as well as live entertainment and other events. Farther afield is McKee Botanical Garden featuring several themed gardens including a tropical rainforest and a water lily garden, plus other exotic and native plants and trees on 18 acres with a library, cafe and gift shop (350 US-1, 772-794-0601). Transportation required.

The city's excellent free bus system, the GoLine (772-569-0903) runs between the beach and riverfront as well as around town, making Vero a perfect stop to get off the boat and get things done. A West Marine is located at 474 21st St. (772-562-2166).

SOUTHERN EDITION

Chapter 4 — Space Coast Area

district, both only 1 mile away. From town you can access the city's free public transit system GoLine (www.golineirt.com), making Vero Beach an excellent provisioning and repair stop for cruisers.

Inexpensive and well-maintained city-owned moorings are available above and below the Vero Beach City Marina. These moorings are very popular and it can get quite crowded in the busy season. Moorings are assigned by the dockmaster of the municipal marina. (Reservations recommended.) Be aware that even if moorings are reserved, boaters may still be expected to share them; boats traveling together are encouraged to make arrangements to raft together. Otherwise, the first boat at a mooring is asked to put out fenders and accept whatever raft is assigned. It is well protected in this area and rafting is rarely a problem. Crews of moored boats enjoy all the marina amenities including showers, a lounge, trash disposal and use of the dinghy dock.

Anchorage: Vessels have been observed anchored in a small pocket between the Wabasso Bridge and the Environmental Learning Center to the west of the ICW at Mile 943.4 with 10- to 12-foot MLW depths. Be aware of charted underwater cables close to the bridge. Dinghy dockage is available at the Environmental Learning Center dock or at a small beach to the north. Depth at the dock is approximately 5 feet MLW. These are public docks but you must stay clear of the center's pontoon boat, which operates inside the "T" on both sides.

There is a good anchorage between Pine and Hole in the Wall Island red daybeacon "112" at Mile 946.5. Turn between the islands with 10 feet MLW all the way up the back of Pine Island with good holding, wind and wake protection for several boats. You can dinghy ashore but beware the live oysters that may cut your inflatable and your dog's feet! This may be your last secluded anchorage when southbound.

Another option is behind Barker Island south of Pine Island. Sound your way in from south of ICW red daybeacon "110" staying closer to the docks than the small island. Anchor in 6 feet of water over firm mud bottom with excellent holding. Very pleasant anchorage surrounded by nice homes and natural areas.

Most of the areas outside the ICW channel and near the mangrove islands above and below Vero Beach are shallow. Boats can anchor between the little islands but need to stay clear of the moorings and watch for shoals, which can be difficult in this area. If carefully negotiated, the area north of the mooring field at Vero Beach provides a protected anchorage with 6 feet MLW. Anchored boats are allowed to use the facilities at Vero Beach City Marina but must register at the office and pay a fee on a daily basis.

■ NEXT STOP

Boaters proceeding south will next encounter Fort Pierce. It has a number of marine facilities and its deep ocean inlet provides access to run outside to points south.

St. Lucie River Area

Chapter 5

Chapter 5: St. Lucie River Area

ICW Mile 952-Mile 988

TO THE CROSSROADS

No Wake Zones, Idle Speed Zones and various Speed Limit restrictions are in effect throughout the waterways included in this chapter. Exercise diligence in knowing the regulations by observing signs and other markers. Enforcement is always present. As always, be courteous to other vessels and avoid manatees and other marine life.

To Fort Pierce–ICW Mile 952 to Mile 965

Some of the spoils islands scattered along this stretch are blanketed in the spring by nesting pelicans, cormorants, herons and egrets. Enjoy watching them but do not disturb their nests.

Also keep a lookout for manatees farther south at the Peter B. Cobb Memorial (SR A1A) Bridge, which is another favorite lounging area for the gentle creatures. If staying in Fort Pierce you may also find manatees visiting the docks and walkways of the Fort Pierce City Marina.

NAVIGATION: Use NOAA Chart 11472. South of Vero Beach the Indian River widens and the dredged ICW channel begins to straighten out for the 13 miles to Fort Pierce. The river's expanded width is deceptive; the actual navigable channel remains narrow. The project depth along this stretch is 12 feet MLW but the actual controlling depth is 8 feet MLW or less. Just beyond the edges of the marked channel depths in many places are 2 feet or less MLW. The tidal range on the Indian River at Vero Beach is 1 foot. Another factor is that with the river's increased width there is also increased fetch in crosswinds, which can produce some chop. Take care to stay in the channel through this section by occasionally looking behind to make sure you are maintaining course alignment.

From green daybeacon "155" (Mile 955.5) to green daybeacon "173" (Mile 961), the Manatee Speed Zone varies from seasonal to year-round. Observe the posted speeds through each of these zones.

You will pass through a busy section starting with the **SR A1A North Causeway (Banty Saunders) Bridge** with 26-foot closed vertical clearance at Mile 964.8. The restricted bridge only opens on signal on the hour and half hour. This is sometimes referred to as North Pierce Bridge. Watch for current and boat traffic here. This can be an awkward place to wait for an opening. Note depths are less than charted northeast of the bridge span despite the marked, small-boat channel to the east.

South of the entrance to Taylor Creek at Mile 965.1 the ICW intersects the Fort Pierce Inlet at Mile 965.6. Just south of the intersection with the inlet at Mile 965.8 is the high-level **Peter B. Cobb Memorial (SR A1A) Bridge**, which is sometimes referred to as the "South Bridge."

Dockage: The accommodating Heritage Boat Yard & Marina is just north of the SR A1A North Causeway (Banty Saunders) Bridge at Mile 964.1. Access is provided via a well-marked channel west from the ICW with reported 6-foot MLW depths. The marina offers a full range of services including an on-site, fully stocked marine store, a mechanic shop, a ship's carpenter, fiberglass repair and painting and in-house welding. Call ahead to check slip availability. The remarkably well-stocked Marine Connection Liquidators (772-465-6460) is just a short walk north.

Just north of the SR A1A North Causeway (Banty Saunders) Bridge is Fort Marine, located on the former site of a historical fishing village. Today the multi-use marina provides various services ranging from boat dockage and storage to fuel, ice, and bait sales.

Immediately south of the Banty Saunders Bridge, a well-marked channel to the west leads to Taylor Creek where several facilities are located. The entrance channel

---

HERITAGE BOAT YARD & MARINA

Formerly dba Riverside Marina
Specializing in Custom Wood and Marine Painting
Do-it yourself Yard
Yard Personnel Available
Steel, Wood, Fiberglass Repairs
Mechanic in Yard (Gas & Diesel) & Outboards
Electrical & Plumbing Repairs
Supplies • 110 & 220 • Showers
75-Ton Marine Travelift 22' Wide & Forklift

Dry Storage All Sizes

2350 Old Dixie Hwy.
Fort Pierce, FL 34946
Phone (772)464-5720
Fax (772)464-1623
riverside2350@hotmail.com

www.riversidemarinaftpierce.com

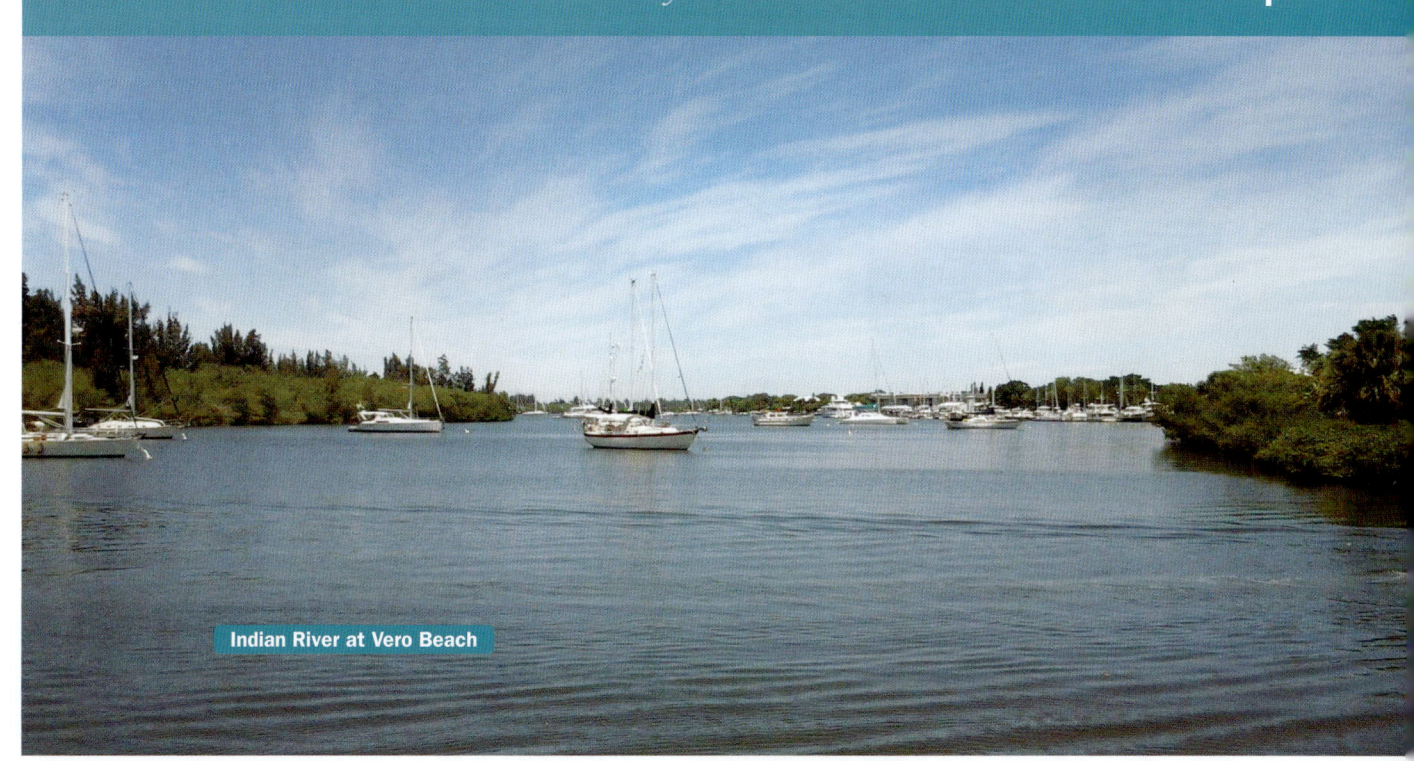
Indian River at Vero Beach

holds 8 to 9 feet MLW but shoaling is reported nearby. Verify depths when calling for reservations. The well-regarded Safe Harbor Harbortown is on the north side of the creek. This is a large, full-service marina and boatyard with a tropical atmosphere. Known for its exceptional hospitality, the facility also boasts a pool, shoreside dining and a calendar of vibrant social events. The island-themed Skippers Cove Bar & Grill (772-429-5303) is located on site as is Sunnyland Canvas (772-489-4850), specializing in marine canvas and upholstery.

Anchorage: At Mile 961.7, turn east at red daybeacon "174" into the privately maintained channel. Follow the channel until you are 200 yards past the small spoil island to your south and 200 yards before green daybeacon "3" and red daybeacon "4" of the private channel. Turn south-southeast in 4 feet MLW for about 300 yards or until you are between the small spoil island and Garfield Point. Anchor in clear water with a hard mud bottom and 4 to 5 feet MLW.

There is an anchorage convenient to Fort Pierce between the Banty Saunders Bridge and the Peter B. Cobb Memorial Bridge at Mile 964.8. Turn westward just north of Fort Pierce R184 to find slightly less than the charted 8 feet MLW off Safe Harbor Harbortown. Depths shallow near the bascule bridge where there is a charted Cable Area. From here you can dinghy to the marina and if you pay for dinghy dockage, the fee may be applied towards marina services or ice.

Fort Pierce Inlet

Fort Pierce Inlet is the only break in the barrier islands between the Sebastian Inlet and the St. Lucie Inlet. The Fort Pierce Inlet channel crosses the ICW at Mile 965. The 22-mile long Hutchinson Island lies to the south and 28-mile long Orchid Island (also known as North Hutchinson Island) lies to the north. These great distances help create strong tidal currents is the inlet. It is best to pass through with the tide or at slack tide as standing waves are possible.

NAVIGATION: Use NOAA Chart 11472. Fort Pierce Inlet is wide and deep with two stone jetties, an inner channel (30-foot MLW depths) and a turning basin (28-foot MLW depths). This is a big ship inlet and one of the best and easiest on Florida's east coast. The channel is marked with ranges and buoys (both lighted and unlighted).

Tidal currents in the inlet are strong averaging 3 to 4 knots. Where the inlet channel crosses the ICW down to the Peter B. Cobb Memorial (SR A1A) Bridge (Mile 965.8), strong crosscurrents exist with a set to the south on the flood and to the north on the ebb. Currents are strongest through the narrow neck of the channel inside the barrier islands near flashing green buoy "9." In strong east winds swells can create rough conditions inside the jetties (especially on ebb tides).

America's Waterway Guide Since 1947 — Chapter 5

> ⚠ **CAUTION:** In the Fort Pierce Inlet entrance channel there is an area of shallow shoals along the north jetty near flashing red buoy "8." These shoals are a popular weekend hangout for local boaters and fishermen. Be aware of traffic in this area.

Many cruisers make Fort Pierce Inlet their exit or entry point for an outside run. It's a 65-nm north run to Cape Canaveral Inlet and 45-nm south run to Lake Worth Inlet. The proximity of the Gulf Stream to this safe, deep inlet makes it an attractive area for deep-sea fishing. Fort Pierce is also a popular inlet when making landfall returning from West End Point on Grand Bahama Island. (The Gulf Stream gives a boost to cruisers heading north.)

Dockage/Moorings: Several dockage options line the south shore of Fort Pierce Inlet. Near green buoy "11" is family-owned Dockside Marina & Resort with ample deep-water slips. You have to approach into the current and sailboats are tied to the end of the piers. These are fixed docks and a tidal difference of 3 feet can make it a bit of a climb on low tide. Amenities include two large swimming pools, pet-friendly facilities, all-day coffee, a bait and tackle shop and picnic areas equipped with barbecue grills.

In the small basin near green buoy "13" (Faber Point) is Pelican Yacht Club, which is private but welcomes transients with fitst-class amenities. In the same basin is Fort Pierce Inlet Marina with 39 boat slips for vessels to 90 feet. Both facilities primarily cater to large sportfishing vessels and are within walking distance to shopping and other amenities.

South of the Peter B. Cobb Memorial Bridge at ICW Mile 966.5 (west shore) is Fort Pierce City Marina with ample transient space on floating docks for vessels to 150 feet.

To approach the marina turn west into the well-marked, dredged entry channel just south of the high-rise bridge. (Note the entry channel has been relocated from where it appears on older charts.) Prior to entering the channel, hail the Fort Pierce City Marina on VHF Channel 16. The staff will then acknowledge you and have you switch to VHF Channel 17. Large yachts use this facility so keep the radio on to check for Sécurité warnings. The channel is narrow and cross-currents can be significant. Four manmade rock islands protect the basin from ocean surge and wakes. The municipal marina has full amenities plus two restaurants and a well-known Farmers' Market on site. The city's investment in recent years has turned this into a beautiful facility, and the historic downtown is just steps away. Groceries, restaurants and a beach are all within biking/walking distance.

A privately marked channel east of red daybeacon "188" leads to additional marinas along the south shore of Causeway Island. This channel is initially shallow at the entry where the chart shows 7- to 8-foot MLW depths but it quickly deepens. The first facility is the large (43 acre) Causeway Cove Marina & RV Park with 198 wet slips and 10 mooring balls that accommodate boats of all sizes. They also offer full amenities and there is constant activity at the RV campground, which adds to the fun.

Farther east along this channel in a protected basin is Harbour Isle Marina at Hutchinson Island, which has well-maintained floating slips (with full finger piers) surrounded by luxury condos and resort amenities include a pool, fitness center and tennis courts.

Anchorage: A popular day anchorage for staging for a dawn departure is at Fort Pierce Channel. Be sure to put out scope appropriate for the conditions. There is a ripping current. From here you can dinghy to the small (unnamed) island or cross the channel to the free Museum Pointe Dinghy Dock. Trash disposal is available and this is a nice place to walk the dog.

There are several anchoring options off Causeway Island's south shore. These are accessed using the same privately marked channel that serves the marinas here. One is south of the marked channel to the east of Causeway Island R4 and another is just south of Causeway Island G9. Both anchorages offer at least 6 feet MLW with excellent holding and protection from northwest to east winds. If these anchorages are crowded, sound around the edges carefully with the dinghy as the boundary of deep water to the south is different than shown on the chart. Anchored boats may use the Fort Pierce City Marina dinghy dock, which is long and roomy.

For a peaceful anchorage with excellent all-round wind protection shoal-draft boats can proceed into beautiful Faber Cove with room for 3 to 4 boats. There is no place to land a dinghy and shore access is not permitted due to the private homes surrounding the cove. Going in proceed with caution as you round

SOUTHERN EDITION

Chapter 5: St. Lucie River Area

GOIN' ASHORE
FORT PIERCE, FL

ATTRACTIONS

1. **A.E. Backus Museum & Gallery**
   Features the works of Florida artist A.E. Backus as well as other regional and national artists at 500 N. Indian River Dr. (772-465-0630).

2. **Downtown Farmers' Market**
   Local vendors offering diverse selection of food, produce, handmade crafts and live music every Saturday at 101 Melody Ln. (772-940-1145).

3. **Manatee Observations and Education Center**
   Hands-on exhibits and boat tours to explore manatees, dolphins, pelicans and terns. The on-site Vanishing Mermaid Gift Shop is worth a look (480 N. Indian River Dr., 772-429-6266).

4. **St. Lucie County Aquarium Attraction**
   Offers exhibits on local marine life including touch tanks where visitors can interact with stingrays and other creatures (420 Seaway Dr., 772-462-3474).

5. **Sunrise Theater**
   Historic theater with a variety of live performances including plays, musicals and concerts. Opened its doors in 1923 and was completely renovated in 2006. Hosts 100 events per year at 117 S. 2nd St. (772-461-4775).

Fort Pierce was originally founded as a military supply depot during the Second Seminole War. Today Fort Pierce is the center of the Indian River citrus industry. Just along the Fort Pierce Inlet north jetty is Fort Pierce Inlet State Park, featuring a beautiful beach with swimming, surfing and picnicking. The park also has hiking and biking trails and visitors can rent kayaks and paddleboards to explore the nearby mangroves.

North of Fort Pierce Inlet State Park at 3300 N. Hwy. A1A is the U.S. Navy SEAL museum (772-595-5845), honoring the history and contributions of the Navy SEALs through exhibits on training, equipment and missions. (Transportation required.)

The downtown area features a variety of shops, restaurants and art galleries. Visitors can also take a walking tour of the historic buildings and murals, or head south to Heathcote Botanical Gardens, featuring a variety of plants from around the world including a Japanese garden, a herb garden and a cactus and succulent garden at 210 Savannah Rd. (772-464-4672).

SERVICES

6. **Holy Family Vet**
   709 US 1 (772-242-8320)

7. **Seven Gables House/Visitor Information**
   482 N. Indian River Dr. (772-468-9152)

8. **St. Lucie County Library**
   101 Melody Ln. (772-462-1615)

9. **Whole Family Health Center**
   725 US 1 (772-468-9900)

MARINAS

10. **Cracker Boy Boat Works**
    1602 N. 2nd St. (772-465-7031)

11. **Fort Pierce City Marina**
    1 Marina Way (772-464-1245)

12. **Heritage Boat Yard**
    2350 Old Dixie Hwy. (772-464-5720)

13. **Safe Harbor Harbortown Marina**
    1936 Harbortown Dr. (772-466-7300)

14. **Taylor Creek Marina**
    1600 N. 2nd St. (772-465-2663)

America's Waterway Guide Since 1947

Chapter 5

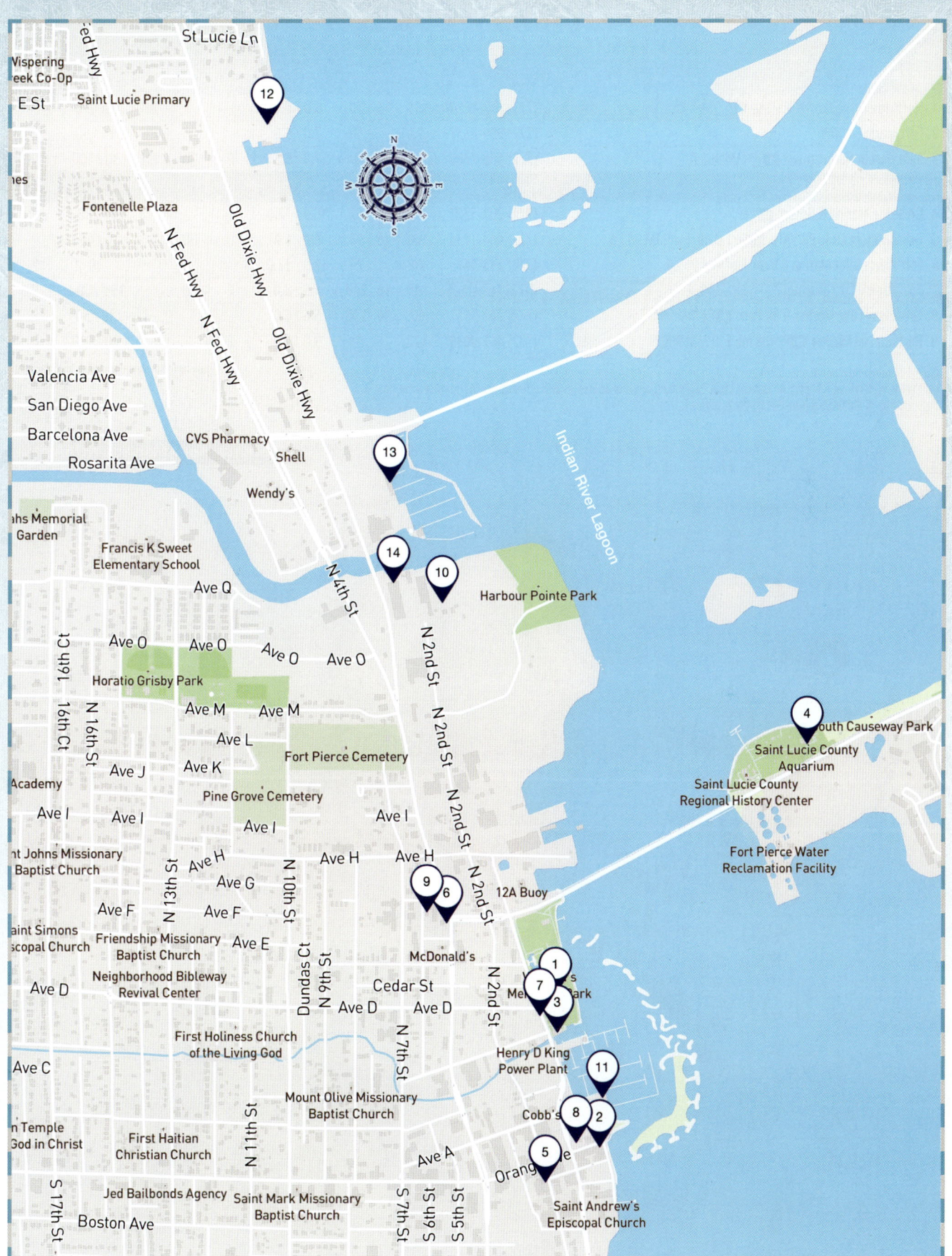

SOUTHERN EDITION

Chapter 5: St. Lucie River Area

Fort Pierce Inlet Area, FL

FORT PIERCE		Largest Vessel	VHF	Total Slips	Approach/ Dockside Depth	Floating Docks	Gas/ Diesel	Repairs/ Haulout	Min/Max Amps	Pump-Out Station
1. Heritage Boat Yard & Marina WiFi MM 964.1	(772) 464-5720	105	16	70	6.0 / 6.0			RH	30 / 50	P
2. Fort Marine WiFi	(772) 999-8357	80		50	7.0 / 6.5			RH	15 / 50	
3. Safe Harbor Harbortown WiFi MM 965.0	(772) 466-7300	160	16	344	7.5 / 6.5	F	GD	RH	30 / 100	P
FORT PIERCE INLET AREA										
4. Dockside Marina & Resort WiFi	(772) 201-5773	140	16	57	16.0 / 12.0				20 / 200+	P
5. Pelican Yacht Club-PRIVATE WiFi 1.0 mi. E of MM 965.6	(772) 464-1734	100	16	93	6.0 / 6.0		GD		30 / 100	P
6. Fort Pierce Inlet Marina 0.8 mi. E of MM 965.6	(772) 236-3675	90		39	12.0 / 12.0				30	P
7. Fort Pierce City Marina WiFi MM 966.5	(772) 464-1245	140	16	247	7.6 / 8.0	F	GD		15 / 200+	P
8. Causeway Cove Marina & RV Park WiFi MM 966.3	(772) 242-3552	60	16	198	5.6 / 6.0				30 / 50	P
9. Harbour Isle Marina WiFi 0.8 mi. E of MM 966.5	(772) 461-9049	120	16	63	9.0 / 9.0	F			30 / 100	P

WiFi Wireless Internet Access
Visit www.waterwayguide.com for current rates, fuel prices, website addresses and other up-to-the-minute information.
(Information in the table is provided by the facilities.)

Scan here for more details:

Source: Aqua Map and NOAA data

green "13" where you will only have 5 to 6 feet MLW. Note that charted green daybeacon "15" has been removed to make room for new docks; swing wide here towards red daybeacon "14" to avoid shoaling to the north.

Fort Pierce to The Crossroads–ICW Mile 965 to Mile 988

Below Fort Pierce the Indian River is deceptively wide. For the most part the ICW follows a deep, natural channel but the navigable channel narrows in many sections where you will see birds walking atop the shoals just outside of the dredged channel. Keep markers lined up ahead and astern through these narrow sections.

> NOTE: This is another good stretch to keep a watch out for wildlife. You may see rays, dolphin and sea turtles along this section of the Indian River.

NAVIGATION: Use NOAA Chart 11472. The natural channel of the Indian River opens up south of green daybeacon "191" allowing some additional maneuvering space, but watch for a series spoils shoals to the east of the ICW that run the entire length of Hutchinson Island. Proceed cautiously past the overhead power cables for the St. Lucie Power Plant, which stands on Herman Bay Point at Big Mud Creek (90-foot authorized overhead clearance at the main channel) just north of red daybeacon "206."

Another area deserving extra attention is between green daybeacons "203" and "205" at about Mile 973.5, where private markers to Big Mud Creek head off to the east. (Do not mistake private green daybeacon "1" located in shallow water up Big Mud Creek for an ICW marker.)

The channel appears to open up as you approach the high-rise **Jensen Beach Causeway (Frank A. Wacha/SR 707A) Bridge** at Mile 981.4 but shoaling is a chronic problem heading south from the bridge to past red daybeacon "220." South of the high-rise **Ernest Lyons (SR A1A) Bridge** at Mile 984.9 there is dangerous shoaling on either side of the channel from north of red daybeacon "228" to red daybeacon "230." Stay in the middle for 7 feet MLW.

> NOTE: This area is popular with windsurfers and small powerboats, so best to pay attention for traffic from here to The Crossroads.

Dockage/Moorings: Nettles Island Marina is located near the southeast corner of Nettles Island north of Jensen

Chapter 5: St. Lucie River Area

Fort Pierce Inlet

Beach. An access channel carrying 8 to 10 feet MLW leads east from the ICW at Mile 979.2 between flashing red "214" and green daybeacon "215." The channel's start is marked by private green daybeacon "1." (Note some of these private markers are difficult to see.) There is a well-stocked grocery/general store with a bakery, a large selection of wines, marine supplies, hardware, bait, and fishing supplies plus a boutique, hair salon, spa and an on-site restaurant in this gated community. The dockmaster doesn't always monitor the VHF so call ahead (772-229-2811).

The first of the many waterfront facilities in and around Stuart start to appear at the Jensen Beach Causeway Bridge. There are 56 moorings at Jensen Beach Mooring Field for vessels to 50 feet. Services and amenities include a dedicated mooring field dinghy dock, clean restrooms and shower facilities, weekly pump-out service, trash receptacles and recycling.

Sun Dance Marine Jensen Beach/Stuart just to the south can be approached from the body of deeper water extending south from the bridge. It is best to pass well south of red daybeacon "220" to avoid shoaling before turning for the facility. This is primarily a brokerage and repair facility that maintains some transient slips.

Directly to the south at Mile 982.8 a marked channel (8 feet MLW reported) exits the ICW west from red daybeacon "222" and leads to the Four Fish Inn & Marina with transient slips in a park-like setting. On-site accommodations are available should you choose to get off the boat for a night.

Anchorage: You can anchor at Nettles Beach east of red daybeacon "210" at Mile 976. Expect depths from 5.5 to 6.5 feet with good holding in mud and wind protection from northeast to southeast. This is a very quiet anchorage.

Between the mainland and the ICW, you will find good anchorages north and south of the Jensen Beach Causeway Bridge. Pick your spot to maximize wind protection but avoid the charted pipeline and cable areas. The tidal range here is only 1 foot, although currents can be significant. Expect wakes. The area of deep water north of the bridge is fairly small as depths

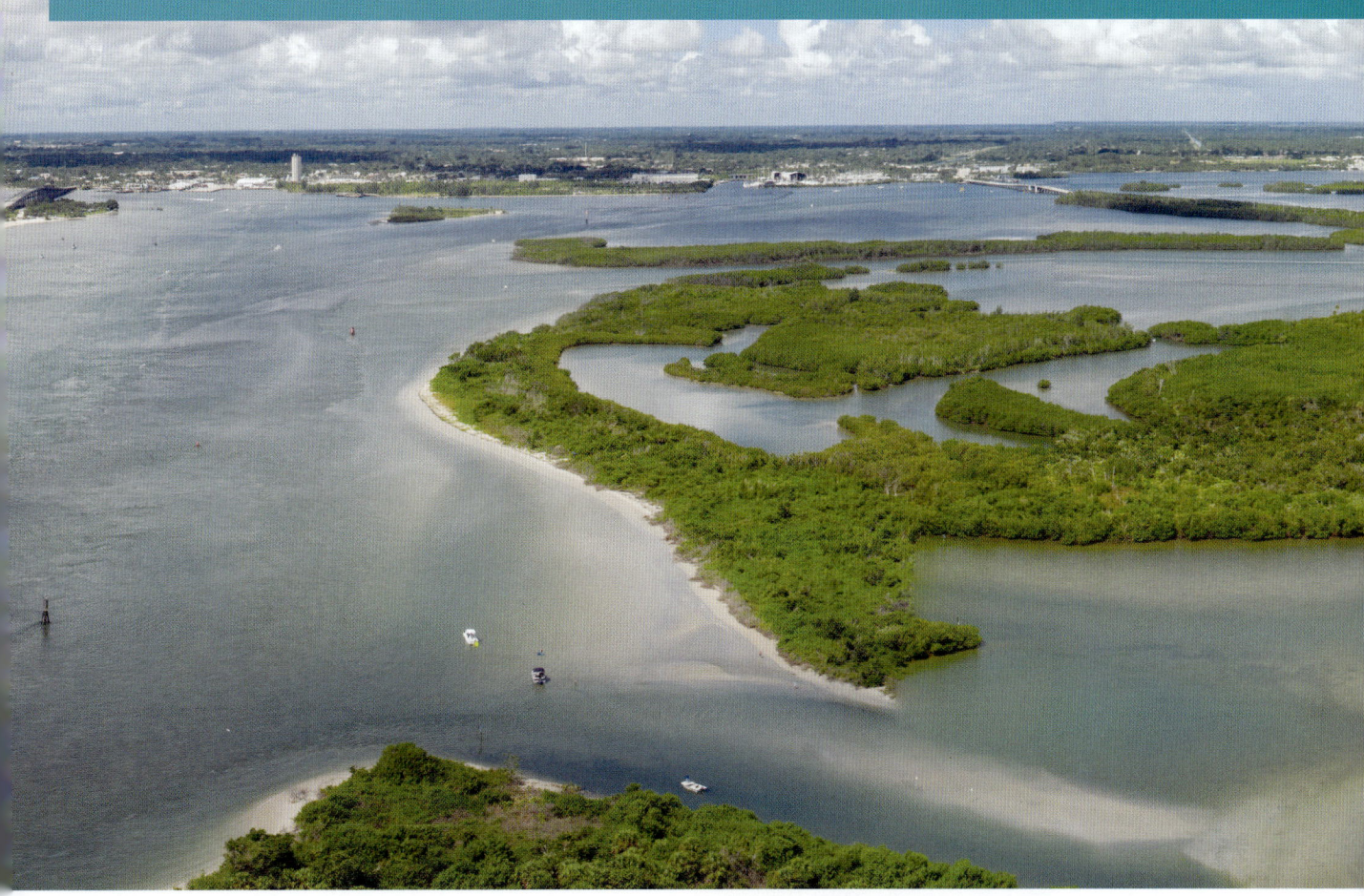

are less than charted. The anchorage to the south is larger with depths of 7 feet MLW but it is often crowded with boats, some of which are permanent residents. To avoid shoals blocking the top of the south anchorage you must enter from a point midway between red daybeacon "220" and green daybeacon "221" and proceed west and then north towards the causeway.

There are dinghy landing options on both the south and north sides of the Jensen Beach Causeway Bridge. Shore access is also available at the thatched-roof Conchy Joe's Seafood Restaurant (772-334-1130), which is just north of the bridge. Dining patrons in dinghies and boats drawing less than 2 feet are welcome at their dinghy dock but call ahead to check availability. Follow the shallow approach channel carefully.

There are additional anchorages outside the charted Cable Areas that follow alongside the Ernest Lyons Bridge. You can anchor in 6 feet MLW north or south of the east causeway. Ease your way in as depths may be less than charted. To approach the south anchorage pass through the first pair of private channel markers and exit south to anchor.

Side Trip: Hutchinson Island

Hutchinson Island is a 22-mile long barrier island protecting the ICW between the Fort Pierce Inlet and the St. Lucie Inlet. Visitors from the mainland can reach Hutchinson Island and its gorgeous beaches via three long causeways. At the west end of the Jensen Beach Causeway a park with a large pier has restrooms, a picnic area and a playground. Currents at the north end of the island will be more affected by the Fort Pierce Inlet tides and at the south end by St. Lucie Inlet tides.

Dockage: Just southeast of the high-rise Ernest Lyons Bridge, the 77-slip Hutchinson Island Marriott Beach Resort & Marina can accommodate vessels to 125 feet (on T-head when available) with resort amenities. Visiting boaters may access the laundry, pool, tennis courts, golf course, spa, restaurant and tiki bar.

It is a short dinghy ride to the beach access on Indian River where coral surrounds an area that is great for swimming or snorkeling. Access is through a public access dock to the southeast of the marina. It is just a 1-mile walk to the ocean beach and 2 miles to St. Lucie Inlet, making this a convenient jumping off spot for a trip to the Bahamas.

Chapter 5: St. Lucie River Area

The Crossroads–ICW Mile 988

At Mile 988 the ICW intersects the St. Lucie River. To the east, the St. Lucie Inlet opens into the Atlantic Ocean and to the west, the Okeechobee Waterway follows St. Lucie River upstream. Locally this intersection is known as "The Crossroads." This point defines Mile Zero on the Okeechobee Waterway's route to Florida's Gulf Coast. Here mariners have a choice of three routes:

1. Follow the ICW south to the resort areas on Florida's southeast coast and the Florida Keys.

2. Follow the St. Lucie Inlet to the Atlantic Ocean for crossing to the Bahamas (or to take "outside" routes north or south in the Gulf Stream).

3. Travel upstream along the St. Lucie River, down the South Fork, traverse the Okeechobee Waterway across Lake Okeechobee and on to Fort Myers and Florida's Gulf Coast.

CAUTION: Note that you can only navigate the Okeechobee Waterway if your draft is shallow enough to do so and you have an airdraft of less than 49 feet. This is detailed in the "Side Trip on the Okeechobee Waterway" chapter.

NAVIGATION: Use NOAA Chart 11472 (inset) or NOAA Chart 11428 (inset). Boaters on the ICW may experience strong crosscurrents at the St. Lucie River. The set depends on tidal phase–westerly on flood or easterly on ebb. Also allow for the crosscurrents when making a turn at The Crossroads. Pay close attention to boat traffic in this area. You will most likely encounter fast-moving fishing boats heading to and from the St. Lucie Inlet, particularly between Manatee Pocket and the ocean.

The 16-foot-high flashing red buoy "240" (ICW marker) at The Crossroads marks the beginning of the Okeechobee Waterway westward. The westbound channel is prone to shoaling here and its markers are often repositioned to indicate the deepest water.

NOTE: Southbound ICW traffic should note that the marker numbering sequence resets here and continues with red markers to starboard (if southbound).

Look up the natural channel to the south for red daybeacon "2" and flashing green "3" located 0.25 miles south of red buoy "240" and split these markers to proceed south. You will find them past a white sign ("DANGER–SHOAL") on the west side of the ICW, which should be kept well to starboard when southbound.

Mind your set as you pass through The Crossroads to maintain a straight course. This route picks up in the next chapter. Shoaling is less of a problem for mariners turning into the St. Lucie Inlet towards the Atlantic. To find the start of this channel look for green daybeacon "17."

Whichever route you take through The Crossroads expect heavy boat traffic, particularly along the St. Lucie River. Channels are narrow and many boats pass closely at high speed. This is not an area known for boater etiquette.

St. Lucie Inlet

NAVIGATION: Use NOAA Chart 11428 (inset) or 11472 (inset). St. Lucie Inlet is used by sport fishermen, megayachts and offshore sailors. The 2-mile run from the ICW to the ocean is subject to continuous shoaling, currents may be strong and markers may be off station. Most markers are unlit; therefore, nighttime navigation is not recommended. The inlet is conveniently located and frequently dredged but requires caution due to problematic shoaling. A jetty to the north and a small breakwater to the south offer protection once inside, although protection from the south is marginal in east to southeast winds. The USCG has placed temporary markers denoting best water. Avoid this inlet in an east wind (over 15 knots) on an outgoing tide.

Martin County begins just north of the Jensen Beach Causeway Bridge. Zoning laws restrict most buildings to a maximum of four stories so local captains returning from the Bahamas are said to locate St. Lucie Inlet by merely aiming for the "valley" midway between the high rise buildings of St. Lucie County to the north and Palm Beach County to the south.

■ SIDE TRIP: THE ST. LUCIE RIVER

From its intersection with the Atlantic ICW at The Crossroads (Mile 0 of the Okeechobee Waterway) the channel heads initially westward and then curves northward starting at Okeechobee Mile 0.5 (near the opening to Manatee Pocket).

Aids to navigation are often relocated and additional markers established to indicate the best water in this area. Keep red markers to starboard when heading upstream. Take time to observe all aids and don't be surprised if their

America's Waterway Guide Since 1947

Chapter 5

Indian River, FL

HUTCHINSON ISLAND		Largest Vessel	VHF	Total Slips	Approach/ Dockside Depth	Floating Docks	Gas/ Diesel	Repairs/ Haulout	Min/Max Amps	Pump-Out Station
1. Nettles Island Marina WiFi MM 979.3	(772) 229-2811	115	16	65	7.0 / 10.0		G	RH	30 / 100	P
2. Hutchinson Island Marriott Beach Resort & Marina WiFi MM 985.0	(772) 225-6989	125	16	77	7.0 / 7.0		GD		30 / 50	
JENSEN BEACH										
3. Jensen Beach Mooring Field WiFi	(772) 320-3184	50			7.5 / 8.5	F				P
4. Sun Dance Marine Jensen Beach/Stuart MM 982.2	(772) 675-1913	45	16	10	8.0 / 4.0		G	RH	30	
5. Four Fish Inn & Marina MM 982.8	(772) 469-2782	90	16	30	8.0 / 6.0	F	GD	RH	30 / 50	P

WiFi Wireless Internet Access
Visit www.waterwayguide.com for current rates, fuel prices, website addresses and other up-to-the-minute information.
(Information in the table is provided by the facilities.)

Scan here for more details:

Source: Aqua Map and NOAA data

SOUTHERN EDITION 235

Chapter 5: St. Lucie River Area

positions or sequence differ from what's on your chart. Tidal range is only about 1 foot here but currents can be strong. These weaken proceeding up the St. Lucie River. Expect heavy boat traffic until you are through Hell Gate.

Manatee Pocket

Manatee Pocket is about 0.6 miles from The Crossroads and comes up quickly in the busy channel. It is often visited by cruisers traveling north and south on the ICW. Considered an all-weather anchorage this is a delightful basin where you can usually find dockage in a lake-like setting. Port Salerno, a small town at the head of Manatee Pocket, features several restaurants and also has a marine electronics store and grocery store. Manatee Pocket is also home to the Chapman School of Seamanship, which has courses and programs for recreational boaters and also offers vocational programs for careers in various maritime fields.

NAVIGATION: Use NOAA Chart 11428 (inset) or NOAA Chart 11472 (inset). Heading west from The Crossroads toward Stuart and the Okeechobee Waterway flashing red buoy "2" and green can buoy "3" (located just southwest of flashing red "240") mark the channel entrance. Shoaling between 5 to 7 feet MLW has been observed over a bar between these two markers. Favor the green side of the channel to flashing green "7." There is a channel straight up the middle of Manatee Pocket approximately 100 feet wide with a depth of 10 to 12 feet MLW.

Be particularly alert for large wakes when traveling between The Crossroads area and the entrance to Manatee Pocket where the channel starts to deepen. This short but narrow stretch is often crowded with powerboats speeding to or from the ocean via the St. Lucie Inlet.

NO WAKE ZONE

All of Manatee Pocket is a No Wake Zone. Proceed accordingly.

Dockage: The family-owned and operated Sailfish Marina of Stuart is the first marina on the right upon entering Manatee Pocket and is the closest marina to the St. Lucie Inlet. This well-maintained facility offers transient dockage to 85 feet and a full-service boatyard. It is home to several businesses including Fish Head's Bait and Tackle and Ellie's Deli.

Next on the right, Mariner Cay Marina accepts transients and has all the usual amenities. The marina's fixed docks are set in a gated community with 24-hour security.

Farther along the west shore is Pirate's Cove Resort & Marina, an "Old Florida" inn with a full-service marina.

America's Waterway Guide Since 1947 — Chapter 5

They cater to sport fishing vessels and an on-site Bait & Tackle Shop are among the amenities. On the opposite shore Hinckley Yacht Services Stuart has a reputation for superior marine carpentry, fiberglass, hull and engine repair work. They have just four reserved transient slips so call ahead.

At the split in the pocket is the friendly Stuart Corinthian Yacht Club (on the eastern branch), which is private but accepts transients if space is available. Both A & J Boat Works (western branch) and Port Salerno Marine on the western shore are repair/service yards and do not accept transients. Manatee Marina has a seawall for transients.

Anchorage: A 10-foot MLW channel is well marked to the south end of Manatee Pocket. Anchor in 5.5 to 6 feet MLW in the wide area between Mariner Cay Marina and Pirate's Cove Resort & Marina or in 5 feet MLW beyond Pirates Cove. You can tie up the dinghy at the small park dock south of Pirates Cove. Anchoring in Manatee Pocket is limited to 72 hours and the restriction is enforced. This can be a very crowded anchorage so be sure to have an alternate plan.

Stuart & the St. Lucie Canal

The City of Stuart, tucked back along the south shore of the St. Lucie River, is as well equipped as almost any port city on the Atlantic coast and supports a sizable winter boat colony. While the quaint city has some modern development, it retains an "Old Florida" feel and offers some respite from the high-rise development along the Florida coastline. Marine facilities and shore activities are a vital part of the community.

Beyond Stuart the Okeechobee Waterway follows the South Fork and then turns westward into the St. Lucie Canal and Lock and, ultimately, the Gulf of Mexico.

NAVIGATION: Use NOAA Chart 11428. Proceeding upstream on the St. Lucie River from the entrance to Manatee Pocket a close pack of makers line the channel on both sides as it gradually curves north towards the "Hell Gate" narrows (as noted on the NOAA chart). The shallowest spots are between red daybeacons "8" and "10." Turn wide around these marks.

Shoaling is continual through the curve to "Hell Gate," particularly on the red side, and navigation aids are regularly being added and moved in an effort to

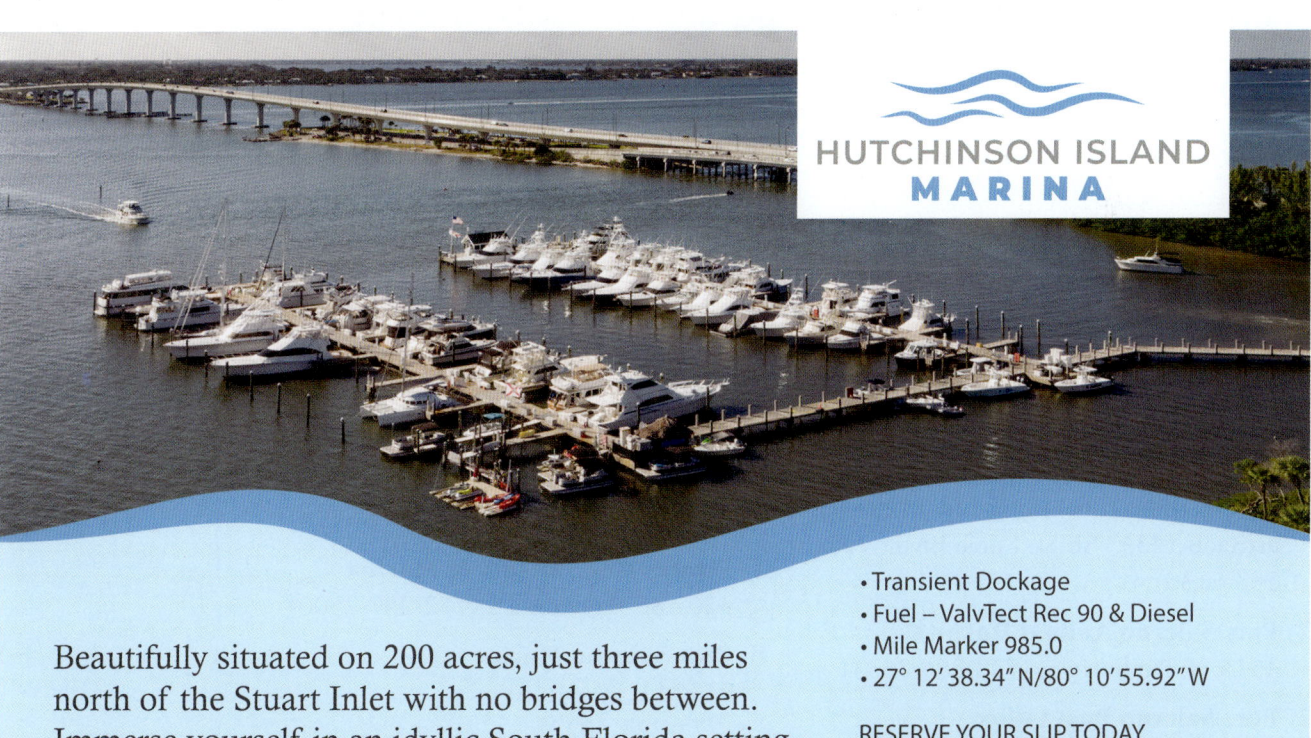

HUTCHINSON ISLAND MARINA

Beautifully situated on 200 acres, just three miles north of the Stuart Inlet with no bridges between. Immerse yourself in an idyllic South Florida setting.

Managed by USMarinaGroup.com

- Transient Dockage
- Fuel – ValvTect Rec 90 & Diesel
- Mile Marker 985.0
- 27° 12' 38.34" N/80° 10' 55.92" W

RESERVE YOUR SLIP TODAY
HutchinsonIslandMarina.com
772-225-6989
555 NE Ocean Boulevard, Stuart, FL

Chapter 5: St. Lucie River Area

GOIN' ASHORE
PORT SALERNO, FL

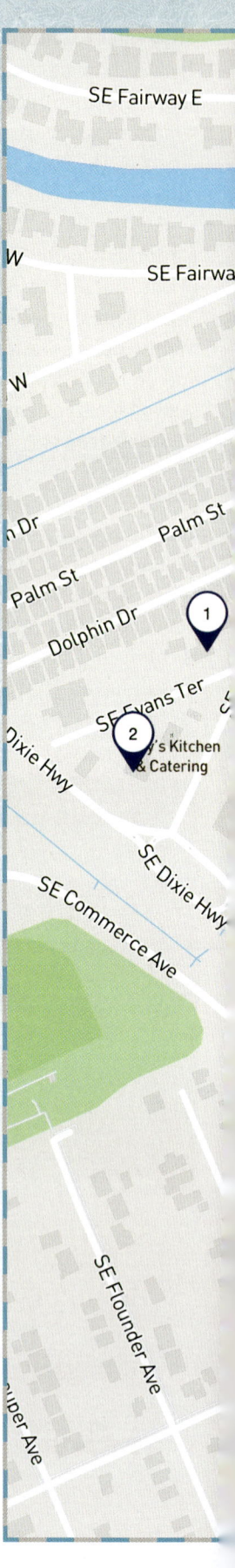

SERVICES

1. **Chapman School of Seamanship**
   World-class boat training school with donated boats for sale, a maritime library and a collection of maritime artifacts (4343 SE St. Lucie Blvd., 772-283-8130).

2. **Port Salerno Animal Hospital**
   4515 SE Dixie Hwy. (772-286-3833)

3. **Port Salerno Post Office**
   4755 SE Dixie Hwy. (772-463-8307)

MARINAS

4. **A&J Boatworks**
   4800 SE Anchor Ave. (772-286-5339)

5. **Hinkley Yacht Services Stuart**
   4550 SE Boatyard Dr.
   (772-287-0923)

6. **Manatee Marina**
   4905 SE Dixie Hwy. (772-283-6714)

7. **Pirates Cove Resort & Marina**
   4307 SE Bayview St. (772-287-2500)

8. **Port Salerno Marine**
   4715 SE Desoto Ave.
   (772-223-5022)

9. **Stuart Corinthian Yacht Club**
   4725 SE Capstan Ave.
   (772-221-1900)

Chapter 5
America's Waterway Guide Since 1947

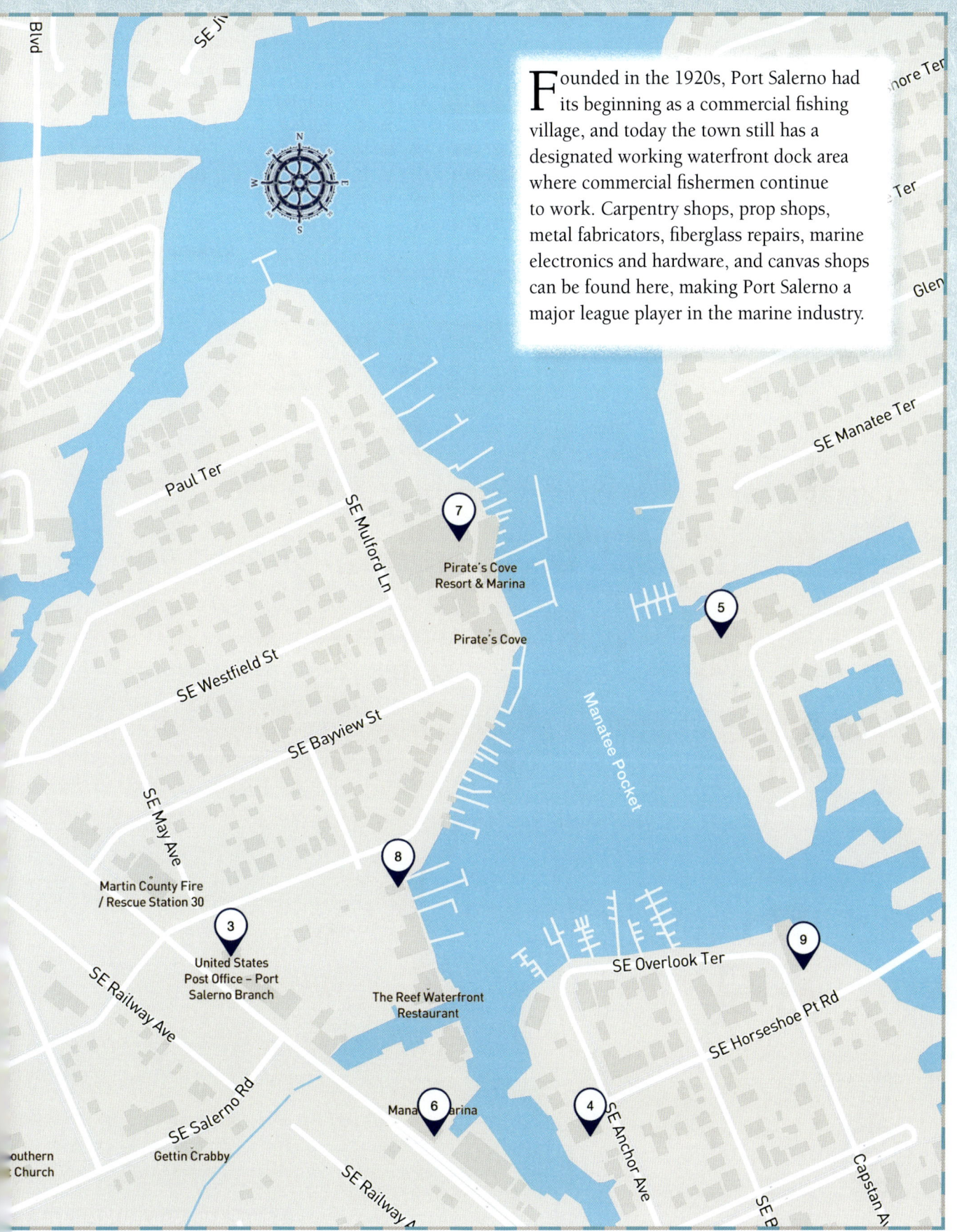

Founded in the 1920s, Port Salerno had its beginning as a commercial fishing village, and today the town still has a designated working waterfront dock area where commercial fishermen continue to work. Carpentry shops, prop shops, metal fabricators, fiberglass repairs, marine electronics and hardware, and canvas shops can be found here, making Port Salerno a major league player in the marine industry.

Chapter 5: St. Lucie River Area

St. Lucie River, FL

MANATEE POCKET AREA		Largest Vessel	VHF	Total Slips	Approach/ Dockside Depth	Floating Docks	Gas/ Diesel	Repairs/ Haulout	Min/Max Amps	Pump-Out Station
1. Sailfish Marina of Stuart WiFi 0.8 mi. W of MM 987.8	(772) 283-1122	85	16	55	12.0 / 10.0		GD	RH	30 / 100	
2. Mariner Cay Marina WiFi 1.1 mi. W of MM 987.8	(772) 287-2900	70	16	48	6.0 / 6.0		GD		30 / 50	P
3. Pirate's Cove Resort & Marina WiFi 1.8 mi. W of MM 987.8	(772) 287-2500	100	68	50	7.0 / 6.0		GD		30 / 100	
4. Hinckley Yacht Services Stuart WiFi MM 989.0	(772) 287-0923	115	16	80	10.0 / 6.5	F	GD	RH	15 / 100	
5. Stuart Corinthian Yacht Club-PRIVATE MM 989.0	(772) 221-1900	45	16	25	8.0 / 5.0				50	
6. Manatee Marina 2.2 mi. E of MM 987.8	(772) 283-6714	53		40	7.0 / 5.0		GD	RH	30 / 50	

WiFi Wireless Internet Access

Visit www.waterwayguide.com for current rates, fuel prices, website addresses and other up-to-the-minute information. (Information in the table is provided by the facilities.)

Scan here for more details:

Source: Aqua Map and NOAA data

better mark the natural channel and the ever-encroaching shoals. (Some markers may not be shown on older charts.)

CAUTION: Starting at Hell Gate Point marked by flashing green "15" the channel completes the turn northward around flashing green "17" and green can "17A." Keep all three of these markers well to port as you turn as there are shoals west of them. Favor the natural channel along Sewalls Point as the charted channel west of flashing green "17" has shoaled. You should end the curve halfway between green can "17A" and river's east shore.

Once through Hell Gate, the St. Lucie River opens up and the long finger of Sewall Point stretches along on the east shore. Parallel the shore of Sewalls Point keeping at least 100 yards off. The high ground is heavily wooded with estates and landscaped terrain. The western shore is equally attractive and is fronted by many private docks.

After approaching flashing green "19" the waterway heads northward on a straight-line course and passes under the high-rise **Evans Crary (SR A1A) Bridge** at Okeechobee Mile 3.4. This area was dredged in 2021 and maintains good depths. Continue on the straight-line course towards flashing green "21" keeping it to port. Once past this marker (located off Hoggs Cove) turn west towards flashing red "22." It's another straight-line course to the next turn at flashing green "23A."

Give green "23A" a wide berth and head southwest for the highest span of the 65-foot fixed vertical clearance **Roosevelt (US 1) Bridge**. This is one of three bridges that are clustered together within a distance of 800 feet. The other two are the **Florida East Coast Railroad Bridge** in Stuart (with a 7-foot closed vertical clearance) and the **Old Roosevelt (Dixie Highway) Bridge** (with a 14-foot closed vertical clearance).

The Florida East Coast Railroad Bridge is normally open but closes when a train approaches. It is an unmanned automated bridge that

Full-Service Marina & Boatyard

Protected Dockage on the Manatee Pocket

Sailfish Marina of Stuart
772-283-1122
www.sailfishmarinastuart.com
Email: sailfishmarina@bellsouth.net

CLOSEST MARINA TO THE ST. LUCIE INLET

FULL SERVICE MARINA

- Discounts to BoatU.S. & Sea Tow members
- High-speed diesel pumps
- Fresh diesel & non-ethanol gas
- Fuel dock hours: 6am-7pm summer; 6am-6pm winter
- 55 wet slips, deep water
- Overnight dockage
- Free WiFi
- Clean restrooms & showers
- Laundry facilities
- Full service boat yard
- 50-ton Travel lift
- Family owned and operated
- Fish Heads Bait & Tackle
- Ellie's Deli - Wed-Sun

3565 SE St. Lucie Blvd.
Stuart, FL 34997

Chapter 5: St. Lucie River Area

Goin' Ashore: STUART, FL

ATTRACTIONS

1. Lyric Theatre
Restored theater offering performance art, concerts and art cinema (films, documentaries, independent films and international cinema) at 59 SW Flagler Ave. (772-286-7827).

2. Stuart Green Market
Weekly community-based market featuring local produce, crafts as well as live entertainment and other events at Flagler Park (201 SW Flagler Ave., 772-285-0502).

3. Stuart Heritage Museum
More than 10,000 artifacts from the 1880s located in the Stuart Feed Store (circa 1901). Open daily from 10:00 a.m. to 3:00 p.m. at 161 SW Flagler Ave. Call ahead for hours and fees (772-220-4600).

SERVICES

4. Tourist Information Center
101 SW Flagler Ave. (772-288-5451)

5. Claunch Animal Hospital
665 SW Pine Ave. (772-221-1680)

6. Cleveland Clinic Martin Health
200 SE Hospital Ave. (772-287-5200)

7. Stuart Post Office
801 SE Johnson Ave. (772-288-0846)

8. Surfside Pet Hospital
812 SE Osceola St. (772-219-8022)

MARINAS

9. Sunset Bay Marina & Anchorage
615 SW Anchorage Way (772-283-9225)

America's Waterway Guide Since 1947 — Chapter 5

Stuart's claim to being the "Sailfish Capital of the World" is sometimes disputed by other Florida cities, but no one would deny that both its outside and inside waters offer outstanding fishing grounds. Along with fishing Stuart is famed for its historic and pedestrian-friendly downtown. A fountain in the shape of a sailfish marks the start of a group of unique galleries, cafés, restaurants, and shops along Flagler and Osceola Streets. One street over is the two-mile-long wooden Riverwalk, where you can enjoy free concerts on the weekends, fishing off the pier and check out the waterfront's restaurants and shopping.

Annual events include the Stuart Air Show with aerial demonstrations and displays and the Stuart Boat Show featuring a variety of boats and marine equipment, as well as other vendors and entertainment.

SOUTHERN EDITION

Chapter 5: St. Lucie River Area

works in concert with the Dixie Highway Bridge, which opens on signal. (Note: This schedule was provided to us by the bridgetender and is different than the published schedule.) If you have concerns, call ahead to 772-692-0321. The railroad bridge will signal via a flashing light and repeating five blast siren for 8 to 10 minutes prior to lowering. It takes about 10 minutes for a train crossing.

The Florida East Coast Railroad Bridge has a horizontal clearance (width) of only 50 feet compared to the Dixie Highway Bridge with a horizontal clearance of 80 feet. With little in the way of a turning basin prior to the bridge and with marine traffic and currents running, passage through the two bridges can be tricky, especially from the wider Dixie Highway Bridge to the narrower railroad bridge. Exercise care. Vessels with a wider beam may want to issue a Sécurité call on VHF Channels 9 and 16.

A turn to the north after passing through the Dixie Highway Bridge takes you off the Okeechobee Waterway and up the North Fork of the St. Lucie River. This can be a very pleasant side trip if your cruising schedule allows you the time.

Turn south to continue on the waterway toward Lake Okeechobee. At the opening to the South Fork the channel weaves around Arbeau Point and then Bessy Point. The waterway narrows into a dredged channel south of green daybeacon "25A."

CAUTION: At Okeechobee Mile 9.5 the 54-foot fixed vertical clearance **Palm City (SR 714) Bridge** crosses the waterway setting the air draft for the Okeechobee Waterway to Indian Town.

After entering the St. Lucie Canal, the **Southwest Martin Highway Bridge** (with 55-foot fixed vertical clearance) crosses at Okeechobee Mile 10.9. From here

From your dock to your destination... take Waterway Guide with you

Scan to subscribe now at www.waterwayguide.com

Chapter 5: St. Lucie River Area

St. Lucie River, FL

		Largest Vessel	VHF	Total Slips	Approach/ Dockside Depth	Floating Docks	Gas/ Diesel	Repairs/ Haulout	Min/Max Amps	Pump-Out Station
STUART										
1. Safe Harbor Harborage Yacht Club WiFi NW of MM 987.8	(772) 692-4000	90	16	300	8.0 / 6.0	F	GD		30 / 100	P
2. Sunset Bay Marina & Anchorage WiFi MM 8.0	(772) 283-9225	120	16	198	8.0 / 8.0	F	GD		30 / 50	P
3. HMY at Waterway Marina WiFi MM 7.7	(772) 692-7900	65		50	7.0 / 6.0				50	
NORTH FORK										
4. Sandpiper Bay Marina WiFi	(772) 335-7875	150	16	65	8.0 / 8.0		GD	R	15 / 50	P
SOUTH FORK										
5. Meridian Marina & Yacht Club MM 9.6	(772) 221-8198	40	5	2	6.0 / 5.0	F	G	RH	30	
6. Loggerhead Marina - Riverwatch Marina MM 9.6	(772) 286-3456	80		28	6.0 / 5.0	F	GD	RH	30 / 50	

WiFi Wireless Internet Access
Visit www.waterwayguide.com for current rates, fuel prices, website addresses and other up-to-the-minute information. (Information in the table is provided by the facilities.)

Scan here for more details:

Source: Aqua Map and NOAA data

Chapter 5 — St. Lucie River Area

you can opt to continue on to the Okeechobee Waterway or backtrack to the ICW and points south.

Dockage/Moorings: Just before the Roosevelt Bridge on the north shore is Safe Harbor Harborage Yacht Club. The 300-slip marina has space for transients on their floating docks with first-class amenities. They also offer complimentary transportation downtown.

Immediately past the Dixie Highway Bridge on the south shore is Sunset Bay Marina & Anchorage with 60 transient slips and 69 moorings. There is a popular restaurant on the premises called Sailor's Return (772-872-7250) serving seafood, steaks and spirits. Dine inside or out. The marina also offers loaner bikes and shuttle service.

Past the Stuart bridges at the start of the North Fork along Britt Point are Apex Marine–Stuart (a no-frills working boatyard) and HMY at Waterway Marina, a yacht brokerage with some reserved transient slips. Call ahead to check slip availability.

Located 3.7 miles northwest of the Dixie Highway Bridge up the North Fork is Sandpiper Bay Marina. They offer some supplies (including beer and wine) and can accommodate vessels to 150 feet. Visitors (including those who anchor off and dinghy in) can purchase discounted daily entrance passes from the co-located Club Med Sandpiper Bay that include access to all services. The all-inclusive resort has several restaurants and bars, swimming pools, a golf course (green fees extra) and a spa plus numerous water activities. For travel weary cruisers this can be a vacation within a vacation.

Before reaching the Palm City Bridge (54-foot fixed vertical clearance) on the South Fork, a channel on the western shore marked by private daybeacons leads to Meridian Marina & Yacht Club. It is primarily a repair and storage facility with extremely limited transient space on the fuel dock (two slips).

On the east shore just south of the Palm City Bridge a marked channel leads into Loggerhead Marina–Riverwatch Marina. The full-service marina features 373 dry storage and wet slips, a comprehensive marine service department, a fuel dock and a boat club. Limited transient dockage is available but be sure to call in advance.

Anchorage: Boats anchor on the southwest side of Sewall Point at Hooker Cove near green daybeacon "19" in 7- to 8-foot MLW depths. Make sure that your anchor is set. Currents tend to run swiftly here. Expect lot of boat traffic early and late in day.

North of the Evans Crary Bridge in Hoggs Cove holding is good in thick mud opposite flashing green "21" and there is protection from north and east winds. Watch the charted rocky shoal off Pisgah Hill and set the anchor in 7 to 9 feet MLW.

For short visits to Stuart or for dinghy access Stuart Riverside Pier offers free dockage for up to 4 hours with 5-to 6-foot MLW depths. Beyond the bridges at Stuart it is possible to anchor almost anywhere in the North Fork but the best anchorage is by red daybeacon "6A." Kitching Cove, located past Sandpiper Bay Marina, is a fine anchorage in 6 to 7 feet MLW. At the north end of the anchorage you can take a scenic dinghy trip to the headwaters of the river where you reach groceries and other needs.

On the South Fork of the St. Lucie River you will find very good holding in thick mud at Pendarvis Cove. This is a popular anchorage with both cruisers and liveaboards. Across the river there is an excellent dinghy dock just inside Frazier Creek that is a 0.5-mile walk to a grocery store, a laundry, restaurants and a hardware store. You can tie your dinghy to the wall at Frazier Creek Park and walk the dogs. There is water at the fish cleaning station and a dumpster in the park.

> **NOTE:** The Martin Ship Pump Out Operation Program (*M.S. Poop*) will come to your boat in Stuart. Service is available Monday through Friday from 8:00 a.m. to 3:00 p.m. and services boaters' requests on a weekly basis. To schedule a pump out, please call 772-260-8326 and leave a message on the operator's phone detailing when you need service. We encourage you to take advantage of this service. Not only does it benefit the waterways but the Martin County Sheriff's Department conducts surprise inspections and can levy hefty fines for noncompliance.

■ NEXT STOP

Those wishing to continue the journey on the Okeechobee Waterway should continue to Chapter 6: "Side Trip on the Oceechobee Waterway." If you plan to return to the Atlantic ICW for the trip south, skip to the next section, Florida's Lower East Coast.

Side Trip on the Okeechobee Waterway

Chapter 6

SOUTHERN EDITION

Chapter 6: Side Trip on the Okeechobee Waterway

NAVIGATION NOTES

The Okeechobee Waterway (OCWW) provides a shortcut from the Atlantic Ocean to the Gulf of Mexico and divides central and south Florida. It starts at the ICW in the mouth of the St. Lucie River at Mile 0 and ends 154 miles later at Mile 0 on the Gulf ICW (GIWW) at San Carlos Bay south of Cape Coral. This efficient route allows boats to pass across the state from the ocean to the Gulf without having to make the long trip down around the Keys and up across Florida Bay.

The OCWW offers a chance to see rural Florida with small towns preserved much as they were early in the last century. Along the waterway ranches and big commercial farms alternate with moss-hung wilderness, while bustling boom towns coexist alongside sleepy villages that have been around since way before Miami.

The Caloosahatchee River was once the only way to get from the Gulf of Mexico to Central Florida via small steamers and freighters. Some still consider the 76.6-mile-long Caloosahatchee to be the most scenic part of the OCWW. For the boater the OCWW and Lake Okeechobee provide a stark transition from the busy coastal cities.

The OCWW is described here according to its three distinct sections:

1. From Mile Zero (the intersection of the OCWW and the ICW at St. Lucie Inlet down the South Fork of the St. Lucie River to the St. Lucie Canal to Lake Okeechobee.
2. Lake Okeechobee (either the "open-water route" directly across the lake or the "rim route" along the lake's south shore).
3. The Caloosahatchee River to the end of the OCWW in San Carlos Bay at Mile 0 of the GIWW heading north.

Cruising Conditions

CAUTION: Hurricane Ian caused widespread damage across southwest Florida after making landfall on Cayo Costa Island as a Category 4 hurricane in September 2022. Many of the communities in this chapter were affected in major ways and rebuilding will be a long process. Call ahead for status prior to arrival.

Lake Okeechobee can be likened to a saucer full of water. It is shallow with normal depths from 7 to 11 feet MLW depending on the season and annual rainfall onto the drainage area to the north and the lake itself. The Army Corps of Engineers and the South Florida Water Management District manage the level of the lake.

The depths charted in Lake Okeechobee are based on a datum of 11.50 feet. If skippers know the lake level they can determine the difference between the datum and the current level and modify the charted depths accordingly. Depths in the sections between dams on either side of the lake vary slightly with lake level changes but the differences are seldom enough to affect navigation.

Note that water levels vary dramatically from season to season, month to month, and sometimes even day to day. Rainfall is the driving force behind the water level fluctuations but lake levels can also be affected by strong southerly winds, which will lower the water level. Daily water levels and route depths are available online from the U.S. Army Corps of Engineers. During a drought, lockage may be restricted depending on water supply. You can also call the Army Corps of Engineers in Clewiston (863-983-8101) for the latest updates.

St. Lucie Lock

Check during your pre-cruise planning and again at the first lock to make sure the *entire* OCWW is open before proceeding. Maintenance on the locks is normally conducted each summer and through-passage from the East Coast to the Gulf Coast may not be possible for as long as several months. During such times Lake Okeechobee may be accessible from one side or the other (but not both).

With the exception of a lake crossing in less than perfect weather passage along the OCWW is easy, piloting is simple and navigational aids are adequate for daytime running. Aids to navigation are numbered in several sequences from east to west all the way across. Even-numbered red aids are on the starboard side (as they are southbound along the Atlantic ICW). Conversely, leave red aids to port eastbound on the OCWW as you would when northbound on the ICW. Yellow squares and triangles are shown on daybeacons and buoys.

Nighttime navigation is not recommended as shoals and deadheads (partially submerged objects) are obscured. Fortunately, ample facilities and occasional anchorages make after-dark travel unnecessary.

Currents are not a problem on the OCWW except for the turbulence that occurs when locks are opened. Average tides at the mouth of the St. Lucie River are 1.1 feet, 1.3 feet at Fort Myers and 2.4 feet at Punta Rassa (at the western end of the waterway) near Mile 0 of the GIWW heading north. There is no tide in the lake itself.

No Wake Zones, Idle Speed Zones and various Speed Limit restrictions are in effect throughout the waterways included in this chapter. Exercise diligence in knowing the regulations by observing signs and other markers. Enforcement is always present. As always, be courteous to other vessels and avoid manatees and other marine life.

Weather

Central Florida weather is generally mild. In winter the prevailing wind on Lake Okeechobee is north to northeast as opposed to summer, when wind is normally east to southeast with very little rain except when cold fronts from the north pass through.

Summer days are calm in the mornings with occasional patchy fog. Winds pick up at about 10:00 a.m. Afternoons often bring showers and thunderstorms, particularly late in the day, so it is a good idea to plan on getting in early. Hurricanes do occur in season–June through November–as well as other times and can affect the lake.

Lake Okeechobee is the second largest freshwater lake located wholly in the continental U.S. (Lake Michigan is the largest) and it can get nasty. You should know the forecast before you leave port. The continuous NOAA marine weather comes from West Palm Beach and Fort Myers on VHF Channel WX-3 and from Belle Glade on WX-2.

Using NOAA Charts

NOAA Chart 11428 covers the area from the intersection with the Atlantic ICW to Fort Myers, while NOAA Chart 11427 continues down the Caloosahatchee River to the GIWW and the Gulf of Mexico. From that point cruisers have the option of moving north on the GIWW to the Sun Coast, outside in the Gulf to the Big Bend or the Panhandle or south to southwest Florida and the Keys.

Note that much of NOAA Chart 11428 is at a scale of 1:80,000, which is different from the charts adjoining at either end–NOAA Charts 11472 and 11427–both of which are at 1:40,000 or the usual ICW scale. NOAA Chart 11428 has two insets at its eastern end and one where it reaches Lake Okeechobee plus an extension at its western end; all of these are at various larger scales.

OCWW Bridges & Locks

The OCWW has five modern, spacious and well-handled locks and more than 20 bridges ranging from electronic controlled to hand operated. Some of the OCWW bridges operate daily from 6:00 a.m. to 10:00 p.m. and require a minimum of 3 hours notice to open at any other time. Phone numbers are posted on each bridge; calls are best made during normal office hours. You can use adjacent dolphins for tie-ups. Note that tying up to the dolphins can be tricky and the dolphins are there for commercial boats and tugs with barges to use in case of any delays. They always have priority.

Chapter 6: Side Trip on the Okeechobee Waterway

CAUTION: The Florida East Coast Railroad Bridge at Mile 38 sets the 49-foot controlling vertical clearance (when open) of the OCWW. If you have any questions about clearance call the Army Corps of Engineers at Clewiston (863-983-8101).

Sailboaters can have their mast unstepped at Stuart or wait and have it done at the Indiantown Marina, which is closer to the Florida East Coast Railroad Bridge (also known as Port Mayaca Bridge).

The water level in Lake Okeechobee is higher than anywhere on the Atlantic Ocean or Gulf ICW. Whether you are headed east or west you ascend through the locks to Lake Okeechobee and then descend after you leave. Typically locks operate between 7:00 a.m. and 5:00 p.m. with the last lockage beginning at 4:30 p.m. Note that the lockage schedule varies depending on lake levels. Allow approximately 15 minutes once inside a lock.

NOTE: The Army Corps of Engineers requires boat operators to turn off radar units during lockage to avoid exposing lock personnel to possible radiation risks. It is recommended, however, that engines be left running.

The OCWW locks are easier to transit when you are the only boat locking through and the lock attendant will give you the windward dock line first when winds are strong. Gusty winds can set up a surge in the locks so use caution. The attendant also might warn you that you could be locking through with a manatee or an alligator.

When you reach the mooring dolphins and the sign Arrival Point before each lock contact the lockmaster on VHF Channel 13. If you receive no response on the VHF sound two long and two short blasts of your horn.

Give your vessel's name and direction and request lockage. At that time they will inform you of the current lockage status and your estimated wait time. The lockmaster will instruct you "port-to" or "starboard-to" indicating which side of the lock to steer to and how to arrange your fenders. The lockmaster will then indicate for you to enter when the traffic light is green.

Unlike in other locks the lockmasters will hand or drop down to you (depending on the water level) a bow line and a stern line, or the lines may be hanging down from the top of the lock's sidewall in which case you will have to steer to them and pick them up. (Keep a boathook handy.)

Port Mayaca Lock

The locks of the OCWW are different from all other locks in North America in that they do not use valves to let water in to the lock. Instead, the front gates on the high side of the canal are opened about a foot and the water pours into the lock. In actuality it is not much worse than locks with valves; however, it can be a little disconcerting the first time you experience this.

Two people can safely handle a small or medium-sized boat but an extra pair of hands is always useful on larger boats. Single-handing through the locks is not safe and is strongly discouraged. Remember that the first boat into the lock should be the first boat out of the lock. Don't be too anxious.

Anchoring in approach areas to some of the locks is possible and the lockmasters can provide local knowledge concerning depths and conditions. Reservations are recommended at any marina on the OCWW.

CAUTION: Anchoring anywhere along the waterway is limited to 24 hours in any one location. This is enforced by the Army Corps of Engineers and applies to the OCWW between the St. Lucie Lock and the W.P. Franklin Lock including all of Lake Okeechobee (OCWW miles 15 to 121.4).

ST. LUCIE CANAL

St. Lucie Lock to Indiantown–OCWW Mile 15 to Mile 28

The OCWW departs the South Fork and continues as the start of the St. Lucie Canal with the St. Lucie Lock at Mile 15 of the OCWW. The small community of Indiantown, located less than 1 mile north of the river, has some lots of citrus groves and some amenities including The Seminole Inn and Restaurant built in 1925 by S. Davis Warfield, a railroad executive. If you want to eat at The Seminole you need to make reservations ahead of time (772-597-3777). Ask at the Indiantown Marina for other dining options and suggestions on transportation.

NAVIGATION: Use NOAA Chart 11428. The canal carrying the OCWW up to Lake Okeechobee itself is deep and easy to traverse and was dredged in spring 2021. On the way to the St. Lucie Lock you will pass under the **Southwest Martin Highway Bridge** at Mile 10.9, the **I-95 Twin Bridges** at Mile 14 and the **Florida Turnpike Bridges** at Mile 14.5. All of these fixed bridges have at least 55-foot vertical clearance.

The **St. Lucie Lock** at Mile 15.1 operates on request from 7:00 a.m. to 5:00 p.m. (Last lockage is at 4:30 p.m.) Radio ahead or call the lock (772-287-2665) prior to your departure for current schedules. This first lock of the system lifts you approximately 13 feet. When approaching the No-Wake Zone entrance area check the light system. If the light is red and a call on VHF Channel 13 or 16 does not get a response give two long and then two short blasts then wait well downstream in the standby area to avoid the discharge from the dam and lock.

Many boats arrive at the lower side of this lock and then turn around and go back without locking through so the lockmaster does not assume, even if he sees you arrive, that you wish to lock through. You must call him via VHF or horn. On each side of each lock of the St. Lucie Lock system there is a sign marked "Arrival Point." Enter slowly on the green signal and be prepared to accept lines fore and aft from the lockmaster. Have fenders ready on the south side of your boat for locking. As the water level rises maintain your position with care.

NOTE: The OCWW plays host not only to many varieties of fish but also to manatees (an endangered species), alligators and turtles of all sizes. The manatees frequently are "locked through" so take extra care if they are reported in the area.

Approaching Indiantown from the east you will first pass under the **SR 76A Bridge** at Mile 17.1 then the **Indiantown (SR 710) Bridge** at Mile 28.1. Both of these fixed bridges have at least 55-feet of vertical clearance. Just past the Indiantown Bridge is the **CSX Transportation Railroad Bridge** with a 7-foot closed vertical clearance. The railroad bridge opens on signal except between 10:00 p.m. and 6:00 a.m., when a 3-hour notice is required. (Call 772-597-3822.) The operator may anticipate you but if it is closed call on VHF Channel 09. If a train is approaching you may be delayed as the train always has the right-of-way.

Dockage: St. Lucie South Campground & Marina at the St. Lucie Lock offers waterfront RV and tent sites, plus boat slips. The docks are short and fairly shallow with space for vessels less than 40 feet. Amenities are what you would expect for a campground, complete with a hiking trail. Call ahead for slip availability.

Chapter 6: Side Trip on the Okeechobee Waterway

St. Lucie Canal, FL

ST. LUCIE LOCK AREA		Largest Vessel	VHF	Total Slips	Approach/ Dockside Depth	Floating Docks	Gas/ Diesel	Repairs/ Haulout	Min/Max Amps	Pump-Out Station
1. St. Lucie South Campground & Marina	(772) 287-1382	38		6	/				30 / 50	P
2. River Forest Yachting Center - Stuart WiFi MM 16.0	(772) 287-4131	150	16		10.0 / 9.0			RH	30 / 100	P

WiFi Wireless Internet Access
Visit www.waterwayguide.com for current rates, fuel prices, website addresses and other up-to-the-minute information.
(Information in the table is provided by the facilities.)

Scan here for more details:

Source: Aqua Map and NOAA data

The well-regarded River Forest Yachting Center–Stuart is located in a protected basin west of the St. Lucie Lock and offers a full range of on-site repair, maintenance and installation services. Be sure to call well in advance for availability of transient dockage. This is one of two freshwater locations (the other is in LaBelle) with climate-controlled indoor storage buildings. The marina also offers a members-only Hurricane Club to offer boat owners safe harbor during hurricane conditions in both Stuart and LaBelle.

A short distance beyond the Seaboard System Railroad Bridge in Indiantown is the 34-slip Indiantown Marina. For those intending to cross Lake Okeechobee via the direct route, this is the last marina until Clewiston, which is 35 miles away. This is a well-protected hurricane hole offering transient slips as well as long-term boat storage with a DIY and full-service boat yard. As with any of the marinas on the OCWW skippers planning to overnight here should call ahead for availability. It is best to take a slip in Indiantown as there is no viable anchorage.

Anchorage: To reach the anchorage at Four Rivers Loop leave the channel at green daybeacon "37" (Mile 11.2) and tuck behind the unnamed island in 5 to 7 feet MLW. Directly across the OCWW from the Army Corps of Engineers slips at Mile 15 at the entrance to a narrow bay is a quiet overnight anchorage for one boat with 8 feet and good holding in mud on the north side of the St. Lucie Lock. You can tie to the St. Lucie dolphins just south of the lock. They are spaced 50 to 100 feet apart so this will take some creative line work.

To Port Mayaca–OCWW Mile 28 to Mile 38

NAVIGATION: Use NOAA Chart 11428. At Mile 38.0 the Florida East Coast Railroad Bridge with 49-foot open vertical clearance sets the controlling overhead clearance for the OCWW. Elsewhere, at least 54 feet of overhead clearance can be carried. The bridge has 7-foot closed vertical clearance but is usually open displaying flashing

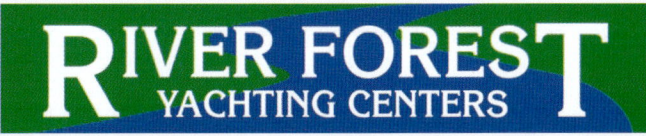

STATE OF THE ART YACHT STORAGE & EXPERT MARINE SERVICE CENTERS

✵ Climate and Non-Climate Controlled Inside Storage for Yachts Up to 85 ft & 82 US Tons in Hurricane Rated Buildings

✵ Land Storage with Tie-Downs Long-Term or Hurricane Club® Memberships

✵ Fresh Water Basins with Broadside Dockage for Safe Harbor & Cruising Boaters

✵ Complete Repair & Maintenance Services by ABYC Certified Technicians

✵ Authorized Dealer for Mercury, Cummins, Yanmar & Volvo Penta Engines, HamiltonJet Drives, Fischer Panda & Onan Generators and Dometic A/C & Head Systems

SECURE A STORAGE OR SERVICE RESERVATION TODAY!

PROVIDING EXCEPTIONAL YACHT STORAGE & SERVICE SOLUTIONS

www.RiverForestYC.com

STUART, FL
9150 SW Pennsylvania Ave. | Stuart, FL 34997 | (772) 287-4131

LABELLE, FL
1992 Williams Road | Moore Haven, FL 33471 | (863) 612-0003

Chapter 6: Side Trip on the Okeechobee Waterway

St. Lucie Canal, FL

INDIANTOWN		Largest Vessel	VHF	Total Slips	Approach/ Dockside Depth	Floating Docks	Gas/ Diesel	Repairs/ Haulout	Min/Max Amps	Pump-Out Station
1. Indiantown Marina WiFi MM 29.4	(772) 597-2455	120	16	34	8.0 / 8.0	F	GD	RH	30 / 50	P

WiFi Wireless Internet Access
Visit www.waterwayguide.com for current rates, fuel prices, website addresses and other up-to-the-minute information. (Information in the table is provided by the facilities.)

Scan here for more details:

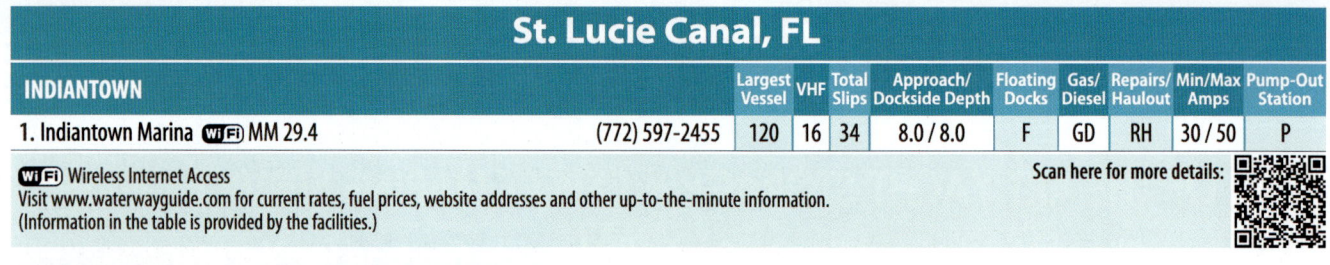

green lights to indicate that vessels may pass (unless a train is coming).

Be sure to stay south of red daybeacon "52" as a ledge of rocks and submerged pilings runs from the marker to the northern bank of the canal. The high-rise **US 98/441 Bridge** at Mile 38.8 and the Port Mayaca Lock just a short distance ahead serve as the entrance to the lake. Mooring dolphins provide the only place to make fast before reaching the lock but they may be in use by barges.

At certain water levels the **Port Mayaca Lock** is open at both ends and on the flashing (or steady) green (or yellow) light you may proceed through cautiously. You should contact the lockmaster on VHF Channel 16 or 13 before entering or if you have any questions. Operating hours are 7:00 a.m. to 5:00 p.m. with a last lock opening at 4:30 p.m. (561-924-2858).

Eastbound boats may experience some difficulty with adverse winds and resulting seas. Under these conditions entering the Port Mayaca Lock and making fast can be tricky. Until the lock is closed waves tend to ricochet from wall to wall. Heading westbound is considerably easier but if the winds are brisk be prepared for a choppy exit.

Anchorage: Be warned that anchoring beyond the Port Mayaca Lock is precarious. A layover elsewhere would be a better plan. The Port Mayaca dolphins before the lock are a possibility for tie-up if not occupied by barges. The east side is reportedly better. This is exposed to wind but if tied properly this won't be an issue: Tie a very long bow line to forward piling cluster, back down to aft piling cluster and tie long line to it. Then take in slack on forward line and your boat will be tied between the two dolphins with no drift, drag or swing. There is no current or tide here. There is also no shoreside access.

America's Waterway Guide Since 1947 — Chapter 6

Florida East Coast Railroad Bridge

LAKE OKEECHOBEE

Lake Okeechobee Routes

Lake Okeechobee is completely enclosed by an impressive levee system, officially named the Herbert Hoover Dike. The dike's construction began during the Hoover administration as a result of two disastrous hurricanes in the 1920s when the lake was literally blown out of its banks. During periods of strong winds the lake becomes choppy and turbulent with short, steep seas typical of shallow water.

> NOTE: The OCWW is 154 or 165 statute miles from the Atlantic Ocean to the Gulf of Mexico depending on whether you cross Lake Okeechobee (Route 1) or take the Rim Route (Route 2) along the lake's southern shore.

Route 1 is a 34-mile open-water crossing of the lake. Be sure you have all needed provisions with you before you start the trek across the lake as you will have few options once on the lake. The controlling depth varies but can be as little as 5 feet. The depth on this route is shallowest just after leaving the Port Mayaca Lock for about 0.5 mile then you will encounter 10 to 14 feet across the lake. At daybeacon "9" approaching Clewiston the depth will come up to 8 feet and remain there until you turn into the channel heading toward Moore Haven. Although 10 miles shorter, note that this route can get nasty in strong winds.

The more scenic Rim Route (Route 2) is 44 miles and follows the shoreline south from Port Mayaca Lock on the eastern shore. This route is subject to extensive shoaling and becomes impassable during periods of low water. The shallowest water is right at the beginning of the route when heading west. After about 1.5 miles the water gets deeper (10-plus feet).

> ⚠️ CAUTION: A low-hanging fiber optic cable at the Torrey Island is estimated to be 35 feet above the water. High-masted vessels are encouraged to use Route 1 until the cable is raised to 52 feet. Recreational and commercial boaters are asked to use caution when navigating through these sections of waterway.

Occasionally, the Rim Route will be closed to navigation because of vegetation in the water. These closures will be announced in the *Local Notice to Mariners* (www.navcen.uscg.gov).

Route 1: Crossing Lake Okeechobee to Clewiston

The open water crossing is normally an enjoyable run and Clewiston is a worthwhile stopover point. If the lake level and season are right expect to see hundreds of beautiful white pelicans bunched together on the half-dozen offshore spoil islands that line the Clewiston approach

SOUTHERN EDITION

Chapter 6: Side Trip on the Okeechobee Waterway

Warning: Blue Green Algae

The U.S. Army Corps of Engineers advises the public, marinas and those operating commercial and recreational vessels through the Okeechobee Waterway that there is the potential of encountering Blue Green Algae. Visitors should be aware that water from areas with blue-green algae can make animals and people sick and should be avoided. This algae may be blue, bright green, brown or red and can have a strong odor like rotting plants. People who are very sensitive to smells may have respiratory irritation. If you come into contact with blue-green algae, get out of the area and wash off with soap and water. See your doctor if you think blue-green algae has made you sick.

The following precautions should be taken if you see algae:

- Do not swim at this location.
- Avoid getting water in your eyes, nose or mouth.
- Do not eat shellfish from affected area.
- Rinse fish fillets with tap or bottled water. Cook fish well.
- Keep pets and livestock away from affected location.

For more information about algal blooms, visit The Florida Department of Environmental Protection online or call 850-245-2118.

channel. Unlike brown pelicans, which plunge-dive from high above the water for their meals, white pelicans scoop up fish by merely submerging their heads and necks while swimming.

NAVIGATION: Use NOAA Chart 11428. Crossing the southern portion of Lake Okeechobee entails a 25-mile-long passage after departing from the Port Mayaca channel in a southwesterly direction. The first run of 15 miles has just one aid to navigation, flashing red "6," which is located about 7 miles out. This will help you compensate for a slight magnetic anomaly in this area, which might affect your compass. About 3 miles out from the Port Mayaca Lock there is a visible wreck to starboard. Do not be led off course. Your GPS chartplotter or radar could be useful on this stretch if visibility is compromised.

As you approach flashing green "7" on the eastern edge of Rocky Reef note what appears to be a cluster of markers and the remains of a platform. Sort things out beforehand and follow the chart's magenta line carefully. After clearing the cut through the reef stick to the charted course. The apparent shortcut due west, a charted auxiliary floodway channel, is shoaled in and obstructed with large boulders (particularly noticeable at low lake levels). *This cut should not be attempted by cruising boats.*

Entering the Clewiston approach channel, marked by a private concrete cylinder and numerous lights and daybeacons, is simple. Westbound green daybeacon "1" is difficult to spot. If the water level is low or the winds are brisk pay strict attention to course keeping. This is where the controlling depth (5 feet) for Route 1 applies. The channel is lined on both sides with rocks and spoil areas. Exercise special care in the area between red daybeacons "4" and "6." This is another area in which the use of your GPS chartplotter will come in handy.

Close to Clewiston be aware that fishnets and traps are a way of life here and their small markers are sometimes difficult to see. Some of the fishermen in high-speed bass boats or skiffs also add to the obstacles.

Directly before reaching the Clewiston Lock the channel makes a hard 90-degree turn to the northwest. There are no nearby channel markers on this northwesterly stretch and a sign on the levee pointing to Moore Haven is difficult to read. The intersection can be confusing but don't go through the lock unless you wish to visit Clewiston.

Lake Okeechobee

The Clewiston Lock is not technically part of the OCWW and is not equipped with a VHF radio but if lake levels are not unusual the lock is left open. If the traffic light is green proceed through. If you wish passage and the lockmaster does not wave to you use two long and two short blasts of your horn or whistle.

Route 2: The Rim Route to Clewiston

If you are not pressed for time or if the lake crossing is questionable due to weather the Rim Route (10 miles longer) can be an interesting alternative if the water level allows it. While open to Lake Okeechobee for about 15 miles the exposure is from west through north. Unless winds are from this quadrant (and in the small craft advisory category) this part of the passage should be pleasant.

NAVIGATION: Use NOAA Chart 11428.

CAUTION: Use the Rim Route (Route 2) at your own risk due to commonly present debris and low water depths (as low as 3 feet). Conditions can change rapidly, especially if tropical storms or hurricanes pass over Lake Okeechobee. Call the Army Corps of Engineers in Clewiston (863-983-8101) for the latest conditions.

From Mile 55 on to Clewiston (where it joins Route 1) and on to the Caloosahatchee Canal entrance the course stays between the mainland levees surrounding Lake Okeechobee and the regular and spoil islands lining the rim. Depths vary according to lake levels and wind conditions. The shallowest stretch has been observed in the easternmost 4 miles; depths increase significantly beyond that.

The local harbor at Pahokee (OCWW Mile 50.6) can be reached from red entrance daybeacon "2," which is opposite red channel daybeacon "62." If the wind is strong from the northwest or north waves from Lake Okeechobee will be reflected back from the breakwater and, when combined with the incoming waves, can result in an uncomfortable or even dangerous situation for boats in the channel as they pass the breakwater.

Near red daybeacon "78" (Mile 54) there is a charted, straight, well-marked channel that leads out through the shallows bordering the Rim Route to the deeper lake water (charted at 7 feet). The section of the OCWW from Mile 55 to Mile 75.7 has always been one of the more interesting stretches on the trip. However, hyacinths and water lettuce grow in profusion, sometimes even clogging the channel. If you must pass through them do it slowly. Should you clog your prop and rudder, back down and then push ahead.

Chapter 6: Side Trip on the Okeechobee Waterway

The **Belle Glade Dike (CR 717) Bridge** has only an 11-foot closed vertical clearance at normal lake levels. The fixed span just west of the swing span has a vertical clearance of 13 feet, which may be an advantage if you only require 12 feet of clearance. This bridge is hand-operated and it takes awhile for the operator to get in place to open the span so be sure to call ahead on VHF Channel 09 and give the operator an estimate as to the time of your arrival. Hours are from 7:00 a.m. to 6:00 p.m. Monday through Thursday, and from 7:00 a.m. to 7:00 p.m. Friday through Sunday (fishing days). The bridge remains closed at night. It also need not open if winds are in excess of 20 mph.

From Belle Glade the OCWW first heads south for several miles then angles northwest past such communities as Bean City and Lake Harbor. A road parallels the OCWW most of the way but you will not see it since it is behind the ubiquitous levee.

Hurricane Gate 3 at about Mile 67 (behind Ritta Island) is usually closed. Continue to follow the markers along the way. At red daybeacon "94" (Mile 70), the channel is narrow and straightforward. As you approach Clewiston be alert for small fishing boats anchored off and in the channel.

Anchorage: Marinas along this route are for small boats only. Some anchoring room is west of the **Torry Island Swing Bridge** (with 8-foot depths). This Torry Island anchorage is good if you want an early start, but note that early risers also include many small boat fishermen who may not show concern for anchored craft.

> NOTE: See navigation alert above about low-hanging (35-feet above the water) fiber optic cable at the Route 2 Bridge at Torry Island.

A better bet is to anchor in South Bay Basin at Mile 63. To reach it leave the OWW just west of the launch ramp and head north into the kidney-shaped basin. Here you will find over 8 feet at the entrance and 10 to 25 feet in the basin. Islands, both natural and spoil, offer protection from winds off the lake along this route, although if the water level is high, it can get a bit unpleasant. There is room for several boats (plus lots of birds, alligators and bugs). From here you can easily dinghy back to the boat ramp. Torry Island Town Dock is an 8-foot floating dock but it is posted as no overnight dockage.

Clewiston

Route 1 (open water route) joins Route 2 (rim route) at Clewiston, a point about halfway between Stuart and Fort Myers. Clewiston bills itself as the "Sweetest Town in America" due to its role in sugarcane production. Mileage from this point on is based on the lesser "cross lake" figure of Mile 65. The rim mileage of 75.7 stops here.

NAVIGATION: Use NOAA Chart 11428. On an eastbound trip from Clewiston heading toward Indiantown the Port Mayaca entrance markers may be hard to pick out. Power company stacks are clearly visible at the port from many miles out and a heading directly toward them will bring you almost directly to the channel entrance.

A hurricane gate and the 50 feet wide by 60 feet long **Clewiston Lock** allows access through the levee into Clewiston Harbor. This lock is not equipped with a VHF radio so contact with the lockmaster must be made visually (waving is the method of choice) or by whistle signals–two long and two short. The schedule calls for an open lock if the water level is low and the lock is usually open for direct passage. Otherwise, the hours are 7:00 a.m. to 5:00 p.m. Check the traffic light to see if it is green or red.

After entering the lock grab the lines hanging from the top of the chamber and hold on. Lock personnel may help with the lines but the change in water level as the lock opens and closes usually will not result in excessive turbulence.

Dockage: Roland and Mary Ann Martins Marina & Resort at Clewiston is a popular spot for transients and boat clubs (particularly bass fishing groups) to spend a weekend or more. Reservations are a must. The channel is very narrow and can be difficult to maneuver but the helpful staff will be glad to give you a hand. This is a full service marina offering boat rentals, fishing guides, airboat tours, an RV park and a swimming pool. There are also two on-site eateries (The Galley and Scotty's Tiki Bar).

Several Clewiston dolphins on the channel's edge northwest of Clewiston can be used for making fast. The main street of this town is only 3 blocks away and includes a small grocery store, a hardware store, an auto parts store and a pharmacy.

America's Waterway Guide Since 1947 — Chapter 6

Lake Okeechobee, FL

CLEWISTON		Largest Vessel	VHF	Total Slips	Approach/Dockside Depth	Floating Docks	Gas/Diesel	Repairs/Haulout	Min/Max Amps	Pump-Out Station
1. Roland and Mary Ann Martins Marina & Resort WiFi MM 75.6	(800) 473-6766	130	16	15	8.0 / 7.0	F	GD	R	30 / 50	
MOORE HAVEN AREA										
2. Moore Haven City Docks MM 78.4	(863) 946-0711	300			6.0 / 6.0				30 / 50	
3. River House Marina WiFi MM 78.5	(863) 946-0466	125		7	5.0 / 5.0				20 / 100	

WiFi Wireless Internet Access
Visit www.waterwayguide.com for current rates, fuel prices, website addresses and other up-to-the-minute information. (Information in the table is provided by the facilities.)

Scan here for more details:

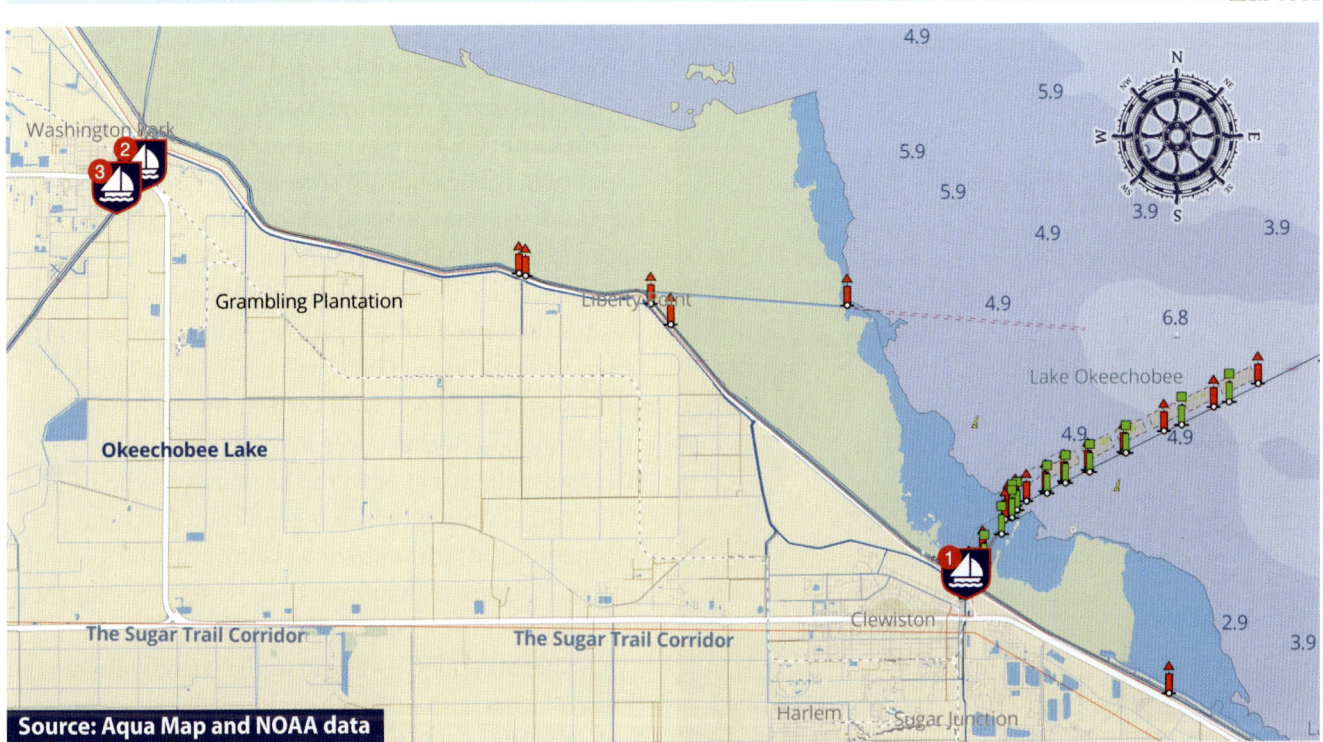

Source: Aqua Map and NOAA data

Moore Haven–OCWW Mile 78

From Clewiston to Moore Haven and the entrance to the Caloosahatchee Canal the OCWW is fairly wide and deep. Fast boats frequent this route and small-boat fishermen anchor or drift fish in the cuts and channel. Several facilities for small fishing boats are along the way and, at times, fishing activity is intense. If it is a sunny day, have your camera ready because this canal is probably one of the best places to see alligators sunning themselves on shore.

Be aware that strong southern winds can significantly lower water depths between Clewiston and Moore Haven. This is more severe during droughts. As noted previously hyacinths and water lettuce can clog the channel as well as your prop and rudder here.

NAVIGATION: Use NOAA Chart 11428. After transiting the 13-mile Caloosahatchee Canal the entrance to the **Moore Haven Lock** at Mile 78 is directly to port and easy to see and negotiate. Because it is in a protected canal it is even easier to pass through than the St. Lucie Lock with equally capable locktenders. If Hurricane Gate 1 is in use during discharge of high water turbulence on the "down" side of the lock can be considerable.

Stay well back from Moore Haven Lock until the green light comes on and enter carefully. Remember that you are now being lowered with the water level so do not tie off your bow or stern lines and be prepared for some surge as you drop. Wait for the gates to open completely before releasing the lines and then proceed slowly out of the lock. The lock operates from 7:00 a.m. to 5:00 p.m. with a last lock opening at 4:30 p.m. Call ahead to find

SOUTHERN EDITION

Chapter 6 — Side Trip on the Okeechobee Waterway

Did You Know?

Manatees only breathe through their nostrils since while they are underwater their mouths are occupied with eating! A manatee's lungs are two-thirds the length of its body. Manatees take up residence primarily in Florida's coastal waters during winter but some individuals migrate as far north as the Carolinas or as far west as Louisiana in summer. Manatees have swum as far north as Cape Cod, MA, in recent years.

out on which side to place fenders (863-946-0414). Information about conditions farther on can also be obtained from the lockmaster.

Immediately beyond the lock are two bridges. The first is the **Seaboard System Railroad Bridge** at Mile 78.3, which has 5-foot closed vertical clearance but is usually open. If closed it will open on signal except from 10:00 p.m. to 6:00 a.m., when it need not open. Signal before you leave the lock. The bridge is hand-operated and the delay can be considerable. Use the eastern draw. The **Moore Haven (US 27) Bridges** have a fixed vertical clearance charted at 55 feet but there are no clearance gauges or fendering system.

Dockage: On the west side of the Caloosahatchee Canal (where the OCWW runs nearly north to south) the Moore Haven City Docks provide alongside dockage for 3 or 4 (depending on size) visiting yachts. Normally space is available but during peak travel seasons the early bird scores. Use minimum space for tie-up so that the next boat will have room. This is a well-constructed dock with vertical rubber bumpers on the pilings. Dockage fees may be paid at City Hall across the street or to the dockmaster who calls in the early evening (and is a good source of local information). Restrooms/showers are available behind City Hall during regular operating hours. You can get a key from the dockmaster.

Just beyond the City Docks is the friendly River House Marina with 400 feet of alongside transient dockage. Dockage fees are collected on the "honor system" (with an envelope dropbox). At the far edge of these docks there is an overhead telephone or television cable (not a power line) crossing. Clearance seems quite adequate but specific height is not charted or known.

Anchorage: If you arrive at the east side of the Moore Haven Lock late in the day and would prefer not to lock through until morning you can proceed past the turn into the lock and anchor in the canal northwest of the lock or you can make fast for the night between the mooring dolphins located on the lake side of the OCWW just before the canal turns into the lock. Be sure to show an anchor light and also be aware of the limited swing room.

America's Waterway Guide Since 1947 — Chapter 6

Caloosahatchee Canal & River, FL

LA BELLE AREA		Largest Vessel	VHF	Total Slips	Approach/Dockside Depth	Floating Docks	Gas/Diesel	Repairs/Haulout	Min/Max Amps	Pump-Out Station
1. The Glades Marina WiFi MM 89.0	(863) 673-5653	90		23	8.0 / 8.0	F			30 / 50	P
2. River Forest Yachting Center - LaBelle WiFi MM 92.8	(863) 612-0003	150	6	20	9.0 / 8.0	F		RH	30 / 100	
3. Port LaBelle Marina WiFi 100.0	(863) 675-2261	80	16	100	5.0 /	F	GD			P
4. LaBelle City Dock 102.6	(863) 673-1191	60	16	8	6.0 / 6.0				30 / 50	

WiFi Wireless Internet Access
Visit www.waterwayguide.com for current rates, fuel prices, website addresses and other up-to-the-minute information. (Information in the table is provided by the facilities.)

Scan here for more details:

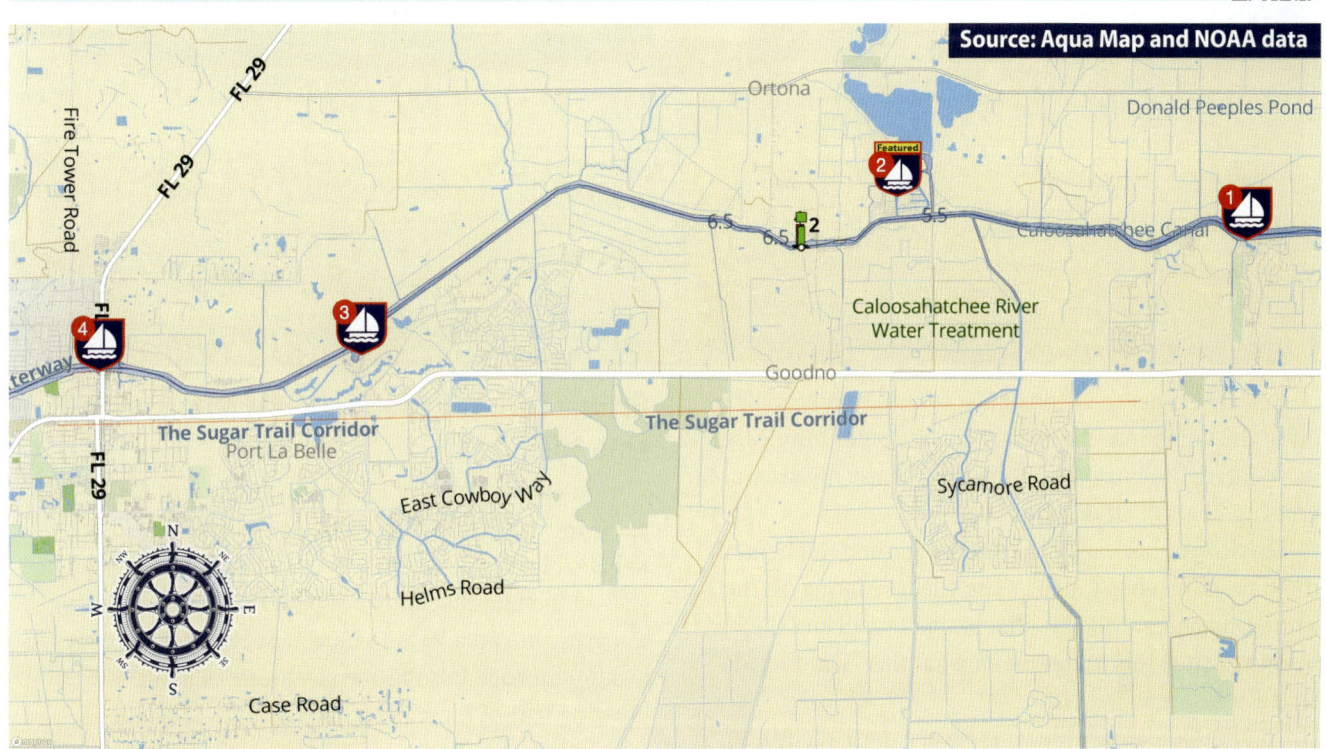

Source: Aqua Map and NOAA data

CALOOSAHATCHEE CANAL & RIVER

CAUTION: Hurricane Ian caused widespread damage across southwest Florida after making landfall on Cayo Costa Island as a Category 4 hurricane in September 2022. All of the communities in this section were affected in major ways and rebuilding will be a long process. Call ahead for status prior to arrival.

To Ortona Lock–OCWW Mile 93.5

Early morning fog and mist sometime curtail an early departure but normally the Caloosahatchee Canal is straightforward, wide and deep, with no surprises. At about Mile 82.5 the channel passes through shallow Lake Hicpochee where again you may encounter small fishing boats anchored along the shore. Watch your wake as a matter of both prudence and courtesy.

NAVIGATION: Use NOAA Chart 11428. Like the Moore Haven Lock, the smooth concrete walls of the

Ortona Lock are a vast improvement over timbered sides that invariably catch fenders and rub rails. Tie-up dolphins are located outside both ends of the lock; boats normally make fast to the south wall. The lock operates the same as the others. Be prepared for some surge as the water is let out. The change in level varies but 8 to 10 feet is normal depending on lake level. The lock operates from 7:00 a.m. to 5:00 p.m. with a last lock opening at 4:30 p.m. (863-675-0616). Call ahead to find out on which side to place fenders.

SOUTHERN EDITION   263

Chapter 6: Side Trip on the Okeechobee Waterway

Ortona Lock

Before you get to Ortona Lock several small canals lead off to the north into the Turkey Creek community. Most of its residents are boaters and their docks usually are full of cruising boats of all descriptions.

Dockage: Just past Lake Hicpochee and the bend in the Caloosahatchee Canal is The Glades Marina on the southern bank at Mile 89. The basin is small and dockage is limited (just four transient slips) at this "Old Florida" style RV resort.

At approximately Mile 93 is River Forest Yachting Center–LaBelle, which is owned by the same people who own the River Forest Yachting Center–Stuart. This facility is very similar to the one on the eastern side of the lake except it is twice as large (at over 100,000 square feet). The marina has been constructed to withstand hurricane winds. Transients are welcome but be sure to call in advance for dockage availability.

Anchorage: At Mile 92.5 just before Turkey Creek there is a narrow canal that leads into Lollipop Lake. It is small but if you go all the way into the lake you will find ample room for anchoring in very protected water. The water in the canal is 8 to 9 feet and much deeper (30-plus feet) once inside the basin. This is a nice, out-of-the-way spot to spend an evening on the hook. Chirping birds, mooing cows and the occasional alligator will keep you company.

Ortona Lock to LaBelle–OCWW Mile 93.5 to Mile 103

The quiet river town of LaBelle dates back to the early 1800s. The Swamp Cabbage Festival is held in LaBelle during the last full weekend in February. The festival includes live music, a parade, a rodeo, a fishing tournament and a Swamp Queen & Princess Pageant. Swamp cabbage (also known as hearts of palm) is the growing part of the sable palm and joins alligator as a local delicacy.

LaBelle is also known as the "Honey Capital." The Harold P. Curtis Honey Company (863-675-2187) is located directly across from the LaBelle Heritage Museum (863-674-0034) on the south side of the bridge. The company maintains about 1,000 beehives and will permit you to sample different types of honey (including Orange Blossom, Palmetto, Wildflower, Seagrape, and Mangrove) in the store, which also carries honey candy and candles.

NAVIGATION: Use NOAA Chart 11428. The **LaBelle (SR 29) Bridge** at Mile 103.0 with 28-foot closed vertical clearance opens on signal except from 7:00 a.m. to 9:00 a.m. and 4:00 p.m. to 6:00 p.m., Monday through Friday (except federal holidays), when the bridge need not open. The bridge will open on signal between 10:00 p.m. and 6:00 a.m. if at least a 3-hour notice is given. Call 866-335-9696 for an opening during these hours.

Dockage: At Mile 100 an entry channel leads off to the south into the Port LaBelle Marina with limited transient slips to 80 feet (no power/electrical). Note there is a 30-foot minimum applied to all reservations. Just to the east there is another cove (sometimes called Tranquility Cove) that is an extension of the marina.

Just beyond the LaBelle Bridge on the south side, LaBelle City Dock has dockage (no longer free) with electric and water. There is a 3-day limit and room for just 8 boats. These docks are usually full on the weekends and are on a first-come, first-served basis. They have mooring posts making it more difficult to off-board for smaller boats. Expect bridge noise. Provisioning needs are within walking distance.

The municipal Bob Mason Waterfront Park is on the north side of the canal and offers free dockage alongside a 50-foot aluminum dock with 7-foot MLW approach and dockside depths. Fender carefully to avoid errant shards of metal. There are no amenities or services.

Anchorage: An easy anchorage is just outside the channel at LaBelle in thick, black mud in 20 feet of water. The channel is wide with a slight downstream current. Some small boat traffic from adjacent ramp. We have received reports of citations being issued to anchored vessels that have encroached on the channel. Keep this in mind when anchoring.

To Franklin Lock–OCWW Mile 103 to Mile 121.4

These are the scenic headwaters of the Caloosahatchee River, once a major transportation artery for the Calusa Indians and other early settlers to Fort Myers. Today powerboats and sailboats traverse the 67-mile-long river, which is an important link the OCWW. The Caloosahatchee River and its meandering tributaries are bordered by lush, towering ferns, stately oaks dripping with moss and verdant vegetation along every shore.

NAVIGATION: Use NOAA Chart 11428. Where the Caloosahatchee River once wandered is now a series of straight sections punctuated by gentle turns and numerous intriguing oxbows and streams. The water runs quite deep to the banks. Swinging room on the river, even at its widest points, is limited and anchoring is not recommended unless you can keep your vessel from swinging into the channel.

Some of the oxbows are deep enough if you feel adventurous but snags or shoals and even low-hanging power cables are prevalent. At about Mile 106.6, well out from the northern bank, red daybeacon "2" marks a shoal.

Two bridges cross this section of the Caloosahatchee River. **Fort Denaud Bridge** at Mile 108.2 has a 9-foot closed vertical clearance. The bridge opens on request and arrows indicate which side of the draw to use. It is closed from 10:00 p.m. until 6:00 a.m. and requires a 3-hour notice to open during those hours (call 866-335-9696).

The **Alva Drawbridge** at Mile 116 has a 23-foot charted closed vertical clearance and likewise opens on signal except from 10:00 p.m. until 6:00 a.m. when a 3-hour notice is required. Use VHF Channel 09 or call 866-335-9696.

The final lock on the Okeechobee Waterway is at Olga. The **W.P. Franklin Lock** normally operates on request from 7:00 a.m. to 5:00 p.m. daily. (Last lockage at 4:30 p.m.) Enter on the green light and remember not to tie off your lines tightly as the level will drop about 3 feet. Wait until the lock is fully open before casting off and exit slowly. Sometimes eastbound boats are waiting nearby to enter. Please note that low water levels in Lake Okeechobee may result in schedule changes at the lock. Be sure to call in advance to check schedules (239-694-5451 or VHF Channel 13).

Dockage: Immediately east of the W.P. Franklin Lock on the north shore at Mile 121.4 is the Army Corps of Engineers marina (W.P. Franklin Campground-Boat-In Docks), which is closed indefinitely while rebuilding from hurricane damage.

Anchorage: You can drop the hook in Hickey Creek at Mile 119.5 behind an unnamed island, where you will find all-around protection from wakes in 7 feet MLW. Another protected anchorage is just west of the Franklin Lock next to the Army Corps of Engineers campground where there is enough room for a couple of small boats to anchor.

Fort Myers to Cape Coral–OCWW Mile 121.4 to Mile 142

While Fort Myers is not actually the western end of the OCWW, most cruisers consider it to be. Like most of Florida the city boasts a growing population, especially if you include the Cape Coral area, which is across the river on the north shore.

Chapter 6: Side Trip on the Okeechobee Waterway

Caloosahatchee River, FL

FORT MYERS AREA		Largest Vessel	VHF	Total Slips	Approach/Dockside Depth	Floating Docks	Gas/Diesel	Repairs/Haulout	Min/Max Amps	Pump-Out Station
1. W.P. Franklin Campground-Boat-In Docks MM 122.0	(239) 694-8770	40		8	/				30 / 50	
2. C-10 Caloosa Marina WiFi 124.2	(239) 694-2708	200	16	15	23.0 / 8.0		GD		30 / 50	
3. Sweetwater Landing Marina WiFi MM 126.0	(239) 694-3850	200	16	65	9.0 / 5.0		G	R	30 / 50	P

WiFi Wireless Internet Access
Visit www.waterwayguide.com for current rates, fuel prices, website addresses and other up-to-the-minute information. (Information in the table is provided by the facilities.)

Scan here for more details:

NAVIGATION: Use NOAA Charts 11428 and 11427.

> ⚠️ **CAUTION:** Although the Caloosahatchee River is a navigable river coming in from the Gulf of Mexico, it is not marked with the conventional "red-right-returning" system with numbers increasing as one proceeds inland. The daybeacons, lights and such are a continuing part of the OCWW system; therefore, numbers increase as you cruise westward and the "reds" are on your right side even though you are going downriver. This can be confusing if you do not understand the system.

The Caloosahatchee River has many aids to navigation beginning with red daybeacon "2" just downriver from the W.P. Franklin Lock. From here to Fort Myers there are several bridges to consider. The first is **Wilson Pigott Drawbridge** at Mile 126.3 with a 27-foot closed vertical clearance. The bridge opens on signal except between 10:00 p.m. and 6:00 a.m., when it requires at least a 3-hour notice to open.

> NOTE: At Mile 127.5, the scale of Chart 11428 changes to 1:40,000 for its final section, an inset marked "Fort Myers Extension."

The **I-75 Bridges** cross the OCWW at Mile 128.9 with a 55-foot fixed vertical clearance. The **SCL Railroad Bridge** at Mile 129.9 at Beautiful Island is normally open unless a train is due. The closed vertical clearance is only 5 feet so signal or call on VHF Channel 9 for an opening and then hold well off until the train has passed and the bridge is fully opened. (Note that the overhang is 55 feet when the bridge is open.)

Beautiful Island lives up to its name but do not get too close due to depth concerns. There are some areas, particularly on the south side, where you can leave the channel but do so very cautiously after examining your chart.

There are two high-level bridges in Fort Myers–the **Edison Bridges** at Mile 134.6 in North Fort Myers and the **US 41/Caloosahatchee River Bridge** at Mile 135. These bridges have at least 55-foot fixed vertical clearance.

At Mile 138.6 is the **Midpoint Memorial Bridge** followed by the **Cape Coral Bridge** at Mile 142. Both are charted at 55 feet. Note that water levels in the lake will affect bridge heights.

Frequent groundings occur in the Caloosahatchee River west of Cape Coral near Mile 143. Be sure to use front and rear ranges.

CAUTION: Due to the widespread damage inflicted by Hurricane Ian, do not plan to dock here without calling ahead for status. Every marina was affected in some way and many were destroyed. You are welcome to anchor in the waters clear of any navigable channel waterway but be aware of underwater obstructions. Refer to Waterway Explorer (www.waterwayguide.com) for the latest updates.

Dockage: Fort Myers area dockage begins west of the W.P. Franklin Lock (Mile 121.4). C-10 Caloosa Marina (formerly Calusa Jacks Marina) offers side tie only (no slips). Sweetwater Landing Marina is a dry-service storage facility that has 10 reserved transient slips. Call ahead for slip availability. Manatee tours and sunset cruises leave from here.

Owl Creek Boat Works at Mile 125.5 offers a full range of repair and maintenance services including fine yacht refinishing. If you need to re-step a mast, this is a good time to do so although this can also be done in Fort Myers.

Before the Edison Bridges on the north bank of the river is Old Bridge Marina, which is primarily a liveaboard marina with few amenities. Call ahead for approach directions and slip availability.

On the north bank at Mile 135 beside flashing red "52" look for the flashing green "1" and red daybeacon "2" of the well-marked channel to Hancock Creek, where you will find 5- to 7-foot MLW depths. Be aware of shoaling in the section of the channel that parallels the shore between green daybeacons "17" and "21" where the channel carries only 4 to 4.5 feet MLW with a soft mud bottom. Marinatown Yacht Harbour is around the first bend above green daybeacon "25." They also cater to liveaboards but may have some transient space. Call in advance. There are restaurants on site as well as kayak and paddleboard rentals.

City of Fort Myers Yacht Basin is situated on the south shore of the Caloosahatchee River between the westernmost span of the Edison Bridges and the US 41/Caloosahatchee River Bridge. This facility is within walking distance of a large grocery store, a library, multiple restaurants and other amenities. The full-service marina can accommodate vessels both large and small but reserve your slip ahead to make sure space is available when you arrive.

OWL CREEK
BOAT WORKS & STORAGE INC.
Southwest Florida's Finest Yacht Refinishing

- 3 Lifts for Hauling up to 150 Tons
- Awlgrip & Imron Refinishing - 6000 sq. ft. Spray Booth
- Custom Fiberglass fabrications
- Custom Woodworking, Alterations and Modifications. Specializing in older wood yacht hulls
- Bottom Painting, Gelcoat & Blister repair
- Complete Gas & Diesel Engine Sales & Service
- B&L Marine Electronics - Complete Sales & Service

BEST BOTTOM PAINT PRICING!

SINCE 1953
WWW.OWLCREEKBOATWORKS.COM
Ft. Myers, FL
239-543-2100
ASK ABOUT OUR SPECIAL DOCKAGE & STORAGE RATES

Chapter 6: Side Trip on the Okeechobee Waterway

Caloosahatchee River, FL

FORT MYERS AREA		Largest Vessel	VHF	Total Slips	Approach/Dockside Depth	Floating Docks	Gas/Diesel	Repairs/Haulout	Min/Max Amps	Pump-Out Station
1. Old Bridge Marina WiFi MM 134.0	(239) 995-2155	56	16	53	6.0 / 4.5	F			30 / 50	P
2. Marinatown Yacht Harbour WiFi MM 135.0	(239) 997-7711	68		135	6.0 / 5.0			R	30 / 100	P
3. City of Fort Myers Yacht Basin WiFi MM 134.5	(239) 321-7080	300	16	241	10.0 / 7.0		GD		30 / 100	P
4. Legacy Harbour Marina WiFi MM 135.5	(239) 461-0775	120	16	131	7.0 / 7.0	F			30 / 50	P
5. The Marina at Edison Ford WiFi MM 136.5	(239) 895-7703	80	16	45	7.0 / 5.0				30 / 50	P

WiFi Wireless Internet Access
Visit www.waterwayguide.com for current rates, fuel prices, website addresses and other up-to-the-minute information.
(Information in the table is provided by the facilities.)

Scan here for more details:

Source: Aqua Map and NOAA data

The entrance to Legacy Harbour Marina is on the east side of the marina. Look for the piling with a white marina flag by the OCWW. Turn at that piling leaving it to starboard and head for the south shore. You will be headed toward a restaurant with a green roof (Joe's Crab Shack). Make a right into the marina basin. Legacy Harbour Marina has concrete floating docks that can accommodate vessels up to 120 feet with resort-style amenities. One of the largest floating breakwaters in the Gulf of Mexico protects the marina from the wakes of the river traffic. Grocery, shops and restaurants are within walking distance in the Historic Downtown River District.

The Marina at Edison Ford has slips to 80 feet and an on-site restaurant (Pinchers).

Anchorage: Because the Caloosahatchee River is more than 1 mile wide it can get rough in nasty weather so anchoring, although possible, could be unpleasant. To reach the oxbow at OWW Mile 124.3, leave the waterway west of the oxbow and head southeast into the loop. Anchor in 5 feet.

Across from flashing green "13" at Mile 128 is the last good anchorage before Fort Myers. Locally known as Power Plant Slough, the western channel is reached by entering southwest of the manatee sign about halfway between the sign and shore. Continuing in the deepest water (at least 8 feet MLW) is about 100 feet off the western shore. The eastern channel of the slough is narrower, shallow and more difficult to follow. Manatees love it here too so be mindful that you will likely be sharing this space.

Turn north off the waterway at red daybeacon "52" into the marked channel leading to condominiums at North Ft. Myers. Follow the marked channel to red daybeacon "26" then turn to port into Hancock Creek. Proceed 100 yards and anchor in 7 to 8 feet of water.

Cape Coral Area

Southwest of Fort Myers the Caloosahatchee River continues somewhat circuitously for another 15 miles to San Carlos Bay (Mile 149). On the way it passes Cape Coral, the second largest city in Florida, which was once swampland known as Redfish Point.

Fort Myers

Chapter 6: Side Trip on the Okeechobee Waterway

Goin' Ashore: FORT MYERS, FL

Strolling through the downtown area of Fort Myers is a great way to spend an afternoon or evening. Art lovers are sure to find events of interest throughout the year, including an Art Walk held on the first Friday of each month all year long.

Farther afield is Six Mile Cypress Slough Preserve, which offers a boardwalk trail that winds through 3500 acres of wetlands and offers views of local wildlife, including alligators and birds. Or continue south to take in a game at JetBlue Park, the spring training home of the Boston Red Sox.

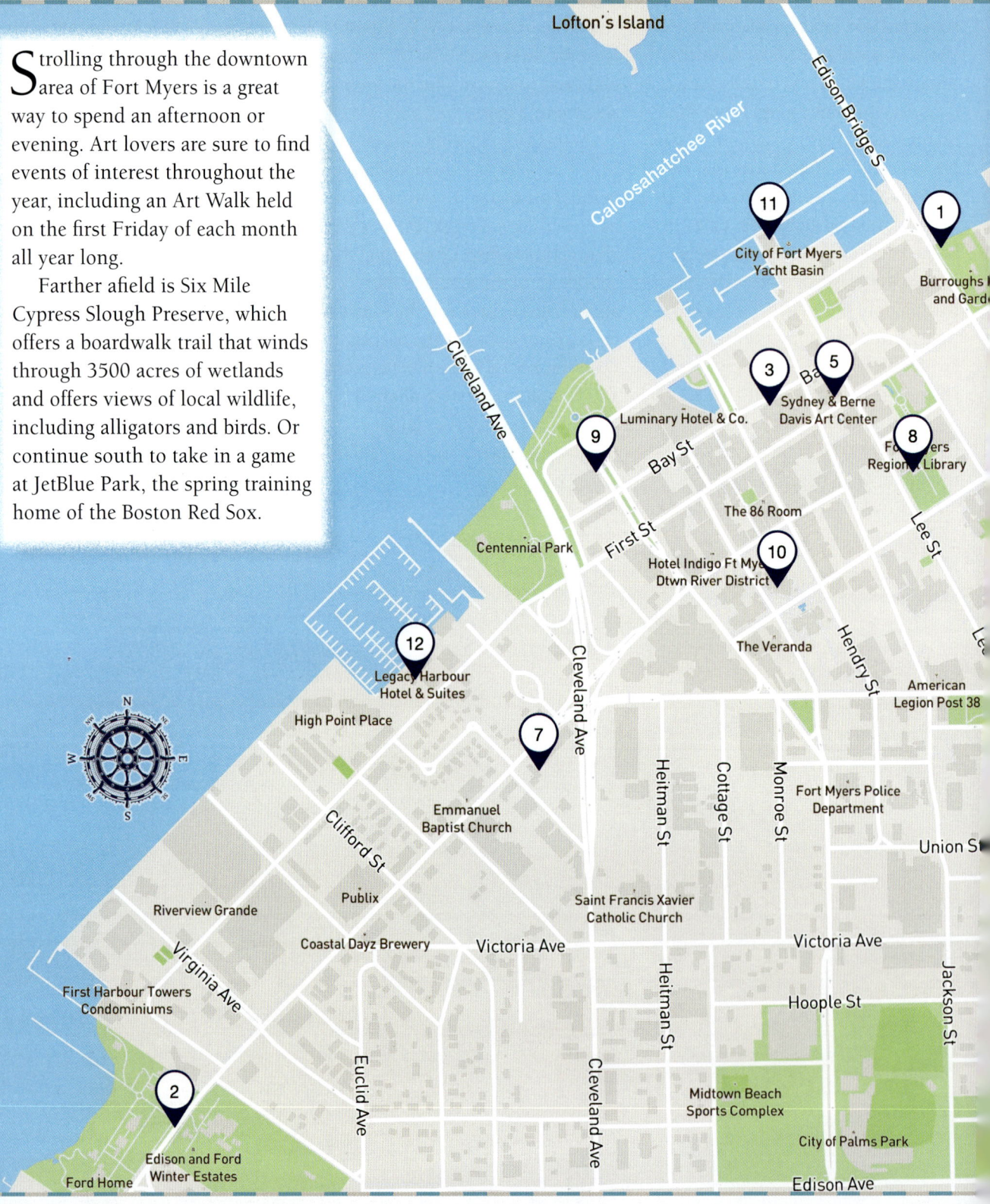

America's Waterway Guide Since 1947 — Chapter 6

ATTRACTIONS

1. **Burroughs Home & Gardens**
   This Georgian Revival Mansion (circa 1901) overlooks the Edison Bridge at 2505 First St. and is open for guided tours. Reservations required (239-337-9505).

2. **Edison & Ford Winter Estates**
   These side-by-side estates have been restored to their original grandeur and are open to the public. Edison's 14-acre riverfront estate is lined for 15 miles with 2,000 royal palms (2350 McGregor Blvd., 239-334-7419).

3. **Florida Repertory Theater**
   Storied 1917 venue for plays, musicals and more produced by a regional professional theater company on the waterfront at 2268 Bay St. (239-332-4488).

4. **IMAG History & Science Center**
   Interactive science museum featuring over 60 hands-on exhibits on a variety of topics from space exploration to physics, including a hurricane simulator (2000 Cranford Ave., 239-243-0043).

5. **Sidney & Berne Davis Art Center**
   Art center housed in Neoclassic Revival architecture at 2301 First St. (239-333-1933).

6. **The Shops at the Butterfly Estates**
   Over 3600-square-foot lass butterfly conservatory that is home to hundreds of colorful butterflies, as well as a botanical garden and gift shop at 1815 Fowler St. (239-690-2359).

SERVICES

7. **Edison Park Animal Hospital**
   2035 McGregor Blvd. (239-689-3525)

8. **Fort Myers Regional Library**
   2450 First St. (239-533-4600)

9. **Fort Myers Post Office**
   1350 Monroe St. (239-332-3696)

10. **Lee County Visitor & Convention Bureau**
    2201 Second St. (239-338-3500)

MARINAS

11. **City of Fort Myers Yacht Basin**
    1300 Lee St. (239-321-7080)

12. **Legacy Harbour Marina**
    2044 West 1st St. (239-461-0775)

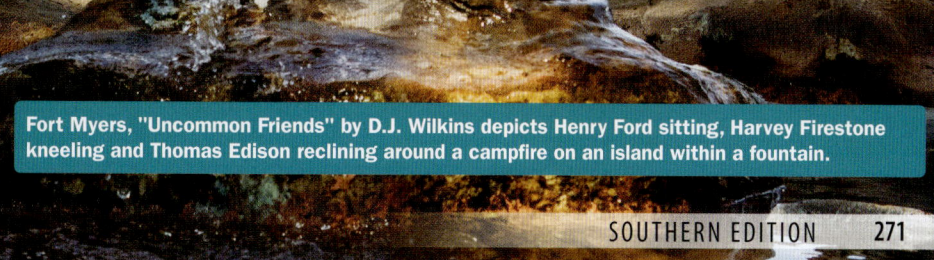
Fort Myers, "Uncommon Friends" by D.J. Wilkins depicts Henry Ford sitting, Harvey Firestone kneeling and Thomas Edison reclining around a campfire on an island within a fountain.

SOUTHERN EDITION

Chapter 6: Side Trip on the Okeechobee Waterway

Caloosahatchee River, FL

CAPE CORAL AREA		Largest Vessel	VHF	Total Slips	Approach/Dockside Depth	Floating Docks	Gas/Diesel	Repairs/Haulout	Min/Max Amps	Pump-Out Station
1. St. Charles Yacht Club WiFi MM 146.0	(239) 264-6008	78	16	65	5.0 / 5.0	F	GD		30 / 50	P
2. Tarpon Point Marina	(239) 549-4900	120	16	225	7.0 / 8.0	F	GD			P
SOUTH FORT MYERS										
3. Safe Harbor Cape Harbour WiFi MM 147.0	(239) 945-4330	60	16	76	6.0 / 6.0		D	H	30 / 50	P

WiFi Wireless Internet Access
Visit www.waterwayguide.com for current rates, fuel prices, website addresses and other up-to-the-minute information.
(Information in the table is provided by the facilities.)

Scan here for more details:

Source: Aqua Map and NOAA data

Luxurious Resort Marina With Direct Gulf Access

Tarpon Point Marina is just a few miles from the Gulf of Mexico and some of the best cruising and fishing grounds in Florida. Our sheltered deepwater harbor accommodates vessels to 120 feet and is accented with luxurious resort amenities, fine dining, spas, and boutiques. Come for a day and you may just stay for a lifetime!

www.tarponpoint.com

239-549-4900

From your dock to your destination... take Waterway Guide with you

Subscribe today for the full package
(Guidebook of your choice, mobile app & online subscription)

Scan to shop now at www.waterwayguide.com

Chapter 6: Side Trip on the Okeechobee Waterway

Cape Coral is 114 square miles and its numerous canals total more mileage than those of Venice, Italy. This is a boating-oriented area and the traffic is reminiscent of downtown Fort Lauderdale.

Dockage: Continuing on the south shore, the 186-slip Gulf Harbour Marina is part of a yacht and country club community with resort amenities. All boaters are welcome. The marina can accommodate boats up to 100 feet. The Landings Marina to the north is strictly private.

East of flashing green "85" a marked channel (starting with green daybeacon "1") leads southward to St. Charles Yacht Club. This club is a member of the Florida Council of Yacht Clubs and recognizes reciprocity.

At red daybeacon "92" a channel leads behind Cattle Dock Point to the north, where markers guide you into the well-appointed Tarpon Point Marina, which is part of a gated community in Cape Coral. They can accommodate vessels to 120 feet and offer kayak and pontoon boat rentals as well as sight-seeing excursions. Reservations are a must.

Just past Tarpon Point signs will guide you to a small lock that provides access to Safe Harbor Cape Harbour. The marina offers transient dockage to 60 feet in a condominium setting. A laundry, pool and competitive fuel pricing make this a popular stop. Be sure to call well in advance as this marina is usually full.

Anchorage: At red daybeacon "84A" there is a well-marked channel off to starboard that will lead you into the well-protected Bimini Basin. You need to stay in this channel and make a 90-degree turn to port when you get to green daybeacon "25." Then keep the red markers on your port side (we know that this is different but it is very important) until you come to the canal that will lead you into the anchorage. This is a handy spot to get to a couple of supermarkets and West Marine plus a very large hardware store as well as a variety of other services. There is a dinghy dock at Four Freedom's Park but no overnight dockage. You must register your boat with the harbormaster (239-574-0809).

Glover Bight, just behind Cattle Dock Point at Mile 147, is another excellent, all-weather anchorage. You will find good protection from all points with 10 to 12 feet at MLW with good holding in mud.

Tarpon Point Marina will let you tie up at the restaurant dock for 2 hours and charges a mandatory landing fee for skiffs and dinghies that are used to ferry passengers from vessels that are not tenants of the marina. The landing fee is refundable with proof of purchase from the nearby Marina Village Shops.

■ NEXT STOP

Should you choose to continue your journey westward to the Gulf, our coverage continues in Chapter 12: "Sanibel Island to Sarasota Bay." Otherwise, we will return to the ICW traveling south in Chapter 7: "The Crossroads to Pompano Beach."

Cape Coral

Chapter 7: The Crossroads to Pompano Beach

Chapter 7

  Mile 988–Mile 1056

■ TO THE CROSSROADS

This journey begins at "The Crossroads," where the St. Lucie River intersects the ICW. All the waterways experience high-traffic here. Study your charts in advance and have a courseline planned before you pass through. Below St. Lucie Inlet the coastline becomes truly tropical with a profusion of palm trees and exotic flowers. Here the laid-back Treasure Coast gives way to the bustling Gold Coast with its burgeoning development and fewer anchorages than you might wish.

You will also notice an increase in population–both on and off the water–as well as an increase in boat and home size. Large estates with manicured lawns line the waterways in Hobe and Jupiter Sounds and they get more opulent in Palm Beach, where there are more "yachts" than "boats." The "water highway" widens at Lake Worth and continues past Boynton and Delray Beaches.

NO WAKE ZONE

No Wake Zones, Idle Speed Zones and various Speed Limit restrictions are in effect throughout the waterways included in this chapter. Exercise diligence in knowing the regulations by observing signs and other markers. Enforcement is always present. As always, be courteous to other vessels and avoid manatees and other marine life.

Manatee speed zones occur with increasing frequency south of the St. Lucie Inlet. From green daybeacon "13" (Mile 990) to green daybeacon "15" you will encounter a Manatee Zone for approximately 1 mile through a narrow cut. If you pay attention, you will see a lot of manatees swimming around. They may look like floating coconuts.

St. Lucie to Hobe Sound– ICW Mile 988 to Mile 995

NAVIGATION: Use NOAA Chart 11472 (inset) or NOAA Chart 11428 (inset).

> NOTE: Southbound ICW traffic should note that the marker numbering sequence resets here but stay consistent with the rest of the ICW and continue to keep red markers to starboard when heading south.

The 16-foot-high flashing red buoy "240" (ICW marker) at The Crossroads marks the beginning of the Okeechobee Waterway westward. Look for channel entry markers red daybeacon "2" and flashing green "3," located 0.25 mile south of flashing red "240" inside Rocky Point. Split these markers proceeding south. The course is approximately 160° magnetic from flashing red "240." You will find these markers past a white sign on the west side of the ICW reading, "DANGER–SHOAL." Favor the green side through to green daybeacon "5" when southbound as a series of dangerous shoals flank the east shore of Rocky Point.

When traversing Great Pocket south from Horseshoe Point watch for shoaling and use caution; it is quite shallow outside the marked channel. In particular watch for extreme shoaling at the west edge of the channel between red daybeacon "12" and flashing red "14." Leaving Great Pocket the ICW enters a cut just south of paired green daybeacon "13" and flashing red "14." (Note that long docks and piers are on both sides of Great Pocket and are not shown on the chart.) The cut ends at paired flashing green "15" and red daybeacon "16" and enters Peck Lake.

There is shoaling on the west (red) side at flashing red "16" to red daybeacon "18" to 5 feet MLW. Favor the green side of the channel for 7 feet MLW. Peck Lake has depths throughout of 6 to 12 feet MLW from the ICW channel to close to shore. Depths are extremely shallow outside the marked channel through most of the lake.

The ICW between Peck Lake and Hobe Sound is a pleasant run through a series of dredged channels and cuts. The ICW channel is sparsely marked on this stretch but fairly obvious. South from Peck Lake favor the west side of the channel for better water. Consistent with Martin County's bylaws, buildings are restricted to four stories here. While development is less imposing, there are a number of side channels so expect increased boat traffic.

Dockage: On the mainland side of Peck Lake near the south end is Loblolly Marina. Don't be scared off by the "Private" signs. Transient and long-term dockage is available in this gated golf course community in a very protected basin with the usual amenities. This quiet location is surrounded by lush mangroves and offers easy access to the beach on Jupiter Island. You can easily dinghy, kayak or paddle from the marina across Peck Lake to the Hobe Sound National Wildlife Refuge.

SOUTHERN EDITION 277

Chapter 7: The Crossroads to Pompano Beach

Hobe Sound, FL

PECK LAKE		Largest Vessel	VHF	Total Slips	Approach/Dockside Depth	Floating Docks	Gas/Diesel	Repairs/Haulout	Min/Max Amps	Pump-Out Station
1. Loblolly Marina WiFi MM 992.2	(772) 546-3136	110	16	77	7.0 / 7.0	F			30 / 100	

WiFi Wireless Internet Access
Visit www.waterwayguide.com for current rates, fuel prices, website addresses and other up-to-the-minute information.
(Information in the table is provided by the facilities.)

Scan here for more details:

Source: Aqua Map and NOAA data

Anchorage: Low dunes, uninhabited beaches and sparkling ocean waters beckon and dredging of Peck Lake and lake access has made anchoring less of a challenge than in the past. Deep water access into Peck Lake is found to the south of flashing green "19" at Mile 992.2. The anchorage is very close to the ICW channel and can be subject to large wakes. Take it slow and head toward the "Danger" sign marking shoaling to the south. You will find 6 to 12 feet MLW in a narrow strip with room for half a dozen boats or more. There is the possibility of debris on the bottom so exercise caution when choosing an anchoring spot and we recommend use of a trip-line.

Even though Peck Lake is well protected on all sides and a no wake zone you will still encounter wakes from some passing boats. The anchorage is often busy during the week and becomes even more crowded on weekends. Once anchored, a dinghy ride to shore brings you to within a short distance over the dunes to a beautiful, unspoiled ocean beach that is part of Hobe Sound National Wildlife Refuge.

Side Trip: St. Lucie Inlet Preserve State Park

A bit of natural wilderness is preserved just south of the inlet in the St. Lucie Inlet Preserve State Park and adjoining Hobe Sound National Wildlife Refuge (officially the Nathanial P. Reed National Wildlife Refuge). The two reserves combined run for 5 miles starting at the north tip of Jupiter Island from Mile 988.5 to Mile 993.5. The state park ends and the wilderness seashore begins at the south end of the cut between Great Pocket and Peck Lake. The reserves are known for their fine beaches, kayaking, trails and boardwalks.

The reserves can be accessed from a dock on Great Pocket or a beach on the east shore of the ICW in Peck Lake. An elevated boardwalk with restrooms and picnic pavilions at either end takes visitors from the Great Pocket docks at Mile 989.3 through mangrove forests and hammocks of live oaks, cabbage palms, paradise trees and wild limes to a neatly preserved Atlantic beach.

Location: situated at Loblolly, a distinguished private residential community on the west shore of Peck's Lake at Hobe Sound between Palm Beach and Stuart, Florida; forty minutes north of Palm Beach International Airport.

Convenience: close by Stuart offers complete marine services; the St. Lucie Inlet is only 3 bridgeless miles north for access in minutes to some of the world's greatest game fishing, cruising, and sailing waters.

New state of the art floating docks.

LOBLOLLY MARINA

Facilities: secure, safe, and able to accommodate craft up to 110 feet in length. Surge protected 30, 50 and 100 amp electrical service, and softened water. Restrooms, showers, wireless internet service, laundry facilities, and full yacht concierge services available. We also offer a private beach shuttle to the adjacent Hobe Sound National Wildlife Refuge and over 3 miles of dedicated bike paths. A limited number of slips are available to transients and on an annual or seasonal basis.

7407 S.E. Hill Terrace, Hobe Sound, Florida 33455•Telephone (772) 546-3136 • espoelstra@loblollyinfo.com
A Limited Number of Marina Memberships Are Available.
We monitor Channel 16 • ICW MM 992.2

A portion north of the crossover path is closed in the spring and early summer months to protect nesting Least Terns (*sterna antillarum*, the smallest of the American terns). South of this path the beach is available for walking and swimming. Note that dogs are allowed on the walkway but not on the beach. Also, when temperatures are above 60 degrees, with little or no wind, sand gnats (commonly called "no-see-ums") can be a problem.

Dockage: A floating dock and a long pier with slips for smaller boats are near the north end of the St. Lucie Inlet Preserve State Park, which is accessible only by boat. Watch for shoaling between the dock and the ICW channel. There is a lot of shallow water in this area. Come out of the channel right by the big dock sign that reads "St. Lucie Inlet Preserve Park" for the deepest water. On the way back out be sure to turn into the channel right away. If you venture too far west, you will find shoaling.

There is an unmarked, shallow channel (4-foot MLW depths) that is best accessed by dinghy. Don't anchor near the docks as they lie in a charted Pipeline Area. It's best to anchor in Peck Lake, farther south through the cut. Tie off carefully as powerboats often pass without slowing causing heavy wakes. A small fee is collected on the honor system for use of the park.

Hobe Sound to Jupiter Inlet–ICW Mile 995 to Mile 1004

The Native American Jove tribe (pronounced "Ho-bay") gave Hobe Sound its name. This highly exclusive area is sometimes compared with Palm Beach due to its grand mansions and manicured lawns along the eastern shore of the channel. The natural wilderness of Hobe Sound National Wildlife Refuge on the western shore at about Mile 997 provides a striking contrast with the sculptured lawns on the opposite shore.

NAVIGATION: Use NOAA Chart 11472. The **Hobe Sound (CR 708) Bridge** crosses the ICW at the northern end of Hobe Sound (Mile 995.9). The bridge has a closed vertical clearance of 21 feet at the center and opens on signal. For the most part both sides of the well-marked channel through Hobe Sound have good depths but it's best not to stray too far from the centerline as there are

Chapter 7 — The Crossroads to Pompano Beach

Jupiter Inlet Area, FL

JUPITER AREA (NORTH)		Largest Vessel	VHF	Total Slips	Approach/ Dockside Depth	Floating Docks	Gas/ Diesel	Repairs/ Haulout	Min/Max Amps	Pump-Out Station
1. Blowing Rocks Marina WiFi MM 1002.2	(561) 746-3312	70	16	60	6.0 / 5.0	F	GD	RH	30 / 50	P
2. JIB Yacht Club Marina WiFi MM 1004.2	(561) 746-4300	70	16	30	8.0 / 8.0		GD		30 / 50	P

WiFi Wireless Internet Access
Visit www.waterwayguide.com for current rates, fuel prices, website addresses and other up-to-the-minute information.
(Information in the table is provided by the facilities.)

Scan here for more details:

Source: Aqua Map and NOAA data

some dangerous shoals. In particular watch for bars that extend from the points jutting from the west shore. Give red markers a wide berth as most mark shoals at the edge of the channel and carefully watch depths near red daybeacons "40" and "44." A Slow-Speed/Minimum-Wake zone is in effect year-round for all vessels between red daybeacon "44" and green daybeacon "49."

The ICW leads into Jupiter Sound at Mile 1002, where the estates of Hobe Sound give way to only slightly more modest homes. Nearby spoil areas and shoals demand careful attention; stay in the channel! Jupiter Inlet at Mile 1004 marks the confluence of Jupiter Sound to the north, Lake Worth Creek to the south and the Loxahatchee River to the west. The inlet is known for its red brick lighthouse and aquamarine-colored waters.

Jupiter Inlet fights a constant battle with shifting sand. Despite frequent dredging, the inlet is cited by the Coast Guard as "not navigable without current local knowledge." The inlet channel is unsafe for all but small boats with local knowledge and very shallow draft. A short jetty protects the inlet entrance to the north and a steel barricade extends halfway into the inlet from the south bank. The mouth of the inlet has strong currents, eddies, turbulence and breaking seas over sandbars that extend from the south side of the inlet offshore towards the northeast. The average tidal range is 2.5 feet.

Shoals also flank the east edge of the channel south from green daybeacon "57" to the **Jupiter Island (CR 707) Bridge** at Mile 1004.1. The bridge has a 25-foot closed vertical clearance and opens on signal. If your vessel is lightly powered, mind the swift current here while waiting for the bridge. Contact the bridgetender prior to your arrival and allow for the set of the current passing through.

Dockage: At Mile 1002 family-owned Blowing Rocks Marina has wet slips and dry storage for boats to 70 feet with limited space (2 slips) for transients. The open-air Tiki 52 restaurant and bar has a Caribbean atmosphere and a tasty menu. The JIB Yacht Club Marina just south of the Jupiter Island Bridge on the east side of the ICW welcomes transients to 70 feet. The facility has 24/7 security and controlled access including private beach access. Call ahead for slip availability.

Anchorage: Because there is a 25-mph speed limit in the Hobe Sound channel almost all anchorages here are susceptible to annoying boat wakes. There are numerous anchorages with 8 to 9 feet MLW west of the ICW channel between red daybeacon "38" and green daybeacon "49." Shore access to the wildlife refuge is easy at several sandy beaches and the sunrises are outstanding.

A favorite spot is the large lobe of deep water north of Mile 999 on the west side of the channel between red Hobe Sound daybeacons "38" and "40" and others north or south of red daybeacon "44," where the speed restrictions apply. Be careful here as shoaling extends from shore to red daybeacon "44." Mind your depth as you leave the channel. Passing vessels and water skiers may throw some wake your way in the daytime but nights are generally peaceful. Do not be surprised by a routine boarding from local marine police and be sure to show an anchor light.

A fair anchorage is by green daybeacon "49." This anchorage is in front of large homes in an expensive Jupiter golf community with docks and quite a few large motor yachts. There's room for three boats in 10 to 12 feet MLW. Anchor as far north as possible.

Hell Gate Cove at Mile 1002.3 is a nice anchorage for a quick night. ICW wake are an issue until sunset. Expect good holding in 6 feet MLW.

Lake Worth Creek–ICW Mile 1004 to Mile 1012

NAVIGATION: Use NOAA Chart 11472. The ICW intersects the Loxahatchee River at Mile 1004.5. The Jupiter Inlet runs to the east and the ICW continues to the west. The ICW route south begins a sharp reverse S-curve, first to starboard (west) up the Loxahatchee River passing under the **U.S. 1 (Jupiter) Bridge** at Mile 1004.8, then to port (south) out of the Loxahatchee River and into Lake Worth Creek. The bridge has 26-foot closed vertical clearance and opens on signal. This is a high-traffic area and obstructions come up quickly so slow down! Large vessels may want to issue a Sécurité call on VHF Channels 09 and 16. Watch currents through the entire S-curve and make the blind turn into Lake Worth Creek cautiously.

The route appears to dead end shortly after in a false lead created by the **Old Dixie Highway Bridge** with a 25-foot fixed vertical clearance and the **Loxahatchee Railroad Bridge**, both on the Loxahatchee River. The railroad bridge is normally open except during train traffic. The ICW actually turns south before the bridges, starting a long sweeping curve at green daybeacon "7" where the ICW leaves the Loxahatchee River and enters Lake Worth Creek. Note that you will not see the opening

Jupiter Inlet

Chapter 7: The Crossroads to Pompano Beach

Jupiter Inlet Area, FL

JUPITER AREA (SOUTH)		Largest Vessel	VHF	Total Slips	Approach/ Dockside Depth	Floating Docks	Gas/ Diesel	Repairs/ Haulout	Min/Max Amps	Pump-Out Station
1. Jupiter Yacht Club & Marina-PRIVATE MM 1006.5	(561) 741-3407	65		79	5.0 / 5.0				30 / 50	
2. Loggerhead Marina - Jupiter Marina MM 1006.8	(561) 747-8980	100	16		7.0 / 6.0	F	G	R		P
3. Admirals Cove Marina WiFi MM 1007.8	(561) 745-5961	170	16	65	11.0 / 10.0	F	GD		30 / 100	P
4. Loggerhead Marina - Palm Beach Gardens WiFi	(561) 627-6358	120	16	136	8.0 / 8.0		GD		30 / 100	P

WiFi Wireless Internet Access
Visit www.waterwayguide.com for current rates, fuel prices, website addresses and other up-to-the-minute information. (Information in the table is provided by the facilities.)

Scan here for more details:

southbound into Lake Worth Creek until you are almost in it, and boats coming from the south will not be visible until after you are well in to the turn. A slow, wide turn is advised.

CAUTION: Construction is underway for the replacement of both the U.S. 1 (Jupiter) Bridge and the Loxahatchee Railroad Bridge. To facilitate launching barges, a temporary access bridge will constructed on the northwest corner of the railroad bridge. The access bridge may extend slightly into the northern edge of the ICW channel. Check ahead for waterway restrictions and/or closures at 305-535-4317.

To assist with the increase in vehicle traffic during closures at the Jupiter Bridge, the **Indiantown (SR 706) Bridge** at Mile 1006.2 will remain closed to navigation daily from 7:00 a.m. to 9:00 a.m. and from 4:30 p.m. to 6:30 p.m. from March 13 to September 7, 2023. The bridge has a 35-foot closed vertical clearance and normally opens on the hour and half-hour, 24 hours a day, 7 days a week. This is an enforced No-Wake Zone.

Donald Ross Bridge (35-foot closed vertical clearance) at Mile 1009.3 opens on the hour and half-hour. Less than 1 mile south of the bridge there is an ongoing barge loading operation at a bend in the ICW that sometimes blocks the east side of the channel, constricting passage and blocking the view around the corner for oncoming traffic. Consider a "Blind Bend" (one long) whistle signal.

Lake Worth Creek bustles with boats of all sizes and the shore gleams with condominiums and houses set among beautifully manicured lawns. But do not let your eye stray too far from mid-channel and check the depth and boat speed frequently.

Dockage: All slips at the private Jupiter Yacht Club & Marina are individually owned. Limited slips are available for sale or rent by the slip owners. This protected harbor is tucked away in a tranquil, tropical setting.

On the west side of the waterway at Mile 1006.8 is Loggerhead Marina–Jupiter Marina offering secure wet or dry storage. Amenities include a pool and a well-stocked Marine Center. Call ahead for slip availability.

The private Admirals Cove Marina is located at a private golf course resort at Mile 1007.8 The marina accepts transients to 170 feet and is considered a natural weather refuge for yachts. The Bluffs Marina at Mile 1008 is a "dockominium" marina that will accommodate short term stays of two to three weeks but not overnight transients.

Loggerhead Marina–Palm Beach Gardens at Mile 1009 is just south of the Donald Ross Bridge in a well-protected basin off the ICW. Loggerhead can accommodate transient boats up to 120 feet plus offers resort-like amenities and easy access to restaurants, shopping, golf, tennis and other activities.

Anchorage: There is a shallow anchorage north of Indiantown Bridge on the east side past flashing green "11." This area is full of small boats permanently moored, along with a public boat ramp and a floating hot dog stand on weekends (in season). There are not a lot of anchoring opportunities on Lake Worth Creek due to the number of private docks lining both shores.

PALM BEACH AREA

A concentration of marinas offering all kinds of services and repairs is located on the ICW stretch from just north of the PGA Boulevard Bridge in North Palm Beach to Palm Beach. All are convenient to the area's famous shopping. With this increase in services expect an increase boat activity. While Lake Worth seems expansive, most to the traffic is confined to the narrow, dredged ICW channel. Expect wakes to be high and boater etiquette to be low on the lake.

For those waiting for a weather window for a Gulf Stream crossing or an "outside run" the Lake Worth area offers some excellent anchorage opportunities. Unfortunately, there are few dockage facilities for dinghies and a provisioning run may necessitate a marina stay. Boat traffic on Lake Worth can be extremely heavy. It's best to anchor in an area with speed restrictions. Noise can be an issue near Peanut Island, particularly on weekends.

> NOTE: Always stay up to date on the most current Florida anchoring laws. They are challenged almost every year in the state legislature.

North Palm Beach– ICW Mile 1012 to Mile 1016

NAVIGATION: Use NOAA Chart 11472. The ICW continues south on an easy run through a wide cut to Lake Worth. There are no aids to navigation in the cut and few hazards. The North Palm Beach Waterway forks off the ICW to the southwest at the apex of the curve between the **PGA Boulevard Bridge** and **Parker (U.S. 1) Bridge**. The PGA Boulevard Bridge at Mile 1012.6 has 24-foot closed vertical clearance and opens on the hour and half-hour. Just over 1 mile south and around a blind curve the Parker Bridge at Mile 1013.7 has 25-foot closed vertical clearance and opens on the quarter and three-quarter hour.

> **NO WAKE ZONE**
> This waterway serves a heavily developed area so expect increased boat traffic here. The extra traffic justifies a Slow-Speed/Minimum-Wake Zone that continues to the opening into Lake Worth at Mile 1014.2.

At Mile 1014 just south of the Parker (U.S. 1) Bridge the ICW enters the open waters of Lake Worth. The lake is long and broad but shallow outside the ICW channel. Do not confuse the ICW markers leading south with those splitting off to the east and then north to Safe Harbor Old Port Cove and the upper end of Lake Worth (and on to Little Lake Worth, a separate body of water). Lake Worth is crowded with boats, marinas and private docks so damage from wakes can be severe.

Dockage: Soverel Harbour Marina is tucked away in a protected basin and welcomes transients on its floating docks. This well-known "hurricane hole" rents slips by the season, for the day or for a couple of hours to access the many restaurants within walking distance. Port 32 Palm Beach Gardens to the south has dry storage, wet dockage and commercial marine sales. This is also home to River House, a venerable local institution with a tiki bar offering steak and seafood with water views on two levels. Call ahead.

Chapter 7 — The Crossroads to Pompano Beach

Lake Worth Area, FL

NORTH PALM BEACH		Largest Vessel	VHF	Total Slips	Approach/Dockside Depth	Floating Docks	Gas/Diesel	Repairs/Haulout	Min/Max Amps	Pump-Out Station
1. Soverel Harbour Marina	WiFi MM 1011.9	(561) 691-9554	100	16	146	12.0 / 8.0	F	GD		30 / 50	P
2. Port 32 Palm Beach Gardens	WiFi MM 1011.9	(561) 626-0200	120	16	30	8.0 / 8.0		GD	RH	30 / 50	
3. Safe Harbor North Palm Beach	WiFi MM 1013.7	(561) 626-4919	150	16	107	10.0 / 8.0	F	GD	R	30 / 100	P
4. Safe Harbor Old Port Cove	WiFi MM 1014.0	(561) 626-1760	200	16	203	12.0 / 15.0	F	D		30 / 200+	P

WiFi Wireless Internet Access
Visit www.waterwayguide.com for current rates, fuel prices, website addresses and other up-to-the-minute information. (Information in the table is provided by the facilities.)

Scan here for more details:

Source: Aqua Map and NOAA data

Just south of the Parker Bridge is Safe Harbor North Palm Beach. This facility is located in a secluded, sheltered keyhole-shaped harbor and can accommodate vessels to 150 feet. The marina features a fully stocked Ship Store and pump-out service at every slip in addition to the usual amenities.

At flashing green "27" turn east into a privately marked channel leading into the north lobe of Lake Worth for Safe Harbor Old Port Cove. Hail "Old Port Cove" on VHF Channel 16 to be directed to a slip. This marina offers resort amenities including a restaurant, a fitness room and indoor laundry facilities. Larger boats will likely be directed to the north basin, which has less protection and is a longer walk to on-site amenities. A West Marine and provisioning options are nearby. Call in advance.

Anchorage: Some cruisers have reported adequate depths for anchoring in the lagoons off the North Palm Beach Waterway. They are reached by turning to starboard at the bend just before Parker (US 1) Bridge. The canal is charted at 7 feet MLW with 6-foot MLW depths in the first basin and 8 feet MLW in the second. This is a high-end residential community; dinghy landings are not permitted.

Another well-protected anchorage is located in the north lobe of Lake Worth opposite Safe Harbor Old Port Cove at Turtle Cove. Continue north past the marina into the lake's deeper basin. You can drop the hook in 9- to 14-foot MLW depths and have plenty of swinging room. This anchorage is surrounded by a residential neighborhood and the only potential dinghy landing is a small patch of sand north of the Little Lake Worth (A1A) Bridge. A Publix and a microbrewery are a few hundred yards west along PGA Boulevard but be aware that attempts have been made to close this landing in recent years.

> NOTE: Turtle Cove can be a problem anchorage based on local law enforcement's interpretation of the regulations and where vessels choose to anchor. The cautionary note is vessels must know where navigation channels are and anchor well out of those channels. Some homeowners is the area complain about boats being anchored near their docks, which can lead to a visit from law enforcement.

Riviera Beach Area–ICW Mile 1016 to Mile 1018

NAVIGATION: Use NOAA Chart 11472. Lake Worth is broad in the first stretch leading to the high-rise **Blue Heron (SR A1A) Bridge** (65-foot fixed vertical clearance) at Mile 1017.2 but depths outside the dredged channel are shallow. Stay in the marked channel even if you see small craft taking other routes. The City of Riviera Beach has two bodies of land split by the waters of Lake Worth and the ICW. Parts of the city lie at each end of this bridge.

> ⚠️ *CAUTION:* While the Blue Heron (SR A1A) Bridge is charted at 65-foot fixed vertical clearance, actual clearance at high tide will be lower. Check the clearance boards on the bridge.

The channel is narrow and a Slow-Speed/Minimum-Wake applies from the Blue Heron Bridge to the turning basin. Considerable chop can build in Lake Worth and watch the set of your course in a strong crosswind.

Just through the Blue Heron Bridge you must make a decision. Directly ahead is Peanut Island and one of the most congested areas on the ICW. If you plan to continue south on the ICW, alter course to starboard following the ICW around Peanut Island on the west side. On weekends

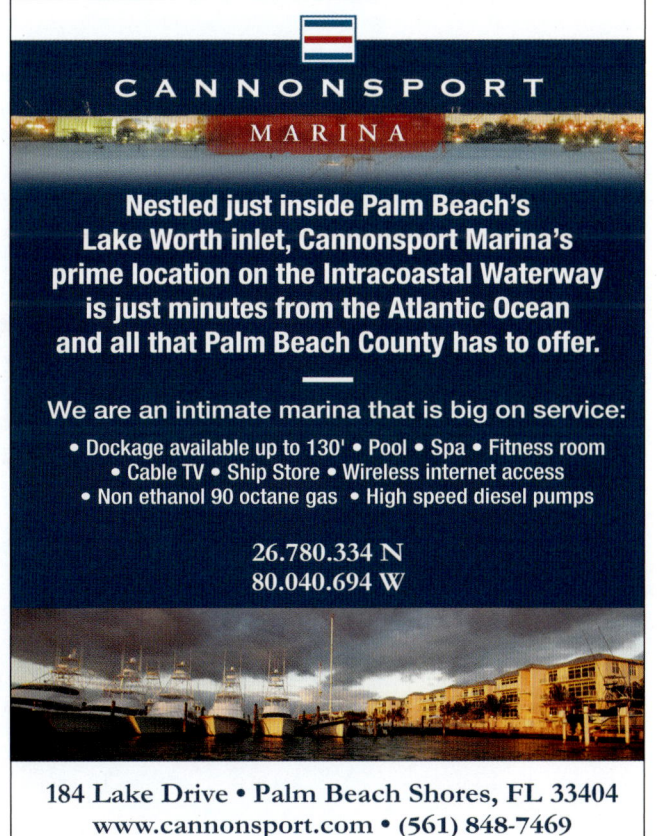

CANNONSPORT MARINA

Nestled just inside Palm Beach's Lake Worth inlet, Cannonsport Marina's prime location on the Intracoastal Waterway is just minutes from the Atlantic Ocean and all that Palm Beach County has to offer.

We are an intimate marina that is big on service:
- Dockage available up to 130' • Pool • Spa • Fitness room
- Cable TV • Ship Store • Wireless internet access
- Non ethanol 90 octane gas • High speed diesel pumps

26.780.334 N
80.040.694 W

184 Lake Drive • Palm Beach Shores, FL 33404
www.cannonsport.com • (561) 848-7469

Chapter 7: The Crossroads to Pompano Beach

Lake Worth, FL

	Largest Vessel	VHF	Total Slips	Approach/Dockside Depth	Floating Docks	Gas/Diesel	Repairs/Haulout	Min/Max Amps	Pump-Out Station
RIVIERA BEACH									
1. Lake Park Harbor Marina WiFi MM 1016.2 (561) 881-3353	80	16	112	6.0 / 5.5	F	GD		30 / 50	P
2. Loggerhead Marina - Riviera Beach Marina MM 1017.0 (561) 840-6868	47		300	6.0 / 6.0	F	GD		30 / 50	P
3. Safe Harbor New Port Cove WiFi MM 1017.4 (561) 844-2504	80	16	49	5.0 / 5.0	F	GD	R	30 / 50	P
4. Riviera Beach City Marina WiFi MM 1018.0 (561) 842-7806	275	16	180	8.0 / 7.0	F	GD		30 / 200+	P
PALM BEACH SHORES									
5. Cannonsport Marina WiFi MM 1017.5 (561) 848-7469	130	16	54	10.0 / 8.0		GD		30 / 100	P
6. Buccaneer Marina WiFi MM 1017.6 (561) 842-1620	85	16	16	12.0 / 12.0		GD		30 / 50	
7. Sailfish Marina Resort WiFi MM 1017.7 (561) 844-1724	180	16	74	8.0 / 8.0	F	GD		15 / 100	

WiFi Wireless Internet Access
Visit www.waterwayguide.com for current rates, fuel prices, website addresses and other up-to-the-minute information. (Information in the table is provided by the facilities.)

Scan here for more details:

Source: Aqua Map and NOAA data

286 WATERWAY GUIDE 2024 www.waterwayguide.com

it can be difficult to discern the channel markers from the mayhem surrounding Peanut Island. Reduce speed here.

There are two channels leading to Lake Worth (Palm Beach) Inlet. The most direct route is via a channel that hugs the shore of Singer Island. After passing under the Blue Heron Bridge, turn east and follow the marked channel, which ends at the Lake Worth (Palm Beach) Inlet. Keep green markers to starboard while traveling southbound on this channel and out of the inlet. Be sure to stay to the north (red) side of the channel as that is where you will find the deeper water. You will pass close to the marinas on the shore of Singer Island so watch your wake. Also note the charted large bar extending east from Peanut Island towards the inlet.

A deeper and wider route passes around the west side of Peanut Island and enters the deepwater Turning Basin at the shipping wharves. From here you follow the Main Ship Channel through to the ocean or continue south on the ICW.

Dockage: North of the Blue Heron Bridge on the west shore at Mile 1016.2 is the friendly Lake Park Harbor Marina. The well-maintained municipal facility has 112 boat slips to 80 feet dispersed throughout an expansive park-like setting. The town sponsors a Sunset Celebration at the marina on the last Friday of every month. This fun event features live music, dancing, food vendors, arts and crafts, and more. You don't want to miss it.

The 300-slip Loggerhead Marina–Riviera Beach Marina is also on the west shore just north of the Blue Heron Bridge (Mile 1017). It's easy to spot its two towers and huge (hurricane-rated) dry storage facility. The marina offers club-type amenities with close proximity to waterfront restaurants, shopping, golf, beaches, tennis and nightlife. Call ahead for slip availability.

South of the Blue Heron Bridge marine facilities are abundant both north and south of Lake Worth (Palm Beach) Inlet. On the west shore beginning at Riviera Beach are repair yards capable of handling boats of any size. Boat Owners Warehouse is also nearby and well worth a visit.

RIVIERA BEACH MARINA VILLAGE

200 E. 13th Street
Riviera Beach, FL 33404
(561) 842-7806
VHF Channel 16
rivierabeachmarina.com

PASSAGE TO PARADISE
FLOATING DOCKS FOR BOATS FROM 30' TO 200'

- 170 Slips with 2,800 Feet of Face-Dock for Wide Beam Yachts & Catamarans.
- 5-Minute No Wake to Deep-Water Lake Worth Inlet with No Bridges.
- Transient, Monthly, Seasonal and Annual Boaters are Welcome.
- ValvTect Marine Diesel Fuel and 90 Octane Non-Ethanol Gasoline.
- 32,000 lb. and 40,000 lb. Boatlifts with 24/7 x 365 Access.
- Rafiki Tiki Restaurant and Bar on-site.
- Peanut Island Shuttle Boat Operating 365-days, weather permitting.
- Parasailing, Sport Fishing, Drift Fishing, Sailing and Scuba Charters on-site.
- 49-Passenger Powerboat and 49 Passenger Sailing Catamaran Charter Boats.
- Sunset Cruises, Intra-Coastal Cruises with Optional Beverage Packages.
- Small Boat & Waverunner Rentals, Kayaks, Paddleboards & More.

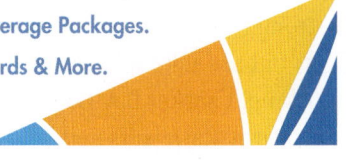

Chapter 7: The Crossroads to Pompano Beach

Safe Harbor New Port Cove has a state-of-the-art dry stack storage system and wet slips with ample upscale amenities. They also have a well-stocked Ship Store. Call ahead for slip availability.

Continuing south is the Riviera Beach City Marina at Mile 1018 (across from Peanut Island), which is part of the Riviera Beach Marina Village, where paddleboard rentals, kayak rentals, wave runner rentals, boat rentals, fishing charters, diving charters, eco tours, and more are available on site. The facility offers dockage to 120 feet including catamaran slips. This is a busy marina with fishing charters and pump-out service at every slip. Crosscurrents can be strong here and maneuvering space gets tight so take some care while docking. Cracker Boy Boat Works is nearby for repairs and maintenance. They allow DIY and also have on-site contractors should you need a hand.

On the east shore the resort area of Palm Beach Shores across the waterway is crowded with houses, motels, docks and restaurants. There is a strong current at all the marine facilities so exercise care while docking. The 54-slip Cannonsport Marina is the northernmost facility. This is an intimate marina that caters to sportfishing vessels but welcomes all transients (to 130 feet).

The iconic Buccaneer Marina at Mile 1017.6 may have space for you. This is billed as a "fisherman's paradise" and has been around well over 50 years. The facility is growing and is under construction so call ahead. Sailfish Marina Resort located just north of the Lake Worth (Palm Beach) Inlet also caters to sportfishing vessels but is an all-transient facility with a popular on-site restaurant. A water taxi is based here for easy trips to Peanut Island.

Anchorage: Northeast of Blue Heron Bridge you can drop the hook in 8- to 13-foot MLW depths over the "Discontinued Spoil Area." There are a number of derelict boats and a few sunken ones here; beware of wreckage on the bottom. It is best to wait and anchor in Lake Worth. Note that anchor lights must be used in all Lake Worth anchorages. South of Blue Heron Bridge is a nice anchorage in 10 feet MLW with a sandy bottom. There are a few boats here on permanent moorings. Safe Harbor Marina will not let you park your dinghy, but there is a public boat ramp located to their south.

Lake Worth (Palm Beach) Inlet

Wide, well-marked and protected by jetties, Lake Worth (Palm Beach) Inlet boasts a deep straightforward big ship channel that is one of the easiest to enter on the Atlantic coast. The meandering Gulf Stream is closer here than at any point in the U.S. (sometimes as close as 1 mile offshore but usually out about 8 to 12 miles) and both commercial and recreational craft give the Lake Worth (Palm Beach) Inlet heavy use. It is located approximately midway between Fort Pierce Inlet (53 miles north) and Port Everglades (40 miles south), making it popular with boaters who prefer to travel offshore.

Lake Worth (Palm Beach) Inlet is a favorite point of departure for boats bound to and from the Bahamas Islands. It's the closest U.S. point to the West End on Grand Bahama Island and boats returning from Bimini can enjoy a boost from the Gulf Stream door-to-door.

NAVIGATION: Use NOAA Chart 11472. To access the ocean continue on the ICW around the west side of Peanut Island to the Turning Basin and then pick up the main Lake Worth (Palm Beach) Inlet channel and follow it to the ocean. It is deep and well marked.

The Coast Guard establishes fixed and moving security zones at the Port of Palm Beach for the protection of passenger vessels (cruise ships), vessels carrying cargoes of a particular hazard and vessels carrying hazardous gases. A moving security zone activates when such a vessel passes red and white buoy "LW" when entering the port and becomes a fixed zone when the ship is docked. These zones cover the waters within 100 yards all around the subject vessels and no craft can enter without prior permission. Patrol craft may be contacted on VHF Channel 16 for the status of these security zones.

> NOTE: For a live view of the Lake Worth (Palm Beach) Inlet visit the online Lake Worth Inlet Webcam.

Anchorage: There are several anchorages in the vicinity of Lake Worth (Palm Beach) Inlet. This is a high-traffic area and anchor lights should be used in all Lake Worth anchorages. When entering any anchorages pay strict attention to your depth sounder as there are several areas of shallow water and measured depths may not be as charted. Avoid the cable area shown on charts when anchoring at Lake Worth R2. This area is subject to tidal currents from the inlet, so observe proximity of other anchored vessels and their anchor set.

Popular Peanut Island

Peanut Island was originally created in 1918 as a result of material excavated when the Lake Worth (Palm Beach) Inlet was created. Originally just 10 acres Peanut Island today comprises approximately 80 acres due to continued maintenance dredging of the inlet and the ICW. Peanut Island is a public park that is popular with small powerboaters who anchor around its perimeter and party in the shallow, sandy-bottom water that extends out into the ICW. (There are also boat slips available for day use only.)

Swimming areas, kayaking lagoons and terrific snorkeling are among the draws of Peanut Island. There are paved walkways with scenic outlooks. A bomb shelter on the south side of the island that was abandoned after JFK's assassination in 1963 was close to ruin when the Palm Beach Maritime Museum took over in the 1990s. Island facilities include picnic shelters, restrooms and a dredged boat basin on its northwest side for dinghy tie-up. Note there is no food or rental concession located on the island.

Water taxi service is available from Palm Beach Water Taxi (561-683-8294) and Peanut Island Shuttle Boat (561-723-2028). Call the water taxi on VHF Channel 16.

Chapter 7: The Crossroads to Pompano Beach

West Palm Beach to Palm Beach–ICW Mile 1018 to Mile 1026

Before entering the ICW south from the Lake Worth (Palm Beach) Inlet cruisers should consider their passage options and the dimensions of their vessel. There are 21 bascule bridges in this stretch and one of them–Southern Boulevard (SR 700/80) Bridge)–is a major construction project at the moment. If your air draft is over 25 feet you will be looking at scheduling openings at 19 of the bridges.

Comfort can also be an issue. Ocean waves may prove less irritating than the wakes from power boats when confined in the narrow, 30-mile-long canal below Lake Worth. Because of this, many choose to take the 40-nm "outside passage" to Ft. Lauderdale. Both the Lake Worth (Palm Beach) Inlet and the Port Everglades (Fort Lauderdale) Inlet are all-weather channels with fully lighted aids to navigation.

The main drawback to the outside route south is the close proximity of the Gulf Stream to shore off Palm Beach, although this factor goes in the plus column if making a northbound passage. Weather conditions and tides are also important factors. There are no intermediate ports of call between the two main inlets. Favorable weather and an early start should be considered essential conditions to making this passage in either direction.

Lake Worth is open south of the Lake Worth (Palm Beach) Inlet and Peanut Island and the ICW channel follows the lake's western shore. The waterway is well marked and maintained and the lake bed is pocked with patches of deep water mainly along the eastern shore with Palm Beach, as well as some shoals and spoils areas. Palm Beach remains a winter ocean resort-town of elegance and charm.

The West Palm Beach shore is mostly given over to marinas, boatyards and yachting amenities. In other places any one of these would be outstanding in size, quality of work and service; here, however, mariners can be overwhelmed by the choices. Not all the services available are confined to the waterfront. A phone call or a short walk can put you in touch with just about every known kind of nautical specialist–sailmakers, electronic sales and services, boat designers, boat maintenance and cleaning and diving services. Supplies of all kinds are also close at hand.

America's Waterway Guide Since 1947 — Chapter 7

Lake Worth, FL

WEST PALM BEACH		Largest Vessel	VHF	Total Slips	Approach/ Dockside Depth	Floating Docks	Gas/ Diesel	Repairs/ Haulout	Min/Max Amps	Pump-Out Station
1. Safe Harbor Rybovich WiFi MM 1019.5	(561) 840-8308	330	16	60	18.0 / 18.0	F	GD	RH	30 / 200+	P
2. Palm Beach Yacht Club & Marina-PRIVATE WiFi MM 1022.9	(561) 655-1944	150	16	47	13.0 / 13.0		GD	H	30 / 100	
3. Palm Harbor Marina WiFi MM 1022.0	(561) 655-4757	250	16	200	11.0 / 11.0	F	GD		30 / 200+	P
PALM BEACH										
4. Town of Palm Beach Marina WiFi 1022.8	(561) 838-5463	294	16	84	9.0 / 12.0				50 / 200+	P

WiFi Wireless Internet Access
Visit www.waterwayguide.com for current rates, fuel prices, website addresses and other up-to-the-minute information. (Information in the table is provided by the facilities.)

Scan here for more details:

Downtown West Palm Beach and Rosemary Square, an upscale outdoor mall surrounding an open-air plaza, are near the marinas. In this festive commercial and cultural district you will find live entertainment, shopping, theaters, restaurants, groceries and art galleries. A free trolley runs from Clematis St. in West Palm Beach to the downtown area.

> NOTE: West Palm is the home of the Palm Beach International Boat Show usually held in March. The event includes hundreds of boats from inflatables to megayachts, plus tents full of the latest electronics and accessories, seminars and fishing clinics for kids.

NAVIGATION: Use NOAA Charts 11472 and 11467. There are three bridges connecting the mainland and Palm Beach. At Mile 1021.8 is the **Flagler Memorial (SR A1A) Bridge** with 21-foot closed vertical clearance. The bridge opens on the quarter and three-quarter hour. The second crossing is the **Royal Park (SR 704) Bridge** at Mile 1022.6, which has a 21-foot closed vertical clearance and opens on the hour and half-hour. (These schedules are always subject to change if the Coast Guard establishes a security zone.) The third bridge is the (new in 2022) **Southern Boulevard (SR 700/80) Bridge** at Mile 1024.7, which has 25-foot closed vertical clearance and opens on the quarter and three-quarter hour.

Dockage: On the mainland side just before Mile 1020 privately maintained green daybeacon "1" and red daybeacon "2" flank the entrance to Safe Harbor Rybovich, a full-service superyacht marina and marine service facility. They can accommodate vessels to 330 feet with resort-style amenities.

North of the Flagler Memorial Bridge at Mile 1022.9 is the private Palm Beach Yacht Club & Marina, which is open to the public on a "first-come first-served" basis with resort-style amenities for vessels ranging up to 150

Source: Aqua Map and NOAA data

SOUTHERN EDITION

Chapter 7: The Crossroads to Pompano Beach

feet. Just south of the bridge on the mainland side is Palm Harbor Marina, which has ample transient berths and resort amenities that include a private clubhouse for guests with a fully equipped lounge, fitness center, business center and shower and restroom facilities.

Town of Palm Beach Marina on the ocean side below the Royal Park (SR 704) Bridge at Mile 1024.5 can accommodate power and sailing vessels up to 260 feet in length. Transient slips may be reserved with a 48-hour advance notice of arrival. An online form makes this easy. Gated docks and concierge service are among the amenities that set this apart from other municipal facilities.

Anchorage: The anchorages close to the Palm Beach Inlet have become busier and busier, with more "private" moorings taking up the space. North of the Flagler Memorial (SR A1A) Bridge at Mile 1020.9, you can find 5-6 feet MLW east of the ICW at Palm Beach Currie Park. Day docks are close by at Currie Park on the west shore, which has several boat ramps and separate "staging" docks for loading/unloading. Pharmacies and small family groceries can be found in the neighborhoods bordering the park.

Farther south but still north of the bridge at Mile 1021 is the Palm Beach North anchorage. This anchorage is fairly protected, but as with all ICW locations, expect to experience boat waves. Easy dinghy ride to the small sandy beach under the bridge at Bradley Park.

At Mile 1022 there are two municipal day docks located north of the Royal Park (SR 704) Bridge (on western side). The docks offer complimentary dockage for visits during the daytime hours of 5:00 a.m. to midnight. There is no overnight dockage but you can drop the hook between the docks in the West Palm Beach anchorage. Free shuttles are available for provisioning and getting the dog off the boat is easy.

Palm Beach to Lantana–ICW Mile 1026 to Mile 1032

Lake Worth may be wide in this area but south of Palm Beach the water is shallow outside the ICW channel. Small islands (many of them originating as spoils banks) break the open expanses and are overgrown with foliage. Estates border most of the eastern shore and tall condominiums appear with increasing frequency on both banks. Even though the Atlantic Ocean is barely 0.5 mile away in places you will find it hard to see among the proliferation of houses, motels, high-rise apartments and condominiums that line the route.

NAVIGATION: Use NOAA Chart 11467. Starting from Mile 1027 (just south of red daybeacon "24") the ICW route is confined to a dredged channel south to Boynton Beach where the waterway enters a cut and Lake Worth ends. There is some shoaling along the edges so stay centered and watch your channel alignment in strong crosswinds. The **Lake Ave. (SR 802) Bridge** with 35-foot closed vertical clearance is at Mile 1028.8 and opens on signal.

Lantana is the next town southbound on Lake Worth. The **E. Ocean Avenue (Lantana) Bridge** (21-foot closed vertical clearance) at Mile 1031 connects Lantana on the mainland with Hypoluxo Island and South Palm Beach on the ocean side. The bridge has scheduled openings on the hour and half-hour.

Dockage: In Bryant Park on the west shore just north of the Lake Ave. Bridge, the Lake Worth Free Dock has five slips for day use only at Snook Islands. The park also has a public launch ramp with a dock south of the bridge that can accommodate dinghy landings.

Three marinas are clustered on the mainland side just north of the E. Ocean Avenue (Lantana) Bridge. Loggerhead Marina–Lantana Marina is at Mile 1030.2 with dry rack storage and wet slips (including catamaran slips) for vessels up to 100 feet. Just to the south is Loggerhead Marina–South Lantana, which has transient dockage to 120 feet. Located in a residential and commercial development, this location has a club atmosphere and amenities and is convenient to groceries and restaurants.

Located between the two Loggerhead facilities is Murrelle Marine, which is a full-service boatyard with an index of specialist contractors to help with your boat maintenance. They also welcome transients to 55 feet.

Anchorage: Just to the southwest of the E. Ocean Avenue (Lantana) Bridge there is room for a half dozen boats in 8 to 10 feet MLW. The Lantana anchorage at Mile 1031.1 is best for winds out of the north; it's rocky with a south wind. Anchoring here is limited to 18 hours. There is shore access at the public dock by the anchorage. Nearby The Old Key Lime House has a dinghy dock if you eat there (561-582-1889). Pets are not allowed at the restaurant. There is an Aldi Supermarket 1 mile west of the dock.

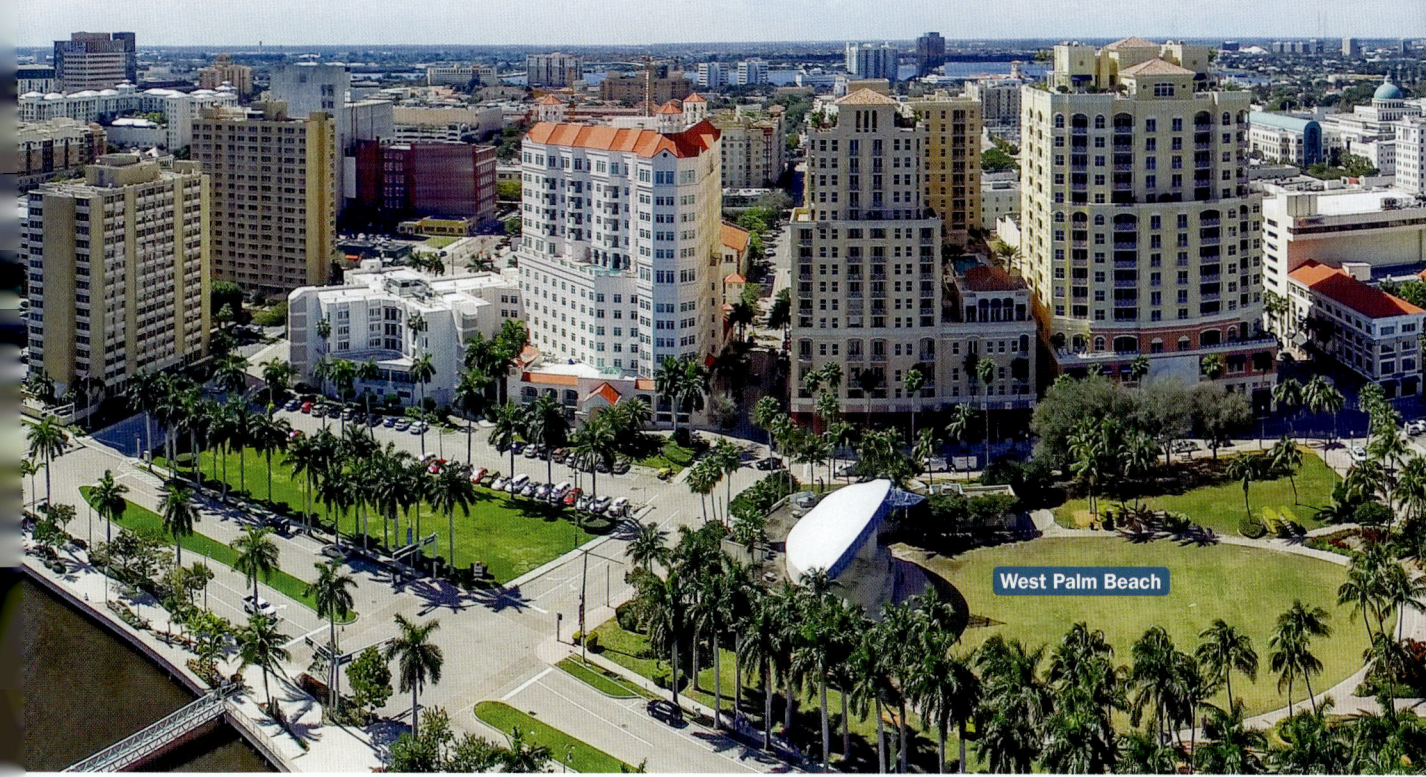
West Palm Beach

Chapter 7: The Crossroads to Pompano Beach

Lake Worth, FL

LANTANA		Largest Vessel	VHF	Total Slips	Approach/Dockside Depth	Floating Docks	Gas/Diesel	Repairs/Haulout	Min/Max Amps	Pump-Out Station
1. Loggerhead Marina - Lantana Marina WiFi MM 1030.4	(561) 582-4422	100	16	83	6.0 / 8.0		G	R	30 / 50	
2. Murrelle Marine WiFi MM 1030.5	(561) 582-3213	55	16	36	4.5 / 5.0			RH	30 / 50	
3. Loggerhead Marina - South Lantana WiFi MM 1030.6	(561) 582-4422	120	16	80	5.0 / 7.0		G		30 / 50	

WiFi Wireless Internet Access
Visit www.waterwayguide.com for current rates, fuel prices, website addresses and other up-to-the-minute information. (Information in the table is provided by the facilities.)

Scan here for more details:

Source: Aqua Map and NOAA data

To Boynton Beach– ICW Mile 1032 to Mile 1036

Continuing south over the next 30 miles the ICW alters its configuration and becomes a narrow land cut in the vicinity of Boynton Beach. Lined with residences and spanned by numerous bridges the ICW truly looks like a "water highway" here. The numerous bridges slow progress and anchorages are in short supply. Passage south will require some planning.

NAVIGATION: Use NOAA Chart 11467. South from the Lantana Bridge the route enters the Boynton Inlet approach area.

CAUTION: Watch your course carefully when crossing the Boynton Inlet area, as the current can push vessels out of the channel. Deeper draft vessels should seek local knowledge. Do not be confused by green can "1" to the east or the green buoys marking a channel leading in to the western shore; these are not ICW markers. Note there is some charted shoaling on both sides from just north of red daybeacon "52A" to just south of green daybeacon "53." Hold the channel center and monitor depths.

Boynton Inlet (also known as South Lake Worth Inlet) at Mile 1034 is popular with local fishermen but it is narrow, shallow and crossed by the fixed **Boynton Inlet Bridge** with an 18-foot vertical clearance. The Coast Guard does not recommend passage through the inlet without complete local knowledge of all the hazardous conditions that exist. A seawall helps stabilize Boynton Inlet's shoreline but currents run swiftly and bad tidal rips develop in strong easterly winds.

Past the inlet at Mile 1035 is **E. Ocean Avenue (Boynton Beach) Bridge** with 21-foot closed vertical clearance, which opens on the hour

Boynton Inlet Area, FL

BOYNTON BEACH		Largest Vessel	VHF	Total Slips	Approach/ Dockside Depth	Floating Docks	Gas/ Diesel	Repairs/ Haulout	Min/Max Amps	Pump-Out Station
1. Palm Beach Yacht Center WiFi MM 1032.7	(561) 588-9911	80	16	100	6.0 / 6.0		GD	RH	30 / 50	P
2. Boynton Harbor Marina WiFi MM 1035.0	(561) 735-7955	40	16	23	12.0 / 6.0		GD		30 / 100	

WiFi Wireless Internet Access
Visit www.waterwayguide.com for current rates, fuel prices, website addresses and other up-to-the-minute information. (Information in the table is provided by the facilities.)

Scan here for more details: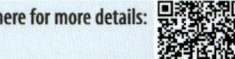

and half-hour. Bridge restrictions apply 24 hours a day, 7 days a week. Less than 1 mile further south, the **E. Woolbright Road (SE 15th Street) Bridge** (25-foot closed vertical clearance) crosses the ICW at Mile 1035.8 and opens on signal.

Dockage: Family-owned and -operated Palm Beach Yacht Center is in a protected basin at Mile 1032.7. This facility has both in-and-out rack storage (to 38 feet) and wet slips (to 80 feet). They also have a 5-acre paved, full-service repair yard.

Just north of the E. Ocean Avenue (Lantana) Bridge in Boynton Beach the friendly Boynton Harbor Marina (Mile 1035) may have a slip for you on a face dock with the usual amenities. They offer a multitude of water activities and waterfront dining. A shopping center and supermarket are within walking distance

■ TO POMPANO BEACH

Lake Worth ends just south of the Boynton Canal at Mile 1034. South from here the ICW becomes a canal with concrete bulkheads lining its borders. Two small, shallow lakes–Wyman and Boca Raton–and a brief stretch of the Hillsboro River are the only naturally formed bodies of water along this route. This area is well-developed with town following town and beautiful homes surrounded by subtropical growth provide the scenery. Even though the Atlantic Ocean is barely 0.5 mile away in places, you will find it hard to see among the proliferation of houses, motels, high-rise apartments and condominiums that line the route.

NO WAKE ZONE

Traveling south from Lake Worth keep an eye out for the many Slow-Speed/Minimum-Wake Zones. They increase with greater frequency the closer you get to Fort Lauderdale.

Source: Aqua Map and NOAA data

Chapter 7: The Crossroads to Pompano Beach

Hillsboro River, FL

DELRAY BEACH		Largest Vessel	VHF	Total Slips	Approach/ Dockside Depth	Floating Docks	Gas/ Diesel	Repairs/ Haulout	Min/Max Amps	Pump-Out Station
1. The Seagate Yacht Club WiFi MM 1039.9	(877) 673-6564	120	16	44	6.5 / 6.5		D		30 / 100	
2. Delray Beach City Marina WiFi MM 1039.8	(561) 243-7250	55		24	/ 10.0	F			30 / 50	P
3. Delray Harbor Club Marina WiFi MM 1040.7	(561) 276-0376	200	16	44	8.0 / 8.0	F	GD	RH	30 / 100	

WiFi Wireless Internet Access
Visit www.waterwayguide.com for current rates, fuel prices, website addresses and other up-to-the-minute information.
(Information in the table is provided by the facilities.)

Scan here for more details:

Source: Aqua Map and NOAA data

Be ready to call on VHF Channel 09 or whistle signal (two blasts: one prolonged, one short) for the opening of many of the 31 bridges that span the channel between Lake Worth and Government Cut at Miami Beach. Schedule a little extra time to allow for restricted openings, occasional bridge malfunctions and No-Wake Zones.

Boynton Inlet to Delray Beach–ICW Mile 1036 to Mile 1044

Delray Beach is a first-class resort destination and a diverse, vibrant, community situated on the Atlantic Ocean between Boca Raton and West Palm Beach. The area has diverse restaurants, a great art museum housed in a 1913 schoolhouse (Cornell Art Museum) and the quirky Silverball Museum, which is dedicated to the preservation of the vintage arcade. In this arcade you pay by the hour, not with tokens or quarters. They also sell food at this marvelous rainy day diversion.

From Delray Beach a confined 25-mile-long canal runs south to Fort Lauderdale. Smaller boats and those bothered by the constant buffeting of the irregular chop caused by wakes might consider traveling on weekdays when traffic is lighter. Wakes on this narrow channel retain their energy between opposing cement bulkheads bouncing back and forth for some time after the passing of a vessel. If weather permits, you may just want to make the outside run from Lake Worth (Palm Beach) Inlet to avoid the numerous bridges and boat wakes.

NAVIGATION: Use NOAA Chart 11467. The first Delray Beach bridge you will encounter (Mile 1038.7) is the **George Bush Boulevard Bridge** with 9-foot closed vertical clearance. This bridge opens on signal. The next bridge (Mile 1039.6) is the **Atlantic Avenue (SR 806) Bridge** with 12-foot closed vertical clearance, which opens on the quarter and three-quarter hour. The **Linton**

Boulevard Bridge at Mile 1041.0 has a charted 30-foot closed vertical clearance (at center). Low steel clearance is 26 feet. Opens on the hour and half-hour at all times.

Dockage: Boating amenities at Delray Beach range from restaurants with dockage to full-service marinas and repair shops. Just north of the Atlantic Avenue Bridge is the municipal Veterans Park at Mile 1039.5 (mainland side). Park amenities include lawn bowling, shuffleboard and complimentary daytime dockage along the seawall for visitors (2-hour limit, no overnight docking).

South past the Atlantic Avenue Bridge on the mainland side at Mile 1035.8 is the well-respected Delray Beach City Marina. The municipal marina provides 24 rental slips for boats to 55 feet in a nicely landscaped environment with restrooms, showers, washer and dryer, and an ice machine. Directly across the waterway The Seagate Yacht Club has slips for vessels to 140 feet with resort accommodations including a sun pool, lounge area and multiple dining options.

In a basin to the south (Mile 1040.5) is the friendly and accommodating Delray Harbor Club Marina with dockage (to 200 feet) and various services. The marina is within walking distance of car rentals, grocery stores, drug stores, pet supply stores, restaurants, and more.

Anchorage: At Mile 1040.5, there is a small anchorage adjacent to the ICW at Delray Beach South with 6 to 7 feet MLW and good holding in mud. Delray Harbor Club Marina may let you tie up there for an hour or two (if you ask nicely).

At about Mile 1042 the round basin to the west of the ICW is locally known as Pelican Harbor. This is a well-protected, 24-hour only anchorage (by order of the town of Delray Beach). Enter in the center of the channel for 6 feet MLW at the bar then deepening to 10-foot depths in the basin. There is room for four or five boats. The bottom is soft mud so you should make sure your anchor is properly set and be prepared to spend some time washing mud off your chain and anchor in the morning.

To Boca Raton—ICW Mile 1044 to Mile 1050

The area now known as Boca Raton is shown on old Spanish navigational maps charts as *Boca de Ratones*, meaning "mouth of the harbor of the hidden rocks." It appears that the name was originally applied to Biscayne Bay near Miami Beach, but early mapmakers moved the name to the present location. The construction of the Florida East Coast Canal (today's ICW) and the Florida East Coast Railway in the 1890s brought pioneers and farmers to the area. In 1925, eccentric architect Addison Mizner was hired to design a world-class resort community. His exclusive hotel, known as the Cloister Inn, was completed in 1926, and remains a landmark as the Boca Raton Resort and Club.

NAVIGATION: Use NOAA Chart 11467. The **Spanish River Boulevard Bridge** at Mile 1044.9 has 25-foot closed vertical clearance and opens on the hour and half-hour, 24 hours a day. There are some spots of shoaling along the channel's edges between red daybeacon "54" through Lake Wyman to flashing green "61." Stay to the well-marked channel's center for this stretch. Lake Wyman is a broad, shallow lake with numerous, unmarked shoals. Exercise caution and stay in the marked channel. Be on the lookout for water skiers and swimmers in the water.

Leaving Lake Wyman southward the ICW route leads into Lake Boca Raton through a cut bordered by beautiful homes. Before entering the lake the ICW passes under **Palmetto Park Bridge** (19-foot closed vertical clearance) at Mile 1047.5. The bridge opens on the hour and half-hour. The opening under the bridge is extremely narrow so expect strong currents. When running with the current in a lightly powered vessel be sure to avoid being carried into the bridge or being carried by eddies into the concrete walls and docks along the sides.

During weekends (particularly in season), many small boats mill around the boat ramp next to the southwestern bridge abutment at Silver Palm Park, adding to the confusion. This is usually a very busy area and extra caution should be taken.

The ICW traverses Lake Boca Raton along its western shore and continues south through the **Camino Real Bridge** at Mile 1048.2 (9-foot closed vertical clearance). It opens on the hour, and at 20 and 40 minutes past the hour, 24 hours daily. This is the only restricted bridge in Palm Beach County that opens more than twice an hour, attesting to the large number of boats passing through. This is also the southernmost bridge in Palm Beach County.

When heading south through these two bridges, keep in mind that the current usually reverses in the ICW as it passes the Boca Raton Inlet. The current is not particularly strong and poses little difficulty even for lightly powered vessels, but be aware of it, particularly on an incoming

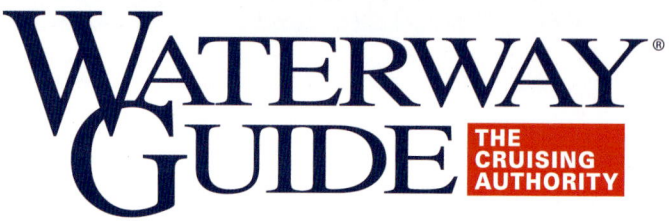

Scan to subscribe now at
www.waterwayguide.com

Navigate with the Cruising Authority

tide. Traffic can be quite busy, especially on weekends in season.

The ICW channel through Lake Boca Raton is an Idle-Speed/No-Wake Zone and the local marine police make a point to strictly enforce it. It is busy with tour boats and water taxis ferrying passengers between the Boca Raton Resort & Club and its private beach.

The Boca Raton Inlet is not recommended for passage without local knowledge due to shoaling to 4 feet MLW. The inlet's entrance has short jetties marked by private lights and the continuous shoaling and shifting sandbars make depths unreliable. The inlet channel and markers are not charted and transit is considered dangerous. Water depths in the main channel, approximately 140 yards outside the jetties, have been reported as low as 2 to 4.5 feet MLW. All mariners are advised to use extreme caution when transiting the area. The **Boca Inlet (Haven Ashe) Bridge** crosses the inlet with 23-foot closed vertical clearance. It opens on signal.

Dockage: Boca Raton Resort & Club is located at Mile 1048.2 on Lake Boca Raton. The pink hotel is a local landmark and offers dockage to 170 feet with a 50-foot minimum. They have a pool with waterslides, a lazy river and a FlowRider wave simulator (surf on land). They also have a private beach and various watersport rentals.

The Cove Waterfront Restaurant & Tiki Bar and Marina is just south of the **Hillsboro Boulevard (SR 810) Bridge** on the ICW. They have 5 reserved transient slips for vessels to 65 feet. Call ahead for reservations. The restaurant has a fun seafood, steak and pasta menu and a popular Friday Night Happy Hour.

Anchorage: Triangle-shaped Deerfield Island Park (charted) is on the west side of the ICW where the Hillsboro Drainage Canal intersects the ICW route. The park has picnic areas and nature walks. A short distance up the Hillsboro Drainage Canal the park boat dock can accommodate dinghies and small runabouts up to about 16 feet.

Just south of the Palmetto Park Bridge (Mile 1047.5) a small anchorage is located at the northeastern end of Lake Boca Raton. Enter north of flashing green "65"

Danger sign at Boca Raton Inlet

Chapter 7: The Crossroads to Pompano Beach

Hillsboro River, FL

BOCA RATON AREA		Largest Vessel	VHF	Total Slips	Approach/Dockside Depth	Floating Docks	Gas/Diesel	Repairs/Haulout	Min/Max Amps	Pump-Out Station
1. Boca Raton Resort & Club MM 1048.2	(561) 447-3000	170	16	32	12.0 / 10.0				50 / 100	
2. The Cove Waterfront Restaurant & Tiki Bar and Marina MM 1050.1	(954) 427-9747	65	16	31	7.0 / 7.0		GD		30 / 50	

🛜 Wireless Internet Access
Visit www.waterwayguide.com for current rates, fuel prices, website addresses and other up-to-the-minute information. (Information in the table is provided by the facilities.)

Scan here for more details:

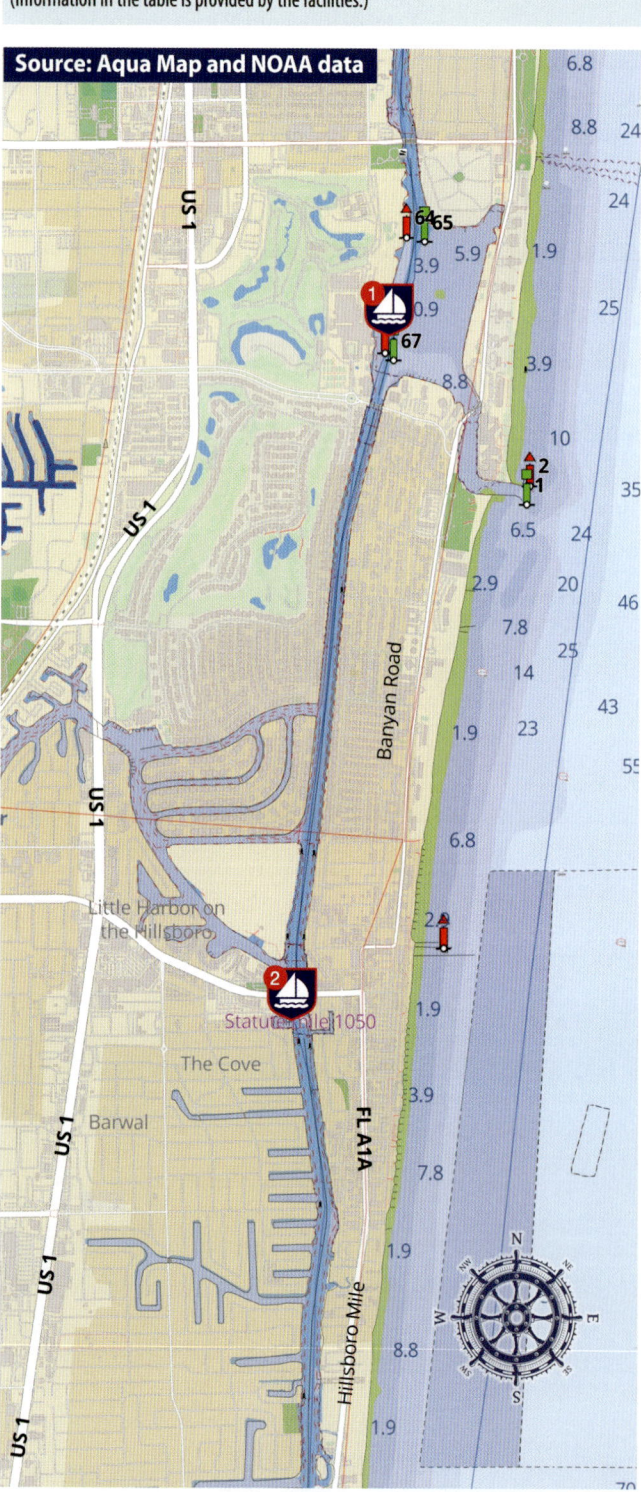

Source: Aqua Map and NOAA data

and anchor in 8-foot MLW depths north and east of the charted shoal areas. An unmarked channel runs through the anchorage area and along the eastern shore to the Boca Raton Inlet. For southbound cruisers it's 10 miles and four bridges to the next anchorage at Lake Santa Barbara.

Boca Raton to Hillsboro Inlet–ICW Mile 1050 to Mile 1053

NAVIGATION: Use NOAA Chart 11467. The ICW leaves Lake Boca Raton through the Camino Real Bridge at Mile 1048.2 (described above) and then enters a straight cut with some side canals. At Mile 1050 the

ICW enters the Hillsboro River with its many bridges and speed restrictions.

Deerfield Beach is the next city, closely followed by the Lighthouse Point area, Hillsboro Inlet and Pompano Beach proper. A maze of manmade canals shoots off the ICW in all directions and from here southward consider that each of these canals contributes to ICW traffic.

NO WAKE ZONE

Along this stretch Manatee Zones and Boating Safety Zones are frequent and often overlap. Where they do the more restrictive limitation applies. Some are seasonal (November 15 through March 31), some are year-round, some are weekends only, some are for the full width of the water and some are more restrictive within a specified distance from the shore. The official signs are well placed and repeated at intervals and may vary in only small details. You must keep a sharp lookout and read each sign carefully. The speed and wake limits are enforced by state, county and municipal police boats.

Near Deerfield Beach the Hillsboro Drainage Canal enters the ICW from the west at Mile 1049.9. During times of high flow (recent heavy rainfall) from the canal strong currents are created only 100 yards from the Hillsboro Boulevard Bridge at Mile 1050. The bridge (21-foot closed vertical clearance) opens on the hour and half-hour at all times. Southbound boats approaching the bridge should not proceed past the canal until the bridge is fully open and should maintain adequate headway to avoid being pushed into the east bridge fender by the canal crosscurrents.

At Hillsboro Inlet the 136-foot-tall lighthouse for which the area is named has one of the most powerful beacons on the coast (visible from 28 miles at sea). The fast-operating **SR A1A (Hillsboro Inlet) Bridge** (13-foot closed vertical clearance) spanning the inlet approach from the ICW opens on signal except from 7:00 a.m. to 6:00 p.m., when it need only open on the hour and at 15, 30 and 45 minutes past the hour. (Note that this bridge is not on the ICW proper.) If you are planning on using the Hillsboro Inlet be sure to get up-to-date information regarding the status of the bridge. The current runs swiftly

Boca Raton Inlet

Chapter 7: The Crossroads to Pompano Beach

beneath the bridge. Wait for the bridge to open completely before approaching.

Although shoals at Hillsboro Inlet shift rapidly, dredging is frequent and local boats and the large fleet of charter fishing and head boats heavily travel the passage here. Swells and/or tidal rip on the ebb against an easterly wind will decrease the available depth. Under good weather conditions, boats with 5-foot drafts or less can run Hillsboro Inlet safely by observing the constant flow of local boats going in and out. A southeast wind against a tide situation can kick up a short, vicious chop that can set an unwary boater onto the shoals to the south of the inlet.

Proceed all the way to the red-and-white sea buoy "HI" before turning south to avoid shoals. A rock jetty extends southeast from the north side of the inlet and is submerged at the outer end. It is wise to seek local knowledge before running this inlet.

Just south of Hillsboro Inlet the ICW swings wide around a projecting point that builds out from the eastern shore. For 1.5 miles south from the inlet spots of shoaling occur along the edges of the ICW channel. The speed limit is Slow-Speed/Minimum-Wake to just before the **NE 14th Street Bridge** where an Idle-Speed/No-Wake Zone begins. Beyond that bridge a sign lists the complex speed restrictions that prevail for the next 2.5 miles.

Dockage: Lighthouse Point Yacht Club at Mile 1052.2 is private but welcomes transients to 100 feet with club amenities and offers a mobile fueling service. Port 32 Lighthouse Point to the south features 102 wet slips that can accommodate vessels to 80 feet. Amenities include a well-stocked Ship Store and the popular Nauti Dawg Marina Cafe.

Anchorage: There is a very popular day anchorage at Hillsboro Inlet for local smaller vessels with access to the beach. Although overnight anchoring is permitted, be aware that your scope will likely be very limited due to the number of boats anchored here. For longer stays, we recommend continuing south to the Lettuce Lake or Lake Santa Barbara anchorages.

Hillsboro Inlet

America's Waterway Guide Since 1947 — **Chapter 7**

Hillsboro Inlet Area, FL

		Largest Vessel	VHF	Total Slips	Approach/ Dockside Depth	Floating Docks	Gas/ Diesel	Repairs/ Haulout	Min/Max Amps	Pump-Out Station
HILLSBORO INLET (NORTH)										
1. Lighthouse Point Yacht Club WiFi MM 1052.2	(954) 263-8281	100	16	78	10.0 / 8.0				30 / 100	P
2. Port 32 Lighthouse Point WiFi MM 1053.7	(954) 941-0227	80	16	100	7.0 / 7.0		GD		30 / 50	P
POMPANO BEACH										
3. Sands Harbor Resort & Marina WiFi MM 1056.2	(954) 942-9100	120	16	50	10.0 / 10.0		GD	R	30 / 100	P

WiFi Wireless Internet Access
Visit www.waterwayguide.com for current rates, fuel prices, website addresses and other up-to-the-minute information.
(Information in the table is provided by the facilities.)

Scan here for more details:

Hillsboro Inlet to Pompano Beach–ICW Mile 1053 to Mile 1056

Pompano Beach equates to "fishing." Even its name was inspired by one of the more popular species found in its waters. When some native folks served the local game fish to a group of surveyors who were mapping the area, the name of the pompano fish was added to the map and the name has stuck to the spot ever since. Pompano Beach has abundant boating services on protected side canals or in enclosed basins along the ICW. Almost anything the yachtsman might want in the way of service, supplies, convenience or outright luxury is available in the immediate area.

> Every April the Pompano Beach Seafood Festival brings together arts and crafts, non-stop live entertainment and great seafood. During the summer "Music Under the Stars" sponsors a variety of free concerts throughout the city.

NAVIGATION: Use NOAA Chart 11467. Two bascule bridges cross the ICW in Pompano Beach, both with 15-foot closed vertical clearance. The northernmost, the **NE 14th Street Bridge**, crosses the ICW at Mile 1055. The bridge opens on the quarter hour and three-quarter hour. The **Atlantic Boulevard (SR 814) Bridge** at Mile 1056 opens on the hour and half-hour. Both bridges monitor VHF Channel 09.

Dockage: Loggerhead Marina–Hidden Harbour Marina (located at the end of a well-protected canal off the ICW) is a dry storage facility that does repair work and offers some services. They may be able to accommodate you in a pinch. Call ahead.

Two side-by-side facilities are just north of the Atlantic Boulevard (SR 814) Bridge on the ocean side. Sands Harbor Resort & Marina (Mile 1056.2) is a hotel marina with dockage for 50 boats to 120 feet. Boaters have access to three restaurants, a resort pool and numerous

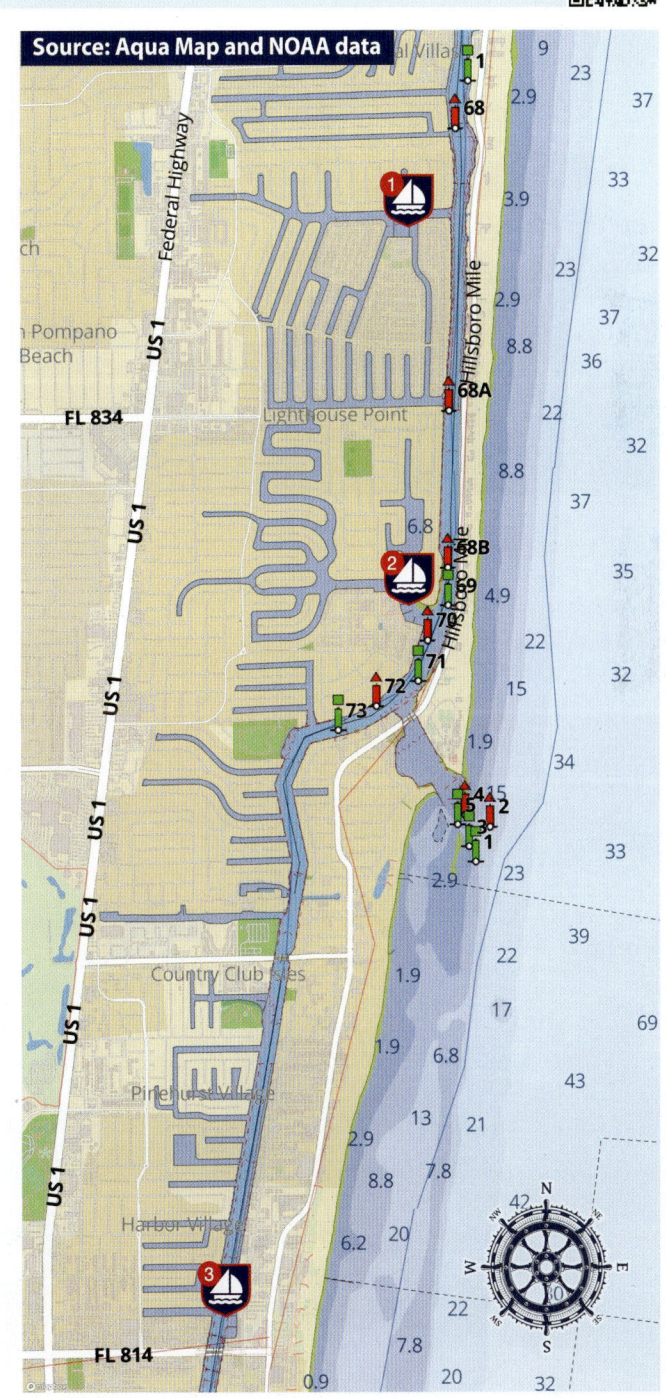

Source: Aqua Map and NOAA data

Chapter 7 — The Crossroads to Pompano Beach

Williams Island Marina
Located 10 miles south of Port Everglades on the ICW at MM1076.6

Please see our ad in chapter 8 North Miami, Miami Beach section

4100 Island Boulevard, Aventura, Florida 33160
305.937.7813 o | 305.936.5713 f
www.WilliamsIslandMarina.com
dockmaster@WilliamsIslandMarina.com

other marine businesses on the property including laundry services, boat maintenance/repairs, small boat/jet ski rentals, yacht brokerage, fishing charters, scuba certifications and dive trips to shipwreck park.

Anchorage: While you can anchor in Lettuce Lake at Mile 1056.8 but holding is reportedly poor. A much better option exists on the west side of the ICW in Lake Santa Barbara. Enter the lake in the middle of the channel and then favor the south shore to go back to a well-protected anchorage. Large enough for at least six boats with excellent protection and good holding in sand and shells in 6 to 15 feet MLW. Expect company on the weekends and a significant amount of boat traffic during the day. Traffic dies down at dusk. There is a small park on the north side by the multi-level townhomes. Although there is no dinghy dock, you can tie up to the metal railing for short periods.

■ NEXT STOP

Just to the south lies a world-class yachting center, Fort Lauderdale. If you're Bahamas bound, check out "Crossing to the Bahamas" at the end of Chapter 9 of this guide for headings from either Hillsboro Inlet or Port Everglades Inlet to Grand Bahama or Bimini.

Pompano Beach

Fort Lauderdale to Hollywood

Chapter 8

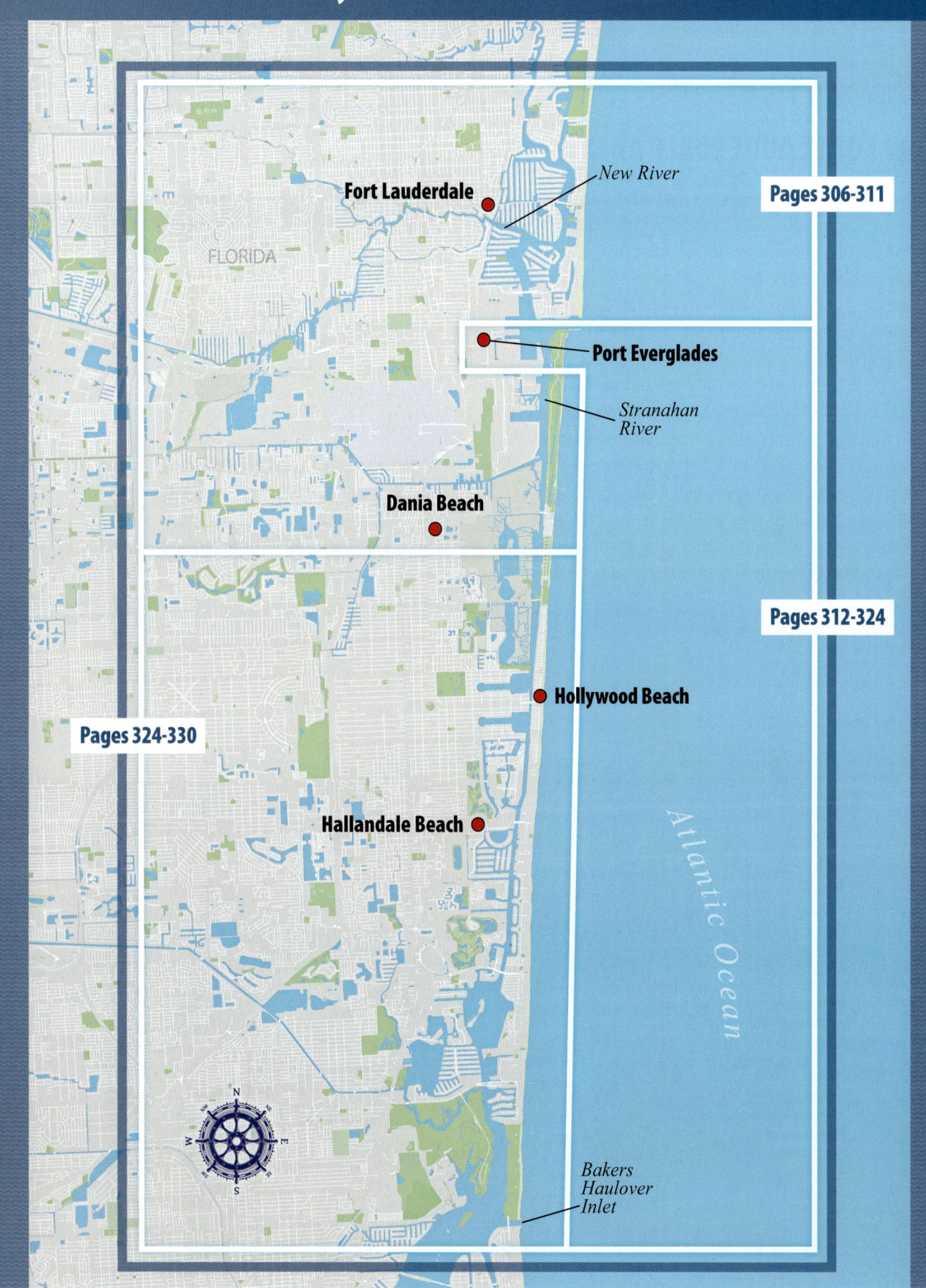

SOUTHERN EDITION

Chapter 8: Fort Lauderdale to Hollywood

 ICW Mile 1056-Mile 1080

■ FORT LAUDERDALE AREA

Nearly 300 miles of mostly navigable inland waterways carve through the Fort Lauderdale area making it the "Venice of America." With the Atlantic Ocean surf to the east and the traffic-laden ICW running north and south the city is conspicuously water-oriented. The New River and its tributaries cut through the center of town and manmade side canals sprout in all directions.

Well known as a yachting center Fort Lauderdale harbors more recreational boats than any other port in Florida. Not surprisingly the marine industry ranks second only to tourism. The city boasts more than 800 marina-related businesses—including a collection of marinas, yacht services, sailmakers, boatyards, yacht brokers, dinghy manufacturers and marine supply stores—and the craftspeople here are some of the best in the business.

Although the entire city of Fort Lauderdale has the look of a huge yachting center, most boating amenities and services are concentrated in three main areas: the main ICW channel, the New River and the Dania Cut-Off Canal.

NO WAKE ZONE

No Wake Zones, Idle Speed Zones and various Speed Limit restrictions are in effect throughout the waterways included in this chapter. Exercise diligence in knowing the regulations by observing signs and other markers. Enforcement is always present. As always, be courteous to other vessels and avoid manatees and other marine life.

Pompano Beach to East Las Olas Boulevard Bridge–ICW Mile 1057 to Mile 1064

This section of the ICW runs through a man-made canal to the junction with Middle River in Fort Lauderdale. Mostly residential development lines the sides of the canal with the exception of the wilderness of Hugh Taylor Birch

Fort Lauderdale

Fort Lauderdale, FL

FORT LAUDERDALE AREA (EAST)		Largest Vessel	VHF	Total Slips	Approach/ Dockside Depth	Floating Docks	Gas/ Diesel	Repairs/ Haulout	Min/Max Amps	Pump-Out Station
1. Coral Ridge Yacht Club-PRIVATE WiFi MM 1062.3	(954) 566-7886	100		58	10.0 / 8.0				30 / 50	P
2. Sunrise Harbor Marina WiFi MM 1062.3	(954) 667-6720	180		19	10.0 / 8.5	F			50 / 200+	
3. Hall of Fame Marina WiFi MM 1063.8	(954) 764-3975	175	16	43	8.0 / 9.0	F			50 / 200+	P
4. Bahia Mar Yachting Center WiFi MM 1064.5	(954) 627-6309	300	16	240	16.0 / 16.0	F	GD		30 / 200+	P

WiFi Wireless Internet Access
Visit www.waterwayguide.com for current rates, fuel prices, website addresses and other up-to-the-minute information.
(Information in the table is provided by the facilities.)

Scan here for more details:

State Park opposite Sunrise Bay. While some areas along this stretch look like potential anchorages, local bylaws restrict overnight stops for most. Keep in mind these restrictions are updated constantly and you may want to check with local authorities before planning a stop.

NAVIGATION: Use NOAA Charts 11467 and 11470. Between Mile 1057 and Mile 1064 are four bridges, all with restricted schedules (i.e., do not open on signal):

- **Mile 1059: Commercial Boulevard (SR 870) Bridge** has 15-foot closed vertical clearance and opens on the hour and half-hour.

- **Mile 1060.5: Oakland Park Boulevard Bridge** has 22-foot closed vertical clearance and opens on the quarter-hour and three-quarter hour.

- **Mile 1062.6: East Sunrise Boulevard (SR 838) Bridge** has 25-foot closed vertical clearance and opens on the hour and half-hour.

- **Mile 1064: East Las Olas Boulevard Bridge** has 24-foot closed vertical clearance and opens on the quarter and three-quarter hour.

In this stretch the ICW runs through a cut, making its course straight and obvious (with no need for aids to navigation). The shores are densely populated and the waterway is heavily traveled. At Mile 1061.5 residential development is broken by the 180-acre Hugh Taylor Birch State Park, which stretches for about 1 mile along the east side of the ICW opposite the yacht club and marina in Sunrise Bay. The park is a pleasant, wooded oasis that offers rental canoes on a quiet lagoon and a swimming beach for a tropical picnic. Unfortunately, the park has no docks on the ICW. The Fort Lauderdale Water Taxi does stop at the park. Local marine police frequently patrol the ICW here and vigorously enforce the speed limit.

Source: Aqua Map and NOAA data

BAHIA MAR
A SUNTEX EXPERIENCE

Your Premiere Destination

Who wouldn't want to spend their days enjoying first-class amenities at this spectacular waterfront destination while being treated like a VIP? Featuring a DoubleTree by Hilton hotel, you can relax with an array of amenities, including tennis, shops, restaurants and lounge, live music, pool, the beach, and activities for the whole family!
Bahia Mar is also the home to the world-renowned Fort Lauderdale International Boat Show.

Whether you stay for a day, a week, or longer, we will make sure that you have a great time along with a safe, comfortable and stress-free experience.

250 slips for vessels up to 300' • 3,000 foot parallel dock • Over 5,000' of floating docks • High speed fueling
Free WiFi • Cable TV • In slip sanitary pump-out • Marine Store • Dive shop • Marine maintenance provider

801 Seabreeze Blvd,
Fort Lauderdale, FL 33316
(954) 627-6309

SUNTEX MARINAS
YOUR PLACE IN THE SUN

#yourplaceinthesun
bahiamaryachtingcenter.com

North of the East Sunrise Boulevard Bridge near Mile 1062 the channel starts to zigzag past the private Coral Ridge Yacht Club and Sunrise Harbor Marina and associated condominiums to the west. Stay close to the western bank from here until you reach the first aid to navigation, flashing green "3" where the channel heads southeast.

At flashing green "5" the channel turns back southwest. Make a gentle turn giving the mainland point opposite flashing green "5" a wide berth. The next marker, flashing red "8," can be hard to find in the seemingly large pond here. It is just off the western shoreline located just north of the East Las Olas Boulevard Bridge. There is an area of privately rented slips from here to the bridge.

Dockage: Numerous restaurants just above and below the Oakland Park Boulevard Bridge have docks for their customers. On weekends several of the livelier drinking and dining spots on the east side have boats rafted out six or more deep into the ICW.

Just north of the East Sunrise Boulevard Bridge (Mile 1062.6) are Coral Ridge Yacht Club followed by Sunrise Harbor Marina. The Yacht Club is private but accepts reciprocals from Florida Council of Yacht Clubs and the American Registry of Yacht Clubs if there is space. The 22-slip Sunrise Harbor Marina caters to megayachts (up to 200 feet) and has upscale amenities including a health and fitness center, spa, tennis courts and two heated pools. It also provides easy access to world-famous beaches, golf, theatre, shopping and dining.

To reach the long-term dockage areas at Isle of Venice and Hendricks Isle turn west off of the ICW at Middle River between flashing green "3" and "5." These canals are the last three straight, north-south canals in the Nurmi Isles section. Many properties rent private slips on these two islands. Most are long-term rentals but some are rented out on a daily basis. The docks are various sizes with unique shoreside amenities and are priced accordingly. The best way to find a slip here is to stop elsewhere temporarily and then visit the area to check availability. Slips are hard to find here during the winter season.

Anchorage: Anchor at your own risk. The anchoring ban does not appear to be enforced here, but we recommend you seek local knowledge. Should you decide to take the risk, Sunrise Bay offers a well-protected anchorage just north of the Yacht Club and across from Hugh Taylor Birch State Park. You can pull fairly close to the houses deep in the bay for 7 feet MLW. The state park has a dinghy dock, so you can get off the boat and explore the area.

> *CAUTION:* Florida legislation bans overnight anchoring in the section of the Middle River at Mile 1063.4 from NE 21st Street to the ICW. It is illegal to anchor at any time during the period between one-half hour after sunset and one-half hour before sunrise. Revisions to the anchoring laws in Florida have continued to include this restriction, despite widespread opposition by boaters.

To Port Everglades–ICW Mile 1064 to Mile 1066

Between the East Las Olas Boulevard Bridge and the SE 17th Street (Brooks Memorial) Bridge there is a concentration of marinas close to the bridges. Canals branch off in all directions and are lined by spectacular homes with yachts docked in their back yards. Many of these residences have been "remodeled" and expanded in size numerous times.

The Fort Lauderdale oceanfront between Bahia Mar and Sunrise Blvd. is limited to one-way north-bound traffic and features bike trails, sidewalks and landscaping, all creating an attractive setting. A large number of high-rise luxury condominium resorts, quite conspicuous from offshore, line the strip between Sunrise and Las Olas Boulevards. Many of these offer upscale shopping and dining experiences on their lower floors.

NAVIGATION: Use NOAA Charts 11470 and 11472. East Las Olas Boulevard Bridge has 24-foot closed vertical clearance and opens on the quarter and three-quarter hour. SE 17th Street (Brooks Memorial) Bridge at Mile 1065.9 has a vertical clearance of 55 feet and opens on the hour and half-hour as needed for sailboats and large motor yachts. Northbound vessels waiting for a bridge opening should stay clear of the turning basin and cruise ship berths as well as any government patrol boats.

> NOTE: Marine Police boats are active here and it is necessary to maintain the slowest possible speed through this area to avoid a warning or ticket. Do not be tempted to speed up to make a bridge opening.

Chapter 8: Fort Lauderdale to Hollywood

For those with the time to spend a few days in Fort Lauderdale a side trip up New River is strongly recommended. You will pass directly through the city's vast Historic District and find easy dockage right next to Fort Lauderdale's active Arts & Museum district with premier dining and shopping areas nearby.

Dockage/Moorings: Although jam-packed with permanent year-round or seasonal boats most marinas reserve some space for transients so the visiting cruiser is almost certain to find a berth at one place or another. At the height of the season you must reserve a berth in advance of arrival.

The first concentration of marine facilities southbound begins at the East Las Olas Boulevard Bridge on the eastern side of the ICW. (The western side is residential except for the small anchorage and mooring area just south of the bridge.) The municipal Las Olas Marina is closed for property renovations (possibly for several years). The town is now managing the Fort Lauderdale Mooring Field at Mile 1064.7. Pick up an empty mooring (no reservation required) and call 954-828-5423. Boaters can also check in and complete the appropriate forms downtown at 2 South New River Drive East, Suite 103. This location is accessible with a dinghy. They are open between 8:00 a.m. and 4:00 p.m. You can pay by check or with a credit card.

Stroll across A1A to the beach while your boat is safe and secure at Hall of Fame Marina. Located in the heart of all the sun, shopping, and dining in Fort Lauderdale, this pristine marina accommodates yachts up to 170'. Watch as the renovation of the world-class Swimming Hall of Fame, which hosts the world's largest outdoor swimming complex, becomes a reality.

Bahia Mar Yachting Center offers 250 slips capable of handling vessels up to 300 feet along its 3,000-foot parallel dock and more than 5,000 feet of floating docks. This facility offers high-speed fueling, in-slip pump-out service, a marine store and dive shop. In addition, slip holders have full access to all of the resort amenities located within the property and the hotel including restaurants, shopping, a pool and tennis courts directly across the street from a pristine sand beach. This is home to the world-renowned Fort Lauderdale International Boat Show.

The second concentration of marinas begins just north of the SE 17th Street (Brooks Memorial) Bridge. Heading south on the ICW the private Lauderdale Yacht Club welcomes individuals sponsored by members. (Call ahead for slip availability.)

Next on the western side is the Lauderdale Marina/15th Street Fisheries, which has been providing accommodation to yachts–large and small–since 1948. Slips are open to the public on a first-come, first-served basis. They also offer boat sales, service and parts. The award-winning Fifteenth Street Fisheries Restaurant is here as well as a 365-foot fuel dock. There is often a line of boats waiting for fuel, especially on weekends. Boaters should try to come in against the current, take up as short a space as possible and fuel up quickly.

The deep-water 17th Street Yacht Basin at the Hilton Marina Hotel accommodates megayachts up to 300 feet along a facewall directly on the ICW and smaller vessels in a quiet basin off the canal. Guests of the marina have access to the hotel amenities including a waterfront cocktail bar, restaurant, pool and fitness center. Farther west along the same canal is Marina Boathouse of Fort Lauderdale, which offers traditional slips but also has a unique fully covered, mega-yacht dockominium and that can accommodate vessels to 200 feet. The facility is walking distance from shopping, restaurants and bars.

Just north and south of the SE 17th Street (Brooks Memorial) Bridge on the east side of the ICW are Pier Sixty-Six Marina and Pier Sixty-Six South. The facilities feature 5,000 linear feet of dockage with 164 slips, welcoming vessels up to 400 feet. High-speed fueling, resort amenities and dockside concierge service add to the appeal.

Anchorage: Lake Sylvia south of Bahia Mar Yachting Center is your best bet now for anchoring in this area. Leave the intracoastal headed east at flashing green "13." Hug the east shore for 6-foot MLW depths into lake. Once in the lake alter course west-southwest to avoid a shallow area and anchor in 8 to 9 feet MLW where space permits. Luxurious homes surround the anchorage. On weekends Lake Sylvia is full of local boats, many rafted for the night. It is also a favorite spot for water skiers.

There is not a dinghy landing in Lake Sylvia but water taxis stand by on VHF Channel 68 and will pick up or drop off passengers at locations throughout Fort Lauderdale along both the ICW and the New River. A pass provides the passenger with unlimited stops and rides for the whole day.

Fort Lauderdale, FL

FORT LAUDERDALE AREA (WEST)		Largest Vessel	VHF	Total Slips	Approach/ Dockside Depth	Floating Docks	Gas/ Diesel	Repairs/ Haulout	Min/Max Amps	Pump-Out Station
1. Lauderdale Yacht Club-PRIVATE MM 1066.0	(954) 527-2209		16	64	5.0 / 5.0				30	
2. Lauderdale Marina/15th Street Fisheries WiFi MM 1065.0	(954) 523-8507		16	60	10.0 / 8.0	F	GD	RH	30 / 200+	
3. 17th Street Yacht Basin at the Hilton Marina Hotel WiFi	(954) 527-6766	300	16	35	20.0 / 10.0				30 / 200+	
4. Marina Boathouse of Fort Lauderdale WiFi MM 1065.0	(954) 306-1056	200		10	14.0 / 12.0			R	50 / 100	P
5. Pier Sixty-Six Marina WiFi MM 1065.0	(954) 728-3578	400	16	157	16.0 / 25.0		GD		30 / 200+	P
6. Pier Sixty-Six South WiFi MM 1065.9	(954) 728-3578	500	16	20	45.0 / 24.0	F	GD		30 / 200+	

WiFi Wireless Internet Access
Visit www.waterwayguide.com for current rates, fuel prices, website addresses and other up-to-the-minute information. (Information in the table is provided by the facilities.)

Scan here for more details:

Source: Aqua Map and NOAA data

Chapter 8: Fort Lauderdale to Hollywood

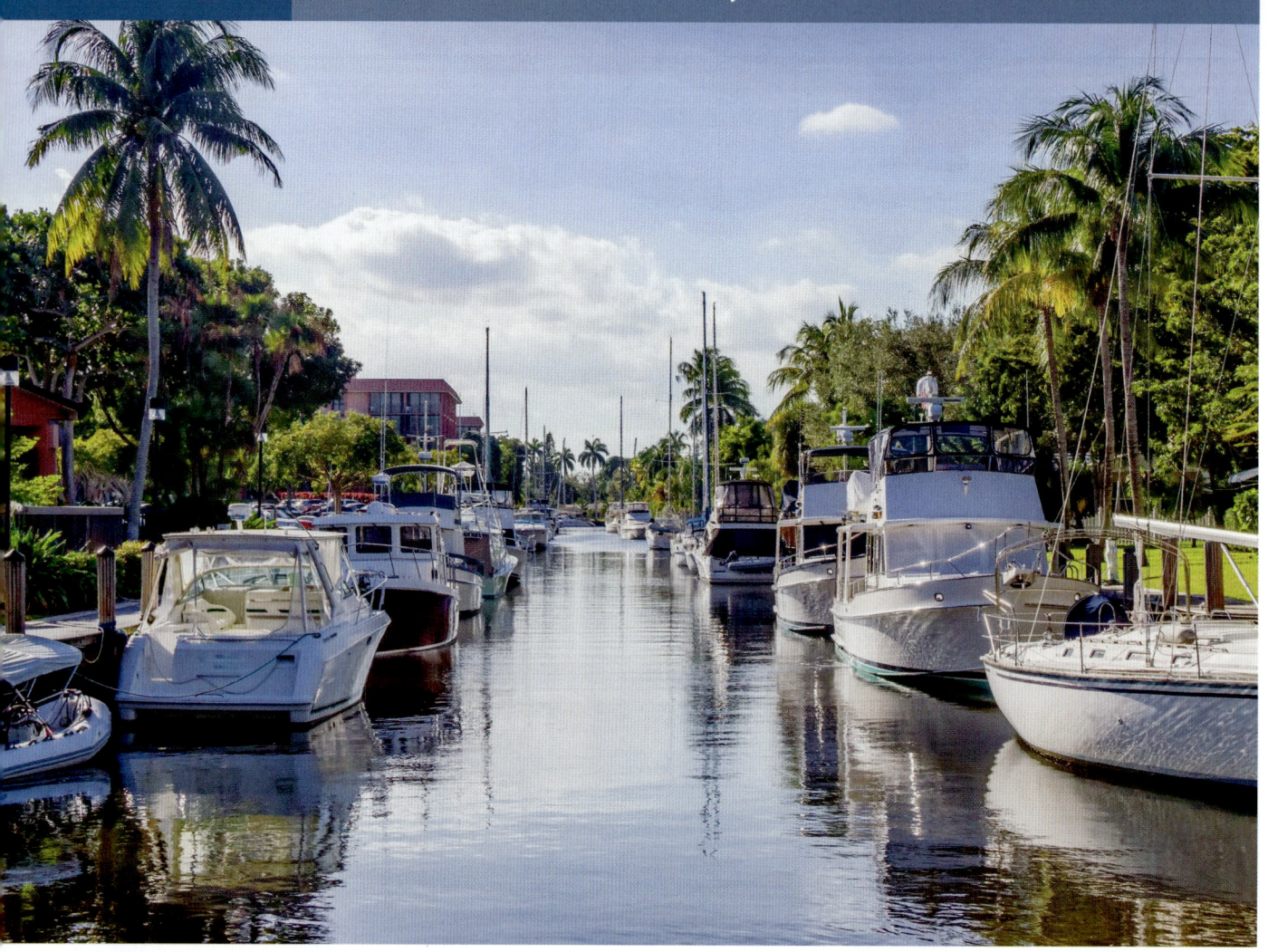

■ SIDE TRIP: NEW RIVER

The gently curving, meandering New River bisects the heart of Fort Lauderdale and serves as another major waterway and yacht service area. The New River is Fort Lauderdale's yachting center with some of the finest facilities for building, repair, haul-out and storage on the entire East Coast. Even if you don't need anything it is worth taking a trip–by boat, dinghy or one of the regularly scheduled sightseeing craft–just to see the contrast of the old and new Fort Lauderdale.

Just beyond its mouth the New River wanders lazily through a short stretch edged by fine lawns and some of the area's older, grander and more gracious homes. Entering the commercial area you pass over south Florida's only traffic tunnel, which carries U.S. Hwy. 1 beneath the river. This area was Fort Lauderdale's original business district and its original marine-services center. Attesting to Fort Lauderdale's long-standing prominence in the marine industry, New River's wooded riverbanks were lined with docks long before World War II much as they are today.

Riverwalk Fort Lauderdale lines both the north and south banks of the New River. The extraordinary waterfront park lies in the heart of downtown and offers lush tropical landscaping and winding brick walkways that link attractions, restaurants and shops. Most cruisers thoroughly enjoy this stretch of river frontage and find this a pleasant place to tie up for a day or two.

Water traffic is heavy on weekends and extra fenders are desirable, although wake action is not nearly as noticeable as you might expect. Every manner of watercraft will pass by and the sights and sounds of this traffic are fascinating. You may also spot the broad back of a manatee or the bulging eyes of an alligator. Nearby Las Olas Blvd. offers excellent restaurants, gourmet food shops, fashionable boutiques and specialty shops. Fort Lauderdale's well-preserved historic districts are all within an easy walk.

The New River forks beyond the William H. Marshall (7th Avenue) Bridge into the North Fork and the South Fork of the New River. The North Fork is residential while the South Fork serves as the principal channel that leads to the heart of Fort Lauderdale's marine-services hub and additional marinas.

NAVIGATION: Use NOAA Charts 11470 and 11467. Entrance to the New River from the ICW has two approaches and entry instructions depend on whether you are southbound or northbound. Southbound ICW traffic enters New River via the approach at Mile 1065 near flashing red "16." The New River approach channel follows a northwesterly course, while the ICW turns southwest. Care should be taken to keep the red-over-green junction daybeacon "A" to port on entry. The water is very shallow immediately behind this daybeacon and you will run aground if you pass it on the wrong side.

Continuing northwest observe daybeacons "1" through "4," which clearly mark the channel. Just inside the approach entry, a white-and-orange DANGER daybeacon marks a shoal. Keep that well to port as you pass.

Northbound ICW traffic enters New River via the south approach at Mile 1065.5 between two red ICW markers. Take red daybeacon "22" to port and keep flashing red "20" to starboard for the New River approach channel, which follows a northerly course. (The ICW turns northeast at this junction). Beware of a rock just outside the channel at red daybeacon "22." Favor the bulkhead-lined western shore from flashing red "20" to green daybeacon "5" in the river's mouth. Northbound vessels should study the chart closely and sort out the confusing transposition of buoys and colors before trying this entrance.

CAUTION: Tarpon River Bend is a blind S-turn at the river's mouth at green daybeacon "11." To make matters worse the last New River marker, red daybeacon "12," marks a hard shoal extending into the channel at Tarpon Bend. There is another blind corner in a narrow section of the river at "Danger Bend" just before the SE 3rd Avenue Bridge. We suggest signaling with a horn when approaching this area so oncoming traffic knows you are coming.

The strong tidal current should be considered when transiting the New River because there is always congestion, especially at the bridges and along the Las Olas Riverfront dining and entertainment area. All of the bridges open on signal with some restrictions.

- **SE 3rd Avenue Bridge** (16-foot closed vertical clearance): Opens on signal except from 7:30 a.m. to 9:00 a.m. and from 4:30 p.m. to 6:00 p.m., Monday through Friday (except federal holidays), when the draw need not open.

- **Andrews Avenue Bridge** (21-foot closed vertical clearance): Opens on signal except from 7:30 a.m. to 9:00 a.m. and from 4:30 p.m. to 6:00 p.m., Monday through Friday (except federal holidays), when the draw need not open. The bridge will not open if the FEC Railroad Bridge is closed.

- **Florida East Coast Railroad Bridge** (4-foot closed vertical clearance): Usually open unless train approaching. It is remotely operated.

- **William H. Marshall (7th Avenue) Bridge** (20-foot closed vertical clearance at center): The draw opens on signal except from 7:30 a.m. to 9:00 a.m. and from 4:30 p.m. to 6:00 p.m., Monday through Friday (except federal holidays), when the draw need not open.

Where the New River forks beyond the William H. Marshall (7th Avenue) Bridge, the narrow and shallow North Fork is residential and has only one bridge (**11th Avenue Bridge**). The hand-operated swing has 3-foot closed vertical clearance and opens on signal. This branch is best explored by dinghy.

The stretch between the William H. Marshall (7th Avenue) Bridge and the South Fork is a good place to wait for coming around the S-curve from the south ("Little Florida"), which can be difficult in a strong current. A Sécurité call may be in order here.

New River's South Fork continues from the junction as a wide channel with 8-foot MLW controlling depths. Development flanking the South Fork is residential for a distance but the waterway serves as the principal channel that leads to the heart of Fort Lauderdale's marine-services hub and additional marinas. A 2-mile stretch of boatyards, service shops and freshwater storage begins less than 1 mile above the **Davie Boulevard Bridge**. The bridge

Chapter 8: Fort Lauderdale to Hollywood

Goin' Ashore

FORT LAUDERDALE (NEW RIVER), FL

America's Waterway Guide Since 1947 — Chapter 8

The New River area of Fort Lauderdale is an extraordinary visitor destination. Spanning the north and south banks of the river is the Riverwalk Park, a waterfront park in the heart of downtown. The lush tropical landscape and winding walkways link attractions, restaurants and shops and is the epicenter for special events, including a Jazz Brunch, held the first Sunday of every month in the Bubier Park area of Riverwalk.

ATTRACTION

1. Broward Center for the Performing Arts
The center is home of the Florida Grand Opera, plus ballet and dance performances, music and theater at 201 SW 5th Ave. (954-462-0222)

2. History Fort Lauderdale Museum
The museum displays history of the area with exhibits and artifacts housed in Broward County's oldest standing hotel at 231 SW 2nd Ave. (954-463-4431).

3. Historic Stranahan House Museum
Museum that offers tours and events in first permanent residence converted to first permanent residence at 335 SE 6th. Ave., (954-524-4736).

4. Museum of Discovery and Science
The museum includes hands-on exhibits and an IMAX 3D Theater 401 SW 2nd St. (954-467-6637) and has a floating dock for those who wish to arrive by boat (for day use only).

SERVICES

5. Broward County Main Library
100 S. Andrews Ave. (954-357-7444)

6. Fort Lauderdale Post Office
1404 E. Las Olas Blvd., Ste. B
(954-523-0327)

7. Greater Fort Lauderdale Convention & Visitors Bureau
101 NE 3rd Ave #100 (954-765-4466)

MARINAS

8. Cooley's Landing Marina
450 SW 7th Ave. (954-828-4626)

9. New River Downtown Docks
2 S. New River Dr. East
(954-828-5423)

SOUTHERN EDITION

Chapter 8: Fort Lauderdale to Hollywood

Fort Lauderdale (New River), FL

NEW RIVER		Largest Vessel	VHF	Total Slips	Approach/ Dockside Depth	Floating Docks	Gas/ Diesel	Repairs/ Haulout	Min/Max Amps	Pump-Out Station
1. New River Downtown Docks WiFi	(954) 828-5423	170	16	100	15.0 / 8.0				30 / 100	P
2. Cooley's Landing Marina WiFi	(954) 828-4626	50	9	30	10.0 / 6.0				30 / 50	P

WiFi Wireless Internet Access
Visit www.waterwayguide.com for current rates, fuel prices, website addresses and other up-to-the-minute information. (Information in the table is provided by the facilities.)

Scan here for more details:

has 21-foot closed vertical clearance and opens on signal except Monday through Friday from 7:30 a.m. to 9:00 a.m. and from 4:30 p.m. to 6:00 p.m. (except federal holidays), when the draw need not open. Exercise caution at the 90-degree turn past the bridge as there is not room for two vessels to pass in the turn.

The service and storage yards for deep-draft vessels continue up to the **I-95 Twin Bridges** (55-foot fixed vertical clearance) where there the air-draft limitation will block many larger vessels. (There is a fixed 55-foot vertical clearance railroad bridge for Tri-Rail passenger trains running alongside the I-95 Twin Bridges.) The water is brown and murky, tinted by the Everglades' cypress swamps that drain into the river upstream. Floating water hyacinths, coconuts and other debris is often seen here. You may spot the broad back of a manatee or the bulging eyes of an alligator. Another Idle-Speed/No-Wake Zone extends about 500 yards on either side of the I-95 Twin Bridges.

Next is the **SCL Railroad Bridge** with 2-foot closed vertical clearance, which is open except when trains are approaching. You may encounter strong currents near the twin bridges and around the railroad bridge and turning room is limited. Call the bridgetender ahead of time on VHF Channel 09 to see if you will need to wait for a train. Do not attempt to wait for a bridge opening under the I-95 Twin Bridges. Wait in front of the Lauderdale Marine Center boat sheds instead.

The South New River Canal continues to the southwest. Although narrow, it holds good depths but a 50-foot-high cable south of the boatyards restricts vertical clearance here. This is as far as most cruising boats go. The South New River Canal passes under the **SR 84 Bridge** with 21-foot closed vertical clearance (opens only

Yes, You can have it all...only in Fort Lauderdale

Two Great Downtown Locations in One Great City!

The City of Fort Lauderdale's Downtown New River Docks offer secure dockage and ample power for all sizes including mega-yachts, while Cooley's Landing caters to vessels up to 50 feet.

The Downtown Docks are located on the New River in the heart of the City. Renowned Las Olas Boulevard offers upscale shopping, boutiques, restaurants and clubs which are just one block away from the north side of the New River. Groceries are just two blocks away.

Cooley's Landing Is a quaint park tucked away in the City's historic Sailboat Bend District and offers tree-lined walks along the New River to the Museum of Discovery and Science, restaurants, clubs and the Broward Center of the Performing Arts/Florida Grand Opera.

Cooley's Landing

New River Downtown Docks

City Of Fort Lauderdale Marine Facilities
2 South New River Drive East, Suite 103
Fort Lauderdale, Florida 33301
954-828-5423   VHF Channels 9 &16

Amenities Include:

| On-Spot Wi-Fi | Free Pumpout | Boat U.S. Participating Marina | Florida Clean Marinas | Showers | Laundry | Security | Lounge |

Prompt and Courteous Staff

Chapter 8: Fort Lauderdale to Hollywood

with 24-hour advance notice). This unmanned bridge is one of the few in Fort Lauderdale not equipped with a VHF radio. The final bridge before joining the Dania Cut-Off Canal (located 2 miles south) is the 40-foot fixed vertical clearance **I-595 Bridge**.

The navigation charts note that the latest reported depths for the Dania Cut-Off Canal is just 2 feet MLW west of the I-595 Bridge. This passage is surrounded by wilderness and swamp and is suited for small boat exploration only. East of this junction is a water-controlled gate that rises like a guillotine to allow vessels with less than 10-foot vertical clearance to pass beneath. For this reason the Dania Cut-Off Canal is typically entered from the ICW south of Port Everglades. There are several large yards at Port Laudania, where small freighters and cargo ships dock. This is discussed in more detail in the Port Everglades section.

Dockage: Be aware that the current along New River can be swift so take care in docking and ensure mooring lines are secure. Dockage at the municipal New River Downtown Docks are available on a first-come-first-served basis or by advance reservation. The docks (linear docking along the seawall) are located in the heart of downtown beginning a short distance upriver from the SE 3rd Avenue Bridge and extending intermittently to the William H. Marshall (7th Avenue) Bridge near Cooley's Landing. The dockmaster's office is on the south bank just east of the Andrews Avenue Bridge. New River Downtown Docks has ample deep-water dockage, pump-out stations and grassy picnic areas and is within walking distance of grocery stores and the famous Las Olas Blvd., known for its shops, galleries, fine restaurants and cafés.

Cooley's Landing Marina is another municipal marina with slips with the usual amenities. This facility is located on the north bank and is adjacent to the arts and science district featuring the Broward Center for the Performing Arts, the Museum of Discovery and Science and Esplanade Park.

Most of the facilities on the South Fork of the New River are oriented towards providing repair services but some offer transient and long-term dockage. On the north side of the I-95 Twin Bridges is the well-regarded Safe Harbor Lauderdale Marine Center, which specializes in repairs and refits and can accommodate large catamarans. Port 32 Fort Lauderdale (formerly Fort Lauderdale Boatyard & Marina) has been undergoing renovations but may have transient slips available. Call for details (954-895-8360).

Marina Mile Yachting Center is located across the river on the southern shore and is a full-service boatyard with a 6-acre repair facility and dry dockage located inside Marina Bay Resort. They maintain 10 reserved transient slips. Next on the south shore is Marina Bay Yachting Center, which offers luxury resort amenities including an expansive activity center with a resort pool, tennis facilities, private theater and a handball court. Rendezvous Bar & Grill (954-797-0054) is on site.

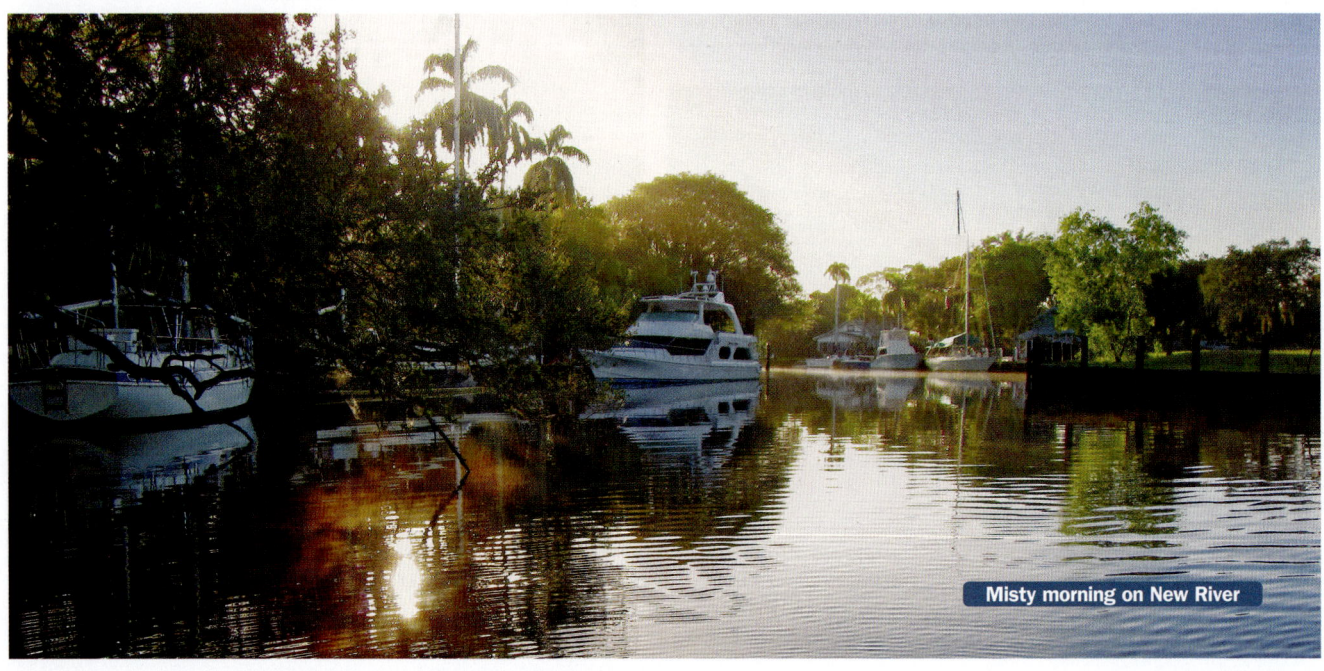
Misty morning on New River

Fort Lauderdale (New River), FL

NEW RIVER - SOUTH FORK		Largest Vessel	VHF	Total Slips	Approach/ Dockside Depth	Floating Docks	Gas/ Diesel	Repairs/ Haulout	Min/Max Amps	Pump-Out Station
1. Safe Harbor Lauderdale Marine Center WiFi	(954) 713-0333	200		89	12.0 / 10.0	F	GD	RH	30 / 100	P
2. Port 32 Fort Lauderdale WiFi New River 1065	(954) 895-8360	120			8.0 / 8.0		GD	RH		
3. Marina Mile Yachting Center WiFi	(954) 583-0053	150		35	12.0 / 10.0	F		RH	50 / 100	
4. Marina Bay Yachting Center WiFi	(954) 791-7600	150		168	12.0 / 45.0	F			30 / 200+	
5. Yacht Haven Park & Marina WiFi	(954) 583-2322	120			10.0 / 6.0				30 / 100	
6. Billfish Marina	(954) 587-6226	130	16	45	14.0 / 9.0	F		RH	30 / 100	

WiFi Wireless Internet Access
Visit www.waterwayguide.com for current rates, fuel prices, website addresses and other up-to-the-minute information.
(Information in the table is provided by the facilities.)

Scan here for more details:

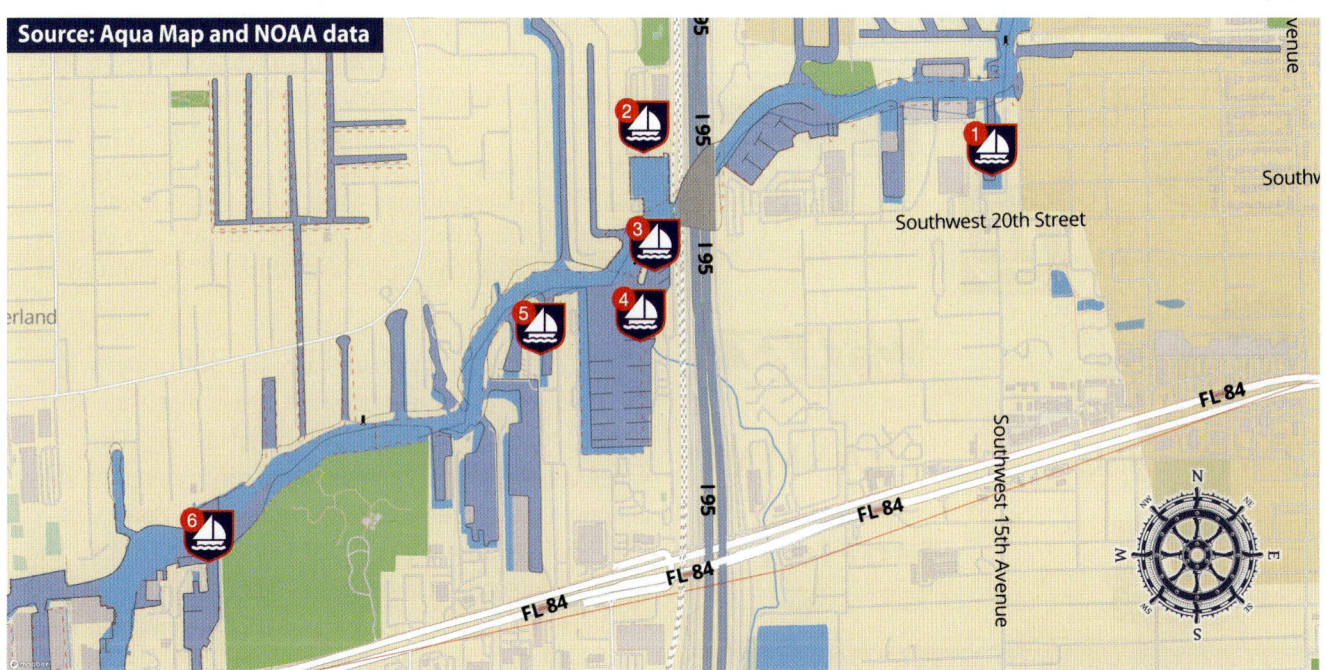

Nearby Yacht Haven Park & Marina is a combination RV park and marina located in a gated 20-acre, park-like setting. This facility welcomes long and short-term boaters with 55 side-tie slips that can accommodate yachts up to 150 feet. A pool and sundeck and a fitness center are among the amenities. The facility requests that larger boats (over 100 feet) call ahead for a reservation.

The next group of marinas and boatyards is about 0.5 mile south just before the SR 84 Bridge. The 45-slip Billfish Marina is a full-service boatyard and marina that can accommodate vessels to 130 feet.

Other boat yards and marine service facilities here include Cable Marine West Yard, Rolly Marine Service, Inc. and Roscioli Yachting Center. Call ahead to see if they have room for you.

Port Everglades (Fort Lauderdale) Inlet

Port Everglades is a modern, deep water harbor and the third of Fort Lauderdale's important boating areas. Expensive waterfront homes overlook the endless stream of cruise ships, recreational craft, tankers, freighters and warships that constantly parade through the Port Everglades (Fort Lauderdale) Inlet. The port is primarily used as a commercial harbor and may be crowded with both commercial and recreational traffic. When military vessels are in port a security cordon is set up for which entry by private craft is prohibited.

When large vessels are docked and secured in the port, boat traffic may still proceed along the ICW provided that they stay to the east of law enforcement craft and cruise ship tenders being used to mark the transit lane. When such vessels are not docked, boats may use the ICW

Chapter 8: Fort Lauderdale to Hollywood

without restriction. Occasionally all traffic may be halted temporarily while ships are docking or leaving. Patrol craft may be contacted on VHF Channel 16 for the status of these security zones. The Coast Guard-established and well enforced Slow-Speed Zone in the Port Everglades Entrance Channel.

NAVIGATION: Use NOAA Charts 11470 and 11467.

CAUTION: Keep clear of large-vessel traffic in the busy inlets, especially Port Everglades (Fort Lauderdale) Inlet, Government Cut (Miami) Inlet and Lake Worth (Palm Beach) Inlet. The Coast Guard establishes a moving security zone for the protection of passenger vessels (cruise ships), vessels carrying cargoes of particular hazard and vessels carrying liquefied hazardous gas when such a vessel passes buoy "PE" to enter the port. Approaching closer than 100 yards to such a vessel is prohibited without prior permission.

The entire Port Everglades area has deep water with the exception of the northeastern corner alongside the marked ICW channel near flashing green "29." Deep water vessel dockage extends to the south along the ship channel that includes the ICW route to the Dania Cut-Off Canal at flashing green "35" (Mile 1068.5) where the ICW marker sequence resumes. (Note there are no ICW markers in the between these two flashing greens.)

One of the best and safest big ship inlets in Florida, Port Everglades (Fort Lauderdale) Inlet is well marked with flashing buoys along the entrance channel. Currents average 0.7 knots with a tidal range of 3.1 feet in the Turning Basin. This is a popular take-off point for cruisers heading to and from the Bahamas, fishermen heading out to the nearby Gulf Stream and skippers cruising north and south along the coast to escape the bridges and speed restrictions.

CAUTION: Vessels with mast heights over 56 feet that are headed south of Miami's Julia Tuttle Causeway Bridge at Mile 1087.2 have no choice but to go outside at Port Everglades. These vessels can then rejoin the ICW via Miami's Government Cut at Dodge Island.

America's Waterway Guide Since 1947 Chapter 8

Port Everglades Inlet

Offshore Buoys for Divers

Broward County has placed buoys at locations of interest in the offshore waters for divers and snorkelers. To protect the coral from damage caused by anchoring, the buoys should be used as moorings. Buoy locations are:

Pompano Drop-Off:
N 26° 13.034'/W 80° 05.028'

Hall of Fame:
N 26° 11.581'/W 80° 05.000'

Anglin's Ledge:
N 26° 11.338'/W 80° 05.246'

Oakland Ridges:
N 26° 09.276'/W 80° 05.072'

The Caves:
N 26° 07.631'/W 80° 05.354'

Barracuda Reef:
N 26° 04.575'/W 80° 05.505

The mooring buoys are maintained by the Natural Resources Planning and Management Division. For more information or to report a problem, call 954-519-1270.

When approaching the port from offshore, the RACON sea buoy will be your best offshore waypoint. Air traffic to and from Fort Lauderdale airport provides an additional visual aid from miles out to sea. If heading north from Port Everglades, you must follow the marked shipping channel offshore for at least 1 nm before turning northwards to avoid the dangerous shoals extending out from shore at the channel's north edge. Also note that the channel markers are spaced at approximately 0.5 nm apart and the jetty ends are not marked. Be sure to maintain a compass course line and maintain alignment on exit or entry.

Dania Cut-Off Canal Area–ICW Mile 1066 to Mile 1070

Named for its early Danish settlers the city of Dania Beach was once the "Tomato Capital of the World." Visitors today can enjoy the beach, the 800-foot-long fishing pier and a remarkable collection of antiques shops. The Dania Marine Flea Market is billed as the largest marine flea market in the world. It is held annually in March. Check online at for general information, dates and location as it moves from year to year. Just about anything for a boat can be found at the event. If you love garage sales, this is the largest one of all and is worth visiting if you are passing through in March.

The Dania Cut-Off Canal, which branches to the west at Mile 1068.5, is a busy marine service area. Businesses here include well-equipped yards, modern marinas, boat builders and marine service specialists.

SOUTHERN EDITION

Chapter 8: Fort Lauderdale to Hollywood

Outside Run to Miami

In ordinary weather an outside run to or from Miami is safe, comfortable and provides some beautiful views of the coastline. With a Gulf Stream boost and by avoiding bridges transit times are generally faster on the outside. Plan your departure and arrival times and wait for a weather window. For most this is an easy and enjoyable passage.

NOTE: Southbound vessels with an air draft in excess of 56 feet must take the outside route to Miami's Government Cut. The Julia Tuttle Causeway Bridge (Mile 1087.2, 56-foot fixed vertical clearance) crosses the ICW between Miami and Miami Beach.

Be sure to plan for your passage and remember to check maintenance issues and tie down deck gear in advance. You are committing to a 20-mile passage south or a 40-mile passage north to the next reliable inlet. Plan to leave early in the day to ensure you arrive before nightfall.

While these inlets can accommodate large commercial ships and are marked with lighted aids to navigation, nighttime arrivals can be difficult and add unnecessary risk. At least 30 minutes before you leave monitor VHF Channel 16 for a Sécurité from large vessels either entering or exiting. Wait until these vessels are safely clear and secure before you enter the inlet channel from either end.

Proceeding out the wide, straight ship channel of the Port Everglades (Fort Lauderdale) Inlet, you will find good water depths in the channel and beyond the entrance buoys. (The last cruise ship through has checked it for you.) But there are submerged hazards beyond the channel's edges north and south. To the south good water extends well inshore and many boaters turn south just beyond flashing green buoy "5."

The Gulf Stream is not a hazard but it does require a strategy. Heading north is simple–angle out (pass flashing red entrance buoy "2") until you detect a course deflection and then turn north to enjoy the ride. Southbound boats want to stay inside the Gulf Stream to avoid the retarding current but also stay well outside the dangerous breakers along the beach. In offshore winds you can travel safely keeping 0.5 mile off the beach; in onshore winds it's best to double that distance. This route keeps you inshore of the Gulf Stream and its approximately 2-knot northerly set. You may even find gentle southward counter-current close to shore but remember to maintain a safe distance from the beach.

The NOAA Weather Stations (Miami, WX-1, serves this area) broadcast the location of the inshore edge of the Gulf Stream from 4:00 p.m. to 8:00 p.m. on Monday, Wednesday and Friday and from 4:00 a.m. to 8:00 a.m. on Tuesday, Thursday and Saturday in the fall and winter. The western edge of the Gulf Stream ranges from as close as 1 nm offshore to more than 10 nm; the width of the Gulf Stream is also stated in the WX broadcasts. NOAA Weather also advises on expected wind conditions and wave height, which can help with finding your weather window.

The Gulf Stream is like a giant moving sidewalk. A sailboat can travel against the Gulf Stream at a good (water) speed without moving "over ground" at all. Coastal cruisers have to factor in the Gulf Stream in East Florida. And sometimes, if they're lucky, southbound cruisers will get a counter-current running close to the shoreline. Now that can make your day!

Dania Canal, FL

DANIA CUT-OFF CANAL		Largest Vessel	VHF	Total Slips	Approach/ Dockside Depth	Floating Docks	Gas/ Diesel	Repairs/ Haulout	Min/Max Amps	Pump-Out Station
1. Harbour Towne Marina 1.0 mi. W of MM 1068.6	(954) 926-0300	200	16	165	17.0 / 7.0		GD	RH	30 / 200+	P
2. Royale Palm Yacht Basin WiFi 1.0 mi. W of MM 1068.6	(954) 923-5900	80		60	7.0 / 7.0			H	50	
3. Seahaven Superyacht Marina WiFi	(954) 416-1860	250	16	30	16.0 / 16.0	F			50 / 200+	P
WHISKEY RIVER										
4. Dania Beach Marina WiFi	(954) 647-8655		16	92	4.0 / 4.0	F			30 / 50	P

WiFi Wireless Internet Access
Visit www.waterwayguide.com for current rates, fuel prices, website addresses and other up-to-the-minute information. (Information in the table is provided by the facilities.)

Scan here for more details:

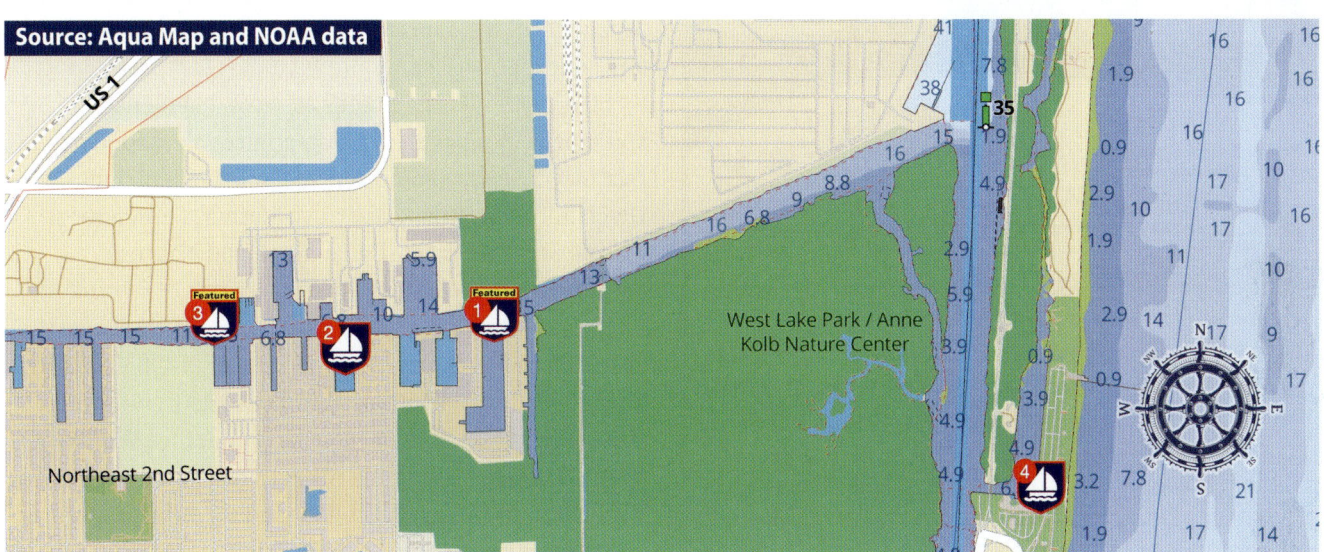

NAVIGATION: Use NOAA Chart 11467. At the point where the ICW crosses the ship channel, keep the Port Everglades (Fort Lauderdale) Inlet and ICW buoys sorted out in your mind. The southbound ICW route takes a straight-line course across the Turning Basin and enters a large ship channel to the south. Once across the Main Turning Basin, vessels southbound on the ICW pass to the west of flashing green "11" (not an ICW marker) and proceed with a close pass of the Fort Lauderdale Coast Guard Station.

South of the Coast Guard Station be careful to avoid the mangroves and partially submerged rocks outside of the channel on the eastern side of the ICW, while keeping the required distance from the cruise ships usually berthed on the mainland side. The ICW route follows the east side of the ship channel as you continue south towards the Dania Cut-Off Canal.

The continuing ICW makers can't be seen from the Main Turning Basin and pick up 1.75 miles south. The first in the continuing sequence south of the inlet is flashing green "35" located directly adjacent the Dania Cut-Off Canal at Mile 1068.5. Favor the west side of the marked channel to Mile 1070.

> NOTE: Remember that ICW markers have a yellow triangle or square above the numerals.

Expect heavy marine traffic as you past the Dania Cut-Off Canal entrance. When approaching the canal from either direction along the ICW keep a sharp lookout for unexpected high-speed traffic swinging out of the canal into the ICW. Also expect traffic entering from Whiskey Creek to the east at Mile 1069.2. Just south of Whiskey Creek is the **Dania Beach Boulevard (SR A1A) Bridge** (22-foot closed vertical clearance). This restricted bridge opens on the hour and half-hour (not on signal).

Dockage: First on the Dania Cut-Off Canal is the 165-slip Harbour Towne Marina with a compliment of over 20 businesses and a wide range of amenities. The marina offers wet and dry storage, can accommodate transient vessels to 200 feet and offers an array of marine services

Chapter 8: Fort Lauderdale to Hollywood

South Florida's Premier Do-It-Yourself Boatyard For Over 40 Years

✓ NO BRIDGES
✓ NO WAITING
✓ NO HASSLES

We are the one-stop location for all of your maintenance and repair needs. Our new 93-ton Marine Travelift® can handle sail or power boats from 27 ft up to 80 ft in length (with a maximum beam of 20ft), and our friendly, experienced staff will haul your boat out, pressure wash the hull below the waterline and block it promptly and professionally. We also provide short hauls for surveys. The yard store carries a full line of quality antifouling paints, primers, zincs, painting supplies and stainless steel fasteners, all at competitive prices. Do the work yourself, or hire one of the approved contractors located on the premises.

PLAYBOY MARINE CENTER

760 Taylor Lane
Dania Beach, FL • 33004
Ph 954-920-0533 • Fax 954-920-0929
www.playboymarine.com
email: playboy_marine@yahoo.com

and repairs. Next on the north bank is Playboy Marine Center, a DIY boat repair facility that also has highly qualified independent contractors should you decide to seek professional services.

On the south bank is Royale Palm Yacht Basin specializing in all aspects of yacht refinishing and with ample transient dockage. Their DIY boatyard and marine service center make this a popular destination.

Seahaven Superyacht Marina on the south shore is specifically designed to cater to mega-yacht clientele. They can accommodate vessels to 250 feet in deep water slips with all the expected amenities plus a fitness center and concierge service.

Boat yards offering marine services, maintenance and repairs along with dry storage areas abound. Ones that may be to accommodate you in a pinch include Derecktor Shipyards, Cozy Cove Marina, Thunderboat Marine Service Center–Dania Beach and Nautical Ventures Marine Center.

Back on the ICW the completely renovated Dania Beach Marina is across from the Dania Cut-Off Canal at Mile 1069.2 on Whiskey Creek. The creek's entrance is crossed by the 18-foot fixed vertical clearance **Whiskey Creek Bridge**. The marina offers transient dockage and is adjacent to the Dania Beach Pier and the beach as well as numerous restaurants.

■ TO BAKERS HAULOVER INLET

Hollywood to Hallandale–ICW Mile 1070 to 1074

South of Dania Beach is an area that has become almost a suburb of Fort Lauderdale and Miami. Hollywood Beach's proximity to Fort Lauderdale makes it a fine alternative when berths are hard to find. Just a short walk from the Hollywood Marina across the Hollywood Beach Boulevard (SR 820) Bridge is beautiful Hollywood Beach and Oceanwalk, a 2-mile-long, brick-lined pedestrian promenade with lots of outdoor dining options. A few miles west in downtown Hollywood you will find extensive shopping and a historic recreated old town with a family-oriented park in the center of Hollywood Circle.

NAVIGATION: Use NOAA Chart 11467. South of Dania Beach the ICW cuts through several broad natural lagoons where the water is spread thinly and the dredged channel is narrow. Pay careful attention to navigation markers and

Hollywood Beach, FL

HOLLYWOOD BEACH AREA		Largest Vessel	VHF	Total Slips	Approach/Dockside Depth	Floating Docks	Gas/Diesel	Repairs/Haulout	Min/Max Amps	Pump-Out Station
1. Hollywood Marina WiFi MM 1072.1	(954) 921-3035	115	16	55	6.0 / 7.0		GD		30 / 50	P
2. Loggerhead Marina - Hollywood Marina WiFi	(954) 457-8557	120	16	190	15.0 / 8.0			H	30 / 100	P
3. Hallandale Beach City Marina WiFi	(954) 457-1653	60		26	/				30	P

WiFi Wireless Internet Access
Visit www.waterwayguide.com for current rates, fuel prices, website addresses and other up-to-the-minute information. (Information in the table is provided by the facilities.)

Scan here for more details:

your depth sounder. The **Sheridan Street Bridge** at Mile 1070.5 has 21-foot closed vertical clearance and opens on the quarter and three-quarter hour (not on signal) and has a dogleg approach.

The channel cuts across from the east close to the western shore before passing under the bridge. Be sure not to stray out of the marked channel. The next bridge is the **Hollywood Beach Boulevard (SR 820) Bridge** at Mile 1072.2, which has a 25-foot closed vertical clearance and opens on the hour and half-hour (not on demand). The **Hallandale Beach Boulevard (SR 858) Bridge** at Mile 1074.0 has 26-foot closed vertical clearance and, like other bridges along this stretch, has restricted openings (in this case on the quarter hour and three-quarter hour).

Dockage: South of the Sheridan Street Bridge the eastern shore is lined with casual restaurants complete with tie-up locations on the bulkhead for dining customers. The municipal Hollywood Marina maintains 15 transient slips plus laundry facilities, showers and restrooms. Controlling depths in the middle of North Lake are reportedly as little as 1.5 to 2.5 feet MLW so stay close to the docks and follow their contour. Call ahead to check availability and approach depths.

Loggerhead Marina–Hollywood Marina offers 190 slips for vessels to 120 feet at red daybeacon "42," just south of the Hollywood Beach Boulevard (SR 820) Bridge. Transient slip holders have full access to the pool and fitness center and the Hollywood Beach boardwalk is just minutes away with restaurants and shopping. The facility requests you call ahead for a reservation.

Hallandale Beach City Marina is located at Mile 1074 on the west side of the ICW in the canal just north of the Hallandale Beach Boulevard (SR 858) Bridge. The city marina has just three reserved transient slips. Be aware that there is a fixed bridge (Three Islands Boulevard Bridge) with 17-foot vertical clearance that must be navigated to reach the marina. Call ahead for approach details.

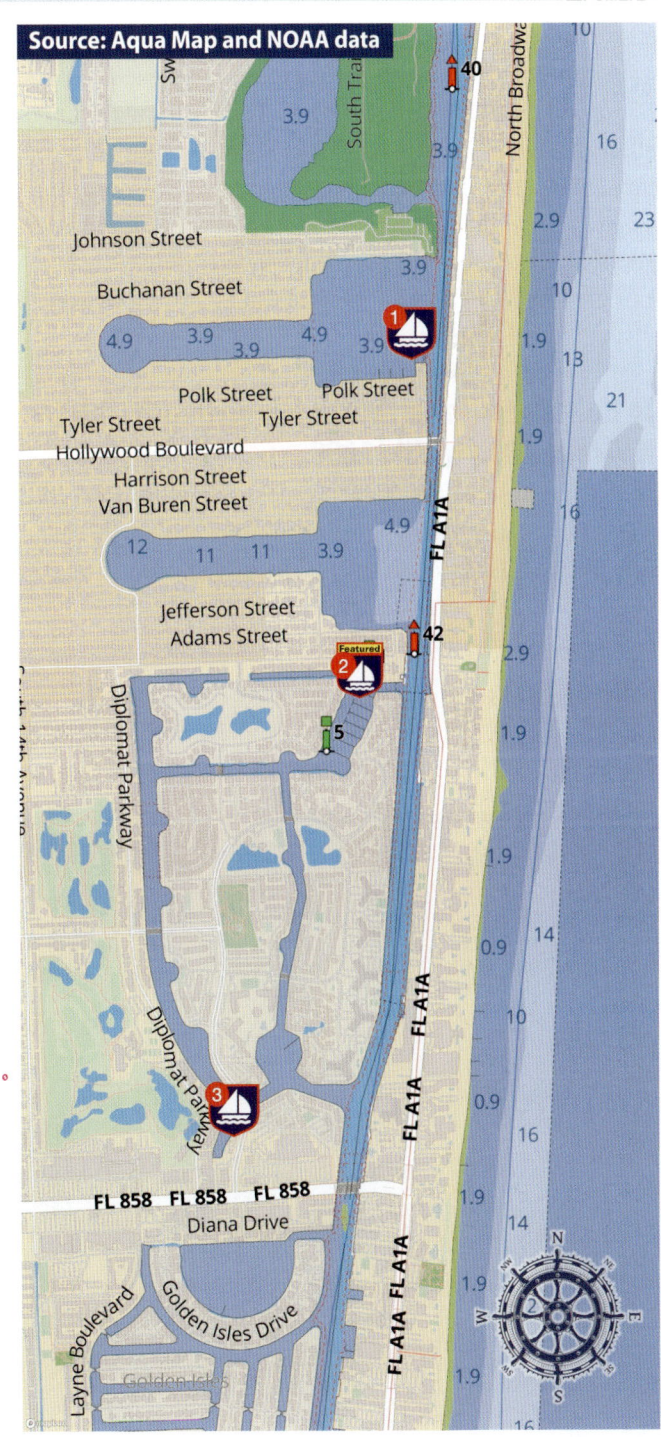

SOUTHERN EDITION

Chapter 8: Fort Lauderdale to Hollywood

Anchorage: Anchorages are available both north and south of the Sheridan Street Bridge, along the east shore. The little cove with the beach north of the Sheridan Street Bridge anchorage is within the boundaries of a park where anchoring is prohibited so be sure you drop your anchor a bit north of the cove for 7-foot MLW depths. South of the Sheridan Street Bridge there is a snug anchorage for one or two boats, north of the line of docks along the edge of the ICW in 9- to 11-foot MLW depths. Dinghy access to the adjacent park is prohibited.

A short distance south of the Hollywood Beach Boulevard (SR 820) Bridge is South Lake. Although the charts show depths of 4 and 5 feet MLW, dredging has increased controlling depths but investigate with caution. There is room for a number of boats and the holding is good but small boats and personal watercraft use the lake as a play area, so expect noise and wakes as they weave through the anchored boats.

To Bakers Haulover (North Miami Beach) Inlet–ICW Mile 1074 to Mile 1080

When you observe the tidal current speeding up along the ICW route you are nearing Bakers Haulover (North Miami Beach) Inlet. This inlet is the northernmost of Miami's inlets from the Atlantic Ocean and is heavily used by recreational fishermen and local boats.

NAVIGATION: Use NOAA Chart 11467. Just about 2 miles past the Hallandale Beach Boulevard (SR 858) Bridge you will encounter the 65-foot fixed vertical clearance **William Lehman Causeway (SR 856) Bridge**, which crosses the ICW at Mile 1076.3. South of Golden Beach the ICW leaves the cut channels and returns to dredged channels through interconnected lagoons beginning with Dumbfoundling Bay.

The lagoon adjoining Dumfoundling Bay is a broad, open and generally shallow body of water with a few deeper patches along its eastern shore. At the lagoon's southern end the marked route crosses over to the western shore. To the north of the Maule Lake entrance, which is popular for anchoring and has dockage facilities, there is a shoal marked by a privately maintained white daybeacon. Give it a wide berth.

Heading south the ICW enters Biscayne Creek, which borders the community of Sunny Isles to the east. At Mile 1078.0 the **NE 163rd Street (SR 826) Bridge** links that community to the mainland. This 30-foot closed vertical clearance bridge opens on signal, except from 7:00 a.m. to 6:00 p.m., Monday through Friday (except federal holidays), and from 10:00 a.m. to 6:00 p.m., on weekends and federal holidays when the draw need only open on the quarter hour and three-quarter hour.

Bakers Haulover (North Miami Beach) Inlet is spanned by the **Bakers Haulover Inlet Bridge** with 32-foot fixed vertical clearance. Jetties are short here and currents are strong (2.0 to 3.0 knots). The inlet can become especially nasty when wind and current oppose. Because of this, it is best to head just 8.3 miles south to Government Cut (Miami) Inlet, a clear, well-marked large ship inlet.

Bakers Haulover Inlet

WILLIAMS ISLAND
Marina

Marina

Berths within a Protected Harbour
10 foot Deep-Water Approaching
Monitored VHF Channel 16/10
106 Yacht Berths | Max 160 Ft/8 Ft Draft
Parallel Docking for Larger Yachts
Floating Docks for Smaller Yachts
Three Phase Electric Dockage
North Marina Slips with Pump Out
Wi Fi Internet & Cable
24 Hour Monitored Security

Marina Office

Staffed with over 37 Years of Experience
Richly Appointed Lobby & Reception
Fully Equipped Business Center
Spacious Conference Room
Boaters Lounge with Smart TV
Top-of-the-line Laundry Facility
Modern Showers and Lockers
Convenient Fitness Center

Club Amenities

27,000 Sq. Ft. Spa & Fitness Center
    with personalized programs
Grand Slam Tennis Center
    16 Hard & HAR-TRU Courts
    Tennis Center with Pro Shop
Island Club - Social Events
Dining
    Island Grille | Overlooking Tennis
    Island Pool Bar | Casual Open Air

Welcome to Williams Island, nestled on 84 acres in Aventura, Florida, mid-way between Miami and Fort Lauderdale. Close to both airports and seaports. Williams Island offers an exclusive, private way of life to those accustomed to the finest of things at one of South Florida's most prestigious addresses. This magnificent Marina enjoys a protected harbour with berth's up to 135 feet and depths of 10 feet approaching the marina and 8 feet within the marina itself, plus a Marine Basin area to help assure a calm, restful environment. Our 106 berths are as comfortable and convenient for our boaters as they are for their vessels.

Marina guests will be treated to an amenity-rich lifestyle that encompasses a luxurious Marina office with richly appointed conveniences: boater lounge, conference room, gym, business center and laundry. A complimentary Williams Island Social Club membership is included in your stay and includes: the 27,000 sq ft Spa and Fitness Center. The Grand Slam-inspired Tennis Center with 16 tennis courts and pro shop that is expertly staffed. Exquisite fine dining and weekly specials are enjoyed at the Island Grille overlooking Center Court. Enjoy a lighter fare at the Island Club Pool Bar your destination for outdoor casual dining and relaxed pool side favorites. Entertainment, Social Events as well as Private Parties are offered at the Island Club.

The Marina is conveniently open daily from 9 am to 6 pm.

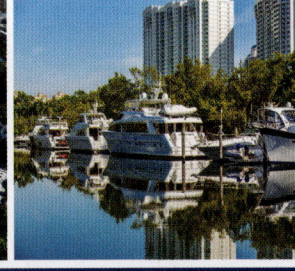

4100 Island Boulevard, Aventura, Florida 33160 | 305.937.7813 office | 305.936.5713 fax
WilliamsIslandMarina.com | dockmaster@WilliamsIslandMarina.com

Chapter 8: Fort Lauderdale to Hollywood

North Miami Beach, FL

NORTH MIAMI BEACH AREA		Largest Vessel	VHF	Total Slips	Approach/ Dockside Depth	Floating Docks	Gas/ Diesel	Repairs/ Haulout	Min/Max Amps	Pump-Out Station
1. Loggerhead Marina - Aventura Marina WiFi MM 1075.2	(305) 935-4295	120	16	100	20.0 / 10.0				30 / 100	P
2. Williams Island Marina WiFi MM 1076.6	(305) 937-7813	160	16	106	10.0 / 8.0	F			30 / 100	P
3. Marina Palms Yacht Club WiFi 54	(786) 707-2629	100	16	112	/ 7.0	F	GD		30 / 100	P

WiFi Wireless Internet Access
Visit www.waterwayguide.com for current rates, fuel prices, website addresses and other up-to-the-minute information. (Information in the table is provided by the facilities.)

Scan here for more details:

Source: Aqua Map and NOAA data

North Miami Beach, FL

BAKERS HAULOVER INLET AREA		Largest Vessel	VHF	Total Slips	Approach/ Dockside Depth	Floating Docks	Gas/ Diesel	Repairs/ Haulout	Min/Max Amps	Pump-Out Station
1. Bill Bird Marina at Haulover Park MM 1079.7	(305) 947-3525	120	16	150	8.0 / 8.5		GD		30 / 100	P
2. Bal Harbour Yacht Club-PRIVATE WiFi	(305) 865-6048	140		35	8.0 / 8.0		G			
3. Keystone Point Marina 1.3 mi. W of MM 1080.8	(305) 940-6236	110	16	26	8.0 / 8.0	F	GD	RH	30 / 50	P

WiFi Wireless Internet Access
Visit www.waterwayguide.com for current rates, fuel prices, website addresses and other up-to-the-minute information. (Information in the table is provided by the facilities.)

Scan here for more details:

Source: Aqua Map and NOAA data

CAUTION: The shoaling problem on the ICW channel west of Bakers Haulover (North Miami Beach) Inlet at Mile 1080 is legendary. Periodically the area south of red daybeacon "6A" is dredged and, inevitably, it fills back in. Markers are moved or added regularly here to indicate the deepest channel; follow the markers as positioned.

If the sun is at the proper angle you can see the path through the shoal area. Watch for a strong set to the west with flood tide and to the east with the ebb. This is a very busy area of the ICW. Proceed with caution.

Dockage: Loggerhead Marina–Aventura Marina across from Golden Beach (Mile 1075.2) accepts vessels to 120 feet in their large, protected harbor. This marina offers many upscale amenities including valet shuttle service and is located within the Waterway Shoppes with open-air shopping (including groceries), dining and entertainment. Turnberry Marina to the south at Mile 1075.5 does not offer transient slips.

At Mile 1076 a straight, narrow and deep canal cuts westward off the ICW to Maule Lake and the large Williams Island Marina, which offers dockage in a well-protected harbor with resort amenities. Nestled on 84 lush acres, this facility offers multiple pools, a spa, 16 tennis courts and several restaurants.

Marina Palms Yacht Club is in a condominium complex on the western shore of Maule Lake with slips to 100 feet and an on-site Boat Club, which offers a full range of activities from jet skiing to kayaking and snorkeling. Reservations should be made in advance.

North of Bakers Haulover Inlet on the east side of the ICW

SOUTHERN EDITION

Chapter 8: Fort Lauderdale to Hollywood

is Bill Bird Marina at Haulover Park with 152 wet slips, accommodating vessels to 120 feet. The dock master building offers a laundry room with coin-operated washers and dryers, vending machines, ice, and restrooms with showers. The private Bal Harbour Yacht Club to the south of the inlet does not offer transient slips.

The mainland opposite the inlet is the start of North Miami. In protected New Arch Creek, there are a number of boating amenities, repair yards and stores that are eager to serve transient mariners including Keystone Point Marina with 10 reserved transient slips to 110 feet. There is a well-marked approach channel leading west from ICW red daybeacon "12." The marina is usually full so call in advance to check on the availability of a slip.

Anchorage: It is possible to anchor in Maule Lake in 8 to 20 feet MLW by exiting the ICW west of red daybeacon "54." Even though this provides all-around protection, the holding is just fair due to the mud and rock bottom. There is shore access at the launch ramp with plenty of shopping within walking distance. (Note that we do not recommend anchoring in Dumfoundling Bay as it is a cable crossing area.)

One of the finest overnight anchorages along this section of the ICW is in the basin across the ICW from the inlet at Bakers Haulover Basin at Mile 1080. The only drawback is its entrance. At high tide you should turn northwest off the ICW (approximately 75 feet north of red daybeacon "6A") and then slowly head directly toward the large, green, rounded roof of the Florida International University athletic building. Proceed slowly between the 3-foot MLW bar to port and the 4-foot-deep spoils area to the north. If you encounter depths of less than 8 feet MLW within the first couple of hundred feet, you are beginning to stray out of the channel.

Once you pass over the bar (soft mud and sand), you will find 8 to 12-foot MLW depths inside. This virtually undeveloped deep-water basin provides serene anchorages protected from all wind directions. The bottom is quite soft and there may be debris in some places. Make sure that your anchor is set well. Visiting boaters are not permitted ashore on the Florida International University's property.

■ NEXT STOP

Next we take you to the Greater Miami area including North Miami, Miami Beach, the Miami River, Key Biscayne, Coconut Grove and Coral Gables. Florida's tropical waters truly begin in Biscayne Bay. A boater's paradise, the bay's shallow, turquoise waters are protected by the accessible barrier islands of Biscayne National Park and are not only a destination themselves, but serve as a gateway to the Florida Keys.

Miami & Biscayne Bay — Chapter 9

SOUTHERN EDITION

Chapter 9: Miami & Biscayne Bay

 Mile 1080-Mile 1111

MIAMI & GOVERNMENT CUT

At 35 miles long and up to 8 miles wide Biscayne Bay ranks as one of North America's great inland waters. Over it's great size the bay also undergoes great variation of scenery, color and development. While not shown on charts, the bay is generally divided into three distinct segments: North, Central and South.

North Biscayne Bay stretches from Bakers Haulover (North Miami Beach) Inlet to Government Cut (Miami) Inlet, the main entrance to the Port of Miami. This segment starts very narrow adjacent to North Miami and gradually widens as it fills the gap between Miami Beach's barrier islands and the mainland. The appearance changes as well. The murky green water and mud bottom of its upper reaches gradually change to a turquoise color with a sandy bottom farther south, just as low-rise development gives way to high-rise on its shores. This segment provides access to Miami Beach, which is a worthy side trip.

Starting south of Dodge Island, Central Biscayne Bay is a boater's paradise. From here south to Cutter Bank, the bay's central segment is wider and its beautiful turquoise waters are deeper. The breadth of the bay here provides boats with room to maneuver but it's barrier islands still create excellent protected anchorages. The high-rise development that flanked the lower reaches of the north segment slowly give way to wilderness and parkland as you enter Biscayne National Park. This land and sea reserve is a treasure and well worth a stop for a walk or snorkel.

No Wake Zones, Idle Speed Zones and various Speed Limit restrictions are in effect throughout the waterways included in this chapter. Exercise diligence in knowing the regulations by observing signs and other markers. Enforcement is always present. As always, be courteous to other vessels and avoid manatees and other marine life.

North Biscayne Bay– ICW Mile 1080 to Mile 1090

The ICW enters the north end of Biscayne Bay at Bakers Haulover (North Miami Beach) Inlet. The area generally referred to as "North Biscayne Bay" stretches from here to Miami's main inlet, Government Cut (Miami) Inlet. As the bay deepens a variety of routes weave past and amongst the man-made causeways and islands. Cruisers can opt to stay in the ICW closer to Miami or leave the ICW via any of several routes for a side trip to explore Miami Beach.

Greater Miami bustles with activity on land and water. The north segment of Biscayne Bay is particularly busy and with its heavy boat traffic, numerous islands and shallow pockets of water, it can be confusing to navigate. Study your charts carefully before attempting to transit this sometimes confusing area.

NAVIGATION: Use NOAA Chart 11467. South from Bakers Haulover (North Miami Beach) Inlet, the ICW maintains a straight course as it angles diagonally across North Biscayne Bay, reaching the western shore just before the **West 79th Street Bridge**. The narrow but well-marked channel parallels the eastern shore until it passes **Broad Causeway Bridge** with 16-foot closed vertical clearance. This is the first of five restricted Miami spans. The span opens on signal except from 8:00 a.m. and 6:00 p.m. when the draw need only open on the quarter hour and three-quarter hour (year-round).

Continuing south from Broad Causeway follow your chart carefully. Starting from green daybeacon "17" there are numerous hazards just outside the marked channel. At flashing red "26" the ICW channel changes course and heads for West 79th Street Bridge at Mile 1084.6 (25-foot closed vertical clearance). The bridge opens on signal, except Monday through Friday (except Federal holidays) from 7:00 a.m. to 7:00 p.m., when the draw need only open on the hour and half hour. Be sure to indicate that you want the "western" span when calling the bridge on VHF Channel 09, rather than the East 79th Street Bridge span for the Miami Beach Channel.

If your intention is to "diverge" from the ICW to explore Miami Beach, you should exit the marked ICW channel just past green daybeacon "15" turning southeast toward Normandy Isle. The relatively well-marked Miami Beach Channel route is described in detail below.

Just south of the West 79th Street Bridge on the western shore is the marked entrance to Little River, which has facilities with various services for transients. South of Little River, the ICW–now narrow and surrounded by shoals–continues on a relatively straight course to the **Julia Tuttle Causeway Bridge**.

> ⚠️ **CAUTION:** The fixed Julia Tuttle Causeway Bridge (charted 56-foot vertical clearance) at Mile 1087.2 sets the limiting overhead clearance for the inside passage from Fort Lauderdale to Miami. A few extra feet may be gained at low tide but study the tide gauge before starting through as there is only a 2-foot tidal range.

South from the Julia Tuttle Causeway Bridge the water outside the channel is slightly deeper but still too shallow for most cruising vessels. Take a moment to consult the charts before approaching the next series of closely packed bridges and channels. The short stretch from Mile 1088.5 to Mile 1089.5 is one of the most complex along the ICW. Over the 1-mile stretch you will pass four bridges, cross the turning basin of Miami's Main Ship Channel and make an abrupt course adjustment.

Note that this segment or the ICW is sparsely marked. Be sure to get aligned from the start to simplify navigation. When centered between green daybeacon "47" and flashing red "48" adjust your heading to thread through the next two bridge openings. This straight-line course continues across the Main Ship Channel's turning basin.

The **Venetian Causeway Bridge (West)** at Mile 1088.6 is first. This bridge has a 12-foot closed vertical clearance and opens on signal, except Monday through Friday (except Federal holidays) from 7:00 a.m. to 7:00 p.m., when the draw need only open on the hour and half hour. Next are the high-rise **MacArthur Causeway Bridges** (65-foot fixed vertical clearance) at Mile 1088.8. Once clear of the bridges you should be headed across the charted turning basin for flashing red "50" (ICW marker) located just west of Dodge Island.

To continue south on the ICW keep flashing red "50" to starboard. Off to port you will see flashing red "20" (Main Channel marker). If your intent is to follow the Main Ship Channel towards Government Cut (Miami) Inlet, keep this marker to port and turn east and out the channel. (No small boat traffic is allowed in the Main Ship Channel when the cruise ships are in and marine police diligently patrol the entrance. Monitor VHF Channel 16 for possible Sécurité warnings.) If the Main Channel is blocked proceed south on the ICW and turn east once past Dodge Island for an alternate route through the Dodge Island Cut.

If continuing south on the ICW, the course changes at flashing red "50." Adjust course to parallel the

Chapter 9: Miami & Biscayne Bay

Upper Biscayne Bay, FL

MIAMI AREA		Largest Vessel	VHF	Total Slips	Approach/Dockside Depth	Floating Docks	Gas/Diesel	Repairs/Haulout	Min/Max Amps	Pump-Out Station
1. Pelican Harbor Marina MM 1084.5	(305) 754-9330	50	16	112	6.0 / 6.0		GD		30 / 50	P
2. Gator Harbor West Marina-PRIVATE 2 mi. E of MM 1084.2	(305) 754-2200	45		20	6.0 / 6.0				30 / 100	
3. Grandview Palace Yacht Club-PRIVATE 1.5 mi. E of MM 1083.8	(305) 300-6828	60	16	118	8.0 / 8.0		G		50	P

WiFi Wireless Internet Access
Visit www.waterwayguide.com for current rates, fuel prices, website addresses and other up-to-the-minute information. (Information in the table is provided by the facilities.)

Scan here for more details:

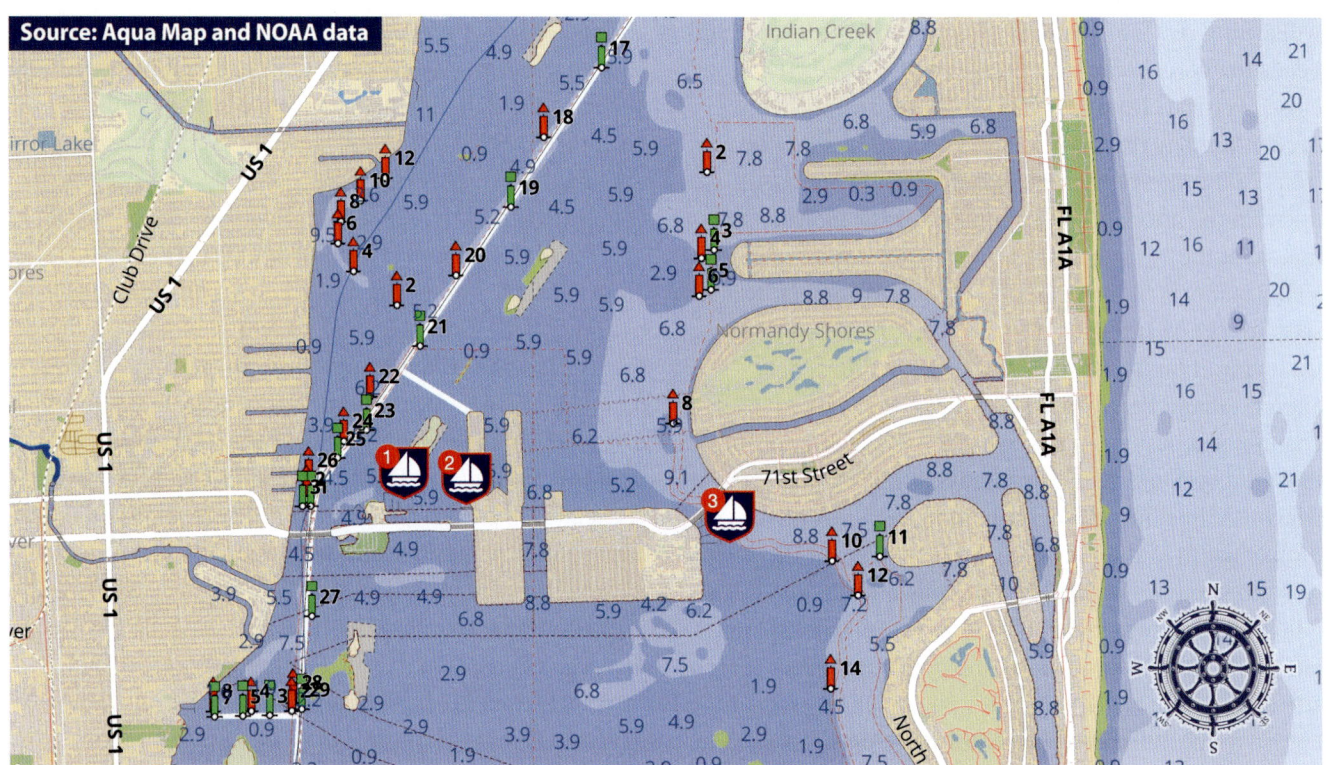

Source: Aqua Map and NOAA data

west wall of Dodge Island as you line up to pass through the next two bridge openings. The closely spaced **Dodge Island Bridge** and **Dodge Island Railroad Bridge** cross the ICW at Mile 1089.3. The fixed Dodge Island Bridge has a 65-foot vertical clearance, while the Dodge Island Railroad Bridge has a 22-foot closed vertical clearance. The railroad bridge is usually in the open position unless a train is approaching.

Once you pass these bridges keep flashing green "53" on you port side. The ICW intersects with two other channels at Mile 1089.8. To the east is Fishermans Channel, which is the alternate route to reach Government Cut (as well as Miami Beach Marina) when the Main Ship Channel is closed. To the west is the entrance to the Miami River. Passage of these routes is described in later sections.

To continue south on the ICW, keep green daybeacon "57" and quick-flashing green "59" to port while preparing to skirt the east shore of Claughton Island.

Dockage/Moorings: You can find transient dockage at Pelican Island, a 10-acre island with covered picnic shelters, barbecue grills, picnic tables and a sand volleyball court (bring your own net and ball). The island is open to the public. The municipal Pelican Harbor Marina is on the north side of the 79th Street Causeway with transient slips (for boats to 50 feet), a sailboat mooring field and a dinghy dock. Call to check for slip availability and approach instructions. The 27 moorings for boats up to 35 feet are available by reservation only.

Gator Harbor West Marina to the east on Harbor Island is strictly private. (No transient slips.) Grandview Palace Yacht Club at the east end of Treasure Island is a

America's Waterway Guide Since 1947 — **Chapter 9**

Upper Biscayne Bay, FL

INDIAN CREEK		Largest Vessel	VHF	Total Slips	Approach/ Dockside Depth	Floating Docks	Gas/ Diesel	Repairs/ Haulout	Min/Max Amps	Pump-Out Station
1. Miami Beach Resort & Spa WiFi	(305) 532-3600	200	16	20	7.0 / 7.0				30 / 50	

WiFi Wireless Internet Access
Visit www.waterwayguide.com for current rates, fuel prices, website addresses and other up-to-the-minute information.
(Information in the table is provided by the facilities.)

Scan here for more details:

membership club open to the public. Transient slips may be available but call in advance to check.

> Port Consolidated-Miami has some of the lowest fuel prices in the area. They are located at 11550 NW 36th Ave.

Anchorage: It is possible to anchor near the West 79th Street Boat Basin at North Bay Island (south side) in 6 to 8 feet MLW with good holding in mud but watch the charted Cable and Pipeline Area. This is open to the south through west and to wakes. You can also drop the hook in 14 feet at MLW north or south of the Julia Tuttle Causeway. This provides minimal protection and is open to ICW wakes.

Side Trip: Miami Beach via Indian Creek

Indian Creek is a waterway that runs between Miami Beach's main island and the jumble of man-made islands immediately to the west. The primary access to Indian Creek is from the channel between Normandy Isle and La Gorce Island. The route northward inside Normandy Isle is restricted to small craft by a series of fixed, low-clearance bridges. The lowest is the fixed 71st Street Bridge with a 5-foot vertical clearance, which connects Normandy Isle to the ocean beach. This can be a pleasant route by dinghy to have a "gander at the grandeur" of the mega-mansions in exclusive Indian Creek Village.

NAVIGATION: Use NOAA Chart 11467. The route south on Indian Creek from La Gorce Island is navigable by larger vessels and leads into the heart of downtown Miami Beach. The controlling depth is charted as 7 feet MLW but check with one of the Indian Creek marinas for local knowledge before entering. There is transient dockage but no anchorage on this route.

Leave the Miami Beach Channel at red daybeacon "10" and hug the shore of Normandy Isle eastward into the opening of Indian Creek. Be sure to stay in the charted deep water to avoid the shoaling closer to La Gorce Island. Continuing south Indian Creek skirts the area's downtown across the road from many of the lavish hotels in Miami Beach's Bar Harbor district. Favor the eastern shore in Indian Creek; shoaling occurs along parts of the western bank of the creek.

Do not try to circumnavigate Normandy Isle unless you do so in a dinghy. The fixed **71st Street Bridge** with a 5-foot vertical clearance connects the island to the ocean beach.

To access the Indian Creek marinas head south on the eastern side of Allison Island through the **63rd Street Bridge**, which connects Allison Island with the beach island. This bridge has 11-foot vertical clearance and opens on signal, except from 7:00 a.m. to 7:00 p.m., Monday through Friday (except federal holidays), when the draw need only open on the hour and half-hour. Additionally, from 7:10 a.m. to 9:55 a.m. and 4:05 p.m. to 6:59 p.m., Monday through Friday (except federal holidays), the draw need not open for the passage of vessels.

SOUTHERN EDITION

Chapter 9 Miami & Biscayne Bay

La Gorce Island

Dockage: Indian Creek is chock-full of hotel and condominium docks as well as Miami Beach Resort & Spa with space for vessels to 200 feet and resort amenities.

To Miami Beach

Whether you take the ICW or the Miami Beach Channel to Miami Beach be sure to allow ample time for sightseeing once you get there. If you travel with a pet aboard, you will find that virtually all the sidewalk restaurants here are extremely pet friendly. The resort potential of Miami Beach's beautiful 9-mile oceanfront was recognized early on. After filling wetlands and taming the barrier island's mangroves, Miami Beach's first hotel was built in 1915, the same year the city was incorporated.

Essentially a creation of the tourism industry, Miami Beach and its islands are mostly man-made and were literally "made for tourists." Today its hip, vibrant image thrives in the Art Deco District with numerous hotels and acclaimed restaurants, as well as the trendy South Beach area. So many people in the entertainment industry have moved here that it has been dubbed "Hollywood East" including the exclusive neighborhood of Indian Creek Village (on Indian Creek Island), home to Miami Beach's rich and famous.

NAVIGATION: Use NOAA Chart 11467. The relatively well-marked Miami Beach Channel runs south along the eastern shore of Biscayne Bay (which is also the western shore of Miami Beach) all the way to Government Cut (Miami) Inlet. Land for homes was created by pumping sand up from Biscayne Bay's bottom and depositing it behind bulkheads. As a consequence, depths of 6 to 7 feet MLW lie almost anywhere near the shore except where indicated on the chart. The open bay outside marked channels, on the other hand, only has depths of 1 to 3 feet MLW.

There are several options for crossing Biscayne Bay to the Miami Beach Channel. The northernmost crossover from the ICW for cruising-size boats is just south of the **Broad Causeway Bridge**. Southbound vessels should exit the marked ICW channel between green daybeacon "15" and red daybeacon "16," turning southeast toward Normandy Isle. This route is sparsely marked but follow the charted deeper water, keeping red markers to starboard. Start with a wide turn southward around flashing red "2" where there is a charted obstruction with no precise location. When approaching Biscayne Point steer to split green daybeacon "3" and red daybeacon "4."

Proceed through the narrow channel splitting green daybeacon "5" and red daybeacon "6" and then hug the shore of Normandy Isle gradually turning southward towards the **East 79th Street Bridge** with 25-foot vertical clearance (opens on signal). Be sure to indicate that you want the "East" span when calling the bridge on VHF Channel 09; there is another span (**West 79th Street Bridge**) for the Miami Beach Channel to the west.

Once past the East 79th Street Bridge continue to skirt the shoreline of Normandy Isle turning eastward until abeam of red daybeacon "10." Here you begin a wide turn southward splitting quick-flashing green "11" and red daybeacon "12," both off La Gorce Island. It is extremely shallow behind the red daybeacons inside this turn. Pass close to red daybeacon "16" to avoid shoaling in the channel to the east where the Biscayne Waterway discharges into the channel.

Vessels with an airdraft of 35 feet or less can continue south of the Julia Tuttle Causeway following the Miami Beach Channel to Government Cut (Miami) Inlet. Turning southwest at red daybeacon "22" head towards green daybeacon "25." Keeping this daybeacon to port enter the narrow channel to pass under the **Julia Tuttle Causeway Bridge (East)** (35-foot fixed vertical clearance) and take a heading to keep red daybeacon "26" just to starboard.

Once clear of the channel parallel the Sunset Islands chain south towards Bell Isle, keeping combined green-over-red daybeacon "S"/red daybeacon "30" to starboard. Turn west just before reaching Belle Isle drawing close to shore and keeping the green daybeacons to starboard and avoiding the charted submerged pilings. The route skirts the north shore of Belle Isle.

There are two more bridges en route to Government Cut. The first bridge is at the **Venetian Causeway Bridge (East)**, which is formed by a chain of man-made islands crossing Biscayne Bay. Belle Isle is the oldest island in Biscayne Bay and is the closest to Miami Beach in the causeway chain. The **Venetian Causeway Bridge (East)** is located midway between Belle Isle and Rivo Alto Island. This bridge has a 5-foot closed vertical clearance and opens on signal except from 7:00 a.m. to 7:00 p.m., when the draw need only open on the hour and half-hour. Be sure to specifically request the "East" bridge on VHF Channel 09, as a bridge with a similar name crosses the ICW to the west.

The channel enters deeper water south of Belle Isle. Swing eastward around the isle and then parallel Miami Beach's main island southward. Keep well east of red daybeacon "2" to avoid shoaling southeast of the Flagler Monument. The final bridge on this route is south of Star Island and connects the east end of the MacArthur Causeway to Miami Beach. The channel runs under the **MacArthur Causeway Bridges** (35-foot fixed vertical clearance) near the U.S. Coast Guard base. After passing under the bridge follow the Meloy Channel to the inner end of Government Cut.

Note some of the dockage and anchorages described in this section can be reached by vessels requiring a higher airdraft by following the marked channel just north of the Venetian Causeway and passing through the Venetian Causeway Bridge (East).

Dockage: In Miami Beach you will find many excellent, upscale marinas with substantial amenities alongside less fancy but somewhat more economical ones. All are convenient to provisioning options, fine dining and shopping.

The Miami Beach Channel leads directly to private Sunset Harbour Yacht Club on two acres fronting Biscayne Bay. This facility is part of an equity club membership program, which allows slip holders access to a fitness center with a heated, Olympic-size pool. A vacant member-owned slips may be available but be sure to call ahead.

Just north of the MacArthur Causeway Bridges (East) is the 16-slip Bentley Bay Marina with transient slips for vessels to 65 feet. Farther south on Meloy Channel (the southern end of Miami Beach Channel) opposite the Coast Guard base is the 400-slip Miami Beach Marina. This facility can accommodate vessels up to 250 feet with full amenities. Friendly Dock Assistants are available to provide assistance in entering and leaving your slip and with delivery of groceries, messages, etc. to and from your yacht.

Note that One Island Park–Miami Beach (IGY adjacent to the Coast Guard station is closed for renovations until 2024.

Anchorage: There are several local restrictions on overnight anchoring in effect for North Biscayne Bay but also lots of available spots close to Miami Beach that provide excellent protection from the prevailing southeast winds.

Chapter 9: Miami & Biscayne Bay

Upper Biscayne Bay, FL

MIAMI BEACH		Largest Vessel	VHF	Total Slips	Approach/ Dockside Depth	Floating Docks	Gas/ Diesel	Repairs/ Haulout	Min/Max Amps	Pump-Out Station
1. Sunset Harbour Yacht Club-PRIVATE WiFi	(305) 398-6800	210	16	125	8.0 / 8.0				30 / 100	P
2. Bentley Bay Marina	(305) 674-0686	65	16	16	10.0 / 8.0				30 / 100	P
3. Miami Beach Marina WiFi 3.0 mi. E of MM 1089.0	(305) 673-6000	250	16	400	13.0 / 12.0		GD		30 / 200+	P
MIAMI AREA										
4. Venetian Marina & Yacht Club WiFi MM 1088.5	(786) 785-1679	110	16	220	13.0 / 10.0		GD		30 / 100	P
5. Yacht Haven Grande Miami WiFi	(305) 531-3747	550	16	50	13.0 / 22.0	F			50 / 200+	P
6. Miami Yacht Club-PRIVATE WiFi MM 1089.0	(305) 377-9877	65		48	7.0 / 6.0			H	30	
7. Miamarina at Bayside MM 1089.5	(305) 960-5180	165	16	130	14.0 / 10.0	F			30 / 100	P

WiFi Wireless Internet Access
Visit www.waterwayguide.com for current rates, fuel prices, website addresses and other up-to-the-minute information.
(Information in the table is provided by the facilities.)

Scan here for more details:

Source: Aqua Map and NOAA data

MIAMI BEACH MARINA
A SUNTEX EXPERIENCE

Your Premiere Destination

- Highest customer satisfaction rating in the hospitality industry
- Dock attendants, security patrol, & surveillance cameras
- Wireless Internet
- Air conditioned restrooms & laundry facilities
- Marine Store open 6 days a week (closed Sundays)

- Premium services and amenities to enhance the customer experience
- 30/50/100 amp single phase/ 100 amp three phase, 480 volt
- 1000+' of floating pier, easy access for small vessels
- In-slip pump-out on most piers
- Adjacent to world famous beaches, Ocean Drive & SoBe Night Life

- Enjoy the valuable personal touch that is delivered by our staff
- Lighted, covered parking
- Gasoline, diesel & high speed diesel
- Golf cart rentals available
- Provisioning from the on-site deli
- On-site casual dining
- Boat lifts for vessels to 40,000 lbs.

SUNTEX MARINAS
YOUR PLACE IN THE SUN

300 Alton Road
Miami Beach, FL 33139
(305) 673-6000

miamibeachmarina.com
VHF: Hail on 16
Working Channel: 68

Chapter 9: Miami & Biscayne Bay

> ⚠️ **CAUTION:** Note that Florida legislation bans overnight anchoring in Sunset Lake and in sections of Biscayne Bay including between Rivo Alto Island and Di Lido Island, San Marino Island and San Marco Island, and San Marco Island and Biscayne Island. It is illegal to anchor at any time during the period between one-half hour after sunset and one-half hour before sunrise. Exemptions include cases of mechanical failure, weather conditions or during certain events. Miami Beach also enforces an ordinance that limits anchoring to 7 days.

On the Miami Beach Channel you can drop the hook at **Tuttle Causeway Bight** south of the east span of the bridge. Here you will find 8 to 9 feet MLW with excellent holding and protection from all directions except west. You can also anchor just off the Sunset Harbour Channel (privately maintained daybeacons and lights) on the northeast side of Belle Isle in 7- to 11-foot MLW depths. Wakes from passing vessels, particularly on weekends, can be disturbing.

A good anchorage is southwest of the small island with the Flagler Monument Island (south of the eastern span of the Venetian Causeway). Approach via the Miami Beach Channel or the cross-bay route south of the Venetian Causeway (on the northern side of the entrance channel) with 6-foot MLW depths. Or try the west side of Star Island, which is well protected from most directions. The bottom is a sand/mud mix and depths are over 8 feet MLW. Expect a few party boats to join you on weekends but they leave when it gets dark. This offers a great view of Miami and the cruise ships.

Finding a place to dock your dinghy to go ashore at Miami Beach can be difficult and rules are constantly changing. You can try the Publix Super Market On the Bay dinghy dock north of Belle Isle and Venetian Causeway (East) or the city-owned dinghy dock at Maurice Gibb Memorial Park to the south of that. We suggest you check with locals or the Marine Patrol (305-673-7959) before using any of the docks.

> **NOTE:** It is unlawful to tie a dinghy to a canal wall to visit the City of Miami Beach. The city also strictly enforces the 20-minute limit for the dinghy dock at the end of 17th Street. These restrictions carry stiff civil fines.

To Government Cut (Miami Inlet) & Fishermans Channel

Government Cut (Miami) Inlet is the primary inlet for the port of Miami. This is a deep-water channel flanked by lighted markers. At its west terminus Government Cut forks into Miami's Main Ship Channel, often clogged with cruise ships, and also Fishermans Channel, which also serves large ships but is generally less congested. If a cruise ship is in port a security zone is established and the Main Ship Channel will be closed requiring you to take Fishermans Channel to get to the ICW. No small boat traffic is allowed in the Main Ship Channel when the cruise ships are in and marine police diligently patrol the entrance. Monitor VHF Channel 16 for possible Sécurité warnings. On either route you must yield to large vessels and ferries.

NAVIGATION: Use NOAA Chart 11467. Government Cut (Miami) Inlet is wide, deep and free of hazards. It runs between Miami Beach (to the north) and Fisher Island (to the south). The Main Ship Channel extends past the end of the Government Cut between Dodge Island and Watson Island to the Turning Basin.

The Main Ship Channel (where cruise ships dock) is often closed for security reasons including when cruise ships are at the Main Ship Channel docks. Closures are announced on VHF Channel 16. Cruisers then must use a route combining Fishermans Channel and the Dodge Channel Cut to skirt the south shore of Dodge Island as an alternative. A short connector channel runs from the west terminus of the Dodge Island Cut to the ICW. The controlling depth is about 12 feet MLW but make sure you identify the markers carefully. Watch for frequent dredging operations in this area and for the numerous ferries headed to and from Fisher Island.

Fishermans Channel and the Dodge Island Cut are similarly free of hazards. When entering the west end of this route from the ICW keep green daybeacon "53A" and flashing green "55" well to port before turning in to the channel due to shoaling extending into the channel. To reach the Dodge Island Cut first split flashing red "18" and green daybeacon "57" (an ICW marker) and then split red daybeacon "16" and flashing green "17." Stay as close to the wharf as is safe as it is quite shallow south of the marked channel. This route is particularly difficult in darkness and it's best to pass at reduced speed. This also serves as the main access to the Miami River and there are several marinas nearby so traffic can be heavy.

Commercial traffic is generally busy here as well and there is a car ferry that runs between Dodge Island and Fisher Island with frequent crossings. You must pay attention in this area and always give the ferry the right of way.

Dockage: The 220-slip Venetian Marina & Yacht Club (north of the Venetian Causeway) is located in the heart of downtown Miami. They can accommodate yachts up to 110 feet with superior amenities. Call ahead for transient space. Yacht Haven Grande Miami is located on the west side of Watson Island just south of the MacArthur Causeway. They cater to super-yachts with deep-water slips to have an outdoor restaurant/lounge (The Deck), laundry service and courtesy cars.

Private Miami Yacht Club is on the east side of Watson Island. Visiting yachts should contact the main office for slip availability. Charges for visiting yachts varies based on club reciprocity. The Miami Yacht Club Youth Sailing Foundation is based here with classes open to everyone (including adults).

The municipal Miamarina at Bayside is south of the Dodge Island bridges at Bayfront Park and may have transient space for vessels (55-foot minimum) on their floating docks. Miamarina is situated within the Bayside Marketplace with an assortment of over 100 stores, shops, restaurants and cafés representing multiple nationalities.

Anchorage: It is also possible to anchor on the east side of Watson Island in 7 to 8 feet MLW. This area falls under the local 7-day anchorage limit.

Long-passage cruisers sometimes follow Fishermans Channel as far as Fisher Island and anchor off its southwestern side (clear of traffic) to get an early start crossing the Gulf Stream. The holding is good here in sand and you should have at least 10 feet MLW. This is open and exposed to the northwest and southeast.

Government Cut to Cape Florida

This section describes the route to the Outside Route (Hawk Channel) leaving Miami harbor through Government Cut (Miami) Inlet. This route is advised for deep-draft vessels and is better suited for operation in darkness.

Departing from the Miami area remember that when there are cruise ships docked at the Port of Miami, the Main Channel is closed to recreational boats. This restriction is strictly enforced. You will have to access the cut through Fishermans Channel located south Dodge Island. To avoid a wait for commercial traffic in one of the shipping channels it may be quicker to proceed south via

Chapter 9: Miami & Biscayne Bay

Miami River

the Inside (ICW) Route, exiting Biscayne Bay south of Key Biscayne. The route through the Cape Florida Channel/Biscayne Channel is actually a shorter route for boats departing from south of Virginia Key.

NAVIGATION: Use NOAA Charts 11451, 11463, 11465 and 11468 (large-scale chart of Miami Harbor). To enter Hawk Channel from North Biscayne Bay you will depart through Government Cut (Miami) Inlet. Access to the in-shore end of the cut may be restricted. Check VHF Channel 16 to see if a security zone is in effect. Government Cut exits the harbor between Miami Beach and Fisher Island, has lighted markers and is flanked by large jetties jutting into the ocean. About 0.5 mile off the north jetty, the ship channel takes a northward dog-leg and proceeds 2 nm seaward through Outer Bar Cut past the charted spoil areas.

An alternate route (weather permitting) is to turn south at flashing green sea buoy "11" once well clear of the south jetty. Pass (but stay clear of) the Miami entrance range markers and the nearby spoils areas and keep well east of the shallows off Virginia Key. From flashing green sea buoy "11" it is a 6.5-nm run southwards on a course of 185° magnetic to flashing red "2" off Cape Florida.

■ SIDE TRIP: MIAMI RIVER

One of Miami's principal yacht service areas is along the Miami River, which flows out from the Everglades and divides the city. From its mouth at Mile 1090 on the ICW the navigable section of the Miami River extends upstream 4 miles to its head of navigation at 36th Street. Most of the operations along the river are primarily repair facilities. Marine services along its banks include custom builders, yacht brokers and boat dealers, sales and service agents, propeller specialists and sailmakers. Along with these are full-service haul-out, repair and storage yards.

NAVIGATION: Use NOAA Chart 11467. The mouth of the Miami River meets the ICW about 0.5 miles south of the Dodge Island Bridges between Bay Front Park and Claughton Island. The ICW follows the shore of Bay Front Park for this stretch and you must execute a sharp turn to starboard (west) to enter the river's mouth at the south end of the park. Give green daybeacons "1" and "3" (the river's only markers) a wide berth and favor the river's north shore (Bay Front Park) upon entry. Shoals extend off the north side of Claughton Island and are at the edge of the marked channel.

Miami River's controlling depth is 14 feet MLW up to the NW 27th Avenue Bridge and then 9 feet MLW up to the 36th Street Dam. Boats proceeding upriver should lower outriggers and antennas for bridge clearance. If land traffic is heavy (and it usually is) bridgetenders will enforce this law.

The stated controlling depths hold for Miami River's more important side branches–South Fork (3 miles from the river's mouth) and Tamiami Canal (1 mile farther on). Both shoot obliquely off to the southwest and, like the main river, each has its own series of boatyards and marine installations. Tamiami Canal is a drainage ditch that parallels the Tamiami Trail Highway to the northwest most of the way across the Florida Peninsula. It is navigable for vessels with up to 6-foot draft (8 feet at high tide) as far as a low-limiting fixed bridge over NW 37th Avenue.

In addition to a wide variety of recreational craft, the Miami River carries considerable commercial traffic. Tugs working in pairs maneuver to place the large oceangoing vessels that line the last mile or so of the river. Give these ships plenty of room.

All lift bridges on the Miami River follow the same restricted schedule (with a few exceptions) and open on signal year-round, except Monday through Friday (not including holidays) from 7:35 a.m. to 8:59 a.m., 12:05 p.m. to 12:59 p.m. and 4:45 p.m. to 5:59 p.m., when the draw need not open. The SW 1st Street Bridge (Mile 0.9) up to and including the NW 27th Avenue Bridge (Mile 3.7) follow the same schedule with one change–they remain operational between 12:05 p.m. to 12:59 p.m. Bridge schedules are always subject to change. If you plan to go upriver, check ahead of time for bridge restrictions.

Most Miami River clearance gauges show the clearance at the fenders instead of the center of the span. There may be a sign indicating the additional clearance available at the center. Charted closed vertical clearances for the bridges in sequence up the Miami River are:

- **Brickell Avenue Bridge** (23-foot clearance)
- **Metro Train Bridge** (75-foot fixed clearance)
- **South Miami Avenue Bridge** (21-foot clearance)
- **Metro Rail/M Path Bridge** (75-foot fixed clearance)
- **SW Second Avenue Bridge** (11-foot clearance)
- **I-95 Twin Bridges** (75-foot fixed clearance)
- **SW 1st Street Bridge** (18-foot clearance)
- **West Flagler Street Bridge** (35-foot clearance)
- **NW 5th Street Bridge** (12-foot clearance)
- **NW 12th Avenue Bridge** (22-foot clearance)
- **Dolphin Expressway Bridge** (75-foot fixed clearance)
- **NW 17th Avenue Bridge** (17-foot clearance)
- **NW 22nd Avenue Bridge** (25-foot clearance)
- **NW 27th Avenue Bridge** (21-foot clearance)

There is one fixed bridge (8-foot vertical clearance) over the South Fork and a swing bridge (erroneously charted as bascule) with 6-foot vertical clearance crossing the Tamiami Canal.

Whenever a big event takes place at Orange Bowl Stadium, home of the University of Miami Hurricanes football team, extra closures are usually imposed. All closures for the regularly scheduled events at the Orange Bowl from August through January are posted online in the *Local Notice to Mariners* starting in late July; they are repeated a week or two before the event dates. These closures usually last only about 2 hours.

Dockage: Behind Claughton Island is the full-service Vice City Marina, a wet storage facility with transient space (30-foot minimum) convenient to the shopping, art and entertainment of Brickell in downtown Miami. As a boutique marina, you won't have charter boats or the other hustle and bustle that comes with some commercial marinas.

There are many repair facilities for the cruising boater on the Miami River but few transient slips. Always call ahead for space availability. Epic Marina is a luxury destination directly on the Miami River with full amenities and two on-site restaurants (Area 31 and ZUMA). The 20-slip marina can accommodate yachts over 300 feet in deep-water slips with no bridges to navigate.

Continuing upriver 5th Street Marina has a seawall capable of berthing up to six mega-yachts with alongside dockage and is co-located with a full-service boatyard, Norseman Shipbuilding Corp. RMK Merrill-Stevens (north of NW 12th Avenue Bridge) is a large shipyard dedicated to yacht refit and repair. They maintain 10 transient slips.

The next group of facilities includes Hurricane Cove Marina & Boatyard, a 150-slip marina, boatyard

Chapter 9: Miami & Biscayne Bay

Goin' Ashore: DOWNTOWN MIAMI, FL

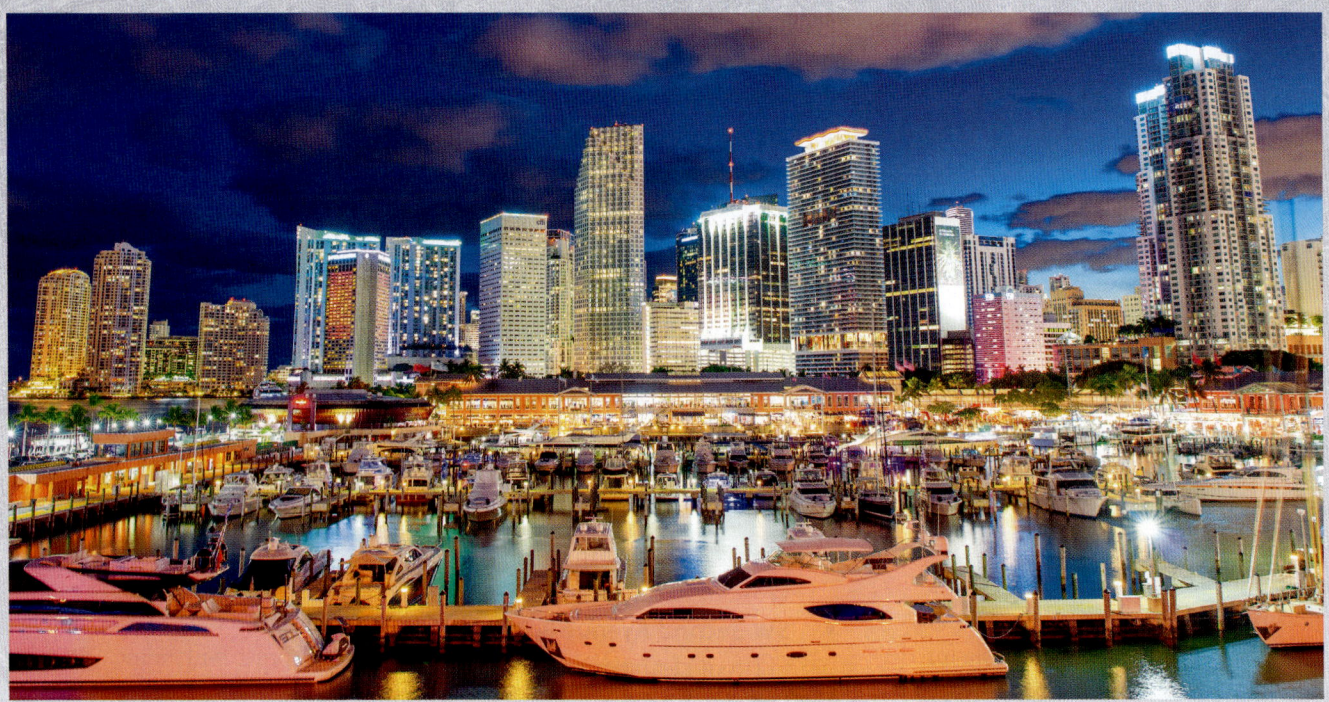

ATTRACTIONS

1. **History Miami Museum** Smithsonian Affiliate with archives, exhibits and area tours exploring Miami's multicultural history (101 W. Flagler St., 305-375-1492).

2. **Pérez Art Museum Miami** Modern and contemporary art museum located in Museum Park overlooking Biscayne Bay. Features a collection of international art from the 20th and 21st centuries (1103 Biscayne Blvd., 305-375-3000).

3. **Phillip and Patricia Frost Museum of Science** Located on 4 acres within the waterfront Maurice A. Ferré Park, the 250,000-square-foot museum explores the process of science and innovation in a campus-like setting. Includes an aquarium and a planetarium at 1101 Biscayne Blvd. (305-434-9600).

4. **Van Gogh: The Immersive Experience** Admire artist Vincent Van Gogh's best work in a 20,000-square foot light and sound exhibit with two-story projections at the Olympia Theater at 174 E. Flagler St. The Olympia Theater is the jewel of South Florida arts and entertainment facilities, providing a unique cultural experience that defies comparison.

SERVICES

5. **Adult Urgent Care** 33 SW 2nd Ave. (Ste. 502), 786-628-0701

6. **Brickell Bay Animal Hospital** 940 Brickell Bay Dr. (786-231-1111)

7. **Greater Miami Convention & Visitors Bureau** 701 Brickell Ave # 2700 (888-766-4264)

8. **Main Library** 101 W. Flagler St. (305-375-2665)

9. **Metro Miami Post Office** 150 SE 2nd Ave. (STE 103), 305-373-7562

MARINAS

10. **Epic Marina** 250 Biscayne Blvd. Way (305-400-6711)

11. **Vice City Marina** 801 Brickell Bay Dr. (305-239-9903)

Chapter 9

America's Waterway Guide Since 1947

The Miami River area has plenty of attractions that make it a great destination for tourists. The easily walkable downtown is home to some of Miami's oldest buildings, which feature a range of architectural styles. It is also known for cultural attractions including museums, galleries and performance spaces. The area hosts a variety of events and festivals throughout the year, celebrating the city's diverse cultures.

SOUTHERN EDITION

Chapter 9: Miami & Biscayne Bay

Miami River, FL

MIAMI RIVER AREA		Largest Vessel	VHF	Total Slips	Approach/ Dockside Depth	Floating Docks	Gas/ Diesel	Repairs/ Haulout	Min/Max Amps	Pump-Out Station
1. Vice City Marina WiFi	(305) 239-9903	80		36	/ 9.0				100	
2. Epic Marina WiFi MM 1090.0	(305) 400-6711	325	16	20	17.0 / 15.0				20 / 200+	P
3. 5th Street Marina	(305) 324-2040	240			15.0 / 13.0			RH	50 / 100	P
4. Norseman Shipbuilding Corp.	(305) 545-6815	90		25	15.0 / 10.0			RH	50	
5. RMK Merrill-Stevens WiFi	(305) 324-5211	250		20	16.0 / 15.0		GD	RH	30 / 100	P
6. Hurricane Cove Marina & Boatyard	(305) 324-8004	85		150	12.0 / 10.0			RH	30	
7. River Cove Marina	(305) 545-5001	60		72	12.0 / 10.0				30 / 50	P

WiFi Wireless Internet Access

Visit www.waterwayguide.com for current rates, fuel prices, website addresses and other up-to-the-minute information. (Information in the table is provided by the facilities.)

Scan here for more details:

Source: Aqua Map and NOAA data

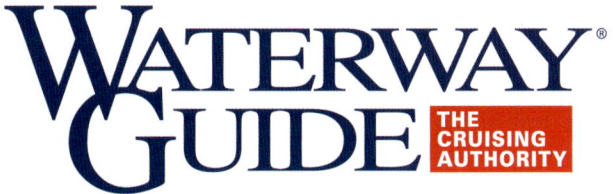

Chapter 9: Miami & Biscayne Bay

and yacht repair facility (both DIY and full service). River Cove Marina has boat slips (to 45 feet) and wet slips (to 60 feet) and has limited transient space. Call ahead.

TO KEY BISCAYNE

When entering Central Biscayne Bay, cruisers will finally feel they have arrived in the tropics. The beautiful turquoise waters and surrounding sand beaches give this area a "postcard" feel. The bay widens and deepens in this segment and provides a protected passage to multiple destinations. Just below Key Biscayne the Cape Florida and Biscayne Channels provide ocean access for either a Gulf Stream crossing east to the Bahamas or a southwest (deep water) route to the Florida Keys along the Hawk Channel.

At the bay's extreme south end are smaller channels to the ocean on the east and the ICW route to the south through Jewfish Creek to Florida Bay and the Upper Florida Keys. On the Bay's western shore are the laid-back communities of South Miami including Coconut Grove, a destination in itself. And, finally, there is Biscayne National Park encompassing both land and sea in all its natural wonder.

To Virginia Key–ICW Mile 1090 to Mile 1092

This section continues the route south on the ICW from the Dodge Island Cut and into Central Biscayne Bay. Navigation on the ICW north from the Dodge Island Cut is particularly complex. Over the first 1.5-mile stretch you will pass four bridges and cross the turning basin of Miami's Main Ship Channel. Review the appropriate section in this guide before reaching Dodge Island.

NAVIGATION: Use NOAA Chart 11467. Flashing green "55" is the final ICW marker before the entrance into the Dodge Island Cut and flashing red "18" is the cut's final marker. To the south the ICW enters a narrow, dredged channel. Observe markers carefully; this section can be particularly confusing in darkness. Starting with green daybeacon "57" and quick-flashing green "59" keep the green markers to port.

When approaching Claughton Island, gradually turn to parallel the island's east shore. The location of the channel is not precisely marked and vessels should proceed at slow speed and use the depth sounder to find and maintain alignment. Depths hold up quite close to shore. If you are reading less than 9 feet MLW, you may have strayed out of the channel.

South of Claughton Island the channel appears to open up but depths at the channel's edge are actually more

Biscayne Bay, FL

VIRGINIA KEY		Largest Vessel	VHF	Total Slips	Approach/ Dockside Depth	Floating Docks	Gas/ Diesel	Repairs/ Haulout	Min/Max Amps	Pump-Out Station
1. Rickenbacker Marina Inc. WiFi MM 1091.5	(305) 361-1900	100	16	200	8.0 / 9.0		G	RH	30 / 50	P
2. Marine Stadium Marina MM 1091.5	(305) 960-5140	43	16		8.0 / 10.0		G	RH		
KEY BISCAYNE										
3. Crandon Park Marina MM 1094.0	(305) 361-1281	80	16	294	6.0 / 5.0	F	GD		30 / 50	P
4. Key Biscayne Yacht Club-PRIVATE	(305) 361-8229	60		100	/		GD	H		P

WiFi Wireless Internet Access
Visit www.waterwayguide.com for current rates, fuel prices, website addresses and other up-to-the-minute information.
(Information in the table is provided by the facilities.)

Scan here for more details:

Source: Aqua Map and NOAA data

SOUTHERN EDITION   349

Chapter 9: Miami & Biscayne Bay

Outside Run From Miami

Coming up on the outside from the south, northbound boats that want to enter inshore waters can take either Cape Florida Channel or Biscayne Channel once they have passed Fowey Rocks Light, or they can continue on to Government Cut. The Miami GPS Differential Beacon (nominal range 75 miles) is located on Virginia Key near the west end of the fixed bridge across Bear Cut.

Coming down along the ocean side of Key Biscayne, southbound boats should stand offshore on the run from Miami. Take a heading due south from the entrance buoys off Government Cut's Outer Bar Cut to pick up Biscayne Channel Light (better known locally as Bug Light), the 37-foot-high spidery pipe structure (flashing white every four seconds) marking the seaward entrance of Cape Florida and Biscayne Channels. Coming in at flashing red "6," you have a choice of two channels leading to Biscayne Bay. Depths in the shared entrance channel to the Cape Florida Channel and the Biscayne Channel are charted at 7 feet at MLW over the bar.

From the sea the right-hand, northern fork is the Cape Florida Channel leading past the prominent lighthouse and the lovely palm-fringed beach. The chart clearly identifies the deep-water passage along the curving shoreline and indicates two shoal spots situated between 0.1 and 0.2 mile southwest of the shore. Hug the shore along the curving concrete bulkhead of the park property to clear the charted shoals, marked by green daybeacon "1." At the inner end bear off to leave red daybeacon "2" and flashing red "4" to starboard. From the outside this is the easiest route to No Name Harbor, the area's most popular jump-off point for mariners awaiting favorable weather for a Bahamas passage.

The southern route, which is better marked and deeper than the unmarked Cape Florida Channel, is known as Biscayne Channel. It is wide, straight, well marked and easy to run. Depths in the channel range from 11 to 16 feet MLW. Even so, the entrance depth from the ocean sometimes limits the channel. At its western end the channel produces good fishing during flood tide.

shallow. You should maintain 9 feet MLW by passing close to quick-flashing green "63," green daybeacon "65" and flashing green "67." For nighttime passage be sure to locate green daybeacon "65" with a searchlight.

South from flashing green "67" it's a straight run to the span of the **Rickenbacker Causeway Bridge** (65-foot fixed vertical clearance), which is sometimes referred to as "the Powell-Rickenbacker Bridge." The older structure is dwarfed alongside its modern replacement and remains in use as a fishing pier that abuts the channel.

> NOTE: Marine Stadium on Virginia Key (northeast of the Rickenbacker Causeway Bridge) was originally built in 1963 to promote powerboat racing. It was considered a modernist icon because of its cantilevered, fold-plate roof and construction of lightweight, poured-in-place concrete, popular in mid-century stadiums. At 326 feet in length (longer than a football field) it was the longest span of cantilevered concrete in the world when it was built. Its eight big slanted columns are anchored in the ground. It has served as the home of the Miami International Boat Show since 2016.

Dockage: The wet slips for Rickenbacker Marina Inc. on Virginia Key are located on the west end of the property. They can accommodate up to 200 vessels with a maximum length of 120 feet (40 foot minimum). This facility offers amazing views of Biscayne Bay and downtown Miami to the west. Marine Stadium Marina is a dry storage facility.

Anchorage: You can anchor at the Marine Stadium for 24 hours only. The anchoring provides good protection in 8- to 12-foot MLW depths with a mud and sand bottom. This anchorage offers a beautiful view of downtown Miami. Jet-skis and wakeboarders use this area on the weekends. There are signs that indicate no dinghy landing and the Miami-Dade Police strictly enforce dinghy landing rules.

Note that the Marine Stadium anchorage is closed from mid-January until after the Miami Boat Show (middle of February) each year.

A popular anchorage is just southeast of Virgina Key in at least 7 feet MLW with good holding in sandy mud. This is open and exposed to the south. Or drop the hook outside the basin north of the Miami Seaquarium at Virginia Key. (Marked on NOAA chart as DOME.)

Shore access to the beach on Virgina Key is difficult. There are signs that indicate no dinghy landing. The Miami-Dade Police strictly enforce dinghy landing rules but drop-offs are possible.

Key Biscayne

While the ICW leads south from Rickenbacker Causeway Bridge, Key Biscayne lies to the east and the Cape Florida Channel, leading to the Atlantic Ocean, skirts its south end. This area offers some well-protected anchorages, access to South Miami and some beautiful barrier islands to explore.

Key Biscayne, site of southern Florida's first town, was founded in 1839. It was also headquarters for a band of renegades who lured ships onto the reefs and "salvaged" their cargo. Today the key is made up of two parks. Crandon Park occupies the northern end of Key Biscayne. This county park boasts a marina (Crandon Park Marina), boat ramp, two miles of ocean beach and excellent picnic grounds. Nearby is the International Tennis Center and an excellent golf course. Bus service is available to the city. Bill Baggs Cape Florida State Park is at Key Biscayne's southern end featuring the restored Cape Florida Lighthouse, the keeper's house with tours, walking trails and another beautiful beach.

> NOTE: Just below Key Biscayne to the east you will see the remaining houses of Stiltsville, an eclectic group of homes on stilts that now belong to the National Park Service. Stiltsville has a colorful history that dates back to the 1930s. At its peak in 1960, there were 27 structures on the flats, but hurricanes, fires and the ravages of being in such an exposed place have taken a toll. There are only a handful of remaining structures visible along the reef.

NAVIGATION: Use NOAA Chart 11467, 11465 and 11451. Cruising south of the Rickenbacker Causeway is easier if you use NOAA Chart 11465 (ICW–Miami to Elliot Key). Although the scale is the same on both charts, NOAA Chart 11465 covers a larger area (as far as Elliot Key) and makes tracing longer courselines simpler. After clearing the Rickenbacker Causeway Bridge at Mile 1091.6 and keeping Virginia Key to the east, you will enter Central Biscayne Bay. Flashing green "69" lies south of the bridge and is the last ICW marker for some distance. There are three approaches to Key Biscayne: (1) Bear Cut, (2) Hurricane Harbor and (3) Cape Florida Channel to "No Name Harbor."

Bear Cut is flanked by Virginia Key on the west and Key Biscayne to the east. It is unmarked at its northeastern end except for red daybeacon "2," which provides an outlet to the ocean for smaller boats that can pass under the Bear Cut Bridge (16-foot fixed vertical clearance). Skippers headed southbound on the ICW should consult their charts and take time to plan their route. Navigation markers are sparse here and can get lost in the expanse of Central Biscayne Bay. While the bay is open and relatively deep, there are some shoals and route planning is essential. Compass headings should be planned and followed for each passage segment.

The channel leading to Hurricane Harbor is at Mile 1095 just past flashing green "1." And the first marker for the Cape Florida Channel is flashing red "4" at Mile 1096. This channel hugs Key Biscayne's southwestern shore.

This is a popular staging area for cruisers waiting for a weather-window to make a "Bahama's Run" across the Gulf Stream. See "BONUS: Crossing to the Bahamas" in the next section for details. This is also the route to the Cape Florida Channel (7 feet MLW), perhaps the easiest route from Central Biscayne Bay to the Atlantic Ocean. This passage is described in detail in "The Florida Keys" chapter of this guide. Follow the route to the No Name Harbor anchorage to take this route.

Dockage/Moorings: Crandon Park Marina at Key Biscayne is best approached from Biscayne Bay by a privately marked natural channel that leads northeastward from the shoal light (flashing white, 4 sec.) off West Point. The marina has slips and moorings (available to sailboats only) in its protected cove with easy access to marina amenities. (Note that the showers are outdoor and cold water only.) This is home to a busy dive boat operation. If you have to do any type of shopping, you will need to arrange for ground transportation as there are no shops or restaurants for several miles.

The use of the facilities at the private Key Biscayne Yacht Club are extended to Members of the Florida Council of Yacht Clubs and reciprocal associations only.

Anchorage: Two of the most popular harbors among boaters waiting for favorable weather to cross over to the Bahamas are Hurricane Harbor near the southwest corner of Key Biscayne and No Name Harbor around the point from Hurricane Harbor (in the Bill Baggs State Park). Hurricane Harbor does not have shore access but is a sheltered spot for inclement weather. Favor the port side as you come in as the starboard side of the channel shoals to 4 feet MLW. Drop the anchor in 5 to 13 feet MLW with excellent holding and some exposure to the northwest.

Chapter 9 — Miami & Biscayne Bay

No Name Harbor has shore access and a fee for overnight anchoring and use of the facilities. Envelopes are provided for depositing the fees in an honor box ashore. There is room for about 25 boats. (Expect lots of company on weekends.) The bottom is hard mud in 11 to 12-foot MLW depths and holding is good with wind protection from all directions except due west (and that is actually not too bad). There are clean restrooms, inexpensive showers and a laundry (although not always operational). Cleats along the seawall make going ashore easy but there is no protection along the raw concrete seawall, so you should rig your own fenders in advance. A pump-out station is located on the southern side of the harbor near the entrance, but it's not always working.

Boaters Grill at the head of No Name Harbor welcomes diners by land or sea with a full menu (including a huge breakfast selection) along with beer and wine (305-361-0080).

When the wind is out of the east, another option is to simply anchor in the lee of the west side of Key Biscayne north of Hurricane Harbor in at least 8 feet MLW. Leave the ICW at Mile 1095 and head due east towards flashing green "3." Head into the small cove to the east located just south of the large (private) yacht club. You will have plenty of swinging room and a great view of the Miami skyline. Do mind the shoals off West Point and stay well south of them. Winds from the west (rare) can set up choppy conditions due to long fetch from mainland coast.

Coconut Grove Area–ICW Mile 1095 to Mile 1098

Once a seaplane base–first for the Pan American clippers flying to the Caribbean and South America and later for the U.S. Coast Guard–Dinner Key is now the site of Miami's premier municipal marina and the old Pan American terminal has been restored and serves as Miami City Hall. The surrounding Coconut Grove area offers a cluster of friendly marine services including yacht clubs, marinas, a boatyard, restaurants, entertainment and shopping. The municipal Dinner Key Marina is a great place to stop for provisioning to get off the boat and stretch your legs.

NAVIGATION: Use NOAA Charts 11467 and 11465. Biscayne Bay changes character south of the Rickenbacker Causeway Bridge, becoming broad, relatively deep (average 10 feet MLW) and natural. Sailing regattas are held in these waters nearly every weekend, while fishing, swimming, water skiing and cruising are everyday activities, year-round. Cruisers will find this part of Biscayne Bay especially inviting. The deep, open water makes a pleasant change from the narrow, dredged sections of the ICW to the north and the sand bottom and clear, turquoise water gives a tropical feel.

On the mainland opposite Key Biscayne lies distinctive Dinner Key, the major center of boating activity for Central Biscayne Bay. Dinner Key is accessed via the well-marked, 1.5-mile-long Dinner Key Channel. Expect 8-foot MLW approach depths to the marina.

No Name Harbor

America's Waterway Guide Since 1947 — Chapter 9

Biscayne Bay, FL

DINNER KEY		Largest Vessel	VHF	Total Slips	Approach/ Dockside Depth	Floating Docks	Gas/ Diesel	Repairs/ Haulout	Min/Max Amps	Pump-Out Station
1. Coral Reef Yacht Club-PRIVATE MM 1094.0	(305) 858-1733	65	71	104	7.0 / 7.0	F		H	30 / 100	P
2. Bayshore Landing WiFi MM 1094.0	(305) 854-7997	100	68	114	5.0 / 6.0	F		H	30 / 100	P
3. Grove Harbour Marina MM 1094.0	(305) 854-6444	150		58	18.0 / 8.0	F	GD	RH	30 / 100	P
4. Dinner Key Marina 1095.0	(305) 329-4755	110	16	582	8.0 / 7.0	F			30 / 100	P

WiFi Wireless Internet Access
Visit www.waterwayguide.com for current rates, fuel prices, website addresses and other up-to-the-minute information. (Information in the table is provided by the facilities.)

Scan here for more details:

Source: Aqua Map and NOAA data

SOUTHERN EDITION

Chapter 9 — Miami & Biscayne Bay

Goin' Ashore

COCONUT GROVE, FL

ATTRACTIONS

1. Barnacle Historic State Park
Five-acre bayfront park that features a former Victorian Estate and gardens as well as beautiful views of Biscayne Bay at 3485 Main Hwy. (305-442-6866).

2. CocoWalk Shopping Center
Upscale outdoor shopping center with a variety of shops and restaurants, as well as a movie theater amid an outdoor courtyard at 3015 Grand Ave. (305-444-0777).

3. Lowe Art Museum
Small museum showcasing art from ancient and Baroque to American with special events and exhibitions. Open Wednesday through Saturday from 10:00 a.m. to 4:00 p.m. at 1301 Stanford Dr. (305-284-3535).

4. Miami City Hall
The Miami City Hall, which serves the Visitor Information Center, is located in the original Pan Am complex on Dinner Key at 3500 Pan American Dr. (305-250-5300). The complex was designed to look like an airplane when viewed from above: Pan Am Drive and Circle represent the body of the plane; the Terminal Building is the cockpit and the hanger buildings represent the wings.

SERVICES

5. Coconut Grove Branch Library
2875 McFarlane Rd. (305-442-8695)

6. Coconut Grove Post Office
3191 Grand Ave. (305-529-6700)

7. Grove Animal Hospital
2803 SW 27th Ave. (786-789-0660)

Part of the City of Miami, Coconut Grove is known to locals as "The Grove." Unlike the rest of Miami, low-key and restful Coconut Grove preserves much of the ambiance of traditional Florida. Take a stroll down the charming streets in an area known for its unique architecture and bohemian vibe. At night, The Grove has a vibrant nightlife scene with plenty of options for dining and entertainment.

Coconut Grove was once a seaplane base for the enormous Pan American clippers flying to the Caribbean and South America. The airport complex took up all of Dinner Key and a large part of the adjacent mainland was designed to look like an airplane when viewed from above.

If you wish to explore further afield (transportation required), the lush Kampong Botanical Garden is to the south with flowering trees and tropical fruit including more than 50 types of mango. This is a great place to relax and take in the scenery (4013 Douglas Rd., 305-442-7169). To the north is Vizcaya Museum & Gardens, a historic estate with formal gardens and sculptures, grottos and a circa-1914 mansion turned museum (3251 S. Miami Ave., 305-250-9133).

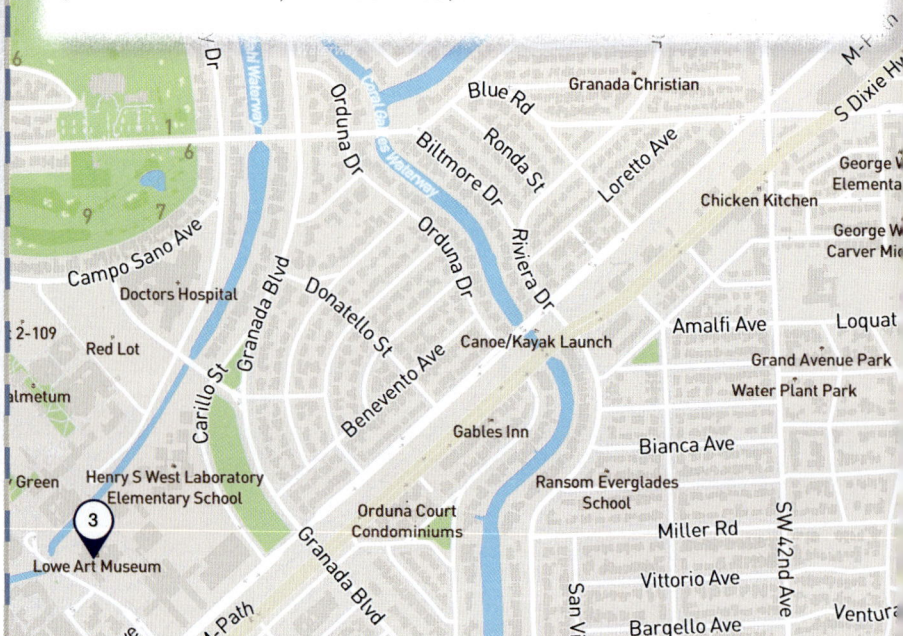

America's Waterway Guide Since 1947 **Chapter 9**

MARINAS

8. Bayshore Landing
2550 S. Bayshore Dr. (305-854-7997)

9. Coral Reef Yacht Club
2484 S. Bayshore Dr. (305-858-1733)

10. Dinner Key Marina
3400 Pan American Dr. (305-329-4755)

11. Grove Harbour Marina
2640 S. Bayshore Dr. (305-854-6444)

Villa Vizcaya Museum

SOUTHERN EDITION   355

Chapter 9: Miami & Biscayne Bay

Dockage/Moorings: Coral Reef Yacht Club uses the same entrance channel from Biscayne Bay as the nearby marinas. Slips are available only by advance reservation with the dockmaster. Space is limited and it is suggested that you contact them at least one day in advance.

Accessible by the same channel is Bayshore Landing, which welcomes transients with full amenities. This is home to local favorite Monty's Raw Bar & Restaurant (305-856-3992) as well as a number of marine-related businesses including a Starbucks, yacht sales and brokerage firms and commercial fishing charter companies.

Grove Harbour Marina in the same basin is a full-service facility run by marine experts. They offer concierge service to take care of all your boating needs. Call ahead for slip availability.

The municipal Dinner Key Marina to the south provides accommodations in a park-like setting to transients and long-term renters in slips or in their large mooring field. Moorings are available on a first-come, first-served basis. Included in the cost of the mooring are pump-out service and a dinghy dock. A free launch service will shuttle you to and from the marina, which is very close to the attractions of Coconut Grove. You can also come in to take on water. This is a popular spot to wait for favorable weather to cross to the Bahamas.

Anchorage: Anchoring is still possible outside of the mooring field at Dinner Key to the north (on the opposite side of the channel) and to the east in 7 to 8 feet MLW. This is open and exposed to the east through southeast. The anchorage is usually crowded so study the area carefully before dropping your hook.

Side Trip: Coral Gables & Homestead

NAVIGATION: Use NOAA Charts 11467 and 11465. Located directly south of Coconut Grove, Coral Gables has its own waterway with a well-marked entrance and 5-foot MLW controlling depths. Since bridges on both branches of this waterway are fixed (most offer about a 12-foot vertical clearance), you will likely have to explore by dinghy. The canals interconnect, wind through residential developments and finally exit to the bay just north of Coral Gables' wide Tahiti Beach.

Dockage: Matheson Hammock Marina is located at Matheson Hammock Park with a sandy beach in Coral

Dinner Key Mooring Field

Biscayne Bay, FL

CORAL GABLES		Largest Vessel	VHF	Total Slips	Approach/ Dockside Depth	Floating Docks	Gas/ Diesel	Repairs/ Haulout	Min/Max Amps	Pump-Out Station
1. Matheson Hammock Marina 3.6 mi. W of MM 1098.0	(305) 665-5475	55		243	5.5 / 5.0	F	GD		30 / 50	P
HOMESTEAD AREA										
2. Black Point Park & Marina MM 1106.0	(305) 258-4092	55	16	200	4.9 / 5.5	F	GD		30 / 50	P
3. Herbert Hoover Marina at Homestead Bayfront Park WiFi MM 1111.0	(305) 230-3033	50	16	174	3.5 / 5.0		GD	H	30 / 50	P

WiFi Wireless Internet Access
Visit www.waterwayguide.com for current rates, fuel prices, website addresses and other up-to-the-minute information. (Information in the table is provided by the facilities.)

Scan here for more details:

Gables. It is one of South Florida's few remaining natural areas with native forest and a lagoon-type atoll beach. Nature trails and bike trails weave throughout the park. At the on-site Redfish Grill you can choose to dine inside a historic coral rock building or outside overlooking the beach and Biscayne Bay. Reservations recommended.

Continuing south (9 miles), Black Point Park & Marina is accessible via a well-marked channel and provides transient dockage, bike and running trails and a dockside restaurant and bar (Black Point Ocean Grill). A jetty that extends 1.5 miles into the Bay enables fishing enthusiasts to cast from shore. In the same basin, Loggerhead Marina–South Miami Marina provides dry storage and has a well-stocked marine store. (No transient slips.)

Five miles south at Convoy Point next to the Biscayne National Park headquarters (south side) is the 174-slip Herbert Hoover Marina at Homestead Bayfront Park. The marina is in a beautiful tropical setting with a beach and an on-site restaurant, La Playa Grill Seafood & Bar, featuring fresh seafood and live music.

It is best to take a slip here, and why not when you can spend the morning on a beautiful beach, hike on a natural trail in the afternoon then enjoy the colors the sunset brings while having dinner at a yummy waterfront restaurant?

■ NEXT STOP

You are now in an ideal position to head either east to the Bahamas or continue south to the Florida Keys and beyond. If you choose the run north outside from Government Cut, the Gulf Stream will provide a boost to Port Everglades and points north. This route also provides a spectacular view of the Miami Beach skyline.

Source: Aqua Map and NOAA data

Chapter 9: Crossing to The Bahamas

PLANNING YOUR TRIP

For vessels crossing between the Florida east coast and the Bahamas, the Gulf Stream is the principal navigational consideration. It is a wide, deep and warm river of fast moving water flowing north, where sea conditions are deeply influenced by the wind. Crossing this river requires careful planning while considering the characteristics of your vessel and crew and the expected wind and weather.

The Gulf Stream current generally begins a few miles out from the Florida coast and extends for approximately 43 nm eastward. The current will gradually increase as you travel east reaching a maximum of roughly 3.6 knots about 8 to 11 miles from the western wall. The current gradually subsides to little or no current at the eastern edge of the Gulf Stream. The average northerly speed over the 43 mile width is 2.5 knots while the average direction of flow is 1° True when north of Lake Worth (Palm Beach) Inlet and about 2° True south of the inlet.

Cruising Conditions

The sea state in the Gulf Stream is largely a function of the prevailing ocean swell in the area, combined with local wind generated waves. The National Weather Service marine forecast provides the Significant Wave Height expected for the Gulf Stream, which is the average height of the highest one-third of the combined swells and wind waves. Be sure to check this when planning your departure. For a useful rule of thumb: south to southeast winds at 10 knots will develop 2-foot seas; 15 knots, 4- to 5-foot seas; 20 knots, 7-foot seas; and 25 knots, 9-foot seas.

For most cruising boats it is generally not advisable to cross the Gulf Stream in winds higher than 15 knots. And it is never a great idea to cross in winds with any significant northerly component as winds against the current cause a very steep, choppy sea. Winds of 10 knots or less offer a relatively comfortable ride for the typical semi-displacement recreational boat 35 to 45 feet in length, provided there are no significant swells in addition to the wind waves.

In winter the location of the Gulf Stream will sometimes be marked by mist rising from its warm waters, which are significantly warmer than the colder coastal water. In winter and whenever a northerly wind is blowing the horizon looking toward the Gulf Stream will often look jagged or saw-toothed. Sailors observing from inshore may say there are "elephants" out there–giant square topped waves kicked up by the Gulf Stream's determination to win its way north against the wind.

In bright sunlight the Gulf Stream is a deep cobalt blue and if the sun is right you may see light dancing in its depths. You will usually see blond-colored patches of Sargasso weed drifting in its waters. Fish will often congregate near and under these patches. You can be sure you have entered the Gulf Stream when the water temperature noticeably increases over a short distance from the near shore ocean temperature. If you are navigating using GPS, you will likely see the effects of the current quickly as your course and speed over ground change significantly.

Planning to Cross

Crossing the Gulf Stream is like traversing a wide, moving walkway–your boat is being steadily pushed northward. The longer you spend in the Gulf Stream, the further north you will be unless you compensate for that movement. Your best strategy is to take advantage of that push by starting as far south (or upstream) of your destination as possible. To the extent that it is possible careful planning and navigation can minimize the time it takes to cross.

NOAA weather broadcasts give daily information about the Gulf Stream including its width, speed, distance offshore at different locations along the Florida coast and its temperature. Many online sources also give daily, detailed maps of the Gulf Stream. For planning purposes a reasonable rule of thumb is to assume the entire distance you have to run from a Florida departure to a point lying along the W 79° 15.000' line of longitude will be subject to an average 2.5-knot, north-flowing current. For faster boats this may have relatively little effect on your course and time to cross but for slower boats, particularly those under sail, the effect is profound and must be taken into account. There are essentially three ways to navigate this challenge:

- In the days before GPS and chartplotters, boats would compute a heading based on the average current and then steer that constant heading. The disadvantage to this approach is that it is based solely on averages while the actual current and wind will vary from day to day and during the crossing. But it generally gets the boat close enough to your destination that it can be recognized.

Chapter 9: Crossing to The Bahamas

- The boat can be steered to stay pointed at the destination waypoint. This works but is not the most efficient method and will take more time.
- For boats equipped with GPS, a chartplotter and preferably autopilot, steer to constantly keep the boat on the route from starting point to destination. The actual heading will vary constantly. You will need to adjust to the actual current and wind drift as you move along the route. This is the most efficient way to navigate the crossing.

There are as many opinions on when to depart Florida and at what time to arrive at your Bahamian waypoint as there are vessels crossing the Gulf Stream. Night crossings are common but they do present the additional challenge of traveling amidst the ever-growing number of freighters and cruise ships in very busy shipping lanes to and from Florida.

Dawn departures provide easier travel in the shipping lanes and arrival in Bahamian waters with the sun behind you. And if you decide to continue across the Banks, night passage will be in many ways easier there than in the Gulf Stream. You should consider your speed of travel, destination and what conditions are expected when you arrive. A vessel departing for and planning to visit North Bimini will have a much different crossing schedule than one headed non-stop to Nassau. Regardless, pay attention to the weather and don't develop forward-only vision.

Be vigilant about frequent checks for other vessels to starboard, port and aft! Don't become another victim rundown by an inattentive skipper traveling on autopilot. And don't forget to file a Float Plan. (A number of free iOS and Android apps allow you to create a float plan and email it to participants or emergency contacts.)

The Constant Heading Table

If you choose the constant heading approach to your passage, the Magnetic Heading & Time-to-Cross table provides for a given boat speed, the single heading to steer and the time to cross on that heading. This data will always be an approximation but is a good estimate for your constant heading and also a good tool for planning passage time if you will be steering to stay on a route line.

The tables are based on the WGS84 datum and 2019 magnetic variation from the National Centers for Environmental Data at NOAA. The results are accurate to within 1° True. The current was assumed to be the average current in the Gulf Stream, which is 2.5 knots. They do not consider wind drift or leeway; compensating for these for your vessel will improve accuracy.

The from/to locations correspond to the waypoints identified in the Departure/Destination Waypoints table. They can be used regardless of your destination but you will have to adjust your total trip plan for additional distances to be run.

For example, assume you want to leave from Lake Worth (Palm Beach) Inlet and go to West End. The fourth entry in the table shows the distance traveled between these waypoints is 55.7 nm at a bearing of 101° magnetic. Also assume you plan to travel at 8 knots boat speed. The table shows that at 8 knots you must steer on average 115° magnetic to arrive near the destination waypoint. The time en route will be approximately 7.2 hours between the two waypoints. So if you plan to leave your anchorage or slip early and arrive at the departure waypoint at 7:00 a.m., you should arrive at the destination waypoint at approximately 2:12 p.m. Of course, you need to allow for the time required to get from there to your final overnight stop wherever that may be.

Chapter 9

Magnetic Heading & Time-To-Cross

Top Number = Heading to Steer (Magnetic)
Bottom Number = Time Between Waypoints (Hours)
Based on Boat Speed (Knots)

Direction (M) / Distance (nm)	From	To	5 kn	6 kn	7 kn	8 kn	9 kn	10 kn	15 kn	20 kn	25 kn
312° / 82.3 nm	West End	Fort Pierce	297° / 14.5	299° / 12.3	301° / 10.6	302° / 9.4	303° / 8.4	304° / 7.6	307° / 5.2	308° / 4.0	309° / 3.2
302° / 67.4 nm	West End	Saint Lucie	283° / 12.4	286° / 10.4	289° / 9.0	290° / 7.9	292° / 7.1	293° / 6.4	296° / 4.3	297° / 3.3	298° / 2.6
282° / 55.7 nm	West End	Lake Worth	259° / 11.9	263° / 9.7	266° / 8.2	268° / 7.1	269° / 6.3	271° / 5.6	274° / 3.7	276° / 2.8	277° / 2.2
101° / 55.7 nm	Lake Worth	West End	124° / 12.3	120° / 9.9	117° / 8.4	115° / 7.2	114° / 6.4	113° / 5.7	109° / 3.8	107° / 2.8	106° / 2.2
65° / 69.3 nm	Port Everglades	West End	83° / 11.9	80° / 10.1	78° / 8.8	77° / 7.8	75° / 7.0	74° / 6.3	71° / 4.3	70° / 3.3	69° / 2.7
111° / 69.0 nm	Lake Worth	Freeport	129° / 15.6	126° / 12.6	124° / 10.6	122° / 9.2	121° / 8.1	120° / 7.2	117° / 4.7	115° / 3.5	114° / 2.8
78° / 74.5 nm	Port Everglades	Freeport	95° / 13.9	92° / 11.7	90° / 10.0	88° / 8.8	87° / 7.9	86° / 7.1	84° / 4.8	82° / 3.6	81° / 2.9
259° / 74.5 nm	Freeport	Port Everglades	242° / 17.6	245° / 14.1	247° / 11.8	248° / 10.2	249° / 8.9	250° / 8.0	253° / 5.2	254° / 3.8	255° / 3.1
291° / 69.0 nm	Freeport	Lake Worth	273° / 13.6	276° / 11.3	278° / 9.6	280° / 8.4	281° / 7.5	282° / 6.8	285° / 4.5	287° / 3.4	288° / 2.7
336° / 74.6 nm	Bimini	Lake Worth	319° / 10.7	322° / 9.3	324° / 8.2	325° / 7.4	327° / 6.7	328° / 6.2	330° / 4.4	332° / 3.4	333° / 2.7
306° / 48.2 nm	Bimini	Port Everglades	279° / 8.6	284° / 7.2	287° / 6.2	289° / 5.5	291° / 4.9	293° / 4.4	297° / 3.0	299° / 2.3	301° / 1.9
281° / 43.8 nm	Bimini	Miami	251° / 9.9	257° / 7.9	260° / 6.6	263° / 5.7	265° / 5.0	267° / 4.5	272° / 2.9	274° / 2.2	275° / 1.8
126° / 48.2 nm	Port Everglades	Bimini	152° / 14.3	147° / 10.8	144° / 8.7	142° / 7.3	140° / 6.3	138° / 5.6	134° / 3.5	132° / 2.6	131° / 2.0
101° / 43.8 nm	Miami	Bimini	130° / 10.2	125° / 8.1	121° / 6.7	119° / 5.8	117° / 5.1	115° / 4.5	110° / 3.0	108° / 2.2	106° / 1.8
87° / 49.8 nm	Lake Worth	Memory Rock	113° / 10.1	108° / 8.3	105° / 7.0	103° / 6.1	101° / 5.4	100° / 4.9	96° / 3.3	93° / 2.5	92° / 2.0
306° / 70.2 nm	Memory Rock	Fort Pierce	288° / 12.6	291° / 10.6	293° / 9.2	295° / 8.1	296° / 7.3	297° / 6.6	300° / 4.5	302° / 3.4	303° / 2.7
105° / 61.7 nm	Fort Pierce	Matanilla Shoal	126° / 13.8	122° / 11.2	120° / 9.4	118° / 8.1	116° / 7.2	115° / 6.4	112° / 4.2	110° / 3.1	109° / 2.5
286° / 61.7 nm	Matantilla Shoal	Fort Pierce	265° / 12.6	269° / 10.4	271° / 8.8	273° / 7.7	274° / 6.8	276° / 6.1	279° / 4.1	281° / 3.1	282° / 2.5

Corrected courses and estimated elapsed times at varying speeds under normal sea conditions

SOUTHERN EDITION

Chapter 9
Crossing to The Bahamas

Departure/Destination Waypoints				
Location	Latitude N		Longitude W	
	degrees	minutes	degrees	minutes
Fort Pierce	27°	28.489	80°	16.216
Matanilla Shoal	27°	20.000	79°	07.500
St. Lucie	27°	10.020	80°	08.530
Memory Rock	26°	55.000	79°	07.000
Lake Worth	26°	46.345	80°	01.879
West End	26°	42.250	78°	59.786
Freeport	26°	30.000	78°	47.060
Port Everglades	26°	05.627	80°	05.416
Miami	25°	45.354	80°	06.888
Bimini	25°	42.630	79°	18.450

Remember that if you use GPS and remain on the route line between points your heading will vary with the current and wind conditions but you will average 115° magnetic over that time. On the other hand, if you steer a constant 115° magnetic, you will deviate from the route line but should end up at or near the destination.

Listen to the Forecast

The Gulf Stream is a relatively constant, predictable force. The weather is not. Listen to the forecasts. Believe the bad ones and don't trust the good ones. Go to the beach if you can and look out over the ocean. What is happening out there? As stated before the most difficult and dangerous time for any vessel to cross the Gulf Stream is when the wind is from the north, including the northeast and the northwest. Whether you are running a 180-foot motor yacht or skippering an 18-foot sailboat, northerly conditions are definitely not the ones in which to cross.

Remember that the Gulf Stream is flowing north at 2.5 knots. When the wind blows from the north, it is like rubbing a cat the wrong way; all the fur kicks up and the results are the "elephants" mentioned earlier. These are high, ugly waves as closely spaced as elephants holding each other's tails in a circus parade. In those conditions the Gulf Stream is not where you want to be.

Weather is available on the VHF NOAA weather channels from numerous online sources and with many weather apps. Pay close attention, plan carefully, pick your weather window and enjoy a pleasant crossing to the wonderful Bahamas.

America's Waterway Guide Since 1947

Skipper Bob Publications

The App from Waterway Guide

No Signal? No Problem!
DOWNLOAD CONTENT

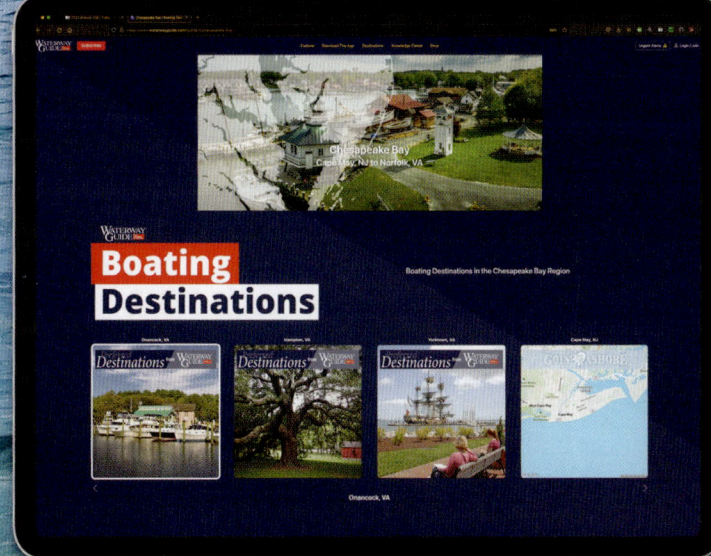

The Explorer web app
waterwayguide.com

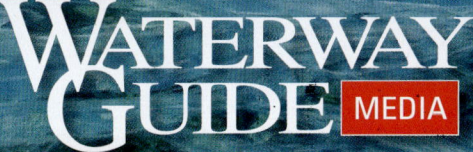

Chapter 10: The Florida Keys

■ NAVIGATION & ANCHORING NOTES

Extending in a sweeping southwesterly curve from Miami and the mainland the Florida Keys offer a cruising experience unlike any other waterway area. In many ways the Keys resemble the islands of the Bahamas except for the main highway and 42 bridges (a total of 18.94 miles of bridges) that tie them together. West of Marathon the Seven Mile (Moser Channel) Bridge–which is actually 6.77 miles long–is the longest in the Keys, while the Harris Gap Channel Bridge at 108 feet is the shortest. The highway runs from the tip of the Florida peninsula to Key West, the nation's southernmost city and one with a year-round carnival atmosphere.

Geologically the Florida Keys are mainly the exposed parts of coral reefs and weathered limestones. Some of the islands have been exposed for so long that sand has built up around them creating barrier islands, while other smaller islands remain as coral atolls. With outstanding natural and artificial underwater reefs, fishermen, snorkelers and divers have found a submarine paradise flanking the southeastern shores of the Keys. Beyond the Keys' northwestern shores lies Florida Bay: a fisherman's heaven and also the gateway to the Everglades National Park. This natural area offers its own unique beauty.

> NOTE: See details on snorkeling and diving, kayaking and paddleboarding, hiking, biking, birding and sportfishing in the "Waterway Guide Florida Keys" edition.

Mariners need to be particularly aware of the wind conditions while navigating the Keys. The region's shallow waters make "wind tide" a serious problem. This is a phenomenon in which strong winds push water from one side of an enclosed basin to another. It is of particular concern on the bay side where operating depths can be a low as 5 feet MLW. In strong northwest winds dockside depths at the marinas can be increased by as much as 1.5 feet, while dockside depths can be reduced by 1.5 feet in strong southeasterly winds.

There are towing services available should you run hard aground and both the Coast Guard and its Auxiliary monitor VHF Channel 16 and have stations along the way. They are not permitted to tow except in a life-threatening situation but they can provide assistance with contacting a commercial towing service (e.g., BoatU.S. or SeaTow). In calm conditions it may be best to wait for a rising tide.

Obviously visual navigation techniques are imperative here and we do not recommend nighttime operation. Your passage plan must be for a series of "achievable daytime hops" allowing travel to end well before nightfall. Luckily the bay side of the Keys offers an excellent selection of marinas, shore facilities and numerous spots to anchor.

Chapter 10: The Florida Keys

Inside or Outside Route?

Cruisers continuing west from Miami to the Florida Keys have two options:

1. Inside Route: Stay on the ICW following Biscayne Bay and the sounds to their western ends then pass under the Card Sound Road Bridge and on into Florida Bay following the chain of the Keys along the bay side.

2. Outside Route: Enter the Atlantic Ocean from Biscayne Bay at either Cape Florida Channel or Angelfish Creek then follow the Hawk Channel westward around Key Largo and continue on along the ocean side of the Keys.

With either choice, cruisers can switch from one route to the other at Channel Five or Moser Channel, on each side of Marathon and west from Marathon.

This choice is not a simple one. Each skipper must evaluate conditions and make the appropriate decision. If taking the inside (ICW) route, slow down and keep a close watch on the depth sounder as depth changes of up the 1.5 feet are common in strong winds in Florida Bay and elsewhere in the Keys. Note that these changes are greater than tidal effects and must be taken into consideration in planning a passage along the ICW on the Inside Route. Obviously in depths of 4 to 5 feet MLW a reduction of 1.5 feet is significant.

Along the bay side stretch of the ICW from Tavernier Creek to Shell Key, you can expect some of the shallowest conditions you will see anywhere on the ICW system with charted depths of 4.5 to 5 feet MLW. To make matters worse the bottom conditions along this stretch are charted as "rocky." For boats that draw over 5 feet we recommend the Outside (Hawk Channel) Route (or "keep to the ocean side" as the locals might say).

Wind strength and direction are other critical considerations. Prevailing winds in the Keys generally have an easterly component. In the summer a southerly component is added, whereas a northerly component is more common in the winter. (Note this is based on probability and is not a prediction.) If winds have either an easterly or southerly component at more than 10 to 15 knots expect choppy conditions in the Hawk Channel (Outside Route). In northwest to north-northeast winds the Outside Route will be the more comfortable route as the westerly curve of the keys will provide more protection.

On the Inside (ICW) Route, cruisers can expect better protection, at least in the closed sounds and basins initially followed by the ICW until things open up north of the Matecumbe Keys. Here the fetch increases and cruisers will experience chop in north to southwest winds. Chop is of particular concern on the inside route as effective water depths will be reduced by the boat's bobbing motion. In east through south-southwest winds the Inside Route is well protected by the unbroken chain of the Florida Keys.

The final consideration, which is well known by seasoned Florida Keys mariners, is that the unbroken chain of the Florida Keys blocks the movement of water as well as waves. The water in the large expanse of the Florida Bay is landlocked on the north, east and south. Strong winds from any of these directions will push the waters of the shallow bay from one side to another creating "wind tide" conditions.

Some cruisers will opt to visit both "sides" of the Keys via a roundtrip. Be aware that depth and clearance restrictions will make some harbors and marinas inaccessible, particularly to sailboats. Careful planning of anchorages and provisioning stops can influence your routing decisions.

NO WAKE ZONE

No Wake Zones, Idle Speed Zones and various Speed Limit restrictions are in effect throughout the waterways included in this chapter. Exercise diligence in knowing the regulations by observing signs and other markers. Enforcement is always present. As always, be courteous to other vessels and avoid manatees and other marine life.

Connections Between the Inside & Outside Route

There are only three major channels between the ICW and Hawk Channel. The first is the Cape Florida (Biscayne Channel) at ICW Mile 1096, which is the northernmost crossover from Biscayne Bay to the Atlantic and also the best marked. The others–Channel Five at ICW Mile 1170 and Moser Channel at ICW Mile 1195–pass under fixed bridges with 65-foot vertical clearances along U.S. Route 1. Several other channels with various limitations exist (including Angelfish Creek) but these are not recommended.

The strong tidal flow in the channels between islands tends to move material from these natural channels and deposit it at the channel mouth, either on the bay side or the ocean side. Near these channels the charted depths are suspect and prudent boaters should reduce speed and keep a close watch on their depth sounder.

Anchoring in the Keys

Anchoring in the Keys has some unique challenges but is well worth the effort. The bottom may be sand, rock or grass and generally offers good holding but, as in any cruising area, attention to depths, tides and general surroundings requires vigilance. The payoff is a night spent under the stars with the gentle lapping of waves on your boat's hull lulling you to sleep!

There are a few key recommendations to keep in mind when anchoring in the Keys:

- Never anchor over coral.
- Anchor as far away from fellow boaters as possible.
- If the shore is covered in vegetation, scrub or mangroves, expect visitors–the kind that bite!
- Be prepared for 180° and 360° swings and strong tidal flows, both of which are common in anchorages in the islands.
- Never use two anchors when one will do. However, if you find yourself in a situation where nothing but two anchors will do, the easiest solution is to set your first anchor and either dinghy out your second anchor or drop back to put down the second anchor and then position yourself between them. Remember that current and tidal flow always win over wind.
- Always try to dive to check that your anchor has set or check it using a dive mask or a glass-bottom bucket from your dinghy. If the bottom is hard-packed sand or rocky, you may have to dive to set an anchor.
- If you run your generator, consider that noise travels better over water and better still at night. Keep use to a minimum and always avoid quiet times when others may not want to hear it such as during breakfast, sunset, dinner time and nighttime.

- Always set an anchor light. Local boats go about their business at all hours of the night often at high speeds. A conventional masthead light is just too high to warn off someone racing along at sea level. Mount an auxiliary anchor light about 10 feet above the water and see how that looks to you from your dinghy. It could be just the most sensible precaution you ever took.
- Take anchor bearings or get a GPS fix and keep them displayed at the helm station. Check them to ensure that you have not dragged. If the risk is high, make out a roster and keep checking through the night. Most modern chartplotters have a built-in anchor alarm feature that can alert you if you have moved more than a set amount of feet from your point of set. Always use these and consider a backup such as a phone App.

Best Ground Tackle

You need to carry two anchors while cruising in the islands (three if you count your tender's anchor). We recommend a plow or spade type and a Danforth. Fit your anchor to your boat length and go oversize if in doubt. When it comes to anchors, BIGGER is always better. In addition, make sure you know the safe working load and the breaking point of your ground tackle.

Chapter 10: The Florida Keys

Depth and Scope

Scope is the length of anchor rode you put out measured from the bow roller into the water to the anchor and it helps determine how well your anchor will hold under most conditions. Generally the greater the scope, the better. With an all-chain rode 5:1 is sufficient in sheltered water. (That is about 5 feet of anchor chain for every 1 foot of depth at high tide.) With nylon and chain 7:1 scope is good. If you are working in meters, take that initial 5-foot figure and work it as 1.5 meters. It is simpler and errs on the side of safety. Don't forget to add your freeboard (the vertical distance from your bow roller to the water surface) to the depth of the water when calculating your scope.

Dive Site Mooring Buoys

There are almost 500 mooring buoys available on a first-come, first-served basis throughout the Everglades National Park Service (www.nps.gov/ever/index.htm). These are provided at no cost to the boater to help protect the coral reef. Boaters can tie off to the 18-inch diameter, blue-striped buoy markers to avoid anchoring on the reef. Run your boat's bow line through the loop of the yellow pick-up line. Cleat both ends of your bow line to the bow of your boat. Never tie the yellow pick-up line directly to your boat as it puts undue stress on the mooring anchor.

> **CAUTION:** Buoys used for marking zones such as sanctuary preservation areas, ecological reserves and special-use research are 30 inches in diameter and yellow. Do not tie your boat to these!

Anchoring on living coral within the sanctuary is prohibited. If no mooring buoy is available and you are outside a no-anchor zone, you may anchor in sand; however, if a mooring buoy is available, you must use it and are not allowed to anchor.

In Severe Storm Conditions

We all dream of idyllic, calm, isolated and uncrowded anchorages. You will definitely find them in the islands; however, you won't have perfection all the time. Your Bahamian anchorage may well turn out to be swept by reversing tidal currents, open to squalls or already crowded with other boats by the time you get there.

If you are unlucky and have to weather a severe storm at anchor, avoid exposed harbors and crowded anchorages. Try to find a hurricane hole or a channel in mangroves where you can secure lines to the sturdy trees. Use every line you have. Make a spider's web of lines allowing 10 feet of slack for tidal surge and use all your anchors fanned out at 90 to 120° to complement your spider's web.

Use chafe protectors on your lines where they come on board. Reduce your windage. Take down any canvas including sails. Lower your antennas, deflate and store your inflatable below deck then lash down everything that must remain on deck. Make the hull as watertight as possible.

If you can't find a hurricane hole (and there are very few that are ideal), you can anchor out to face the wind. Set three anchors in a 120° fan. Ideally lead the three rodes to a swivel and then run line from the swivel to the boat. Try for a 10:1 scope. If you use all chain put a nylon snubber (equal to 10 percent of the chain length) on the chain to absorb shock.

ICW (INSIDE) ROUTE TO BOOT KEY

For boats that draw no more than 5 feet and can take the occasional short, hard chop of shallow water, the Inside (ICW) Route on the bay side provides a relatively well protected and interesting passage option to Islamorada, Marathon and beyond to Key West. This route is clearly marked; however, for certain stretches the markers are far apart and careful attention is required to stay in the controlled channel. In many places you do not have to stray too far out of the channel to find yourself hard aground. Many boats will leave "tracks" (usually just stirred-up, powdery sand) somewhere along this route.

Biscayne National Park

The central segment of Biscayne Bay is its largest and this extraordinary land-and-sea park covers much of it, as well as the adjacent barrier islands and a 3-mile swath of the Atlantic Ocean beyond. Biscayne National Park covers 270 square miles and the ICW runs its entire 20-mile length. Eight miles south of the park's northern boundary (at Mile 1097) a 100-mile-long island chain begins with the tiny Ragged Keys group. This island chain is a world-renowned tourist area known as the Florida Keys.

> SHHHH! Personal watercraft (jet skis) are prohibited in Biscayne National Park, as are generators (after 10:00 p.m.).

NAVIGATION: Use NOAA Charts 11451 and 11463. Central Biscayne Bay runs 25 miles south from Virginia Key to Card Sound. The bay is open and relatively deep. Despite its large size there are only a dozen ICW markers and only eight are visible from the channel. The ICW takes a straight 13.4 nm run at 199° magnetic from flashing green "69," just south of Virginia Key at Mile 1092, to flashing green "3" marking the cut through the Featherbed Bank at Mile 1107. Biscayne National Park boundary flashing yellow light "C" lies exactly on the ICW route at Mile 1102.5 and serves as a helpful intermediate checkpoint on this long run. The four ICW markers in between mark the shoals closest to the designated channel and most are at least 1 mile distant from the ICW.

A well-marked but narrow channel cuts through Featherbed Bank at Mile 1107. Split flashing green "3" and red daybeacon "4" when entering the channel from the north and maintain alignment to split green daybeacon "5" and flashing red "6" to exit south. South from here the ICW takes a straight 7-nm run at 193° magnetic from flashing red "6" to flashing red "8" at Mile 1116.

From flashing red "8" alter your course to split flashing green "9" and red daybeacon "8A." This marker pair frames the entrance to the straight cut through Cutter Bank. Through the cut split the two intermediate marker pairs and keep green daybeacon "13A" well to port to avoid a very shallow shoal behind. Exit the south end of the cut through paired flashing red "14" and green daybeacon "15" and enter Card Sound, the first section of South Biscayne Bay. Passing through the cut you will notice a change in water color from dark turquoise to a murky green.

> NOTE: Anchoring is available anywhere in Biscayne National Park except over coral or sponge beds. Mooring buoys are available throughout the park but use is limited to 4 hours by any one boat for snorkeling and diving.

Side Trip: Boca Chita, Sand & Elliott Keys

Just south of the Ragged Keys lies historic Boca Chita Key followed by Sand Key and Elliott Key beyond. Vessels that draw 5 feet or less can leave the ICW and take a parallel route closer to these barrier islands and stop visit some of the park's wonderful land-based attractions. This side trip doesn't add much distance, offers some excellent anchorages and is well worth the time.

NAVIGATION: Use NOAA Charts 11465 and 11463. To reach the channel to Boca Chita Key southbound vessels should leave the ICW at Mile 1105 on a southeast heading to split green daybeacon "1" and flashing red "2" marking a passage through the northern extremity of the Featherbed Bank. Continue on this course into the center of the small sound to the west of Boca Chita Key and once there, adjust your course to head for the charted "TOWER" on Boca Chita Key. Follow the well-marked but shallow channel to the Key's small harbor, which starts with paired floating markers green "1" and red "2." As you approach shore turn with caution northward into the well-protected harbor.

Tiny Boca Chita Key with its cozy harbor and elegant 65-foot lighthouse (circa 1937) is a popular stop. Note that historic preservation projects and repairs will be conducted on several structures on Boca Chita Key throughout the summer months and may be closed at various times.

About 1 mile west of Boca Chita Key another marked channel crosses the eastern extremity of Featherbed Bank from the mainland. The entrance to this channel is about a 0.5 mile south of the entrance to the Boca Chita Key approach channel. Split flashing green "3" and red daybeacon "4" to cross the bank and access Sand Key and Elliot Key; the channel over the bank carries 5.5 feet

Distances
Inside Route: ICW (Miles from Miami)

LOCATION	STATUTE MILES	NAUTICAL MILES
Miami (Mile 1090)	0	0
Angelfish	30	26.1
Jewfish Creek	43	37.4
Tavernier	60	52.1
Islamorada	69	60.0
Channel Five	80	69.5
Marathon (Sisters Creek)	102	88.6
Moser Channel	107	93.0
Harbor Key Bank Light	128	111.2
Northwest Channel	147	127.7
Key West	154	133.6

(For comparison, Moser Channel to Key West on the Outside Route via Hawk Channel is 40 statute miles versus the 47 shown here.)

Chapter 10 — The Florida Keys

Biscayne Bay, FL

BOCA CHITA KEY

		Largest Vessel	VHF	Total Slips	Approach/Dockside Depth	Floating Docks	Gas/Diesel	Repairs/Haulout	Min/Max Amps	Pump-Out Station
1. Boca Chita Key - Biscayne National Park 3.0 mi. E of MM 1106.0	(305) 230-7275	35	16		4.0 / 4.0					

WiFi Wireless Internet Access
Visit www.waterwayguide.com for current rates, fuel prices, website addresses and other up-to-the-minute information. (Information in the table is provided by the facilities.)

Scan here for more details:

Source: Aqua Map and NOAA data

MLW. Continuing south, the route inside Elliot Key is well protected and has better depths, although there are a few unmarked shoals.

Elliott Key, lying about 3 miles east of the ICW, is another popular attraction in Biscayne National Park and is open to the public. Graced with a hardwood jungle and a shell-laden ocean beach, Elliott Key is the largest of the 25 keys encompassed by the park.

South of Elliott Key there are a few navigable creeks that lead to Hawk Channel that are often used by cruisers to get access to the Outside Route or start a "Bahamas Run" across the Gulf Stream. The ocean-side approaches to these creeks have charted depths of 4 feet MLW and we recommend you seek local knowledge before attempting passage.

Dockage: The entry channel to the Biscayne National Park facility at Boca Chita Key has charted depths of 4 feet MLW but closer to 5 foot MLW has been observed. Proceed with caution and adjust for wind-tide or chop. The channel is marked with three pairs of floating buoys. Docking availability is on a first-come, first-served basis (reservations not accepted). There is a flat marina use fee per night that includes one campsite on the island. There are no services available (electricity, water, trash removal, etc.) but there are restrooms on shore.

NOTE: Pets are not allowed on the island or on boats (including while docked) with the exception of service animals as defined by the ADA.

While the Biscayne National Park service maintains docks for small boats (less than 20 feet) on Elliot Key, there is no marked approach channel to the boat basin and dockside depths may be as little as 2 feet MLW. This is strictly dinghy territory for most cruisers and there are two dinghy landings. Showers and restroom facilities are at the campground close to the docks but only non-potable water is provided. Potable water is available from a faucet nearby.

While ashore on Elliot Key, pets must be on an attended leash that is no longer than 6 feet in length. Be sure to bring lots of bug spray because you will encounter mosquitoes and no-see-ums. Visitors are requested not to (purposely) feed the wildlife.

Anchorage: An anchorage at Ragged Keys, located north of Boca Chita Key has 7 to 8 feet MLW with good holding in grass and mud. It is, however, exposed to northwest through southwest winds.

Two miles south, the Sands Key (inner) anchorage has excellent holding in 6 to 7 feet MLW and all-around protection. The shallow approach (with spots as shallow as 4 feet MLW) restricts this spot to all but shoal-draft boats. The approach is a little tricky so you might have to wait for high tide to either enter or exit. There are a few rocks but you should find a place to drop your hook.

If you can't manage the inner anchorage, you can anchor outside on the west side of Sands Key in 5 to 6 feet MLW with good holding in grass and mud. This is exposed to north through southwest winds.

Cruising vessels typically anchor in deeper water well offshore at Elliot Key. During summer months with the prevailing winds from the southeast, this is a popular anchorage

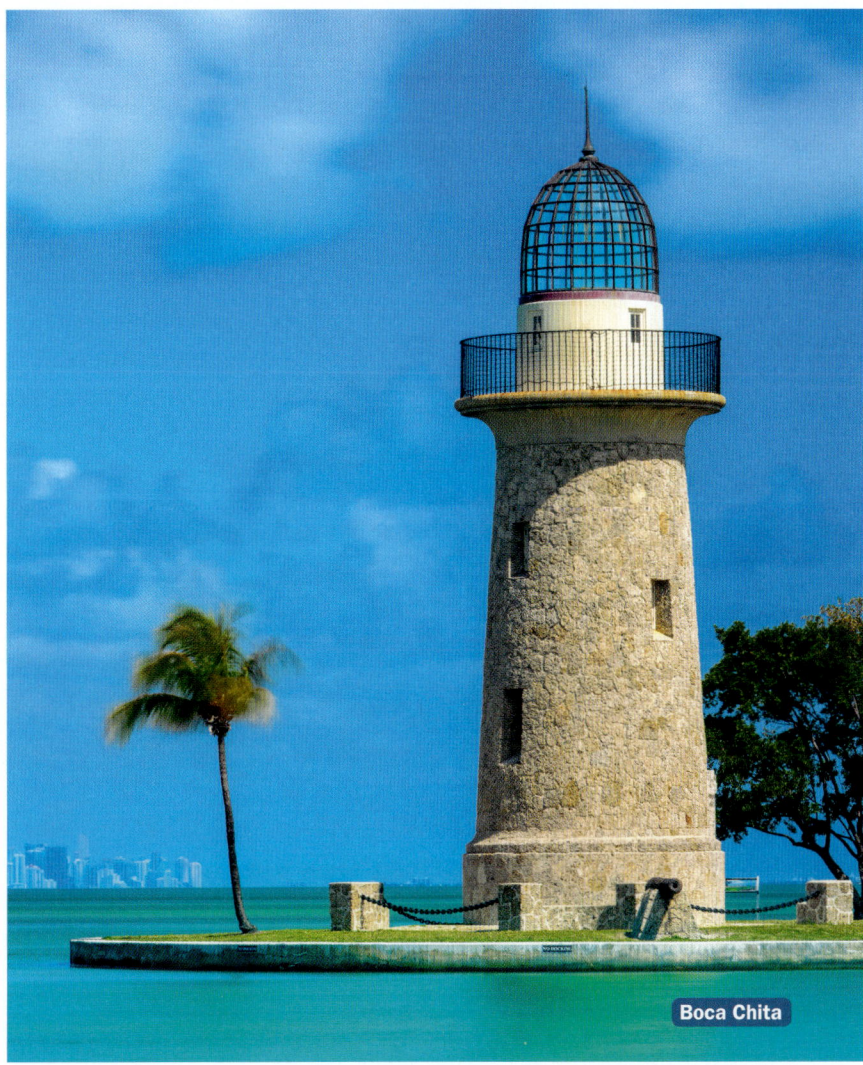

Boca Chita

hosting hundreds of boats. Keep an eye out for storm systems during the summer. Far fewer boats will visit this beautiful area during the winter because frequent northerlies can make anchoring here risky and downright uncomfortable.

Caesar Creek winds around tiny Adams Key with 7- to 12-foot MLW depths and shore access at the ranger station docks. You are free to tie up your dinghy (but not overnight) and walk your dog in the lawn area of the park. Anchor on the north edge of the channel. Access to Caesars Creek requires careful planning as the eastern path in only has less than 4 feet MLW. With a tide of over 1 foot, you can expect 5 feet of depth. The eastern exit into the ocean has 4.5 feet MLW.

A southern spur of Caesar Creek leads to an anchorage between Rubicon and Reid Keys. The approach depths to this anchorage are only about 3 feet MLW; however, you should have up to 12 feet MLW once inside. This provides protected from everything but a direct north wind. The bottom is a mixture of grass, mud or a light covering of sand over coral rock. Note amount of current and anchor accordingly.

Chapter 10: The Florida Keys

Card Sound–ICW Mile 1120 to Mile 1127

Card Sound marks the upper segment of South Biscayne Bay. South from here the water is a murky green and the bottom changes to mud and grass much like the sounds of Florida Bay. These sounds have shorter fetch and are less prone to chop than the larger segments to the north. Depths are good but expect some local shoaling at the ends of the cuts through the banks.

NAVIGATION: Use NOAA Charts 11451 and 11463. South from Cutter Bank it's a 4.6 nm run at 234° magnetic from flashing red "14" to marker pair flashing green "17" and red daybeacon "16" that frame the north entrance of the cut through Card Bank. Pass through the intermediate marker pair and then exit the cut splitting flashing red "20" and green daybeacon "21" and into Little Card Sound. It's just over 1 mile southwest to the next ICW marker (flashing red "22"), which sets alignment for the bridge immediately to the south.

From Card Sound there is a channel that runs between the adjacent keys east to the ocean that is popular with local fishermen. In favorable weather Angelfish Creek is a heavily used passage between the ICW and Hawk Channel. For vessels wanting to maximize the Gulf Stream's powerful boost for a transit to Bimini in the Bahamas, the 1.8-nm-long Angelfish Creek provides a more southerly approach than Miami, despite the added 14 nm distance (56 nm versus 42 nm) some argue a quicker passage time.

Entering from Card Sound at flashing red buoy "14," the depths will increase quickly to 7 to 10 feet MLW, then to over 13 feet MLW until you approach the exit to the Atlantic. At red buoy "4" you will see three green daybeacons ahead. Favor the red side as you approach flashing red buoy "2" and proceed slowly through to the Atlantic while watching your depth. There is a cross current here; pay attention to your track so that you don't get pushed out of the channel.

Anchorage: In a north wind some protection can be found south of Long Arsenicker located between Biscayne Bay and the northeast corner of Card Sound near the south end of Midnight Pass (Mile 1120). Don't anchor too close to the land to avoid no-see-ums and plan to use your screens.

To the southeast at Mile 1121 south of Angelfish Creek is a well-known rendezvous and anchoring spot in the lee of small Pumpkin Key. ICW cruisers frequently congregate here, some waiting to cross the Gulf Stream via Angelfish Creek and others just to enjoy a quiet stop en route. Drop the anchor in 7 to 9 feet MLW with excellent holding in grass and mud. (No shore access.) Little Pumpkin Creek, just below the mouth of Angelfish Creek, is another "locals spot" and can get busy on weekends. Locals also regard it as a hurricane hole.

The southernmost anchorage in Card Sound is off Jew Point near the very south pocket of the sound, about 1.5 miles east of the mouth of Steamboat Creek (Mile 1125). The anchorage has 7 to 9 feet MLW with good holding in grass and mud and protection from all but north winds.

It is possible to anchor in Little Card Sound but because of its small size it's tough to get out of the wakes of boats passing on the ICW. Boat traffic can be busy here, even at night.

Barnes Sound–ICW Mile 1127 to Mile 1133

NAVIGATION: Use NOAA Charts 11451 and 11463. From Cutter Bank Pass set a course of 234° magnetic for about 4.6 nm to flashing green "17" (located just south of distinctive Card Point) marking the entrance to a narrow cut through Card Bank to Little Card Sound. Watch for shoaling at the well-marked north entry of the cut.

The **Card Sound Road Bridge** (fixed 65-foot vertical clearance bridge) at Mile 1126.9 serves as the next landmark. This is the first of two highway bridges linking Key Largo with the mainland. The channel under the bridge is marked and dredged, but it shallows rapidly at its south exit into Barnes Sound so follow markers closely. Once you are through the channel and on to flashing red "26" in Barnes Sound, minimum 8 foot MLW depths hold for the straight 4.5-mile run to the end of Barnes Sound where flashing green "29" marks the entrance to Jewfish Creek. Depending on wind direction, the chop can build in Barnes Sound and it can get sloppy.

Jewfish Creek in the southeast corner of Barnes Sound leads to Blackwater Sound. This can be a high traffic area. During the winter season, you will likely encounter commercial stone crabbing or lobster boats in addition to the usual menagerie of sport fishermen and ICW cruisers. There is good fishing in Barnes Sound and you can dinghy through the mangroves.

Anchorage: You can drop the hook south of Card Sound Bridge in a calm and protected anchorage with good holding in mud. It is an easy dinghy ride from here

America's Waterway Guide Since 1947 — Chapter 10

Upper Keys, FL

KEY LARGO AREA		Largest Vessel	VHF	Total Slips	Approach/ Dockside Depth	Floating Docks	Gas/ Diesel	Repairs/ Haulout	Min/Max Amps	Pump-Out Station
1. Gilbert's Resort and Marina WiFi MM 108	(305) 451-1133	105	16	50	6.0 / 15.0		GD		30 / 50	
2. Anchorage Resort & Yacht Club WiFi MM 1134.2	(305) 451-0500	180	16	20	6.0 / 8.0				30 / 50	

WiFi Wireless Internet Access
Visit www.waterwayguide.com for current rates, fuel prices, website addresses and other up-to-the-minute information. (Information in the table is provided by the facilities.)

Scan here for more details:

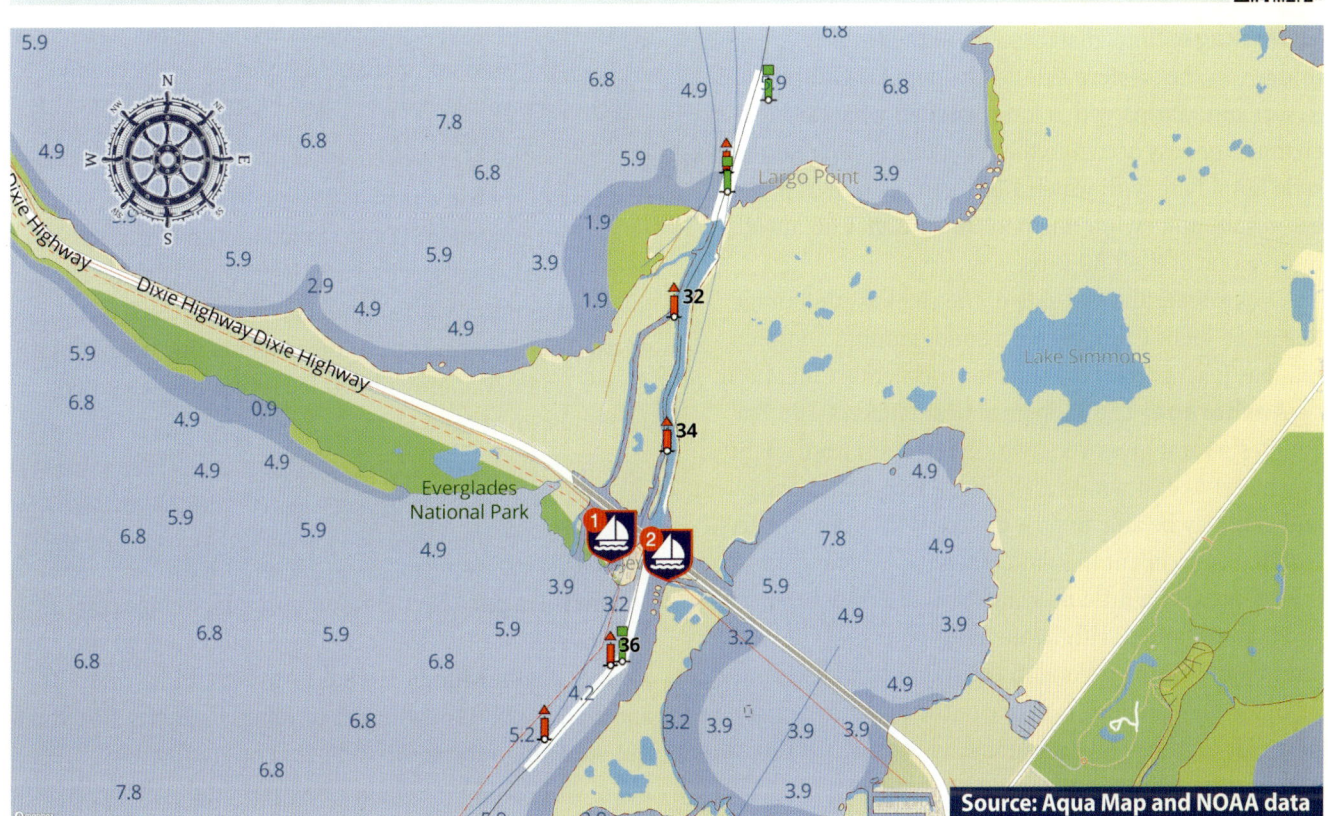

Source: Aqua Map and NOAA data

to lively Alabama Jack's on the causeway. The restaurant is renowned for its conch fritters, live music and breezy atmosphere.

In the northeast corner of Barnes Sound near Steamboat Creek is a protected cove with 7 to 9 feet MLW. It offers protection from the north through east winds only. (Shoal-draft boats can ease in farther for 5-foot MLW depths and find better protection from northeast winds.)

Thursday Cove in the southeast corner of Barnes Sound has been a well-kept secret (until now). Expect excellent holding in 6 feet MLW and wind protection from northeast to southwest winds. As always, don't get in too close to the mangroves or the mosquitos will eat you. Should the weather turn, a good hurricane hole is at nearby Cross Key. Head west into the narrow creek by red daybeacon "32" for 8 feet and all-around protection.

Jewfish Creek–ICW Mile 1133 to Mile 1134

At about Mile 1133 you enter a well-marked, deep channel through Jewfish Creek. Key Largo lies to the east and offers many sites of historical, geological and romantic interest along its 30-mile length. Some sites are close to the marinas but if this is a first visit, it's best to arrange for land transportation so you can explore the area fully.

NAVIGATION: Use NOAA Charts 11451 and 11463. Jewfish Creek itself is a favorite fishing spot and small boats often congregate in the area. The numerous anchored or slow-trolling small fishing boats occupying this narrow channel require a close watch and it's best to throttle back Idle-Speed/No-Wake here. Be prepared to navigate carefully and defensively here. Also expect watercraft around the surprisingly active docks at the south end of the creek. The creek passes under the

SOUTHERN EDITION

Chapter 10   The Florida Keys

Jewfish Creek (US 1) Bridge at Mile 1134.1 (with 65-foot fixed vertical clearance).

If accessing the marina/anchorage from Jewfish Creek, proceed to red daybeacon "38" before turning to starboard. Water depths are less than charted with 3 to 4 feet MLW starboard of the channel. Steer to the northwest of the marked wreck on most charts before turning in towards the resort.

Dockage: Immediately south of the Jewfish Creek Bridge (on the western side) is the popular Gilbert's Resort and Marina with a long, wooden wharf along the channel for easy access to the fuel pumps. There is a Keys-style hotel here with waterfront rooms as well as a tiki bar, restaurant, swimming pool and beach. Call ahead to reserve one of their 50 slips.

Opposite on the east side of the creek is Anchorage Resort & Yacht Club, part of a condominium complex that has just six reserved slips for transients. Call ahead.

Anchorage: The anchorage near Gilbert's Tiki Bar and Restaurant gives good wind protection from slightly northwest to east winds. Cell phone reception is excellent, and you may be able to pick up free WiFi from Gilbert's. Holding is excellent in sand/coral with sea grass. Try to find an area with little/no sea grass if visibility permits. You'll be rewarded with frequent dolphin visits next to your boat. Fishing is good in the sound as well as in the mangroves. Watch for manatee in the mangrove channels in cooler months. Take advantage of the opportunity to kayak or row through the mangroves and explore Lake Surprise. (The lake has a 3-foot MLW entrance channel and is not a viable anchorage for cruising vessels.)

Blackwater Sound–ICW Mile 1134 to Mile 1039

After exiting Jewfish Creek, the ICW meets the southeast corner of Everglades National Park and skirts the park's southern boundary for the next 41 miles westward. In the past sporadic signs marked the park boundary that were useful for navigation but few of these signs remain. Be sure to check park regulations before entering. Everglades National Park is famous for its vast expanses of water, mangrove forests and marshy grasslands.

NOTE: The boundary for Everglades National Park is marked on charts as "PARTICULARLY SENSITIVE SEA AREA" (PSSA). Landings are not allowed at any of the Keys within the park except where specifically designated and charted by park authorities. Other restrictions may apply.

Considered the upper reaches of Florida Bay by some, Blackwater Sound is a completely enclosed basin. The sound has considerable fetch and you may see some chop here.

NAVIGATION: Use NOAA Charts 11451 and 11464.

CAUTION: There is a shallow sandbar to the north side of the marked channel between red daybeacon "36" and flashing red "38" just before Mile 1135. This may not be shown on your charts.

Leaving Jewfish Creek at flashing red "38" set a course of 223° magnetic for 1.7 nm to the mouth of the creek with charted depths as low as 4 feet MLW. Throttle back here and monitor your sounder. Some cruisers have advised diverging east from the magenta line here to find deeper water. Mangrove-lined Dusenbury Creek enters Tarpon Basin at Mile 1138.5.

NOTE: The fishing on the expansive shallow flats here is outstanding but catch and licensing regulations are in effect and enforcement is strict.

Anchorage: There are numerous anchorages on the eastern side of Blackwater Sound. Sexton Cove at the northeast end (Mile 1135) has 6- to 7-foot MLW depths and a grassy bottom with fair holding. Farther south you can snug up to the south of Stellrecht Point in 6 to 7 feet MLW with good holding in grass and mud with protection from winds with an easterly component.

At the southeast end of Blackwater Sound you can drop the hook near Dusenbury Creek in 6 to 7 feet MLW with good holding and protection from south winds.

NOTE: The local radio station in this area is WCTH-FM 100.3 with up-to-date local weather information and music.

Tarpon Basin–ICW Mile 1139

NAVIGATION: Use NOAA Charts 11451 and 11464. From Blackwater Sound the ICW snakes through mangrove-lined Dusenbury Creek (Mile 1138) to Tarpon Basin. The narrow creek carries good depths but small powerboats pass through here full-throttle so slow down and proceed with caution around the blind corners.

The expanse of Tarpon Basin is deceptive. The basin is very shallow outside the dredged channel (charted at

5 to 6 foot MLW) and it is best to maintain a low speed around the tight curve in the channel. Dangerous shoals (with 2.5-foot MLW depths) line the channel's edge on the outside of the turn from red daybeacon "42" through flashing red "48." Favor the markers on the inside of this tight curve. Straighten up at flashing red "48" and head directly for red daybeacon "48A" and then on to flashing red "50." Westbound traffic should keep red daybeacon "52" to starboard at the entry to narrow Grouper Creek.

Depths are shallow at both ends of the creek so maintain channel alignment. After exiting the creek between green daybeacon "53" and red daybeacon "52A" head straight for flashing red "54," which leads on into Buttonwood Sound.

Anchorage: Tarpon Basin offers good anchoring opportunities due to short fetch. Just be aware that holding is just fair due to the grassy bottom. (Some flat rock has also been reported.) The most popular area is just south of the large shoal in the center of the basin. To enter proceed all the way to Tarpon Basin red daybeacon "48A" and then head south from this marker to find the charted deeper water. Watch your depth and anchor with care. Some also anchor north of red daybeacon "48A" in the pocket with 7- to 8-foot MLW depths.

Signs at the Nelson Government Building prohibit overnight parking without a county permit, tying up to the dock or trees or mooring within 25 feet of the dock. If you do drop a hook here be sure to seek local knowledge about the mangrove tunnels that you can explore from the comfort of your dinghy.

Buttonwood Sound– ICW Mile 1140 to Mile 1147

Buttonwood Sound is not fully enclosed and once here you are officially in Florida Bay. Snook's Bayside Restaurant and the Grand Tiki is located in Buttonwood Sound with an excellent "happy hour" and great food. They also host a nightly sunset celebration. The Upper Keys Sailing Club is to the northeast at nearby Point Pleasant. This is a private sailing club but you can ask for permission to tie up for a short stop and wander down to town, which isn't more than a 0.5-mile walk. A liquor store, some good restaurants and Publix are nearby.

NAVIGATION: Use NOAA Charts 11451 and 11464. While Florida Bay is expansive and the fetch can be very long, the bay's shallow depths reduce chop, which

Mangrove Shorelines

Nearly every inch of the Florida Keys natural shoreline is covered in mangrove trees. There are actually three types of mangrove that live in the Keys: red, black and white. The most commonly recognized is the red mangrove, which grows along the shoreline standing on a web of prop roots. Black mangroves are almost the opposite; their roots shoot straight up a few inches above the surface. White mangroves are inland trees that grow around tropical hardwood hammocks and are found on drier land.

Mangroves are extremely salt tolerant. Their roots absorb water from the sea and their waxy leaves excrete the excess salt. Mangroves grow all over the world but are sensitive to cold weather and are only found in tropical climates like those of Florida, Mexico and Central America.

Of course, mangroves encompass so much more than just species of trees. They thrive in conditions that other plants cannot and create entire ecosystems with their roots and structure. The biodiversity found in mangrove swamps is astounding, with hundreds of algae, crustacean, mollusk, fish, reptile and insect species present. Their roots provide shelter for smaller animals that live their entire lives there or that just visit for spawning. Mangroves are sometimes referred to as the nurseries of the coral reefs.

For the islands of the Florida Keys mangroves also provide shelter and protection. Mangroves form a natural barrier to erosion and especially to the damaging storm surge that comes with hurricanes. For this reason, mangroves are protected in Florida and especially in the Keys. Without mangroves the Florida Keys would be washed away.

Chapter 10 — The Florida Keys

is typically light even in moderate winds. But winds can cause other effects. Although the normal 1-foot tidal range is modest here strong winds can cause "wind tide" conditions raising or lowering normal water levels by up to 1.5 feet. Strong north to east winds reduce water levels in Florida Bay and strong west to south winds can raise them. If you detect depths below what is charted or expected, throttle back and consider postponing your passage. Winds can also affect course alignment and auto pilot settings.

The ICW markers are widely spaced for many sections along this route. Glance astern occasionally to check your actual course heading, which can differ significantly from your compass heading.

> **CAUTION:** Depths are as shallow as 5 feet MLW in the stretch from flashing red "54" (Mile 1141) to flashing green "55" in the marked ICW channel. Some cruisers choose to diverge slightly east here and parallel the ICW channel in the charted 7-foot MLW depths.

The ICW leaves Buttonwood Sound through Baker Cut. Flashing green "55" marks the entrance to the cut at Mile 1143. Initially the ICW continues along this shallow stretch through a well-marked but narrow dredged channel, which carries 7 feet MLW initially but drops to 6 feet MLW at flashing red "58." Spots of shoaling flank both sides of the channel from the cut to flashing red "60." Maintain the center of the marked channel through here. Once past flashing red "60" some cruisers will diverge north into the charted deeper water adding some wiggle room but the markers are widely spaced and channel alignment is difficult.

Groundings are common. If your draft is more than 5 feet, seek local knowledge. Another option may be to wait for a favorable wind tide; strong southwest winds can improve depths in upper Florida Bay.

Anchorage: To the east of Baker Cut lies Sunset Cove. Turn to port between daybeacons red "54" and green "55" and proceed towards the beach for best depth and holding. The anchorage has minimal tide but is exposed in north and west winds. You will not be alone. There are always numerous boats anchored here.

Cowpens Cut–ICW Mile 1145 to Mile 1153

NAVIGATION: Use NOAA Charts 11451 and 11464. At quick-flashing green "61" (Mile 1147.5) just past Pigeon Key, the ICW turns abruptly south towards quick-flashing red "62" and Hammer Point beyond. Take a gentle turn around red daybeacons "62A," "64" and "64A" keeping 50 feet off the markers to maintain 7 feet MLW. Avoid a little (unnamed) island and surrounding shoals to the north. Several groundings have been reported here so don't cut the corner between markers and watch your depth. The ICW route continues westward past flashing green "65" and through well-marked Ramshorn Cut. Stay centered in the cut to carry 6 feet MLW as the edges shallow quickly.

Approaching Tavernier Creek things get confusing as the markers for the two channels are placed close together. Although the chart shows the magenta line passing between red daybeacon "18" and green daybeacon "17," note that these markers are for the Tavernier Creek channel. The ICW passes north of this marker pair, closer to the charted PSSA boundary of Everglades National Park. You pass the shallowest spot (5.5 feet MLW) near flashing green "71" but the exit of Tavernier Creek is prone to shoaling. Slow down and find your way carefully. There have been numerous groundings reported here. If it starts getting shallow, move north to gain better depth.

From Tavernier Creek proceed straight toward flashing green "73" at the opening of Cowpens Cut. Enter the cut with caution as its east entrance has a charted depth of 5 feet MLW. You will find deeper water closer to the green side of the entrance. Maintain center channel in the cut through the "Cross Bank" to flashing red "78."

Dockage: The 102-slip Mangrove Marina hosts many liveaboard boaters, both transient and long term to 70 feet. Access is provided via a short, privately marked channel. Once past ICW red daybeacon "64A" look south and see a little bay (next to charted "Community Hbr") and private markers. The water depths just off the channel are 6 feet MLW and shallow to 4 feet as you get closer to shore. Call ahead for specific navigation directions. The facility is in a natural "hurricane hole" surrounded by hearty mangroves and spread over 20 acres, offering two bathhouses with showers, dock carts, bicycle racks and gardens.

Tavernier Creek Marina north of the fixed **Tavernier Creek Bridge** (15-foot vertical clearance) is primarily a boat storage facility with

America's Waterway Guide Since 1947 — Chapter 10

numerous on-site services including marine detailing, engine repair and yacht sales as well as a bait and tackle shop, dive shop, fishing charters and a restaurant. They maintain a few transient slips to 36 feet (not available during holidays, weekends and special events).

Anchorage: You can anchor on the south side of Butternut Key at Mile 1146 in 5 to 6 feet MLW. This provides fair holding with no protection from the south. At Mile 1150 the Community Harbor at Plantation Key offers a fair anchorage with 4 to 5 feet MLW. There is no protection here from the north.

To Islamorada–ICW Mile 1154 to Mile 1162

This leg of your trip will take you past popular Islamorada. The village of Islamorada is actually made up of five islands: Tea Table Key, Lower Matecumbe Key, Upper Matecumbe Key, Windley Key and Plantation Key.

NAVIGATION: Use NOAA Charts 11451 and 11464. Southwest from flashing red "78" (Mile 1153.5) it can be difficult to find the ICW route. It appears as if the ICW ends here because the yellow squares and triangles no longer appear on aids to navigation and the daybeacons and lights appear in a different section of the *Light List* published by the USCG (www.noaachartmap.com/uscg-light-lists). Also the magenta line and mileage bars have been removed from the most recent NOAA Charts. NOAA, however, considers the ICW to continue on to Key West and coverage in the *Coast Pilot Vol 4* chapter on the ICW does, in fact, continue to Key West. From this point to Key West, this guide will provide either a compass heading and/or visual reference points for the ICW route.

CAUTION: From Cotton Key at ICW red daybeacon 80 (Mile 1158) to Steamboat Channel, the ICW passes through what is perhaps the shallowest part of the entire route. Remember, touching a sandy bottom at slow speeds is rarely dangerous but at high speeds can do considerable damage to your props. There just isn't enough water here to take any chances.

The ICW route parallels the charted PSSA boundary line for another 20 miles where the marker numbering sequence next resets at flashing green "1" (Mile 1173)

Chapter 10: The Florida Keys

Goin' Ashore: ISLAMORADA, FL

America's Waterway Guide Since 1947

Chapter 10

ATTRACTION

1. 1935 Hurricane Monument
Memorializes the 408 people who perished in the 1935 hurricane, which hit Islamorada and the Florida West Coast (1831 Old Hwy.).

2. History of Diving Museum
Compact, unique museum with relics, exhibits and equipment showcasing the evolution of diving at 82990 Overseas Hwy. (305-664-9737)

3. Keys History & Discovery Center
Located at Islander Resort with a model of Indian Key the way it looked in 1840, a "legends of the line" fishing exhibit and numerous historical photos of the area (82100 Overseas Hwy., 305-922-2237).

4. Redbone Gallery
Specializing in fine original angling and island art with portions of all original art sales benefiting The Cystic Fibrosis Foundation. Unique paintings, sculptures and jewelry (much related to saltwater fishing) are among the offerings at 200 Morada Way. Open daily except Sunday (305-664-2002).

5. Worldwide Sportsman
Large destination owned by Bass Pro Shop with fishing tackle and some boating supplies (81576 Overseas Hwy., 305-664-4615). Be sure to check out the tarpon swimming in the pen alongside the dock.

SERVICES

6. Islamorada Post Office
82801 Overseas Hwy. (305-664-4738)

7. Island Paws Veterinary Hospital
81581 Old Hwy. (305-664-0142)

8. Keys Medical Center
81990 Overseas Hwy. #101 (305-664-2488)

9. Monroe County Public Library
81830 Overseas Hwy. (305-664-4645)

MARINAS

10. Coral Bay Marina
601 Mastic St. (305-664-3111)

11. Islamorada Yacht Basin
96 Madeira Rd. (305-664-2692)

12. Worldwide Sportsman Marina
81576 Overseas Hwy. (305-664-3398)

Islamorada (which translates as Purple Isle) is a flourishing village spread across five islands along the Overseas Highway. Arriving from the north are: Plantation Key, Windley Key, Upper Matecumbe Key and Lower Matecumbe Key. Teatable Key (or Tea Table Key to some), lies south of the highway and can't quite decide on a name. Nearby Indian Key, Shell Key and Lignumvitae Key are only accessible by boat and are part of Florida's State Park System.

SOUTHERN EDITION

Chapter 10: The Florida Keys

Upper Keys, FL

TAVERNIER		Largest Vessel	VHF	Total Slips	Approach/ Dockside Depth	Floating Docks	Gas/ Diesel	Repairs/ Haulout	Min/Max Amps	Pump-Out Station
1. Mangrove Marina WiFi MM 91.7	(305) 852-8380	50		111	4.5 / 4.5		GD	H	30 / 50	P
2. Tavernier Creek Marina 1.4 mi. SE of MM 1151.7	(305) 852-5854	36		21	5.0 / 5.0		G	RH	30	
PLANTATION KEY										
3. **Plantation Yacht Harbor Marina** WiFi MM 1154.6	(305) 852-2381	80	16	85	5.0 / 5.0		GD		30 / 100	P
4. IslaMarina WiFi MM 1156.0	(305) 664-3636	60	16	12	5.0 / 6.0		GD		30 / 50	

WiFi Wireless Internet Access

Visit www.waterwayguide.com for current rates, fuel prices, website addresses and other up-to-the-minute information.
(Information in the table is provided by the facilities.)

Scan here for more details:

Source: Aqua Map and NOAA data

America's Waterway Guide Since 1947 — Chapter 10

located at the north end of Old Dan Bank. As previously mentioned, the PSSA line charts the Everglades National Park boundary and there may be some signage along this route reading "National Park Boundary."

> NOTE: Proceeding west, floats for lobster and stone crab traps fill the ICW channel and surrounding water in season. Be careful not to foul your propeller. Traps and floats are usually removed during the off-season (May 15 to October 15) making navigation simpler but many stray traps remain requiring a sharp lookout.

The Cowpens Cut through Cross Bank (at Mile 1153) leads into Cotton Key Basin. As mentioned above the magenta line showing ICW channel centerline is not shown on recent NOAA charts. For this segment the ICW runs immediately south of the charted PSSA boundary line indicating the southern boundary of the Everglades National Park. From flashing red "78" at the exit from Cowpens Cut the ICW "channel" runs a straight-line course of 250° magnetic for 4.2 nm across the Cotton Key Basin to flashing green "81" northwest of Cotton Key. The only intermediate marker is red daybeacon "78A," positioned midway on the run.

The segment to Cotton Key is very shallow even though there is some evidence that Cotton Key Basin has been scoured-out by recent storms. The latest charts show an additional foot of depth along the designated ICW route, which was confirmed by our Cruising Editor. Caution through to flashing red "90" is suggested as minimum depths may be less than the charted 5 feet MLW in spots. Reduce speed, watch your course and monitor depth readings carefully.

Markers are spaced about 2 miles apart in Cotton Key Basin and course alignment can be a challenge. Glance behind occasionally to check for leeway traversing the shallow basin. Remember that wind-tide is a factor in Florida Bay and depths may be shallower than charted minimums. In a strong southeast breeze you may have to anchor and wait for a change in conditions.

At flashing green "81" adjust course to 235° magnetic and follow the straight-line defined by closely spaced red daybeacons "80" through "86" keeping them well to the north. While Barley Basin has deepened in recent years, measured depths in the channel were slightly less than charted (5.5 feet MLW). Also note there are still some extremely shallow shoals just north of the channel. The ICW continues to parallel the charted Everglades National Park PSSA boundary line along the National Park.

Enter the narrow Steamboat Channel at flashing green "87" and aim for flashing red "90" at the west end. Maintain center

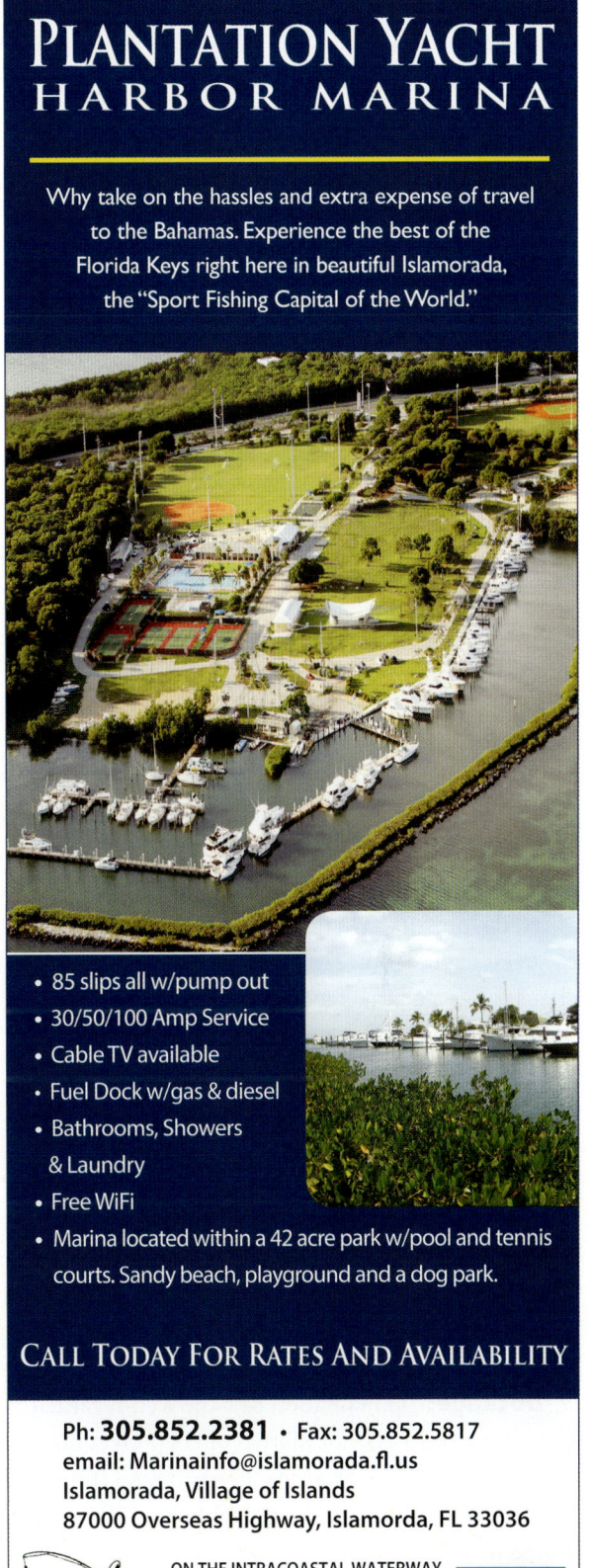

PLANTATION YACHT HARBOR MARINA

Why take on the hassles and extra expense of travel to the Bahamas. Experience the best of the Florida Keys right here in beautiful Islamorada, the "Sport Fishing Capital of the World."

- 85 slips all w/pump out
- 30/50/100 Amp Service
- Cable TV available
- Fuel Dock w/gas & diesel
- Bathrooms, Showers & Laundry
- Free WiFi
- Marina located within a 42 acre park w/pool and tennis courts. Sandy beach, playground and a dog park.

CALL TODAY FOR RATES AND AVAILABILITY

Ph: 305.852.2381 • Fax: 305.852.5817
email: Marinainfo@islamorada.fl.us
Islamorada, Village of Islands
87000 Overseas Highway, Islamorda, FL 33036

ON THE INTRACOASTAL WATERWAY, BETWEEN MM 78 AND MM 78A
TURN 150° AT 24° 59.263/ 80° 35.070

CLEAN MARINA

SOUTHERN EDITION

Chapter 10: The Florida Keys

through the channel. Birds standing on the shallow shoals on each side will supervise your progress. Once in the Lignumvitae Basin the ICW channel deepens considerably westward and the shallowest depths are behind you. A course of 247° magnetic should keep you in the channel running parallel to the charted Everglades National Park PSSA boundary line.

South from red daybeacon "78A" a side channel leads to Snake Creek, which is a very shallow route to Hawk Channel on the ocean side. Local knowledge is advised before attempting passage. This poorly marked channel begins with flashing red "12" at its northern end. (Note that the aids on this channel are numbered from the ocean side.) The **Snake Creek Bridge** (27-foot closed vertical clearance) spans the creek with Plantation Key to the east and Windley Key to the west. The bridge opens on signal except from 8:00 a.m. to 6:00 p.m. when it need only open on the hour. South of the bridge the channel has shoaled on the ocean side and passage is not recommended.

Whale Harbor Channel separates Windley Key and Upper Matecumbe Key, both part of the village of Islamorada. The 10-foot fixed **Whale Harbor Channel Bridge** gives dinghy access to the ocean side. At Upper Matecumbe Key a second access channel off Barley Basin leads to the village of Islamorada. One nautical mile south of red daybeacon "84" the Shell Key Channel is flanked by green daybeacon "21" and red daybeacon "22." The channel has a charted controlling depth of 6 feet MLW but this area is prone to shoaling and it is best to check locally for more recent soundings. This well-marked channel connects with Teatable Key Channel, which offers a dinghy route to Islamorada's ocean-side.

At the south end of Upper Matecumbe Key, **Upper Matecumbe Key Bridge** (7-foot fixed vertical clearance) crosses a shallow (not navigable) channel. Just south is **Teatable Key Channel Bridge** (10-foot fixed vertical clearance) crossing the (initially) shallow Teatable Key Channel to the ocean side.

Dockage: On Plantation Key the well-regarded Plantation Yacht Harbor Marina offers protection from all but hurricane-force winds. If westbound from flashing red "78" continue toward red daybeacon "78A" for 1 mile then alter course to about 150° magnetic and continue about 1 mile toward shore. You will spot a red and white horizontally striped lighthouse at the end of the marina's breakwater. Leaving it to starboard make a sharp starboard turn around the lighthouse and follow the marked channel. The jetty protecting the marina is a popular snorkel spot so keep a sharp eye out. The village of Islamorada owns the 42-acre Founder's Park in which the marina is located. In addition to slips and the regular cruiser amenities, the park offers a swimming pool, a dog park, sandy beaches and walking trails.

IslaMarina is at the south end of Snake Creek with slips to 60 feet and a well-stocked Ship Store. They also rent fishing gear and floatables. The facility is located north of the restricted Snake Creek Bridge (27-foot closed vertical clearance). Seek local knowledge before attempting.

From red daybeacon "84" steer a course of 150° magnetic cross through the middle the reasonably deep Barley Basin to Islamorada Yacht Basin-Lorelei Restaurant. This tight, well-protected yacht basin (4.5-foot MLW controlling depth) only maintains 3 transient slips (to 45 feet) so call ahead. The Lorelei Restaurant and Cabana Bar is the draw here. They have an expansive menu, a fun tiki bar and the best sunset views in the Keys. The restaurant hosts daily happy hour specials from 4:00 p.m. to 6:00 p.m. and nightly sunset celebrations with live entertainment.

To the south a set of white stakes mark the entrance to the full-service Coral Bay Marina, which is full-service marina offering haul-out, pressure spraying, bottom painting and repairs as well as transient slips.

Farther south in Little Basin is World Wide Sportsman/Bayside Marina located at the popular Bass Pro Shop sporting goods retailer. The marina can accommodate vessels to 40 feet. It's a great place to watch large fish and other sealife feeding around the pilings.

Safe Harbor Islamorada on Yellow Shark Channel is primarily a dry storage facility. The marina also has a dive center, restaurant and service center. Call ahead for slip availability. Located one channel to the south is the private Safe Harbor Angler House, which has charter fishing, floating villas and resort-style amenities. What it does not have is transient slips.

Anchorage: The charted Cowpens anchorage at Mile 1155 has 5- to 6-foot MLW depths with good holding in grass and mud. This anchorage is open and exposed to the west. Cowpens North is a bit quieter with excellent wind protection. From here you can dinghy to Marker 88 for lunch and dinner.

The Windley Key anchorage is in a shallow basin with good wind protection from the northeast through

Upper Keys, FL

MATECUMBE KEYS		Largest Vessel	VHF	Total Slips	Approach/ Dockside Depth	Floating Docks	Gas/ Diesel	Repairs/ Haulout	Min/Max Amps	Pump-Out Station
1. Islamorada Yacht Basin WiFi 2.2 mi. S of MM 1160.2	(305) 664-2692	45	16	15	4.5 / 4.5				30 / 50	P
2. Coral Bay Marina WiFi 2.2 mi. S of MM 1160.2	(305) 664-3111	62	16	35	5.0 / 6.0			RH	50	P
3. World Wide Sportsman / Bayside Marina MM 1160.0	(305) 664-3398	40		43	3.0 / 5.0		GD		30 / 50	P
4. Safe Harbor Islamorada WiFi	(305) 664-8884	50		14	5.0 / 4.5		GD	RH	30 / 50	

WiFi Wireless Internet Access
Visit www.waterwayguide.com for current rates, fuel prices, website addresses and other up-to-the-minute information.
(Information in the table is provided by the facilities.)

Scan here for more details:

Chapter 10 — The Florida Keys

southwest. Depth is about 6 feet MLW with good holding in grass and sand. The Oceanview Inn & Sports Pub has a small boat dock to access the restaurant or supplies. This is one of the few places that will let you dock a dinghy in Islamorada.

You can also anchor in 5 to 6 feet MLW south of Cotton Key at Mile 1158 in Barley Basin. This provides protection from the east through southeast with excellent holding in at least 5-foot MLW depths. Most boats anchor close to Lorelei's on the west end of Barley Basin. However, if you want to get away from others, reduce boat wakes and kayak through some beautiful shallows, Barley Basin (north) is a good spot. This anchorage also provides some protection from northeasterlies. While surrounded by private property with no access to shore, this spot does bring you closer to a dinghy ride to the Islamorada sandbar.

The Upper Matecumbe Key inside anchorage is located offshore from Islamorada Yacht Basin Lorelei Restaurant. Dinghies from anchored boats are welcome at the docks of World Wide Sportsman/Bayside Marina and The Beach Café at Morada Bay. The Lorelei dinghy dock is reserved for diners (and this is enforced).

Lignumvitae Basin to Channel Five– ICW Mile 1162 to Mile 1170

Lying between Steamboat Channel (Mile 1161) on the east and Bowlegys Cut (Mile 1165) to the west, the Lignumvitae Basin offers improved controlling depths (7 foot MLW) reducing keel scuffs for sailors and saving props for power boaters.

Three shallow channels weave through the islands that border the basin's southeast flank and connect Lignumvitae Basin to the ocean side. These channels are strictly dinghy territory as they are blocked by entry shoals and low clearance fixed bridges.

NAVIGATION: Use NOAA Charts 11451 and 11464. Once clear of the southwest end of Steamboat Channel (marked by flashing red "90") adjust to a course of 247° magnetic, once again paralleling the charted Everglades National Park PSSA boundary line. You should see some small signs marking the park's boundary with the basin on the north as you cross. Continue on this course for the 3 nm to the north end of Bowlegys Cut, which is marked by flashing green "93." Line up for the cut well before entry and stay center channel through to flashing red "98" at the south end. This is the last marker before the numbering sequence resets.

Cruisers have a choice of two viable routes at this point. To continue west through Florida Bay on the Inside Route (ICW) to Marathon steer a course of 247° magnetic for 6nm from flashing red "98" (at the south entrance to Bowlegys Cut) to flashing green "1" marking the north tip of Old Dan Bank (Mile 1173.8). Alternately, turn southwest to a course of 214° magnetic for the 4-nm run to the **Channel Five Bridge** (fixed 65-foot vertical clearance) and then on to Hawk Channel ocean side for the Outside Route.

Of the three well-marked channels directly from Lignumvitae Basin to the ocean side only **Indian Key Channel Bridge** offers significant fixed vertical clearance (27 feet). The **Teatable Key Channel Bridge** at the end of the Race/Shell Key Channel has just 10 feet fixed vertical clearance, as does the **Lignumvitae Channel Bridge** to the south.

> ⚠️ **CAUTION:** The shallow turtle grass flats in this area are clearly marked. The flats are all closed to boats with internal combustion engines (gas or diesel, inboard or outboard). State law enforcement officers police the area and violators (particularly those who have damaged the grass with their props) are subject to stiff fines.

Anchorage: The anchorage at Matecumbe Bight at Mile 1167 is large and wide and provides excellent holding and protection (unless the wind is out of the north). Expect 6 to 7 feet MLW.

Side Trip: Lignumvitae Key

At just 18 feet above sea level Lignumvitae Key has the highest elevation of the Keys and is named for one of the hardest woods in the world. Lignumvitae State Botanical State Park is a worthwhile visit. Park hours are Thursday through Monday, 8:00 a.m. to 4:00 p.m., and a ranger collects the $2.50 entry fee. The park has mooring balls and a dinghy dock but a strict "no pets" policy. The park suggests visitors bring shoes and mosquito repellent.

Dockage/Moorings: Lignumvitae Key Dock & Moorings can accommodate medium-size cruising craft (4-foot MLW depths), although no docking is permitted after 5:00 p.m. and pets are not allowed ashore. They also have complementary moorings off the northwest side of the island for stays of up to one week.

Long Key to Boot Key–ICW Mile 1168 to Mile 1196

This section covers the stretch between the Florida Key's two major crossovers: Channel Five and the Moser Channel. There are some shallow spots along this route. Most are shoals associated with one of the numerous sinewy banks that extend northward from the Keys. Shoals bordering the channel are marked and navigation is straightforward here. Remember to keep red markers to the right. Mariners straying from the designated route should exercise caution.

NAVIGATION: Use NOAA Charts 11449, 11451 and 11453. The ICW continues west flashing green "1" off Old Dan Bank on a course of 247° magnetic for about 4.8 nm with depths between 6 and 9 feet MLW to reach flashing green "5" off the Channel Key Banks, running north of Duck Key. These banks are extremely shallow where they cross the ICW. Deeper-draft boats should stay on the ICW route over this stretch. There are rocky shoals charted at 5 feet MLW just north of the course line about 1 mile west of flashing green "1" (at Mile 1174). These are unmarked as they are within the range of controlling depths, but they do pose a threat.

A more dangerous shoal at Mile 1178 is marked by red daybeacon "4." The course line passes well south here and this is a good place to verify your alignment. This shoal is the first in a series that make up the Channel Key Bank. It is essential that you follow the narrow Channel Key Pass through the banks. Be sure to split green daybeacon "7" and red daybeacon "8" to stay in the narrow dredged cut at Mile 1178.8. Favor red daybeacon "8" as you thread through this pass.

The **Long Key Viaduct Bridge** with 23-foot fixed vertical clearance lies southeast of the ICW at Mile 1176. Boats with lower airdraft can take this channel to reach Duck Key on the ocean side. Local knowledge is needed as the charted (and uncharted) shoals in this channel are not marked. Given the close proximity to the Channel Five Bridge, this channel poses unnecessary risks.

Once clear of the Channel Key Bank, the ICW follows a heading of 257° magnetic for a 6.5 nm straight-line run from red daybeacon "8" to flashing green "13." On this

Side Trip: Sombrero Key Reef

If you are waiting around for a mooring in Boot Key Harbor, a trip to Sombrero Key is a good way to bide your time. Sombrero Key Reef is one of the Florida Key's prime snorkeling sites. Reef visitors will see all manner of reef fish, stingrays, lots of barracudas and the occasional nurse shark. Barracuda are particularly plentiful under the 142-foot Sombrero Key Lighthouse (circa 1858). Clearest conditions are found the day after calm weather. But get there early, as this popular snorkeling site can get busy.

The route to the reef is a straight line 4 miles due south from flashing green "1" in the Boot Key Channel entrance. Just aim for the big tower. Pick up a mooring ball to the south of the reef (offshore side).

Mooring balls are plentiful, but anchoring is allowed only if all mooring balls are in use. You must anchor well clear of the reef, which can make a snorkeling visit difficult. It's better to wait for a mooring ball to free up.

Chapter 10 — The Florida Keys

route you must pass north of flashing green "11" marking the north end of the Grassy Key Bank (Mile 1182), which projects northerly from long, low Grassy Key. Be aware that Grassy Key Bank has water depths below 1 foot MLW to the south of this marker. Also note some rocky shoals with 5 feet MLW in a patch north of Bamboo Key. These pose no threat if you are on the designated ICW course.

Some cruisers seeking bay-side services in Marathon often leave the designated ICW either at flashing green "11" or "13," passing north of Bamboo Key then skirting Stirrup Key for the first route, or south of the Rachel Bank towards Rachel Key for the second. There is sufficient depths for most cruising vessels in these waters but plan compass course lines that avoid the rocky shoals in this area. For those continuing to Moser Channel under the **Seven Mile Bridge**, the ICW route is shorter and the shoals are better marked.

Cruisers heading on to Moser Channel and Boot Key change course back to 247° magnetic at flashing green "13" for the 5.9-nm run to flashing red "20" marking Bethel Bank. This segment is well marked. Daybeacons "14" and "18" assist with course alignment and mark threats. Pass close to these markers to avoid the hazards to the south. In particular, when passing Rachel Bank we advise rounding north of the bank's charted shallows and a charted obstruction as a precaution. Pass through flashing red "20" and green daybeacon "19" keeping south of Bethel Bank.

> NOTE: If continuing to Key West on the inside route, adjust course to 259° magnetic at flashing red "20" for the 5.5 nm run to red daybeacon "26" at ICW Mile 1200. This route passes close to red daybeacons "22" and "24."

Anchorage: At the start of this stretch there are some excellent anchorages near Fiesta Key (Mile 1172). You can find good protection in Jewfish Hole west of Fiesta Key (7- to 8-foot MLW depths) or in 6 feet MLW between Fiesta Key and Jewfish Bush Banks, which is protected by a causeway.

Seven Mile Bridge

HAWK CHANNEL (OUTSIDE) ROUTE TO BOOT KEY

The deepest and only viable route for vessels with a draft of 5 feet or more is the Hawk Channel running from Biscayne Bay to Key West. Not "officially" part of the ICW system, Hawk Channel tracks southwest 1 to 3 nm off the ocean side of the Keys. Taking the form of a somewhat protected "channel," it runs over the flat banks (Florida Platform) between the Keys and Florida's barrier reef to the southeast. In ordinary weather it is a pleasant sail or an easy run for the entire length of the Keys.

The prevailing southeasterly winds can provide a nice boost for a long reach on an outside run under sail. However, with numerous breaks in the outer reef it can offer its share of rough water should the wind be strong from either the southern or southwestern quarter.

Navigation Notes

Hawk Channel is relatively wide; nevertheless, navigation should be precise as aids to navigation are typically spaced far apart and can be difficult to spot. Unlike on the ICW, NOAA charts show no magenta line or mile markers for the Hawk Channel so skippers must plan each passage segment. A compass heading for every course segment should be the rule, as should following prudent piloting practices. An autopilot can be very helpful on some of the long tedious runs (particularly under power) but this route is busy with recreational and commercial traffic so the helm must be attended at all times. A GPS will be extremely useful on this passage particularly during times of poor visibility as numerous shoals pose a hazard along this route.

Expect a controlling depth of 9 feet MLW (but generally closer to 20 feet MLW for most of the route) and all major shoals along the route are marked. The route is generally well protected from north through west wind conditions when the channel is in the lee of the Keys themselves. It is important to be aware that if you run aground in the Keys and hit coral heads, coral reefs or sea grass beds, you could be levied a large fine in addition to any towing or repair costs.

CAUTION: Anchor in designated areas only. Also avoid entering designated "Marine Sanctuaries." These are restricted areas and should never be considered "cruising grounds" or traversed as part of a planned passage route.

Boats destined for the Florida Keys that draw over 4.5 feet must stay on the ocean side at least as far as Channel Five (Mile 1170), which is just southwest of Lower Matecumbe Key. For a passage on the Outside Route, Hawk Channel is well marked and provides some protection in most winds. Eastbound vessels often make an ocean leg, riding the Gulf Stream outside the reefs, but most cruisers prefer the comfort and convenience of the Hawk Channel in both directions.

While nighttime operation is an option on the Hawk Channel many markers are not lighted and we recommend that a passage be broken into a series of "achievable daytime hops." Consider appropriate stops and plan to complete each day's run well before dark. Skippers who do plan for nighttime operation should be aware the Florida Keys are strewn with hazards to navigation and a well-developed set of nighttime operation skills are mandatory here. Fortunately both anchorages and marinas can be found at reasonable intervals throughout the Keys.

For nighttime operation, and if weather allows, many skippers will choose a run off the Florida Platform in the open ocean beyond the reefs. This puts cruisers further from hazards and can simplify navigation. Be warned: Once this choice is taken there are few viable places to switch to the Hawk Channel along this 44-mile route.

In heavy easterly weather beam seas are the rule amplified by current and counter-current in the stretches abeam the numerous gaps in the Florida reef. Sailboats might like this weather but powerboats may wish to sit it out or move inside to the ICW. Conditions quiet down when winds slacken and veer to the southeast and south. With slack winds sailboats may choose to motorsail or make short close-hauled runs. Powerboats may still roll a bit but the journey will be generally enjoyable.

Central Biscayne Bay to Cape Florida

This section describes the route from Central Biscayne Bay through the Cape Florida Channel/Biscayne Channel and has a controlling depth of 7 feet MLW at the ocean-side entrance. This is the shorter route for boats departing from the Coconut Grove area south of Virginia Key. There is actually a choice of two channels: the Cape Florida Channel closer to Key Biscayne or

Chapter 10: The Florida Keys

the more southerly Biscayne Channel. The two channels converge at 12-foot flashing red "6" located south of Cape Florida's lighthouse. Current charts and local knowledge should be obtained before attempting these channels for the first time.

NAVIGATION: Use NOAA Charts 11451 and 11465.

> ⚠️ **CAUTION:** Some variation in channel markers has resulted from frequent storms so navigate carefully using the latest charts.

Heading seaward in either channel remember that green markers are to starboard until past flashing green "1" on the ocean side. Ocean-bound vessels enter Biscayne Channel (7 feet MLW) through paired markers flashing red "20" and flashing green "21" located 1 nm east of the ICW (Mile 1097.8). Follow the well-marked channel and be sure to pass between the paired markers green daybeacon "7" and red daybeacon "8" (positioned oddly). Turn northeastward through this pair toward flashing red "6" keeping green daybeacon "7" to starboard. This is a well-marked channel but watch for shallow spots.

Eastbound vessels taking Cape Florida Channel (6 to 7 feet MLW), leave the ICW at Mile 1095.8 and head east 0.7 nm to flashing red "4" off the southwest tip of Key Biscayne. While rounding red day beacon "2" gradually turn to the northeast, keeping green daybeacon "1" to starboard and head towards Key Biscayne. Turn east to follow the shoreline keeping at least 100 yards off (in 7 feet MLW) for approximately 1.5 nm until adjacent to the southernmost tip of Key Biscayne near the lighthouse then head towards flashing red "6" to avoid nearby shoals.

The merged channel follows a path from flashing red "6" to flashing green "3" to flashing green "1." When exiting hold course for 0.5 nm past flashing green "1" before turning south. It is 3 nm due south from here to the entry to the Hawk Channel.

> ⚠️ **CAUTION:** Shoaling to 6 feet MLW have been reported along the entire merged channel from around flashing red "6" to flashing green "1." Proceed with caution and note depths can be less than charted in high wind or surge conditions.

Keeping 0.5 nm off flashing red "2" marking the entrance to Biscayne Channel head due south for 3 nm to the start of the Hawk Channel. The matched pair of daybeacons–red "2" and green "3"–mark the channel's entrance. The pair's center is about 1.5 nm west of the Fowey Rocks Light (flashing white every 10 seconds). From this point to Channel Five is approximately 74 miles south-southwest.

> **NOTE:** Hawk Channel markers generally follow red-right-southbound (the same as the ICW).

Cape Florida to Angelfish Creek

This section continues the trip south from Cape Florida for vessels entering the ocean from either Government Cut (Miami) Inlet or the Cape Florida (Biscayne Bay) Inlet. Immediately south from Cape Florida and Key Biscayne the waters are open and depths should exceed 15 feet MLW. The first Hawk Channel markers are 3 nm south of the Cape Florida (Biscayne Bay) Inlet entry markers and the Florida Keys begin at the Ragged Keys another 3 nm south.

The Hawk Channel narrows considerably approaching the Ragged Keys with shoals flanking the channel's edges and depths shallow to 12 feet MLW in spots. Most of the markers on Hawk Channel are un-lit and cruisers should take particular care if operating in darkness. Many opt to move an additional 5 miles off the barrier islands through this stretch and operate in the deeper water

Distances
Outside Route: Hawk Channel
(Miles from Miami)

LOCATION	STATUTE MILES	NAUTICAL MILES
Miami (Government Cut)	0	0
Miami (Cape Florida)	8	6.9
Fowey Rocks Light	14	12.0
Angelfish Creek	28	24.0
South Sound Creek	51	44.0
Tavernier	63	54.7
Islamorada	70	60.8
Channel Five	82	71.0
Duck Key	92	79.9
Marathon (Sisters Creek)	102	88.6
Moser Channel	109	94.7
Key West	151	131.0

(several hundred feet) beyond the edge of the Florida Platform. The drop-off is quite close to the barrier islands here and the Hawk Channel can be re-entered 45 miles south at Mosquito Bank. This section passes Caesar Creek and Angelfish Creek, the last two crossovers (for shoal-draft vessels) between the Hawk Channel and Biscayne Bay. Below Angelfish Creek, Key Largo, the largest of the Florida Keys, extends 33 miles southwest to Tavernier Creek.

NAVIGATION: Use NOAA Charts 11451 or 11465, 11463, 11464 and 11449 (when heading southwards). This route will be described as a series of course segments, each with a compass heading. Starting just east of flashing green "1" marking the east entry of the Cape Florida (Biscayne Bay) Inlet run for 3 nm at a course of 180° magnetic to red daybeacon "2." Paired red daybeacon "2" and green daybeacon "3" frame the entry of the Hawk Channel (approximately 1.5 nm to the east you should see the Fowey Rocks Light). Continue 5.4 nm south at a course of 198° magnetic from red daybeacon "2" to flashing red "8" near Bowles Bank Light lying off Sands Key.

A series of dangerous shoals flanking both sides of Hawk Channel starts at Bowles Bank and continues 29.5 nm south to Mosquito Bank. Sailboats that are close-hauled will want to plan their course carefully in this area as there is little room to tack. At flashing red "8" adjust course to 205° magnetic and run 7.7 nm to flashing red "20" marking the opening to Caesar Creek. When passing the mouth of the creek continue on this heading for another 2.4 nm to flashing red "22" off the Old Rhoads Bank. There is a series of green daybeacons and one flashing green marking dangerous shoals to the east of the channel through this stretch. Operation is darkness here can be challenging and a close watch is required.

At flashing red "22" the channel bends to the south-southwest as the westward curve of the Florida Keys commences. (The northernmost point of Key Largo is about 2 nm west of the marker.) Adjust course to 219° magnetic and run 9.3 nm to flashing green "31." Continue to watch for un-lit daybeacons close to the channel on this stretch. At flashing green "31" make a slight course adjustment to 217° magnetic and continue 10.2 nm to flashing green "35" at Mosquito Bank. South of Mosquito Bank the Hawk Channel opens up and hazards are fewer and farther from the marked channel.

Caesar Creek at the southwest end of Elliott Key is the first crossover to the ICW. Flashing red "20" is at the entrance to the National Park Service's marked channel. It is open to shoal-draft vessels only due to the shallows on the western end of the cut. The channel is well marked but narrow and bounded by 1 to 2-foot MLW depths. Pay attention to the wind direction as it will affect depths. Pass in daylight to enable visual navigation. Use extreme caution when transiting this area. We suggest you obtain local knowledge before using this as a crossover.

Angelfish Creek to Largo Sound

For vessels wanting to take advantage of the Gulf Stream for a transit to Bimini Island in the Bahamas, Angelfish Creek provides a more southerly approach than Miami. Be aware that the 1.8-nm-long inlet adds 14 nm to the Bahamas trip making it 56 nm instead of 42 nm.

NAVIGATION: Use NOAA Charts 11451 and 11463. Local skippers often use well-marked Angelfish Creek (located about 3 nm south of Caesar Creek) to cross between Biscayne Bay and the ocean. (Study your chart carefully and avoid Broad Creek to the north, which is shoaled at the entrance.) There are shoals at both the east and west ends of Angelfish Creek but for boats that draw 5 feet or less it is a fairly simple passage. Boats with drafts greater than 5 feet should use the channel on a rising tide. Note the tidal range in this area is approximately 1 foot. Stay well out from the entrance until the channel markers are lined up. Just inside the entrance from Hawk Channel is a rocky ledge with 5-foot MLW depths; avoid this area in rough conditions.

Keep dead center in Angelfish Creek at low tide and maintain enough speed to prevent leeway. Do not enter if another boat is coming out. You need to able to stay on the centerline. Once inside the controlling 5-foot MLW depth creates no problem and you can often find deeper water. Depths of at least 7 feet MLW along the creek are the rule rather than the exception. Side creeks offer anchorages but note that the bottom is rocky and currents are strong.

Dockage: South of the ocean side entrance to Angelfish Creek is the private Ocean Reef Resort & Yacht Club, which accepts only members and sponsored guests. Other facilities along the Hawk Channel cater to transients although many are oriented primarily to charters and sport fishermen. Average approach depths to

Chapter 10: The Florida Keys

America's First Underwater Park

As early as the 1930s work had begun to protect the reefs of the Upper Florida Keys. When Everglades National Park was first proposed the intent was to protect all of the connected ecosystems found in South Florida, including the mangroves, seagrass beds and coral reefs off the Keys. Local property owners and business protested and when Everglades National Park was created in 1947, it did not include areas south of Florida Bay.

But by the late 1950s residents of the Keys were becoming more and more concerned about the future of the reefs. Coral, starfish, sea horses and many other living creatures were being harvested and sold as souvenirs. In 1960 President Dwight D. Eisenhower proclaimed the reefs off Key Largo as the Key Largo Coral Reef Preserve. Later when adjacent lands on Key Largo were acquired by the State of Florida, the present state park was formed absorbing responsibility for the underwater reefs as well. John D. Pennekamp, an editor for the *Miami Herald* and a supporter of the efforts to protect the Everglades and the reefs, helped lead the effort to create both Everglades National Park and the park that now bears his name in Key Largo.

The John D. Pennekamp Coral Reef State Park opened in 1963 as the first underwater park in the U.S. The park includes the visitor center and concessionaire complex at MM 103 in Key Largo, where several beaches, trails, a campground, a boat ramp and a marina are located. The park extends 3 miles offshore over the flats of the Florida Platform and covers 70 square nautical miles. It protects the unique ecosystems of the Upper Keys and is Florida's most visited state park.

many of these privately marked channels are 5 feet or less MLW. Be sure to call ahead for channel depths.

A little over 10 nm to the south Garden Cove Marina has a well-marked channel that begins at red daybeacon "32" (at Rattlesnake Key). Sound your way into their channel. The approach depth is about 4 feet MLW. There is plenty of water once you get into the basin where you will find slips to 35 feet and the Buzzard's Roost Restaurant (305-453-3746) serving lunch, dinner and Sunday brunch. They will even cook your catch!

John Pennekamp Coral Reef State Park

The John Pennekamp Coral Reef State Park in Largo Sound offers glass-bottom boat tours, scuba gear rentals and instruction, boat rentals, a campground and a Visitor's Center with a 30,000-gallon saltwater aquarium. There are 50 miles of natural mangrove trails to explore by kayak or stand-up paddleboard (available for rent) and the underwater park contains 178 square miles of mangrove swamps, sea grass beds and coral reef including the larger of the two living reefs that lie in Florida waters. Abundant reef fish live around the coral and there are several shipwrecks creating an underwater paradise for divers and snorkelers. Only hook-and-line fishing is permitted in the park.

NAVIGATION: Use NOAA Charts 11451, 11463 and 11464. Hawk Channel crosses the John Pennekamp Coral Reef State Park north boundary at green daybeacon "23" (off Angelfish Creek). The park's land attractions are located 20 miles southwest in Largo Sound, which is about midway down Key Largo. To visit by boat enter through South Sound Creek southwest of Largo Sound and less than 2 nm north of Mosquito Bank, which is marked by flashing green "35." The entrance to South Sound Creek is marked by flashing red "2." Do not cut inside this marker. There are shoals to the north. The channel carries 6-foot MLW depths but 5-foot MLW depths have been reported inside Largo Sound. It is best to contact the park ranger in advance to confirm approach depths.

Dive and sightseeing boats use this channel frequently so be prepared to move but not too far as 3-foot MLW depths have been observed outside of the channel. Because of the narrow channel and blind turns commercial vessels will make a Sécurité call on VHF

America's Waterway Guide Since 1947 — Chapter 10

Upper Keys, FL

KEY LARGO AREA–OUTSIDE		Largest Vessel	VHF	Total Slips	Approach/ Dockside Depth	Floating Docks	Gas/ Diesel	Repairs/ Haulout	Min/Max Amps	Pump-Out Station
1. Garden Cove Marina 1006.5	(305) 451-4694	35	16		4.0 / 14.0		G	RH	30	
2. John Pennekamp Coral Reef State Park	(305) 451-6300	50	16	9	/				30	P
3. Key Largo Harbor Marina WiFi 1.7 mi. E of MM 1141.3	(305) 451-0045	65	16	24	4.0 / 10.0		GD	RH	30 / 50	
4. Marina Del Mar Resort and Marina WiFi	(305) 453-7171	60	16	77	4.5 / 18.0				30 / 50	P
5. Pilot House Marina & Restaurant WiFi MM 1142.0	(305) 451-3142	85	16	50	4.5 / 10.0	F	GD	H	30 / 100	P

WiFi Wireless Internet Access
Visit www.waterwayguide.com for current rates, fuel prices, website addresses and other up-to-the-minute information. (Information in the table is provided by the facilities.)

Scan here for more details:

Source: Aqua Map and NOAA data

SOUTHERN EDITION 391

Chapter 10: The Florida Keys

Channel 16 before entering. Listen for such calls and make your own if appropriate.

Vessels with drafts of 4 feet or less and airdrafts of 14 feet or less can cross over from Largo Sound to Blackwater Sound through a rock cut (charted as Marvin D. Adams Waterway). The cut runs between the southernmost corner of Blackwater Sound and the western shore of Largo Sound. (The shallowest water lies at the two ends of the cut.) If you cannot get your big boat through here, it still makes a worthwhile dinghy trip. Be advised that a strong current runs through the cut.

Dockage/Moorings: John Pennekamp Coral Reef State Park offers nine full-service slips accommodating boats up to 50 feet in length. It is highly recommended you call the dockmaster on VHF Channel 16 to check availability and approach/dockside depths before arrival. This is a busy place. Reservations are recommended and should be made online). For the most up-to-date information, call 305-451-6300.

Although overnight anchoring is prohibited in Largo Sound, about a dozen white mooring balls are located near the park headquarters in the southwest corner of the sound. Simply tie up to a vacant ball and dinghy over to the dockmaster's office (in the Dive Center to check in.

Largo Sound to Hens and Chicks

While Hawk Channel opens up on this stretch there are still a few dangerous shoals skirting the green side. This stretch passes Rodriguez Key off Rock Harbor and Tavernier Key off Tavernier Creek, where 33-mile long Key Largo ends and Plantation Key begins.

NAVIGATION: Use NOAA Charts 11451 and 11464. Continuing southwest in the Hawk Channel it is a 11.7-nm run at 230° magnetic from flashing green "35" at the Mosquito Bank to flashing red "40" marking the Hens and Chickens reef. The reef is designated as a Marine Sanctuary and is quite close to Hawk Channel. This can be a great place to stop for a snorkel but be sure to avoid passage through the marked prohibited area. Note the extremely shallow shoals (3 to 5 feet MLW) marked by "triangles" that flank the green side between green daybeacons "37" to "39."

To the south of Largo Sound is Port Largo Canal offering some dockage options. About 1 nm south from flashing green "35" along Hawk Channel turn northwest and continue 1 nm to flashing red "2." From here take a wide turn around red daybeacons "4" and "6" staying in the deeper water and keeping these to starboard. Once

Angelfish Creek

around red daybeacon "6" start your approach to the canal splitting flashing green "7" and red daybeacon "8." (Keep red to port here.)

Watch your depth as the approach channel is only around 5 feet MLW. Just to the south of Port Largo there is a large tower south of the entrance to the canal leading to Lake Largo. This canal is to port just before red daybeacon "8" for the entrance to Port Largo.

Dockage: The full-service Key Largo Harbor Marina is the first facility (to starboard) on Port Largo Canal with maintenance and repairs. They mostly cater to large sportfishing vessels. Call ahead for slip availability. A bit farther into the canal is the 77-slip Marina Del Mar Resort and Marina offering transient dockage and resort-style amenities. Dockage options include side ties against the canal wall and slips with finger piers. The marina also provides access to snorkeling and diving adventures.

Pilot House Marina & Restaurant is to the south on Lake Largo in the heart of downtown Key Largo. The marina can accommodate power or sailboats up to 85 feet in length. They offer climate-controlled restrooms and showers, laundry facilities and the waterfront Pilot House with a full menu and live music on Friday and Saturday nights.

Anchorage: Rodriguez Key is directly northwest from Hawk Channel marker green daybeacon "37." This is a popular anchorage. Anchor in 5 to 8 feet MLW on whichever side of the island gives the best wind protection. Often the best protection in north winds is between Rodriguez Key and Key Largo closer to (outer) Rock Harbor. The holding is good in grass and sand in 6 feet MLW. Check the tide stage before anchoring as the range is 3 feet.

There are several small marinas and a boat ramp in and around Rock Harbor where you might land your dinghy. Straight out from the anchorage is Molasses Reef with excellent snorkeling. This is a popular stop for boats preparing to cross to the Bahamas or heading on to Marathon.

Hens & Chicks to Channel Five

Over this stretch there are fewer shoals on the seaward side and several hazards between Hawk Channel and the Keys. The Hens and Chickens, Cheeca Rocks or a small shoal 1 mile south of Lower Matecumbe Key can make a pleasant stop for lunch and a snorkel. Passage through charted "Marine Sanctuaries" should be avoided.

NAVIGATION: Use NOAA Charts 11451 and 11464. South from the flashing red "40" marking the Hens and Chickens reef take a course of 236° magnetic for 4.2 nm southwest to green daybeacon "41" located 1 nm seaward from Cheeca Rocks Marine Sanctuary. If leaving Hawk Channel watch for an unmarked 3-foot MLW shoal known as "The Rocks" that is located northwest of the Hen and Chickens.

From green daybeacon "41" proceed 10.5 nm at 246° magnetic to the Channel Five entry marker flashing red "2." Be aware of a shoal that extends 0.5 mile south of the channel entry marker. Continuing on the Hawk Channel proceed 0.7 nm on the same heading past Channel Five to reach flashing red "44" off Long Key. This marks the start of the Middle Keys.

The fixed **Tavernier Creek Bridge** (15-foot vertical clearance) crosses Tavernier Creek at ICW Mile 1151.5. The creek's entrance has charted 3-foot MLW depths but many cruisers anchor outside in the harbor protected by Tavernier Key and take a dinghy ride to visit the bay side.

Snake Creek is a limited crossover to the bay side. The creek is crossed by the **Snake Creek Bridge** with 27-foot closed vertical clearance. The bridge opens on signal, except from 8:00 a.m. to 6:00 p.m., when it need only open on the hour. The channel has shoaled (4 feet MLW reported) on the ocean side and passage is not recommended except by dinghy.

> NOTE: West of Snake Creek is Windley Key Fossil Reef Geological State Park, which has self-guided trails including one along an 8-foot high quarry wall revealing preserved fossilized specimens of a variety of ancient coral animals. Interpretive tours are offered in winter months. This interesting site is open Thursday through Monday from 8:00 a.m. to 5:00 p.m.

West of Windley Key is Whale Harbor Channel (5 feet MLW), which leads to Cotton Key Basin. The 10-foot fixed vertical clearance of the **Whale Harbor Channel Bridge** restricts vessels needing more clearance.

Next is tiny and picturesque Teatable Key on the ocean side off the south tip of Upper Matecumbe Key. This was once a Navy base and is now a private island. Between Teatable Key and Indian Key are two well-marked channels leading to the bay side. Teatable Key Channel's airdraft is restricted by the 10-foot fixed vertical clearance of the **Teatable Key Channel Bridge**. The airdraft restriction of the Indian

Chapter 10: The Florida Keys

Upper Keys, FL

MATECUMBE KEYS–OUTSIDE		Largest Vessel	VHF	Total Slips	Approach/ Dockside Depth	Floating Docks	Gas/ Diesel	Repairs/ Haulout	Min/Max Amps	Pump-Out Station
1. Postcard Inn Marina at Holiday Isle WiFi MM 1157.5	(305) 433-9942	90	16	56	4.5 / 7.0		GD		30 / 50	P
2. La Siesta Resort & Marina WiFi MM 1162.5	(855) 335-1078	30		24	3.5 / 6.0		G			
3. Bud'n Mary's Fishing Marina MM 1162.1	(305) 664-2461	45	77	35	4.5 / 4.5		GD	RH	30 / 50	

WiFi Wireless Internet Access

Visit www.waterwayguide.com for current rates, fuel prices, website addresses and other up-to-the-minute information. (Information in the table is provided by the facilities.)

Scan here for more details:

Source: Aqua Map and NOAA data

Upper Keys, FL

MATECUMBE KEYS—OUTSIDE

	Largest Vessel	VHF	Total Slips	Approach/ Dockside Depth	Floating Docks	Gas/ Diesel	Repairs/ Haulout	Min/Max Amps	Pump-Out Station
1. Caloosa Cove Marina & Resort WiFi MM 1168.0 (305) 664-4455	60		40	4.0 / 4.0		GD	H	30 / 50	

WiFi Wireless Internet Access
Visit www.waterwayguide.com for current rates, fuel prices, website addresses and other up-to-the-minute information.
(Information in the table is provided by the facilities.)

Scan here for more details:

Source: Aqua Map and NOAA data

Key Channel is set by the **Indian Key Channel Bridge** (27-foot fixed vertical clearance).

Lower Matecumbe Key is the midpoint in the run from Fowey Rocks to Key West. At its western tip Channel Two is another restricted crossover restricted by the 10-foot fixed vertical clearance of **Channel Two Bridge**.

Dockage/Moorings: Postcard Inn Marina at Holiday Isle, located at the north end of the Whale Harbor Channel Bridge, caters to sportfishing vessels and sells gas and diesel fuel. There are many fishing charters based here as well as shoreside accommodations, several restaurants and many bars. Their well-known tiki bar is self-proclaimed "home of the Rum Runner." They have 18 transient slips to 90 feet.

At the south end of the Whale Harbor Channel Bridge is Whale Harbor Marina, which is the base for several sportfishing charters and has two on-site restaurants. They do not have transient slips.

On Upper Matecumbe Key a privately marked channel leads to La Siesta Resort & Marina. Call for instructions before entering this channel (reported 3.5-foot MLW approach depths). They have transient slips to 35 feet along with rooms, cottages and houses for rent.

Behind Teatable Key to the east a privately maintained channel (controlling depth of 4.5 feet MLW) leads to Bud'n Mary's Fishing Marina. Pay very close attention when navigating the channel. It is fairly narrow with a rock jetty on the northeast side and a "flat" on the southwest side. This is one of the oldest and most active sportfishing/charter centers in the Keys. Rental skiffs and guided fishing charters are available along with a limited number of transient slips to 45 feet. Call ahead for reservations.

Chapter 10: The Florida Keys

Indian Key has a small boat dock and three complementary moorings (for up to one week) off the southeast side. The Indian Key Moorings are exposed but provide easy access from Hawk Channel. One mooring ball is very close to the island's pretty beach area and wooden dock.

Caloosa Cove Marina & Resort on Lower Matecumbe Key is in a protected basin with 4-foot MLW approach and dockside depths. After a complete rebuilding/renovation, the facilities are better than ever and include shoreside accommodations, a well-stocked general store and two restaurants. They welcome transients to 60 feet.

Anchorage: The harbor at Tavernier Harbor has 4 to 7 feet MLW with good holding in sand and grass. This is open and exposed from the northeast through the east. Closer to Tavernier Key you will find an excellent anchorage in 6 feet of fairly clear water with a sand and grass bottom.

In calm conditions or with light winds from the west through to the north-northeast it is possible to anchor in the sand off Whale Harbor in 5 feet MLW. This is not a particularly good or recommended anchorage but if you do anchor here, you and your dinghy are welcome at the Whale Harbor Inn, which boasts a huge seafood buffet.

Channel Five Crossing (from ocean)

Channel Five is the first major crossover below Biscayne Bay. This channel allows cruisers to cross between the ocean side and bay side or perhaps just to switch sides to get away from weather and find an anchorage. While there are minimal markers, navigation of the wide channel is straightforward. It has a controlling depth of 8 feet MLW. The fixed **Channel Five Bridge** (65-foot vertical clearance) sets the channel's vertical clearance.

NAVIGATION: Use NOAA Chart 11451.

CAUTION: The dangerous shoals that flank both sides of Channel Five are poorly marked and growing. Do not cut close to markers or charted shoals while turning. Monitor depths through the active shoaling area and expect channel minimum 7 feet MLW near flashing red "2."

When entering from the ocean side westbound traffic should continue in the Hawk Channel until flashing red "2" is on the beam. At flashing red "2" turn due north keeping west of red daybeacon "4" and the shoals behind. After pass red daybeacon "4" slowly adjust your course to 025° magnetic to pass through the Channel Five Bridge

America's Waterway Guide Since 1947 — Chapter 10

US 1 bridge over Channel 5 to Key West

center span. After passing under the bridge stay east of the dangerous shoals of the Jewfish Bush Banks.

If joining the ICW eastbound from Channel Five, the heading is 034° magnetic for the 4-nm run to flashing red "98" at the west entrance to Bowlegys Cut (Mile 1165.6).

If joining the ICW westbound from Channel Five, continue on 025° magnetic for at least 1 nm from the Channel Five Bridge span to ensure you are well north of the dangerous Jewfish Bush Banks before turning westward to join the ICW. The first ICW marker is flashing green "1" located at the north tip of Old Dan Bank (Mile 1173.8).

Long Key to Marathon

This section picks up the Hawk Channel route just past Channel Five at flashing red "44" off Long Key. Dangerous shoals flank Channel Five and the southeast shore of Long Key. You must observe Channel Five markers carefully and stay at least 1 nm south of Long Key while operating in this area.

NAVIGATION: Use NOAA Charts 11449, 11451 and 11453. Southwest along the Hawk Channel keep red markers to starboard. From flashing red "44" (marking shoals off Long Key and the Channel Five entrance) set a course of 248° magnetic toward flashing green "45" located just north of East Turtle Shoal (with 5-foot MLW depths). Along this 9.2-nm run there are few hazards although some charted obstructions and an 8-foot MLW shoal lie off the designated courseline.

To avoid East Turtle Shoal head west from flashing green "45" on Hawk Channel at 253° magnetic for the 5.3-nm run toward red daybeacon "48." From this marker southwest the heading for the designated route swings further to the west to 259° magnetic. Hawk Channel continues southwest on this heading for 14.2 nm past Moser Channel and Bahia Honda Key. (Note the controlling depth on this stretch is only 8 feet MLW.) If diverging from the courseline, be wary of East Washerwoman Shoal marked by flashing green "49." This is a dangerous shoal (2 feet MLW) so keep well to the north.

Continuing southwest from Long Key you will begin to see the urban sprawl of Marathon to the north plus Grassy Key, Crawl Key, Fat Deer Key and Vaca Key. (There is a Sea Tow office on Grassy Key should you need it.) Boot Key lies at the end of this chain and is uninhabited and covered with mangroves and the occasional radio tower. Fronting Fat Deer Key is Coco Plum Beach, which is well marked by a 14-story-high condominium tower. This tower serves as an excellent landmark for cruisers on Hawk Channel (and is also the highest building in all of the Florida Keys).

SOUTHERN EDITION

Anchorage: Long Key is the home of Long Key State Park, a 300-acre wild area with a campground, numerous picnic tables and grills. You can drop the hook in Long Key Bight in 4- to 6-foot MLW depths with good holding in sand and grass. If approaching from Hawk Channel, give red daybeacon "2" a wide berth as shoaling extends south to south-southeast with less than 6 feet MLW. This anchorage is open to the northeast but you can relocate south of the island to seek protection in these conditions.

■ BOOT KEY (MARATHON)

While many marine services and anchorages are located in the Marathon area, its principal harbor is Boot Key Harbor, which is entered south of the Seven Mile Bridge either from Moser or Hawk Channels. Marathon's bay-side facilities offer some great options but most visitors to Marathon choose to stay in the city's massive and well-protected Boot Key Harbor.

Cruisers should note that the current is swift in both the Moser Channel and Knight Key Channel. If under sail this can have an extreme effect on your set. Also shoal areas are expanding along north-south lines with the current. Watch your depth and give charted shoal areas a wide berth. Stay 1 mile south of the Seven Mile Bridge while passing the Pidgeon Key Banks then proceed to red daybeacon "2" in Moser Channel before turning for Boot Key.

Boot Key Harbor is a busy place and first-time visitors are always surprised by the number of boats packed inside. Perhaps the best and most heavily populated harbor in the Keys, the harbor has an abundance of marine facilities along the channel and in the harbor beyond. Don't be surprised if a small boat cuts across traffic to get to the fuel docks along the channel's narrow section. Be sure to obey the strictly enforced "SLOW-SPEED/MINIMUM-WAKE ZONE" in effect for the entire harbor. Before entering you should have arranged dockage or a mooring in advance. If you intend to anchor be warned you must be 100 feet outside a mooring field for your entire swing circle.

NAVIGATION: Use NOAA Chart 11453. From the north shore of Marathon and the ICW, you can round Knight Key and head south under the **Knight Key Channel Bridge** (19-foot fixed vertical clearance) to flashing green "1" marking the entrance to Boot Key Channel. This route is impassible for most cruising-size boats and is not recommended. The route is poorly marked, currents run swiftly on either tide and the monofilament lines of multitudes of anglers dangle from the old bridge. Controlling depth is 8 feet MLW but a shallow shoal is evident before the bridge at low tide. Be careful. If you do choose this route, once through to the ocean side, keep well clear of the shoal extending west from Knight Key.

The preferred entry route from the ICW is via Moser Channel to the west, the primary passageway and the last major crossover between the inside (ICW) route and the outside (Hawk Channel) route. Simply maintain your designated course line until the gap in the Old Seven Mile Bridge is on your beam. Then turn 90° towards the center of this gap. This approach stays well clear of the charted shoals that flank Moser Channel but monitor your depth as shoaling in the channel is continual.

As you approach Seven Mile Bridge (65-foot fixed vertical clearance), adjust your course to take a straight-line course through the three sets of bridge pilings. Note that currents can be strong and boat traffic is often heavy in the passage. Check VHF Channel 16 for a Sécurité if large craft are present.

Once under the bridges and south of Moser Channel marker red daybeacon "2," turn east and head towards the distant red daybeacon "2" off Boot Key (2.5 nm east). This is a Boot Key Harbor entrance channel marker. If coming from the Hawk Channel, keep north of flashing green "49," which marks East Washerwoman Shoal. This is a dangerous shoal with only 2 feet MLW so keep well to the north.

To enter Boot Key Harbor use the Boot Key Channel, which starts between Knight and Boot Keys. Enter the Boot Key Channel centered between flashing green "1" and red daybeacon "2" and favor the green daybeacons in to green daybeacon "9." The shoaling to the south is awash at low tide but depth along this route should maintain 9 feet MLW. Keep a close watch. If you see shallower depths, you've turned too soon and must head farther west around the shoals off Boot Key and then turn north. The channel narrows past green daybeacon "9" and depths increase to 10 feet MLW or more.

Continue to favor the green side close to the mangroves along the channel's north edge until centering again after the turn towards the bridge opening. Note the draw of the old Boot Key Harbor Bridge and nearby charted overhead cables have been removed. The bridge

Chapter 10: The Florida Keys

Goin' Ashore: MARATHON, FL

Marathon's waterfront boasts fine restaurants, beautiful beaches and access to world-class diving and snorkeling. It is a cruiser's dream, with extraordinary marine services, comprehensive provisioning opportunities, fine dining and a wonderful community feel. You'll meet dozens who came here to visit and simply could not leave. The marina loans out bikes to visitors who can show evidence of a working lock, and that makes provisioning a breeze. West Marine is conveniently located at 2109 Overseas Hwy. (305-289-1009), while Seamark Electronics is at 2994 Overseas Hwy. (305-743-6633), should you need them.

If you have transportation, the Dolphin Research Center at Vaca Key hosts dolphin shows, dolphin and sea lion interactions and offers educational programs, interactive experiences and guided tours at 58901 Overseas Hwy. (305-289-1121). Stop by Curry Hammock State Park on the way for a beautiful beach, as well as hiking trails, fishing opportunities and a variety of wildlife. Another worthwhile destination is Crane Point Museum & Nature Center to the north, which includes a natural history museum, marine touch tanks and a bird rescue center at 5550 Overseas Hwy. (305-743-3900). Several nature trails wind through the tropical palm forest.

ATTRACTIONS

1. Captain Hooks Marina and Dive Center
Center offers a variety of water sports and activities including scuba diving, snorkeling, fishing and kayaking at 11833 Overseas Hwy. (305-743-2444).

2. Florida Keys Aquarium Encounter
Features interactive exhibits and experiences including diving, snorkeling and feeding activities, as well as touch tanks and a variety of marine life and habitats at 11710 Overseas Hwy. (305-407-3262). Cafe on site as well.

3. Turtle Hospital
Located in a 1940s-era motel at 2396 Overseas Hwy. and committed to the rehabilitation of endangered sea turtles. Offers 90-minute guided tours and a chance to feed the permanent residents. Call for hours and fees (305-743-2552).

SERVICES

4. Fishermen's Community Hospital
3301 Overseas Hwy. (305-743-5533)

5. Marathon Post Office
82801 Overseas Hwy. (305-664-4738)

Chapter 10
America's Waterway Guide Since 1947

6. Marathon Veterinary Hospital
5001 Overseas Hwy. (305-743-7099)

7. Monroe County Public Library
81830 Overseas Hwy. (305-664-4645)

MARINAS

8. Burdines Waterfront Marina
1200 Oceanview Ave. (305-743-5317)

9. Banana Bay Resort & Marina
4590 Overseas Hwy. (305-743-3500)

10. Blackfin Resort and Marina
4650 Overseas Hwy. (305-743-2393)

11. Boot Key Harbor City Marina
800 35th St. (305-289-8877)

12. Capt. Pip's Marina & Hideaway
1480 Overseas Hwy. (305-743-4403)

13. Faro Blanco Resort & Yacht Club
1996 Overseas Hwy. (305-743-1234)

14. Marlin Bay Resort & Marina
3800 Gulfview Ave. (305-731-2207)

15. Safe Harbor Marathon Marina
1021 11th St. Ocean (305-743-6575)

16. Marathon Boat Yard
2059 Overseas Hwy. (305-735-4594)

17. Pancho's Marina & Fuel Dock
1280 Oceanview Ave. (305-743-2281)

18. Skipjack Resort & Marina
19 Sombrero Blvd. (305-600-4281)

19. Sombrero Marina Dockside
35 Sombrero Blvd. (305-743-5663)

SOUTHERN EDITION

Chapter 10 — The Florida Keys

opening is narrow. Be aware that incoming traffic has a bad visibility angle and you may not see outgoing boats on the other side (and vice versa); exercise caution.

> **CAUTION:** There is severe shoaling between red daybeacons "18" and "20" in Boot Key Harbor. The controlling depth has been reduced to 5 feet MLW and there are a few spots in the channel where depths are between 4.5 and 5.0 feet MLW. The deepest water is on the green side of the channel about 50 feet to the south of the white shallow area markers that delineate grass flats. Vessels drawing more than 5 feet should pay close attention to the tides in this part of the channel.

None of the channel markers in Boot Key Harbor are lighted and while ambient light is usually sufficient, night entry is not recommended for first-timers. Should you arrive after dark, an alternate anchorage is outside off the west end of Boot Key.

> **NOTE:** Sister Creek, slicing between Vaca and Boot Keys, has shoaled at its south entrance and is no longer a viable entry into Boot Key Harbor for cruising vessels. Local sportfishing boats that still use the shallow entry report 3-feet MLW depths in ideal conditions but use of this entrance is not recommended.

Dockage/Moorings: The 2-mile stretch west from Rachel Key on the ICW (Mile 1191) is packed with dockage options including some resorts that may make room for you in a pinch. Call ahead.

Blackfin Resort and Marina has 27 slips (20 transient) and good approach depths (8 feet MLW) and has a nice mix of liveaboards, seasonal slip holders, transients and fishing boats. Nearby Banana Bay Resort & Marina is a small marina (34 slips) with a great seasonal community of boaters. The marina is able to accommodate boats up to 56 feet (including transients). Restaurants, grocery stores and a Home Depot are all within easy walking distance.

Marlin Bay Resort & Marina combines access to resort amenities and top-notch service with gated seclusion. Resort amenities include a clubhouse lounge and game room, fitness center, heated pool and hot tub, a pool bar and concierge service. Our favorite feature is comfy Adirondack chairs for spectacular sunset viewing.

Keys Fisheries Marina accommodates vessels up to 55 feet in length and the restaurant provides fresh seafood on the days when you simply don't feel like cooking your own catch.

Also on the bay side is the well-regarded Faro Blanco Resort & Yacht Club welcomes transient vessels of all sizes in their breakwater-protected slips with world-class amenities including 24-hour security, marine concierge services, a marine store, pool and fitness center and first-class accommodations. This is a fine location for a crew change or visit with friends and family.

Several other facilities are located inside Boot Key Channel. Safe Harbor Marathon offers easy in and out, right off the channel (north shore) just before it narrows at green daybeacon "9." This is a premier marina with deep-water slips to 130 feet and a convenient fuel dock. Amenities include a fitness center, a saltwater pool, laundry facilities and a restaurant (Lazy Days South) and tiki bar. This well-maintained boat yard offers either DIY or full service.

Just past the mangrove "hedge" is Pancho's Marina and Fuel Dock. This "mom and pop"-run facility gives you a taste of the old Keys with friendly service and great prices. To the east is Burdines Waterfront Marina offering all-transient slips on floating docks and a large store selling snacks and fishing gear. The restaurant upstairs from the marina store has a great menu and is the place to watch the continuous channel traffic below.

Just inside the remnants of the Boot Key Bridge is the long entry channel to the very well-regarded Marathon Boat Yard. The 20-slip facility handles every aspect of boat repairs and power for vessels to 75 feet and are known for quality workmanship. They maintain just five transient slips; call ahead. A large West Marine is next door.

The friendly municipal Boot Key Harbor City Marina can be hard to locate. The office is next to a thatched roof hut at the end of the channel between the two main mooring fields (or just watch where the dinghies are heading). The facility only has room for 12 boats dockside but manages 211 moorings for boats up to 45 feet and 15 more for boats to 60 feet. They do not take reservations but keep a waiting list when they're full. You must appear in person to get on the list.

A large dinghy dock is adjacent to their shoreside facilities. The mooring rates include showers, a weekly pump-out service and free loaner bikes (if you bring a secure lock). Cruiser's also take advantage of the beautiful park and sports complex next the city marina. Numerous provisioning options are nearby.

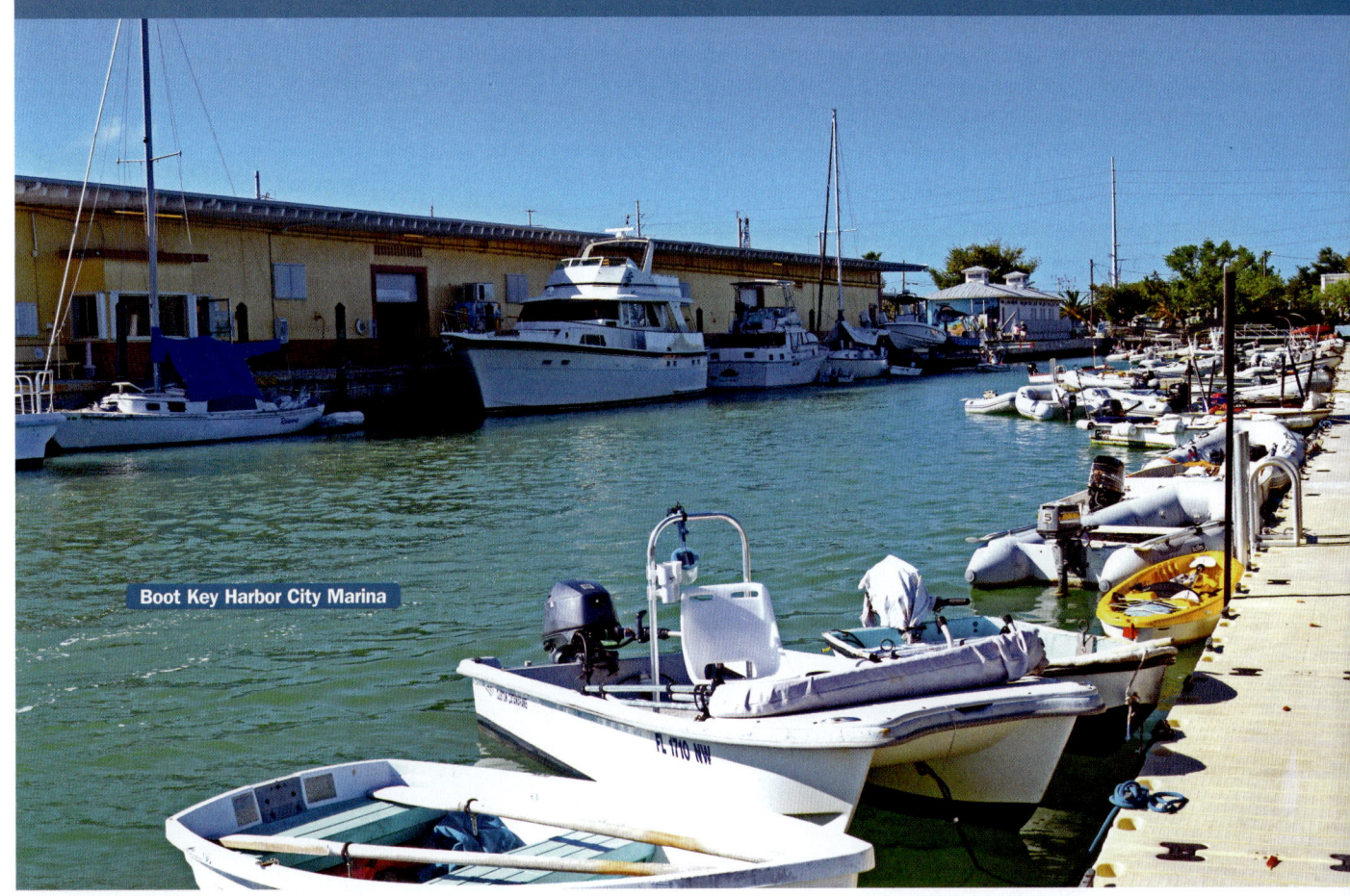

Boot Key Harbor City Marina

Additional marinas are located at the east end of the harbor. On the south shore where the harbor starts to narrow is Sombrero Marina Dockside with ample transient dockage and basic amenities. Dockside Boot Key Harbor is located between the A & B dock offering live music and amazing views (but no slips). For those with clubs on board, Florida Keys Country Club across the street is open to the public.

Farther east up the narrows on the north shore is 54-slip Skipjack Resort Suites and Marina. Cruisers give this facility high marks for the wind protection and free weekly pump-out service. The facility can accommodate vessels to 60 feet and offers full resort amenities. At the end of the protected canal adjacent to Skipjack Resort is the well-protected Yacht Haven Marina with some reserved transient space to 120 feet. This facility is within walking distance to many area services and amenities.

If approaching from Hawk Channel, Captain Hook's Marina & Dive Center–Marathon is on the ocean side of the **Vaca Cut Bridge** (13-foot fixed vertical clearance). The family-owned business offers boat rentals and all types of charters and tours including scuba diving, snorkeling, fishing, paddle sports and sightseeing.

The next set of facilities on the ocean (Hawk Channel) side are to the south in the Key Colony Area. The 14-story Bonefish Towers stands at the eastern edge of the deep channel leading to Key Colony Beach Marina, which maintains some transient slips. Family-friendly White Marlin Marina is located around a 2.5-acre private island on the same channel. It offers excellent weather protection and features a huge tiki area and a fire pit with amazing sunset views.

About 8 nm southwest along Hawk Channel from flashing red "44" is Hawks Cay Resort Marina on Duck Key. The entrance to the Duck Key canal system (known as the Duck Key "moat") is at the Key's southernmost point. Private markers guide you to the entry channel starting with a quick-flashing white and followed by a pair of daybeacons–green "1" and red "2." Once inside the Duck Key moat entrance take the right branch and enjoy deep water on your way to the marina. Observe Idle Speed/No Wake signs.

The upscale Hawks Cay Resort Marina features 85 boat slips accommodating vessels up to 110 feet in length (35-foot minimum) and offers a boat-in/boat-out service as

Chapter 10: The Florida Keys

Boot Key, FL

MARATHON (BAY SIDE)	Phone	Largest Vessel	VHF	Total Slips	Approach/Dockside Depth	Floating Docks	Gas/Diesel	Repairs/Haulout	Min/Max Amps	Pump-Out Station
1. Blackfin Resort and Marina WiFi	(305) 743-2393	40		27	8.0 / 10.0				30	P
2. Banana Bay Resort & Marina	(305) 432-1122	56	16	34	5.0 / 7.0				30 / 50	P
3. Marlin Bay Resort & Marina WiFi	(305) 731-2207	72	16	73	6.0 / 6.0				30 / 50	P
4. Keys Fisheries Marina	(305) 743-4985	38			/		GD			
5. Faro Blanco Marina WiFi	(305) 434-9047	185	16	74	7.0 / 8.0		GD		30 / 100	P
6. Safe Harbor Marathon WiFi MM 1193.0	(305) 743-6575	125	16	111	9.0 / 11.0	F	GD	RH	30 / 100	
MARATHON (INNER HARBOR)										
7. Pancho's Marina and Fuel Dock WiFi MM 1193.0	(305) 743-2281	90	16	20	8.0 / 6.5		GD		30 / 50	P
8. Burdines Waterfront Marina MM 1193.0	(305) 743-5317	120	16	21	10.0 / 7.0	F	GD		30 / 50	
9. Marathon Boat Yard WiFi MM 1193.0	(305) 735-4594	75			8.0 / 20.0			RH	30 / 50	
10. Boot Key Harbor City Marina WiFi MM 1193.0	(305) 289-8877	60	16	12	10.0 / 20.0	F			30 / 50	P
11. Sombrero Marina Dockside WiFi MM 1193.0	(305) 743-5663	85		57	7.0 / 9.0				20 / 50	P
12. Skipjack Resort Suites and Marina WiFi MM 1192.0	(305) 289-7662	65	16	54	10.0 / 15.0				30 / 50	P
13. Yacht Haven Marina	(305) 393-5073	120		42	/				30 / 100	P

WiFi Wireless Internet Access
Visit www.waterwayguide.com for current rates, fuel prices, website addresses and other up-to-the-minute information.
(Information in the table is provided by the facilities.)

Scan here for more details:

Source: Aqua Map and NOAA data

America's Waterway Guide Since 1947 — Chapter 10

Boot Key Harbor

Boot Key Harbor City Marina is a modest community of liveaboards, ranging from year-round residents to transient loopers to cruisers from all over the world. With the City Park located just next door, you can enjoy bocce ball, tennis, basketball, or one of the several events hosted there throughout the year...and walk back to your boat when you're done. We hope to welcome you soon!

Boot Key Harbor City Marina
(305) 289-8877
VHF Channel 16 for Dock or Mooring Assignment
www.cityofmarathonmarina.com

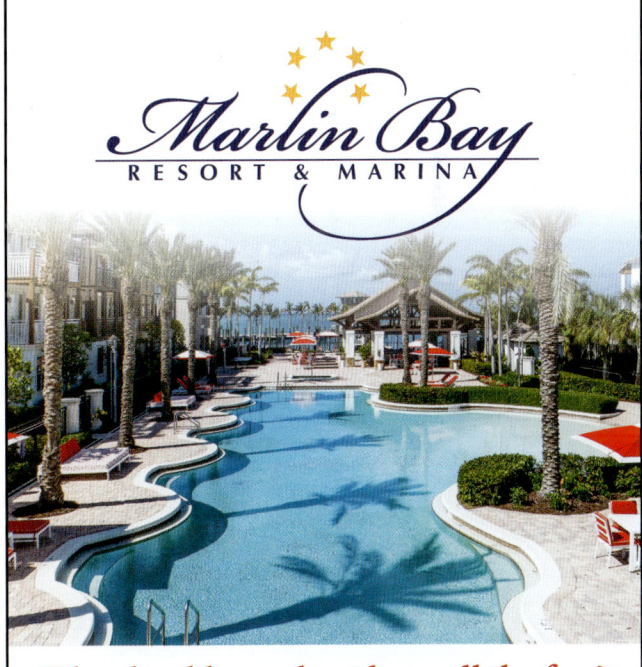

Why should your boat have all the fun?

MODERN MARINA • VACATION RENTALS • HEATED POOL • HOT TUB
FITNESS CENTER • POOLSIDE BAR • CLUBHOUSE • BOAT LIFTS

Marathon, FL
305.731.2207 // marlinbay.com

SOUTHERN EDITION

Chapter 10: The Florida Keys

Boot Key Area, FL

MARATHON AREA (OCEAN SIDE)		Largest Vessel	VHF	Total Slips	Approach/ Dockside Depth	Floating Docks	Gas/ Diesel	Repairs/ Haulout	Min/Max Amps	Pump-Out Station
1. Key Colony Beach Marina WiFi MM 1187.0	(305) 289-1310	120	16	35	12.0 / 8.0		GD		30 / 100	P
2. White Marlin Marina-FL WiFi 53-54 MM	(305) 509-2661	82		27	6.5 / 5.2				30 / 50	P

WiFi Wireless Internet Access

Visit www.waterwayguide.com for current rates, fuel prices, website addresses and other up-to-the-minute information. (Information in the table is provided by the facilities.)

Scan here for more details:

Source: Aqua Map and NOAA data

America's Waterway Guide Since 1947 — Chapter 10

Boot Key Area, FL

MARATHON AREA (OCEAN SIDE)		Largest Vessel	VHF	Total Slips	Approach/ Dockside Depth	Floating Docks	Gas/ Diesel	Repairs/ Haulout	Min/Max Amps	Pump-Out Station
1. Hawks Cay Resort Marina WiFi 3.0 mi. S of MM 1180.0	(888) 974-8469	110	16	85	5.0 / 5.0				30 / 50	P

WiFi Wireless Internet Access
Visit www.waterwayguide.com for current rates, fuel prices, website addresses and other up-to-the-minute information.
(Information in the table is provided by the facilities.)

Scan here for more details:

well as dockage for resort guests and liveaboard boaters. All overnight guests at the marina have access to its restaurants and attractions with a free shuttle service between the marina and the resort.

Anchorage: On the ICW (inside) route, tiny Rachel Key at Mile 1191 offers some protection. Shoal-draft boats can snug in close to shore. Pick the side with best wind protection. There is good holding in sand and 6 to 7 feet MLW. The area just east of Pretty Joe Rock offers the best protection. Holding is only fair in sand and grass from here west along the bay side of the Vaca Key shoreline.

Fanny Keys to the north of Faro Blanco Resort & Yacht Club is an open anchorage with good protection from east winds and good holding. Expect a bit of current.

Finding a place to anchor inside Boot Key Harbor can be a challenge from Thanksgiving through March. This is made more difficult by Florida law that dictates you must stay 100 feet from a designated mooring field. Because of this, most cruisers anchor outside Boot Key. The bottom is sandy and tidal current is significant but you will find excellent holding in sand and grass. The downside is the fair amount of traffic in and out of Boot Key so be prepared for wakes. Shoal-draft vessels can work closer into the charted 5-foot MLW area and avoid some of that. This anchorage is comfortable in northeast through southeast winds, but you will want to move around to the north side of Vaca Key for strong winds out of the south or southwest.

When the mooring field is full, Sisters Creek is a better anchoring alternative than the anchorages in the western or eastern ends of the harbor. The holding is good as is the protection from wind in all directions. The recommended way to anchor here is to drop an anchor about 100 feet from the mangroves on the west side of the

SOUTHERN EDITION

Dive into *relaxation*

Chart a course for waypoint N24° 45' 48' W80° 54' 40' and refuel, reload and relax in an island paradise known for some of the best fishing and diving the world has to offer. Laid back luxury is a way of life at Hawks Cay Marina. Drop your anchor, tie up and indulge in the incomparable amenities and culinary excellence of our world-class resort while docked within reach of the only living coral reef in the continental U.S. Hawks Cay Marina features 85 boat slips, accommodation for vessels up to 110 feet in length, one spectacular resort, five pools, the Key's only saltwater lagoon, award-winning restaurants and a full-service spa.

FIND WHAT *lures you*

HAWKSCAY.COM | (888) 947-8469

Mention the Waterway Guide and
SAVE 10% ON YOUR DOCKAGE!

LIFESTYLE
Preferred
HOTELS & RESORTS

America's Waterway Guide Since 1947   **Chapter 10**

creek and back into the mangroves med-mooring style. Once the stern is secured to the mangroves, tighten the anchor rode to hold the bow steady. During the peak of the season there can be 20 or more boats tied up this way along the length of the creek.

> NOTE: Avoid anchoring near the array of 100,000-watt radio antennas on the east side of the creek, which can interfere with your electronics.

Boot Key Harbor City Marina will provide pump-out services for a nominal fee either at their dock or at your anchored boat in Boot Key Harbor. You can tie up at the marina (for a fee) for full access to their facilities. (Hint: If you are staying for awhile ask about the weekly rates, which are lower.)

ICW (INSIDE) ROUTE TO KEY WEST

Side Trip: Bahia Honda

Two of the nicest beaches in the Keys are located at Bahia Honda State Park. The palm-rimmed Calusa Beach near the concession stand is sheltered and roped off for swimming and snorkeling. There are also three nature trails. The park concession stand sells snacks and ice. There are also tours and scuba charters out of the park. The slowly disintegrating Old Bahia Honda Bridge located at the island's western end is a national historic monument and provides a great view of the park and the Keys. The park can be crowded with "day trippers" so plan accordingly.

NAVIGATION: Use NOAA Charts 11445, 11448, 1451 and 11453. If coming from the ICW, the channel into Florida Bay is deep and wide from the gap in **Old Seven Mile Bridge** about 1 mile west of Pigeon Key. Once clear of the gap set a course of 310° magnetic for the 1.2-nm run to red daybeacon "24." After 0.7 nm adjust course to 253° magnetic on a course to take flashing green "25" to port. Continue on this heading to Bahia Honda Key keeping well off the shallows surrounding the north shore of the island. Once the Bahia Honda Light (flashing white) is on the beam adjust to a course of 235° magnetic towards the high-span of the **Bahia Honda Bridges** (20-foot fixed vertical clearance).

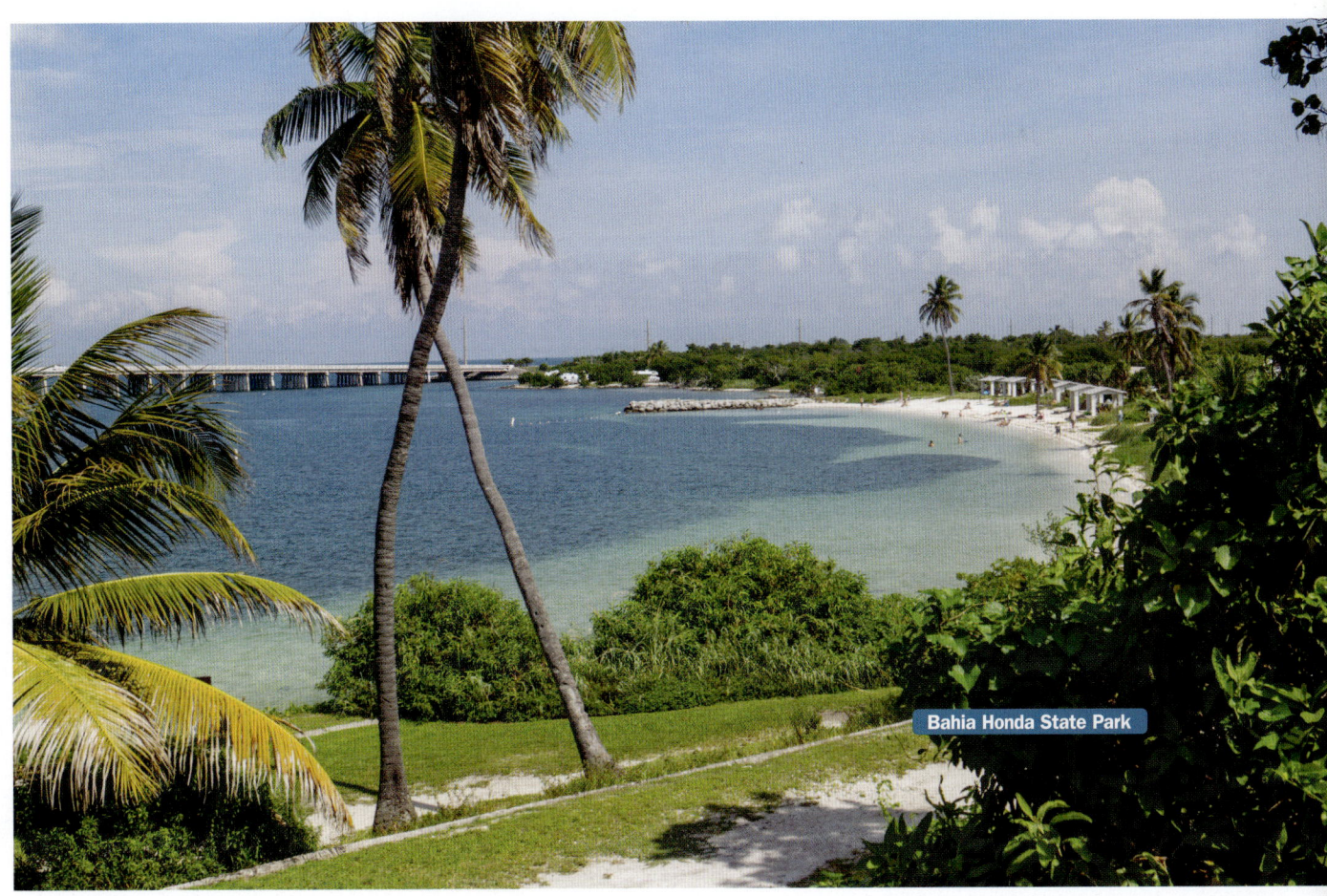

Bahia Honda State Park

SOUTHERN EDITION   409

Chapter 10 — The Florida Keys

Lower Keys, FL

BAHIA HONDA KEY AREA		Largest Vessel	VHF	Total Slips	Approach/Dockside Depth	Floating Docks	Gas/Diesel	Repairs/Haulout	Min/Max Amps	Pump-Out Station
1. Bahia Honda State Park & Marina WiFi MM 1205.0	(305) 872-3210	50	16	19	3.5 / 4.5				30	P

WiFi Wireless Internet Access
Visit www.waterwayguide.com for current rates, fuel prices, website addresses and other up-to-the-minute information. (Information in the table is provided by the facilities.)

Scan here for more details:

NOTE: Sailboats that cannot negotiate the 20-foot fixed bridge will need to go out at Moser Channel and proceed via the Hawk Channel Route. A span of the old bridge has been removed so that sailboats can pass through into the cove between the old bridge and the newer Bahia Honda Bridges (20-foot fixed vertical clearance).

To rejoin the ICW route from the Bahia Honda Bridges via Big Spanish Channel on to Florida Bay head due north for flashing red "32," keeping west of the shoal extending south from Little Pine Key. Here the course picks up the route described below. Remember you are returning to Florida Bay so keep red navigational aids to starboard.

Dockage: Transients can find dockage in the well-protected boat basin at Bahia Honda State Park & Marina. Expect 8 to 10 feet MLW dockside but the entrance is shallow (as low as 3.5 feet MLW) with a tidal range of a little over 1 foot. This is a campground that has boat slips boats, not a resort, although there is a free holding tank pump-out. Bath facilities are shared with the park campground and are clean and well maintained. This is a popular spot so call ahead.

Anchorage: The cove between the old and new bridges west of the park at Bahia Honda Key is a popular anchorage. Be warned that the holding is only fair in sand and grass and the currents are strong. (If you choose to swim off the boat, hang a grab-line off the back just in case you get caught in the current.) It is wise to check your position after a turning tide to avoid a closer look at one bridge or the other. This is a good place to let out extra scope. Once securely anchored you can go ashore to the park (short-term dinghy tie-ups allowed). If going ashore, bring shoes or aqua socks to hike the nature trails and visit the two sandy beaches. You can tie up to the marina wall near the office (for a fee) during park hours. You can bring your trash for disposal in readily available trash cans.

Another popular anchorage for both day boats and overnight anchoring is north of Bahia Honda Key. Anchor in 6 to 8 feet MLW with good protection from south and southeast winds. The bottom is primarily coral, covered with a shallow layer of sand/mud/grasses. Plan to leave the area in heavy northerly blows. It's a short dinghy ride to the park.

Moser Channel to Northwest Channel– Mile 1196 to Mile 1242

> **CAUTION:** Once past the Seven Mile Bridge there are no air-draft restrictions all the way to Key West. However, the controlling depth for the Big Spanish Channel on this route has been reduced to 4.5 feet MLW in recent years. This is strictly shoal-draft boat territory.

NAVIGATION: Use NOAA Charts 11448 and 11442. Can also use NOAA Charts 11445, 11451 and 11453. Keep all red markers to starboard on this route. Starting at the gap in the Old Seven Mile Bridge set a course of 310° magnetic for the 1.2-nm run to red daybeacon "24" where you rejoin the ICW along its run from Bethel Bank. From red daybeacon "24" adjust course to 259° magnetic for the 2 nm to red daybeacon "26." Keeping south of red daybeacon "26" adjust course to 271° magnetic and continue for 4 nm to the southern entrance to Big Spanish Channel. On this leg pass just north of flashing green "27" then split green daybeacon "29" and red daybeacon "30." Keep well south of flashing red "32," which marks dangerous shoals (2 feet MLW) to the north.

The well-marked Big Spanish Channel stretches to the northwest from Mile 1205. Initially the channel is wide and deep (controlling depth 7 feet MLW). Once clear of flashing red "32" proceed 2 nm on a course of 303° magnetic towards red daybeacon "34" then adjust to 316° magnetic towards red daybeacon "36." Once clear of red daybeacon "36" proceed for 2 nm at a course of 326° magnetic towards red daybeacon "38" near Mile 1210. From here the course is 297° magnetic for the 1 nm to red daybeacon "40."

Beyond red daybeacon "40" the Big Spanish Channel narrows and shallows dramatically. Set a course of 305° magnetic for the 1.7 nm from red daybeacon "40" to red daybeacon "42." Continue with caution on this heading for the 0.8 nm onwards to green daybeacon "43." Over this segment expect depths as low as 4.5 feet MLW and shoals just off the designated route as shallow as 3 feet MLW. It is advised that you slow down through this stretch and closely monitor depths. The tidal range is up to 4 feet here; if depths appear too shallow, wait for a high tide.

Passing green daybeacon "43" the winding but well-marked channel narrows further but the controlling depth returns to 7 feet MLW. Continue to follow the closely packed markers as placed through this tight section to green daybeacon "53." (Markers are occasionally repositioned here to reflect the changing alignment of the natural channel.) Once past green daybeacon "53" the channel begins to widen again through to flashing green "57." The course is roughly 340° magnetic for this 2.3-nm leg but you should follow the deep, natural channel into the open Florida Bay.

From here to the Northwest Channel leading into Key West the designated ICW route traverses the open expanse of Florida Bay, paralleling the Lower Keys to the south. You can expect some chop in any winds lacking a southerly component. The course is 251° magnetic for this 28-nm run but it's easier to use the near straight-line alignment of the Keys as a reference. Initially the controlling depth is 8 feet MLW but deepens to 20 MLW beyond Mile 1222.

Note beyond Cudjoe Channel the route picks up on NOAA Chart 11442, which covers to flashing green bell buoy "1" marking the Northwest Channel to Key West (N 24° 38.880'/W 081° 53.960'). There is no reason to stray from your course as you must reach bell buoy "1" before turning south towards Key West. The semi-submerged east jetty and the adjacent shallow flats block any attempts to turn early. The Calda Channel and various other shortcuts are not recommended for use by cruising vessels.

Anchorage: About 8 miles west from green daybeacon "57" the Cudjoe Channel has a controlling depth of 7 feet MLW. This branching channel cuts back to the southeast through the flats of the National Key Deer Refuge. There are some nice options for anchoring here. One favorite is southwest of Crane Key; another is closer to Raccoon Key. Choose a spot that gives the best

Chapter 10 — The Florida Keys

protection. Despite being open this can be a beautiful, quiet anchorage in the right conditions. You are off the beaten track but close enough to it to get underway again with no trouble. The fishing in the deeper channel is great.

Another popular spot is Tarpon Belly Keys. Anchor right up next to the western side of the island in charted tongue of water with at least 8-foot MLW depths. There is good holding and fair protection. There aren't many other anchorage options along the route onward to Key West. Most channels are very shallow (4 to 4.5 feet MLW) and tucked between low-lying mangrove islands.

Northwest Channel to Key West–ICW Mile 1242 to Mile 1245

NAVIGATION: Use NOAA Chart 11441. Note that shoaling on the Frankfort Bank leaves no viable route directly leading from the Northwest Channel into Man of War Harbor. The recommended route is to follow the Northwest Channel south of Tank Island and round into the Main Ship Channel to enter Key West Harbor. The channel provides the only viable entry from the north that leads to Key West Harbor. Do not attempt any shortcuts as there are many submerged hazards here. A shorter but unmarked route may be possible via the shallow channel between Tank and Wisteria Islands but this route is not recommended.

The entry to the Northwest Channel can be quite sloppy in certain conditions. Avoid entry in strong winds in the northwest quadrant if possible. Many channel markers are not lighted and nighttime navigation of this channel is not recommended. To avoid the jetties you must pass green bell buoy "1" on entry or leaving. This is not a place to attempt shortcuts.

Northwest Channel begins at flashing green bell buoy "1." From this point steer a course for red nun buoy "2" and, leaving it to starboard, adjust to a course to split quick-flashing green "3" to port and red nun "4" to starboard. From this pair a course of approximately 132° magnetic should keep you centered to flashing red "10." This approach should keep you safely inside the two submerged (east and west) jetties. (Note that the east jetty is awash at low tide.)

From flashing red "10" a course of approximately 147° magnetic should maintain channel alignment for the 5 nm to Main Ship Channel marker flashing green buoy "15." Here the route turns northward up the Main Ship Channel and into the harbor.

To reach Key West's main yacht harbor in Key West Bight turn east at flashing red buoy "24" towards quick-flashing red "4" at the end of the seawall. Quick-flashing red "4" marks the Key West Bight harbor entrance.

■ HAWK CHANNEL (OUTSIDE) ROUTE TO STOCK ISLAND

Moser Channel to Stock Island

NAVIGATION: Use NOAA Chart 11445. Leaving Marathon you will parallel the Seven Mile Bridge as you head southwest passing the 142-foot Sombrero Key Light to port. Leaving from the Boot Key Channel entrance adjust course to 247° magnetic for 9.5 nm passing south of the Molasses Keys and the nearby shoals. Once directly abeam of the west tip of Bahia Honda Key parallel the Keys at 261° magnetic for 5-nm run to Cook Island at Mile 1212. Tighten the course slightly here to 265° magnetic for the 10-nm run to the Ninefoot Shoal Light (18-foot, flashing white 2.5 sec) at Mile 1225. The shoal is actually charted at 10 feet MLW and is not a hazard for most cruising vessels.

Hawk Channel narrows past the marked lighted Ninefoot Shoal (Mile 1224.5) and passes safely north of West Washerwoman Shoal (Mile 1227). For the 10-nm run from Ninefoot Shoal to the Boca Chica Channel (Mile 1236) the heading changes slightly to 263° magnetic passing the western end of Sugarloaf, the Saddlebunch Keys and the Boca Chica Key air base. On Boca Chica Key the hangers, control tower and radar dome of the Naval Air Station Key West make good landmarks.

Dockage: Transients can find dockage in the well-protected boat basin at Bahia Honda State Park & Marina. Expect 8 to 10 feet MLW dockside but the entrance is shallow (as low as 3.5 feet MLW) with a tidal range of a little over 1 foot. This is a campground that has boat slips boats, not a resort, although there is a free holding tank pump-out. Bath facilities are shared with the park campground and are clean and well maintained. This is a popular spot so call ahead.

> Bahia Honda State Park & Marina is covered in more detail in the "ICW (Inside) Route to Key West" section.

Anchorage: To reach the Molasses Keys anchorage, stay alongside the Seven Mile Bridge until you reach deeper water (7 feet MLW) just north of the larger Molasses Key. From here you can dinghy to the sand flats on the north side of that smaller island. Watch the current in the small channels....It rips.

The cove between the old and new bridges west of the park at Bahia Honda Key is a popular anchorage. Be warned that the holding is only fair in sand and grass and the currents are strong. (If you choose to swim off the boat, hang a grab-line off the back just in case you get caught in the current.) It is wise to check your position after a turning tide to avoid a closer look at one bridge or the other. This is a good place to let out extra scope. Once securely anchored you can go ashore to the park (short-term dinghy tie-ups allowed). If going ashore, bring shoes or aqua socks to hike the nature trails and visit the two sandy beaches. You can tie up to the marina wall near the office (for a fee) during park hours. You can bring your trash for disposal in readily available trash cans.

West of Bahia Honda Key at flashing red "50" lies the Newfound Harbor Channel. The relatively well-marked and well-protected channel leads to what has become an increasingly popular anchorage area. There are several options here in 8 to 16 feet MLW but the approach is quite shallow, particularly in strong north winds when depths can be reduced by over 1 foot. In normal conditions you should have 7 to 8 feet MLW on approach.

> NOTE: About 4.5 miles due north of Newfound Harbor lies the superb snorkeling sites of Looe Key National Marine Sanctuary, which is an excellent snorkeling site.

Shoal-draft boats can anchor in 5- to 6-foot MLW depths just east of the main channel or in 4-foot MLW depths near the channel entrance. Picnic Island in Newfound Harbor is a popular anchorage. Follow the channel for 5.2 feet MLW (at the shallowest spot). Once into the anchorage the depth deepens to 7 to 8 feet MLW. There is better weather protection from wave action than it appears due to the dampening action of the nearby shoals. The island is a local favorite for pet owners; it's like a dog park where pets can run free.

When Picnic Island is too busy, the large area to the northwest provides good protection from winds with a northerly component. Holding in the northwest corner of Newfound Harbor is excellent even though it provides only modest wind protection. Head farther north as room permits during strong northerlies. It is possible to dinghy from here to a few restaurants and dive shops.

On entry to Newfound Harbor at Big Pine Key, give flashing red "2" a wide berth to starboard to avoid shoaling that extends about 100 yards south and west of this marker but don't go too far west as the channel has shoaled there as well.

About 2 nm to the west Niles Channel offers a reasonably well-protected anchorage between Ramrod Key and Summerland Key. Anchor between red daybeacons "4" and "6" in 7 to 10 feet MLW. Be careful to avoid a couple of 2 and 3-foot MLW shoals here. The area is also not well protected from southerlies.

Farther west before Loggerhead Keys and due north of flashing red "50A" a marked shoal-draft channel with the entrance by green daybeacon "1" leads to sheltered although relatively shallow Kemp Channel between Cudjoe and Summerland Keys. This channel only carries 4 to 5 feet MLW. Be sure to monitor your depth sounder.

Saddlebunch Harbor located just east of Boca Chica Key has fair holding in 7 to 8 feet MLW with a grassy and mud bottom. It offers good protection from the east but only limited protection from the south. In east winds snug-in close to shore just north of daybeacon red "8." The current is strong here but the depth holds quite close to land. This is usually a quiet spot and offers easy in and out. Dinghy to the restaurant at Geiger Key Marina.

Chapter 10: The Florida Keys

■ STOCK ISLAND & KEY WEST

Stock Island

NAVIGATION: Use NOAA Charts 11441, 11442 and 11446. Immediately west of Boca Chica Channel (located about 2 miles past flashing red "56") is the charted channel leading to the Stock Island service facilities. Several boat builders, boat storage and fishing docks are here. Provisioning from this location, however, requires ground transportation. Check with marinas as some offer a shuttle service into Key West. Public transit stops are also nearby.

> ⚠️ **CAUTION:** An overhead power cable with an authorized vertical clearance of 60 feet restricts access to the basins for both Boca Chica and the Stock Island anchorage.

Dockage: Full-service Stock Island Yacht Club and Marina, which has transient slips to 110 feet, is in a protected basin off Boca Chica Channel (before the overhead power cable). First-rate amenities include a waterfront pool, dockside restaurant and fitness center. There is also a private beach. Call ahead for slip availability.

The unnamed channel into Oceans Edge Key West Resort & Marina is east of the Stock Island Channel just after green daybeacon "5." The resort is located on 20 acres of palm trees with multiple swimming pools, luxurious guest rooms and slips for boats up to 140 feet. The on-site restaurant serves breakfast, lunch and dinner. Note that the entry channel has an S-shaped curve where it leaves the Stock Island Channel and there are rocks 50 feet off the dock so study your charts.

The Perry Hotel and Marina at the head of the Stock Island Channel can accommodate vessels up to 450 feet. With 288 slips and state-of-the-art floating docks, every type of boat can be accommodated. They offer resort-style amenities and a boutique hotel and several restaurants

Stock Island, FL

STOCK ISLAND		Largest Vessel	VHF	Total Slips	Approach/ Dockside Depth	Floating Docks	Gas/ Diesel	Repairs/ Haulout	Min/Max Amps	Pump-Out Station
1. Stock Island Yacht Club and Marina WiFi	(305) 292-3121	110	16	100	8.0 / 10.0	F	GD	R	30 / 100	P
2. Oceans Edge Key West Resort & Marina WiFi MM 1237.0	(786) 862-6315	140	16	125	20.0 / 12.0		GD		30 / 50	P
3. The Perry Hotel and Marina WiFi	(239) 294-0229	450	10	288	15.0 / 20.0	F	GD		30 / 200+	P

WiFi Wireless Internet Access
Visit www.waterwayguide.com for current rates, fuel prices, website addresses and other up-to-the-minute information.
(Information in the table is provided by the facilities.)

Scan here for more details:

Source: Aqua Map and NOAA data

are on site. The marina also offers shuttle service to downtown Key West. There is a West Marine nearby at 5790 2nd Ave. (305-294-2025).

Anchorage: Anchor among the Boca Chica Spoil Islands for good protection from nearly any direction. Stay out of the channels to the east and north. You can run a line to the mangroves if needed to manage swinging. Note: We have received reports that there is little to no room here due to semi-derelict part- or full-time liveaboards. Seek local knowledge.

Stock Island to Key West

NAVIGATION: Use NOAA Charts 11441, 11442 and 11447. Following the Hawk Channel westward from Stock Island the towers and radar domes of Key West International Airport appear to starboard along with many waterfront hotels and condominiums. Hawk Channel ends at its intersection with Key West's Main Ship Channel.

The channel turns due west off Stock Island and runs 4.7 nm to flashing red buoy "12" (at Mile 1241.7) marking a corner of the Key West's Main Ship Channel. Stay offshore of the quick-flashing green range marker off Whitehead Spit (the southwesterly tip of Key West at Mile 1241) and turn north into the Main Ship Channel at flashing red "12." Keeping red markers to starboard as you enter the well-marked channel.

Continue to follow the Main Ship Channel northwards toward the harbor. Favor the east side of the channel (closer to the docked cruise ships) and keep well off Tank Island (locally known as Sunset Key) and Wisteria Island from flashing green buoy "23" to flashing green "29." There are 1-foot MLW shoals off Wisteria Island and throughout Man of War Harbor. If there is commercial traffic you can follow the markers outside the channel's eastern edge as there is plenty of depth. Pass the cruise ship docks with caution and also note that there is ferry traffic coming out of Margaritaville Harbor at all hours.

The channel has good width and depth but the current and wind can be significant factors here along with the vessel traffic. The abundance of buoys in the area can confuse a first-time visitor, particularly at night. We strongly recommend that first-timers do not attempt a night entry. Day or night, it's prudent to have a "Plan B" in case of traffic conflicts or possible breakdowns in this area.

> *CAUTION:* It is important to monitor VHF Channel 16 in the Main Ship Channel. Larger vessels will issue a Sécurité call before they enter the channel. This is particularly important when the massive cruise ships are on the move (usually in the morning and early evening).

An alternate entry to the Main Ship Channel past the Stock Island Channel is well-marked but rarely used by recreational craft. The channel is marked by lighted red-and-white whistle buoy "KW" located at the reef-line 5 nm south of Key West. It initially follows a range (flashing green over quick-flashing green) aligned with the prominent (and lighted) red-and-white water tank on the western end of the island. The channel takes an abrupt dogleg to the northwest at quick-flashing red "8" and then another dogleg (about 1 nm farther) to the north between quick-flashing green "9" and quick-flashing red "12," which serves at as the entry point for boats southbound on Hawk Channel.

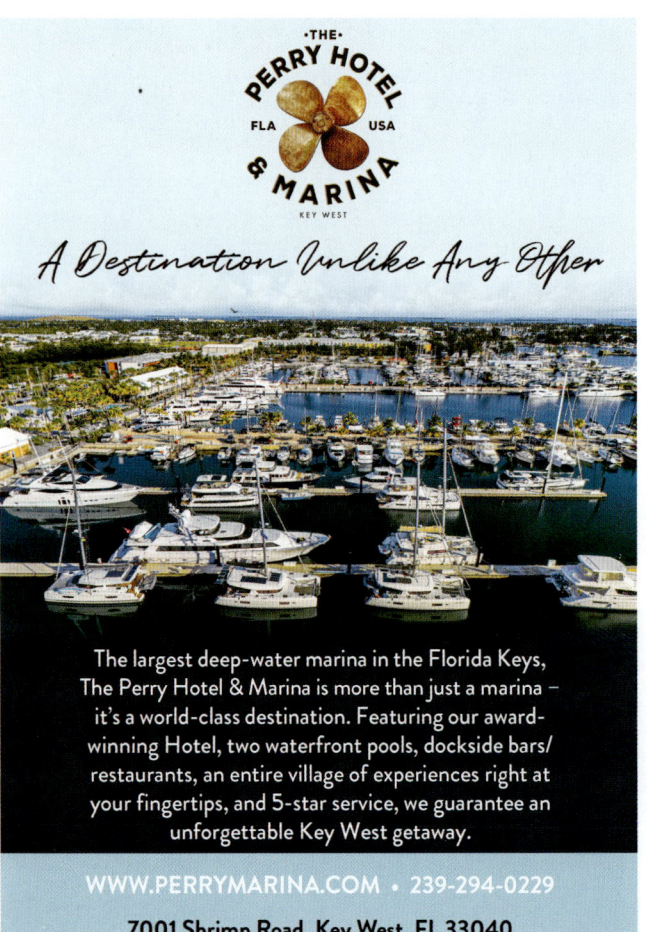

The largest deep-water marina in the Florida Keys, The Perry Hotel & Marina is more than just a marina – it's a world-class destination. Featuring our award-winning Hotel, two waterfront pools, dockside bars/restaurants, an entire village of experiences right at your fingertips, and 5-star service, we guarantee an unforgettable Key West getaway.

WWW.PERRYMARINA.COM • 239-294-0229
7001 Shrimp Road, Key West, FL 33040

America's Waterway Guide Since 1947 — Chapter 10

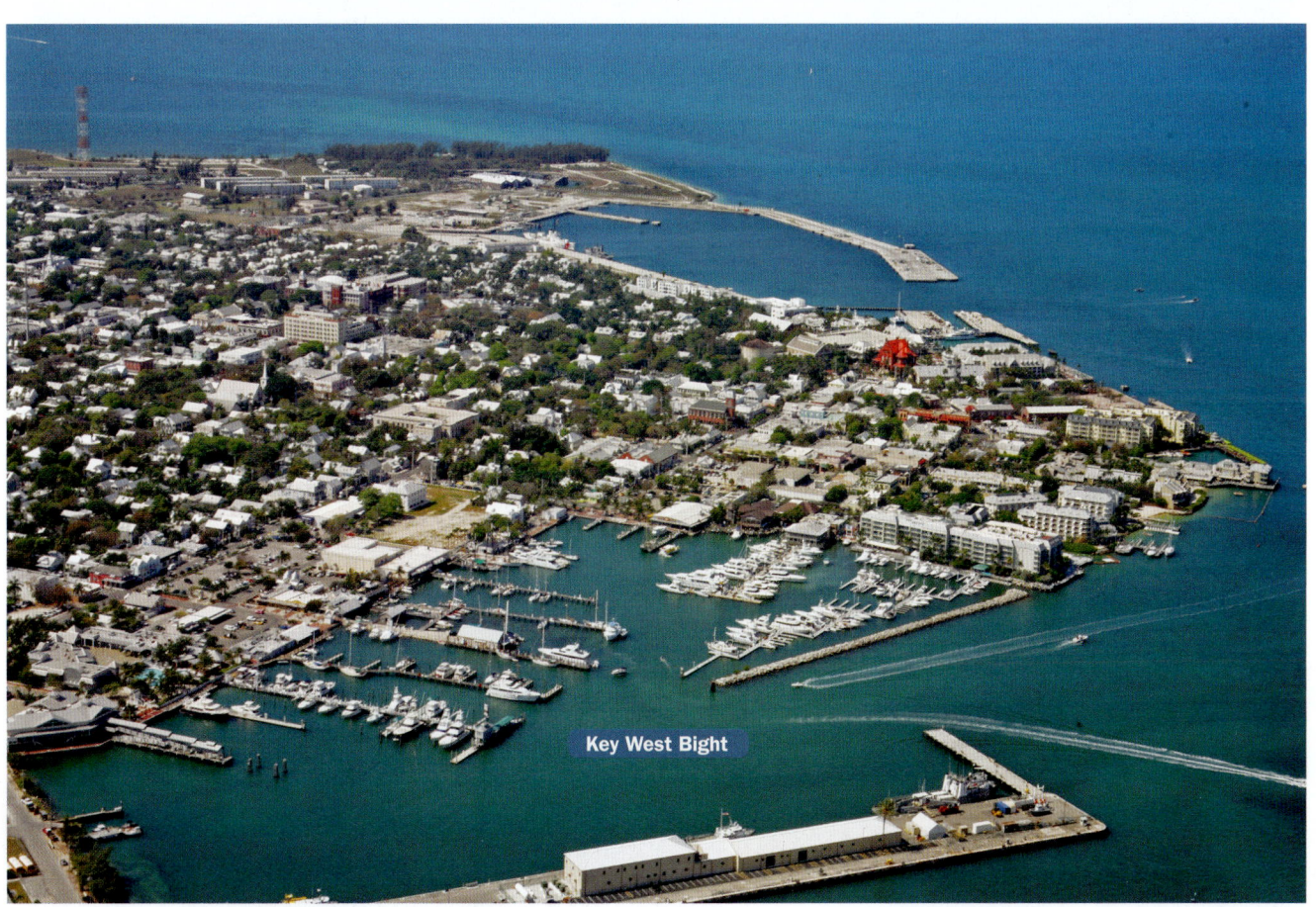

Key West Bight

Side Trip: Sand Key Moorings

If you decide to explore the wonders of the underwater world, you can make the 6-mile trip southwest from Key West to the Sand Key Moorings. This is a great snorkeling site, especially in calm conditions. The nearby Marine Sanctuary sites also offer excellent snorkeling. Exercise caution when transiting this area. Sand Key Light has been extinguished because it was structurally unsound and a temporary light has been established in its place.

Anchorage/Moorings: There are 21 mooring balls for visitors to tie to next to this shallow reef. If a mooring buoy is not available at Sand Key Moorings and you are outside a no-anchor zone, you may anchor in sand but it is a long swim to the reef. It is best to wait for a mooring ball.

Key West

Key West is the sunny, end-of-the-line destination for tourists and travelers of all descriptions. Many are drawn down U.S. 1 and thousands more arrive by cruise ship, all landing at the Key West waterfront. However they get there, visitors quickly confirm to the laid-back local style where casual sailing duds substitute for more formal attire almost anywhere on this island.

Key West is difficult to categorize. It is a unique and irresistible magnet to yachtsmen, long-distance cruisers and sportfishers. The ready availability of amenities and attractions makes the city a great stop for recreation, repairs and provisioning.

NAVIGATION: Use NOAA Charts 11441, 11442 and 11447. Following the Hawk Channel westward from Stock Island the towers and radar domes of Key West International Airport appear to starboard along with many waterfront hotels and condominiums. Hawk Channel ends at its intersection with Key West's Main Ship Channel.

The channel turns due west off Stock Island and runs 4.7 nm to flashing red buoy "12" (at Mile 1241.7) marking a corner of the Key West's Main Ship Channel. Stay offshore of the quick-flashing green range marker off Whitehead Spit (the southwesterly tip of Key West at Mile 1241) and turn north into the Main Ship Channel at flashing red "12." Keeping red markers to starboard as you enter the well-marked channel.

SOUTHERN EDITION

Chapter 10 — The Florida Keys

Goin' Ashore
KEY WEST, FL

Key West's Old Town is the city's main attraction. Beyond the boutiques, wonderful eateries, seasoned drinking holes and countless T-shirt shops, this is a place to find a sitting spot and just watch as the throngs pass by. Be sure to get a few blocks off Duval St. and have a look at the city's beautifully preserved and restored buildings. Pick up a free Key West map before you start out, available at most marinas and many shops. The free "Duval Loop" bus is a great way to get around the downtown. Walk one way and take the bus back. Be sure to stop for a photo-op at the Southernmost Point of the continental U.S. (90 miles north of Cuba).

There is a West Marine at 951 Caroline St. (305-296-0953) and the well-stocked Key West Marine Hardware at 818 Caroline St. (305-294-3425).

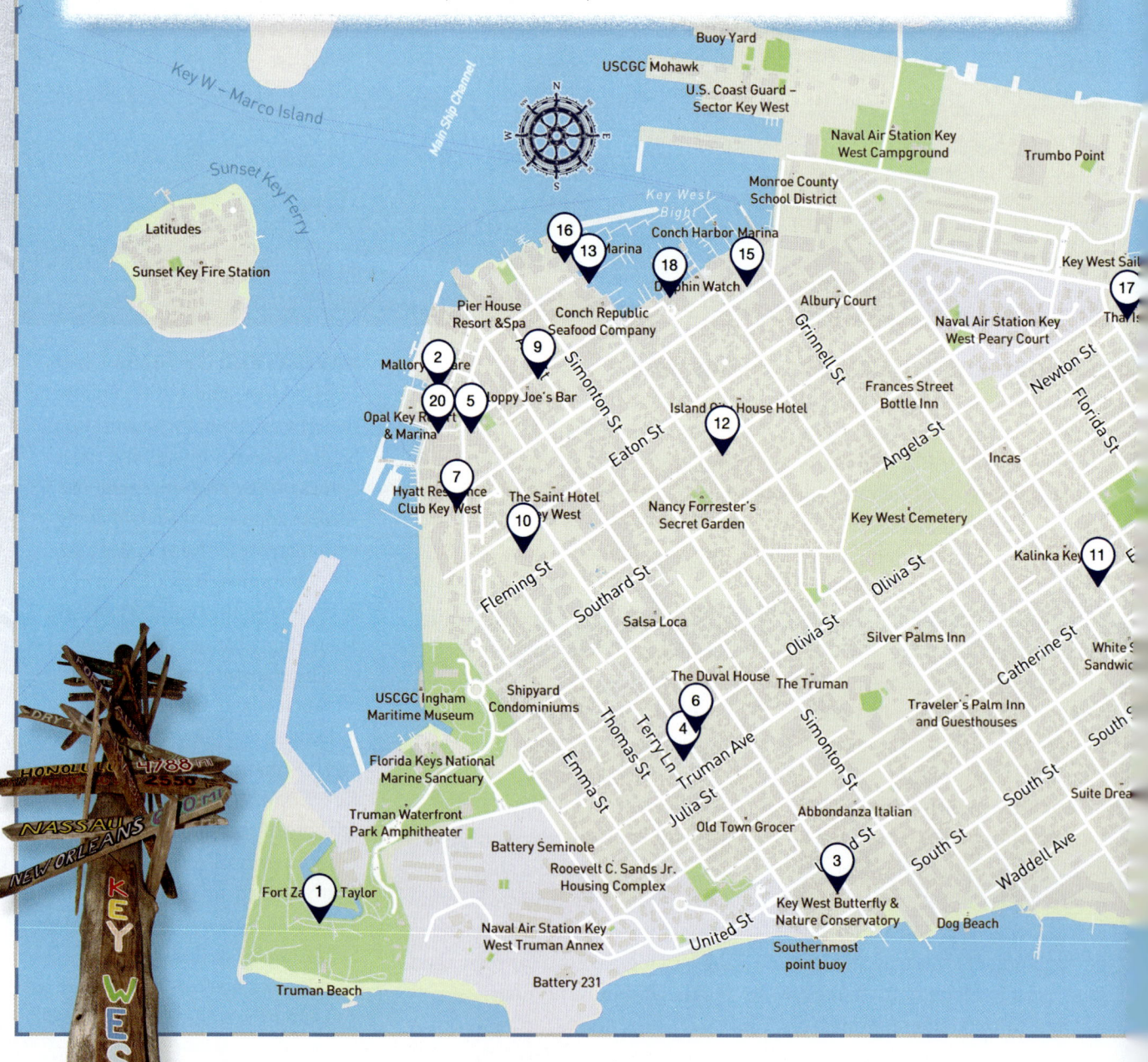

America's Waterway Guide Since 1947 — Chapter 10

ATTRACTIONS

1. Fort Zachary Taylor State Park
Located on the west side of the island with a beautiful beach, a historic fort and nature trails. Predates Civil War and is a National Historic Monument housing the largest cache of Civil War armament in the world. Beyond historical importance, this is the southernmost state park in the continental United States (601 Howard England Way, 305-292-6713).

2. Key West Aquarium
Interactive conservation talks and animal feedings are offered at 1 Whitehead St., home to alligators, jellyfish, sharks, turtles and stingrays (305-296-2051).

3. Key West Butterfly & Nature Conservatory
Glass-enclosed, plant-filled habitat for interactive walks among species of butterflies and birds at 1316 Duval St. (305-296-2988).

4. Key West Lighthouse Museum
Take the 88 steps to the top of the lighthouse for astounding views at 938 Whitehead St. (305-294-0012). The keepers quarters are also on site.

5. Mel Fisher Maritime Museum
This small museum and conservation lab displays artifacts from a 17th-century shipwreck at 200 Greene St. Open daily year-round (305-294-2633).

6. The Ernest Hemingway Home & Museum
Ernest Hemingway lived and wrote at 907 Whitehead St. for more than 10 years. Wander through the lush grounds and enjoy the whimsy of the more than 40 resident six-toed cats (305-294-1136).

7. Truman Little White House
Once the winter residence of President Truman and now a museum showcasing his life and presidency. Guided tours available at 111 Front St. (305-294-9911).

SERVICES

8. Advanced Urgent Care
1980 N. Roosevelt Blvd. (305-294-0011)

9. Key West Chamber of Commerce
510 Greene St. (305-294-2587)

10. Key West Post Office
400 Whitehead St. (305-294-9539)

11. Key West Vets and Pets
1118 White St., Ste. A (305-294-0099)

12. Monroe County Library
700 Fleming St. (305-292-3595)

MARINAS

13. A&B Marina
700 Front St. (305-294-2535)

14. City Marina at Garrison Bight
1801 N. Roosevelt Blvd. (305-809-3982)

15. Conch Harbor Marina
951 Caroline St. (305-294-2933)

16. Galleon Marina
619 Front St. (305-292-1292)

17. Garrison Bight Marina
711 Eisenhower Dr. (305-294-3093)

18. Key West Bight Marina
201 William St. (305-809-3984)

19. Key West Yacht Club
2315 N. Roosevelt Blvd. (305-296-5389)

20. Margaritaville Resort & Marina
245 Front St. (305-294-4000)

Duval Street, Key West

Chapter 10: The Florida Keys

> **CAUTION**: It is important to monitor VHF Channel 16 in the Main Ship Channel. Larger vessels will issue a Sécurité call before they enter the channel. This is particularly important when the massive cruise ships are on the move (usually in the morning and early evening).

Continue to follow the Main Ship Channel northwards toward the harbor. Favor the east side of the channel (closer to the docked cruise ships) and keep well off Tank Island (locally known as Sunset Key) and Wisteria Island from flashing green buoy "23" to flashing green "29." There are 1-foot MLW shoals off Wisteria Island and throughout Man of War Harbor. If there is commercial traffic you can follow the markers outside the channel's eastern edge as there is plenty of depth. Pass the cruise ship docks with caution and also note that there is ferry traffic coming out of the harbor at all hours.

The channel has good width and depth but the current and wind can be significant factors here along with the vessel traffic. The abundance of buoys in the area can confuse a first-time visitor, particularly at night. We strongly recommend that first-timers do not attempt a night entry. Day or night, it's prudent to have a "Plan B" in case of traffic conflicts or possible breakdowns in this area.

To reach the main yacht harbor in Key West Bight turn east at flashing red buoy "24" towards quick-flashing red "4" at the end of the seawall. Quick-flashing red "4" marks the Key West Bight harbor entrance.

Vessels unable to pass under the **Fleming Key Bridge** (18-foot fixed vertical clearance) must proceed northward around Fleming Key to access the municipal mooring field, Garrison Bight Harbor and the north Stock Island facilities east of Fleming Key. The well-marked channel rounds the north end of Fleming Key. If you stay centered in the channel you should carry at least 7- to 8-foot MLW depths.

Dockage: The 37-slip Opal Key Resort and Marina (formerly Margaritaville Resort & Marina) is located just off the east side of the Main Ship Channel opposite flashing green buoy "23" just south of the cruise ship wharf. The 37-slip marina accommodates yachts to 200 feet with full use of resort amenities and facilities The resort has multiple restaurants, a pool surrounded by tropical native plants and lush trees and a private spa and is located just one block away from Old Town Key West.

Several facilities are located in Key West Bight. The entry is marked by quick-flashing red "4" at the east end of the protective seawall. These facilities are adjacent to the Historic Seaport Harbor Walk, which extends to the restaurants and shops on the southeast side of the Key West Bight. Key West Marine Hardware (818 Caroline St., 305-294-3425) is within easy walking distance from the bight and has a complete selection of marine paint and hardware.

The spacious floating docks (finger piers port and starboard) of the Galleon Marina lie at the far west end of the bight inside the seawall. Marina guests have access to all the resort's amenities including swimming pool, patio lounge with tiki bar, private beach, fitness center and restaurants. Reservations are recommended far in advance during high season and especially for regatta weeks and Fantasy Fest. A dockmaster is on duty 24/7.

A & B Marina is also located on the Historic Seaport Harbor Walk. The marina offers transient slips and free laundry facilities. They request that you tie up "stern to" and will help you arrange this. This is a hub for several fishing charter companies.

Transients return again and again to Key West Bight Marina, easily identified by the easily accessible fuel dock and the cluster of schooners available for harbor cruises. This friendly and affordable marina can accommodate vessels to 140 feet in its deep-water transient slips with excellent service and amenities.

In the southeast corner of the bight, Conch Harbor Marina offers slips for vessels to 200 feet on a monthly and transient basis. They have a large pool and two restaurants on site. Slips are reserved well in advance and reservations are required.

Additional transient dockage may be available at Garrison Bight.

> **CAUTION:** Before entering Garrison Bight, be aware that the charted overhead cables crossing the entry channel have an authorized vertical clearance of 50 feet and only 34 feet elsewhere over the north basin. Some local businesses report a higher clearance but no precise measurements were provided. To be on the safe side respect the charted clearance, which effectively blocks all but small sailboats. In addition, overnight anchoring in the Bight is prohibited for all vessels. Note also that the fixed **Garrison Bight Bridge** over the channel to the south basin has a charted vertical clearance of 19 feet.

The private Key West Yacht Club at the east end of Garrison Bight (before the fixed bridge) is a member of the Yachting Clubs of America. Reciprocity is extended to members outside of a 50-mile radius (if space is available). They have a full-service dining room and bar.

City Marina at Garrison Bight has floating docks along both sides of the 19-foot vertical clearance fixed Garrison Bight Bridge. They can accommodate vessels to 70 feet. A good portion of the boats docked here are house boats. Garrison Bight Marina in the inner harbor caters to local small fishing boats (to 40 feet) utilizing the marina's ample dry storage capability. They also have marine service and repairs.

The well-protected Sunset Marina Key West is located in a channel northeast of Sigsbee Island, offering access to Stock Island and Key West. The marina is located at the end of a deep, dredged, well-marked channel. Some slips on the floating concrete dock are privately owned and you can rent through the owners (to 55 feet.)

Moorings: Garrison Bight Mooring Field is east of Fleming Key with daily and monthly rates. Be aware that if the mooring field does not appear full, there may be mooring buoys that are "owned" by monthly or annual customers and not available to transients. City Marina at Garrison Bight administers these. For reservations call 305-809-3981. The east side of Fleming Key has significantly less traffic (and wakes) and is much less bumpy than the west side. It's a short dinghy ride under the Fleming Key Bridge (18-foot closed vertical clearance) to get to the tourist area of Key West.

> **NOTE:** Key West is a federal No-Discharge Zone meaning no waste, even that which has been treated, should be discharged overboard. A pump-out service for boats on moorings, anchored or in marinas is provided by PumpOut Florida Keys (www.po-keys.com) (305-809-3981 or VHF Channel 16) with service available Monday through Saturday, 8:00 a.m. to 4:00 p.m. They will visit marinas but anchored and moored boats take priority.

Key West

Chapter 10 — The Florida Keys

Key West, FL

KEY WEST		Largest Vessel	VHF	Total Slips	Approach/ Dockside Depth	Floating Docks	Gas/ Diesel	Repairs/ Haulout	Min/Max Amps	Pump-Out Station
1. Opal Key Resort and Marina WiFi MM 1243.0	(305) 292-4375	160	16	37	37.0 / 14.0	F			15 / 100	P
2. Galleon Marina WiFi MM 4	**(305) 292-1292**	**150**	**16**	**91**	**12.0 / 9.0**	**F**			**30 / 100**	**P**
3. A & B Marina WiFi MM 1243.0	(305) 294-2535	217	16	50	14.0 / 12.0	F	D		30 / 100	P
4. Key West Bight Marina WiFi MM 1245.0	(305) 809-3984	140	16	145	20.0 / 12.0		GD		30 / 100	P
5. Conch Harbor Marina WiFi MM 1245.0	(305) 294-2933	195	16	40	30.0 / 9.0		GD		30 / 100	P
6. Garrison Bight Marina MM 1243.0	(305) 294-3093	40		280	4.0 / 6.0		G	RH		
7. City Marina at Garrison Bight WiFi MM 1243.0	(305) 809-3981	70	16	245	7.0 / 6.0	F			30 / 50	P
8. Key West Yacht Club-PRIVATE WiFi MM 1243.0	(305) 296-5389	58	16	68	6.0 / 9.0				30 / 50	
9. Sunset Marina Key West MM 1239.0	(305) 296-7101	55	16	120	6.0 / 9.0	F	GD		30 / 50	P

WiFi Wireless Internet Access
Visit www.waterwayguide.com for current rates, fuel prices, website addresses and other up-to-the-minute information.
(Information in the table is provided by the facilities.)

Scan here for more details:

Source: Aqua Map and NOAA data

Key West's Luxurious Resort Marina

The Galleon MARINA

The Galleon's breakwater shielded floating docks have been engineered for maximum protection and security (24 hrs.) for your vessel. The Galleon provides Old Towne Key West's finest accommodations for yachts up to 150 ft. Guests not staying on board may find luxurious two bedroom, two bath suites with complete kitchens at the dockside Galleon Resort . . . all near the exciting nightlife of famous Olde Towne Key West. A full watersports program . . . small boat and jet skis, as well as mopeds and bicycles. Our Harbourmaster is on duty 24 hours, 7 days a week monitoring channel 16. Plenty of fresh water at no extra charge, 50 amp electricity, cable TV, telephones and 9 ft. of water dockside. A warm welcome awaits you!

Marina guests enjoy the pool, fitness center, sauna, outdoor spa, sundecks and the harbor view tiki bar.

619 Front Street, Key West, FL 33040. For additional information call Toll free: 1-800-6MARINA or 305-292-1292

Chapter 10 | **The Florida Keys**

Anchorage: Key West abounds with anchorage possibilities but many locations afford only modest protection from fast-shifting winds and swift currents. Despite its popularity the holding around Wisteria Island (known locally as Christmas Tree Island) is poor. The exposure from north through east can be a problem in unsettled weather. Nevertheless, boats continue to anchor north to the northwest or southeast side of Wisteria Island.

> NOTE: Nearby Sunset Key (identified on the NOAA chart as "Tank Island") is a 27-acre private residential neighborhood and resort island. This tiny island was a Navy fuel tank depot until 1994 (hence the label "Tank Island"). Do not attempt to go ashore.

On the west side of Fleming Key are two anchorages: Man of War Harbor and the west side of Fleming Key. Expect a lot of traffic...everything from parasail boats to excursion schooners to floating tiki bars to cruise ships plus a lot of apparently abandoned (derelict) boats. Strong currents and poor holding add to the challenge.

> *CAUTION:* Note that the charted Restricted Area (150-yard exclusion zone) around the military facilities on Fleming Island have expanded and patrol boats are issuing tickets to violators. Be careful where you anchor.

A less desirable alternative is the area just to the north of the mooring field and Sigsbee Park where there are good depths of 7 to 10 feet MLW and good holding. Make sure you are outside of the mooring field buoys. This anchorage is exposed to the north but has much less current and boat wakes than the others. Even in strong northerly winds the shallow water between here and the Gulf cuts down most of the swells leaving you with wind chop, which can be significant in a strong northerly. Some cruisers have been unable to dinghy back to this anchorage under harsh conditions. Be sure to monitor the weather when you plan to go ashore. If you happen to have access to military facilities, the dinghy dock at the Sigsbee Island Marina is a very short walk from showers at the campground and groceries at the commissary.

Both the Wisteria Island and Fleming Key anchorages are relatively close to the downtown public dinghy dock at Key West Bight Marina and the one at City Marina at Garrison Bight. It's about a 1-mile walk from Garrison Bight to downtown. The dinghy dock is located immediately in front of Turtle Kraals Restaurant and allows vessels up to 13 feet. The fee for tying up your dinghy is payable to the City Marina at Garrison Bight. (Discounts are available for longer stays.) The dinghy dock has two sections—one with reserved spots with numbers (outer dock) and another (more chaotic inner dock) for everyone else. Expect shenanigans if you tie up in the wrong space.

■ SIDE TRIP: TO THE DRY TORTUGAS

Seventy nautical miles from the nearest settlement in Key West the Dry Tortugas are the westernmost of the Florida Keys, the most remote and, in some respects, the most fascinating and beautiful. With careful preparation a voyage to the Dry Tortugas can be most rewarding.

Before departure from Key West skippers should consult the most up-to-date *Local Notice to Mariners*. In addition to changes in aids to navigation in the area, check on any military operations in the restricted area west of the Marquesas Keys. The Coast Guard can be reached on VHF Channels 16 and 22A in Key West.

Because of erratic and sometimes severe weather in the area (unpredicted fronts packing high winds are not that unusual) passage to the Dry Tortugas requires planning for the unexpected. Weekend trippers, Caribbean-bound cruisers and fishermen alike often find themselves holed up for a week or more in the modestly protected harbor off Garden Key in persistent 25- to 35-knot winds from stalled fronts in the Gulf of Mexico or off the Cuban coast. If weather conditions are less than ideal a trip to the Dry Tortugas should be postponed. (Or opt for a seaplane ride!)

In all conditions boats bound for the Dry Tortugas should be equipped at a minimum with a VHF radio, depth sounder and GPS unit. Careful checking with NOAA radio forecasts before and during such a trip is essential for your safety. The National Park Service posts daily NOAA weather reports at the docks at Garden Key.

NAVIGATION: Use NOAA Charts 11420, 11434 and 11439. One route to the Dry Tortugas runs south of the Marquesas and the other to the north. The southern route permits easy access to the best anchorage in the Marquesas. Check your charts for shoal areas and stay clear of both keys. Boca Grande Key is approximately 12 nm west of Key West.

The southern route leaves Key West southbound via the Main Ship Channel and enters the Southwest Channel at flashing green "15." From flashing green "15" take a heading of 236° magnetic for the 5.3 nm run to point north of green daybeacon "3" marking shoal charted as Middle Ground. From this point adjust your course to 277° magnetic for 10.3 nm

Fort Jefferson

Chapter 10: The Florida Keys

through West Channel to the southern terminus of the Boca Grande Channel, about 2.5 nm north of Coalbin Rock. This leg runs south of Man Key and Boca Grande Key and north of Parsonage Shoal. The route to the Dry Tortugas continues for another 42 nm to the Southeast Channel approach.

The Boca Grande Key anchorage is to the north. Watch for shoals off the key's west flank on approach. Continuing west it is about 4 nm from the Boca Grade Channel at 277° magnetic to the Marquesas Keys. Keep well north of Coalbin Rock. The passage to the Dry Tortugas continues at 277° magnetic for another 10 nm passing south of the Marquesas and The Quicksands.

Anchorage: If you choose to take the southern route you can stop off and anchor to the northwest of Boca Grande Key near green daybeacon "17" in 10 to 16 feet at MLW. This site can accommodate boats with deeper drafts. Choose your location based on wind direction. There are no other intermediate anchorages, facilities or supplies of any kind after leaving Key West.

Stopover: The Marquesas Keys

The beautiful Marquesas Keys lie along the route to the Dry Tortugas and are only 21.6 nm west of Key West. An interesting stopover with a fairly well-sheltered but shallow lagoon the Marquesas are made up of numerous small keys arranged in the shape of a South Seas atoll. Use binoculars to locate a suitable entrance. If you have a shoal-draft boat, a high tide and an overhead sun, then you might want to try it; otherwise, don't risk it and anchor outside. You are likely beyond VHF range for assistance.

NAVIGATION: Use NOAA Chart 11439. The Marquesas atoll can be approached from either the northern route or the southern route. You can switch between these routes using the north-south Boca Grande Channel located approximately 2 nm west of Boca Grande Key and identified by green daybeacon "1" to the north and red daybeacon "2" to the south. There are some promising-looking entrances to the Marquesas Keys lagoon on the charts. Only extreme shoal-draft vessels should attempt entry and be prepared to get yourself off the bottom if you run aground. You are likely out of VHF range for assistance here.

Anchorage: At the Marquesas Keys try to figure out the winds and then anchor in the lee of the islands. The NOAA chart shows Mooney Harbor Key as having room for several boats but that is deceiving. Shallow draft boats can snug up due west of the island in at least 4 feet MLW with exposure from the south. It is shallow but you will find excellent holding here. An anchorage on the western side of the atoll is comfortable in winds from an easterly quadrant. Depths of 8 to 13 feet MLW can be found fairly close to shore.

Enjoy a dinghy ride through the maze of passages in the Marquesas atoll but do not go ashore. This is a marine sanctuary and signs on the shore prohibit you from landing. This area is known for the famous Spanish treasure ship, *The Atocha*, which sank just to the west of the Marquesas in the Quick Sands. Many boat captains from Key West bring their clients here to bonefish or angle for tarpon.

The Marquesas Keys to the Dry Tortugas

Dry Tortugas National Park was dedicated in 1992. Its boundary now marked by an elliptical circuit of 10 large yellow buoys. Touring Fort Jefferson on your own is an option but a ranger-guided tour provides many interesting and unusual facts that will enhance your visit and understanding of life at the fort. It is the largest and best-preserved fort of the 19th-century U.S. coastal defense perimeter (8-foot-thick brick walls, standing 50 feet high and surrounding a 17-acre quad).

NAVIGATION: Use NOAA Charts 11420, 11438 (for harbor details) and 11439. Heading west from the Marquesas Keys the southern route continues at 277° magnetic for another 10 nm passing south of The Quicksands. At this point adjust to 290° magnetic for the 28-nm run to flashing red "2" that marks the entrance to Southeast Channel just east of Long Key in the Dry Tortugas. Plot a course to pass well south of Halfmoon Shoal and Rebecca Shoal along this route. The flashing red lights on these shoals can be useful as waypoints.

Once 0.3 nm west of flashing red buoy "2" adjust course (approximately 315° magnetic) to split flashing green "3" marking Iowa Rock and red daybeacon "4" marking Hospital Key. Then turn due west passing flashing green "3" south of charted Middle Ground. Once west of Garden Key and the associated shoals turn southwest towards the harbor entry channel.

The northern route from the Marquesas starts at the Ellis Rock light located 2 nm northwest of the Marquesas atoll. It is a straight 35-nm run at 272° magnetic to flashing red "2" marking the Southeast Channel approach to the Dry Tortugas. There are some markers in the shallows south along this route. Pass south of the flashing white on the western edge of New Ground shoal (4 second, 19 feet high).

Pass north of the flashing red markers for Halfmoon Shoal and Rebecca Shoal. You should maintain 20 feet MLW on this segment. As you approach the eastern edge of the Dry Tortugas you can pick out Bush Key and Garden Key with Fort Jefferson dominating the island landscape. This route joins the southern route at flashing read "2."

The channel to the anchorage is entered by splitting red daybeacon "2" and green daybeacon "3." Visual navigation is required here and entry should not be attempted in darkness. The course swings southeast after passing the entry markers so keep south of green daybeacon "7." Rounding green daybeacon "7" turn east into the Garden Key anchorage.

Vessels approaching from the south are advised to use Southwest Channel running between Loggerhead Key and Garden Key. Keep green markers to port on this channel and enter east of green can buoy "1." At red daybeacon "6" take a wide turn to the southeast and follow the closely spaced markers on both sides of the deep channel into the Garden Key anchorage.

> **CAUTION:** Note that a solid isthmus between Bush Key and Garden Key has formed in recent years. We suggest that you refer to print-on-demand charts to get the most recent published information on the channels in and out of the Garden Key anchorage at Fort Jefferson.

Keep in mind the shoals can change in a single storm so visual shallow water techniques will be required in and around the Dry Tortugas. Entry in good light is advised.

Anchorage: The best anchorage is found in front (to the east) of the deteriorated steamship docks at the southern end of Garden Key. There is variable holding in 15 to 20 feet MLW. Be careful outside the channel as charted depths are about 1 foot MLW. Find a sandy patch, power back, test the set and then perform a visual check or an anchor dive to make sure. In this relatively confined and exposed area there are almost always at least half a dozen boats and often more than twice that number during a blow.

> NOTE: Park regulations restrict overnight anchoring to within 1 mile of Garden Key Harbor Light. During nesting season you may want to anchor away from Bush Key to avoid the nighttime noise of the Sooty Terns.

When visiting Garden Key by private boat you must check in at the National Park Service Visitor Center inside Fort Jefferson upon arrival. Rangers will provide a copy of the park's brochure with maps and regulations and the latest weather report. There are restrooms at the docks and beach space for dinghy landings.

The park is a No-Discharge Zone and park rangers may check your vessel's Y-valve. The park has picnic tables, a few charcoal grills and a beautiful designated swim beaches. No services or supplies are available and all trash must be carted back to your boat.

■ NEXT STOP

Next up is the eclectic West Coast of Florida where the alligators, fish camps and seagrass of the Everglades give way to the fast-paced urban life of the Tampa Bay area to the north. Take your time and consider a stop in Everglades National Park on the way. The scenery and wildlife are spectacular.

Chapter 10: The Florida Keys

■ KEYS ANCHORAGES

ICW ROUTE

Ragged Keys (Mile 1106). East of the ICW, 7-foot approach, 8 feet to shoal west of Keys. Holding fair to good in grassy mud. Limited protection from northeast through southeast.

Sand Key (Mile 1108). East of the ICW, 6.5-foot approach, 5 feet in area west of northern portion of the key. Holding fair to good in grassy mud. Protected from south to northeast.

Elliott Key (Mile 1109 to Mile 1114). East of the ICW, 5-foot approach, 5 feet to shoal anywhere along west side of the key. Holding fair to good depending on rocky to grassy mud bottom. Protection from northeast through southeast.

Caesar Creek (Mile 1115). East of the ICW, anchorage open to both routes. Four-foot approach from ICW; 12 feet in best area between Rubicon and Reid keys. Holding good; mud and some grass. Well protected.

Angelfish Creek (Mile 1120). East of the ICW, anchorage open to both routes. Five-foot approach from both ends. Anchorage in side creeks north of channel is 5 feet deep. Holding mixed: some rocky areas, some hard. Strong currents. Well protected.

Pumpkin Key (Mile 1122). East of the ICW, 9-foot approach, 7 feet to shoal anywhere in lee of key depending on winds. Holding fair to good in grassy mud with some rocks.

Steamboat Creek in Card Sound (Mile 1125). East of the ICW, 9-foot approach, 7 feet to shoal north and in mouth of creek off Jew Point. Holding good in grassy mud. Protection only from southwest to east.

Manatee Bay in Barnes Sound (Mile 1132). West of the ICW, 5-foot approach and 5 feet to shoal in area near marked channel leading into Manatee Creek. Holding good in hard bottom. Protection fair to good except in strong winds from north to northwest.

Thursday Cove, Barnes Sound (Mile 1133). East of the ICW, 7-foot approach, 5 to 7 feet between Largo Point and Thursday Point. Holding good in grassy mud. Protection only from southwest to northeast.

Sexton Cove (Mile 1135). East of the ICW, 7-foot approach, 6-foot depth to shoaling close in. Holding fair in grass and hard bottom with some rocks. Protection from northwest through southeast.

Stellrecht Point (Mile 1136). Southeast of the ICW, 7-foot approach, 6 feet to shoal just south of the point. Holding fair to good in grassy mud. Protected from northeast through south.

Tarpon Basin (Mile 1139). Southeast of the ICW, 7-foot approach, anchor in 5-6 feet south of shoal in center of the basin. Holding fair to good in grassy mud over rock. All-round protection.

Sunset Cove, Buttonwood Sound (Mile 1143). Southeast of the ICW, 5-foot approach, 4 feet or less close in, 5 feet near Pelican Key and near Upper Keys Sailing Club docks. Holding fair to good. Protection depends on location.

Butternut Key (Mile 1146). Northwest of the ICW, 6-foot approach, 5 feet near eastern Butternut Key just north of marker "60." Holding fair in soft bottom. Protection only from northwest to north. (Note this anchorage is in Everglades National Park.)

Tavernier Community Harbor (Mile 1150). South of the ICW, 5-foot approach, 5 feet outside basin, 4 feet inside. Holding poor to fair in dense, grassy bottom. Protection fair to good in all but strongest north winds.

Cowpens Anchorage (Mile 1155). Southeast of the ICW, 5-foot approach and depth. Numerous spots to anchor in Cowpens Anchorage area. Fair to good holding in soft bottom, some grass. Protection from east through west, depending on exact anchoring spot.

Cotton Key (Mile 1157). South of the ICW, 7-foot approach and 5 feet in the anchorage. Leave ICW at red day-beacon "86." Protection from north through southeast. Holding fair in grassy mud bottom.

Upper Matecumbe Key (Mile 1160). South of the ICW, 6-foot approach and 5 feet in the anchorage off of the restaurant/bar. Protection from south through southeast. Holding fair in soft bottom.

Shell Key (Mile 1161). Southeast of the ICW, 7-foot approach from the west. Can drop anchor close to shore for good protection from east winds. Holding good in grass and sand.

Lignumvitae Key (Mile 1164). Southeast of the ICW, 7-foot approach to either side of key. DO NOT ANCHOR; use the heavy moorings provided. Protection is dependent on being in the lee of the key.

Long Key Bight (Mile 1170). On ocean side of Channel Five Bridge, 7-foot approach, shoaling to 5 feet at center. Anchor as far in as draft allows. Holding good in grassy mud. Protection from all but east winds.

Fiesta Key (Mile 1171). On bay-side of Channel Five Bridge, 9-foot approach, 6 feet at anchor. Anchor as close to causeway as draft allows. Holding good in sand and grass. Protection west through southeast.

Rachel Key (Mile 1190). Southwest of the ICW, south of Rachel Bank, 7-foot approach, 5 feet in area southwest of Rachel Key and southeast of charted shoal. Holding fair to good in sand and grass. Anchoring in the bight southeast of Rachel Key is also possible. Protection fair to good depending on exact location.

Boot Key Harbor (Mile 1195). East of the ICW, accessible through Knights Key Channel or Moser Channel, then east to Boot Key Channel. See details in anchorages for Hawk Channel route.

Bahia Honda Area (Mile 1205). Southwest of the ICW in charted cove, 7-foot approach, 7 feet to shoal inside 6-foot line. Holding fair in grassy mud. Protection from east through southwest only. You can, with care, anchor just outside the park basin in 8 feet if you can get under the 20-foot clearance at the bridge.

Crane Key (Mile 1225). Enter through Cudjoe Channel in good light. Eight-foot approach, 6 feet at anchor. Anchor as close to key as draft allows. Holding good in grassy mud. Protection from northeast through southeast.

HAWK CHANNEL ROUTE

Caesar Creek (Mile 1118). Anchorage open to both routes. Seven-foot approach from Hawk Channel, 4 feet from ICW. Anchorage best between Rubicon and Reid keys. Twelve-foot depth, holding good. Well protected.

Angelfish Creek (Mile 1122). Anchorage open to both routes. Five-foot approach from both channels. Anchorage in side creeks north of channel. Five-foot depth, holding mixed, some hard and some rocky areas. Strong currents, well protected.

Largo Sound (Mile 1141). Five-foot approach, some 5-foot depths near the channel, but 3 feet is the norm. Holding fair, some grass, well protected.

Rodriguez Key (Mile 1145). Seven-foot approach, 7 feet or less close in. Anchor in lee as required for protection. Holding good. Note wrecks north of key and shoal to the west.

Rock Harbor (Mile 1144). Seven-foot approach, anchor as close in as draft will permit. Protection from north to northeast. Mandalay Restaurant (cash only) has a dinghy beach.

Tavernier Key (Mile 1150). Six-foot approach, less close in. Anchor in Tavernier Harbor area. Holding good. Some protection from northwest to north, southwest through south.

Whale Harbor (Mile 1158). Five-foot approach, 5 feet in anchorage. Anchor in lee relative of keys to north and to small key to southwest near marker "5A." Holding fair, some grass. Protection fair northwest through east. Note shoals.

Chapter 10: The Florida Keys

Indian Key (Mile 1165). Seven-foot approach, 7 feet or less at anchorage close in. Anchor on southeast side of key in lee. Holding good in sand and sea grass. Protection fair from northwest through northeast.

Long Key Bight (Mile 1172). Nine-foot approach, shoaling to 5 feet in center. You can anchor as far in as draft allows. Holding good in some sea grass. Good protection from all but due east.

Boot Key Harbor (Mile 1193). Seven-foot approach from Sister Creek, 7-foot approach from Boot Key Channel. Eleven feet to shoaling near head of harbor. Holding good. Good protection for 360° except in severe east-northeast winds. Little room to anchor outside of mooring field. Alternative is to harbor outside, just west of Boot Key in 5 to 8 feet.

Bahia Honda Key (Mile 1207). Ten-foot approach, 9 feet or less close in between bridges. Holding fair to good. Fair to good protection. Strong tidal currents. Anchor checks on tide swings are advised.

Newfound Harbor (Mile 1215). Seven-foot approach. Most anchor in the cross-bar of the "H" etched by the deeper channels in 7 to 8 feet. Or in 9 feet or less close in toward highway bridge. Holding good. Fair to good protection in all but worst southerly winds.

Niles Channel (Mile 1215). Seven-foot approach, depths of 7 to 21 feet in sand and grass. Holding fair to good in mud and grass. Fair to good protection in all but worst winds from the south.

Saddlebunch Harbor (Mile 1228). Six-foot approach through narrow channel between Saddlebunch Keys and Pelican Key. Anchor in 7 to 8 feet close to mangroves on east shore. Holding fair. Strong currents. Buoy your anchor. Fair to good protection.

Key West (Mile 1245). Anchoring is not permitted in Garrison Bight. Many of the best spots in Key West are taken by liveaboards. Also be wary of submerged wrecks. The anchorages north or east of Wisteria Island are popular but exposed in north and west winds. Holding is fair in a sand and grass with depths of 7 feet to shoal near shore. West of Fleming Key is another alternative but not within 150 yards of the military facilities on Fleming Island. This anchorage is adjacent and contiguous to the harbor and is exposed to the wash and wake of passing vessels. Holding is good with a fairly hard bottom with protection from east and south winds and partially by the shoals to the north. Alternately, proceed around the north end of Fleming Key and find limited protection north of the mooring field and off of Sigsbee Park.

Section 3: Florida's West Coast

Chapter 11: Florida Keys to Fort Myers Beach **Chapter 12:** Sanibel Island to Sarasota Bay
Chapter 13: Tampa Bay to Tarpon Springs

SOUTHERN EDITION

Chapter 11: Florida Keys to Fort Myers Beach

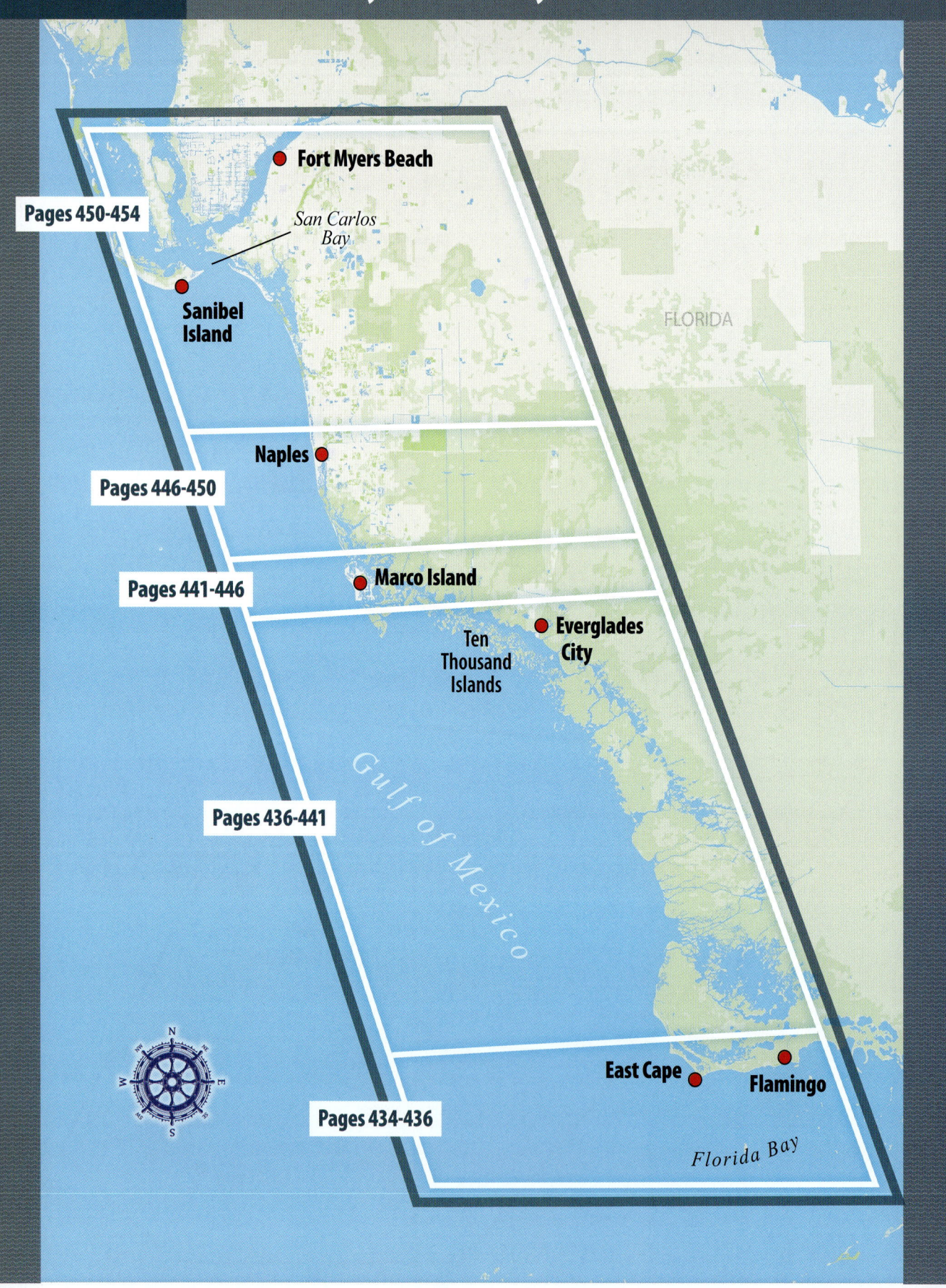

NAVIGATION NOTES

With sugar sand beaches and seashells, tropical hardwoods and Everglades swampland, Florida's lower west coast provides a greater diversity of experiences than the east. Instead of being packed with crowds, cultural communities and glamour, cruising the west coast brings opportunities for relaxation and the kind of casual luxury that is experienced in isolated high-end resorts. The cruising, too, is entirely different as it is less confined by the waterway and offers more open water passages.

The amenities may be more limited and spaced farther apart but Florida's southwestern waters give access to the swampy wilderness of the Everglades, the long sweep of Sanibel and Captiva Islands, picturesque fishing villages, bustling Tampa Bay and the history- and restaurant-rich Greek sponge center of Tarpon Springs. Here cruisers think more about enjoying the ride and less about putting down miles.

The lower half of the coast is alternately wild and developed. At the bottom of the peninsula Cape Sable and the Ten Thousand Islands guard the swampland of the Everglades. Up the coast the shoreline transitions to sandy beaches backed by walls of pine and tropical hardwood jungle. Traveling through the wild and uninhabited expanse of the Everglades cruisers are enveloped in nature and learn to respect its power at the same time. There are no services between Marathon and Everglades City and you must plan the passage carefully. For most this will enhance the experience but this is true cruising and crews must be self-reliant and prepared.

Heading north through the natural beauty of the Everglades and the Ten Thousand Islands, you may wonder if you are still in Florida. The natural diversity and seclusion of Florida's west coast is a gunkholer's dream and makes cruising here a draw for the adventuresome.

The tropical barrier islands emerge at San Carlos Bay. Deep water moves in closer toward shore and resort communities begin to appear. Mile 0 of the Gulf Intracoastal Waterway (GIWW) whets the appetite for travel at the mouth of the Caloosahatchee River, where the Okeechobee Waterway ends for westbound traffic and begins for those heading east.

From Marco Island northward the west coast sees increasing development, boat traffic, marinas and shore activity. The wilderness that defines the Everglades shoreline is relegated to protected pockets and south Florida's dominant mangroves increasingly give way to extensive shoreside development.

Gulf Coast Cruising Conditions

CAUTION: Hurricane Ian caused widespread damage across southwest Florida after making landfall on Cayo Costa Island as a Category 4 hurricane in September 2022. Many of the communities in this chapter were affected in major ways and rebuilding will be a long process. Call ahead for status prior to arrival.

Much of the shoreline of the lower half of Florida's west coast remains undeveloped and natural. Most significant is the 65 nm of Everglades National Park shoreline from Flamingo to Everglades City. This navigable coastal area is uninhabited, is only accessible by boat and offers no services. This shoreline does, however, provide well-provisioned cruisers access to a natural paradise.

Farther north along the west coast there are 14 aquatic preserves, 40 state parks, 14 national wildlife refuges and the over 100,000-acre Rookery Bay National Estuarine Research Reserve–one of the few remaining undisturbed mangrove estuaries in North America. Florida's west coast is wonderful destination for cruisers hoping to explore some of Florida's natural habitat.

No Wake Zones, Idle Speed Zones and various Speed Limit restrictions are in effect throughout the waterways included in this chapter. Exercise diligence in knowing the regulations by observing signs and other markers. Enforcement is always present. As always, be courteous to other vessels and avoid manatees and other marine life.

Offshore Routes

Unlike Florida's east coast there is not a continuous inland waterway running the full length of the Gulf Coast. For most cruising boats it will be an open ocean passage for the 125 nm from Marathon (in the Florida Keys) to the start of the GIWW at Cape Coral on San Carlos Bay. There are anchorages along the way that allow cruisers to break up the trip

Chapter 11: Florida Keys to Fort Myers Beach

but cruisers will need to complete several ocean passages of 40 nm or more.

Although they might seem worse to the inexperienced, most tidal currents are less than 2 knots here. At 1 to 3 feet the tidal range is relatively small and water depths tend to be governed more by wind than by tide. When winds blow from the northeast the water is driven out of the bays, while strong winds from the southeast and southwest push water in. Under northeast wind conditions there is generally less water in the bays than the charted mean low water. Be especially wary when a spring low tide combines with a fresh northeast breeze. Be prepared with the latest charts and up-to-date weather advisories and make sure your boat and equipment are in top shape.

If you have a vessel large enough to cruise offshore, a faster boat or are comfortable with a longer duration passage, then hugging the shore of Cape Sable is just adding extra miles to your trip. Routes that hug the Everglades coast eventually have to head westward to avoid the Cape Romano Shoals that extend south from Marco Island.

Basically, if the weather is right and your objective is to reach Naples or points north, you may want to take a direct route passing well offshore of the Everglades. We describe "Offshore" and "Coastal" routes separately below.

Note that offshore routes are longer and slower craft will need longer than 12 hours to complete the passage necessitating nighttime operation for many. There are hazards on these routes and caution should be exercised for operation in darkness. Offshore depths are consistent but numerous fishing boats operate in these waters and there are typically a multitude of lobster pots in the area. Be sure that you have a sufficient weather window (with a 24-hour buffer) before attempting an overnight passage.

■ TO EAST CAPE

Regardless of whether you choose an inland passage or an offshore passage, there are three practical departure points northward from the Keys. The most easterly is the Yacht Channel north from the Channel Five Bridge. The most central is via Moser Channel from the Marathon area. And many leave directly from Key West via the Northwest Channel (or from the Cudjoe Channel if an intermediate stop is planned).

Should you choose to try a side trip to Flamingo, realize this is small boat territory only. Call ahead for up-to-date information and conditions. Taking it slow and easy is recommended when exploring this area. Follow the buoys and daybeacons carefully; depths outside the channel are 1 to 2 feet MLW. Play the tides if your draft is over 3 feet.

Route 1: From Long Key via Yacht Channel

NAVIGATION: Use NOAA Charts 11449, 11431, 11429 and 11452. This route is not recommended for vessels with drafts exceeding 5 feet or for passage in poor light. Expect depths to be shallower than the charted nominal depths of 5 to 6 feet MLW, especially if the wind has a strong easterly component. Particular caution should be exercised crossing the Arsenic Bank and the Sprigger Bank.

The route is the same as for the coastal route to flashing red "2" located south of East Cape. From here it's a heading of 321° magnetic north-westward for 60 nm to clear the Cape Romano shoals. Turning north at this point paralleling the shore of Marco Island for 11 nm to the Capri Pass entrance.

Route 2: From Vaca Key via Moser Channel

NAVIGATION: Use NOAA Charts 11442, 11453, 11431, 11429 and 11452. Depths on this route should maintain 7 to 8 feet MLW. From the Moser Channel gap in the **Seven Mile Bridge** the course is initially due north magnetic. Several shoals flank the route on both sides until clear of the Bullard Bank approximately 7 nm north of the bridge, and your course must be adjusted to keep red markers to starboard and green markers to port. From flashing green "17" off the Bullard Bank shoal it's a heading of 327° magnetic for 70 nm to clear the Cape Romano shoals. Turning north at this point paralleling the shore of Marco Island for 11 nm to the Capri Pass entrance.

Route 3: From Key West via Northwest Channel

NAVIGATION: Use NOAA Charts 11442, 11431, 11429 and 11452. It is a single 80-nm leg at 008° magnetic from flashing green "1" marking the northern terminus of Key West's Northwest Channel to flashing red "2" marking the entry to the Capri Pass south of Naples. The minimum depth is 14 feet MLW and is much deeper offshore.

Flamingo, FL

FLAMINGO		Largest Vessel	VHF	Total Slips	Approach/ Dockside Depth	Floating Docks	Gas/ Diesel	Repairs/ Haulout	Min/Max Amps	Pump-Out Station
1. Flamingo Marina	(239) 695-2945	40	16	26	1.0 / 3.5		G	H	30	P

WiFi Wireless Internet Access
Visit www.waterwayguide.com for current rates, fuel prices, website addresses and other up-to-the-minute information.
(Information in the table is provided by the facilities.)

Scan here for more details:

Source: Aqua Map and NOAA data

Despite being an offshore route, you must man the helm on this passage as numerous fishing boats operate in these waters and it is littered with lobster pots.

Side Trip: Flamingo & Cape Sable

The Flamingo Basin forms the northern reach of Florida Bay and its navigable waters allow cruisers to explore the bay's shallows and provides shore-access to the Everglades National Park. The Cape Sable structure is Florida's southernmost mainland feature and has some beautiful, isolated beaches that have been formed by coastal storm action.

The cape's relatively high elevation (by Everglades standards) provides the dry land site of the Flamingo Visitors Center. The Visitor Center offers canoe, kayak and bike rentals in addition to daily tours and a small museum that highlights the park's unique plant and animal life. For activity schedules, trail guides, a backcountry trip planner, natural history and more, visit Flamingo Visitors Center or call 239-695-2945.

> NOTE: The 65 nm of Everglades National Park shoreline runs from Flamingo to Everglades City. All visitors to Everglades National Park are required to pay an entrance fee. Digital passes may be purchased online. Be prepared to show your hard copy pass or digital pass on your mobile device.

NAVIGATION: Use NOAA Charts 11433 or 11451. This is shoal-draft boat territory and "wind tide" can be significant. The dredged access channel to Flamingo has a charted design depth of 4.5 feet MLW but is unreliable. Before you venture into Flamingo we suggest that you call ahead for up-to-date information and conditions. Most larger cruising vessels anchor in Florida Bay at the end of the access channel north of Murray Key (close to red daybeacon "8") and dinghy in. Taking it slow and easy is recommended when exploring this area.

The turn to reach Flamingo either for a daytime visit or an anchorage is at flashing red "2," which is 1.95 nm on a bearing of 178° magnetic from East Cape on Cape Sable. From flashing red "2" keep red markers to starboard and green markers to port. The channel passes south of the Middle Ground shoals. It is 8.5 nm from East Cape to the Flamingo access channel marked by flashing green "9." The shallow access channel runs north-northeast for a little over 1 mile to the Flamingo harbor but is only passible by extreme shoal draft vessels.

> **CAUTION:** Follow the buoys and daybeacons carefully. Depths outside the access channel are 1 to 2 feet MLW. Play the tides if your draft is over 3 feet. The chart shows 4.5 feet MLW in the entry channel but the date of the sounding data is quite old. Be sure to refer to the most up-to-date charts.

Chapter 11: Florida Keys to Fort Myers Beach

Dockage: Flamingo Marina is open year-round with electric and water hookups. There is a marina store with limited supplies. The channel will accept a 4-foot maximum draft at high tide. The channel is approximately 2 feet deep at MLW.

Anchorage: It is possible to anchor outside the breakwater immediately south of the Flamingo Visitors Center in 4 to 5 feet MLW with good holding in mud. Flamingo Basin provides all-around protection. Larger vessels must anchor in Florida Bay north of Murray Key at the end of the access channel. Depths drop off quickly on the Dan Foy Bank so anchor just outside the marked channel in 5 to 7 feet MLW. The protection is only fair but the chop is limited by the surrounding shallow waters. A mild breeze is welcome as it will reduce the mosquito annoyance.

■ TO TEN THOUSAND ISLANDS AREA

East Cape to Fort Myers Beach–Outside Passage

It is approximately 115 nm from Flamingo to Fort Myers Beach. Many skippers with faster craft choose to travel this distance offshore. From flashing red "2" located south of East Cape a heading of 321° magnetic north-westward for 60 nm should allow you to clear the Cape Romano Shoals. Once north of Cape Romano adjust to 340° magnetic and parallel Florida's west coast for the 40-nm run to San Carlos Bay. From here you can pass under the **Sanibel Causeway Boulevard 'B' Span Bridge** and enter the Gulf Intracoastal Waterway (GIWW).

North from East Cape–Inland Passage

NAVIGATION: Use NOAA Charts 11425. The coastal (inland) route continues northward inside the 3-mile limit and parallels the Everglades National Park shoreline. First passing Cape Sable and then into the Ten Thousand Islands, which begin near the mouth of the Chatham River. It's about 16 nm from East Cape to Little Shark River and another 19 nm to Little Turkey Key at the start of the Ten Thousand Islands. This island group stretches for about 26 nm to Cape Romano. Primitive, remote and uninhabited, these islands form the northern shoreline of the Everglades National Park.

Cape Sable has three distinct prominences: East Cape, Middle Cape and Northwest Cape. The southernmost,

East Cape, is also the most southerly point of mainland Florida. The cape's beautiful, pristine beaches make a wonderful stop for cruisers but don't expect complete solitude; they are inhabited by American Crocodiles.

> NOTE: Middle Cape Canal just north of Middle Cape is reported to be a good fishing spot but you will need a freshwater license if you intend to dip the rod in Lake Ingraham.

NAVIGATION: Use NOAA Charts 11429, 11431, 11433 and 11451. To avoid the shoals extending from East Cape, keep south and west of green daybeacon "1A" as you turn north. (Note the charted submerged pile near the daybeacon.) You will encounter thousands of lobster and crab pot markers if you leave the marked boundaries of Everglades National Park. It's best to parallel the shoreline about 2 miles off.

Pay close attention to your chart and the depth sounder while underway as several sandbars extend from shore. Enter waypoints or follow courselines on your chartplotter to keep a safe distance offshore and to avoid hazards. If you are planning to head for Cape Romano, Marco Island or Naples, set your course to remain well offshore of the Cape Romano Shoals some with depths below 1 foot MLW. These shoals begin 10 nm south of Cape Romano.

Heading north to round Cape Romano and its extensive shoal system courselines run offshore and you are exposed to winds from the entire northern sector. "Holing up" in a blow is recommended. Even in the summer squall lines or simply strong prevailing southeasterlies can stir things up. NOAA weather reports on VHF Channel WX2 or WX3 should keep you informed so you can make the passage safely.

Anchorage: If the winds have an easterly component and are light you can anchor off the beautiful Cape Sable beaches that extend from East Cape to Northwest Cape. East Cape Sable north of Middle Cape is particularly pleasant. You can dinghy ashore but watch for the American Crocodiles that inhabit this area and keep pets on a leash. These animals are more aggressive than alligators but typically enter the ocean when humans approach. Everglades National Park rangers report that incidents with the crocodiles are rare but you may want to avoid swimming here.

Depths will depend on your chosen location. Be sure to test your hold in the sand and grass bottom as a wind shift could leave you awash on the beach. This is open northwest through south. The area provides excellent beach combing opportunities and you will have little competition as few people anchor here.

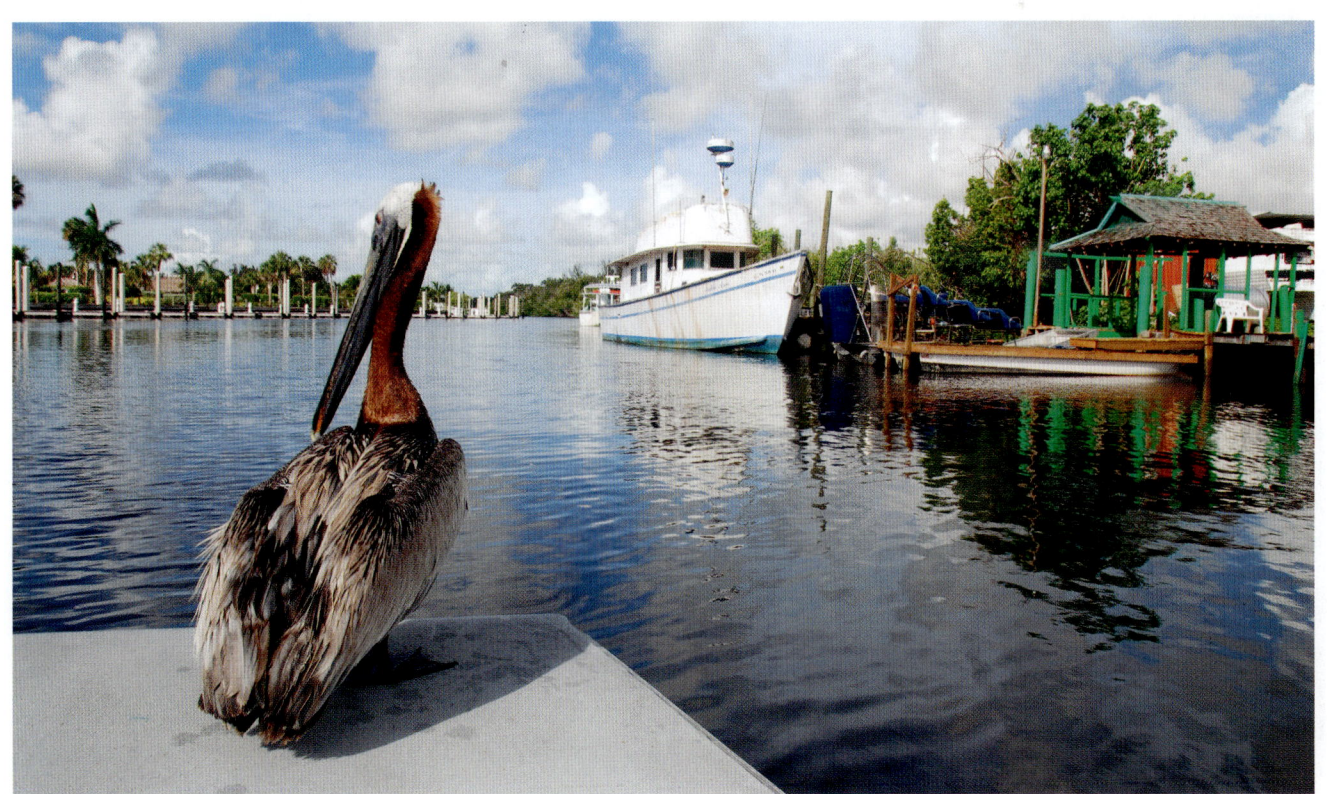

Chapter 11: Florida Keys to Fort Myers Beach

Little Shark River

The well-protected Little Shark River anchorage a popular stop for cruisers in slower craft that are breaking up the journey from the Florida Keys to Naples. The river is also an access route to Everglades Wilderness Waterway, Oyster Bay and the park's inner regions.

NAVIGATION: Use NOAA Charts 11431 and 11432. About 6 miles above Northwest Cape pick up the marked entrance to the Little Shark River off the tip of Shark River Island just south of Ponce de Leon Bay. Note that some of Shark River Island has been eroded away in storms and may not appear exactly as charted.

Little Shark River is a gateway to the inner regions of the Everglades National Park and can provide access to the Everglades Wilderness Waterway connecting Flamingo and Everglades City. This route is not recommended for vessels requiring more than 18 feet of clearance nor those that have high cabins and/or windscreens because of the narrow channels and over-hanging foliage in some areas.

Marked channels lead into coffee-colored wide and shallow bays or up narrow rivers through hundreds of islands and winding waterways. Uncharted snags and bars are common in these waters so operate with caution here. Remember navigating this type of course requires knowing where you are at all times. It is easy to get lost in the numerous channels many of which seem to dead end.

The in-shore waters north of Little Shark River are riddled with shoals and spots of very shallow water (2 to 3 feet MLW). Your depth sounder and your chartplotter will be your friend. It's best to follow your "cookie crumbs" when reversing course in shallow waters.

Anchorage: If you are looking to wait out nasty northerly weather or just wanting to break up your passage into daylight hops, getting the hook down in the Little Shark River and out of the waves is a good option. The water is deep (10 to 15 feet MLW) and the scenery is beautiful. Mariners have been waiting out bad weather here for many years. Many cruising boats anchor in the first mile or so of the Little Shark River, which is protected by a 60-foot-high mangrove forest.

A popular spot to anchor is in the bend in the river north of red daybeacon "4." This area has shoaled in with mud/shell and may be more shallow than the charted depth of 4 to 12 feet MLW. Slowly feel your way in but be sure to sound out your entire swing radius as tidal currents are strong. Make sure your anchor is well set. Snags are a potential problem here; use of a trip line is advised.

A second option is north of Shark River Island. You can get much closer to shore than the charts indicate and still have 8 to 10 feet MLW. This is a good spot to get out of southerly winds. Definitely take out your dinghy or kayaks for some exploration.

If your boat is not screened in, keep plenty of bug repellent handy. (On second thought, keep some handy even if you do have screens.) Those with keen eyes can spot alligators along the banks or in the water. At night a flashlight shone into the wilderness will usually reveal dozens of little red eyes that belong to alligators. This is a definite "no swimming" area!

The pelicans work this area quite often and are fun to watch. A crab line dropped overboard and carefully hauled in will supply the galley with a magnificent meal. Fishing is good but licenses are required and limits must be carefully observed. Leave the area as you found it. There are no shoreside facilities in this area.

If you don't want to go all the way to Everglades City for your next stop, you can anchor behind New Turkey Key in depths of 3 to 6 feet MLW (so only shoal draft boats can find refuge here). This anchorage is just south of the Chatham River and approximately 19 nm north of Ponce de Leon Bay. Make sure you set your anchor well as the currents are strong in this area.

Side Trip: Everglades City

Everglades City's history dates back more than 2,000 years to the age of the coastal Calusa mound dwellers, who had a major settlement on Chokoloskee Island. This island has one of the highest elevations in the Everglades achieving 20 feet above sea level. The island's abnormal elevation is artificial and the result of the discard of shells by the indigenous inhabitants over their 2000-year occupation. Europeans established a settlement here in the late 1800s and the local economy was based on trade, fishing and shellfishing. As more settlers arrived the community gradually evolved into a shipping port for produce and seafood.

Seafood is still a major economic factor in the area but is following the decline of the produce market and tourism has become the area's major economic driver. The city is the northern terminus of the Everglades Wilderness Waterway and offers water-based tours of all types

Ten Thousand Islands, FL

EVERGLADES		Largest Vessel	VHF	Total Slips	Approach/Dockside Depth	Floating Docks	Gas/Diesel	Repairs/Haulout	Min/Max Amps	Pump-Out Station
1. Everglades Rod & Gun Club	(239) 695-2101	100	16	17	5.5 / 6.0				50	
2. Everglades Isle Marina WiFi	(239) 695-2600	60		100	/	F	G		20 / 100	P

WiFi Wireless Internet Access
Visit www.waterwayguide.com for current rates, fuel prices, website addresses and other up-to-the-minute information. (Information in the table is provided by the facilities.)

Scan here for more details:

Source: Aqua Map and NOAA data

including airboats, kayaks, canoes and swamp buggies. A bike ride to the ancient Calusa settlement site on nearby Chokoloskee Island can be an interesting experience.

Unique to Everglades City is The Everglades Rod and Gun Club (239-695-2101). Once a trading post that opened in the late 1800s the club has hosted many famous faces who come for the renowned hunting and fishing including former U.S. presidents, Mick Jagger and Ernest Hemingway. The rambling wood frame home is now a delightful marina, restaurant, with nearby cottages right on the Barron River. The old clubhouse, which was constructed in the early European period, is well worth a visit.

NAVIGATION: Use NOAA Charts 11429, 11430 and 11432. A sparse series of Everglades National Park boundary signs and flashing red markers parallel the coastline north from Little Shark River. Along this stretch it is advisable to roughly follow the Three Nautical Mile Line outside these markers to avoid the wide and shallow mouth of Ponce de Leon Bay and other obstructions closer to shore.

Several channels break the coastline. Some are deep enough to attract shoal-draft boats and skippers seeking more remote anchorages and good fishing. These passes and rivers have numerous sandbars and shoals and aside from Indian Key Pass are unmarked. Operation here requires careful, experienced navigation. Small-boat operators may be able to provide local knowledge for those adventuresome cruisers planning side trips and excursions off the main channels. No sign of civilization will be evident other than a remote ranger station.

The entrance to the Indian Key Pass (leading to Everglades City) is marked by 16-foot-high flashing white light "IK" located about 3.5 nm offshore of flashing green "1" at Indian Key. Flashing green "1" can be difficult to pick out from offshore. Use GPS coordinates to guide you in. Well-marked Indian Key Pass starts as a natural channel but quickly narrows into a dredged channel. You

SOUTHERN EDITION 439

Chapter 11 Florida Keys to Fort Myers Beach

Everglades City

should maintain 6-foot MLW depths but be careful to maintain alignment as the channel is flanked by shoals on both sides. Some markers are lighted but entry in darkness is not recommended. Tidal range is approximately 3 feet and, in addition, "wind tide" can be a factor here in a strong northeast blow.

> ⚠️ **CAUTION:** Between the flashing red "22" and the red "30" where the channel crosses the Chokoloskee Bay there is a strong lateral current from the south during the ebb and to the north during the flood. The channel is deep but narrow and you need to watch the marks ahead and behind as it is easy to drift out of the channel and into depths of 2 to 3 feet MLW.

In Everglades City between the red daybeacons "44" and "46" (past The Everglades Rod and Gun Club) the marked channel cuts off a natural bend in the river. Depths at the bend are charted at 7 to 8 feet MLW but it has shoaled to less than 6 feet MLW. Be sure to stick to the marked channel.

Dockage: Up the Barron River, Everglades Rod & Gun Club has dockage with limited facilities. Water is available at the dock but is not potable. (Potable water is available at the lodge.) Payment is cash only. We suggest you call ahead.

Everglades Isle Marina is 0.5 mile north on the Barron River. Just after passing the Everglades Rod & Gun Club, take the channel to port of red daybeacon "44." Exercise caution! An inflowing tide will draw craft toward this marker, so give it a wide berth and maintain sufficient speed to counteract the current. Continue up the Barron River channel following the charted marks to green daybeacon "55." The marina is a combination marina/Class A RV resort with 30-foot boat slips are located in a basin with a controlling depth of 5 feet MLW. The grounds are beautiful and the high-end club house includes a movie theater and a spa. Golf cart rentals are available to explore the small town.

Anchorage: You can anchor shortly after entering Indian Key Pass on the north side of Indian Key in 6 to 7 feet MLW. Good protection from south winds. There is significant current in the channel and you may experience wind against current creating some small waves. Dolphins may join you.

Just northwest of flashing green "7" on Indian Key Pass is Russell Pass, where you can drop the hook in at least 7 feet MLW. For more wind protection, proceed farther up Russell Pass to where it opens up to the south for 7- to 8-foot MLW depths. Make sure you avoid the uncharted pocket or you could find yourself on the bottom at low tide.

America's Waterway Guide Since 1947 — Chapter 11

Ten Thousand Islands, FL

TEN THOUSAND ISLANDS AREA		Largest Vessel	VHF	Total Slips	Approach/ Dockside Depth	Floating Docks	Gas/ Diesel	Repairs/ Haulout	Min/Max Amps	Pump-Out Station
1. Port of the Islands Marina WiFi	(239) 389-0367	65	16	175	5.0 / 6.0	F	G		30 / 50	P

WiFi Wireless Internet Access
Visit www.waterwayguide.com for current rates, fuel prices, website addresses and other up-to-the-minute information. (Information in the table is provided by the facilities.)

Scan here for more details: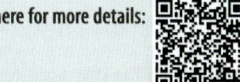

Panther Key north of West Pass has 7 to 10 feet MLW with good holding in soft mud. This is somewhat exposed to the south. Anchor for best wind protection. This is wilderness. Don't expect amenities but you can dinghy to a beach.

Side Trip: Faka Union River

NAVIGATION: Use NOAA Charts 11429 and 11430. Seven miles west of Everglades City as the crow flies lies the shallow Faka Union River, home of Port of the Islands Marina. Heading northwest from Indian Key proceed to green daybeacon "3" off Gomez Point at the tip of Panther Key. This marks the entrance to the 5-mile-long, mangrove-fringed channel on the Faka Union River to the marina. The straight channel to the marina is well marked by daybeacons beginning with green daybeacon "3" and red "4." Charted depths in the channel are 5 to 6 feet MLW. This is a year-round manatee zone so proceed at idle speed only.

Dockage: The remote Port of the Islands Marina located at the head of the Faka Union River provides "full immersion" in the Everglades. The marina offers transient boat slips on concrete floating docks, pump-out boat and a Ship Store with convenience store items. Amenities are limited. Call ahead on VHF Channel 16 to verify available space and for advice on tide and channel conditions. (Tides in this area are from 1 to 3 feet MLW.)

■ TO MARCO ISLAND

Two routes are available to travel from the Ten Thousand Islands area to Marco Island and beyond: the Outside Passage and the Inland Passage. The Inland Passage is only viable for extreme shoal-draft vessels with an air-draft of less than 55 feet. It's a long back-track to avoid the Cape Romano Shoals so it's best to plan your route before entering Gullivan Bay. Most cruising size vessels take the Outside Passage.

Source: Aqua Map and NOAA data

Chapter 11: Florida Keys to Fort Myers Beach

Ten Thousand Islands to Marco Island–Outside Passage

Most cruising vessels take this route. Set course waypoints in advance to ensure you pass west of the dangerous Cape Romano Shoals.

NAVIGATION: Use NOAA Charts 11429 and 11430. To reach Marco Island from Everglades City or points farther north in the Gulf you must pass outside the Cape Romano Shoals and well offshore of the Cape itself. Charts record isolated spots with depths of as low as 1-foot MLW at the Three Nautical Mile Line. Your course should take you at least 3 to 4 miles west of Cape Romano, whether coming from the south or north. Use your GPS and enter a good standoff waypoint south of the finger shoals. If using radar Cape Romano will be prominently displayed as you run offshore to avoid it.

The shoals extend 9.5 nm south from Cape Romano where a flashing white light marks the southernmost finger shoal. If approaching from Everglades City this light is 12 nm southwest of Indian Key. From Little Shark River it's a course of 310° magnetic to clear the light.

Once clear of the southern extremity of the finger shoals a course of 335° magnetic will lead past Marco Island to the Capri Pass. This is the main entrance to the Marco Island marinas and the inland channel to Naples. When approaching Capri Pass from the south, pass west of 16-foot-high flashing red buoy "2" before turning for entry to stay clear of the shoaling near Big Marco Pass. Coconut Island, once located in Capri Pass, just south of the green-over-red daybeacon is now submerged and has been removed from recent charts; however, it lies just under the surface.

Follow the markers carefully through Capri Pass. Head from flashing red "6" to split quick flashing green "9" and red daybeacon "8" while favoring the green side. There is plenty of room but traffic can be heavy on weekends and the markers are confusing where the inside channel to Naples splits off northward at the green-over-red daybeacon.

CAUTION: Shoaling has been observed from the north side of Capri Pass. Stick closer to red daybeacons "4" and "6" when going in and out.

Ten Thousand Islands to Goodland–Inland Passage

Situated on a small peninsula of a large island and marsh complex the village of Goodland is a laid-back fishing village with good but unpretentious restaurants, fishing supplies and limited groceries.

NAVIGATION: Use NOAA Charts 11429 and 11430. If your draft is 3 feet or less and your air-draft requirement is less than 55 feet, you may save some time by taking the protected inside route to Marco Island. Vessels with slightly deeper drafts may take this route, if they have the flexibility to schedule their passage at high tide.

The route begins about 6 miles west of Faka Union Bay at the head of Gullivan Bay off Coon Key where Coon Key Light, a 22-foot-high flashing white light, marks the entrance to Coon Key Pass. Stay 400 to 500 yards east of the light and head north up the east side of Coon Key towards red daybeacon "2" (on the west side of Tripod Key). Next proceed through well-marked Coon Key Pass (if heading north, leave red markers to starboard) to the village of Goodland, which is east of Marco Island. The route is quite shallow in spots and charted depths are unreliable. Fortunately, the bottom is reported to be soft mud.

Local boats frequently use this passage (some at high speed) so ask for latest channel conditions and then make your own decision. The fixed **Goodland Bridge** (55-foot vertical clearance) sets the bar as the lowest bridge for the rest of this route.

Dockage: The full-service Walker's Coon Key Marina south of Goodland Bridge offers repair services with factory-trained technicians and a fully stocked marine parts and accessories department. They also offer dry storage and boat rentals and maintain a few transient slips. Safe Harbor Calusa Island (west of Coon Key Pass red daybeacon "6") has ample transient space (to 70 feet) plus a full array of convenient amenities and services. Call ahead to these facilities for slip availability.

Anchorage: You can anchor in Blue Hill Creek to the west of Goodland in 7 to 10 feet MLW and dinghy to town. In the northeast corner of Goodland Bay there's a deep water hole (at least 8 feet MLW) northeast of green daybeacon "7." To the southeast at Tripod Key you can anchor at the intersection of Sugar Bay at Coon Key Pass in 5 feet MLW.

America's Waterway Guide Since 1947 — Chapter 11

Ten Thousand Islands, FL

TEN THOUSAND ISLANDS AREA		Largest Vessel	VHF	Total Slips	Approach/ Dockside Depth	Floating Docks	Gas/ Diesel	Repairs/ Haulout	Min/Max Amps	Pump-Out Station
1. Walker's Coon Key Marina	(239) 394-2797	60	16	40	8.0 / 6.0	F	GD	RH	30	
2. Safe Harbor Calusa Island WiFi	(239) 394-3668	70	16	84	5.0 / 6.0	F	GD	R	30 / 50	P

WiFi Wireless Internet Access
Visit www.waterwayguide.com for current rates, fuel prices, website addresses and other up-to-the-minute information.
(Information in the table is provided by the facilities.)

Scan here for more details:

Goodland to Marco Island–Inland Passage

NAVIGATION: Use NOAA Chart 11430. The route through Goodland Bay to the Big Marco River requires considerable care even for those who have traveled it before. Seek local knowledge in Goodland or over the VHF radio. Markers are moved when necessary to reflect shifting shoals and may not be exactly where the chart shows them. Many prefer to pass through on a rising tide for obvious reasons.

Maintain a close watch on the depth sounder and use a pre-set alarm if possible. To get oriented it's a good idea to study your charts and GPS carefully after you have gathered some local knowledge. This is a scenic and viable route for some shoal-draft vessels. Refer to NOAA online charts for the most up-to-date information.

After you have passed Goodland at red daybeacon "10" you will need to make a sharp turn to the north, staying close to the marker and pass under the Goodland Bridge (55-foot fixed vertical clearance). After passing under the bridge you will find deeper water for a short time. Just beyond daybeacon "16" there is a very shallow area (as low as 3 feet MLW) when approaching daybeacon "18."

Once past "18" the water deepens again. When you pass green daybeacon "25" make sure you do not head straight for the bridge open span. You will need to veer further west and head for daybeacon "26." It will appear as if you are going completely off track because daybeacon "26" is almost to shore on the west side of the river. Don't be fooled by smaller boats that go straight to the bridge; it gets extremely shallow!

The **Judge Jolley (SR951) Memorial Bridge** (locally known as the **Marco Island Bridge**) crosses the waterway here with 55-foot fixed vertical clearance.

> NOTE: Just past the Marco Island Bridge the channel markers reverse. Northbound boats will now have green to starboard and red to port until you reach the Gulf of Mexico.

Source: Aqua Map and NOAA data

Chapter 11: Florida Keys to Fort Myers Beach

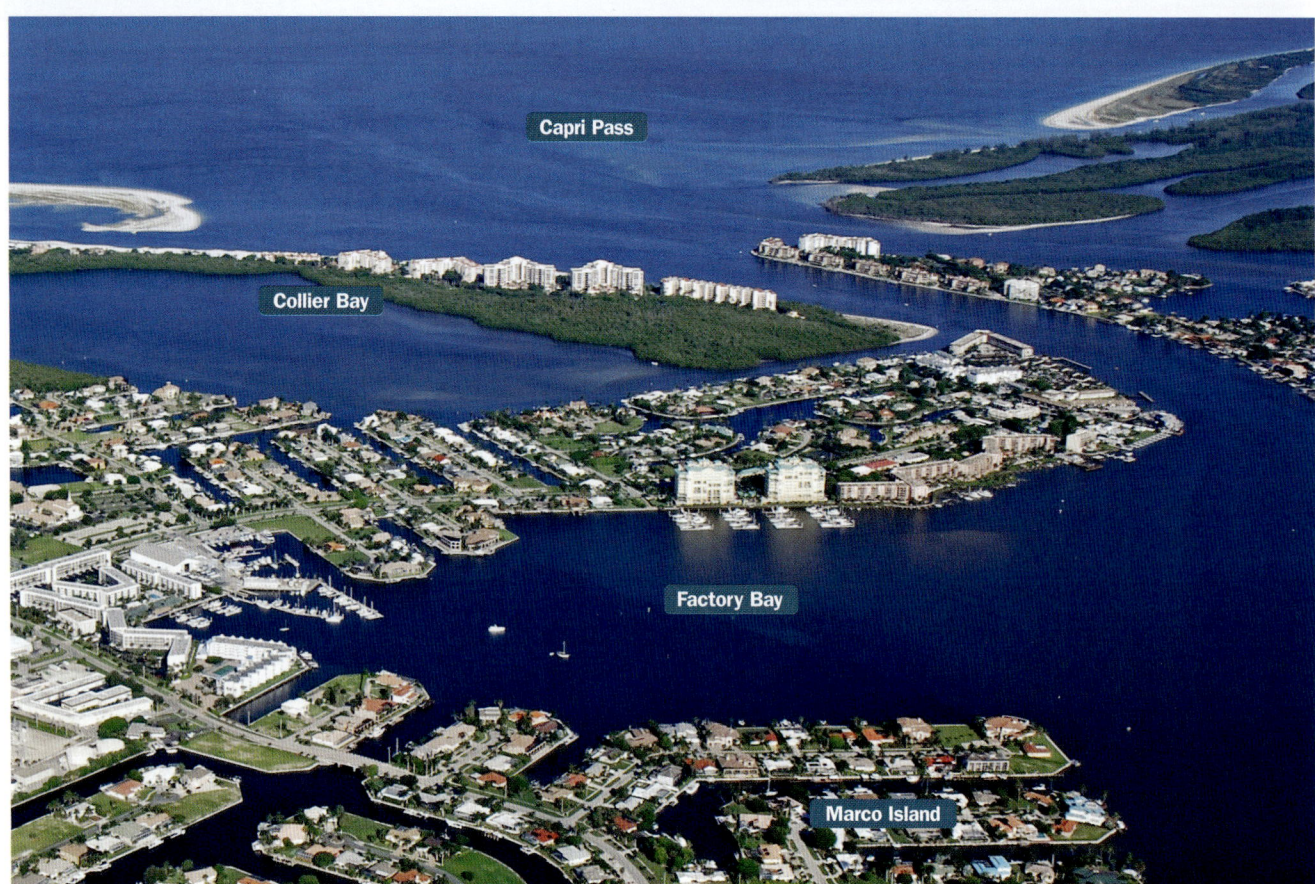

The next marker for the main channel is green daybeacon "15" not to be confused with nearby green daybeacon "1," which starts the northern channel into Factory Bay. Those heading directly to the Gulf continue north and then west through Capri Pass. When passing through Capri Pass be warned that the markers in the pass can be confusing and there are several sand bars. Check the notes on the Outside Passage for a description of Capri Pass.

Dockage: Continue north on Isle of Capri Pass for Pelican Bend Restaurant & Marina, which has three reserved transient slips to 60 feet. The Tarpon Club Marina looks to be adjacent to Pelican Bend at first glimpse but a closer look at the chart reveals that it is located on Tarpon Bay, accessible from the Big Marco River (not Isle of Capri Pass). This is primarily a storage facility but may have space for you. Call ahead.

If you approach Marco Island from the Isle of Capri Pass, Collier Bay will be to starboard, which leads to the 77-slip Esplanade Marina. The marina is tucked inside Smokehouse Bay, which is tricky to get into but once inside is well protected (360°). Between red daybeacons "12" and "14," turn south and follow the shallow but well-marked channel to Collier Bay. Continue southwest to red daybeacon "6" and make a sharp eastward turn leaving green daybeacon "7" to the north and heading into Smokehouse Bay. The marina has 6-foot MLW approach and dockside depths alongside their floating docks. Two great restaurants are on site and a grocery store is across street.

Snook Inn on the Big Marco River has been a landmark for more than 30 years and offers dockage for patrons and waterfront dining inside or out at the tiki bar. They have live entertainment 7 days a week and happy hour from 4:00 to 6:00 p.m. The marina can accommodate vessels up to 60 feet. (They also offer free transportation from other marinas.)

Marina at Factory Bay is on the Big Marco River past Collier Bay (if heading to the bridge). Past flashing red "14" and the Snook Inn, pick up the side channel at green daybeacon "1." The marina is between green daybeacons "3" and "5." Hail the dockmaster for assistance tying up and to arrange a long-term or transient stay on their floating docks. Transients are placed on the end of one

Marco Island, FL

MARCO ISLAND AREA		Largest Vessel	VHF	Total Slips	Approach/ Dockside Depth	Floating Docks	Gas/ Diesel	Repairs/ Haulout	Min/Max Amps	Pump-Out Station
1. Pelican Bend Restaurant & Marina	(239) 394-3452	60	16	18	5.0 / 7.0		GD		30	
2. The Tarpon Club Marina	(239) 417-6802	36	16	140	4.0 / 5.0	F	G		50	
3. Esplanade Marina WiFi	(239) 394-6333	66	16	77	6.0 / 6.0	F			30 / 50	P
4. Snook Inn	(239) 394-3313	60		20	15.0 / 6.0					
5. Pelican Pier Marina WiFi	(239) 389-2628	55	16	5	10.0 / 10.0	F	G			
6. The Marina at Factory Bay WiFi Marker 3A	(239) 389-2929	107	6	72	10.0 / 15.0	F			30 / 100	P
7. Rose Marina WiFi	(239) 394-2502	160	9	109	7.0 / 8.0	F	GD	RH	30 / 100	P
8. Marco Island Marina WiFi	(239) 776-2986	110	16	121	7.0 / 6.5	F			30 / 100	P
9. Riverside Marina at Marco Island Yacht Club WiFi	(239) 399-0199	125	16	27	7.0 / 6.0	F			30 / 200+	P

WiFi) Wireless Internet Access
Visit www.waterwayguide.com for current rates, fuel prices, website addresses and other up-to-the-minute information.
(Information in the table is provided by the facilities.)

Scan here for more details:

Source: Aqua Map and NOAA data

SOUTHERN EDITION 445

Chapter 11: Florida Keys to Fort Myers Beach

of the T docks, which makes for a easy approach and docking. There is limited transient dockage (35-foot minimum) so do call ahead.

The busy Rose Marina is in the southwestern corner of Factory Bay and may be hailed on VHF Channel 16 for reservations and directions. They have slips to accommodate all varieties and lengths of vessels including wider catamarans with a 30-foot minimum. They have a well-stocked store and are busy with rental boats coming and going as well as the Key West Jet Express, which runs out of this facility.

If you are looking for quiet surroundings, Marco Island Marina on the south side at the Marco Island Bridge is a very nice stop. The well-marked entrance is approximately 3 miles from Capri Pass past the stanchion of power lines and has 7-foot MLW approach depths. They welcome transients to 110 feet with all the expected amenities. A walk of less than 1 mile leads to groceries, a Post Office and a West Marine (1089 N. Collier Blvd., 239-642-7060).

The new docks at Riverside Marina at Marco Island Yacht Club have transient slips plus owners may rent out slips to 125 feet. This provides access to all Yacht Club facilities including restaurants and bars.

Anchorage: Once you work your way into Collier Bay proceed to daybeacon "7" and then enter the protected anchorage with good holding in Smokehouse Bay. There is 10 feet MLW and very good holding. Just follow channel markers closely and stay nearer the docking side of the channel for more depth. This anchorage is located in a residential neighborhood. Grocery shopping is easily accessed by passing under the west span of the Marco Island Bridge and landing at the convenient dinghy dock located beside the Winn-Dixie Supermarket.

You can also anchor in the Big Marco River to the northwest of flashing green "15" in 10 to 12 feet MLW. This is fairly exposed; expect wakes. Holding here is very good with a muddy sand bottom with some small shell.

Factory Bay also has good holding with 10 to 12 feet MLW. A sandbar splits the bay but there is plenty of water around the edge. Anchor in the southeast side by red daybeacons "2" and "4" for good protection. Nearby Rose Marina offers free pump-out service and a dinghy landing (for $5) for access to town.

■ TO NAPLES

From Marco Island to Naples is another opportunity to choose between an Inland Passage and an Outside Passage. Again, the Inland Passage is only viable for extreme shoal-draft vessels with an air-draft of less than 55 feet. Most cruising size vessels take the Outside Passage.

To Naples–Outside Passage

Naples is known for high-end shopping, sophisticated dining and an abundance of golf courses. The Naples Pier is a popular fishing and dolphin-spotting destination and the miles of fine white "sugar" sand and calm waters make the beaches here especially desirable.

NAVIGATION: Use NOAA Chart 11430. The 7-nm passage outside is fairly straightforward. Exiting Capri Pass be sure to clear flashing green "3" before turning northward to avoid the shoals extending off Sea Oat Island. Parallel Keewaydin Island to the well marked but slightly tricky entrance to Gordon Pass. It is best to line up for the channel well offshore. Use flashing reds "4" and "6" as a range on entry. A rock jetty on the south side of Gordon Pass extends 100 yards into the Gulf of Mexico. Favor the south side of the channel along the jetty. With onshore

Marco Island

winds and outgoing tide it can be challenging for slow or underpowered vessels. The encroaching shoals and jetties make this narrow entrance a bad place for an engine failure. Pass close to flashing red "6" on entry then turn north once clear of green daybeacon "7" to avoid the shoal off the northern spit (visible at low tide).

To reach Naples turn north up the Gordon River at green daybeacon "21." Shoals fringe the dredged channel so stay within the well-marked channel.

To Naples–Inland Passage

Naples is known for high-end shopping, sophisticated dining and an abundance of golf courses. The Naples Pier is a popular fishing and dolphin-spotting destination and the miles of fine white "sugar" sand and calm waters make the beaches here especially desirable.

For shoal-draft vessels the inside route from Capri Pass to Gordon Pass is delightful. The route of protected by a series on barrier islands and traverses some nature reserves. There is limited development along this route and during breaks in the sometimes-heavy boat traffic you will feel you've stumbled into a wilderness area. But this passage is not known for boater courtesy and you may experience some wakes from boats passing close by at full throttle.

About halfway along (red daybeacon "46") you pass Rookery Bay National Estuarine Research Reserve, a major wildlife sanctuary. Many cruisers choose to anchor in Rookery Channel to enjoy the natural beauty. This channel initially has good depth and provides some refuge from the wakes of passing powerboats. Birdwatchers should keep the binoculars handy.

NAVIGATION: Use NOAA Chart 11430.

CAUTION: Big Marco Pass is too shallow for passage by most vessels. The viable route into Marco Island is via well-marked Capri Pass just to the north. To enter pass close to flashing red "2" offshore and align to the channel.

The route northward starts by taking the north branch at the green-over-red daybeacon in Capri Pass initially towards the Iles of Capri Pass. Beware of the shifting sandbar to port near green daybeacon "1." Reduced speed is advised until the turn north. At green daybeacon "3" turn north as the channel deepens near Johnson Island. You will find deeper water closer to Cannon Island as you proceed through Calhoun Channel. There are spots as shallow is 3.5 feet MLW but with the 2- to 3-foot tidal range deeper vessels can pass through the 9-nm route on

Chapter 11: Florida Keys to Fort Myers Beach

Naples Bay, FL

NAPLES AREA		Largest Vessel	VHF	Total Slips	Approach/ Dockside Depth	Floating Docks	Gas/ Diesel	Repairs/ Haulout	Min/Max Amps	Pump-Out Station
1. Hamilton Harbor Yacht Club-PRIVATE	(239) 775-0506	60	16	36	7.0 / 7.0	F	GD	H		P
2. South Pointe Yacht Club and Marina-PRIVATE Naples	(239) 774-0518	70	16	72	5.0 / 5.0					

WiFi Wireless Internet Access
Visit www.waterwayguide.com for current rates, fuel prices, website addresses and other up-to-the-minute information.
(Information in the table is provided by the facilities.)

Scan here for more details:

a rising tide. You may also experience a "sleigh ride" on a rising tide for the passage north.

The channel shallows abruptly between green day beacons "17" and "19" where you may find 4-foot MLW depths. Look back occasionally to check channel alignment through this dredged segment. Expect some shoaling inside the marked channel through to green daybeacon "33." Pay strict attention to the channel markers (although some may be missing). Between green daybeacons "33" and "47" the route follows a deeper, natural channel.

At green daybeacon "47" the route again enters a narrow, dredged channel. Expect the shallowest parts of the passage in Dollar Bay between red daybeacons "64 and 68," where you may encounter spots with depths as low as 3 feet MLW. For most cruising vessels passage is only possible if you past this stretch near high tide.

A no wake zone extends from flashing red "34" (south of the Naples Yacht Club) to the US 41 Bridge on the Gordon River although, it is frequently ignored by "weekend warriors."

Dockage/Moorings: Dock space is usually available at Naples' numerous marinas but local marina operators recommend calling ahead for slip or mooring reservations particularly during the peak periods (holidays and weekends). Hamilton Harbor Yacht Club and South Pointe Yacht Club and Marina south of Naples are strictly private.

Farther north after flashing red "32" is Naples Yacht Club with slips (to 130 feet). The club practices reciprocity with other clubs but requests you make reservations ahead of time.

Naples Bay, FL

NAPLES AREA		Largest Vessel	VHF	Total Slips	Approach/Dockside Depth	Floating Docks	Gas/Diesel	Repairs/Haulout	Min/Max Amps	Pump-Out Station
1. Naples Yacht Club-PRIVATE WiFi	(239) 262-7301	130	16	88	8.0 / 6.0	F	GD		30 / 200+	P
2. Naples City Dock	(239) 213-3070	200	16	79	9.0 / 9.0	F	GD		30 / 100	P
3. Naples Boat Club Marina WiFi	(239) 263-2774	110	16	47	8.0 / 8.0	F	GD	RH	30 / 100	P
4. Naples Sailing & Yacht Club-PRIVATE WiFi 40	(239) 774-0424	65	16	75	6.0 / 6.0	F	GD		30 / 100	
5. Marina at Naples Bay Resort WiFi	(239) 530-5134	90	68	97	5.5 / 5.5	F	G		30 / 50	P

WiFi Wireless Internet Access
Visit www.waterwayguide.com for current rates, fuel prices, website addresses and other up-to-the-minute information.
(Information in the table is provided by the facilities.)

Scan here for more details:

Naples City Dock can accommodate vessels of various sizes with slips, a 400-foot face dock as well as 12 moorings in two well-protected coves. You are required to pump out and get your valve tag to lock down your discharge valve before going to the mooring ball. There is easy access to the pump-out at the fuel dock. You cannot stay more than four days at the dock or on a mooring in accordance with a city ordinance. The floating dinghy dock is on the same side of the pier as the mooring field.

In a convenient location on Naples Bay at red daybeacon "40" is the full-service Naples Boat Club Marina with wet slips, dry rack boat storage plus a restaurant, yacht sales and service. Amenities include a clubhouse with bar, billiards bayside pool and great views of Naples Bay.

Naples Sailing & Yacht Club at the south end of the island in the Gordon River welcomes visiting members from American Register of Yacht Clubs. Marina at Naples Bay Resort on the east side of the river has resort amenities. There are multiple restaurants on the marina grounds and they offer kayak, stand-up paddleboard and bicycle rentals.

Anchorage: Shoal-draft vessels can drop the hook in the old ICW channel at Johnson Bay red daybeacon "14" in 4 feet MLW. You can avoid some wakes by tucking in between Little Marco Island and Keewaydin Island south of Little Marco Island green daybeacon "33." The anchorage east of Rookery Channel green daybeacon "47" is a popular spot. The deepest water (6 to 8 feet MLW) is about 0.5 mile in. From here you can explore the nature reserve by dinghy.

Gordon Pass north of red daybeacon "10" and "12" is an option if you can handle the charted bar with 4-foot MLW depths that crosses the entrance. Enter the first canal to the east and anchor in a well-protected cove in 9-foot MLW depths among beautiful homes. There is no

Chapter 11: Florida Keys to Fort Myers Beach

place to land a dinghy. A second option is to proceed into Gordon Pass green daybeacon "21" and turn northwest and then southwest into the first cove. You will be well protected from all sides in 7-foot MLW depths. There is no shore access here but you may find beach access just east of red daybeacon "22."

■ TO FORT MYERS BEACH

> **CAUTION:** Due to the widespread damage inflicted by Hurricane Ian, do not plan to dock here without calling ahead for status. Every marina was affected in some way and many were destroyed. Refer to Waterway Explorer (www.waterwayguide.com) for the latest updates.

Gordon Pass to Big Carlos Pass

There is no protected inside route between Naples and Estero Bay. Be sure you have adequate daylight and favorable weather before embarking on the 19 nm passage from Gordon Pass to Big Carlos Pass (23.5-nm passage from Gordon Pass to the deeper Matanzas Pass entrance).

NAVIGATION: Use NOAA Charts 11427 and 11430. There are a few obstructions and hazards along this coastline so stay about 2 nm off the beach. In particular expect some shoals extending from the inlets along the coast. In good weather the Gulf of Mexico is calm and easy to transit but in winter months, when the winds are often out of the northwest or north it can get rough. If the winds are northwest at more than 12 knots, you may want to wait it out in Naples. Pick your weather wisely and there should be no problem.

Controlling depths in the marked channel from New Pass to Big Carlos Pass are reported to be 4 feet MLW with a 2.5-foot tidal range. Note there is a fixed bridge with a vertical clearance of 30 feet on this route. For vessels drawing 4 feet or less daybeacons lead from Wiggins Pass for a distance of just under 0.5 mile into the Cocohatchee River where dockage is available.

> **CAUTION:** Due to significant and seasonal low tide conditions, the private aids to navigation in Wiggins Pass are no longer reliable. Permanent fixed private aids to navigation dayboards have been removed and unmarked structures may still be present. Temporary floating private aids to navigation have been established to mark best water. Mariners are advised to exercise caution while transiting the area.

Dockage: Once through Wiggins Pass controlling channel depths to the marinas are 4 to 5 feet MLW. Pelican Isle Yacht Club just inside Wiggins Pass is a private members-only club. Directly across from Pelican Isle is the municipal Cocohatchee River Park Marina, which has slips for boats 30 feet or smaller. This is a 7-acre property with paddling trails.

Anchorage: About 5.7 miles north of Gordon Pass narrow Doctors Pass can serve as a harbor of refuge. The area is well marked; favor the center. Once inside, Moorings Bay has 3 to 6 feet MLW with good holding and all-around protection. There are no services for transients.

Mangrove Islands along Big Carlos Pass

Cocohatchee River, FL

WIGGINS PASS		Largest Vessel	VHF	Total Slips	Approach/ Dockside Depth	Floating Docks	Gas/ Diesel	Repairs/ Haulout	Min/Max Amps	Pump-Out Station
1. Pelican Isle Yacht Club-PRIVATE	(239) 566-1606	55	16	190	5.0 / 4.5	F	GD		30 / 50	P
2. Cocohatchee River Park Marina	(239) 514-3752	30	16	39	6.0 / 6.0		GD		30 / 50	P

WiFi Wireless Internet Access
Visit www.waterwayguide.com for current rates, fuel prices, website addresses and other up-to-the-minute information. (Information in the table is provided by the facilities.)

Scan here for more details:

Big Carlos Pass to Fort Myers Beach– Outside Passage

NAVIGATION: Use NOAA Chart 11427. From Big Carlos Pass set a course for the flashing white Morse (A) 16-foot-high marker "SC." From that point you should be able to pick out 16-foot flashing red buoy "2" approximately 1 mile to the north-northwest and quick flashing red "4" beyond. Keep red markers to starboard entering San Carlos Bay. Beware of the dangerous shoals that extend 3 nm south from Sanibel Island. This shoal structure has been growing in recent years and depths may be shallower than charted in this area.

Due north from quick flashing red "4" lies the well-marked entrance channel leading off from San Carlos Bay into Matanzas Pass, which begins with flashing green "1." Keep red markers to starboard southbound through the pass. Starting at red daybeacon "6" the channel makes a large U-turn to the south behind the northwestern hook of Estero Island. The channel runs close to Estero Island. There are spoils areas and shoals to the east.

Currents can be swift in the Matanzas Pass channel depending on the tide. Expect heavy marine traffic

Chapter 11 — Florida Keys to Fort Myers Beach

Fort Myers Beach, FL

FORT MYERS BEACH AREA		Largest Vessel	VHF	Total Slips	Approach/ Dockside Depth	Floating Docks	Gas/ Diesel	Repairs/ Haulout	Min/Max Amps	Pump-Out Station
1. Loggerhead Marina - Fish-Tale Marina WiFi	(239) 463-3600	80	77	100	4.0 / 8.0	F	G	RH	30 / 50	P
2. Snook Bight Marina WiFi	(239) 221-2800	70	16	74	6.5 / 6.5	F	GD	RH	30 / 50	P

WiFi Wireless Internet Access
Visit www.waterwayguide.com for current rates, fuel prices, website addresses and other up-to-the-minute information.
(Information in the table is provided by the facilities.)

Scan here for more details:

Source: Aqua Map and NOAA data

Fort Myers Beach, FL

FORT MYERS BEACH AREA		Largest Vessel	VHF	Total Slips	Approach/ Dockside Depth	Floating Docks	Gas/ Diesel	Repairs/ Haulout	Min/Max Amps	Pump-Out Station
1. Pink Shell Beach Resort and Marina WiFi	(239) 463-8620	120	16	41	15.0 / 8.5	F		R	30 / 100	P
2. Moss Marina 17	(239) 765-6677	160	16	51	12.0 /	F	GD	R		
3. Matanzas Inn Bayside Resort and Marina WiFi	(239) 463-9258	60	16	16	12.0 / 8.0				30 / 50	P
4. Salty Sam's Marina WiFi	(239) 463-7333	225	16	130	14.0 / 12.0	F	GD	RH	30 / 100	P

WiFi Wireless Internet Access
Visit www.waterwayguide.com for current rates, fuel prices, website addresses and other up-to-the-minute information.
(Information in the table is provided by the facilities.)

Scan here for more details:

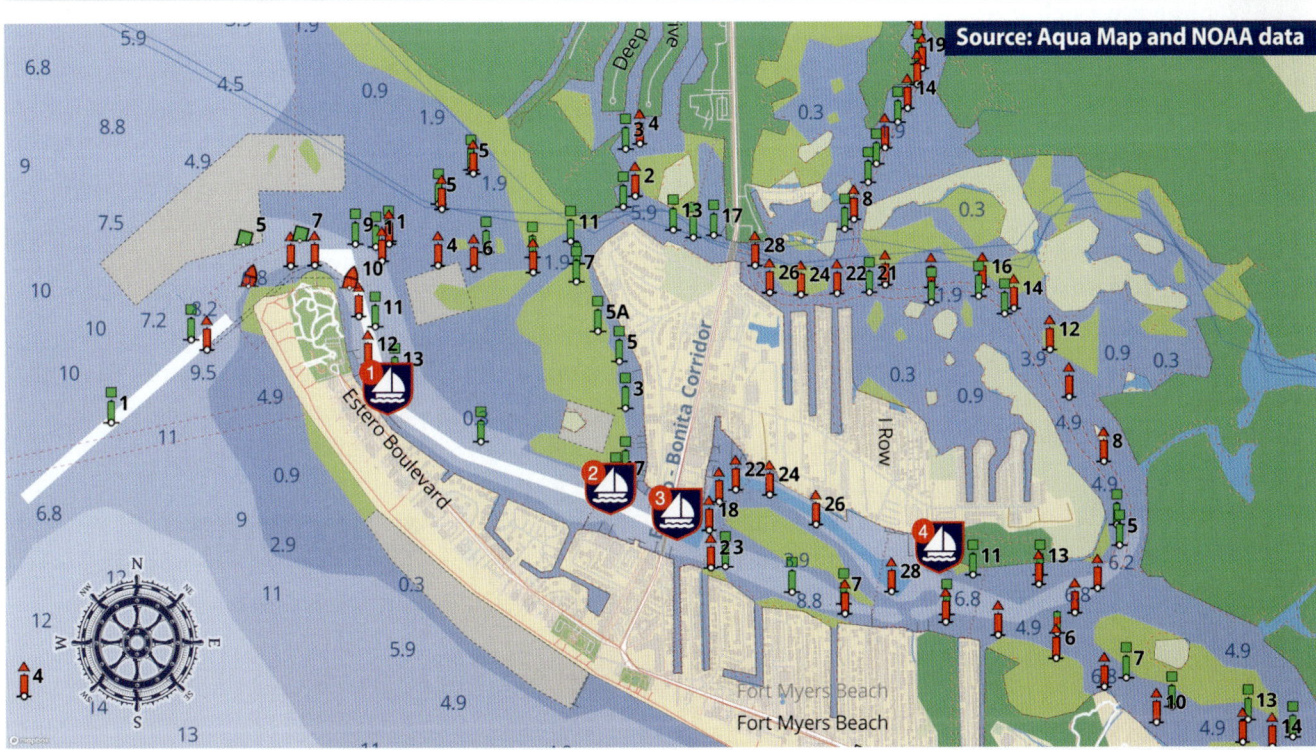

between Estero Island and San Carlos Island. **SR 865 Matanzas Pass Bridge** (65-foot fixed vertical clearance) crosses the channel about 2 nm from the entrance.

Big Carlos Pass to Fort Myers Beach–Inland Passage

NAVIGATION: Use NOAA Chart 11427. If you are hugging the coastline about 1 nm offshore from Naples, you should be aware that shoals project well offshore from Big Carlos Pass. If you are trying to reach Estero Bay and Fort Myers Beach, you can enter at Big Carlos Pass but the channel location moves and you may want to wait for a lead-in boat to follow. Although charts indicate controlling depths of 4 to 6 feet MLW some claim the channel carries about 8 feet MLW. While the bottom here is constantly shifting reports suggest the channel follows the contour lines of Lovers Key on approach from the south. It is best to call ahead to nearby Estero Bay Boat Tours (VHF Channel 79) for an update on directions and controlling depths.

Big Carlos Pass (SR 865) Bridge (23-foot closed vertical clearance) opens on signal except from 7:00 p.m. to 8:00 a.m. daily, when it need not open. Once past Carlos Point and under the bridge daybeacons guide your passage either north or south through the natural and historic beauty of Estero Bay. To reach Fort Myers Beach turn north between green daybeacon "67" and red daybeacon "68." This channel is well marked but note that you must keep red markers to port heading northward.

The route north follows the northeast shore of Estero Island to the Matanzas Pass, which leads on to Fort Myers Beach. There are numerous hazards outside the marked channel so take care to maintain alignment.

Chapter 11: Florida Keys to Fort Myers Beach

Dockage/Moorings:

CAUTION: Due to the widespread damage inflicted by Hurricane Ian, do not plan to dock here without calling ahead for status. Every marina was affected in some way and many were destroyed. You are welcome to anchor in the waters clear of any navigable channel waterway but be aware of underwater obstructions. Refer to Waterway Explorer (www.waterwayguide.com) for the latest updates.

Loggerhead Marina–Fish Tale Marina is a small marina and restaurant on Estero Island in a channel behind Coon Key. They report 4-foot MLW approach depths. Call ahead for slip availability. Approximately halfway along Estero Island you will encounter the full-service Snook Bight Yacht Club & Marina. The marina offers ample boater services and amenities including repair, maintenance and restoration; waterfront dining; and a well-stocked Ship Store.

The first marina you will encounter before Matanzas Pass is the family-friendly Pink Shell Beach Resort and Marina, which is set on 12 lush acres. The marina can accommodate vessels up to 120 feet on floating docks. Guests at the marina are welcome to the resort's numerous amenities including the pool and beach club, a fitness center and water sport rentals. (Be sure to ask about their grocery service.) They are also a stop on the shuttle route for easy access to the island. As always call in advance for reservations.

The complex of white buildings of Moss Marina is highly visible to the south adjacent to daybeacon "17." Transient berths are available on their floating docks but make advance reservations particularly during the winter months. They also have multiple fueling stations. It is a short walk to fine dining and the beach.

Soon after you pass under the bridge on the south shore is Matanzas Inn Bayside Resort and Marina with 16 slips for boats up to 60 feet. There are two fields (East and West) at Matanzas Pass Mooring Fields, which is managed by the city. Check in at the Mooring Office across the street from the dinghy dock. Open 9:00 a.m. to 1:00 p.m. Showers and laundry room are provided with (flat rate) fee.

A little farther along the channel is Ballard Oil Co., a fuel dock with gas and diesel fuel at great prices. At the end of the harbor (beyond the shrimp fleet) is Salty Sam's Marina, which specializes in dry storage, boat rentals and boat detailing services. They welcome transients or tie up for a bite at the waterfront Parrot Key Caribbean Grill or the Original Shrimp Dock Bar & Grill, both of which are dog friendly!

Anchorage: There is an easy-access, open anchorage at Big Carlos) with depths of 9 to 12 feet. Anchor to avoid the charted power line on the north side of the channel as well as the small boat channel to the east. Bass and pontoon boats are frequent but only during the day.

You can drop the hook in 8 feet of water at the entrance to the Matanzas River. There is some mild current and the area is a no wake zone. Easy access to the Gulf and getting into Ft. Myers Beach by dinghy if needed.

You can also anchor in 5 to 7 feet MLW east of Matanzas Pass red daybeacon "4" on the north side of the unnamed island.

■ NEXT STOP

Fort Myers Beach is a genuine nautical crossroad. It is a pivotal location for vessels making passages farther north up the west coast of Florida or entering the Okeechobee Waterway and cruising all the way to its east coast terminus at the ICW in Stuart.(The Okeechobee Waterway is covered in detail in Chapter 6 of this guide.)

Matanzas Pass Bridge

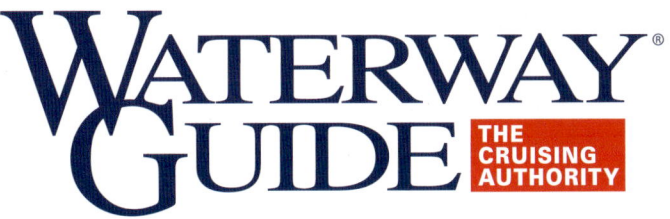

Scan to subscribe now at
www.waterwayguide.com

Navigate with the Cruising Authority

Chapter 12: Sanibel Island to Sarasota Bay

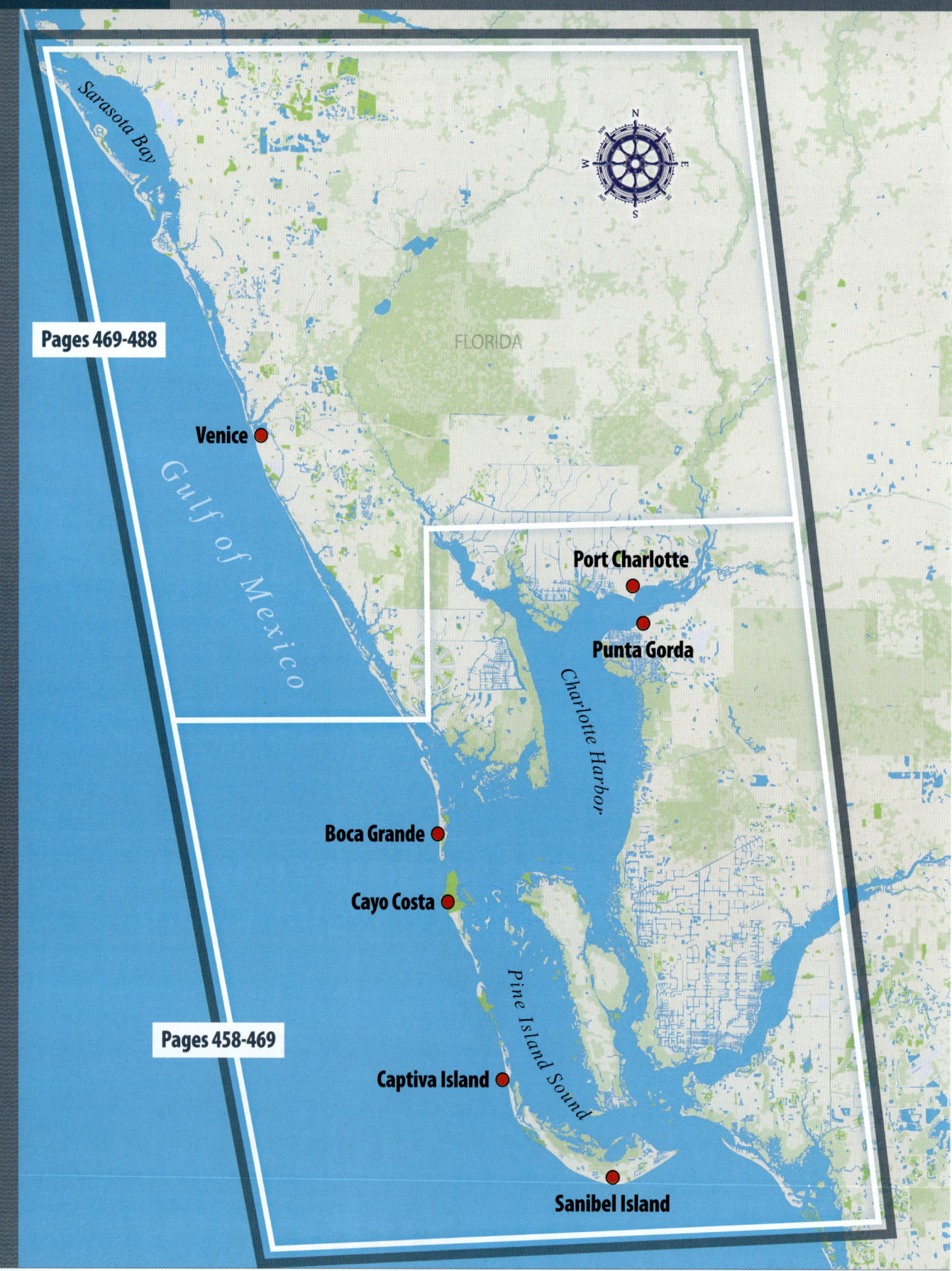

NAVIGATING THE GIWW

The GIWW runs from Cape Coral FL, to Brownsville, TX, with an open-water gap between Tarpon Springs and Carrabelle, FL. The traditional way to describe your direction of travel is to declare that you are "eastbound" if you're traveling from Texas towards Carrabelle, FL, and "westbound" if traveling the other direction. (This book is written as though you were traveling westbound from Florida to Texas.) Distances are measured in statute miles east or west of the Harvey Lock in New Orleans. It is a good idea to switch your GPS to statute miles when cruising these waters.

The GIWW is either a dredged channel behind barrier islands or a passage through one of Florida's large Gulf Coast bays. Much of the waterway is constrained to a narrow marked channel with shoals lurking just outside the buoys. While the option of an "inside route" is reassuring, many cruisers make the trip northward as a series of open ocean hops. Seas are generally manageable in the shallow off-shore waters and refuge can be sought at regular intervals. Be sure to check for a suitable weather window and plan your passage based on inlets with sufficient depth.

Unless you must hurry to meet a deadline and are in a powerboat that can hit high double numbers we suggest you take the protected and infinitely more interesting GIWW route inside. There are fewer bridges on the GIWW than the ICW, most are bascule or swing bridges and many operate on a fixed schedule. The air-draft for the GIWW is 65 feet and is set by fixed bridges. The minimum authorized overhead cable clearance is 85 feet.

Shoals flank much of the marked route similar to the ICW on Florida's east coast. The Army Corps of Engineers' project depth for the length of the GIWW is purported to be 9 feet MLW but do not count on having that much water. Keep an eye on the depths here, especially in winter when northerly winds push the water out of bays and channels. Even under optimum conditions shoaling is so chronic in certain spots (noted in the text) that boats must slow down and gently ease their way through.

Heading north on the GIWW leave red daybeacons to starboard and green to port. As with the Atlantic ICW, GIWW channel markers are green or red with small yellow triangles on red markers and squares on green markers (and an occasional yellow stripe) in addition to the numbers and/or letters. Another way to remember this is that the red marks delineate the mainland side of the GIWW channel.

> DO NOT pass a cable-operated pontoon bridge or cable operated ferry crossing unless you are SURE the cable is on the bottom.

Bridges respond on VHF Channel 13 and sometimes VHF Channel 16, except in Florida where they use VHF Channel 09 and VHF Channel 16. Locks use VHF Channel 14. Specific channel information is listed behind each lock and bridge listed in this guide. Tell them you are a pleasure craft and make your request. If appropriate, announce your intentions. Locks sometimes ask for your documentation or state registration number, so have that information handy.

NO WAKE ZONE

No Wake Zones, Idle Speed Zones and various Speed Limit restrictions are in effect throughout the waterways included in this chapter. Exercise diligence in knowing the regulations by observing signs and other markers. Enforcement is always present. As always, be courteous to other vessels and avoid manatees and other marine life.

Chapter 12: Sanibel Island to Sarasota Bay

 GIWW Mile 0–Mile 78

■ TO CHARLOTTE HARBOR

CAUTION: Hurricane Ian caused widespread damage across southwest Florida after making landfall on Cayo Costa Island as a Category 4 hurricane in September 2022. All of the communities in this section were affected in major ways and rebuilding will be a long process. Call ahead for status prior to arrival.

Option: Outside (Gulf) Route

NAVIGATION: Use NOAA Charts 11425, 11426 and 11427. Mariners running the Gulf of Mexico to Charlotte Harbor or points north need only to choose the best weather and go. The only complications along this route are the shoals and bars that extend out from many areas of the shoreline and form an integral part of virtually every pass and inlet on Florida's West Coast. Be sure you are standing sufficiently offshore to clear them, which may make the trip somewhat longer than cutting up Pine Island Sound. Staying 3 to 4 nm off the coastline should get the job done.

To reach the Gulf for the trip north head south down the marked channel that goes underneath Sanibel Causeway Boulevard 'A' Span Bridge. Well-charted shoals extend most of the way from Point Ybel south to the San Carlos Bay Morse (A) marker "SC," where it becomes safe to turn west as long as the weather and water won't sweep you into the shallow areas. Curve north with the sweep of Sanibel Island and lay a course that will take you to the Boca Grande flashing red buoy "2" (roughly 4.5 nm outside the entrance to Charlotte Harbor; GPS coordinates: N 026° 39.846'/W 082° 19.565').

If not planning to stop at Charlotte Harbor, entering a target waypoint just offshore of your target destination will provide the distance and after a close double-check along the path a "stay outside" line for quick visual reference. Venice provides a clean, well-marked inlet if visiting Sarasota. Using the two passes closest to Sarasota (New Pass and Big Sarasota Pass) definitely requires local knowledge.

Sanibel Island

A string of barrier islands including Sanibel, Captiva, North Captiva and Cayo Costa separate Pine Island Sound from the Gulf of Mexico. Together the islands form a shallow crescent lying at an angle to the currents. That accident of shape and location causes what are said to be the world's most prolific shell deposits and the resultant "Sanibel stoop" of the island's visitors. More than 300 varieties of shells have been found on these beaches. The best shelling is at low tide after a storm when winds and waves have washed a new supply up on the beaches.

> **NOTE:** Sanibel Island law prohibits collectors from taking live shells, living starfish and sand dollars.

The best way to see Sanibel Island is on the miles of bicycle paths. Rental bikes are readily available from numerous sources on the island. You will want to visit the historic Sanibel Lighthouse at Point Ybel (1884) southeast from the marina and its beach and a fishing pier. The tree-lined main thoroughfare, Periwinkle Way, takes you to the Sanibel Historical Village and Museum (239-472-4648), which showcases the island's history. Tours (for a fee) are held at 10:30 a.m. and 1:30 p.m. based on docent availability.

The only public landing on the island other than dropping the hook and landing by dinghy is at Sanibel Marina. If you want to explore the island by land you will need to obtain permission to tie up your dinghy at the marina.

NAVIGATION: Use NOAA Chart 11426 or 11427. To reach the GIWW from Fort Myers Beach head west from Matanzas Pass. If your vessel requires more than 26 feet of vertical clearance, you will have to go through **Sanibel Causeway Boulevard 'A' Span Bridge** (70-foot fixed vertical clearance) on the Punta Rassa (northeast) side of the bay. If you can navigate the 26-foot fixed vertical clearance you can use the **Sanibel Causeway Boulevard 'C' Span Bridge**. **Sanibel Causeway Boulevard 'B' Span Bridge** has 9-foot fixed vertical clearance.

To reach the high span ('A') from flashing green "1" at Matanzas Pass steer a course of 282° magnetic to flashing red "6" indicating the start of the channel to the Caloosahatchee River and the Okeechobee Waterway. Follow the channel from flashing red "6" through the bridge and then to flashing red "14" leaving it to the east. Shortly past that red lighted aid watch for green daybeacon "15" to

San Carlos Bay, FL

PUNTA RASSA		Largest Vessel	VHF	Total Slips	Approach/ Dockside Depth	Floating Docks	Gas/ Diesel	Repairs/ Haulout	Min/Max Amps	Pump-Out Station
1. Sanibel Harbour Yacht Club- PRIVATE	(239) 333-4200	48	16	4	/ 6.0					
2. Royal Shell Port Sanibel Marina WiFi	(239) 437-1660	65	16	95	4.0 / 5.0		GD	H	30 / 50	P
SANIBEL ISLAND										
3. Sanibel Marina (Open-call ahead) WiFi	(239) 472-2723	70	16	65	6.0 / 6.0		GD	R	50	P

WiFi Wireless Internet Access
Visit www.waterwayguide.com for current rates, fuel prices, website addresses and other up-to-the-minute information.
(Information in the table is provided by the facilities.)

Scan here for more details:

Chapter 12: Sanibel Island to Sarasota Bay

the southwest and flashing green "101" to the northeast, which mark the end of the Okeechobee Waterway and the beginning of the GIWW (Mile 0). Turn southwest at green can "1" and pick up the well-marked channel as described above.

If you plan on transiting span 'C' (26-foot fixed vertical clearance) from Matanzas Pass, set a course of 265° magnetic from flashing green "1" when leaving the Matanzas Pass channel to flashing red "2" on the Sanibel Island side of the entrance to San Carlos Bay a distance of about 2.75 nm. Once under the 'C' span and about 2.5 miles up the well-marked channel you will pick out the 16-foot high, quick flashing green "11" for the GIWW channel.

A little less than 1 mile to the southwest you will see red daybeacon "2" marking the entrance to the channel to Sanibel Marina. Be careful making your approach. The sandy bottom is always shifting. It is best to enter at half-tide or better and call ahead for the latest local information. Enter the channel heading south and stay to the west side to avoid the obvious shoal at the first canal to the east. Continue south for Sanibel Marina's fuel dock.

Dockage: Just north of the eastern end of the fixed bridge (span 'A') west of Punta Rassa you may find a berth at Royal Shell Port Sanibel Marina, an "Old Florida" style marina. Guests can enjoy a mile-long nature boardwalk that meanders through a pristine mangrove forest. They report 4-foot MLW approach depths; call ahead for assistance with directions. They also offer charters and boat rentals so expect traffic. Nearby Sanibel Harbour Yacht Club is private.

A snug harbor is available at the full-service Sanibel Marina, the only marina on the island. The well-protected marina monitors VHF Channel 16 and has transient slips for vessels up to 70 feet in an unhurried, palm-fringed setting. They have all the usual amenities plus laundry and some of the best water in the area, thanks to a reverse-osmosis water treatment system. There is a Ship Store on site with a large inventory of boat necessities and clothing. The on-site Gramma Dot's may have space for you while you eat lunch. Call ahead to the dockmaster on VHF Channel 16 or 239-472-8138.

Anchorage: The Point Ybel anchorage just off Sanibel Marina has 9 to 14 feet MLW. This offers easy access to the shore but expect some current. There is a pocket of deeper water to the northeast in Matanzas Pass that has easy access, good depth and good holding. It is exposed to wind from the south but is perfectly acceptable for short stops.

Vessels often anchor in the deeper water slot between Kitchel Key and Fisherman Key in 7 to 11 feet MLW. Watch the shoal to starboard when entering. Boats also anchor north on the outside of Punta Rassa Cove with at least 8-foot MLW depths. Both of these anchorages are fairly exposed but will suffice during settled weather.

Side Trip: J.N. "Ding" Darling National Wildlife Refuge

The 6,354-acre J.N. "Ding" Darling National Wildlife Refuge takes up much of 12-mile-long Sanibel Island mainly along the northern (Pine Island Sound) side. The refuge also serves as headquarters for several small wildlife refuges on nearby islands. During the nesting season mariners are asked not to land on these rookery islands. The refuge offers nature walks and an interpretive center. Even the most casual visitor will inevitably see alligators, anhinga ("snakebirds"), roseate spoonbills, snowy egrets, wood storks and great blue herons. Pink flamingos are seen quite often as well. The park is open daily from 10:00 a.m. to 4:00 p.m. For more information visit J.N. "Ding" Darling National Wildlife Refuge or call 239-472-1100.

Anchorage: J.N. "Ding" Darling National Wildlife Refuge offers an excellent anchorage possibility during settled weather in the cove due south of flashing red "16" (situated south of York Island). It is exposed to east through north winds with room for several boats. This is easily accessed off the channel. Watch your charts while entering for one shallow shoal. Holding is excellent in sand and mud close to Sanibel Island's mangrove shoreline in at least 6 feet MLW with good holding. It's a very scenic anchorage and a great spot to explore.

To North Captiva Island–GIWW Mile 4

Liberally dotted with small islands and protected from the open Gulf of Mexico by a string of barrier islands Pine Island Sound runs about 15 miles to the mouth of Charlotte Harbor at Boca Grande Pass. Many of the small islands in the sound are part of the Pine Island National Wildlife Refuge and are closed to public access to protect the wildlife. Along this stretch you will see many ospreys tending their large nests.

America's Waterway Guide Since 1947 Chapter 12

Pine Island Sound, FL

CAPTIVA ISLAND		Largest Vessel	VHF	Total Slips	Approach/ Dockside Depth	Floating Docks	Gas/ Diesel	Repairs/ Haulout	Min/Max Amps	Pump-Out Station
1. 'Tween Waters Island Resort & Spa MM 11.0	(239) 472-5161	100	16	41	6.0 / 6.0		GD		30 / 50	P
2. Jensen's Twin Palm Cottages and Marina WIFI MM 12.0	(239) 472-5800	25	16	20	5.0 / 5.0		G			
3. South Seas Marina WIFI MM 13.6	(855) 777-3625	120	16		6.0 / 6.0		GD		30 / 100	P

WIFI Wireless Internet Access Scan here for more details:
Visit www.waterwayguide.com for current rates, fuel prices, website addresses and other up-to-the-minute information. (Information in the table is provided by the facilities.)

NAVIGATION: Use NOAA Charts 11426 and 11427. Sailors in auxiliary-powered sailboats know the "Miserable Mile" well. Here the tide sweeps in and out directly across the arrow-straight channel and strong crosscurrents are likely. Allow for the set and line up markers fore and aft. The channel is well marked and easy to follow.

Be especially careful crossing south of Matlacha (pronounced "Mat-la-shay") Pass. The channel cuts off to the northwest just past green daybeacon "5" (when headed west). Do not stray too far to the west into 2 to 3 foot MLW. The currents are very strong and the channel is prone to silting around flashing green daybeacons "5" and "9." One nautical mile farther west the problem worsens near where the channel bends to the northwest around the south end of Pine Island. Northerly winds tend to encourage the buildup of silt in the area.

The channel runs a jagged course often at an angle to the swift current through pools of relatively deep water interspersed with great shallow bays. Exercise caution. Stay to mid-channel, take navigational aids in order and do not try any shortcuts. In Pine Island Sound between flashing green "23" and red daybeacon "24" at about Mile 8 power lines cross the channel with a charted vertical clearance of 95 feet at the main channel.

Just to the north of Sanibel is Captiva Island, about 6 miles long and separated from Sanibel Island by Blind Pass, which is crossed by a 7-foot fixed vertical clearance bridge. Heading north up Pine Island Sound at red daybeacon "38" a course of about 215° magnetic brings you back through shoal water to the little village of Captiva where cruisers will find marinas and amenities. Look for the marked channel beginning at flashing red "2" leading into town.

Shifting, shoaling Redfish Pass divides Captiva Island from North Captiva Island. This pass should only be used with current local knowledge. If you choose to exit or enter the Gulf of Mexico here call South Seas Island Resort

SOUTHERN EDITION

Chapter 12: Sanibel Island to Sarasota Bay

& Marina for advice. Remember that currents are strong in this area and shoaling persists. Boca Grande Pass, a good exit to the Gulf of Mexico, is the preferred pass and is only 6 miles to the north.

North Captiva Island is accessible only by boat. A marked channel runs north from Captiva Pass across the GIWW toward Charlotte Harbor but do not use it as a shortcut unless yours is a very shallow-draft boat. This channel shoals in its upper reaches to about 5 feet MLW. In the rest of the channel depths run 7 to 13 feet MLW with occasional spots for anchoring. Although used by fishers with local knowledge Captiva Pass–between North Captiva Island and Cayo Costa–is unmarked and subject to change.

Dockage: Honor the red markers (controlling depth is 6.5 feet MLW) for 'Tween Waters Island Resort & Spa tucked in behind Buck Key. To reach the 41-slip marina turn west at red daybeacon "38" of the GIWW and proceed on a course of 215° magnetic (for about 1.0 mile) to locate Roosevelt Channel's flashing red "2." Follow that to green daybeacon "19." (Better yet, call ahead for directions and follow them.) Transients have free access to the resort including beach access, a pool complex, spa and lively pub-style bar (with entertainment most nights). They also have kayak and stand-up paddleboard rentals as well as loaner bikes to get you to the main commercial area on the island, which is about a mile away. Farther up the channel is Jensen's Twin Palm Cottages and Marina, a small boutique inn with a laid-back, relaxed atmosphere. Call ahead for slip availability.

A channel marked with daybeacons leads from the GIWW between red daybeacon "38" and flashing green "39" to South Seas Island Resort & Marina. The channel leading into the marina is well marked and they can accommodate vessels to 120 feet. This is a first-rate facility with resort amenities. All vessels must announce entry upon arrival at the entrance marker on VHF Channel 16.

Anchorage: At the southern tip of Pine Island sits the central point for fishing on the lower sound, St. James City. Fishing camps and small boat marinas abound here along with shallow water and numerous private markers that can be confusing to the stranger. You can anchor south of St. James City by the mangroves in 8 to 9 feet MLW and dinghy to shore. There are also several restaurants directly on the main (Monroe) canal you can dinghy to for a visit.

Chino Island to the north in Pine Island Sound offers protection from easterly and northerly winds with good holding. Leave the GIWW at flashing green "23" and you will find 7- to 8-foot MLW depths almost to the shore. You may receive a few wakes from vessels traveling the GIWW and locals who use this area for fishing and a shortcut to nearby canals. You can anchor anywhere off the channel in Pine Island Sound where deeper water is indicated on the charts.

Two anchorage areas are located behind Buck Key at Captiva Island. You can also drop the hook at green daybeacon "21" or at green daybeacon "17" in 4 to 5 feet MLW. The anchorage at the northern tip of North Captiva Island is a beautiful location in fair weather but is fully exposed from northeast through south-southeast. North Captiva has no cars, just sand roads for foot, bike and golf cart traffic. Off the southeast tip of Cayo Costa Key an anchorage is within a dinghy-pull of the beaches at both North Captiva Island and Cayo Costa. Both anchorages have 7 to 10 feet MLW.

Side Trip: Cabbage Key

Just west of the GIWW channel Cabbage Key lies in the lee of Cayo Costa. This delightful and unspoiled island is accessible only by boat and offers ample opportunity for observing nature in all its forms. For bird and nature enthusiasts the bird watching and nature walk should not be missed. It is best to begin at the top of Cabbage Key's walk-up water tower for an overview of the island. Easily followed trails traverse Cabbage Key's connected shell mounds, revealing representative varieties of subtropical trees, shrubs, plants and bird life. Nesting ospreys are abundant as are telltale signs of the Florida gopher tortoise.

A great exploration by dinghy gives you access to the front beach of Cabbage Key by way of The Tunnel. If you are anchored northeast of flashing red "60" proceed south around Cabbage Key to Murdock Bayou. Go almost to the end of Murdock Bayou and you will see a small, open area in the mangroves on the west side. There is enough room to tie a couple of dinghies to the mangroves. Walk through the tunnel of mangroves to the path that leads to the beach. (Watch for alligators.) It is a great place to picnic and enjoy the white sandy beach. In north winds depths through The Tunnel and Murdock Bayou may be too shallow even for dinghies.

Pine Island Sound, FL

CABBAGE KEY		Largest Vessel	VHF	Total Slips	Approach/ Dockside Depth	Floating Docks	Gas/ Diesel	Repairs/ Haulout	Min/Max Amps	Pump-Out Station
1. Cabbage Key Inn WiFi MM 21.5	(239) 283-2278	85	16	25	8.0 / 6.0				30 / 50	
PINE ISLAND										
2. Cayo Costa State Park	(941) 964-0375	35			6.0 / 6.0	F				

WiFi Wireless Internet Access
Visit www.waterwayguide.com for current rates, fuel prices, website addresses and other up-to-the-minute information.
(Information in the table is provided by the facilities.)

Scan here for more details:

Source: Aqua Map and NOAA data

Chapter 12: Sanibel Island to Sarasota Bay

Dockage: Reached by the privately marked entry channel just west of green daybeacon "61" is the classic old Florida island retreat, Cabbage Key Inn, which sits upon a 38-foot-high Calusa shell mound. One hundred acres of tropical vegetation surround the historic restaurant, inn and rental cottages. The marina sits at the base with 25 slips.

Opposite Cayo Costa north of the GIWW at about flashing red "60" is the private island of Useppa. Accessible only by water, Useppa Island Club has been established as a private club. They do not accept transients; you must be a member or a guest of a member.

Anchorage: A large, popular anchorage is available off the GIWW between flashing red "60" and red daybeacon "62" near the west side of Useppa Island. This anchorage can sometimes be uncomfortable from wakes of passing boats, especially on weekends but the scenery is beautiful. It is also somewhat exposed to wind so caution should be used when anchoring. The advantages of this anchorage far outnumber the disadvantages.

Cayo Costa–GIWW Mile 19

Spanish fishermen from Havana gave 6-mile-long Cayo Costa its name (translated as "Coastal Key"). Located at the north end of Pine Island Sound on the south side of Boca Grande Pass, this almost-uninhabited island (home to a herd of feral pigs) is accessible only by boat.

Both Punta Blanca Island and Cayo Costa are part of Cayo Costa State Park. At the northern end of Punta Blanca Island (between the two islands) is Pelican Pass and Pelican Bay. Although the Pelican Pass entrance may at first appear a bit dicey, it is well worth the effort. With caution and a little help from the tide boats drawing up to 5 feet can normally get through Pelican Pass into Pelican Bay.

NAVIGATION: Use NOAA Chart 11427. To reach Pelican Bay from red daybeacon "74" travel southwest toward the tip of the beach on Cayo Costa. Stay to within about 75 feet of the sand beach and just past the little sign in the water turn slightly east and follow the beach up into Pelican Bay. You will find 5 to 6 feet MLW in the pass. When inside Pelican Bay pay attention to your depth sounder as there are several very shallow areas.

If feeling particularly adventuresome, take your dinghy and look for the unmarked small but deep creek on Cayo Costa that opens into a small lake of about 200 yards in diameter. The depth in the creek is more than adequate for dinghies. There is a small dock on the lake that was once used for loading supplies on the island. You can land your dinghy there and explore. It is very pretty and worth the effort!

Dockage: Cayo Costa State Park remains closed until further notice due to hurricane damage and landing on the grounds is not permitted (as of summer 2023). When operational, it provides 10 free slips for vessels 30' and under on a first-come, first-served basis. The longer pier at the end is for the ferry and not to be used by cruisers.

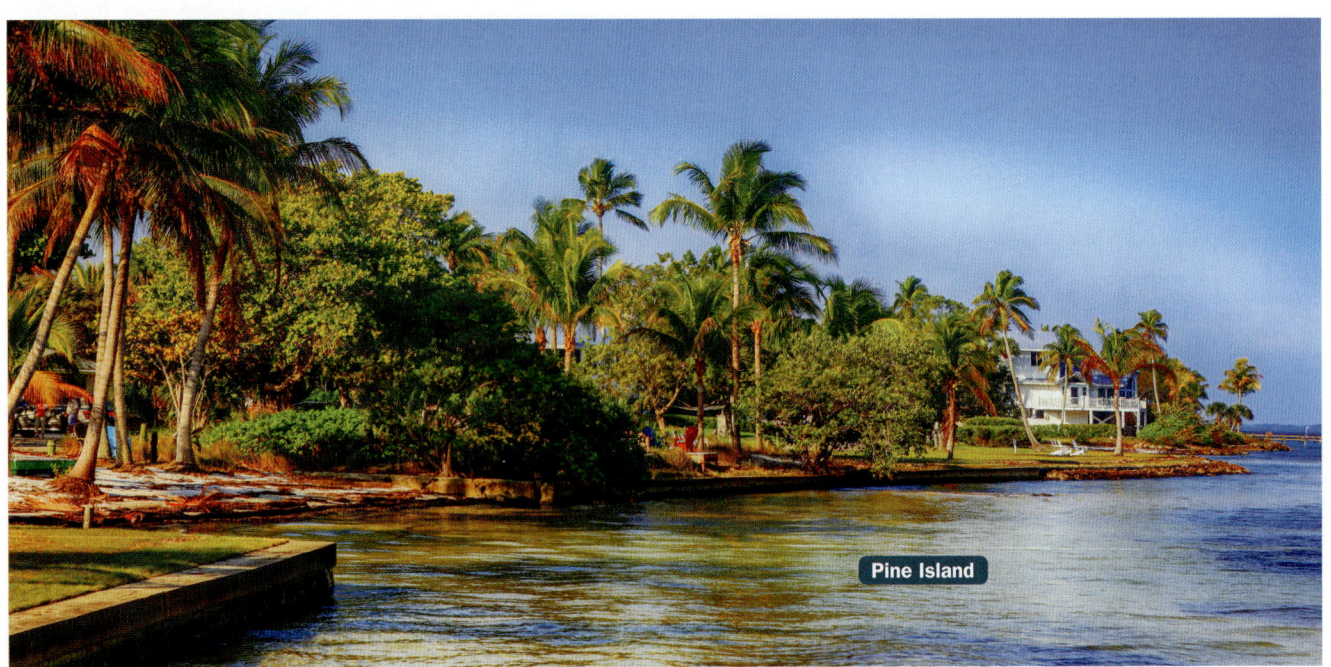
Pine Island

Pine Island Sound, FL

PINE ISLAND		Largest Vessel	VHF	Total Slips	Approach/Dockside Depth	Floating Docks	Gas/Diesel	Repairs/Haulout	Min/Max Amps	Pump-Out Station
1. Safe Harbor Pineland	(239) 283-3593	38	16	30	4.5 / 7.0		GD	RH		

WiFi Wireless Internet Access
Visit www.waterwayguide.com for current rates, fuel prices, website addresses and other up-to-the-minute information. (Information in the table is provided by the facilities.)

Scan here for more details:

The island is virtually all a State Park with walking trails, cabins and tent sites, restrooms, and even two cemeteries. Dogs are not permitted in some parts of the park. Transportation across the island is by foot, tram or rental bike. The beaches on the Gulf side are very popular for shelling.

Anchorage: At Mile 22.5 at the southern tip of Punta Blanca Island is a bowl of deep water that provides an attractive anchorage. The adventurous skipper can take up to a 6-foot draft vessel completely around the point where there is an exceptionally cozy anchorage. The downside of the equation is that this anchorage has poor ventilation and is best in winter months.

Another option is Punta Blanca North Cove at the opposite end of the island, which is convenient for taking the dinghy over to the state park (when open).

You can anchor in Pelican Bay in 7 to 8 feet MLW with plenty of swinging room and really good holding. This is a very popular anchorage so it can get crowded on weekends. The seasonal manatee population is robust and there are many places to explore in the dinghy.

Pine Island (North)–GIWW Mile 25

The largest island off Florida's Gulf Coast Pine Island offers a small-town atmosphere amid mangroves, three aquatic preserves and acres of palm, tropical plants and fruit groves. The waters of Pine Island Sound provide not only some of the finest fishing in Florida but are a haven for birdwatchers and nature lovers. The heart of Pine Island is a collection of homegrown shops, galleries, fish markets and residences.

Chapter 12: Sanibel Island to Sarasota Bay

Pine Island Sound, FL

MATLACHA		Largest Vessel	VHF	Total Slips	Approach/ Dockside Depth	Floating Docks	Gas/ Diesel	Repairs/ Haulout	Min/Max Amps	Pump-Out Station
1. Olde Fish House Marina	(239) 282-9577	38			12.0 / 5.0					
2. Four Winds Marina WiFi 6 NE of 19	(239) 283-0250	32	16	89	3.5 / 4.0	F	G	R	30 / 50	

WiFi Wireless Internet Access
Visit www.waterwayguide.com for current rates, fuel prices, website addresses and other up-to-the-minute information.
(Information in the table is provided by the facilities.)

Scan here for more details:

NAVIGATION: Use NOAA Chart 11427. Matlacha Pass carries a marked but shallow, crooked channel north between Pine Island and the mainland to Charlotte Harbor. Controlling depth is about 3 feet MLW and a 32-foot-high power cable and the **Matlacha Pass (SR 78) Bridge** cross the pass. The bridge has 9-foot closed vertical clearance but opens on signal. This passage is not recommended but can be safely explored from the northern entrance.

Dockage: At the northwestern end of Pine Island is Wilson Cut, which leads to Safe Harbor Pineland. They have slips but you may access some skinny water on your way in. Wait for a high tide if you require more than 30 inches. Be sure to go follow all the marks on the way in or out...Don't cut corners. A very good marina for smaller boats (under 34 feet) is Four Winds Marina at the north end of Pine Island. At Matlacha Pass just before the bridge is Olde Fish House Marina. Originally a fish packing house, this marina, seafood market and full-service restaurant is family-owned and -operated. Call ahead for slip availability.

Charlotte Harbor–GIWW Mile 25

About 60 miles southeast of Tampa Bay, Charlotte Harbor is a wide, elbow-shaped bay carrying 9-foot MLW depths to Punta Gorda at the mouth of the Peace River. Stretching 20 miles long and 10 miles wide, Charlotte Harbor offers a lot for the cruising boater.

Charlotte Harbor is formed by the confluence of the Peace and Myakka Rivers. Tidal range averages 2 feet but winds from the west reportedly can increase water levels as much as 5 feet. The open sweep and relatively uniform depths of

Charlotte Harbor, FL

PUNTA GORDA AREA		Largest Vessel	VHF	Total Slips	Approach/Dockside Depth	Floating Docks	Gas/Diesel	Repairs/Haulout	Min/Max Amps	Pump-Out Station
1. Safe Harbor Burnt Store WiFi	(941) 637-0083	100	16	525	8.0 / 8.0	F	GD	RH	30 / 100	P

WiFi Wireless Internet Access
Visit www.waterwayguide.com for current rates, fuel prices, website addresses and other up-to-the-minute information. (Information in the table is provided by the facilities.)

Scan here for more details:

water in Charlotte Harbor provide a welcome change from the narrow, shoal-bordered GIWW. The high sandbars that protect the shoreline limit opportunities for gunkholing but both the Peace and Myakka Rivers compensate for that weakness by offering opportunities for scenic dinghy trips.

On the southern shore of the Peace River is the charming boating community of Punta Gorda. It comprises 60 miles of canals that meander through well-kept neighborhoods and lead to Charlotte Harbor. The city has a historic district with over 150 significant historical residential and commercial structures along its brick-lined streets. Along the Punta Gorda coastline of Charlotte Harbor is Harborwalk, a scenic pedestrian- and bicycle-friendly riverside walkway lined with palm trees, brick pavers and park amenities.

Charlotte Harbor is a good place for daysailing and has variable winds. Yacht clubs in the area are involved year-round in sailboat racing and offer privileges to members of reciprocating clubs. When entering any marina in Charlotte Harbor be sure to stay inside the well-marked channels. The water can be very shallow outside of them.

NAVIGATION: Use NOAA Chart 11426. The Peace River enters Charlotte Harbor from the northeast. It is very shallow (7 to 8 feet MLW) and marked for only about 6 miles but its channel is navigable to the town of Hull located 15 miles upriver. With just 3-foot MLW depths this stretch calls for local knowledge and the snags and heavy growths of hyacinths in the upper river require extra caution. Two 45-foot fixed vertical clearance bridges (**Tamiami Trail Bridges** and **I-75 Bridges**) cross the Peace River at the entrance. If you can get under the lower bridge, the 60-foot overhead power lines won't be an issue. The CR 761 bridge, with 12-foot fixed vertical clearance, may restrict some boats from proceeding past the town of Platt.

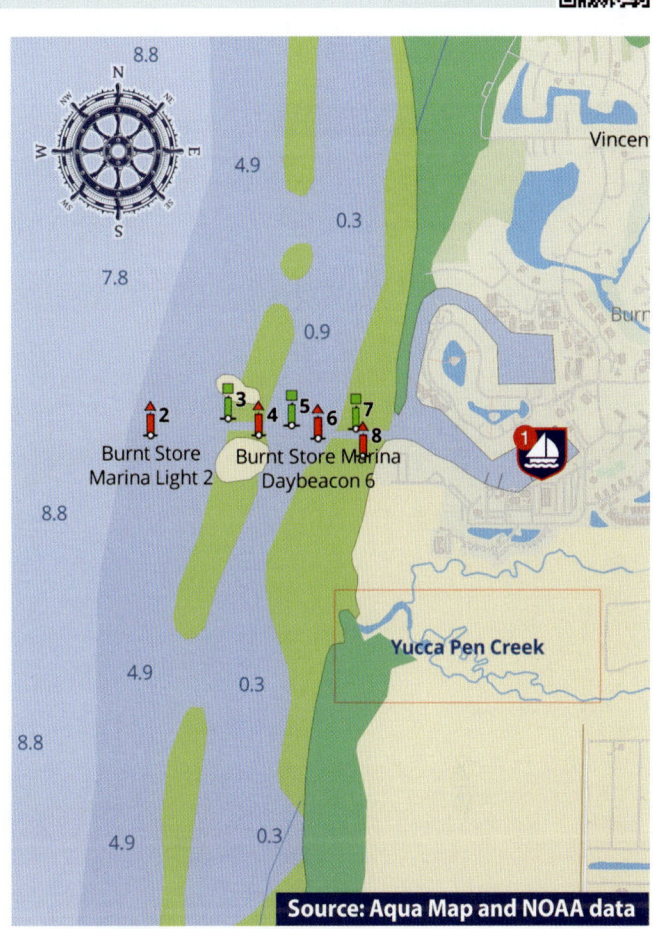

Source: Aqua Map and NOAA data

Wandering through dense woodland the Myakka River runs from the northwest from Myakka Lake to Charlotte Harbor. Boats drawing 3 feet or less with less than 25-foot clearance and armed with local knowledge can travel about 17 miles up the Myakka River. Three nautical miles up the river the **SR 776 Bridge** sets the 25-foot fixed vertical clearance limit. Past Myakka State Park in the upper reaches of the Myakka River there is a wilderness reminiscent of the Everglades. This is home to large alligators, feral hogs, eagles, deer, rattlesnakes and even the very rare Florida panther.

Dockage/Moorings: Opposite Boca Grande Channel and midway up the eastern shore of Charlotte Harbor, the large (525-slip) Safe Harbor Burnt Store

Chapter 12: Sanibel Island to Sarasota Bay

Charlotte Harbor, FL

PUNTA GORDA AREA		Largest Vessel	VHF	Total Slips	Approach/Dockside Depth	Floating Docks	Gas/Diesel	Repairs/Haulout	Min/Max Amps	Pump-Out Station
1. Fishermen's Village Marina WiFi	(941) 575-3000	125	16	111	7.0 / 5.0		GD		30 / 100	P
2. Charlotte Harbor Yacht Club WiFi	(941) 629-5131	55	16	18	4.0 / 6.0		G		30 / 50	P
3. Laishley Park Municipal Marina WiFi	(941) 575-0142	80	16	94	7.0 / 7.0	F			30 / 50	P

WiFi Wireless Internet Access
Visit www.waterwayguide.com for current rates, fuel prices, website addresses and other up-to-the-minute information.
(Information in the table is provided by the facilities.)

Scan here for more details:

Source: Aqua Map and NOAA data

is a very popular stop. Flashing red "6" leads off the approach from Charlotte Harbor and is then followed by flashing red "2" and a series of daybeacons into the protected harbor. The inlet channel has been dredged and ongoing maintenance is evident. This is more to this facility than its dockage and restaurant (Cass Cay). This is home to a tight-knit community of boaters who return year after year. Taxis are available for the relatively lengthy ride to Punta Gorda for provisioning.

Fishermen's Village Marina is located on upper Charlotte Harbor with no bridges or other restrictions to the Gulf of Mexico and is within walking distance of Historic Punta Gorda. This is a very popular spot for transients to spend the winter and spring months. The well-kept marina also has courtesy docks for day-trippers and a long dinghy dock.

Laishley Park Municipal Marina has floating concrete slips and a mooring field just past the Tamiami Trail Bridges. Be sure to call in advance for availability. A pump-out boat comes twice a week to the mooring field. They also have a day use-only dock. Laishley Park is the site of many festivals and activities throughout the year. On the north side of the Peace River at the mouth is Charlotte Harbor Yacht Club, which recognizes reciprocity from other clubs. They have a beautiful clubhouse with a restaurant and bar, a secure harbor with slips for sail and power boats, tennis/pickelball courts and many social activities. Call ahead for availability.

Marine repair and storage facilities (no transient slips) can be found on a series of canals (6 miles long) off the Santa Cruz Waterway on the Myakka River located on the northwestern shore of Charlotte Harbor. The depth inside is less than 4 feet MLW. Fuel Buddy To Your Boat has convenient fuel service. Schedule your fuel delivery and they will come to you.

Anchorage: You need to be adventuresome to anchor on the Peace River. If you travel beyond the 12-foot fixed vertical clearance bridge, you will find plenty of anchorages in at least 4 feet MLW and miles of unspoiled natural scenery. Be sure to stay in the channel.

A protected anchorage lies on the Myakka River near green daybeacon "9" (at the beginning of the Santa Cruz Waterway). Here you will find 5 to 7 feet MLW with protection from the north and west.

TO SARASOTA BAY

Those running north on the GIWW will find the bays beginning to narrow somewhat. Shores are closer and more developed and you should watch the markers carefully. The channel from Boca Grande and Charlotte Harbor winds sufficiently to maintain interest. Channel depths average 7 to 11 feet MLW although depths are extremely shallow outside the marked channel where the birds are often able to walk in the shallows.

The inside route from Charlotte Harbor to Sarasota Bay is well marked and not too heavily congested with manatee or boating safety areas.

NO WAKE ZONE

The 25-mph speed zone in the GIWW channel ("Slow-Speed/Minimum-Wake" within a specified distance from the shore) is more the rule than the exception. Pay close attention to posted signs in these slow-speed restriction areas.

Option: Outside (Gulf) Route via Boca Grande Pass

NAVIGATION: Use NOAA Chart 11425. From Boca Grande Pass, shoal-draft boats (5-foot draft or less) can use the shortcut route (known locally as "The Swash Channel") to Big Sarasota Pass. The channel leads to deep water well inshore of the big ship route. To follow The Swash Channel around the tip of Gasparilla Island you should proceed west in Boca Grande Pass until you reach the end of an old concrete pier, bearing 340° magnetic. Pass the pier about 50 to 100 feet out in 8- to 9-foot MLW depths avoiding the long shoal that runs off to the south-southeast. Once clear of the shoal you will find 10- to 11-foot MLW depths.

Note that if you are returning to Charlotte Harbor from the Gulf of Mexico in a brisk northwesterly with an outgoing tide, Boca Grande Pass can appear reasonably docile until you are almost next to the piers when you can be in breaking waves before you know it. (The waves break away from you and are hard to recognize.) It is wise to avoid The Swash Channel in such conditions because there is no "wiggle room" there. Current local knowledge is advisable.

The safer approach to entering Charlotte Harbor particularly if the water is rough is to enter via the ship

Chapter 12: Sanibel Island to Sarasota Bay

channel. The shoals along the ship channel particularly on the northwest side need to be monitored carefully as the charted channel runs very close to them. If entering Boca Grande Channel from the north, take care to come all of the way to green buoy "3" and red nun buoy "4" before turning in to avoid the shoal entirely. You will be at about the Three Nautical Mile line. Deeper water lies to the south side of the channel if you need to get out of the way of commercial vessels.

Big Sarasota Pass has reasonably good depths for most cruising boats but is subject to shoaling. Follow the charted marks. Be sure to call ahead for local information. Towing services are really good about giving information as is the Sarasota Yacht Club website.

Boca Grande Area– GIWW Mile 27 to Mile 36

Boca Grande on the south end of Gasparilla Island makes a good stop. In a bygone era Boca Grande was a winter resort and fishing retreat for northern socialites and tycoons. For the most part the gracious old homes they once occupied have been faithfully maintained, preserving the elegance of the past.

Those in the entertainment business seem to favor the Gasparilla Inn for its privacy and good manners as well as the absolutely charming atmosphere. (You must book a room to dock there.) This is a wonderful stop and shouldn't be missed if time permits (941-964-4620).

NAVIGATION: Use NOAA Chart 11425. The Boca Grande Channel, one of the primary inlets from the Gulf, runs between Cayo Costa and Gasparilla Island forming the entrance to Charlotte Harbor. The channel is easy to navigate, deep, well marked and lighted and is one of the primary, important passes on the stretch between Naples and Tampa.

To cross Boca Grande Channel from the GIWW inside, flashing red "76" (off the northeast point of Cayo Costa) and flashing green "1" (off the eastern shore of Gasparilla Island) are the important markers. If heading north, follow a bearing of about 350° magnetic after leaving flashing red "76" to the east. The channel carries 10 to 12 feet MLW and is well marked.

Located about a quarter of the way up Gasparilla Island when you are headed north is what is designated on some charts (e.g., Navionics) as "yacht basin." This is not a business but the location of Boca Grande Marina. Use 16-foot flashing green "1" to line up red daybeacon "2" and green daybeacon "3" to enter the channel into the harbor. The channel carries 7 to 9 feet MLW. On entering the Boca Grande Bayou to starboard, flashing green "7" should be given a wide berth because of the encroaching sandbar. Controlling depths are 6 feet MLW in Boca Grande Bayou.

Continuing north on the GIWW and Gasparilla Sound near the town of Placida the waterway channel doglegs farther west toward a pair of bridges at green daybeacon "19." Pass through the permanently opened railway bridge just past green daybeacon "21" then leave green daybeacon "1" to the south as you approach the Boca Grande Swing Bridge at GIWW Mile 34.3.

Boca Grande Swing Bridge (22-foot closed vertical clearance) opens on signal except 7:00 a.m. to 6:00 p.m., Monday through Friday, when the draw need only open on the hour and half-hour. On Saturdays, Sundays and federal holidays the draw opens every 15 minutes. Vessels must request an opening. Be sure to check the Coast Guard *Local Notice to Mariners* for schedule changes or use VHF Channel 09 to get in touch with the bridgetender.

> *CAUTION:* When approaching from the Gulf, Gasparilla Pass is not recommended. This is an access used by local fishers with a lot of local knowledge and very shallow-draft boats. The area around the pass is riddled with charted 2- to 3-foot MLW spots and the entire north side of the pass has a 1-foot MLW bar on its border. Use Boca Grande Pass instead.

Dockage: Boca Grande Marina has secure berths and a full range of amenities for visiting boaters inside the yacht basin. Guests will enjoy friendly dockside assistance, a well-stocked Ship Store and waterfront casual dining (inside or out). This facility is located just 0.5 mile from downtown and offers golf cart rentals. Just to the north, The Gasparilla Inn & Club hosts a full-service marina that is open to the public. It is located on the bayou behind The Inn with slips and miscellaneous boating supplies in the on-site Ship Store.

Arriving at the northern tip of Gasparilla Island along the GIWW from the south transients can find

America's Waterway Guide Since 1947 — **Chapter 12**

Gasparilla Sound, FL

BOCA GRANDE AREA		Largest Vessel	VHF	Total Slips	Approach/ Dockside Depth	Floating Docks	Gas/ Diesel	Repairs/ Haulout	Min/Max Amps	Pump-Out Station
1. Boca Grande Marina WiFi MM 28.5	(941) 964-2100	150	16	20	6.5 / 6.5		GD		30 / 100	P
2. The Gasparilla Inn & Club MM 29.5	(941) 964-4620	50		24	6.0 / 4.5	F	GD	RH	50	
3. Uncle Henry's Marina WiFi MM 32.8	(941) 964-0154	90	16	58	6.0 / 9.0		GD		30 / 200+	P

WiFi Wireless Internet Access
Visit www.waterwayguide.com for current rates, fuel prices, website addresses and other up-to-the-minute information. (Information in the table is provided by the facilities.)

Scan here for more details:

dockage at Uncle Henry's Marina. Turn southwest between the open railroad bridge and the Boca Grande Swing Bridge. (Note that private green daybeacon "1" may be missing.) The quiet, attractive marina can accommodate vessels up to 80 feet. There is a covered patio and grill and Kappy's Market is adjacent for groceries and golf cart rentals

The entrance has 6 to 7 feet MLW and a 1.5- to 2-foot tidal range. With a wind out of the north depths will be less. Pay attention to the tide tables; deep-draft vessels should call Uncle Henry's (941-964-0154) for a current report. There has been some silting along both sides of this access passage so honor all markers and stay as close to center channel as possible. Nearby Gasparilla Marina across the waterway at Placida no longer offers transient slips.

Anchorage: Anchorage is limited around Gasparilla Island and any available space is often filled with local boats on permanent moorings. You may be able to find a spot in the harbor at Boca Grande or farther north at Jack Point. Enter directly west of green marker "5" with good protection in a residential area. Docks to east are private. Easy dinghy ride to restaurants at Boca Bayou. At Mile 36 Cape Haze offers a quiet, protected anchorage northeast of red daybeacon "30" in 7- to 9-foot MLW depths surrounded by private homes. Set your anchor carefully as the bottom is soft mud. There is a small canal that leads to the north and the tidal current may swing you more than the wind. There is only enough room for two or three boats to anchor comfortably. In short, watch your depths, set your anchor well and, if there are three boats already there, proceed north to Blue Heron Cove at Mile 37.3 or Don Pedro Island at Mile 37.0 for a comparable anchorage with room for five or six boats. At green daybeacon "3" turn toward the mangroves and watch your depth. About halfway between the marker and the shore you'll find 8 to 10 feet in good holding with protection from nearly all wind.

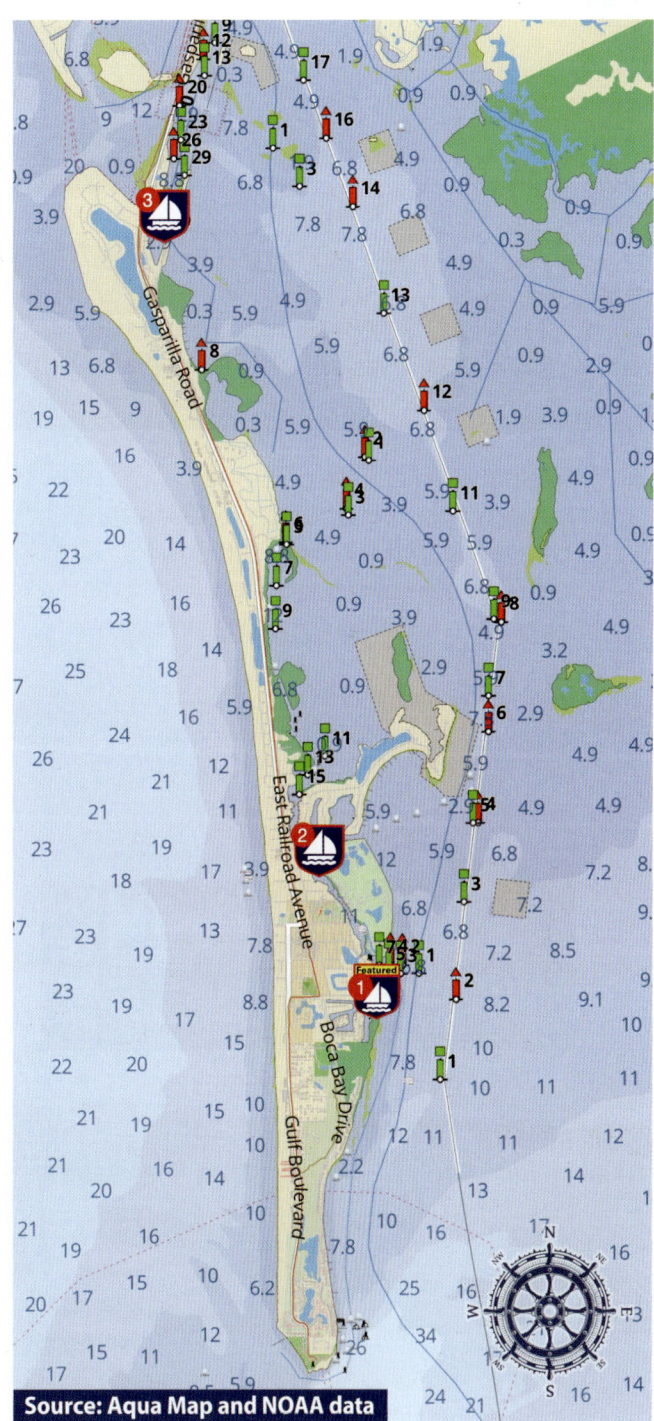

Source: Aqua Map and NOAA data

SOUTHERN EDITION 471

Boca Grande Marina

N 26° 44.832 W 82° 15.378   VHF-16

We provide transient dockage, accommodating boats up to 130 feet, and are located walking distance to historic downtown Boca Grande. Numerous restaurants, galleries, boutiques, and beautiful Gulf beaches are only steps away!

- **Two waterfront restaurants**
- **Friendly & knowledgeable dock attendants**
- **30/50/100 AMP shore power**
- **Ethanol-free gas & diesel**
- **Updated restrooms and laundry**
- **Fully-stocked ship store**
- **Wi-Fi & pumpout service**
- **Golf cart rentals**

Enjoy exceptional fine dining at Eagle Grille, or a more casual experience at Miller's Dockside, both onsite and waterfront. The Eagle Grille and Bellamy Lounge are also available for special events.

941-964-8000 | EagleGrille.com

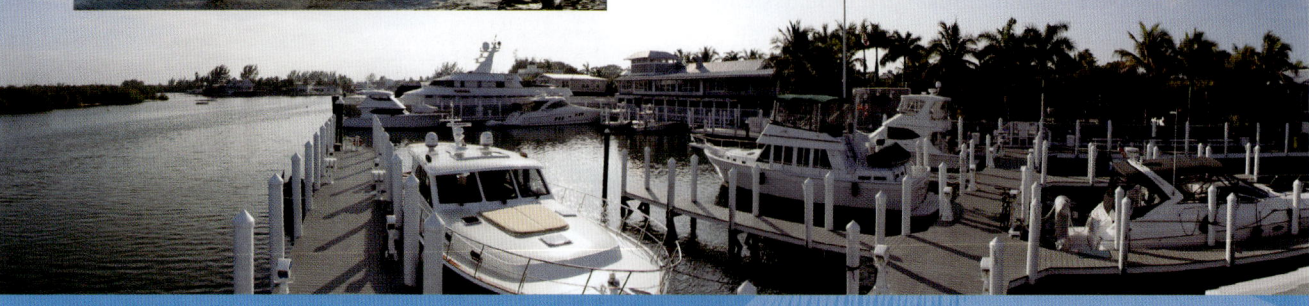

941-964-2100   BocaGrandeMarina.net

Chapter 12

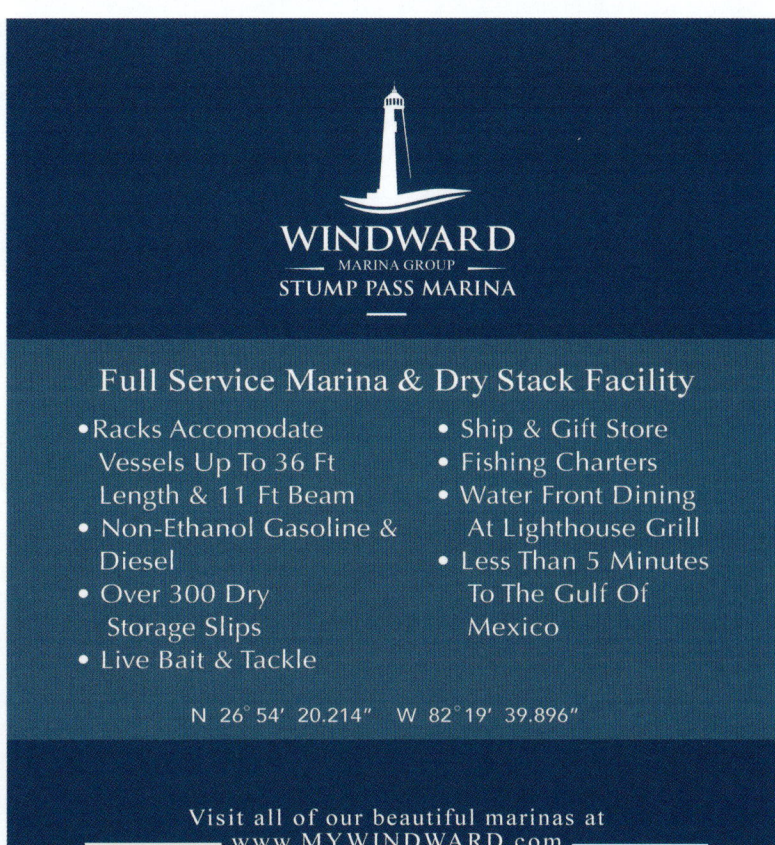

Chapter 12: Sanibel Island to Sarasota Bay

Lemon Bay, FL

LEMON BAY AREA		Largest Vessel	VHF	Total Slips	Approach/Dockside Depth	Floating Docks	Gas/Diesel	Repairs/Haulout	Min/Max Amps	Pump-Out Station
1. Loggerhead Marina - Palm Harbour Marina WiFi MM 38.5	(941) 697-4356	65	16	90	7.0 / 6.0		GD	RH	30 / 50	P
2. Cape Haze Marina MM 39.0	(941) 698-1110	70	16	105	6.0 / 9.0	F	GD	RH	30 / 50	P

WiFi Wireless Internet Access
Visit www.waterwayguide.com for current rates, fuel prices, website addresses and other up-to-the-minute information. (Information in the table is provided by the facilities.)

Scan here for more details: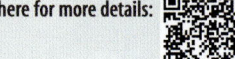

Source: Aqua Map and NOAA data

Lemon Bay, FL

LEMON BAY AREA		Largest Vessel	VHF	Total Slips	Approach/ Dockside Depth	Floating Docks	Gas/ Diesel	Repairs/ Haulout	Min/Max Amps	Pump-Out Station
1. Royal Palm Marina WiFi	(941) 475-6882	80	16	230	6.0 / 9.0		GD	RH	30 / 50	

WiFi Wireless Internet Access
Visit www.waterwayguide.com for current rates, fuel prices, website addresses and other up-to-the-minute information. (Information in the table is provided by the facilities.)

Scan here for more details:

Source: Aqua Map and NOAA data

To Lemon Bay–GIWW Mile 36 to Mile 50

NAVIGATION: Use NOAA Chart 11425. Beyond Little Gasparilla Island and Placida Harbor the GIWW threads through a series of small islands to a narrow 2.25-mile straight stretch called The Cutoff, leading into Lemon Bay. Once in Lemon Bay the GIWW swings to the northeast shore and opens up for a 7.5-mile narrow straightaway through shallow water to the end of the bay. Green daybeacon "17A" keeps you on the straight and narrow where other daybeacons indicate the channel leading to Stump Pass, which opens to the Gulf. Private navigational aids are relocated as channel conditions change in Stump Pass, which requires local knowledge.

At GIWW Mile 43.5 is the 26-foot closed vertical clearance **Tom Adams Bridge** (also known as the Manasota Key Bridge), which opens on signal. The **Manasota Bridge** (26-foot closed vertical clearance) at Mile 49.9 also opens on signal.

Dockage: Marinas in Lemon Bay tend to be small, unpretentious and friendly but are geared to handle cruising boats. Two marinas are located near Mile 38 before the GIWW enters Lemon Bay at The Cutoff. The sheltered Loggerhead Marina–Palm Harbour Marina located on the mainland side near green daybeacon "7" is a boutique, resort-style marina with upscale amenities including the popular seafood restaurant, Leverock's. The marina features dry stack storage for up to 40 feet and wet slips up to 65 feet.

Just to the north is full-service Cape Haze Marina in a protected basin with a narrow, dredged channel. The marina has transient dockage and can accommodate vessels to 70 feet. Their Cabana pool and spa is a great place for relaxing and enjoying the sun. Winward Stump Pass has dry storage and fuel available at Mile 40.8.

Chapter 12: Sanibel Island to Sarasota Bay

Lemon Bay

Royal Palm Marina is tucked away to the north at Mile 45.8 with dry and wet boat storage, transient dockage, supplies, bait and full services "from mast to motor." The on-site Snook's Bayside Bar & Grill (941-475-3712) is open daily for lunch and dinner and has panoramic views and a waterfront tiki bar.

Anchorage: Anchorages in the area include one at the north end of Thorton Key and one on the south side of Manasota Key at Peterson Island (Mile 40.9). Both offer good holding and protection.

At Mile 43.3 on the west side of the GIWW is a large, quiet anchorage with 7- to 10-foot MLW depths at Englewood Beach at Manasott Key. The anchorage is reached by heading southwest between lighted red daybeacon "22" and the Tom Adams Bridge. Buildings around the anchorage help to protect visiting yachts from buffeting winds. If you continue south hugging the mangroves, you will be sheltered from all directions. Watch depths closely. A convenience store and souvenir shop, dive shops, restaurants and the beach are across the street. To the north of Tom Adams Bridge is an anchorage at Lemon Bay with 6 feet MLW and excellent holding at Mile 44.5 east of red daybeacon "26."

To Venice–GIWW Mile 50 to Mile 65

About 15 miles south of Sarasota, Venice is one of Florida's younger towns. You will find boutiques, a theater and a variety of dining options around a central green, which was planned in the 1920s with a Mediterranean theme. As you can imagine there are several good Italian restaurants here. You shouldn't leave Venice feeling hungry. It is a short walk to one of the widest and loveliest beaches on Florida's west coast from the marinas. Fossilized sharks' teeth–either gray or black and with a triangular shape–are abundant here.

NAVIGATION: Use NOAA Chart 11425. Past Lemon Bay at Mile 53 the GIWW becomes a long, high-banked land cut, which runs through a corner of the Venice Municipal Airport. Watch for water-soaked debris in the cut. There is little tidal flushing action to move it out and it can be a nuisance.

At GIWW Mile 54.9 the **Tamiami Trail (Circus) Bridges** (25-foot vertical clearance) open on signal. This is followed by the **Venice Avenue Bridge** at Mile 56.6 (30-foot vertical clearance), which opens on signal except from 7:00 a.m. to 4:30 p.m., Monday through Friday, when it opens at 10, 30 and 50 minutes past the hour. (Note that the bridge need not open between 4:35 p.m. and 5:35 p.m.)

> ⚠ **CAUTION:** A well-marked shoaling area is at Mile 56.5.

Entering Venice waters the first bridge is the **KMI (Hatchett Creek) Bridge** at GIWW Mile 56.9, which has 30-foot closed vertical clearance and restricted openings year-round. It opens on signal except from 7:00 a.m. to 4:20 p.m., Monday through Friday (except federal holiday), when the draw need only open on the hour and at 20 and 40 minutes past the hour (except between 4:25 p.m. and 5:25 p.m. when the bridge need not open). On weekends and holidays it opens from 7:30 a.m. to 6:00 p.m. on the hour and at 15, 30 and 45 minutes past the hour. Call ahead on VHF Channel 09.

After leaving the land cut the GIWW runs through Roberts Bay. Lightly powered vessels should be cautious of the strong currents flowing in and out of Venice Inlet, which cross the route and create some navigational challenges. Shoaling is a recurrent condition even though the Army Corps of Engineers advises that 9-foot MLW depths are maintained in Venice Inlet. The inlet is jettied and easily navigable except when strong westerly winds oppose an ebbing tide.

North of Venice the GIWW continues its sheltered path behind Casey Key through the **Albee Road Bridge** (14-foot closed vertical clearance) at Mile 59.3. Boaters who require an opening should radio ahead on VHF Channel 09 before entering the channel.

Blackburn Bay outside the GIWW at Mile 60 is very shallow and has only limited tie-ups. Proceed with caution and definitely do not attempt transiting this area at night. The course crosses Little Sarasota Bay, the approach to Sarasota.

The **Blackburn Point Bridge** (9-foot closed vertical clearance) at Mile 63 is a swing bridge and opens on signal. Note that the bridgetender has to walk out to the middle to turn (open) the bridge. Passage through both bridges is on an angle in tight quarters (51-foot horizontal clearance) with little maneuvering room on either side so use caution.

Overall the GIWW is well marked and maintained and if you keep to the middle of the channel, you should encounter no problems.

Chapter 12: Sanibel Island to Sarasota Bay

Venice Inlet, FL

VENICE AREA		Largest Vessel	VHF	Total Slips	Approach/ Dockside Depth	Floating Docks	Gas/ Diesel	Repairs/ Haulout	Min/Max Amps	Pump-Out Station
1. Fisherman's Wharf Marina of Venice WiFi MM 57.0	(941) 486-0500	100	16	57	8.0 / 7.0	F	GD		30 / 100	P
2. Venice Yacht Club MM 57.5	(941) 483-3625	100	16	67	10.0 / 10.0		GD		30 / 100	P
3. Crow's Nest Marina & Restaurant WiFi MM 58.0	**(941) 484-9551**	**140**	**16**	**34**	**12.0 / 12.0**		**GD**		**30 / 100**	**P**
4. Escape at Casey Key Resort & Marina MM 59.0	(941) 218-3199	50		14	10.0 / 4.0				30 / 50	

WiFi Wireless Internet Access
Visit www.waterwayguide.com for current rates, fuel prices, website addresses and other up-to-the-minute information. (Information in the table is provided by the facilities.)

Scan here for more details:

Source: Aqua Map and NOAA data

Chapter 12

Little Sarasota Bay, FL

SIESTA KEY AREA		Largest Vessel	VHF	Total Slips	Approach/Dockside Depth	Floating Docks	Gas/Diesel	Repairs/Haulout	Min/Max Amps	Pump-Out Station
1. Bayfront Yacht Works & Marina MM 48	(941) 349-9449	50		25	5.0 / 5.0		G	RH		
2. Safe Harbor Siesta Key	(941) 349-1970	34			/		GD	R		

WiFi Wireless Internet Access
Visit www.waterwayguide.com for current rates, fuel prices, website addresses and other up-to-the-minute information.
(Information in the table is provided by the facilities.)

Scan here for more details:

Source: Aqua Map and NOAA data

SOUTHERN EDITION 479

Chapter 12 — Sanibel Island to Sarasota Bay

Dockage: Marine supplies are available at GIWW Mile 55.1 at MarineMax of Venice with a well-stocked Ship Store and repairs. They do not, however, have transient slips. Well-maintained Fisherman's Wharf Marina at GIWW Mile 57 has been serving the boating community since 1949. They offer all amenities and floating docks for monthly and yearly rentals and might be able to make room for you for a night or two but do call ahead. They have a pet-friendly restaurant on site and Fisherman's Wharf Tiki Hut is on the water near the docks for your fishing and boating needs. It is just a short walk over the bridge to historic downtown Venice.

At Mile 58 between quick-flashing green "13" and red daybeacon "14" a privately marked channel leads west toward the private Venice Yacht Club (with reciprocal privileges for members of the Florida Yacht Council only).

Conveniently situated just inside the Venice Inlet, Crow's Nest Marina & Restaurant can accommodate boats up to 140 feet and offers the usual cruiser amenities plus a laundry and a very popular on-site restaurant. It is an easy walk to the beach and rental bikes are available for the 1.5-mile ride to town (well worth the ride). The tidal current can be strong, but the experienced dockhands will be standing by to help. Call ahead.

Note that Gulf Harbor Marina is just south of the Albee Road Bridge at Mile 59 with repairs but no transient dockage. This is strictly a storage facility. On the north side of the Albee Road Bridge is Escape at Casey Key Resort & Marina. Two slips (to 50 feet) are available for non-hotel guests as well as those staying at the resort. Resort amenities include a heated pool, a fully-appointed clubhouse (with kitchen) and access to kayaks, stand-up paddleboards and bicycles. It is best to plan to take a slip here as this area is somewhat exposed to the north and east and to GIWW wakes.

America's Waterway Guide Since 1947 — Chapter 12

To Little Sarasota Bay– GIWW Mile 65 to Mile 72

Writers and artists congregate on the slender, heavily wooded Siesta Key between Venice and Sarasota. Large private estates and deluxe condos line the waterway, each with their own dock. Siesta Beach is a favorite and facilities include picnic areas, restrooms, concession stands, a playground, trails and tennis and volleyball courts.

Behind Siesta Key the narrow, dredged GIWW runs up the center of Little Sarasota Bay until the bay narrows to the north. At the **Stickney Point (SR 72) Bridge** at GIWW Mile 68.6 (18-foot closed vertical clearance) the route moves over to the western shore then swings out into the middle again at Roberts Bay. At the northern end of Siesta Key at GIWW Mile 71.6 is the **Siesta Drive Bridge** (25-foot closed vertical clearance). Both bridges follow the same schedule and open on signal except from 6:00 a.m. to 7:00 p.m., when the draw need only open on the hour and half hour (daily).

Dockage: There are several small marinas along this stretch of the GIWW that cater to small center consoles and pontoon boats. Marinas with facilities and slips to handle transient cruisers are largely located in Venice and in Sarasota Bay. Bayfront Yacht Works & Marina at Mile 66 is a Suntex Marina offering boat rentals and an array of services, as well as dry storage. Call for details. Just south of the Stickney Point Bridge is Safe Harbor Siesta Key with boat rentals, sales and storage. Call ahead for slip availability.

Anchorage: You can anchor at White Beach at Mile 67.4 west of green daybeacon "55" in 5 to 6 feet MLW with good holding. This is somewhat exposed to wakes from passing boats. There is another anchorage west of green daybeacon "79" at Mile 71 at Siesta Key. Here you will find good holding in 5 to 6 feet MLW. In the busy season expect jet skis, wake boarders and boats towing all manner of floats.

Sarasota

Sarasota Bay Area– GIWW Mile 72 to Mile 78

At Siesta Key off to port heading north after clearing Little Sarasota Bay the Sarasota area officially begins around Mile 71 and then continues for about 15 miles. The passage starts with a well-marked stretch through the shoals of Roberts Bay and ends with the exit through Longboat Key Pass to the north of Sarasota Bay.

This section of the GIWW traverses a sophisticated, fast-growing region and is a popular layover spot for cruising boats. As such, facilities are plentiful, ranging from fishing camps to marina resorts, and all manner of boating needs and repairs can be handled here. As the mainland's focal point for a cluster of offshore island resorts (linked to it by causeways) Sarasota acts as the hub of an important agricultural and cattle-ranching district but is most proud of its cultural image.

The low purple building on the east side of Sarasota Bay just north of the causeway is the Van Wezel Theatre of Performing Arts (pronounced "Vann WAY-zull"). At about Mile 77 also on the east side you can see the coral-colored mansion of John Ringling (of circus fame).

NAVIGATION: Use NOAA Chart 11425. After traversing Roberts Bay the GIWW widens amidst a variety of marine facilities and then passes under the **Ringling Causeway (SR 789) Bridge** at Mile 73.6 with a fixed vertical clearance of 65 feet. Ringling Causeway crosses three Sarasota Bay keys (Bird, Coon and St. Armands) to link Lido Key to the mainland. The bridge span between Bird Key and Coon Key is fixed with

SOUTHERN EDITION

Chapter 12: Sanibel Island to Sarasota Bay

Sarasota Bay, FL

SARASOTA AREA		Largest Vessel	VHF	Total Slips	Approach/Dockside Depth	Floating Docks	Gas/Diesel	Repairs/Haulout	Min/Max Amps	Pump-Out Station
1. Marina Jack Yacht Basin WiFi MM 73.5	(941) 955-9488	180	16	298	8.0 / 8.0	F	GD		30 / 100	P
2. Bird Key Yacht Club WiFi	(941) 953-4455	50	16	42	12.0 / 8.0		GD		30 / 50	P
3. Sarasota Yacht Club WiFi	(941) 365-4191	120	16	113	16.0 / 10.0		GD		30 / 50	P
4. Sarasota Sailing Squadron	(941) 388-2355		72	4	/					

WiFi Wireless Internet Access
Visit www.waterwayguide.com for current rates, fuel prices, website addresses and other up-to-the-minute information.
(Information in the table is provided by the facilities.)

Scan here for more details:

Source: Aqua Map and NOAA data

only a 10-foot vertical clearance. From flashing green "13" north of the causeway Sarasota Bay opens up both in width and–in certain areas–depth.

After New Pass (not recommended due to shoaling) Longboat Key shields Sarasota Bay from the Gulf of Mexico and opens wide with central controlling depths of 7 to 12 feet MLW. Watch out for strong crosscurrents to and from Longboat Pass. The 17-foot closed vertical clearance **Longboat Pass (SR 789) Bridge** crosses the pass (opens on request). A call to a towboat captain for local knowledge is wise.

In this area the GIWW runs a straight line down the middle of Sarasota Bay with markers along this stretch spaced about 2 miles apart. At flashing green "17" (near the midpoint of Longboat Key at Mile 80) the route turns sharply west and Sarasota Bay narrows. Along this stretch the GIWW follows a dredged path through shoal water (1- and 2-foot MLW depths outside the channel). You must observe all aids to navigation very carefully!

Dockage/Moorings: Many of Sarasota's marine facilities are on the mainland near the Ringling Causeway, in Whittaker Bayou and clustered around New Pass. Repairs and service are readily available.

Tucked in behind Island Park, Marina Jack (a Suntex Marina) welcomes transients at the doorstep to downtown Sarasota. Full amenities include laundry facilities, concierge service, a shuttle and a well-stocked Ship Store. There are several on-site options for waterfront dining.

The Sarasota Mooring Field has 85 moorings for vessels to 80 feet. It is run by Marina Jack and includes all the marina amenities and access to a dinghy dock.

South of the Ringling Causeway before Lido Key are Bird Key Yacht Club and Sarasota Yacht Club, both of which may have transient space for reciprocating yacht club members only. Be sure to call ahead.

Sarasota Sailing Squadron on Lido Key is private but welcomes visiting sailors. Facilities include shower facilities, temporary mast-up storage and docking, boat ramps and hoist, and beachfront access.

To get farther from the crowd take a slip at the large Longboat Key Club Moorings. To reach its channel

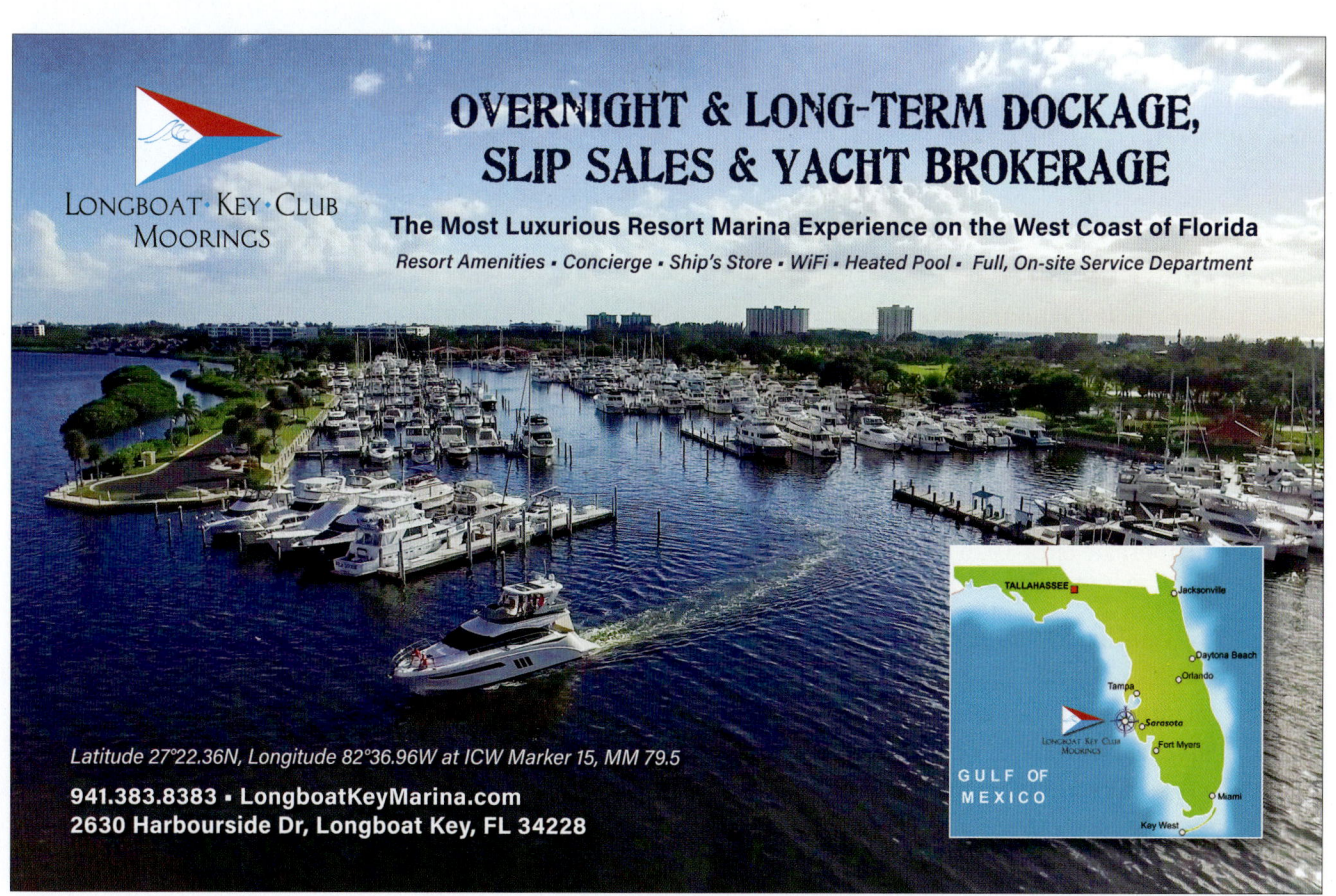

Chapter 12: Sanibel Island to Sarasota Bay

GOIN' ASHORE
SARASOTA, FL

In 1929, John Ringling chose Sarasota as winter headquarters for his "Greatest Show on Earth" circus, and even though the circus has moved on, the Ringling legacy is very much alive here. The Ringling Museum of Art is a Renaissance-style palace that the circus king built to house his art collection. In addition to the 31 galleries of art, the Ringling includes a 66-acre bayfront garden, the Ringling's 56-room mansion and a circus museum. Next to his museum, Ringling reconstructed an 18th-century Italian theater with stones brought piece by piece from Asolo, Italy. Throughout the year, visitors can see plays and operas in the playhouse built for Queen Catherine (5401 Bay Shore Rd., 941-359-5700).

ATTRACTIONS

1. **Marie Selby Botanical Gardens**
   Bayfront oasis with tropical plants, a conservatory and a garden museum at 900 S. Palm Ave. (941-366-5731).

2. **Sarasota Opera House**
   Familiar and unusual opera productions performed in an ornate circa-1926 theater (61 N. Pineapple Ave., 941-328-1300).

3. **Unconditional Surrender**
   One in a series of sculptures replicating an iconic photo taken of a sailor and nurse kissing in Times Square at the end of World War II. Located on the way to City Island on Bayfront Dr.

SERVICES

4. **Animal Medical Clinic at Rosemary**
   650 Central Ave. #2 (941-955-0136)

5. **Sarasota County Visitor Information Center**
   1945 Fruitville Rd. (941-706-1253)

6. **Sarasota Memorial Hospital**
   1700 S. Tamiami Trail (941-917-9000)

7. **Sarasota Post Office**
   1661 Ringling Blvd. (941-331-4221)

8. **Selby Library**
   1331 1st St. (941-861-1100)

9. **Veterinary Center of Sarasota**
   311 S. Washington Blvd. (941-952-1900)

MARINAS

10. **Marina Jack**
    2 Marina Plaza (941-955-9488)

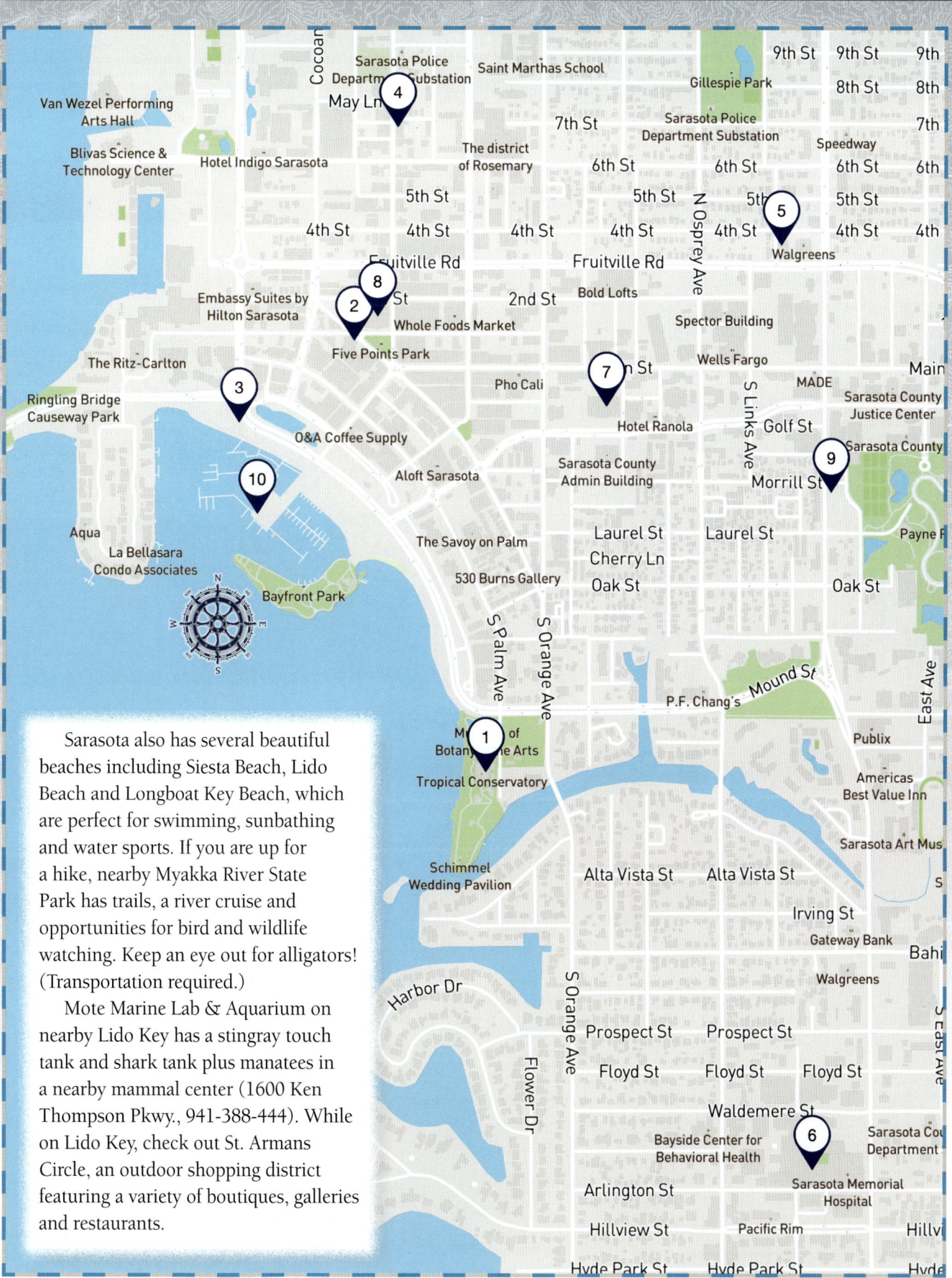

Chapter 12: Sanibel Island to Sarasota Bay

Sarasota Bay, FL

SARASOTA AREA			Largest Vessel	VHF	Total Slips	Approach/Dockside Depth	Floating Docks	Gas/Diesel	Repairs/Haulout	Min/Max Amps	Pump-Out Station
1. Longboat Key Club Moorings	WiFi 2.5 mi. NW of MM 76.0	(941) 383-8383	145	16	287	8.0 / 20.0		GD	R	30 / 100	P
2. The Dock on the Bay	WiFi 2.0 mi. SW of MM 80.5	(941) 376-1999	45		20	7.0 / 5.0				30	

WiFi Wireless Internet Access

Visit www.waterwayguide.com for current rates, fuel prices, website addresses and other up-to-the-minute information. (Information in the table is provided by the facilities.)

Scan here for more details:

Source: Aqua Map and NOAA data

Sarasota Bay, FL

SARASOTA AREA		Largest Vessel	VHF	Total Slips	Approach/ Dockside Depth	Floating Docks	Gas/ Diesel	Repairs/ Haulout	Min/Max Amps	Pump-Out Station
1. Ramada by Wyndham Sarasota WiFi 1.5 mi. NE of MM 78.5	(941) 203-6439	70		78	4.0 / 6.0	F		R	30 / 50	P
2. Sara Bay Marina WiFi 1.5 mi NE of MM 78.5	(941) 359-0390	50		60	4.0 / 4.0	F		RH	30 / 50	P

WiFi Wireless Internet Access
Visit www.waterwayguide.com for current rates, fuel prices, website addresses and other up-to-the-minute information.
(Information in the table is provided by the facilities.)

Scan here for more details:

Source: Aqua Map and NOAA data

steer 255° true from flashing green "15." On this course point toward the one farthest south of the three high-rise condominiums where you will encounter the privately maintained entrance channel to the 291-slip facility. Dockage provides access to the resort facilities (some for a fee) including tennis and a spa as well as the on-site Portofino Ristorante & Bar.

The 20-slip The Dock on the Bay is also on Longboat Key in the Buttonwood Harbor area and may have transient space for vessels to 45 feet with basic amenities and a pool. Call ahead.

At red daybeacon "16" in Sarasota Bay, steer a course of 038° magnetic for 1.5 nm to access the entrance markers to the Ramada by Wyndham Sarasota, which has a long seawall for tie-ups and an on-site restaurant.

Sara Bay Marina is nearby and may have space for you. Call ahead.

Anchorage: Many transient and local boats anchor in Sarasota Bay. Privately owned Bickel's Bayou is offered for transient cruiser use and is located on the north (mainland) side of the Ringling Causeway (SR 789) Bridge. Be sure to anchor only in the area exposed to the west and not in the rest of the basin. The access channel has a controlling depth of about 6 feet MLW. Approach from the GIWW directly eastward towards the basin where you will find 9 feet MLW. Leave enough space in the central channel for other boats to access the rest of the basin. Shallow-draft vessels should leave the deeper areas for those with deeper keels. There is no shore access here. Please do not trespass on private land.

Dinghy access is available at the Ringling Bridge Causeway Park or the public boat ramp at 10th Street to the north of the anchorage. Anchor light regulations are enforced after dark.

An established anchorage with several long-term boats is at City Island (Lido Key), where you will find at least 6 feet MLW with good holding in sand and mud with all-around protection.

Off New Pass Cove is a lovely anchorage in well-protected New Pass Cove at green daybeacon "9." Coming from the GIWW you must be able to pass under the **New Pass (SR 789) Bridge** (23-foot closed vertical clearance) or wait for an opening. From 7:00 a.m. to 6:00 p.m. the bridge need only open on the hour, 20 minutes past the hour and 40 minutes past the hour. From 6:00 p.m. to 7:00 a.m., the bridge will open on signal if at least a 3-hour notice is given to the drawtender. There is no more than 4 feet MLW at the entrance to the cove. Enter between the "No Wake" sign and the shore nearest the bridge. Once you enter there is 9 feet MLW and some crab pots to dodge.

Closer to the north end of Longboat Key at Mile 78.4 there is an anchorage west of green daybeacon "15" where you will find 7 to 11 feet MLW with good holding in sand and mud. Just before red daybeacon "40" to the north a good anchorage in 13-foot MLW depths lies behind the tip of Longboat Key just off Longbeach. A restaurant is within dinghy range. You can take the dinghy almost all the way down Bishop Bayou from the Long Boat Key anchorage and tie up to the cement wall on the left side to access a shopping plaza with groceries, a liquor store, a Post Office and a restaurant.

■ NEXT STOP

Continuing north, cruisers will next encounter Anna Maria Island and the popular Tampa-St. Petersburg area. Beyond that, Clearwater and its famous resort beaches beckon.

Siesta Key

Tampa Bay to Tarpon Springs

Chapter 13

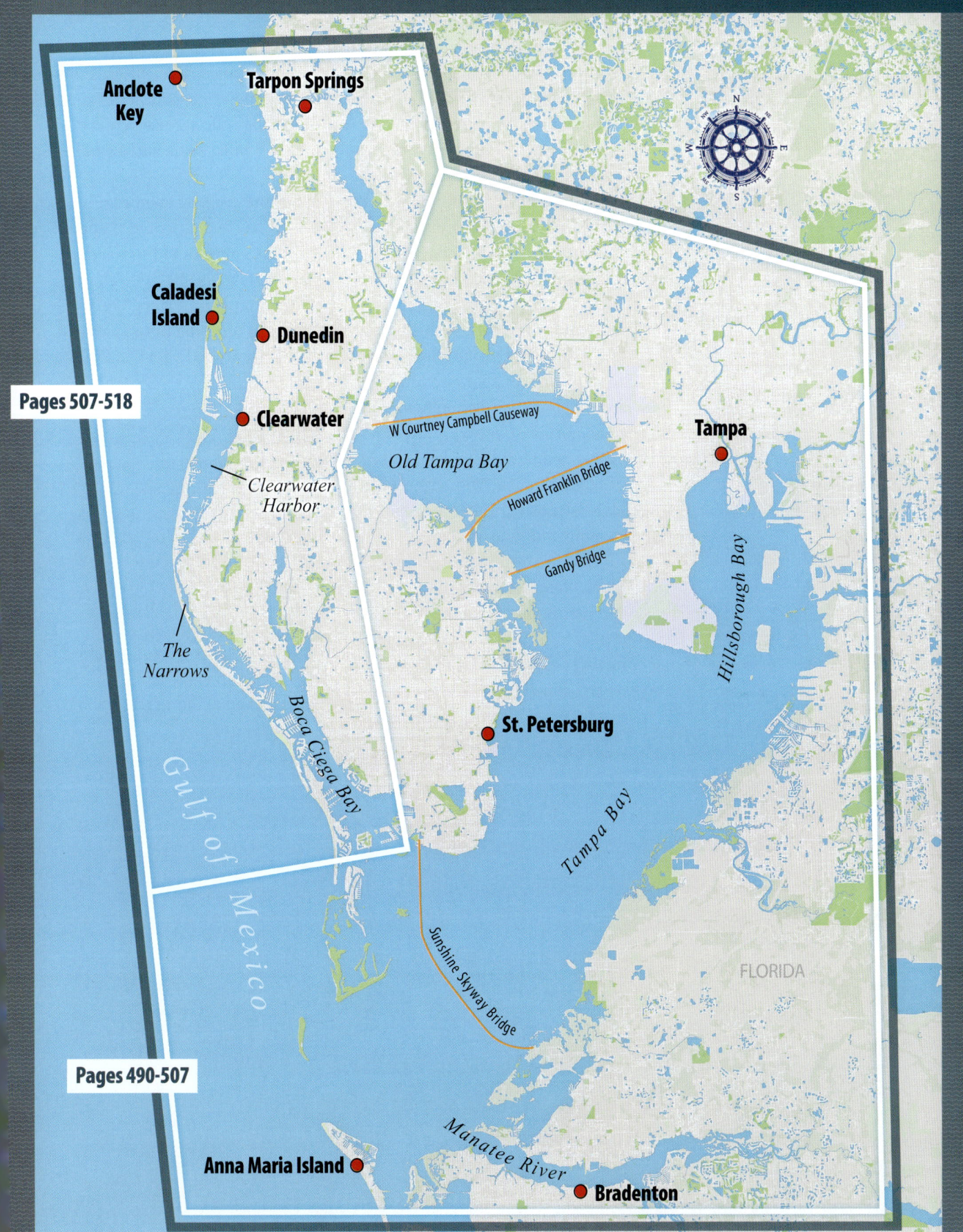

Chapter 13: Tampa Bay to Tarpon Springs

GIWW Mile 78 to Mile 150

■ TAMPA BAY AREA

One of the great natural harbors of the world Tampa Bay extends about 25 miles north to south and about 10 miles east to west. It has two major cities (Tampa and St. Petersburg) and several large rivers that meander in from the east and north. Fringing the west side of the coast and extending northward is a pencil-thin chain of barrier islands with resort communities famous for their Gulf shore beaches.

Tampa Bay comprises three vast bodies of water–Tampa Bay proper, Old Tampa Bay to the northwest and Hillsborough Bay to the northeast–all providing excellent cruising. Lower Tampa Bay opens to the Gulf of Mexico but enjoys the protection of barrier islands. Old Tampa Bay reaches northwest from Tampa Bay to the shoal water around Safety Harbor and Mobbly Bay. Hillsborough Bay branches off to the northeast between Interbay Peninsula and the mainland to serve the city of Tampa, Ybor City and Davis Islands with their extensive shipping and industrial areas.

From the open mouth of Tampa Bay, St. Petersburg lies due north with metropolitan Tampa to the northeast. Each dominates one of the two big peninsulas that pierce the bay. Pinellas to the west extends about 45 miles from the southern edge of St. Petersburg almost to Tarpon Springs. MacDill Air Force Base occupies the southern tip of Interbay, the second peninsula (about 3 miles wide and 10 miles long).

For the cruising skipper Tampa Bay is a welcome change from the confines of the GIWW. Here there are some 300 square miles of cruising waters, Gulf fishing, interesting ports, pleasant anchorages, good yacht facilities and superb sailing.

NO WAKE ZONE

No Wake Zones, Idle Speed Zones and various Speed Limit restrictions are in effect throughout the waterways included in this chapter. Exercise diligence in knowing the regulations by observing signs and other markers. Enforcement is always present. As always, be courteous to other vessels and avoid manatees and other marine life.

Bradenton Beach pier, Anna Maria Island

Anna Maria Sound, FL

BRADENTON BEACH AREA		Largest Vessel	VHF	Total Slips	Approach/Dockside Depth	Floating Docks	Gas/Diesel	Repairs/Haulout	Min/Max Amps	Pump-Out Station
1. Bradenton Beach Marina WiFi MM 87.2	(941) 778-2288	60	16	40	6.0 / 4.0		GD	RH	30 / 50	P
2. Loggerhead Marina - Cortez Village Marina	(941) 795-3625	38			/	F	G	RH		
3. Seafood Shack Marina, Bar & Grill WiFi MM 87.2	(386) 643-5555	120	68	68	14.0 / 12.0		GD		30 / 50	

WiFi Wireless Internet Access
Visit www.waterwayguide.com for current rates, fuel prices, website addresses and other up-to-the-minute information.
(Information in the table is provided by the facilities.)

Scan here for more details:

Anna Maria Island–GIWW Mile 89

Lovely Anna Maria Island is noted for its white sandy beaches, good tarpon fishing and premium restaurants. The island lies between Sarasota Bay on the south, Anna Maria Sound (separating the island from the mainland at the towns of Cortez and Bradenton) and Tampa Bay on the north. Cruisers can reach Tampa Bay and points north either directly from the Gulf of Mexico or via the inside GIWW route from Sarasota Bay.

NAVIGATION: Use NOAA Charts 11415 and 11425. Traveling north from Sarasota Bay there is no "quick" route north by going out into the Gulf of Mexico at Longboat Pass. Just stay on the inside. Even with a couple of bascule bridges that will have to open on the GIWW you will save time and fuel. The inside route will bring you into Tampa Bay at red daybeacon "68."

Two bascule bridges cross the GIWW on this stretch before reaching Tampa Bay: the **Cortez (SR 684) Bridge** at Mile 87.4 (22-foot closed vertical clearance) and the **Anna Maria (SR 64/Manatee Avenue West) Bridge** at Mile 89.2 (24-foot closed vertical clearance). Both open on signal except from 6:00 a.m. to 7:00 p.m. daily, when the draw need only open on the quarter hour and three quarter hour. The GIWW channel cuts through shoals in much of Anna Maria Sound and at red daybeacon "52" starts swinging toward Perico Island just south of the Anna Maria Bridge.

A back range at Mile 90 helps you stay in the center of the channel until you reach the sand bar charted as "The Bulkhead," which is marked by flashing red "64" at Mile 92. After leaving red daybeacon "68" the water is deep and you can head into Tampa Bay, go up the Manatee River to the east or turn due west for the continuation of the GIWW across the bay. You can also head into the channel through Key Royale Bar to Bimini Bay on the northeast end of Anna Maria Island.

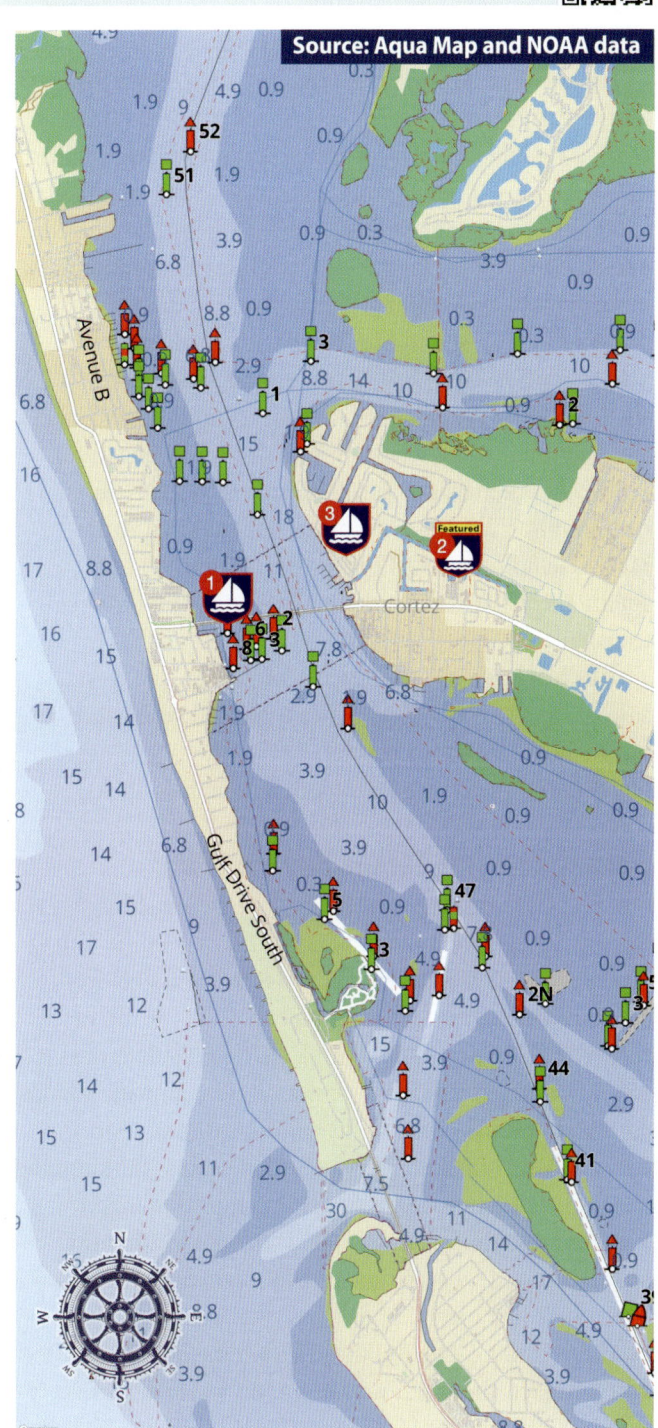

Source: Aqua Map and NOAA data

Chapter 13: Tampa Bay to Tarpon Springs

Dockage: To the west of the GIWW on the south side of the Cortez Bridge is the full-service Bradenton Beach Marina, which has 15 reserved transient slips and an on-site boatyard. This a busy location with many tours and activities.

Immediately after the Cortez Bridge a dredged channel on the eastern shore leads to Loggerhead Marina–Cortez Village Marina. They offer dry storage slips with valet boat service, wet slips with lifts (to 38 feet), an on-site service department and a boat brokerage.

Shortly after flashing red "48" and the Cortez Bridge on the eastern shore is Seafood Shack Marina, Bar & Grill, a popular waterfront restaurant and marina with transient slips. The helpful dockmaster answers on VHF Channel 16. They also offer over 400 feet of dedicated dockage for restaurant guests (two hour complimentary mooring while you dine). To the north is the very protected Cove Sound Moorings with slips to 50 feet.

Safe Harbor Pier 77 at Perico Island boasts a drystack building rated to withstand 175 mph winds. They also maintain some wet transient slips. Call ahead for availability. Waterline Marina Resort & Beach Club, Autograph Collection in a protected basin on Anna Maria Island offers 50 slips for boats up to 45 feet. Galati Yacht Basin is home to a brokerage and offers transient space to 105 feet.

Anchorage: It is possible to anchor on the west side of the Cortez Bridge in 4 to 8 feet MLW. Be sure not to swing into the channel. The anchorage is near restaurants, a dive shop and commercial fish docks.

Option: Crossing Tampa Bay via GIWW

On clear days the high-level Bob Graham Sunshine Skyway Bridge, the span of which forms a 15-mile-long highway across lower Tampa Bay, is clearly visible from The Bulkhead. The span is 425 feet high at the top of the two cable towers and it has a charted fixed vertical clearance of 180 feet at the center. Small manmade islands (called dolphins) flank the 12 columns that support the Bob Graham Sunshine Skyway Bridge nearest the shipping channel. Their function is to deflect ships that might wander out of the channel. Half of the old southbound span, damaged when struck in 1980, remains on both sides as fishing piers.

After crossing The Bulkhead at red daybeacon "68" you will face about 4.5 miles of open water across Tampa Bay to the continuation of the GIWW on the north side of the bay. Flashing red "70" near Mile 95 is a useful checkpoint on this open-water run. When crossing the main shipping channel remember that commercial shipping traffic has the right-of-way and stay alert. With its long fetch this stretch can kick up an uncomfortable chop.

The Sunshine Skyway Channel is on the opposite side of the main (Mullet Key) channel and is marked by flashing green "1." Exercise caution when crossing the busy channel.

CAUTION: Shoaling to 5 feet MLW has been observed in the Sunshine Skyway Channel. The shoaling extends 40 to 50 feet into the channel to the southwest of red daybeacon "14." Deep-draft vessels should exercise caution while transiting the area.

Side Trip: Egmont Key–GIWW Mile 95

Square in the middle of the entrance to Tampa Bay lies Egmont Key, 3 miles off the tip of Anna Maria Island. The island is a bird sanctuary and you will also see a lot of gopher tortoises, which are on the endangered species list. Unfettered wandering is discouraged. Egmont Key is a popular daytime anchorage that gets crowded on the weekends in the summer. You can anchor close to shore on the southeast end of the island and dinghy in. As an overnight anchorage the waters on the east side off Egmont may be uncomfortable when an evening breeze kicks in and creates a lee shore. The bottom is hard sand with good holding.

The Manatee River (Bradenton)

Manatee River's main city, Bradenton, is a popular layover port for those who want to explore the river and other waters. The protected marina basin has good depths and includes slips for liveaboards and weekenders alike.

NAVIGATION: Use NOAA Charts 11415 and 11425. From the exit at The Bulkhead in Anna Maria Sound, a sharp turn to the east around red daybeacon "68" leads to the mouth of the lovely Manatee River, one of Tampa Bay's finest cruising and gunkholing areas.

The almost-tropical Manatee River has a well-marked, deep channel (8-foot MLW depths), interesting side

Chapter 13

Anna Maria Sound, FL

ANNA MARIA ISLAND		Largest Vessel	VHF	Total Slips	Approach/ Dockside Depth	Floating Docks	Gas/ Diesel	Repairs/ Haulout	Min/Max Amps	Pump-Out Station
1. Safe Harbor Pier 77 WiFi 53/54	(941) 761-4200	50	16	55	/	F	GD		30 / 50	P
2. Galati Yacht Basin 1.0 mi W of MM 91.8	(941) 778-0755	105	16	60	7.0 / 7.0		GD	RH	50	P

WiFi Wireless Internet Access
Visit www.waterwayguide.com for current rates, fuel prices, website addresses and other up-to-the-minute information.
(Information in the table is provided by the facilities.)

Scan here for more details:

Source: Aqua Map and NOAA data

SOUTHERN EDITION

Chapter 13: Tampa Bay to Tarpon Springs

Manatee River, FL

PALMETTO AREA		Largest Vessel	VHF	Total Slips	Approach/ Dockside Depth	Floating Docks	Gas/ Diesel	Repairs/ Haulout	Min/Max Amps	Pump-Out Station
1. Bradenton Yacht Club-PRIVATE WiFi	(941) 722-5936	185	16	52	/				30 / 50	
2. Tropic Isles Marina	(941) 729-8128	30			10.0 / 9.0		G			

WiFi Wireless Internet Access
Visit www.waterwayguide.com for current rates, fuel prices, website addresses and other up-to-the-minute information.
(Information in the table is provided by the facilities.)

Scan here for more details:

streams to explore by dinghy and friendly towns to visit. The entrance channel threads through shoals but a series of ranges are strategically placed to keep the mariner from finding those shoals.

When traveling in from the north be aware of the shoal that is north of quick-flashing red "4" stay close to the buoy but inside the channel. Follow the markers closely until you are past DeSoto Point marked by flashing red "12" where there is ample water. Continuing up the river be aware of flashing red "14" and green daybeacon "15" as there are shoals growing in and around the markers. Give them a wide berth.

At Bradenton three bridges cross the Manatee River within 1 mile of each other. The first is the **8th Avenue West Bridge** (known locally as the Green Bridge), which has 41-foot fixed vertical clearance; the second (**CSX Railroad Bridge**) is untended and usually open (5-foot closed vertical clearance); and the third (**Hernando Desoto Bridge**) has 40-foot fixed vertical clearance.

The upper Manatee River east of these three bridges offers some cruising options and holds depths of 10 feet MLW or better to the I-75 Bridges at Ellenton (40-foot fixed vertical clearance). After that depths shallow considerably and venturing farther is not recommended.

The Braden River opens to the south 2 nm beyond the last of the bridges. This is a lush and scenic stream with plenty of wildlife but it is unmarked and full of shoals. Slim water and a fixed bridge with 10-foot vertical clearance limit exploration by bigger boats but offer fine gunkholing by dinghy.

Manatee River, FL

PALMETTO AREA		Largest Vessel	VHF	Total Slips	Approach/ Dockside Depth	Floating Docks	Gas/ Diesel	Repairs/ Haulout	Min/Max Amps	Pump-Out Station
1. Safe Harbor Regatta Pointe WiFi	(941) 729-6021	120	16	350	10.0 / 10.0		GD		30 / 50	P
2. Twin Dolphin Marina WiFi	(941) 747-8300	105	16	225	12.0 / 9.0	F	GD		30 / 100	P
3. Riviera Dunes Marina WiFi	(941) 981-5330	110	16	219	9.0 / 18.0	F	GD		30 / 100	P

WiFi Wireless Internet Access
Visit www.waterwayguide.com for current rates, fuel prices, website addresses and other up-to-the-minute information.
(Information in the table is provided by the facilities.)

Scan here for more details:

Source: Aqua Map and NOAA data

Dockage: The friendly Bradenton Yacht Club east of McKay Point (northeast of red daybeacon "14") welcome members of reciprocal yacht clubs. They offer elegant as well as casual dining in its spacious formal dining room.

Between Snead Island and Palmetto a land cut beside the Bradenton Yacht Club leads into Terra Ceia Bay. This channel has depths of about 5 feet MLW and a fixed bridge with a 13-foot vertical clearance restricting access for some to the small boat facilities beyond the bridge including Tropic Isles Marina, which caters to power boats to 30 feet.

Directly on the Manatee River west of the Hwy. 41 Bridge is the well-equipped and well-appointed Safe Harbor Regatta Pointe, which accommodates transient guests with upscale amenities and three waterfront restaurants. Bicycles are available for loan at the marina store to get to the grocery store located a few blocks away.

Directly across the river and close to downtown Bradenton is Twin Dolphin Marina with transient dockage at floating docks. The marina is located at green daybeacon "21" and red daybeacon "22." The marina has a single-opening entrance configuration through its breakwaters. Be sure to sound your horn going in or coming out.

On the opposite (north) shore is the full-service and well-maintained Riviera Dunes Marina, which can accommodate vessels to 120 feet (30 feet minimum) with resort amenities, including two heated pools. Riviera Dunes Dockside offers casual upscale cuisine and live entertainment Wednesday through Sunday.

Chapter 13: Tampa Bay to Tarpon Springs

Tampa Bay, FL

LITTLE MANATEE RIVER		Largest Vessel	VHF	Total Slips	Approach/ Dockside Depth	Floating Docks	Gas/ Diesel	Repairs/ Haulout	Min/Max Amps	Pump-Out Station
1. Little Harbor Marinas WiFi	(813) 645-2288	65	16	200	6.0 / 10.0	F	GD	R	30 / 50	P
2. Shell Point Marina WiFi	(813) 645-1313	60	9	45	6.0 / 9.0	F	GD	RH	30	P

WiFi Wireless Internet Access
Visit www.waterwayguide.com for current rates, fuel prices, website addresses and other up-to-the-minute information.
(Information in the table is provided by the facilities.)

Scan here for more details:

There are two supermarkets, banks, a pharmacy and an auto parts store within walking distance.

Anchorage: Follow the channel past flashing red "12" then turn west into the cove behind Desoto Point (Holy Hole), being mindful of the charted shoal in the center of the cove. (This is called "holy hole" due to the three crosses on shore.) There is plenty of room for several boats to anchor despite the shoal. This anchorage is protected except from the east and carries 9 to 10 feet MLW. You can land your dinghy to visit the DeSoto National Memorial Park.

A second anchorage is across the river at McKay Point east of Snead Island Boat Works Inc. Depths range from 6 to 9 feet MLW but protection is good only from north winds.

Farther upriver boats anchor just west of the bridge on either the Bradenton side (near red daybeacon "22") or the Palmetto side (east of red daybeacon "18"). Both have good holding in mud in a least 7 feet MLW. Expect a strong current.

Little Manatee River & Apollo Beach

NAVIGATION: Use NOAA Chart 11416. About 15 miles north of Manatee River on Tampa Bay is Little Manatee River. From the Manatee River channel follow the main ship channel to flashing red "6D" and head for lighted "LM" at the mouth of the river. Head north for Little Harbor and south for Shell Point. Apollo Beach is just to the north on Tampa Bay and is approached on a southeasterly course from the Cut "C" Channel range light.

Hillsboro Bay, FL

APOLLO BEACH

		Largest Vessel	VHF	Total Slips	Approach/Dockside Depth	Floating Docks	Gas/Diesel	Repairs/Haulout	Min/Max Amps	Pump-Out Station
1. Apollo Beach Marina	(813) 645-0720	40		12	8.0 / 5.0			H	30	

WiFi Wireless Internet Access
Visit www.waterwayguide.com for current rates, fuel prices, website addresses and other up-to-the-minute information.
(Information in the table is provided by the facilities.)

Scan here for more details:

Source: Aqua Map and NOAA data

SOUTHERN EDITION

Chapter 13: Tampa Bay to Tarpon Springs

Dockage: Suntex manages Little Harbor Marinas in a protected canal off the Little Manatee River. Dual facilities offer dry storage and dockage and repairs with full amenities and multiple restaurants. This is in a protected basin surrounded by multi-story condos making it a great hurricane hole. A beach is within walking distance. To the south near the mouth of the Manatee River, Shell Point Marina provides wet slips and amenities with "old Florida charm" as well as dry storage, bottom jobs and marina services (including DIY).

Apollo Beach Marina is approached from the north via the Big Bend Channel. This facility is usually full with long-term rentals so be sure to call first for transient availability.

There is no room for anchoring in these tight harbors. It's best to take a slip here or continue north to Boca Ciega Bay if you must anchor out.

City of Tampa

One of the great natural harbors of the world Tampa Bay extends about 25 miles north to south and about 10 miles east to west. It has two major cities (Tampa and St. Petersburg) and several large rivers that meander in from the east and north. Fringing the west side of the coast and extending northward is a pencil-thin chain of barrier islands with resort communities famous for their Gulf shore beaches.

Tampa Bay comprises three vast bodies of water–Tampa Bay proper, Old Tampa Bay to the northwest and Hillsborough Bay to the northeast–all providing excellent cruising. Lower Tampa Bay opens to the Gulf of Mexico but enjoys the protection of barrier islands. Old Tampa Bay reaches northwest from Tampa Bay to the shoal water around Safety Harbor and Mobbly Bay. Hillsborough Bay branches off to the northeast between Interbay Peninsula and the mainland to serve the City of Tampa, Ybor City and Davis Islands with their extensive shipping and industrial areas.

St. Petersburg lies due north from the open mouth of Tampa Bay with metropolitan Tampa to the northeast. Each dominates one of the two big peninsulas that pierce the bay. Pinellas to the west extends about 45 miles from the southern edge of St. Petersburg almost to Tarpon Springs. MacDill

Hillsboro Bay, FL

TAMPA AREA		Largest Vessel	VHF	Total Slips	Approach/ Dockside Depth	Floating Docks	Gas/ Diesel	Repairs/ Haulout	Min/Max Amps	Pump-Out Station
1. Davis Island Yacht Club-PRIVATE	(813) 251-1158	55		114	10.0 / 8.0	F		H	30	
2. Marjorie Park Yacht Basin WiFi	(813) 259-1604	90		32	21.0 / 9.0	F	GD		30 / 50	P
3. Tampa Convention Center Transient Marina	(813) 444-7728	160		19	19.0 / 19.0	F			30 / 50	
4. Marriott Tampa Water Street Hotel & Marina WiFi	(813) 204-6361	60	16	32	19.0 / 19.0	F			30 / 50	

WiFi Wireless Internet Access
Visit www.waterwayguide.com for current rates, fuel prices, website addresses and other up-to-the-minute information.
(Information in the table is provided by the facilities.)

Scan here for more details:

Source: Aqua Map and NOAA data

Chapter 13: Tampa Bay to Tarpon Springs

Old Tampa Bay, FL

PORT TAMPA AREA		Largest Vessel	VHF	Total Slips	Approach/ Dockside Depth	Floating Docks	Gas/ Diesel	Repairs/ Haulout	Min/Max Amps	Pump-Out Station
1. Port 32 Tampa WiFi	(813) 831-1200	80	16	25	25.0 / 12.0	F	GD	RH	30 / 50	P
2. Oasis Marinas at Westshore Yacht Club WiFi	(813) 831-7002	150	16	149	25.0 / 8.0	F			30 / 100	

WiFi Wireless Internet Access
Visit www.waterwayguide.com for current rates, fuel prices, website addresses and other up-to-the-minute information. (Information in the table is provided by the facilities.)

Scan here for more details:

Air Force Base occupies the southern tip of Interbay, the second peninsula (about 3 miles wide and 10 miles long).

For the cruising skipper Tampa Bay is a welcome change from the confines of the GIWW. Here there are some 300 square miles of cruising waters, Gulf fishing, interesting ports, pleasant anchorages, good yacht facilities and superb sailing.

NAVIGATION: Use NOAA Chart 11415 and 11416. To get to Tampa from The Bulkhead at the exit of Anna Maria Sound set a course of 022° magnetic for flashing red buoy "70" well out in Tampa Bay at GIWW Mile 95. Continue on the same heading until you pick up quick-flashing red buoy "26" at Mullet Key Channel, the big ship route up Tampa Bay. Go under the center spans of the Bob Graham Sunshine Skyway Bridge (known locally as the Meisner Bridge). You may then follow the Mullet Key Channel the 20 to 25 miles all the way northeast to the City of Tampa.

Most of the marine facilities are on the Seddon Channel between Harbor and Davis Islands. At the end of Davis Islands is a park that offers a small beach area, off-leash area for dogs, picnic area, canoe launch and boat ramps.

Dockage: Nearly all of the dockage at Harbour Island, which is in downtown Tampa, is private. Davis Island Yacht Club at Tampa is private.

The municipal Marjorie Park Yacht Basin located on the channel between Harbor and Davis Islands is a full-service facility with slips and easy access to mass transit.

There are 27 slips at the conveniently located Tampa Convention Center Transient Docks. Tie up at one of two floating docks for a few hours or stay overnight. (Note that North Dock has no power and water but South Dock does.) There are black-out dates due to construction and special events so call ahead for a reservation. This facility is very convenient to the sights, sounds and activities of downtown Tampa and Ybor City.

Marriott Tampa Water Street Hotel & Marina is located on Garrison Channel between the **S. Franklin Street Bridge** and the **S. Meridian Avenue Bridge**, both with charted 10-foot fixed vertical clearance. (According to the marina the vertical clearance is actually closer to 18 feet MLW.) They may have transient slips on their floating docks for those who can navigate the bridge but call well in advance to check availability. This facility offers resort amenities including laundry facilities, a fitness center and a rooftop pool.

Port Consolidated-Tampa has some of the lowest fuel prices in the area with two Tampa locations: 5007 Denver St. and 5020 Santa Fe Rd.

> NOTE: Plan to take a slip. There is no room to anchor in the Seddon or Garrison Channels.

Old Tampa Bay

On the opposite side of Interbay Peninsula from the City of Tampa is Old Tampa Bay, which is crossed by three bridges. Marine facilities are located at Port Tampa before the southernmost bridge (**Gandy Bridges**) with 43-foot vertical clearance.

Dockage: The full-service Port 32 Tampa has wet slips with easy docking and direct access to Tampa Bay. They offer transient dockage, as well as in-water repairs and refits. Oasis Marinas at Westshore Yacht Club is part of a condominium complex that has transient slips on floating docks for vessels up to 150 feet on floating slips. Guests have access to the waterfront Bay Club with a spa, fitness center, pools and restaurant (which will deliver to boats in the marina).

City of St. Petersburg

Facilities of one kind or another line all sides of the peninsula in St. Petersburg (often referred to as St. Pete). Boaters heading up Tampa Bay reach the marinas at the south end first but there are also facilities downtown on the east side of the peninsula and in Boca Ciega Bay on the west side.

NAVIGATION: Use NOAA Charts 11411, 11415 and 11416. Two routes, both clearly marked on NOAA Chart 11416, lead from Anna Maria Sound to St. Petersburg. Starting from The Bulkhead set a course of 022° magnetic for flashing red "70" well out in Tampa Bay at Mile 95. Continue on the same heading until you pick up flashing red buoy "26" at Mullet Key Channel, the big ship route up Tampa Bay.

The western approach to St. Petersburg follows Mullet Key Channel eastward through the high-rise Bob Graham Sunshine Skyway Bridge. Leave the channel at flashing green buoy "3B" with a bearing of about 5° magnetic. After leaving a 27-foot-high quick-flashing red to the east you should pick up the twin, 16-foot-high flashing green "1" and flashing red "2." At quick-flashing green "3" continue north on the marked channel to access the facilities on the east side of the peninsula.

You can head into Bayboro Harbor at flashing green "S." Coast Guard ships and cruise ships come here so the water is deep. Keep north for the marinas at the three yacht basins (North, Central and South).

To continue to Boca Ciega Bay, turn west to flashing green "1" and take the channel under the 65-foot fixed vertical clearance span of the Maximo Bridge until it converges with the northbound channel to St. Petersburg at red daybeacon "14."

Be advised that if you are exiting Boca Ciega Bay and hoping to avoid easterly winds out in Tampa Bay, you will have them right on your nose from green daybeacon "13A." It is several miles to the northbound channel.

> NOTE: In case you haven't guessed, this is a great place for a good set of binoculars for sorting out the different channel markers.

Dockage/Moorings: Renaissance Vinoy Resort Marina near the big pink historic Vinoy Hotel in the North Basin is a Marriott property with 74 concrete boat slips for vessels of up to 130 feet and offering resort amenities. Nearby St. Petersburg Yacht Club is private but recognizes reciprocity with other clubs. Anchoring is not allowed in the North Basin (also known as Vinoy Basin).

The large (650-slip) St. Petersburg Municipal Marina in the Central Basin has a concrete, side-to mooring pier that is 500 feet in length. Berthing space for transients is based on reservations and availability. Reservations are

America's Waterway Guide Since 1947 — Chapter 13

As with most larger cities, St. Petersburg boasts an exciting arts and food scene, professional sporting events, a variety of museums and a serious nightlife. Start your exploration on the very walkable Bayshore Dr., a picturesque street with shops, restaurants and waterfront views. Take a tour of the historic Vinoy Hotel, a beautiful, historic hotel that has been a St. Petersburg landmark since the 1920s. If it's a Saturday, stop by the St. Petersburg Saturday Morning Market, a popular market at 230 1st St. SE that features fresh produce, crafts and live music. At the end of the day, make your way to St. Pete Beach, known for white sand, turquoise waters and stunning sunsets. Nearby Sunken Gardens is a century-old botanical garden featuring over 50,000 tropical plants, a butterfly aviary and a historic flamingo colony at 1825 4th St. N. (727-551-3102).

Not only does St. Pete have the largest public waterfront park system of any U.S. city, it's also an easy city to negotiate by foot or public transportation. The downtown "Looper" trolley (727-821-5166) stops at many of the tourist spots and downtown locations every 15 minutes for a nominal charge. The public bus service (PSTA, 727-540-1800) can get you around the rest of the city in all-electric buses.

Salvador Dali Museum

ATTRACTIONS

1. Museum of Fine Arts
Daily guided tours of expansive fine art and photography collection at 255 Beach Dr. NE (727-896-2667).

2. St. Petersburg Museum of History
Artifacts, photos and an exhibit on the beginning of commercial air travel at 335 2nd Ave. NE (727-894-1052).

3. Sundial St. Pete
Outdoor mall with upscale shopping and dining in the downtown center featuring three-story tall sundial (153 2nd Ave. N., 727-800-3201).

4. The Dali
Houses the largest collection of works of Salvador Dali outside of Europe, including paintings, sculpture, holograms and art glass. Don't miss the hedge maze and melting clock benches (1 Dali Blvd., 727-823-3767).

5. The Mahaffey Theater
Hosts the Florida Orchestra, ballet, performing artists and traveling Broadway plays at 400 1st St. S. (727-892-5767).

SERVICES

6. Downtown St. Pete Vet Clinic
111 2nd Ave. NE, Unit 113 (727-755-7387)

7. Nelson Poynter Memorial Library
140 7th Ave. S. (727-873-4405)

8. St. Pete Store & Visitors Center
100 2nd Ave. N. #150 (727-388-0686)

9. St. Petersburg Post Office
3135 1st Ave. N. (727-322-6632)

MARINAS

10. Harborage Marina
1110 3rd St. S. (727-821-6347)

11. Renaissance Vinoy Resort Marina
501 5th Ave. NE (727-824-8022)

12. St. Petersburg Municipal Marina
500 1st Ave. SE (727-893-7329)

13. St. Petersburg Yacht Club
11 Central Ave. (727-822-3873)

SOUTHERN EDITION

Chapter 13 — Tampa Bay to Tarpon Springs

Tampa Bay, FL

ST. PETERSBURG AREA		Largest Vessel	VHF	Total Slips	Approach/ Dockside Depth	Floating Docks	Gas/ Diesel	Repairs/ Haulout	Min/Max Amps	Pump-Out Station
1. Vinoy Resort Marina WiFi	(727) 824-8022	130	16	74	12.0 / 12.0				30 / 100	P
2. St. Petersburg Yacht Club-PRIVATE WiFi	(727) 822-3227	120	16	60	10.0 / 14.0		GD		30 / 100	
3. St. Petersburg Municipal Marina	(727) 893-7329	125	16	650	12.0 / 12.0		GD		30 / 100	P
4. The Harborage at Waterview Marinas WiFi	(727) 821-6347	300	16	340	24.0 / 12.0	F	GD		30 / 200+	P

WiFi Wireless Internet Access
Visit www.waterwayguide.com for current rates, fuel prices, website addresses and other up-to-the-minute information. (Information in the table is provided by the facilities.)

Scan here for more details:

America's Waterway Guide Since 1947
Chapter 13

taken no more than 30 days prior to arrival, including special events. The trolley system has stops close by but most everything is within walking distance.

The Harborage at Waterview Marinas at Bayboro is around the bend from downtown but close to a trolley stop so you can get around if needed. The mega-yacht marina offers deep-water transient slips protected by an 800-foot breakwater. They also boast a resort-style pool and tiki hut.

Southern Boca Ciega Bay

NAVIGATION: Use NOAA Chart 11411. There are two routes to reach boating facilities on the west side of the Pinellas Peninsula. Those who can clear **Pinellas Bayway Structure 'A' Bridge** (with 18-foot fixed vertical clearance) can use the shortcut east of Indian Key off the straight-line extension of the Sunshine Skyway Channel. Otherwise follow the GIWW channel through the new (in 2021) **Pinellas Bayway Structure 'E' Bridge** (65-foot vertical clearance) and then **Pinellas Bayway Structure 'C' Bridge** (65-foot fixed vertical clearance). The main GIWW channel intersects Pass-a-Grille Channel near Mile 113.

CAUTION: Just north of the Pinellas Bayway Bridges is a shoal spot that sometimes catches the unwary. It is well marked but it is recommended that you stay alert. Flashing red "26" and red "26A" lead past the shoal.

Dockage: Just to the north Loggerhead Marina–St. Petersburg Marina is located in Frenchman Creek. They can accommodate vessels up to 60 feet and provide hurricane-rated dry storage in their well-protected harbor. They also have a pool and this location provides easy access to restaurants, shopping and activities.

South of the Pinellas Bayway Structure 'C' Bridge and just to the west of Pinellas Bayway Structure 'E' Bridge, Tierra Verde Marina has 10 reserved transient slips (to 60 feet) and offers dry storage. The

SOUTHERN EDITION 505

Chapter 13 — Tampa Bay to Tarpon Springs

Boca Ciega Bay, FL

MAXIMO POINT		Largest Vessel	VHF	Total Slips	Approach/ Dockside Depth	Floating Docks	Gas/ Diesel	Repairs/ Haulout	Min/Max Amps	Pump-Out Station
1. Loggerhead Marina - St. Petersburg Marina WiFi	(727) 867-2600	60		143	5.0 / 5.0	F	GD	RH	30 / 50	P
PASS-A-GRILLE AREA										
2. Tierra Verde Marina MM 113.0	(727) 866-0255	42	75	34	20.0 / 15.0	F	GD	RH	30 / 50	
3. Port 32 Tierra Verde WiFi MM 113.0	(727) 867-0400	120	72	115	12.0 / 12.0	F	GD	RH	15 / 50	P
4. The Pass-A-Grille Marina WiFi MM 113.8	(727) 360-0100	50	16	20	20.0 / 15.0	F	GD	RH	30 / 100	

WiFi Wireless Internet Access

Visit www.waterwayguide.com for current rates, fuel prices, website addresses and other up-to-the-minute information. (Information in the table is provided by the facilities.)

Scan here for more details:

Source: Aqua Map and NOAA data

pet-friendly marina also has a retail center with many businesses. To the south off Pass-A-Grille Channel is Port 32 Tierra Verde with dry stack storage, wet slips (to 120 feet) and a full range of services. On the opposite side of the channel is The Pass-A-Grille Marina with slips to 50 feet and limited amenities but in a great location near beaches and shopping.

■ TO TARPON SPRINGS

The GIWW runs from Tampa Bay to Anclote Key via Boca Ciega Bay at the mouth of the Anclote River leading to Tarpon Springs. Tarpon Springs on the Anclote River marks the end of the Florida GIWW at Mile 150.

NOTE: The GIWW picks back up in the The Big Bend section of this guide, where mileages are measured east and west of Harvey Lock, LA, notated as EHL or WHL.

Passes to the Gulf

From Tampa Bay to Clearwater any one of several inlets affords easy access from the GIWW to and from the Gulf of Mexico (in good weather and daylight).

Passage Key Inlet: Follow the charts closely and stay in deep water. Not marked so be aware that there could be hazards. Should only be attempted with local knowledge. A better route is Southwest Channel.

Southwest Channel: Well marked and deep inlet into Tampa Bay. Carries a lot of commercial traffic so stay alert and pay attention. Remember, tonnage rules!

North Channel (just north of Tampa Bay): Well marked and leads from the Gulf to Pass-a-Grille Channel.

Pass-A-Grille Channel: Watch for shoaling and keep clear of the north side.

Johns Pass: Connects with the GIWW between Mitchell and Sunshine beaches and is crossed by **Johns Pass Drawbridge** (with closed vertical clearance of 27 feet at the center of the channel). The bridge opens on request.

> ⚠ *CAUTION:* All vessels operating with more than a 3-foot draft are advised to use extreme caution when transiting inbound and outbound of Johns Pass due to an encroaching shoal to the north in the vicinity of green can "3" in the entry channel from the Gulf. Shoaling has also been observed in the channel between flashing red "8" and "10." The shoaling is from center of the channel towards the red side. This inlet tends to shoal rapidly. Calling for local knowledge from one of the tow services would be wise.

Clearwater Pass: Located about 13 nm north of Johns Pass. Leads right into the heart of Clearwater proper. The 74-foot fixed vertical clearance **Clearwater Pass (SR183) Bridge** spans the pass. This is the preferred channel unless you have solid local knowledge for the others.

Boca Ciega Bay–GIWW Mile 114 to Mile 126

The GIWW runs from Tampa Bay to Anclote Key and the Tarpon Springs area through well-marked Boca Ciega Bay. From Boca Ciega Bay the GIWW is a well-marked, dredged channel that meanders northward through shallows inside the barrier islands referred to as the Holiday Isles–St. Petersburg Beach, Treasure Island and Sand Key.

When approaching bridges in this section bide your time and leave ample room for maneuvering while waiting. Call ahead on VHF Channel 09 if you are in doubt of the opening schedule. There are three bascule bridges on the GIWW with varying restrictions and schedules:

Corey Causeway (SR 693) Bridge (23-foot vertical clearance) opens on signal except from 8:00 a.m. to 7:00 p.m., Monday through Friday, and 10:00 a.m. to 7:00 p.m., Saturdays, Sundays and federal holidays, when the draw need only open on the hour, 20 minutes after the hour and 40 minutes after the hour.

Treasure Island Causeway Bridge (21-foot vertical clearance) opens on signal except from 7:00 a.m. to 7:00 p.m., when the draw need only open on the hour, 20 minutes after the hour and 40 minutes after the hour (Monday through Friday) and on the quarter hour and three-quarter hour on Saturday, Sunday and federal holidays.

Welch Causeway (SR 699) Bridge opens on signal except from 7:00 a.m. to 7:00 p.m., when the draw need only open on the hour and half hour (excludes holidays). While openings are usually prompt, delays can occur.

Dockage: North of the Pinellas Bayway is Isla Del Sol Yacht & Country Club, which is private but welcomes transient members of any reciprocal yacht club to their social and dining facilities. Maximo Marina (IGY) is to the east and just north of Cats Point and the Pinellas Bayway Structure 'A' Bridge. This facility has a mixture of fixed and floating docks (including four megayacht slips), some of which are covered. They have an on-site restaurant (Tiki Docks), a full-service

Chapter 13: Tampa Bay to Tarpon Springs

Boca Ciega Bay, FL

		Largest Vessel	VHF	Total Slips	Approach/ Dockside Depth	Floating Docks	Gas/ Diesel	Repairs/ Haulout	Min/Max Amps	Pump-Out Station
PINELLAS BAYWAY AREA										
1. Isla Del Sol Yacht & Country Club-PRIVATE WiFi MM 114.5	(727) 867-3625	65	16	76	20.0 / 6.0			H	30 / 50	P
2. Maximo Marina (IGY) WiFi 1.5 mi. NE of MM 115.0	(727) 867-1102	110	6	220	8.0 / 8.0	F	GD	RH	30	P
GULFPORT										
3. Gulfport Municipal Marina WiFi 1.5 mi. NE of MM 115.0	(727) 893-1071	45	16	250	7.0 / 6.0	F	GD	R	30 / 50	P
PASADENA										
4. Pasadena Yacht & Country Club-PRIVATE WiFi MM 116.5	(727) 543-4086	110	16	89	8.5 / 10.5				50 / 100	
5. Pasadena Marina WiFi MM 116.0	(727) 343-4500	56		125	6.0 / 6.0				30 / 50	P

WiFi Wireless Internet Access
Visit www.waterwayguide.com for current rates, fuel prices, website addresses and other up-to-the-minute information.
(Information in the table is provided by the facilities.)

Scan here for more details:

yard and dry storage. Within two blocks is a grocery store, several banks and a few other restaurants.

To reach Gulfport and its boating facilities turn to the northeast at GIWW Mile 114.5 just before flashing red "26." Slow down and take care as you round red daybeacon "2" and head carefully for green daybeacon "3." The red flashing light marks a shoal. Gulfport Municipal Marina has a full complement of transient facilities in its well-protected basin. The marina is located on 11 acres and surrounded by residential neighborhoods. It is a short walk to the center of downtown Gulfport and the trailhead for the Pinellas Trail is only 1 mile away.

The friendly Pasadena Yacht & Country Club to the north is private. Reciprocal privileges include dining, dockage and use of the swimming pool, subject to availability. (Golf, fitness and tennis are not included.) The well-maintained Pasadena Marina is quietly tucked away in a picturesque and well protected deep water basin on Boca Ciega Bay. The marina offers 125 full-service slips, both covered and open, accommodating boats up to 55 feet. Call ahead for transient availability.

There are full-service municipal marinas and facilities on both shores from Johns Pass at Mile 121 north to Sand Key including Blind Pass Marina, John's Pass Marina, Madeira Beach Moorings Yacht Harbor & Resort, Snug Harbor Inn and Madeira Beach Municipal Marina. Slips and repairs are available. There are also motels and on-the-water restaurants with dockage while you dine. You can use the Publix Shopping Dock, Treasure Island for shopping by dinghy.

Also nearby is On-Demand Fuel offering truck to dock fuel delivery. Discounts are offered for 100+ gallon orders. They currently only sell gas but plans to supply diesel are in the works.

To the northeast of Turtlecrawl Point between two fixed bridges (32-foot vertical clearance on first bridge) is the friendly Bay Pines Marina with slips and some services and repairs. Like most facilities here, they mostly cater to sportfishing vessels.

NOTE: We have been told that you are only allowed to stay aboard your boat for three days in this area. If you plan to stay longer, call ahead before your arrival.

Chapter 13: Tampa Bay to Tarpon Springs

Boca Ciega Bay, FL

JOHNS PASS AREA		Largest Vessel	VHF	Total Slips	Approach/ Dockside Depth	Floating Docks	Gas/ Diesel	Repairs/ Haulout	Min/Max Amps	Pump-Out Station
1. Blind Pass Marina MM 118.5	(727) 360-4281	40	16	110	8.0 / 6.0				30	P
2. John's Pass Marina WiFi 1 mi. S of MM 121.4	(727) 367-3835	75	16	34	10.0 / 5.0	F	GD		30 / 50	
3. Madeira Beach Moorings Yacht Harbor & Resort WiFi	(727) 440-9108	70	68	44	10.0 / 6.0	F		R	30 / 50	P
4. Madeira Beach Municipal Marina MM 122.2	(727) 399-2631	100	16	80	6.0 / 11.0	F	GD	R	30 / 50	P
5. Bay Pines Marina WiFi 1.5 mi. NE of MM 120.5	(727) 392-4922	50	16	60	5.0 / 7.0	F	G	RH	30 / 50	P

WiFi Wireless Internet Access

Scan here for more details:

Visit www.waterwayguide.com for current rates, fuel prices, website addresses and other up-to-the-minute information. (Information in the table is provided by the facilities.)

Source: Aqua Map and NOAA data

America's Waterway Guide Since 1947 — Chapter 13

Clearwater Harbor, FL

INDIAN SHORES		Largest Vessel	VHF	Total Slips	Approach/ Dockside Depth	Floating Docks	Gas/ Diesel	Repairs/ Haulout	Min/Max Amps	Pump-Out Station
1. Indian Springs Marina MM 129.0	(727) 595-2956	40		48	4.5 / 4.5	F	G	RH	30	
2. Harbourside Marina WiFi MM 129.4	(727) 240-9031	70	16	50	8.0 / 6.0				30 / 50	

WiFi Wireless Internet Access
Visit www.waterwayguide.com for current rates, fuel prices, website addresses and other up-to-the-minute information. (Information in the table is provided by the facilities.)

Scan here for more details:

Anchorage: One popular spot near the Gulfport Municipal Marina has 5 to 7 feet MLW and the other to the northwest has 6 to 10 feet MLW. These offer protection from all but southern blows. Expect lots of weekend boat traffic and snuggle up to the east shore.

To anchor closer to St. Pete Beach, proceed west between green daybeacon "31" and red daybeacon "30" from flashing red "32" then anchor where the chart shows 7- to 8-foot MLW depths. Proceed between the last two "No-Wake" markers to find the best depths. Expect wakes from boats coming inshore via Pass-A-Grille Channel.

Just north of the Treasure Island Bridge, about 200 yards north of green daybeacon "17," turn off the west between the charted spoils area and Isle of Palms for the Treasure Island anchorage with no less than 7 feet MLW leaving the channel and 10 to 12 feet extending all the way along the edge of Isle of Palms to the back of the bay. There is good holding, no current, plenty of swing room, moderate traffic and some road noise from shore. West of the GIWW at St. Pete Beach is the highly visible Don CeSar Hotel, a longtime landmark for mariners.

Finally you can anchor north of the Welch Causeway (SR 699) Bridge (Mile 122.1) in 7 feet MLW with good holding at Welch Causeway Bridge northeast. Dinghy back to the first channel by the bridge (past the American Legion building) to the day dock to access restaurants and shopping.

The Narrows—GIWW Mile 126 to Mile 130

NAVIGATION: Use NOAA Chart 11411. Nine nautical miles south of Clearwater the GIWW enters the well-named Narrows, a deep but narrow channel connecting Boca Ciega Bay to Clearwater Harbor, which is comparatively broad and open. At the northern end of the GIWW approaching Clearwater the waterway tends to narrow and bridges and shoaling become more frequent. Boats with significant draft should be very cautious.

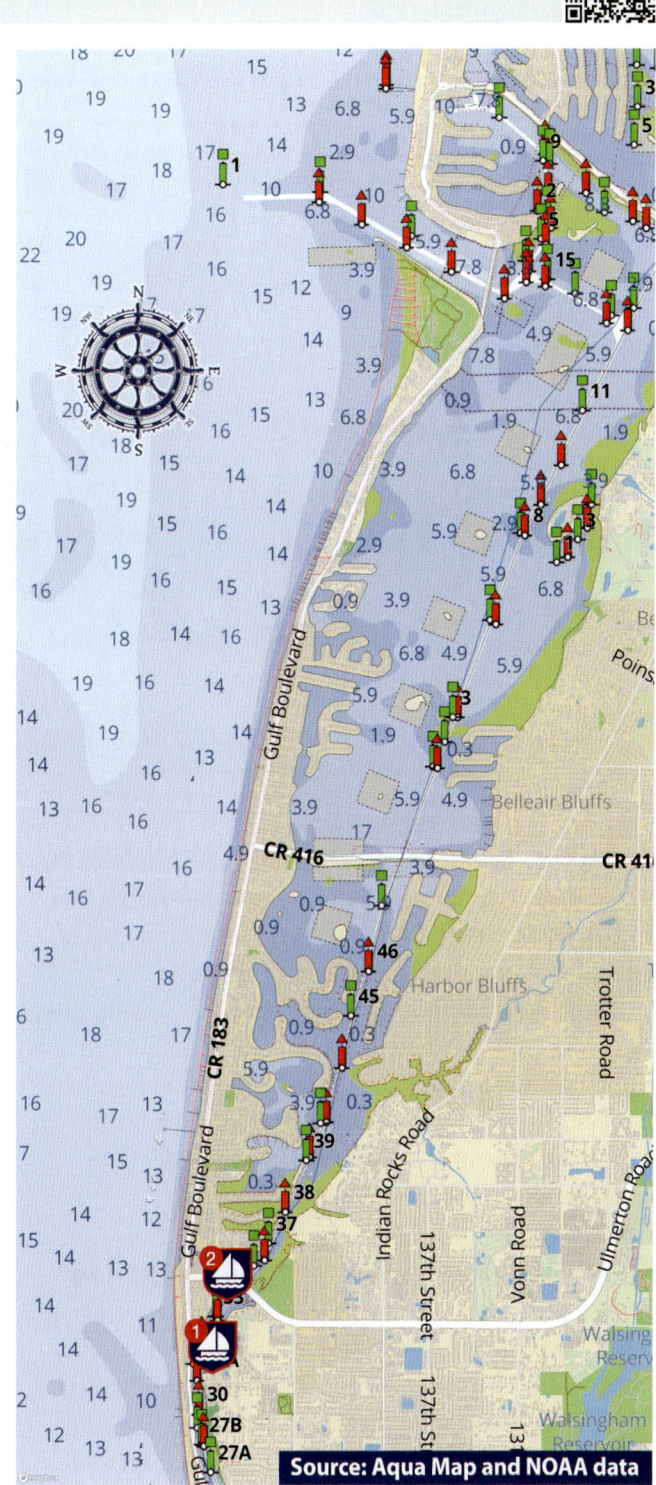

Source: Aqua Map and NOAA data

Chapter 13: Tampa Bay to Tarpon Springs

Clearwater Harbor, FL

CLEARWATER BEACH AREA		Largest Vessel	VHF	Total Slips	Approach/Dockside Depth	Floating Docks	Gas/Diesel	Repairs/Haulout	Min/Max Amps	Pump-Out Station
1. Clearwater Municipal Marinas (Clearwater Harbor Marina) WiFi	(727) 562-4981	125	16	126	7.0 / 7.0	F			30 / 50	P
2. Chart House Marina WiFi	(727) 449-8007			26	7.0 / 7.0				30 / 50	
3. Clearwater Yacht Club–PRIVATE WiFi MM 136.0	(727) 447-6000	70	16	42	7.0 / 7.0				30 / 50	
4. Clearwater Municipal Marinas (Clearwater Beach Marina) WiFi	(727) 562-4955 x2	125	16	207	7.0 / 12.0	F	GD		30 / 100	P
5. Clearwater Beach Marina WiFi	(727) 282-4990	55	16	50	/ 15.0	F			20 / 30	

WiFi Wireless Internet Access
Visit www.waterwayguide.com for current rates, fuel prices, website addresses and other up-to-the-minute information. (Information in the table is provided by the facilities.)

Scan here for more details:

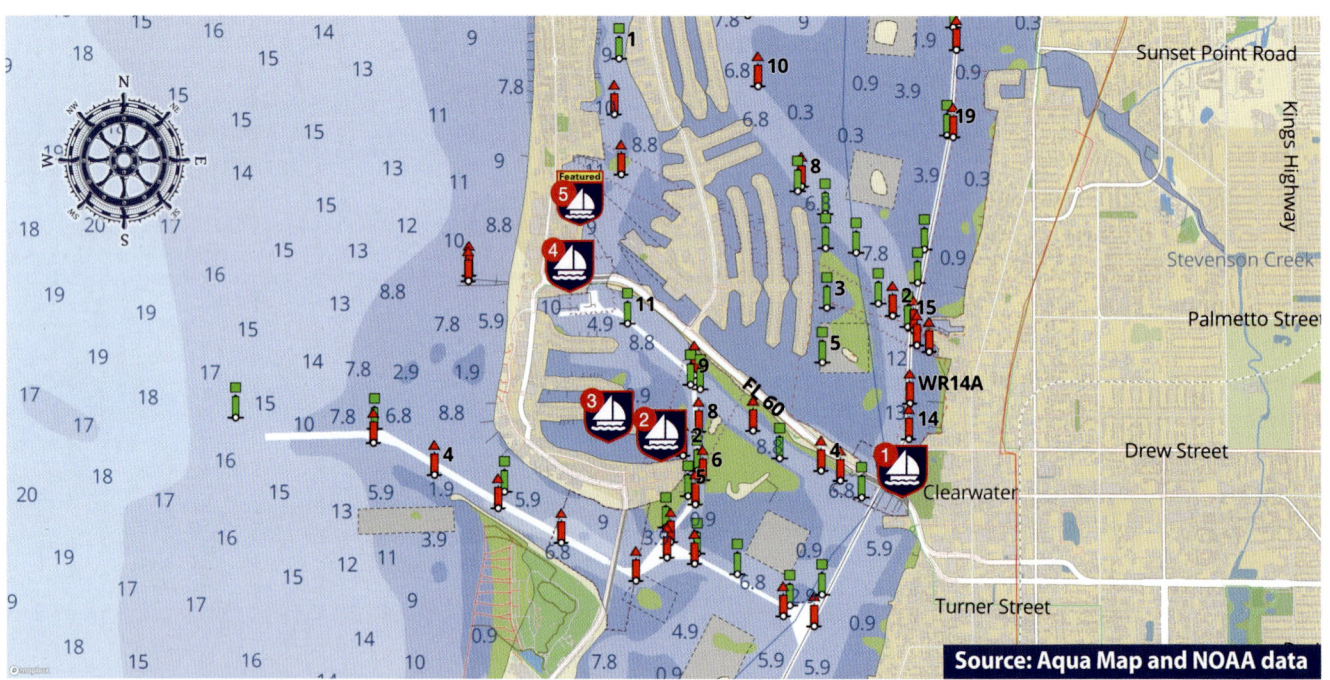

Park Boulevard North Bridge at Mile 126.6 has a 20-foot closed vertical clearance and opens on request. The Indian Rocks Beach Bridge at Mile 129.3 has a 25-foot closed vertical clearance and opens on request.

Dockage: Indian Springs Marina at GIWW Mile 129 is a yacht brokerage and dry boat storage facility with some covered wet slips (to 40 feet). Call ahead for slip availability. Harbourside Marina, part of a Holiday Inn & Suites, is near the Indian Rocks Beach Bridge with transient slips and access to hotel amenities.

Clearwater Area–GIWW Mile 130 to Mile 136

Although divided by the GIWW channel, Clearwater and Clearwater Beach constitute one very boat-minded community. Boaters find it an increasingly important port of call both as a base of operations from which to enjoy the nearby resort attractions and also as a layover stop.

The yacht services and elegant marinas here are mostly deep water and capable of handling the largest boats that travel the GIWW. Marinas and repair installations are busy but transient berths are generally available.

NAVIGATION: Use NOAA Chart 11411. At the northern end of the GIWW approaching Clearwater the waterway tends to narrow and bridges and shoaling become more frequent. Boats with significant draft should be very cautious. The **Belleair Causeway Bridge** at Mile 131.8 has 75-foot fixed vertical clearance. The best access to Clearwater from the Gulf of Mexico is through Clearwater Pass north of the bridge and just south of Clearwater. This is one of the west coast's better daytime passes and it is easy to use in good weather. North of the causeway the channel has shoaled; proceed with caution.

When approaching from Clearwater Pass 16-foot-high, flashing red "8" is followed by the 74-foot fixed vertical clearance **Sand Key Bridge**. At flashing red "14" turn north and into the channel marked by quick-flashing red "2" and green daybeacon "3." A well-marked channel will take you to green daybeacon "9" where you will turn west into the channel leading to the Clearwater Municipal Marinas (Clearwater Beach Marina).

You can also turn east into the well-marked channel running parallel to the causeway to green daybeacon "1" where that channel merges with the GIWW. The next bridge to the north on the GIWW is **Clearwater Memorial Causeway Bridge** (74-foot fixed vertical clearance).

Dockage: Approaching from the GIWW channel, Clearwater Municipal Marinas (Clearwater Harbor Marina) is on the mainland side at green daybeacon "1." A sizable charter boat fleet is berthed here as well as tour and fishing boats of all sizes. The marina takes reservations and the helpful marina staff can usually accommodate transients on the floating docks. The Jolly Trolley (727-445-1200) stops in front of the marina complex and provides a convenient ride to the grocery store or the beach.

On the beach side, facilities include the 26-slip Chart House Marina (part of a hotel complex) and the private Clearwater Yacht Club, which accepts members of reciprocating yacht clubs in Florida with slips and dining options.

A second location of the municipal marina is at the west end of the Clearwater Memorial Causeway (SR 60) Bridge. A second city-owned facility, Clearwater Municipal Marinas (Clearwater Beach Marina), has ample transient space and all the usual amenities. The marina offers access to a variety of boating activities and is home to fishing and sailing charters, sight-seeing boats and dinner cruises and parasailing and personal watercraft rentals. There is also a restaurant, gift shop, barber shop, laundry facilities, mini-mart and bait house.

Courtyard Clearwater Beach Marina has new (in 2022) floating docks and bathrooms with access to the adjacent hotel pool and bars. This are within walking distance of the beach, restaurants and stores.

> The celebration of sunset (much like in Key West) is held nightly at Pier 60 from two hours before until two hours after sunset. The festivities include street performers, crafts, outdoor movies and fabulous sunsets (weather permitting).

Anchorage: There are more anchoring choices in Clearwater Harbor than in Boca Ciega Bay beginning at GIWW Mile 131.9. On the northern side of the Belleair Beach Causeway Bridge (75-foot fixed vertical clearance) you will find 7 to 8 feet MLW with good holding in sand. There is about a 3-foot tide here. Use bow and stern anchors to ride the wakes from the nearby launch ramp and the GIWW.

Looking South to Clearwater Pass

Chapter 13: Tampa Bay to Tarpon Springs

Clearwater Harbor, FL

		Largest Vessel	VHF	Total Slips	Approach/ Dockside Depth	Floating Docks	Gas/ Diesel	Repairs/ Haulout	Min/Max Amps	Pump-Out Station
DUNEDIN AREA										
1. Dunedin Municipal Marina MM 139.3	(727) 298-3030	55	16	192	7.0 / 4.5				30 / 50	P
2. Loggerhead Marina - Marker 1 WiFi 0.5 mi. E of MM 141.8	(727) 733-9324	65	16	150	5.0 / 5.0		GD		30 / 50	P
CALADESI ISLAND										
3. Caladesi Island State Park Marina	(727) 469-5918	46		108	4.0 / 4.0	F			30	
PALM HARBOR AREA										
4. Home Port Marina WiFi	(727) 784-1443	42		187	5.0 / 5.0		GD	RH	30	P
5. Ozona Fish Camp WiFi	(727) 784-0143	37	68		6.0 / 4.0		G		30	

WiFi Wireless Internet Access
Visit www.waterwayguide.com for current rates, fuel prices, website addresses and other up-to-the-minute information.
(Information in the table is provided by the facilities.)

Scan here for more details:

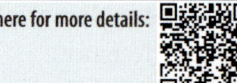

Source: Aqua Map and NOAA data

514 WATERWAY GUIDE 2024 www.waterwayguide.com

Clearwater Yacht Club has an anchorage with 6 to 9 feet MLW. You can also anchor on either side of the west side of the SR 60/Clearwater Harbor Bridge (14-foot fixed vertical clearance) in 6 to 10 feet MLW or Clearwater Beach Causeway.

Dunedin Area–GIWW Mile 136 to Mile 150

St. Joseph Sound is home to Dunedin and several beaches including Honeymoon Island and Caladesi Island State Park (accessible only by boat). Dunedin is one of the few open waterfront communities from Sarasota to Cedar Key where buildings do not completely obscure the view of the waterway and the Gulf of Mexico beyond from the highway. There is also a lack of large commercial signage to obscure the view and no franchise restaurants or chain retail stores.

> NOTE: Pinellas Trail, a 39-mile-long bicycle and pedestrian trail that traverses Pinellas County, bisects downtown Dunedin. A large portion of the trail lies on the former roadbed of the Orange Belt Railway, the first railroad in Pinellas County, which arrived in 1888.

NAVIGATION: Use NOAA Chart 11411. The **Dunedin Causeway Drawbridge** (opens on signal) crosses the GIWW at Mile 141.9. Although the stated clearance at mean high water is 24 feet, the clearance boards will reflect significantly less vertical clearance, sometimes down to below 19 feet. The clearance boards measure to "low steel," which is at the fenders. In the middle of the bridge there is an additional 4 feet of clearance.

As always, it is the captain's responsibility to ensure there is adequate clearance to safely pass under the bridge without asking for an opening. Call the bridge operator on VHF Channel 09 and, if in doubt, err on the conservative side and ask for an opening.

CAUTION: The Coast Guard has made several changes to the aids to navigation in this area that may not be reflected on older NOAA charts. Proceed with caution.

Dockage: Dunedin Municipal Marina has a busy boat ramp, day docks and transient slips and is within walking distance to Dunedin's restaurants and shopping. Limited transient dockage may be available dependent upon slip vacancies. No advance reservations. Four slips are available at the day docks and a designated slip for dinghy access. These slips are free to use on a first-come first-serve basis, with a maximum 4-hour limit.

Loggerhead Marina–Marker 1 Marina offers slips and dry racks and caters to sportfishing vessels. Located immediately south of the Dunedin Causeway Drawbridge, this facility is close to downtown Dunedin with good restaurants and groceries as well as the Pinellas Trail.

To the north of the bridge is Palm Harbor, which is shown on the NOAA chart as "Smith Bayou." This is not large boat territory (slips to 42 feet maximum). To access the facilities here turn east at green daybeacon "17" and follow the privately marked channel toward the large dry stack buildings. Home Port Marina has slips (to 42 feet) and a marine service center and is the site of the popular waterfront Ozona Blue Grilling Co. (727-789-4540).

Ozona Fish Camp to the north is accessed via a marked channel off the GIWW. They can accommodate vessels to 37 feet.

Side Trip: Caladesi Island State Park

Caladesi Island State Park has trails and a quiet beach that is rated among the best in the world. There are 108 slips in the isolated Caladesi Island State Park Marina. To get to Caladesi Island turn west just south of the Dunedin Causeway Drawbridge (green daybeacon "17") and then follow the Honeymoon Island Channel to a separate buoyed channel into Seven Mouth Creek. Only three slips here are wider than 11 feet; however, there are three "T" docks for larger boats.

Average depths on the approach and dockside are reported at 4 feet MLW so you may need to travel at high tide, go slowly and obtain up-to-date local knowledge. This is a great place to tuck away for a day or two or just visit for a night. Call ahead for reservations.

Anclote Key–GIWW Mile 150

About 3 miles north of Clearwater the barrier islands fall away and the GIWW enters unprotected St. Joseph Sound and the approach to Anclote Key. After this final stretch on the GIWW boaters continuing north beyond Anclote Key and the Anclote River have two choices: You may cross the open Gulf of Mexico for about 140 nm to Carrabelle or you can follow a series of several markers relatively close in-shore around the Big Bend section of Florida for about 160 or 165 miles to Carrabelle.

Chapter 13 — Tampa Bay to Tarpon Springs

Anchorage: A popular anchorage in St. Joseph Sound is Three Rooker Bar, a narrow C-shaped island located between Honeymoon Island and Anclote Key about 2.5 miles offshore from Tarpon Springs. Three Rooker's white sand beaches line the north and seaward sides of the island and offer some of the best shelling and beachcombing anywhere. The bay side of the island's shallow water teems with fish and birds. This is a well-protected anchorage from all but east winds.

CAUTION: Enter the anchorage around the north end of the bar, being careful to avoid shoaling encroaching on the navigable channel near red daybeacon "36" where depths as low as 2 to 5 feet MLW have been reported.

Drop anchor in the crescent near the beach in 4- to 8-foot MLW depths over a soft mud bottom. Use the depth sounder and line-of-sight navigation to avoid the white sand bars that run out from the beach. On holiday weekends this normally placid anchorage becomes a maelstrom of activity with jet skis, small outboards and a floating hamburger stand all vying for space.

It is also possible to anchor at Anclote Key (Mile 151) in 8 to 10 feet MLW with excellent holding and protection from the west. Anclote Key Preserve State Park has no provisions but the 403-acre park is home to at least 43 species of birds including the American oystercatcher, bald eagle and piping plover. A picturesque 1887 lighthouse stands as a sentinel on the southern end of the island.

Side Trip: Tarpon Springs

In reality, there are two Tarpon Springs. Both are intimately interrelated and well worth a visit. The sponge docks, the unbroken string of Greek restaurants and charming shops along Dodecanese Boulevard and the marinas are one aspect, while the other (historic downtown Tarpon Springs) is a charming complement to the docks.

From November to early spring you will find manatees make their home in the shallow Spring Bayou close to downtown. Craig Park offers a great vantage point for observing these gentle giants. It only takes a short dinghy ride to get to the Bayou but it becomes a non-motorized area so you will need to row in and around the bayou to view the manatees.

NAVIGATION: Use NOAA Chart 11411. A range helps you through the big offshore shoal around the entrance to the Anclote River. (If you cannot see the onshore light, locate quick-flashing green "1.") Channel markers are no more than 0.75 miles apart. For help in orienting you will see a tall, power plant chimney on the north side of the Anclote River entrance visible from 22 nm at sea (on a clear day). The chimney, illuminated by flashing lights at night, is plotted on NOAA Chart 11411 ("STACK") and mentioned in the *U.S. Coast Pilot*.

Respect the shoal south of Anclote Key. When entering the GIWW south of Anclote Key or entering the Anclote River give flashing green "7" near Mile 150 a wide berth. Older charts may not show the extension of the shoal southward. When traveling in this area it is important to keep your charts current and your depthsounder on. Refer to the latest NOAA charts for the most up-to-date information.

NO WAKE ZONE

Take it easy going upriver the 3 miles to Tarpon Springs and observe the posted Idle-Speed/No-Wake Zone. There are many boats at slips in the river and your wake can cause serious damage.

Commercial fishing and sponging boats also use the channel. The Cut C range's eastern mark is partially obscured by trees. Favor the southern side of the channel to avoid the shoal.

CAUTION: Mariners are advised to exercise extreme caution while transiting the area and stay close to the southern side of the basin as that is where the deeper water lies.

Dockage: Just as you enter the river on the northeast side is the 20-slip Anclote Village Marina with just two transient slips (to 55 feet) and "high and dry" storage for smaller boats. This is a convenient stopping place if you do not have time to go upriver. Only recently open to transients is MAR-MARina, a full-service marina with wet and dry storage and a helpful staff.

Anclote River, FL

TARPON SPRINGS AREA		Largest Vessel	VHF	Total Slips	Approach/ Dockside Depth	Floating Docks	Gas/ Diesel	Repairs/ Haulout	Min/Max Amps	Pump-Out Station
1. Anclote Village Marina WiFi	(727) 937-9737	55		20	5.0 / 7.0	F	GD	R	30 / 50	
2. Port Tarpon Marina WiFi	(727) 937-2200	75	16	58	9.0 / 9.0	F	GD	RH	50 / 100	
3. Anclote Harbors Marina WiFi	(727) 934-7616	45	16	30	9.0 / 6.0		G	RH	30 / 50	
4. Anclote Isles Marina WiFi	(727) 939-0100	85	16	70	8.0 / 7.0				30 / 100	P
5. Belle Harbour Marina WiFi	(727) 943-8489	50	16	18	6.0 / 5.0	F	G	RH	30 / 50	P
6. Tarpon Landing Marina	(727) 937-1100	50		20	5.0 / 6.0		GD	R	30 / 50	P
7. City of Tarpon Springs Municipal Marina WiFi	(727) 946-5658	50	16	21	11.0 / 10.0	F			30 / 50	
8. Spongeorama WiFi	(727) 365-8793	55			/ 6.0				30 / 50	
9. Turtle Cove Marina WiFi	(727) 934-2202	50	16	56	5.0 / 6.0	F	GD	H	30 / 50	P
10. Tarpon Springs Yacht Club—PRIVATE	(727) 934-2136	50		13	/					

WiFi Wireless Internet Access
Visit www.waterwayguide.com for current rates, fuel prices, website addresses and other up-to-the-minute information. (Information in the table is provided by the facilities.)

Scan here for more details:

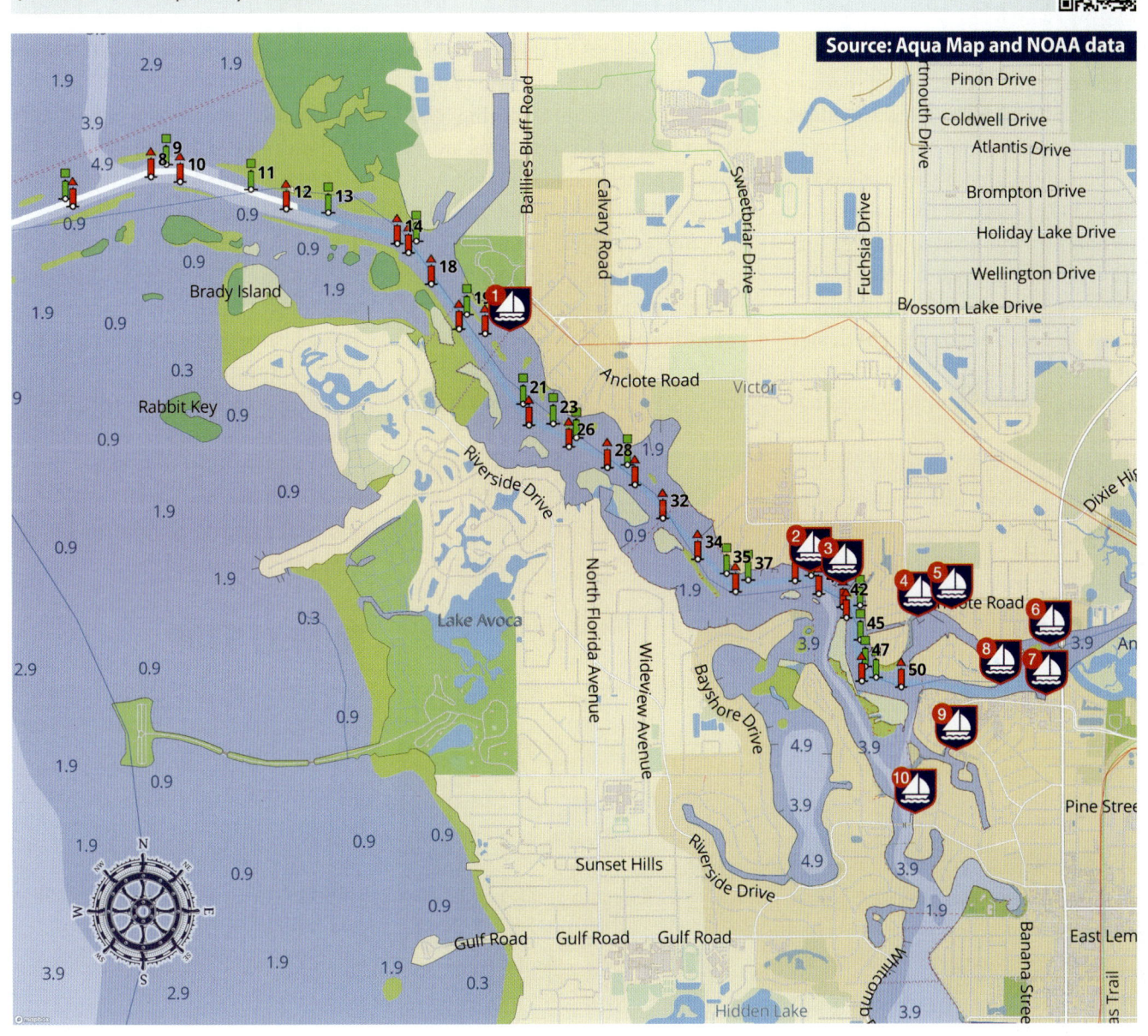

Source: Aqua Map and NOAA data

SOUTHERN EDITION

Chapter 13: Tampa Bay to Tarpon Springs

Opposite green daybeacon "39" on the northeast side Port Tarpon Marina has a convenient fuel dock just off the river channel and offers wet slips (covered and uncovered), high and dry racks and transient berths for boats to 65 feet. Next door, Anclote Harbors Marina welcomes cruising boats up to 45 feet in deep water slips. The buildings, floating docks and restrooms are all clean and well maintained.

In a basin to the east is the quiet and secure Anclote Isles Marina, which can accommodate vessels to 85 feet and has all the usual amenities. The 18-slip Belle Harbour Marina has a few wet slips, storage options and repairs.

Staying at any of the marinas on the north side of the river means you will need to arrange for transportation if you wish to get to the sponge docks and restaurants, most of which are on the south side of the river. The exception is Tarpon Landing Marina from which sponge docks and Greek restaurants are a short walk across the fixed **SR 19 Alternate Hwy. Bridge** to the south side of the river. The marina caters to anglers and weekend boaters with wet slips (to 50 feet), dry storage and marina services. (Call ahead.) Capt'n Jack's Waterfront Bar and Grille (727-944-3346) is at the head of the slips with casual dining in a tropical atmosphere.

At the end of the navigable portion of the river the floating docks of the City of Tarpon Springs Municipal Marina is on the south side of the river. This no-frills marina is in the heart of the sponge-dock area and is an ideal location for exploring Tarpon Springs. Reservations are a must. Spongeorama, a sponge factory with the world's largest collection of natural sponges has hourly and overnight dockage on well-maintained docks.

To the east of Spongeorama River on the south shore is Energy–The New F & Y Inc., an oil company with a 200-foot marine dock for refueling (diesel only). They can accept vessels to 200 feet at their docks for fueling. No transient slips.

To reach the full-service Turtle Cove Marina, turn and follow the channel, favoring the north side. The marina channel (to port) is marked with private floating reds and greens. Stay in the channel. After about 100 yards it opens up into the marina area. This is a full-service facility with floating docks and pump-out service at every slip.

Tarpon Springs Yacht Club, located before the **Beckett Bridge** (25-foot vertical clearance), is private but welcomes members of reciprocating yacht clubs.

Anchorage: An anchorage with 6-foot MLW depths is located by the river's entrance east of green daybeacon "17" at Anclote River just beyond the power plant stack. There is a nearby park with a boat ramp and restrooms.

Up the river in Tarpon Springs some boats anchor in front of the City of Tarpon Springs Municipal Marina but shoaling and traffic may be a problem and it is not recommended.

■ NEXT STOP

Mile 150 at Tarpon Springs on the Anclote River marks the end of the Florida GIWW. The GIWW picks back up in Carrabelle, FL, where mileages are measured from the east (EHL) and west (WHL) of Harvey Lock, LA. Beyond Anclote Key lies the intriguing Big Bend (or Nature Coast).

Spongers of Tarpon Springs Statue

America's Waterway Guide Since 1947

Skipper Bob Publications

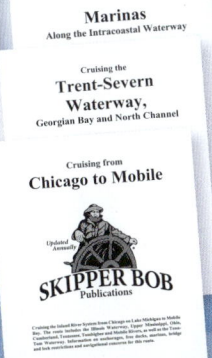

The App from Waterway Guide

No Signal? No Problem!
DOWNLOAD CONTENT

The Explorer web app
waterwayguide.com

Section 4: Upper Gulf Coast

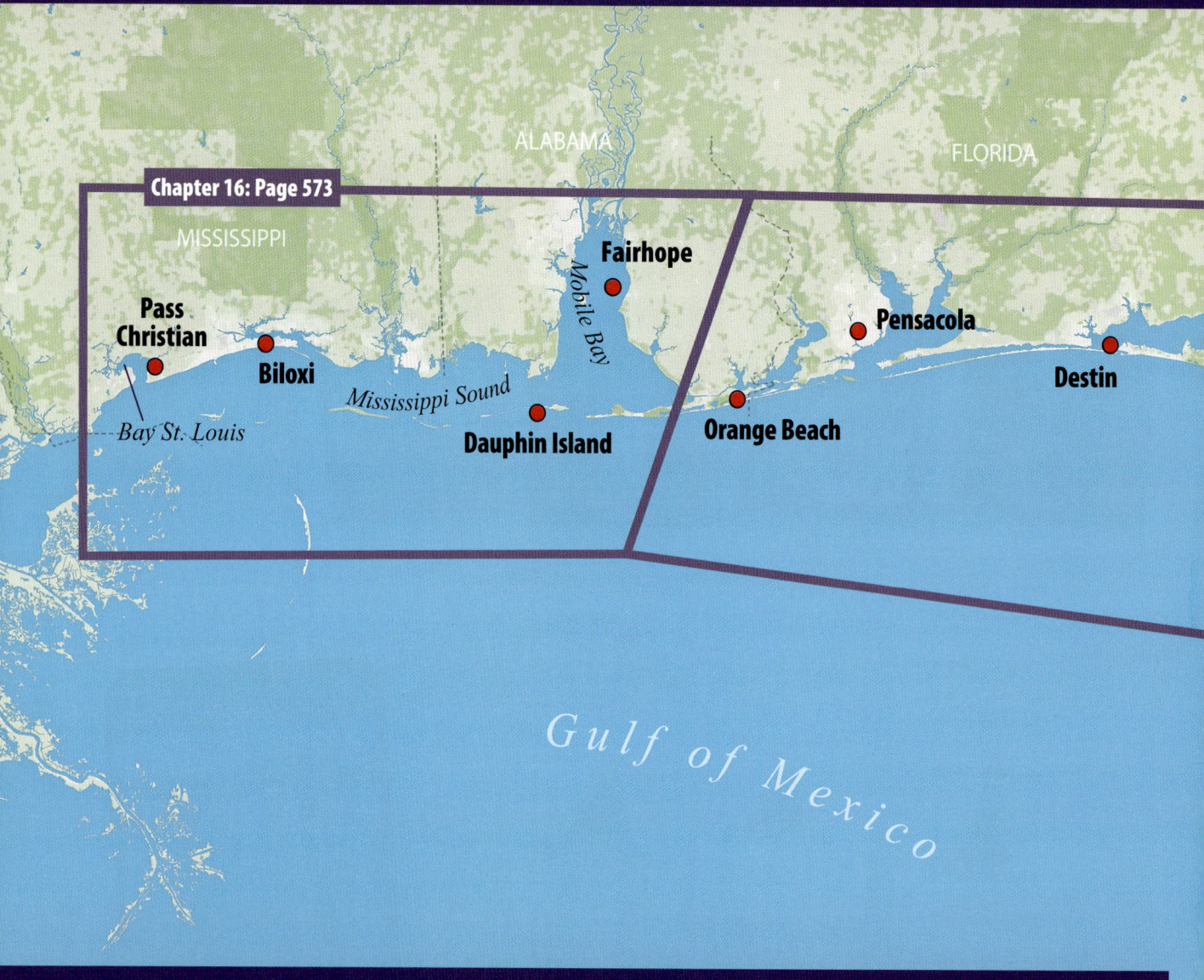

Chapter 14: The Big Bend: Anclote Key to Carrabelle
Chapter 15: The Florida Panhandle
Chapter 16: Mobile Bay Area to Bay St. Louis, MS

Note that the direction of travel for the Waterway Guide content is from south to north along the west coast of Florida and east to west along the northern Gulf Coast as you transit the Gulf Intracoastal Waterway (GIWW). Some sections of the coasts do not have recognized or charted GIWW waterways.

Chapter 14: The Big Bend: Anclote Key to Carrabelle

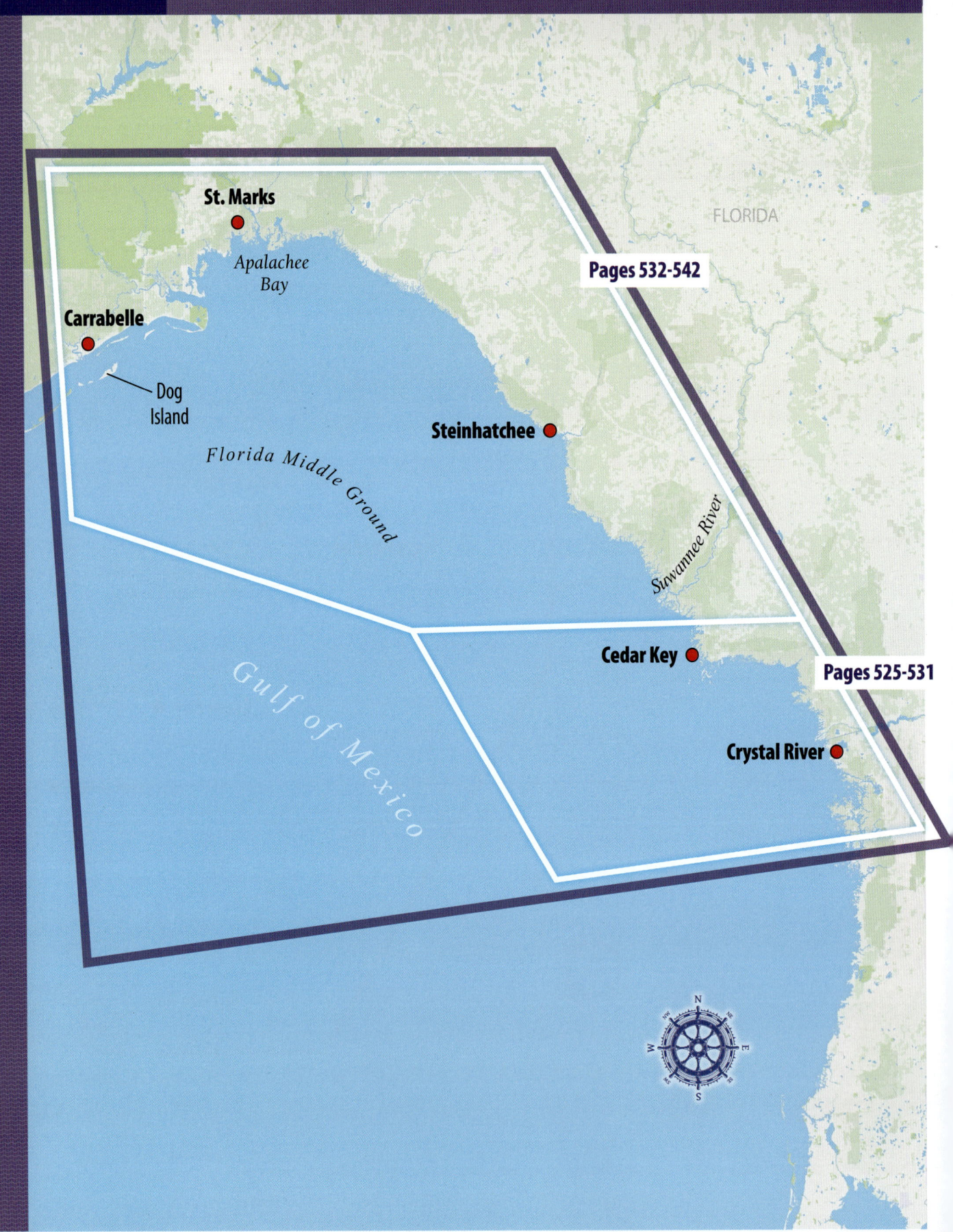

Chapter 14
America's Waterway Guide Since 1947

■ NAVIGATION NOTES

The 350-nm stretch from Anclote Key to Carrabelle across the Big Bend (also called "The Nature Coast") has no protected inside route. To transit the Big Bend area mariners must make the trip across open waters in the Gulf of Mexico. For the second half, from Carrabelle on to Florida's Panhandle, you can travel the GIWW (inside) or continue outside in the Gulf. The more interesting GIWW route connects big bays and sounds that are protected by narrow, wooded barrier islands.

Along the west coast shore from Anclote Key almost to Carrabelle the Gulf of Mexico is relatively shallow and the coastline low and indistinct. It is possible to safely make the Big Bend Passage and never lose sight of land. If you are running along the shore, keep a close eye on the depth sounder and tide charts and the little buoys for crab pots and lobster traps.

This is a fine sailing area but boats with deep drafts should be wary of the shoals and reefs, many of which are oyster bars, some littered with rocks. When sailing in difficult waters for which you have little knowledge and past experience, it may be safer to be farther out than nearer to land.

Brown pelicans are tricky neighbors here. They have a tendency to deface buoy numbers and a pelican perched on a green can buoy may, from a distance, change the outline to that of a red nun buoy. Get in the habit of checking floating marks carefully.

The Coast Guard station on the Withlacoochee River at Yankeetown (about 17 miles southeast of Cedar Key) covers this area and monitors VHF Channel 16. This station also operates and maintains three vessels for emergency search and rescue. In addition to VHF, the station can be reached by telephone at 352-447-6900.

A small change in latitude creates a perceptible difference in the weather of this region compared to southern Florida. The upper Gulf Coast of Florida is the only coastal section of the state that experiences a noticeable winter. Depending on the marine facility and location, the boating season in the Upper Gulf Coast may run from Easter through Columbus Day. If necessary, check with your destinations to determine their off-season operating hours. It gets chilly in the winter but it is still possible to enjoy these uncrowded, clear waters, award-winning beaches and boating-oriented communities.

Planning Your Stops

For vessels traveling along an inside route by day consider the following as possible ports for shelter. Plan your travel to begin after the sun has sufficient elevation to provide visibility on and into the water and to end before the sun gets too low to provide good feedback. Keep a sharp eye for crab pot buoys. All distances are total daily nautical miles from point of departure to an anchorage or marina at the end of each day.

Daily distance of approximately 50 nm:
1. Anclote Key to Hernando Beach*–25 nm
2. Hernando Beach to Crystal River–50 nm
3. Crystal River to Yankeetown–30 nm
4. Yankeetown to Suwannee River–50 nm
5. Suwannee to Steinhatchee–40 nm
6. Steinhatchee to St. Marks–60 nm
7. St. Marks to East Pass–40 nm

(*Note: It is possible to go directly from Hernando Beach to Yankeetown, a distance of 50 nm. The channel is shallow and it can take more time to find deep water and work your way in to the Withlacoochee River.)

Daily distance of approximately 60 nm:
1. Anclote Key to Crystal River–55 nm
2. Crystal River to Suwannee River–55 nm
3. Suwannee River to Steinhatchee–40 nm
4. Steinhatchee to St. Marks–60 nm
5. St. Marks to East Pass–45 nm

(Alternate Route)
Daily distance of approximately 60 nm:
1. Anclote Key to Yankeetown–55 nm
2. Yankeetown to Suwannee–50 nm
3. Suwannee River to Steinhatchee–40 nm
4. Steinhatchee to East Pass–70 nm

Daily distance of approximately 80 nm:
1. Anclote to Suwannee River–75 nm
2. Suwannee River to Steinhatchee–40 nm
3. Steinhatchee to East Pass–70 nm

(Note that it is possible to go directly from Suwannee to East Pass, a distance of 90 nm.)

Chapter 14: The Big Bend: Anclote Key to Carrabelle

No Wake Zones, Idle Speed Zones and various Speed Limit restrictions are in effect throughout the waterways included in this chapter. Exercise diligence in knowing the regulations by observing signs and other markers. Enforcement is always present. As always, be courteous to other vessels and avoid manatees and other marine life.

Choice of Routes

Planning the trip through The Big Bend starts by making a decision about which route you are going to travel. You can go nearer shore with multiple stops or you can go offshore, traveling directly from Clearwater or Tarpon Springs to Carrabelle. The near shore route breaks the trip into multiple legs with daytime travel and multiple nighttime layovers. The trip can be broken into as few as three segments with daily travel of about 70 miles or into as many as seven segments with daily distances of less than 50 miles.

The offshore trip from Clearwater to Carrabelle is about 190 statute miles and as much as 45 miles from shore. A fast boat (averaging 20 mph) can make this trip during daylight hours. A displacement boat (averaging 8 mph) will need an overnight passage of about 23 hours. If you are starting from Carrabelle and going south to Tarpon Springs or Clearwater you should plan your arrival at Anclote red daybeacon "2" or Clearwater green daybeacon "1" after 10 a.m. to avoid early morning sun glare off the water directly in front of you, which can hide crab pot buoys.

Weather is always a serious consideration when boating but it is a primary concern on this trip for several reasons. First, the voyage is over 24 hours long so you will have to look for a minimum of a 48-hour weather window for your trip. Second, "bailing out" is not easy as it may involve as much as 5 hours to get back to land and a potential arrival in the dark through the skinny water that your offshore trip was designed to avoid.

You will need to look at multiple sources of weather information. NOAA's Zone Forecast for the area will give you the general forecast and is a good place to start. Include the 12 hours before and after your passage time in your evaluations. Windy (www.windy.com), PassageWeather (www.passageweather.com) and Buoyweather (www.buoyweather.com) are good resources to supplement NOAA. Look for a degree of agreement among the forecasts and acceptable wind speeds and wave heights covering your expanded passage window. The consensus seems to be a 15-mph maximum wind and 2-foot maximum seas are the "no drama" parameters for the crossing. Finding these conditions will require a degree of flexibility in your schedule and a discipline to not push the envelope.

Navigation

The destination for the northbound passage is Carrabelle flashing red "2" at N 29° 44.541' / W 84° 39.199'. If you are heading south from Carrabelle, you will use the coordinates for the Anclote Key or Clearwater buoys as your destination. Remember to time your arrival at either of these buoys later than 10 a.m. to avoid heading directly into low sun.

NOTE: All open water mileage is measured in nautical miles.

- From Anclote Key flashing red "2" (N 28° 15.089'/ W 82° 52.896'): Set a course 320° degrees magnetic for a 130-nm crossing to Carrabelle flashing red "2."
- From Clearwater green daybeacon "1" (N 27° 58.270'/ W 82° 50.840'): Set a course 323° magnetic for a 142.5-nm crossing to Carrabelle flashing red "2."

Distances—Outside Run
Nautical Miles (approximate) from Anclote Key

VIA GULF OF MEXICO	TO APPROACH LIGHT	FROM LIGHT TO DOCKS
Anclote Keys	0	
St. Martins Light	15	
Homosassa River	30	7
Crystal River	45	20
Withlacoochee River	50	8
Cedar Key	60	4
Steinhatchee River	104	2
St. Marks River	140	4
Carrabelle	145	8

Distances—Gulf Inside Route
Statute Miles (approximate)

VIA GIWW	FROM CARRABELLE
Carrabelle	0
Apalachicola	29
Panama City	86
Fort Walton	155
Pensacola	200

Option: Offshore Crossing to St. George Island

You can travel outside in the Gulf of Mexico by following the coastline all the way to Pensacola. If you don't plan to cruise the Big Bend area, running the 130- to 140-nm rhumb line directly from Tarpon Springs or Clearwater to the St. George Island East Pass entrance buoy for Carrabelle can save a lot of time but only an able boat enjoying good weather should attempt this passage. Many cruisers prefer to follow a route closer to the coastline. The Big Bend markers that provided an inshore route closer to the coastline have been discontinued but there are channel entrance markers that can be used to run a course closer to shore.

Before setting out make sure your boat is seaworthy and your engine is sound. Know your compass error. Have the latest charts on board. There have been numerous changes to the navigation aids in recent years. Plot your courses carefully and stick to them along this route. The land is low lying and it can be a long stretch between the navigation aids as you traverse this coastline. Always track your position by both dead reckoning and GPS. There are some remote sections of this coast and even though you are not far offshore, you may be far from help. A registered Emergency Position Indicating Radio Beacon (EPIRB) is an excellent addition to your safety equipment.

Unless you are very experienced run only in daylight. It is particularly important to have daylight while you are within 20 nm or so off the Florida coast as the crab pots can be very thick.

TO CEDAR KEY

Anclote Key to Homosassa

St. Martins Reef runs along the coast north from Anclote Key for some 40 nm. The shoals of this reef extend over 10 nm offshore. St. Martins Outer Shoal 16-foot high, flashing red "10" marks the outer limit of the shallow water. Many of the rocks and shoals are identified by private markers. Cruisers without local knowledge should approach the coast with care and deep-draft vessels should stand out in deeper waters. Smaller boats with drafts of 3 to 4 feet can usually follow the coast and find smooth water by keeping about 7 nm offshore.

Hernando Beach is a potential stop between Anclote and Crystal River. This is a small community with restaurants within walking distance and Hernando Beach Marina has a small Ship Store.

The Homosassa River is another possible stopover, although it is a comparatively narrow and shallow waterway with winding channels and unforgiving oyster bars and rock beds. It has some great fishing for both salt and freshwater species, thanks to the headwater springs. This phenomenon is possible because the mineral content in the spring water resembles minerals found in salt water.

The village of Homosassa is an attractive fishing center that grows more popular each year. More than 20 fishing guides operate year-round. Fishers should remember that the river qualifies as freshwater so a fishing license is required.

NAVIGATION: Use NOAA Chart 11409. To reach Hernando Beach travel the distance from Anclote Key's 16-foot high, flashing red "2" to St Martins Outer Shoal 16-foot high, flashing red "10" for 11 nm at 350° magnetic. From St. Martins Outer Shoal 16-foot high, flashing red "10" set a course of 64° magnetic for 8.5 nm to the private Oc (Billy Steele Obstruction Light) flashing 14-foot marker. Then proceed 3.5 nm at 58° magnetic to a point where you can turn toward the Hernando Beach Channel. The channel entrance is 1 nm at 142° magnetic. Controlling channel depth is reported as 4 feet MLW; however, mariners with local knowledge say it is common for boats with drafts of 5 feet to use the channel.

For Homosassa from St. Martins Outer Shoal 16-foot high, flashing red "10" set a course of 26° magnetic for 16.5 nm to Homosassa Bay entrance 16-foot high, flashing red buoy "2" at N 28° 41.435'/W 82° 48.641'. Keep a close eye on your depth. Avoid the shoals to the southeast between that and red daybeacon "2A." Steer a careful, direct course between the first three reds as there are shallows to both sides.

> **CAUTION:** Local mariners report depths of 3 feet MLW at what they call "Hells Gate," a very narrow passage close to the entrance of the marked channel to Homosassa. Proceed with great care. Currents can be strong.

Chapter 14: The Big Bend: Anclote Key to Carrabelle

Little Pine Island Bay, FL

HERNANDO BEACH		Largest Vessel	VHF	Total Slips	Approach/Dockside Depth	Floating Docks	Gas/Diesel	Repairs/Haulout	Min/Max Amps	Pump-Out Station
1. Hernando Beach Marina Hernando Beach	(352) 596-2952	45		31	4.0 / 4.0	F	GD	RH	30	
2. Blue Pelican Marina	(352) 610-9999	30		4	4.0 / 4.0	F	G	RH		

WiFi Wireless Internet Access
Visit www.waterwayguide.com for current rates, fuel prices, website addresses and other up-to-the-minute information. (Information in the table is provided by the facilities.)

Scan here for more details:

The route winds its way to the fishing village of Homosassa about 4 miles upriver. The channel into the Homosassa River is narrow and shallow with depths reported from 3.5 to 7 feet MLW. Be aware that you may encounter many fast moving small fishing boats.

Dockage: Hernando Beach Marina provides dry storage, wet slips, boat rentals and sales, boat repairs and maintenance, Ship Store and on-site restaurant. (Be aware that their widest slip is 14 feet.) Blue Pelican Marina is primarily a dry stack facility but may have transient space for smaller vessels (to 30 feet). Call ahead for slip availability and to verify that shoaling is not a problem in this well-marked channel.

MacRae's of Homosassa has slips (to 35 feet) as well as a hotel, bait house (for anglers) and a riverfront tiki bar. They report 3-foot MLW dockside depths so call ahead if that is a concern.

St. Martins Outer Shoal (Homosassa) to Crystal River

Crystal River and Crystal Bay are located 45 nm north of Anclote River and 23 nm southeast of Cedar Key. A marked channel leads from the Gulf through Crystal Bay and the Crystal River 6 nm to Kings Bay and the town of Crystal River. Crystal River is Florida's second largest system of natural springs with a daily flow of about 3 million cubic yards of water at a constant temperature of 72 degrees. When the water temperature drops in the Gulf of Mexico manatees move to the warmer waters of the Crystal River. Crystal River is one of the few places where you can swim with manatees.

NAVIGATION: Use NOAA Chart 11409. From St Martins Outer Shoal 16-foot high, flashing red "10" continue on a course of 358° magnetic for 21.9 nm to Crystal

Chapter 14

Homosassa River, FL

HOMOSASSA		Largest Vessel	VHF	Total Slips	Approach/Dockside Depth	Floating Docks	Gas/Diesel	Repairs/Haulout	Min/Max Amps	Pump-Out Station
1. MacRae's of Homosassa WiFi	(352) 628-2602	35	16	10	6.0 / 3.0	F	G	R	30	

WiFi Wireless Internet Access
Visit www.waterwayguide.com for current rates, fuel prices, website addresses and other up-to-the-minute information.
(Information in the table is provided by the facilities.)

Scan here for more details:

Homosassa River

SOUTHERN EDITION

Chapter 14 — The Big Bend: Anclote Key to Carrabelle

River flashing red buoy "2" at N 28° 47.542'/W 82° 58.571'. From there it is another 14 nm on a course of 65° magnetic to the Crystal River entrance between flashing green "1" and red daybeacon "2." As local channels and rivers go, Crystal River is navigable and King's Bay is worth the trip. Depths are posted from 5 to 8 feet MLW from flashing red buoy "2" through the channel and the river. Local mariners say the depth is actually closer to 6 to 9 feet MLW. Depths can drop dramatically during periods of north winds.

CAUTION: Watch for rocks inside the channel at Crystal River close to red daybeacon "8." Local knowledge advises favoring green daybeacon "7."

Dockage: At the junction of the Salt and Crystal Rivers you will find Twin Rivers Marina. This is the only full-service boatyard in Crystal River. Water depth to the marina and dockside is 5 feet MLW. This is a rural area but what it lacks in amenities it makes up for in natural beauty.

NOTE: Use caution approaching Twin Rivers Marina on the Salt River and check your height; the charted overhead power cables have a 47-foot vertical clearance.

Pete's Pier Inc. is located in the City of Crystal River at Kings Bay. They have some transient slips reserved for vessels to 80 feet on new (in 2022) docks. The marina is the center of Manatee viewing tour operators and has a busy boat launch. There is an on-site bait shop and golf carts for going into town for provisions. A grocery store, fish market, liquor store and a laundry are all about 1 mile from the waterfront. You can get a bite to eat at Crackers Bar and Grill (352-795-3999), which has a fun tiki hut with live entertainment on the weekends.

Anchorage: You can anchor anywhere in the wide part of Kings Bay with good holding and protection with plenty of room to swing. There is a full 3-foot tidal range with 3 feet MLW. From here you can kayak or dinghy to the springs or to Pete's Pier Inc. where there is a dock for small boats at the restaurant.

Side Trip: Withlacoochee River (Yankeetown)

There are two Withlacoochee Rivers in Florida. The other one flows from Georgia and empties into the Suwannee River. Big Bend's Withlacoochee River empties into the Gulf of Mexico 17 nm southeast of Cedar Keys. Yankeetown is the primary boating community on the river. It is a very small fishing and winter resort 3 nm above the mouth. The river is navigable for 8 miles upstream where it intersects with a bridge with a fixed vertical clearance of 10 feet. This is an easily navigable channel and river. The river itself is worth the trip to Yankeetown.

NOTE: You need to work your way through the well-marked confusion of the Cross Florida Greenway into the channel for the Withlacoochee River. Officially named the Marjorie Harris Carr Cross Florida Greenway, this planned conduit was intended to stretch 110 miles from the Gulf of Mexico (GIWW) to St. John's River (and the ICW) in Palatka. Only two sections were completed before the project was abandoned in 1992.

Crystal River, FL

CRYSTAL RIVER		Largest Vessel	VHF	Total Slips	Approach/ Dockside Depth	Floating Docks	Gas/ Diesel	Repairs/ Haulout	Min/Max Amps	Pump-Out Station
1. Twin Rivers Marina WiFi	(352) 795-3552	60	68	53	5.0 / 8.0	F	GD	RH	30 / 50	
2. Pete's Pier Inc.	(352) 795-3302	80	68	92	8.0 / 8.0		GD	H	30 / 50	P

WiFi Wireless Internet Access
Visit www.waterwayguide.com for current rates, fuel prices, website addresses and other up-to-the-minute information.
(Information in the table is provided by the facilities.)

Scan here for more details: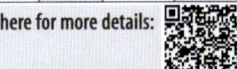

NAVIGATION: Use NOAA Charts 11408 and 11409. Back on your inside course through the Big Bend leave Crystal River flashing red buoy "2" at N 28° 47.542'/W 82° 58.571' on a course of 9° magnetic. Travel with a watchful eye on the depth sounder for 8 miles to the flashing red "4" at N 28° 55.512'/W 82° 58.004'. The Cross Florida Greenway is the northernmost of the two very visible channels (which fork from one) just south of the entrance to Withlacoochee. It runs in an easterly direction. Follow the canal to flashing green "17" where a channel will branch off to the right and a channel will go slightly left or straight. Take the channel straight ahead using flashing red "20" to set yourself in the new channel.

At flashing green "23" take a course of 36° magnetic and make for the 16-foot high, quick-flashing green "1" to take the Withlacoochee River Entrance channel. Green daybeacon "25" will be south as will red daybeacon "26." The channel winds with rocks on both sides. From green daybeacon "3" it is about 8 miles to Yankeetown. Depths for the channel, canal and river are reported to be 5 feet MLW or more. The Withlacoochee definitely fits the bill for those wanting to take the path less traveled.

Dockage: This is a great place to visit off the beaten path but do not expect high-end docks or resort amenities. This is a remote location. Yankeetown Marina has just one transient slip (to 50 feet). It is followed by B's Marina & Campground, which has cabins, pontoon boats, kayaks and bikes for rent. Riverside Marina & Cottages is a family-owned camping and RV resort with covered and open transient slips. They also rent pontoon boats and kayaks for further exploration. Call ahead as there is limited transient dockage here.

Chapter 14 — The Big Bend: Anclote Key to Carrabelle

Withlachoochee River, FL

YANKEETOWN		Largest Vessel	VHF	Total Slips	Approach/Dockside Depth	Floating Docks	Gas/Diesel	Repairs/Haulout	Min/Max Amps	Pump-Out Station
1. Yankeetown Marina	(352) 302-4725	50	16	50	6.0 / 6.0				50	
2. B's Marina & Campground (WiFi)	(352) 447-5888	60		12	12.0 / 12.0		GD		30	
3. Riverside Marina & Cottages (WiFi)	(352) 447-2980	60		15	25.0 / 6.0				30	

(WiFi) Wireless Internet Access
Visit www.waterwayguide.com for current rates, fuel prices, website addresses and other up-to-the-minute information. (Information in the table is provided by the facilities.)

Scan here for more details:

Anchorage: Sailboats have been seen anchoring near the **Hwy. 19 Bridge** (40-foot fixed vertical clearance) on the Cross Florida Greenway.

Crystal River to Seahorse Reef (Cedar Key)

The Cedar Keys are a group of low sandy islets covered with mangrove trees and pelicans...lots of pelicans. The outermost islet is Seahorse Key, where the white tower of an abandoned lighthouse stands on its south side. The lighthouse is visible from offshore.

Cedar Key is a small town on Way Key, located roughly one-third of the way between Anclote Key and Carrabelle. The island was named for the stand of cedar trees that once grew here and are now gone (logged out) and now the town subsists on fishing, both commercial and sport. Cedar Key is the top U.S. producer of farm-raised clams. You can find out more at the museum at the Cedar Key Museum State Park, which offers a nature trail, a 1920s home and artifacts depicting Cedar Key's history as a busy port.

NAVIGATION: Use NOAA Chart 11408. Resume your course for this route at Crystal River flashing red buoy "2" at N 28° 47.542'/W 82° 58.571'. Leave flashing red "2" on a course of 348° magnetic and travel for 17.3 nm to Cedar Key's 16-foot high, flashing green "1" at N 29° 04.000'/W 083° 04.500'. Depths in the channel are at least 7 feet MLW but you must follow the well-marked channel carefully. Study an up-to-date chart in detail before you enter and you should have no difficulty.

Seahorse Reef extends for 11 nm from Seahorse Key and is a dangerous shoal with little depth. The outer end of the reef is marked by a 31-foot high, flashing white tower "Seahorse Reef Light" (N 28° 58.310'/W 83° 09.130'). The shoal between red daybeacons "10" and "12" is building out into the channel. When transiting this area give red daybeacon "12" a wide berth favoring the western (Seahorse Key) side of the channel.

CAUTION: Be careful! Several unwary visitors seeking a shortcut have been grounded by the S-curve in the winding channel.

Also pay close attention at the junction of Ship and Northwest Channels just past Grassy Key. Sorting out the maze of shoals and lights demands serious concentration. Go slowly, attempt no shortcuts and be aware of the currents.

When leaving Cedar Key northbound take Northwest Channel, which leaves the main channel at quick-flashing red "30" about 1 nm from the town dock off Grassy Key. Do not attempt Northwest Channel on a low tide if your draft exceeds 4 feet or during darkness or rough water conditions. Shoaling is particularly acute between green daybeacon "17A" and flashing red "18" and also between flashing green "19" and red daybeacon "20." Prominent landmarks on Cedar Key are a radio tower and 140-foot municipal water tank.

Anchorage: It is possible to anchor in depths around 8 feet MLW on the north side of Atsena Otie Key. Feel your way in cautiously. The island is part of the Cedar Keys National Wildlife Refuge. The cut between the two halves of the island provides a great place to paddle a kayak.

Another alternative is to anchor just southwest of the fishing pier at Cedar Key (out of the channel) in 8 to 14 feet MLW, and then dinghy in under the bridge to the small-boat docking area in the basin. Because of the strong tidal current in the anchorage, you may want to use a two-anchor Bahamian moor.

NOTE: All of these anchorage are exposed to wind and tide with ittle protection. You should only anchor here in fair weather. This is not cruising boat territory.

Swim with the Manatees

Crystal River is Florida's second largest system of natural springs with a daily flow of about 3 million cubic yards of water at a constant temperature of 72°. When the water temperature drops in the Gulf of Mexico manatees move to the warmer waters of the Crystal River. This area may host Florida's largest population of manatees.

Do not leave this area without checking out the spectacular caverns nearby. You can look down from King's Bay and see springs 60 feet under the surface. This is the only place where you can legally swim with manatees in the wild in the U.S. (during designated times). Be respectful of the manatees and remember that you are in their waters.

We recommend going with a local guide who can take you to the manatee "hot spots" and who will also educate you about them, giving you a more full experience and a greater understanding of these gentle creatures.

Another option is to board a free bus tour to Three Sisters Spring during the Florida Manatee Festival, held the third weekend in January in downtown Crystal River. Tours run continuously during the Festival. Manatee boat tours are also available for a nominal charge to take you out into Kings Bay and other favorite hangouts of the manatees.

Chapter 14 — The Big Bend: Anclote Key to Carrabelle

■ TO CARRABELLE

It is just over 83 miles from Cedar Keys to the St. Marks River. Two good stopovers are the Suwanee and Steinhatchee Rivers. The Suwanee River originates in Georgia's Okefenokee Swamp and meanders about 280 miles before reaching the Gulf of Mexico. This is Old Florida territory and you won't find much here except the beauty of the river and the 70-plus springs that feed millions of gallons of water into it every day.

> The tannin-stained water of the Suwanee River was the inspiration for Stephen Foster's Suwannee River from "Old Folks at Home," which is Florida's official state song.

Suwannee River to St. Marks

NAVIGATION: Use NOAA Chart 11408. On approach from the Gulf of Mexico there are three passes or channels into the Suwannee, which can be confusing.

East Pass: Approaching from the south you will pass Derrick Key Gap at the south end of Suwannee Reef and Suwannee Sound. Depths in East Pass are about 2 feet MLW. You may see small fishing boats using the Pass but you shouldn't be tempted to enter.

West Pass: Sometimes referred to as Alligator Pass by local and on charted markers, this is the first marked channel. You may see small boats coming and going from West Pass. At high tide it should carry depths of 4 feet or more but it is not recommended for a cruising boat.

Suwannee River McGriff: Often referred to as Wadley Pass on older charts, this is the northernmost of the three channels and the preferred one. Depths are posted at a controlling depth of 3 feet MLW; however, we have received reports of at least 5 feet MLW. Keep in mind that if a north wind is blowing and a winter front is coming through, depths can drop considerably.

To access Suwannee River McGriff Pass starting at daybeacon green "1" at the entrance of the Crystal River Channel, travel 2 nm on a course of 269° magnetic. Then follow a course of 281° magnetic for 20 nm to the 31-foot white flashing "Seahorse Reef Light" at Sea Horse Reef. Be mindful to avoid the markers as you pass the Cross Florida Greenway.

From Sea Horse Reef travel on a course of 352° magnetic for 20 nm.

Suwannee River

Then navigate to 68° magnetic for 0.5 nm to the entrance channel for the Suwannee River McGriff Pass to the Suwannee River. The total distance from the Crystal River Channel entrance to the Suwannee River McGriff Pass channel entrance is 42 nm. Follow the channel markers into the Suwannee River. Depths in the river average 15 feet MLW.

CAUTION: Shoaling in the Suwanee River channel has been observed between red daybeacon "10" and "12." Entrance during high tide is recommended.

The average cruising boat should be able to enter the river (at high tide) and travel the 34 miles or so upriver to Fanning Springs, where you will encounter the 34-foot fixed vertical clearance **Hwy. 19 Bridge**.

Should you choose to explore the river be wary of the unmarked shoal, Jack's Sandbar, about 13 miles above the river entrance and 3.7 miles north of Fowlers Bluff. The reef occupies about two thirds of the east bank with depths as shallow as 1 foot MLW. Stay close to the west bank where you will find depths of more than 10 feet MLW. The location of Jack's Sandbar is identified on some charts.

NOTE: A 25-mile trip upriver will take you to Manatee Springs and the State Park dock. It is possible to anchor in the river and enjoy all the park has to offer.

Dockage: Gateway Marina is a houseboat community that is always ready to make room for travelers in route. Call ahead for approach depths and space availability. The Suwannee Marina has dry boat storage, covered and open boat slips, a boat ramp, bait and tackle, marine supplies and a popular on-site restaurant. Call ahead.

You can tie up at Salt Creek Restaurant (352-542-7072) at the town of Suwannee (north of Barbree Island on Salt Creek) if you plan to dine there. Choose from the large deck with water views, cozy indoor bar or cool outdoor tiki bar.

Anchorage: Anchorage opportunities are boundless along the Suwannee River. North and west of Hog Island carries at least 5 feet MLW and excellent holding in mud. Salt Creek has 5 feet MLW with good holding in mud. Both provide all-around protection.

Leaping Sturgeons!

The Suwannee River appears to support the largest viable population of Gulf sturgeon according to the Florida Fish and Wildlife Conservation Commission (FWC). Biologists estimate the annual population at 10,000 to 14,000 fish, averaging approximately 40 pounds each.

The sturgeon can be hazardous to boaters as they tend to leap unexpectedly straight up and out of the water, turning sideways and landing with a loud noise. Much like deer hit by cars, jumping sturgeon are sometimes struck by boats. A large sturgeon can weigh more than 100 pounds so impact with a fast-moving boat can cause serious injury to both boat passengers and the sturgeon alike. Numerous people have been injured in accidental collisions with the jumping sturgeon on the Suwannee River.

Sturgeon can leap more than 7 feet out of the water and jumping occurs most frequently in mid-summer (May through August) when sturgeon are fasting. Researchers have determined that the sturgeon jump to communicate with other fish and to gulp air to fill their swim bladders. This allows the sturgeon to maintain neutral buoyancy.

FWC officials have initiated a public awareness campaign to alert boaters to the risks of jumping sturgeon and recommended that boaters slow down to reduce the risk of impact and to have more reaction time if a jumping sturgeon is encountered. And boaters are always encouraged to wear their life jackets at all times while on the water. To report sturgeon collisions call 888-404-FWCC (3922).

Chapter 14 — The Big Bend: Anclote Key to Carrabelle

Suwannee River, FL

SUWANNEE		Largest Vessel	VHF	Total Slips	Approach/Dockside Depth	Floating Docks	Gas/Diesel	Repairs/Haulout	Min/Max Amps	Pump-Out Station
1. Gateway Marina WiFi	(352) 542-7349	70	16	200	10.0 / 6.0	F	GD	H	30	P
2. The Suwannee Marina	(352) 542-9159	38		20	7.0 / 7.0	F	G	R		

WiFi Wireless Internet Access
Visit www.waterwayguide.com for current rates, fuel prices, website addresses and other up-to-the-minute information.
(Information in the table is provided by the facilities.)

Scan here for more details:

Source: Aqua Map and NOAA data

534 WATERWAY GUIDE 2024 www.waterwayguide.com

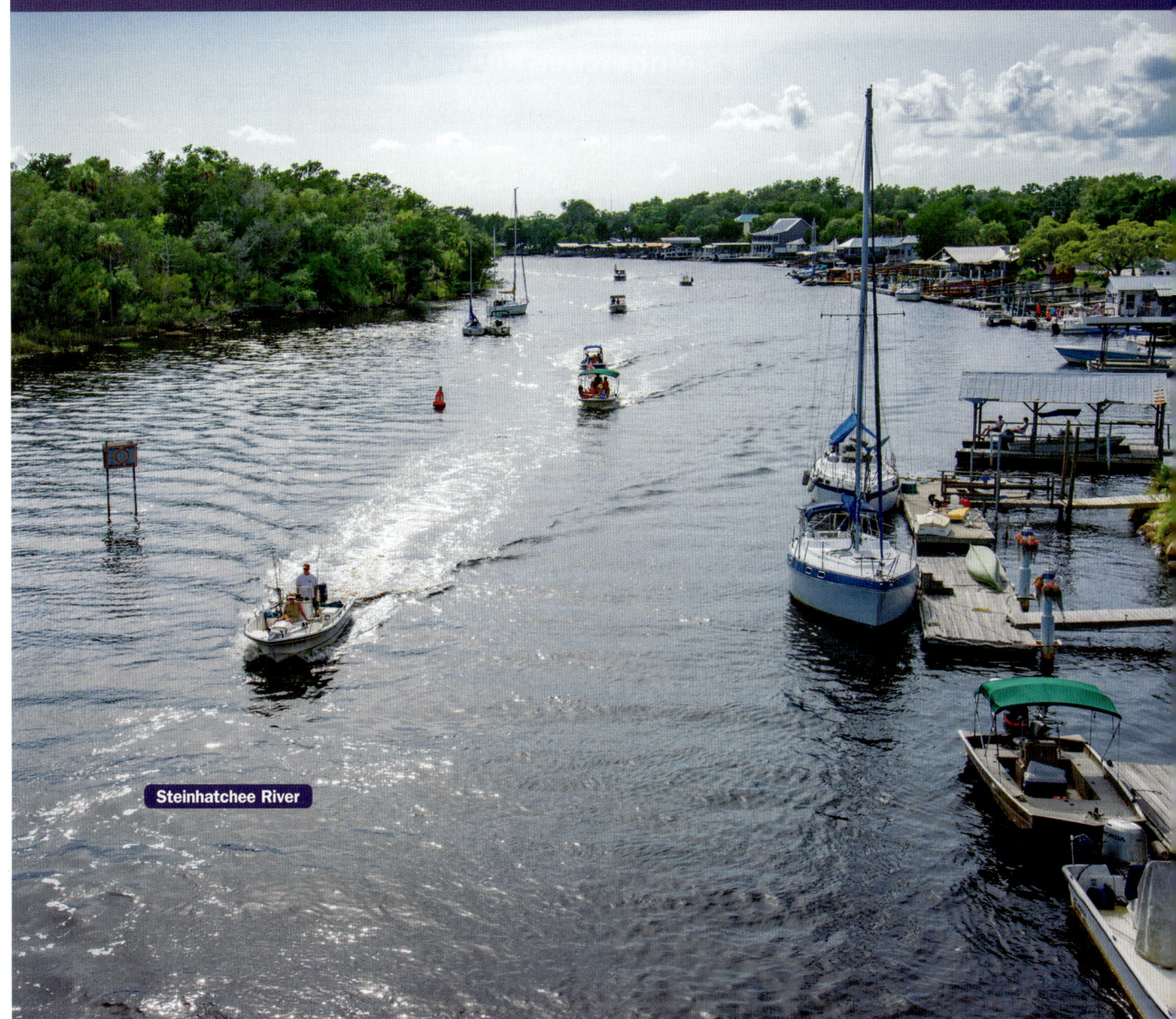

Steinhatchee River

Steinhatchee River

NAVIGATION: Use NOAA Chart 11407. From the inside route through the Big Bend leave the Crystal River red buoy "2" on a course of 335° magnetic. Stay on this course for 40 nm until you are standing out from Bull Cove.

At Bull Cove keep a distance from shore of about 6 nm. Keep a close eye on the depth sounder to make sure you avoid shoals that extend as far as 4 nm from the coast. From Bull Cove change course to 17° magnetic and run 7.5 nm to Steinhatchee River flashing green "1" at N 29° 39.357'/W 83° 27.347', which marks the entrance to the channel for Steinhatchee River. Controlling depth is 5 feet MLW. The channel is narrow in places but depths of 6 feet MLW or more are common.

This one of the more accessible ports of call along Florida's Big Bend. The interesting fishing village of Steinhatchee (pronounced "STEEN-hatchee") supports several seafood plants.

Dockage: Steinhatchee Marina at Deadman Bay is a new (in 2022) and welcome addition to the area. Modern facilities include a marina bar and a well-stocked store that carries some groceries. They have deep-water slips to 60 feet plus offer boat rentals and storage. Sea Hag Marina is able to accommodate a few boats in transient slips to 80 feet. They have a large tackle shop and dive shop, plus renovated motel rooms with a wide selection of rooms and rates. Good Times Motel & Marina across the river has limited transient space (3 slips to 45 feet). There is a motel, bar and grill and a fishing-centered store on site.

Chapter 14: The Big Bend: Anclote Key to Carrabelle

Steinhatchee River, FL

STEINHATCHEE		Largest Vessel	VHF	Total Slips	Approach/Dockside Depth	Floating Docks	Gas/Diesel	Repairs/Haulout	Min/Max Amps	Pump-Out Station
1. Steinhatchee Marina at Deadman Bay WiFi	(352) 578-1900	60		103	/	F	GD		30 / 50	
2. Sea Hag Marina WiFi 46	(352) 498-3008	80	9	70	6.0 / 12.0	F	GD	RH	30 / 50	
3. Good Times Motel & Marina WiFi	(352) 498-8088	45	9	50	9.0 / 9.0	F	GD		30	
4. Steinhatchee River Inn and Marina WiFi	(352) 498-0709	70	10	51	3.5 / 10.0	F	G	RH	30 / 50	P

WiFi Wireless Internet Access
Visit www.waterwayguide.com for current rates, fuel prices, website addresses and other up-to-the-minute information. (Information in the table is provided by the facilities.)

Scan here for more details:

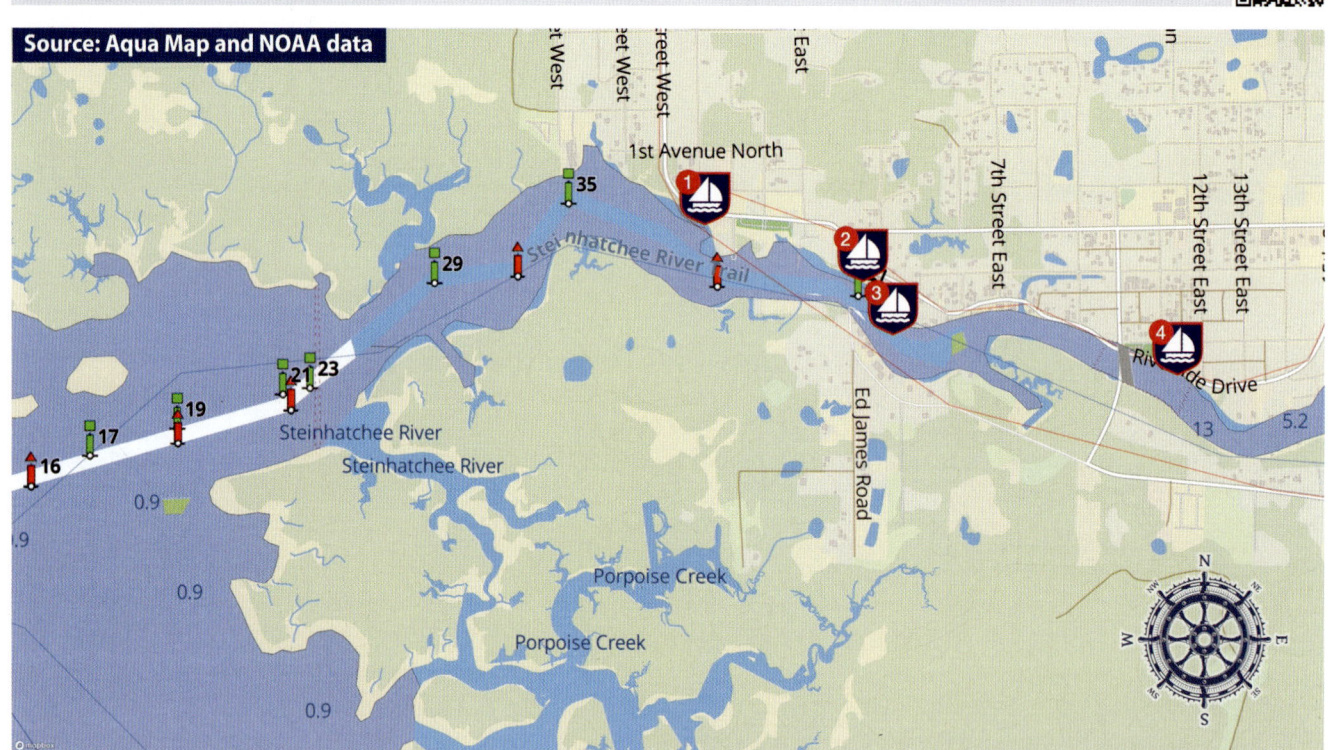

Source: Aqua Map and NOAA data

Steinhatchee River Inn and Marina (formerly River Haven Marina & Motel) is above the 10th Street Bridge (25-foot fixed vertical clearance). They report 3.5-foot MLW approach depths. Call ahead for slip availability, directions and updated knowledge about water depths. They also have a motel and rent small boats and kayaks for exploring the upper reaches of the river.

Anchorage: An anchorage is located on the outside of the bend several hundred feet beyond red daybeacon "36" in 6- to 7-foot MLW depths. The holding is soupy but protection from all directions is excellent. Anchorage is also available just above Sea Hag Marina after daybeacon red "48" (may be missing) before the **10th St. Bridge** (25-foot fixed vertical clearance).

St. Marks

Four rivers flow into the eastern Apalachee Bay: St. Marks, Aucilla, Econfina and Fenholloway. Residential and commercial development is minimal along this part of the coast. This is truly a part of "old Florida." From Cedar Key it is 83 miles to the St. Marks River. The town of St. Marks is 5.5 miles above the river entrance. The Visitor Center is at 15 Old Palmetto Path (850-925-0400) just 1.7 miles from Shields Marina.

Wakulla Springs is less than 10 miles away. This immense freshwater spring reaches a maximum depth of 185 feet and more than 600,000 gallons flow from the spring every minute, literally creating the Wakulla River.

NAVIGATION: Use NOAA Charts 11406, 11407, 11408 and 11405. A good reference for a route to St. Marks is to begin at the Crystal

America's Waterway Guide Since 1947 — Chapter 14

St. George Sound, FL

ST. MARKS		Largest Vessel	VHF	Total Slips	Approach/Dockside Depth	Floating Docks	Gas/Diesel	Repairs/Haulout	Min/Max Amps	Pump-Out Station
1. St. Marks Yacht Club—PRIVATE	(850) 925-6606	50		25	7.0 / 7.0	F			50	
2. Shields Marina	(850) 925-6158	65	16	100	12.0 / 10.0		GD	RH	50	P

WiFi Wireless Internet Access
Visit www.waterwayguide.com for current rates, fuel prices, website addresses and other up-to-the-minute information. (Information in the table is provided by the facilities.)

Scan here for more details:

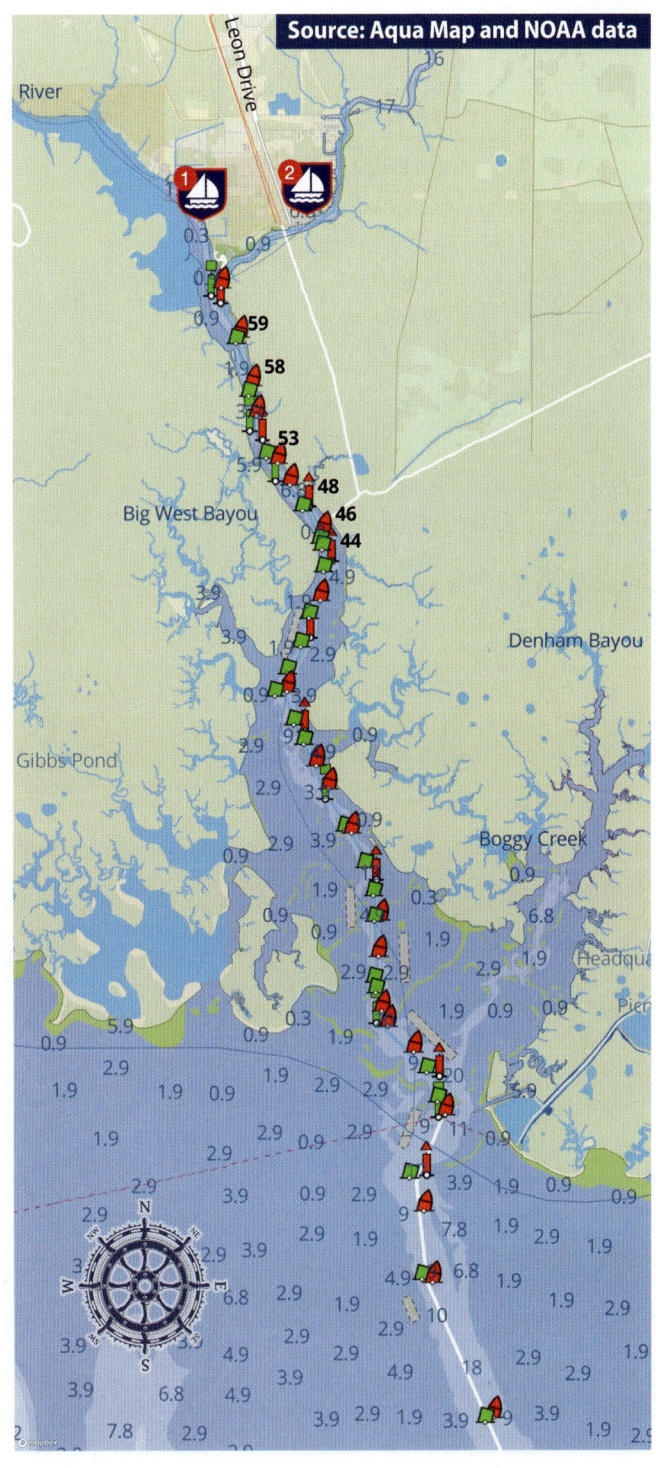
Source: Aqua Map and NOAA data

River approach flashing red "2." Set a course of 322° magnetic for 89 nm to Ochlockonee Shoal's flashing red "24." From there it is 9.5 nm on a course of 3° magnetic to flashing green "1" and red nun buoy "2" at the entrance of the St. Marks Channel.

St. Marks is easily accessible from Steinhatchee. From 30-foot flashing green "1" marking the entrance to the Steinhatchee River Channel, set a course of 278° magnetic for 9 nm to the yellow special purpose buoy at Steinhatchee Reef at N 29° 39.893'/W 83° 37.823'. Depths at the reef are charted at 15 feet at MLW. From Steinhatchee Reef your course is 313° magnetic for 36 nm to flashing green "1" and red nun buoy "2" marking the entrance to the St. Marks River.

Well before arriving at flashing green "1" and red nun buoy "2" you will see the 82-foot-high St. Marks Lighthouse (no longer lighted) on shore but do not shortcut this leg. The well-marked entry channel twists and turns through a maze of shoals. Daylight passage should present no problems but avoid going in at night. The single orange range marker is used in conjunction with the St. Marks Lighthouse. Lining both up will keep you in mid-channel from flashing green "1" to the first dogleg at green can buoy "3A."

St. Marks has a straightforward channel and river. Both are wide, well-marked and carry enough depth (at least 6 feet MLW) to accommodate most cruising boats that have made it this far.

Dockage: Up the St. Marks River is Shields Marina selling new and used boats and motors and renting pontoon boats, kayaks, paddleboards and bikes. Their Ship Store is over 6,000 square feet and sells fishing tackle and gear, as well as electronics, nautical charts and more. They have limited (two) reserved transient slips to 65 feet on floating docks. Two restaurants, a Post Office and a small grocery store are within easy walking distance of the marina.

St. Marks Yacht Club is on the Wakulla River, which branches off the St. Marks River south of the

SOUTHERN EDITION

Chapter 14: The Big Bend: Anclote Key to Carrabelle

Shell Point Area, FL

SHELL POINT		Largest Vessel	VHF	Total Slips	Approach/ Dockside Depth	Floating Docks	Gas/ Diesel	Repairs/ Haulout	Min/Max Amps	Pump-Out Station
1. Marsh Harbor Marina of Shell Point	(850) 819-4300	60		94	/ 9.0	F			30	P

WiFi Wireless Internet Access
Visit www.waterwayguide.com for current rates, fuel prices, website addresses and other up-to-the-minute information. (Information in the table is provided by the facilities.)

Scan here for more details:

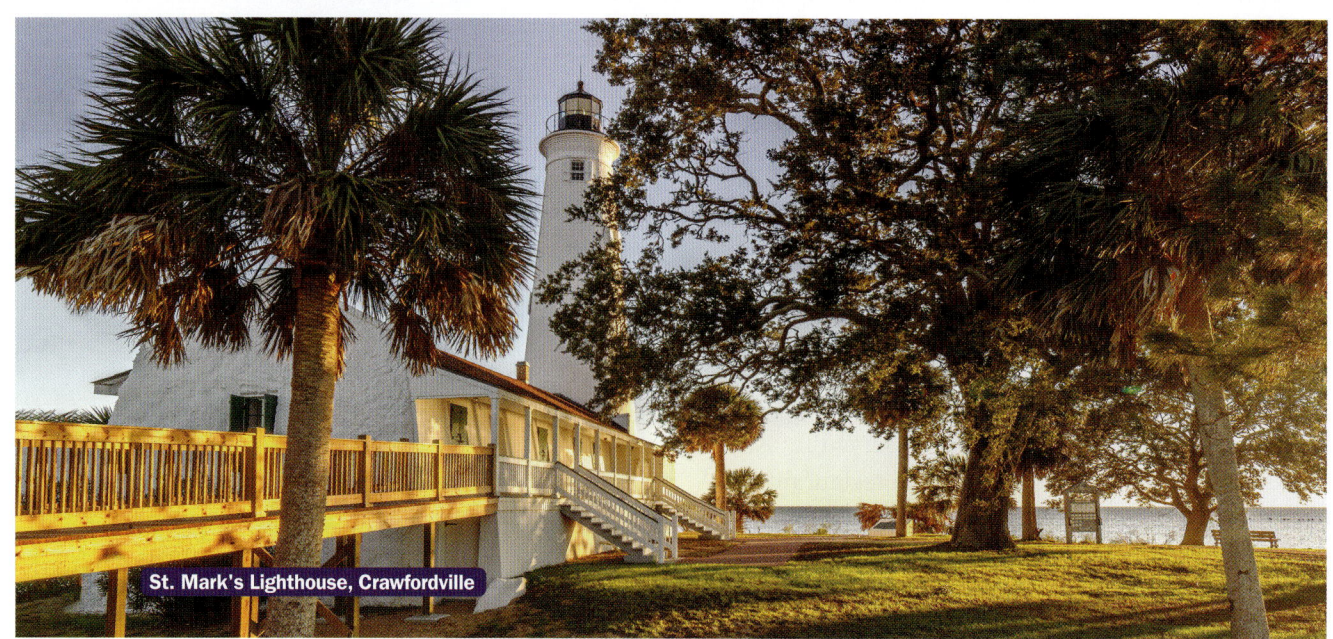

St. Mark's Lighthouse, Crawfordville

St. George Sound, FL

ALLIGATOR HARBOR

		Largest Vessel	VHF	Total Slips	Approach/Dockside Depth	Floating Docks	Gas/Diesel	Repairs/Haulout	Min/Max Amps	Pump-Out Station
1. Windward at Alligator Point Marina WiFi	(850) 349-2511	45		45	4.0 / 5.0	F	GD		30 / 50	

WiFi Wireless Internet Access
Visit www.waterwayguide.com for current rates, fuel prices, website addresses and other up-to-the-minute information. (Information in the table is provided by the facilities.)

Scan here for more details:

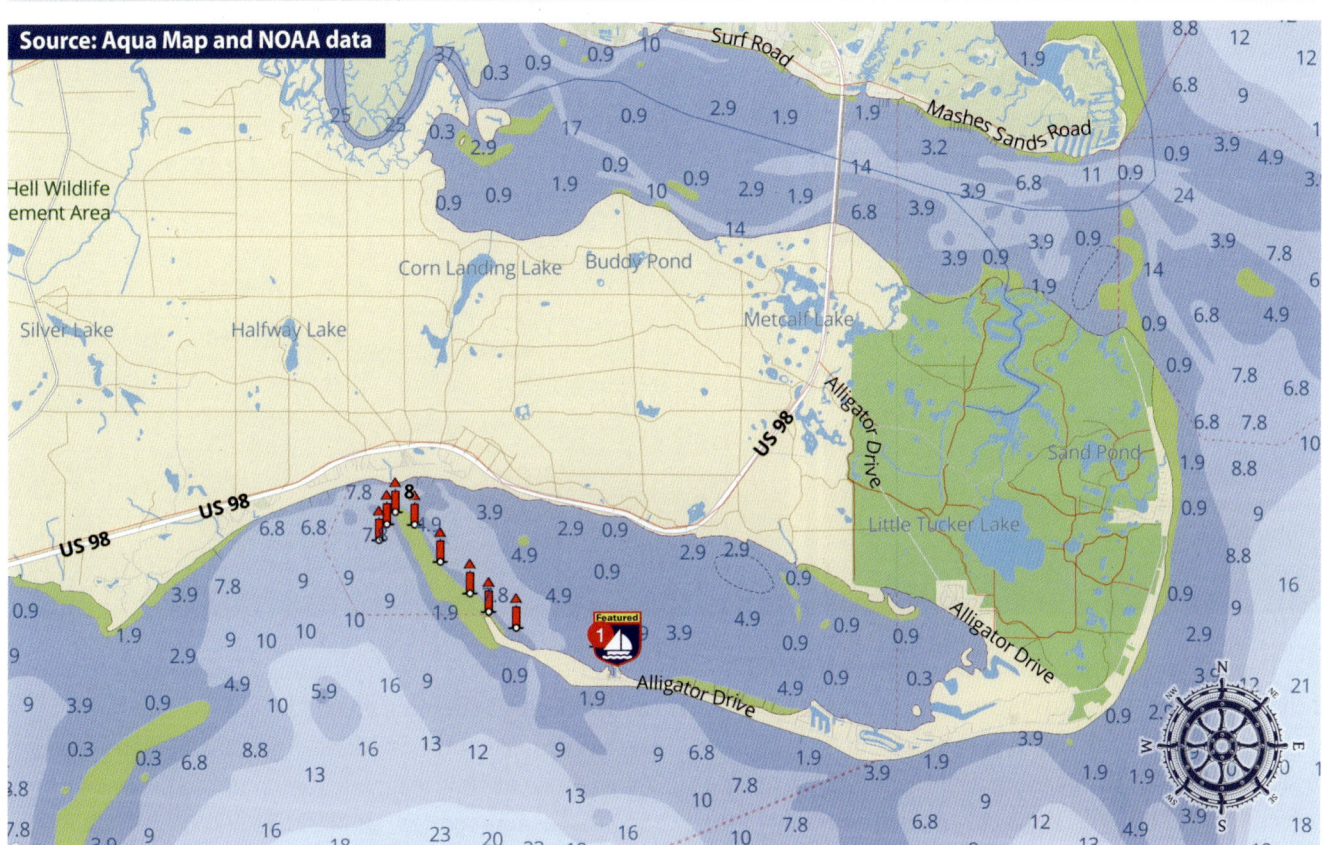

Source: Aqua Map and NOAA data

town. The private club accept non-members if space is available. There are no amenities nearby but the small Wakulla River Park is next door with some trails and a pavilion. A call ahead to the marinas is essential here based on the minimal number of reserved transient slips.

To the west of the St. Marks River is Marsh Harbor Marina of Shell Point, which is under new ownership (in 2023). They offer floating slips to 60 feet with all the usual amenities. Call ahead for slip availability.

Anchorage: About 1 mile above the marinas around the first bend, the St. Marks River offers an anchorage completely different from the usual Gulf Coast beaches. Tropical plants line both riverbanks, wildlife abounds and you can anchor in complete solitude. Be sure to install your screens and apply plenty of insect repellent.

Alligator Harbor

NAVIGATION: Use NOAA Chart 11405. To reach Alligator Harbor take your departure from flashing red bell buoy "26" south of South Shoal. From there take a course of 312° magnetic to flashing green "1" at the northeast end of Dog Island Reef. At this point you can alter course to 358° magnetic. After just more than 3 nm you will pick up flashing red "2" marking the entrance to Alligator Harbor. Follow the daybeacons all the way to the Alligator Point Marina.

Dockage: Watch your depth. Shoals at the entrance to Windward at Alligator Point Marina are charted at 4 to 5 feet MLW. The marina is primarily for small fishing boats but transient slips to 45 feet are available. They have a Ship Store with fishing tackle and boating accessories. The draw here is the white sandy beach. The seasonal on-site

Chapter 14 — The Big Bend: Anclote Key to Carrabelle

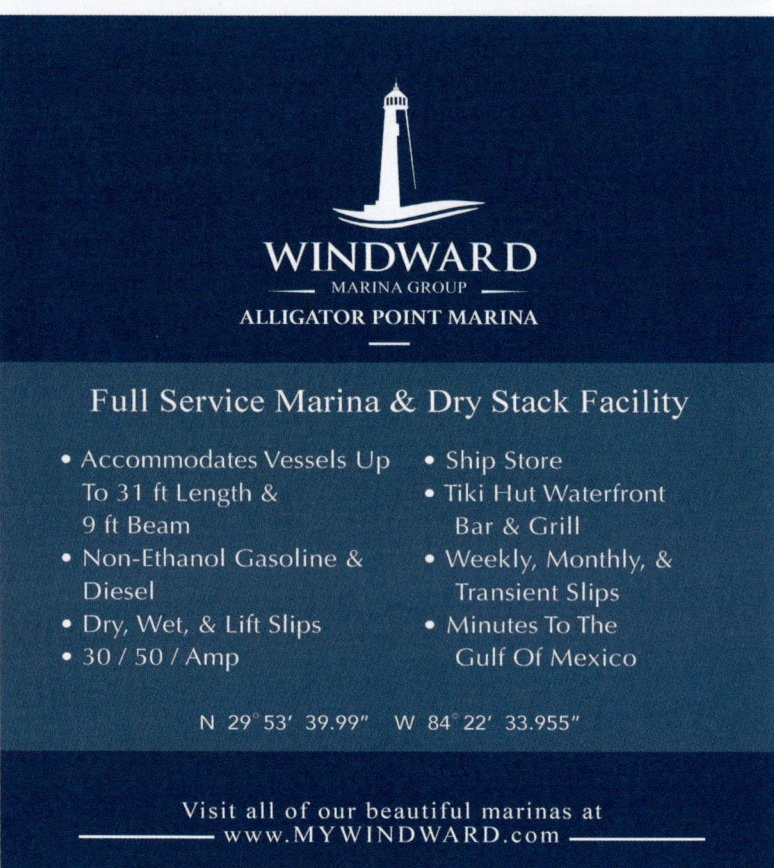

tiki hut will cook your catch on site or you can choose from their (mostly grilled) menu.

Anchorage: A protected anchorage can be found inside Bay Mouth Bar near red daybeacon "22" in at least 7 feet MLW or off Wilson Beach (on the north side of the harbor) in 8 to 10 feet MLW.

St. George Sound to Carrabelle

East Pass into St. George Sound marks the end of the trek across Florida's Big Bend. Once again cruising boats with a vertical clearance of less than 50 feet can choose to travel the GIWW or go offshore in the Gulf of Mexico.

To the west is the port city of Apalachicola and to the east is the port city of Carrabelle. Carrabelle is the closest to East Pass. It is an excellent stop for boats looking for a place to rest after crossing The Big Bend. Carabelle is a friendly fishing village that feels like a step back in time.

NAVIGATION: Use NOAA Charts 11401, 11404 and 11405. The inside route runs from Ochlockonee Shoal's flashing red "24" to the East Pass entrance to St. George Sound and on to Carrabelle.

For the cruising boaters coming from St. Marks, your transit begins at flashing green "1" and red nun buoy "2" at the entrance of the St. Marks River. From there, travel on a course of 183° magnetic for 9.5 nm to Ochlockonee Shoal's flashing red "24" at N 29° 51.500'/W 84° 10.300'.

Next, travel a course of 254° magnetic for 9.3 nm to flashing red "26" at N 29° 47.500'/W 84° 20.000'. From flashing red "26" change course to 265° magnetic for 17 nm to flashing red "2" at N 29° 44.500'/W 84° 39.200' marking the entrance to East Pass and St. George Sound.

East Pass, one of the better Florida west coast passes, leads 5 nm through St. George Sound to the Carrabelle River. Follow the marked channel through East Pass and note the northeastern jog at flashing red "12." Stay in the marked marina channel to Carrabelle. Be aware that the tide here is up to 3 feet and tie up accordingly.

Dockage: Three marinas offer transient dockage 1 mile north of the GIWW on the Carrabelle River. MS Dockside Marina & Boatyard offers slips and boat yard services on Timber Island. Across the river, the friendly C-Quarters Marina has slips for transient boats to 53 feet.

St. George Sound, FL

CARRABELLE

		Largest Vessel	VHF	Total Slips	Approach/Dockside Depth	Floating Docks	Gas/Diesel	Repairs/Haulout	Min/Max Amps	Pump-Out Station
1. MS Dockside Marina & Boatyard	(850) 697-3337	65	16	22	16.0 / 9.0	F		RH	30 / 50	
2. C-Quarters Marina WiFi	(850) 697-8400	80	16	67	12.0 / 9.0		GD	R	30 / 50	P
3. The Moorings of Carrabelle WiFi	(850) 697-2800	150	16	150	15.0 / 9.0		GD		30 / 50	P

WiFi Wireless Internet Access
Visit www.waterwayguide.com for current rates, fuel prices, website addresses and other up-to-the-minute information.
(Information in the table is provided by the facilities.)

Scan here for more details:

Source: Aqua Map and NOAA data

Chapter 14: The Big Bend: Anclote Key to Carrabelle

Their Ship Store is open daily from dawn to dusk. Many locals congregate here in the mornings and evenings on the well-known front porch for coffee or a cold beverage.

The largest marina in Carrabelle, The Moorings of Carrabelle, has transient slips in an enclosed basin plus an on-site hotel, complimentary bicycles and continental breakfast. There is no public transportation but groceries, hardware and several restaurants are easily accessible.

Anchorage: There is an anchorage south and west of green marker "17" at Carrabelle; however, the actual depths are less than the charted 5 feet MLW. There is also a tidal current moving through the anchorage so you will swing. Boats with 3-foot draft may be able to anchor here.

Side Trip: Dog Island

Due south of the Carrabelle River is Dog Island with numerous anchoring possibilities. Just inside the hook of the west end of Dog Island you can anchor at Shipping Cove, an excellent spot in deep water (charted at 17 to 20 feet MLW). A small embayment at the northeast end of Dog Island can provide limited shelter. There are no areas for transient anchoring in Tysons Harbor due to the private docks of Dog Island Yacht Club.

There are no amenities ashore. The island's hospitable owners allow cruising mariners to explore the beaches but please stay off private docks and property. A portion of the island is a bird breeding and nesting area, posted with "Keep Out" signs. Please honor them. (The posted section does not include the beach.)

■ NEXT STOP

Upon entering the Florida Panhandle you will need to decide if you are going to travel outside in the Gulf of Mexico, following the coastline all the way to Pensacola or take the 200-statute mile inside (GIWW) route.

> Fixed bridge heights of 48 feet will prevent most sailboats from using at least parts of the inside route.

The Florida Panhandle

Chapter 15

SOUTHERN EDITION

Chapter 15 — The Florida Panhandle

■ NAVIGATION NOTES

For the cruising boat that reaches St. Georges Sound (and has a vertical clearance of less than 48 feet) it is difficult to recommend an offshore passage to Pensacola. The GIWW distance from Mile 375 EHL to Mile 180 in Pensacola Bay is 195 statute miles through an enjoyable, low-stress section of the GIWW.

The more interesting GIWW route connects big bays and sounds that are protected by narrow, wooded barrier islands. From Carrabelle to Pensacola there are 200 statute miles of inside cruising with occasional passes to the Gulf of Mexico. Actual fixed bridge heights down to 48 feet (as indicated by clearance boards) at the Dupont (US 98) Bridge (Mile 295.4 EHL), the Brooks Memorial Bridge (Mile 223.1 EHL) and the Navarre Beach Causeway (CR 399) Bridge (Mile 206.7 EHL) will prevent most sailboats from using some of the inside route.

Along the panhandle of Florida a rather unique change occurs to tides. West of St. George Sound/Apalachicola Bay, there are only two tides per 24 hours (one high and one low, called diurnal tides), while east of this demarcation the tides are the normal four per 24 hours (two highs and two lows). Very few places on the planet can claim this distinction.

> **NO WAKE ZONE**
> No Wake Zones, Idle Speed Zones and various Speed Limit restrictions are in effect throughout the waterways included in this chapter. Exercise diligence in knowing the regulations by observing signs and other markers. Enforcement is always present. As always, be courteous to other vessels and avoid manatees and other marine life.

Gulf Island National Seashore

The islands located offshore on the Gulf of Mexico from Biloxi, MS (GIWW mile 73.0 EHL) to Destin, FL (GIWW mile 227.5 EHL) are part of the Gulf Islands National Seashore. There are beautiful white beaches, coastal marshes, and thick forests. You can explore 19th century forts, enjoy shaded picnic areas, and hike on nature trails. Many cruisers enjoy exploring these islands and associated beaches.

The National Park Service controls entrance to these areas and certain rules apply. An "entrance pass" is required at most visitor sites and historic displays. The Gulf Island 7-day pass is $15 per person/$25 per vehicle (2023). The National Park and Federal Recreation Lands Pass is also recognized. We recommend that you check the website for the most current pricing/specials.

Have a wonderful time while ashore but keep the following rules in mind:

- No glass containers of any kind are allowed ashore.
- Many areas are closed to pets. If so indicated, do not take your pet ashore.
- Where pets are allowed, they must be on a leash and you must clean up after them.
- You are not permitted to walk on the dunes in some areas and other areas have limited access due to nesting birds.
- Fishing (with the proper license) is generally acceptable.
- Fires are allowed on most (not all) beaches 5' above the high tide line using driftwood. You must extinguish your fire with water and bury the ashes under at least 6" of sand prior to leaving.

The rules may seem strict but they are in place to preserve a true national treasure. Help us all by obeying the rules and paying for your entrance pass.

Offshore Route: East Pass to Pensacola

The offshore passage from East Pass must go around the shoals that extend from Cape St. George and Cape San Blas. The offshore distance from Mile 375 EHL to the entrance at Pensacola Bay is 158 nm. From the flashing red "2" at the end of East Pass set a course of about 230° magnetic for 25 nm to avoid the shoals at Cape St. George and Cape San Blas. Then set a course of about 295° magnetic for 130 nm (for a total distance of 155 nm) to Pensacola.

There are two inlets that will allow you to break the trip into two days to enjoy this part of the Emerald Coast. The well-marked inlet at St. Andrews Bay is 80 nm from East Pass. The channel at Destin is 120 nm from East Pass and is passable but not as well marked. It has a controlling depth of 6 feet MLW and a width of 50 feet. From this channel you can reach marine facilities before the fixed **William T. Marler (US 98/SR 30) Bridge** with 49-foot vertical clearance, which crosses the pass.

America's Waterway Guide Since 1947   Chapter 15

An alternate (and recommended) offshore route is to enter St. George Sound at East Pass and proceed 52 (statute) miles along the GIWW to Port St. Joe. To reach Port St. Joe turn to the southwest at Mile 328 EHL at the Gulf County Canal. (There are signs at this intersection.) The offshore run from Port St. Joe to the entrance at Pensacola Bay is 100 nm on a course of 283° magnetic.

CAUTION: This area of the Gulf is used extensively by the U.S. Air Force. Along the entire route you will be passing by and over areas marked as missile testing, unexploded ordnance and fish havens. Check the latest *Local Notice to Mariners* for updates.

 GIWW Mile 351–Mile 170 EHL

CARRABELLE TO PANAMA CITY

From Carrabelle to Florida's Panhandle you can travel the GIWW (inside) or continue outside in the Gulf. Note that the inside route is in shallow waters! Know where you are going to go, how you are going to get there and the condition of the water all along the route before you leave the dock.

Apalachicola–GIWW Mile 351 EHL
A worthwhile layover along this stretch of the GIWW is Apalachicola with a village-like atmosphere, excellent

Apalachicola

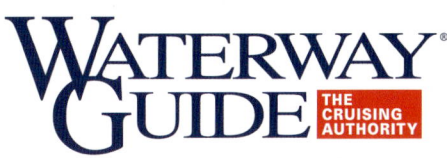

Navigate with the Cruising Authority

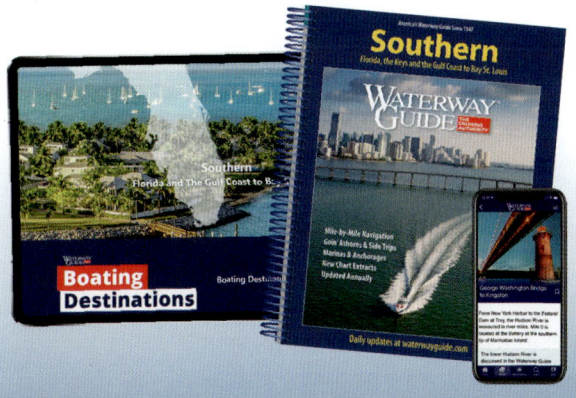

Subscribe today for the full package
(Guidebook of your choice, mobile app & online subscription)

Scan to shop now at www.waterwayguide.com

SOUTHERN EDITION   545

Chapter 15: The Florida Panhandle

Goin' Ashore

APALACHICOLA, FL

As you step off your boat onto the docks in Apalachicola it is impossible not to feel how history infuses the entire town. In the middle of the "Forgotten Coast" of the Florida Panhandle this community of 2,000 inhabitants blends its 4,000 plus years of human history into everyday life. The town still has thriving businesses in oyster, shrimp, crab, sponge, and finfish and echoes of the past ring loud through the town. Couple this with a 21st Century tourism business that is unique to the area and visitors can expect a very pleasant and laid back experience.

Apalachicola has a very low key vibe with a vibrant Old Florida ambiance. There are many funky boutiques, coffee shops, restaurants, raw bars, and even a local brewery. "Fresh caught" takes on new meaning when ordering seafood here. What is really nice is the town is not overrun with visitors. Everything gets done but there is no sense of urgency. The town really grows on you.

Chapter 15
America's Waterway Guide Since 1947

ATTRACTIONS

1. Apalachicola Center for History, Culture & Art
Artist exhibits, events, films, lectures, classes and workshops, cultural events and programs are housed in this restored 1830s cotton warehouse at 86 Water St. (850-653-1458).

2. Apalachicola Maritime Museum
Active boating excursions, adventure programs, boat building and restoration, and educational programs at 103 Water St. (850-653-2500).

3. The Gibson Inn
"Front porch sitting" has been going on since 1907 in this "cracker" style structure characterized by a metal roof and a wraparound porch. Lodging, a bar and fine dining at 51 Ave. C (850-653-2191).

4. Raney House Museum
Local historical artifacts are housed in the 1800s home of cotton-trader David G. Raney at 128 Market St. (850-653-1700).

5. Down Town Books and Purl
Find a wide selection of books and exquisite yarns plus games and diversions at 67 Commerce St. (850-653-1290).

6. The Tin Shed
This literal "shed" contains a comprehensive collection of antique and used nautical equipment and items plus shells, wood carvings and apparel at 170 Water St. (850-653-3635).

SERVICES

7. Apalachicola Bay Chamber of Commerce & Visitor Center
17 Ave. E (850-653-9419)

8. Apalachicola Margaret Key Library
80 12th St. (850-653-8436)

9. Apalachicola Post Office
20 Ave. D, Ste. 101. (850-653-9554)

MARINAS

10. Apalachicola Marina, Inc.
119 Water St. (850-653-9521)

11. Battery Park Marina
1 Bay Ave. (850-653-9319)

12. Scipio Creek Marina
301 Market St. (850-653-8030)

13. Water Street Hotel & Marina
329 Water St. (850-653-3700)

Shrimp boats at port in Apalachicola

SOUTHERN EDITION

Chapter 15 — The Florida Panhandle

Apalachicola River, FL

APALACHICOLA		Largest Vessel	VHF	Total Slips	Approach/Dockside Depth	Floating Docks	Gas/Diesel	Repairs/Haulout	Min/Max Amps	Pump-Out Station
1. Battery Park Marina GIWW 351.0 mi. EHL	(850) 653-9319	50			6.0 / 5.0				50	P
2. Apalachicola Marina, Inc. GIWW 351.0 mi. EHL	(850) 899-3675	100		3	9.0 / 8.0				30 / 50	
3. Water Street Hotel and Marina GIWW 351.0 mi. EHL	(850) 653-3700	55		19	12.0 / 8.0	F			50	
4. Scipio Creek Marina WiFi GIWW 351.0 mi. EHL	(850) 653-8030	100	16	14	12.0 / 10.0		GD	RH	30 / 50	

WiFi Wireless Internet Access
Visit www.waterwayguide.com for current rates, fuel prices, website addresses and other up-to-the-minute information. (Information in the table is provided by the facilities.)

Scan here for more details:

Source: Aqua Map and NOAA data

548 WATERWAY GUIDE 2024 www.waterwayguide.com

local oysters and unique shopping opportunities within walking distance of the marinas. It is a pleasant trip through St. George Sound and Apalachicola Bay to the unique and beautiful City of Apalachicola.

NAVIGATION: Use NOAA Chart 11404. If you go into Carrabelle, you will have to come back out the same way. After exiting the Carrabelle River and retracing your course into St. George Sound pick up flashing red "2" (Mile 374 EHL) just inside East Pass.

Flashing red "6" becomes visible about 2.5 miles to the southwest. From here the GIWW is clearly marked as it jogs south by southwest at flashing red "20" for about 2 miles to flashing red "28" (Mile 365 EHL) where it resumes its southwest direction.

From that point it is a straight shot southwest for about 9.3 miles under the fixed **Bryant Patton (SR 300) Bridge** at Mile 361.4 EHL (65-foot vertical clearance) over Apalachicola Bay at Bulkhead Shoal (red nun buoy "48"). Just east of the bridge there are high tension lines that are marked on some charts as having a 46-foot clearance. If you dig deeper you will find that the clearance in the channel is actually 85 feet so the power lines are not an issue for boaters.

Watch your depths carefully in the area of Bulkhead Shoal where the oyster beds come right to the edge of the channel. The channel is especially narrow on the east side of the bridge so keep an eye on the markers ahead and behind to keep from crabbing into the shallows. The bridge is the boundary of demarcation between St. George Sound and Apalachicola Bay.

After traversing much of Apalachicola Bay at flashing red "76" make a 90-degree turn north and follow the GIWW about 3.5 miles to red nun buoy "24" marking the entrance to the Apalachicola River and the town of Apalachicola.

Dockage: After passing red nun buoy "24" and just south of the fixed **John Gorrie Memorial (US 98/319) Bridge** at Mile 351.4 EHL (65-foot vertical clearance) the Apalachicola municipal marina (Battery Park Marina) is in a basin to port. Transient slips are available to 50 feet with the usual amenities. There are several busy boat ramps here and the docks are open to wakes left by passing boaters so be sure to use ample spring lines and fenders. The park features multiple boat ramps with wooden docks, fishing piers and a community center that hosts events such as the annual Florida Seafood Festival. Apalachicola City Dock is next with 300 to 400 feet of linear space with no amenities. Call ahead for rates and reservations.

The well-regarded Apalachicola Marina, Inc. may be small in size (three total slips on a 150-foot face dock) but it's big on service and sells some marine supplies. A supermarket, drug store and restaurants are within easy walking distance.

Most of the other transient facilities are located farther north along with various fuel docks and a waterfront hotel (Water Street Hotel and Marina) with newly renovated dock space. Their 19 transient slips on floating docks can accommodate power or sailboats up to 55 feet in an Old Florida setting. Features include a welcoming staff, pool and a 30-suite hotel with screened porches on the water. Within walking distance of the center of Apalachicola, the hotel's beautiful turn-of-the-century look captures the solitude of life by the water.

> NOTE: Take care while fueling and docking as the Apalachicola River can have a strong current depending on tidal flow.

If you want to get away from GIWW traffic, Scipio Creek Marina is a popular stopover for cruisers. (The "c" is silent in Scipio.) Boats are docked one behind the other along three long docks. There is less tidal current here than at the facilities located directly on the Apalachicola River. The marina is located to the northwest of the river at green-red can "A" with slips, an on-site store and a restaurant. Motels, more restaurants and provisions are within a three-block walk.

Anchorage: It is possible to anchor at Apalachicola just north of the John Gorrie Memorial (US 98/319) Bridge. Here you will find 9 to 12 feet MLW with good holding. You will be exposed to wakes so be sure to anchor well out of the channel. There are also anchorages at Shell Point on St. George Island (GIWW Mile 365 EHL) in 7 to 10 feet MLW.

To White City–GIWW Mile 351 to Mile 329 EHL

The GIWW leaves Apalachicola Bay and the Gulf of Mexico at Mile 350 EHL and winds along on the scenic Apalachicola River, undulating generally northwest to the **Apalachicola Northern Railroad Bridge** at Mile 347.0 EHL (11-foot closed vertical clearance, usually open). Keep a sharp eye out for tree limbs and other floating debris. *Again, a night passage is not recommended.*

Chapter 15: The Florida Panhandle

NAVIGATION: Use NOAA Charts 11393, 11401 and 11402. From the mouth of the Apalachicola River the GIWW is well marked. Past red daybeacon "30" the Apalachicola River turns north and the GIWW continues along the Jackson River to Lake Wimico at Mile 340 EHL.

You will soon take a hairpin turn to the south past flashing green "9" just west of Mile 345 EHL and about 1 mile later take a sharp curve to the west and proceed to Lake Wimico at Mile 340 EHL and green daybeacon "3" and red daybeacon "4." The course for the straight shot across the lake is about 310° magnetic. Follow the daybeacons carefully as the spoil areas are close to the narrow channel.

At flashing green "15" enter Searcy Creek at the end of Lake Wimico (Mile 335 EHL). Follow the well-marked channel from here about 6 miles to the **Elgin Bayless (SR 71) Bridge** (65-foot fixed vertical clearance) at Mile 329.3 EHL. The waterway is relatively wide and deep and offers an enjoyable view as you traverse swamp country (described on the some charts as "impenetrable," "cypress" and "low swampy area").

A little over 1.5 miles from the bridge you must choose to continue on the GIWW to Panama City or turn southwest on the Gulf County Canal to Port St. Joe, St. Joseph Bay and the Gulf.

Note that there is currently no transient dockage available at White City. The old free wall at White City Dock is no longer safe for use and the newly renovated floating dock is not available for transient traffic. Things may change in the future so stay tuned to Waterway Explorer.

Anchorage: Just after the Jackson River splits off from the Apalachicola there is an excellent protected anchorage in 8 feet MLW at the junction of Saul Creek and the Saul Creek Cutoff (northeast at Mile 345 EHL between green daybeacon "7" and red "8"). There is some shoaling on the left bank when turning in so stay more right of center when leaving the GIWW. Depths exceed 30 feet MLW in much of this lovely creek. For optimum holding use your depth sounder to find an appropriate depth to set the hook. Alligators and birds are abundant.

After exiting Lake Wimico into Searcy Creek, the oxbow around the island at Mile 334 EHL normally carries 10 feet MLW or better and provides an excellent secluded anchorage.

Side Trip: North on the Apalachicola River

Boaters seeking a side trip can follow the Apalachicola River upstream through a few miles of heavily wooded swampland to the St. Marks, East and Brothers Rivers after exiting the GIWW at red daybeacon "30" (GIWW Mile 346 EHL). There is ample depth here for smaller vessels. (Controlling depths of 9 to 10 feet MLW are available to St. Marks Island.) The really adventurous can navigate the river up to the Jim Woodruff Dam at Chattahoochee but obtain local knowledge before embarking.

Option 1: White City to Panama City– GIWW Mile 329 to Mile 290 EHL

NAVIGATION: Use NOAA Charts 11390, 11391 and 11393. From White City the GIWW continues to run clean, wide and deep with no need for navigational aids. At about Mile 318 EHL it becomes the South Prong of Wetappo Creek and continues beneath **Overstreet (SR 386) Bridge** at Mile 315.4 EHL (65-foot fixed vertical clearance) to about Mile 314 EHL where it joins the North Prong and becomes Wetappo Creek.

At this point aids to navigation appear again, starting with green daybeacon "1" at about Mile 313 EHL and continuing down the Wetappo Creek and into Big Cove. At that same green daybeacon "1" eastbound vessels need to stay alert as the channel bends southeast here and the small bay to the south can be confused with the GIWW.

On this part of your journey you will be passing a bay that leads to Sandy Creek just past GIWW Mile 310 EHL and past Raffield Island to the south (at 3 feet mean sea level). During strong southerlies the narrow channel leading west to the sharp turn at GIWW Mile 310 EHL (flashing red "28") can pose serious difficulties to barge traffic. If meeting a tow along this stretch be sure to coordinate on VHF Channel 13 to clarify your intentions. As a matter of practical concern we recommend you have your VHF radio cycling between VHF Channels 16 and 13 on this section of the GIWW.

Study the chart carefully for the run up East Bay to Panama City. Flashing green "29" (Mile 294.2 EHL) off Parker Bayou should be left to starboard here as the GIWW buoy system gives way to the Panama City buoy system (red-right-returning from the Gulf). This can be confusing as red buoys are now on your port side as you travel west switching back to red on the right with flashing red "6" off Buena Vista Point west of Panama City.

Chapter 15

St. Joseph Bay, FL

MEXICO BEACH		Largest Vessel	VHF	Total Slips	Approach/Dockside Depth	Floating Docks	Gas/Diesel	Repairs/Haulout	Min/Max Amps	Pump-Out Station
1. Point South Port St. Joe Marina WiFi GIWW 327.5 mi. EHL	(850) 797-3489	120	16	60	15.0 / 6.0	F	GD		30 / 100	P
2. Captain's Cove Marina WiFi	(850) 227-3357	90		4	15.0 / 12.0		GD	R	30 / 50	

WiFi Wireless Internet Access
Visit www.waterwayguide.com for current rates, fuel prices, website addresses and other up-to-the-minute information.
(Information in the table is provided by the facilities.)

Scan here for more details:

Source: Aqua Map and NOAA data

SOUTHERN EDITION

Chapter 15: The Florida Panhandle

> ⚠️ **CAUTION:** There is a 4-foot-deep MLW shoal charted just northeast of the channel at red daybeacon "38" off Piney Point (Mile 300.75).

The GIWW channel continues southwest from Raffield Island and turns west at red daybeacon "44" to Murray Point. Near GIWW Mile 306 EHL favor the southwestern side of the channel to avoid oyster reefs on the northeast side (generally marked with "Danger" signs).

Just past Long Point on East Bay is the Dupont (US 98) Bridge at Mile 295.4 (50-foot fixed vertical clearance). From here to Panama City the GIWW runs through relatively deep water (25 to 35 and even 40 feet).

Anchorage: Between White City and Panama City on the GIWW a pleasant, protected overnight anchorage is located on Wetappo Creek at GIWW Mile 314.5. Just around the first bend of the creek you can safely anchor over a soft mud bottom in about 10 feet MLW. Due to the strong current a Bahamian moor is appropriate here, preferably on the side of the river by the marshlands.

As you enter the East Bay there are several good overnight choices. Walker Bayou (GIWW Mile 307.5 EHL), California Bayou (GIWW Mile 302 EHL), Laird Bayou (GIWW Mile 299.5 EHL) and Callaway Bayou (GIWW Mile 298.1 EHL) all offer good holding in soft mud with starting depths greater than 7 feet MLW and then shoal as you move farther back in the bayous. Walker has good protection from winds from the south, while the other three have better protection from winds with a northerly component. Be prepared for some tidal current and the swing that it brings.

Option 2: White City to Panama City– Gulf Canal & Gulf Route

NAVIGATION: Use NOAA Charts 11389, 11393 and 11401. About 1.5 miles northwest of White City at about GIWW 328 EHL, the Gulf Canal cuts off 90 degrees to the southwest and extends 5 miles from the waterway to Port St. Joe on St. Joseph Bay. The controlling depth is 8 feet MLW and there is a 75-foot fixed **U.S. 98/SR 30 Bridge** near the exit to St. Joseph Bay.

The channel from Port St. Joe to the Gulf is clearly marked in St. Joseph Bay. Turn northwest at the intersection with the ship channel and then north to get around St. Joseph Point at the tip of St. Joseph Peninsula and out of St. Joseph Bay. You will be doing this incrementally with the last straight run to the southwest until you get into the Gulf of Mexico and 30-plus feet of water.

To get to the entrance buoy (RW "SA") off Panama City, steer northwest. The distance is 21 miles. The "SA" stands for either St. Andrew or St. Andrews depending on whether you are looking at a chart or listening to the locals. It is best to be flexible.

Dockage: Point South Port St. Joe Marina is bringing boaters back to Port St. Joe with great service and amenities including a private pool, complimentary laundry facilities and dockside morning newspaper delivery. Captain's Cove Marina is primarily a dry storage facility but they do maintain four transient tie-ups (for up to one week) alongside the canal. Call ahead.

Mexico Beach Marina to the north of Port St. Joe has been rebuilt but all boat slips are private. They still operate a fuel dock and have a well-stocked Ship Store for bait, ice, tackle, marine supplies and such.

Anchorage: Just north of the Gulf Canal where it intersects with St. Joseph Bay is an anchorage in 8 to 9 feet MLW at Highland View in front of the tank (shown on the NOAA chart).

You can drop the hook in Eagle Harbor on the inland side of St. Joseph Peninsula. This is a beautiful, remote deep-water anchorage. Dinghy into the St. Joseph Peninsula State Park to access the hiking trails and beach.

Panama City–GIWW Mile 290 EHL

It's no surprise that a city with the slogan "Where life sets sail" is a popular boater destination. Panama City welcomes cruisers year-round. Check in with the friendly staff at Destination Panama City Visitors Center at 1000 Beck Ave. (850-215-1700) when you arrive. They can point you to the unique art galleries and specialty shops, a thriving music scene and dining opportunities that range from casual dockside cafés to upscale eateries, with local Gulf oysters as the fare of choice.

Panama City boasts a large year-round charter fishing fleet, party boats, fishing piers, diving and surf fishing. Gulf fishing has greatly improved in the area thanks to conservation efforts and inshore light-tackle catch-and-release fishing on the bay has become very popular. Boaters can also enjoy the area's sparkling white sugar

America's Waterway Guide Since 1947 — Chapter 15

St. Andrew Bay, FL

		Largest Vessel	VHF	Total Slips	Approach/Dockside Depth	Floating Docks	Gas/Diesel	Repairs/Haulout	Min/Max Amps	Pump-Out Station
BUENA VISTA POINT										
1. St. Andrews Marina - FUEL ONLY-NO DOCKAGE GIWW 287.0 mi. EHL	(850) 872-7240	60	16		15.0 / 8.0		GD			P
GRAND LAGOON										
2. Lighthouse Marina WiFi GIWW 289.0 mi. EHL	(850) 625-2728	70	16	50	8.0 / 8.0		GD	R	30 / 50	
3. Treasure Island Marina GIWW 289.0 mi. EHL	(850) 234-6533	70	16	85	8.0 / 6.0		GD	RH	30 / 50	P
4. Pirates Cove Marina WiFi GIWW 289.0 mi. EHL	(850) 234-3939	60	16	400	6.0 / 8.0		GD	RH	30 / 50	
5. Point South Marina Bay Point WiFi GIWW 289.0 EHL	(850) 235-6911	120	16	130	6.0 / 7.0	F	GD	R	30 / 200+	P
PANAMA CITY										
6. Bristol Harbor WiFi	(731) 217-6649	85		49	12.0 / 12.0				30 / 50	P
7. Emerald Harbor Marina WiFi	(731) 217-6649	100			/					P

WiFi Wireless Internet Access
Visit www.waterwayguide.com for current rates, fuel prices, website addresses and other up-to-the-minute information.
(Information in the table is provided by the facilities.)

Scan here for more details:

Source: Aqua Map and NOAA data

Chapter 15: The Florida Panhandle

Panama City

sand beaches, rated as some of the finest in the country.

NAVIGATION: Use NOAA Chart 11389 and 11390. Shell Island, the barrier island forming the southern side of the main pass from the Gulf of Mexico into St. Andrew Bay, provides shelter for Panama City, which is a major harbor for transient yachts. The cut itself is considered one of the best deep-water channels on the Gulf Coast.

St. Andrew Bay, one of Florida's finest bays and home to Panama City, is deep and almost landlocked. The well-marked exit to the Gulf of Mexico is a land cut through St. Andrews Park that has a rock jetty. The Navy operates a lab on the west end of the bay and south of the **Hathaway (US 98) Bridge** at Mile 284.6 EHL (65-foot fixed vertical clearance). You will frequently see helicopters, hovercraft and some esoteric "special ops" equipment here.

Dockage: Panama City is probably the best-equipped harbor north of Tampa and St. Petersburg and berths are usually available except on holiday weekends. There are facilities throughout the area beginning from the east at Watson Bayou (north of flashing green "25") and extending west to flashing red "14" off Dyers Point. However, this area has seen more than its share of hurricanes over the past several years and renovations are ongoing. Because of this, it is a good idea to call ahead and reserve a berth.

Two new (in 2022) facilities are a welcome addition to this area. Newly rebuilt Emerald Harbor Marina is located just off the GIWW at green marker "25" with 6 dedicated transient slips for vessels to 100 feet. They offer power, water and a pump-out at every slip (expected spring 2023) plus a free on-site laundry and courtesy car.

Bristol Harbor is located beyond the **Tarpon Dock Bascule Bridge** in Massalina Bayou. The bridge opens on signal except from 9:00 p.m. until 11:00 p.m. on July 4, when the draw need not open for the passage of vessels. The quaint marina caters to a limited number of well-maintained yachts on brand new fixed docks with full amenities including pump-out service at each slip. This is within easy walking distance to downtown Panama City.

St. Andrews Marina at Buena Vista Point (0.5 mile north of flashing red "6") currently has fuel only (no dockage) due to ongoing hurricane repairs. Call ahead.

Anchorage: Along this stretch of the GIWW from the Dupont Bridge to Panama City virtually any cove well away from the channel offers good anchorage. Pitts Bayou and Parker Bayou on the north side of Long Point are viable anchorages. Pearl Bayou to the south is a nice anchorage that could be considered a hurricane hole.

Watson Bayou also offers 360° protection and good holding in 8 to 10 feet MLW. Farther west of Watson Bayou on the southern side of the GIWW (near flashing red "20"), Redfish Point and Smack Bayou offer protection from southerly winds with good holding in 8 to 9 feet MLW with a sandy mud bottom. You can get in pretty close to shore at Redfish Point for great protection. Expect to hear jets flying over in the mornings. Bunkers Cove is across the water with at least 9-feet MLW depths if you need northerly protection.

West of Watson Bayou you will find some anchoring room in Massalina Bayou. The drawbridge at the entrance (7-foot closed vertical clearance) opens on demand 24 hours a day.

Shell Island has some excellent anchorages off the beach over a hard sand-and-shell bottom. If boat wakes from the channel bother you, head farther east on the island. Be wary of the charted sandbars between Davis Point and Shell Island. If your depth sounder shows less than 7-foot MLW depths you are either too close to the island or too far north over the Camel Humps.

Side Trip: Grand Lagoon

Grand Lagoon, immediately inside and west of St. Andrews Inlet, offers an interesting side trip.

Dockage: Customer-oriented Point South Marina Bay Point has new docks (in 2022), helpful dockhands and spotless restrooms. It's a short walk to dining options. Lighthouse Marina, Treasure Island Marina and Pirates Cove Marina are here. Call ahead for slip availability and amenities.

Anchorage: The anchorage at Grand Lagoon has 10 to 13 feet MLW with good holding in sand. It is open and exposed, however, to the southeast and wakes. Note that jets flying overhead (often early in the morning) is pretty typical of the entire area.

■ TO SANTA ROSA SOUND

From Panama City westbound cruisers will find about 12 miles of relatively trouble-free transit through West Bay then about 16.5 miles of transit through a land cut known to some as the "Grand Canyon" before ending up in wide Choctawhatchee Bay.

To Choctawhatchee Bay–GIWW Mile 253.5 EHL

NAVIGATION: Use NOAA Charts 11385 and 11390. When westbound from Panama City and approaching the **Hathaway (US 98) Bridge** at Mile 284.6 EHL (65-foot fixed vertical clearance) stay well off the 17-foot high, flashing red "14" off Dyers Point (Audubon Island) as shoaling off the small island reaches into the marked channel.

The GIWW opens up after the Hathaway Bridge. Heading north give flashing green "5" at Shell Point a wide berth. From there the GIWW curves northwest through West Bay, cuts under the **West Bay Creek (SR 79) Bridge** at Mile 271.8 EHL (65-foot fixed vertical clearance) and then enters the relatively narrow channel of West Bay Creek, the start of the land cut known as the "Grand Canyon." For purposes of careful navigation, however, you may assume that you are in narrow circumstances at flashing green "15" at GIWW Mile 275 EHL.

While in the Grand Canyon watch aids to navigation and your course carefully as shoal water with depths of 2 to 4 feet MLW runs very close to either side of the channel. The narrow channel persists past green daybeacon "39" (just past West Bay Creek Bridge) where the aids to navigation cease. The channel here runs relatively wide and deep for about 16.5 miles to GIWW Mile 254.5 EHL at the entrance to Choctawhatchee Bay.

Occasionally when high winds are expected on Choctawhatchee Bay you will find westbound barges waiting inside the Grand Canyon at about GIWW Mile 254 EHL for better conditions. Cautious mariners might follow suit. Tying up to a commercial barge here is entirely possible, if you make a proper approach to the towboat's skipper.

In the event of strong crosswinds make it a point to check with any tows (VHF Channel 13) in the channel east of the **Clyde B. Wells & Choctawhatchee Bay (US 331/SR 83) Bridges** at Mile 250.4 EHL (65-foot fixed vertical clearance) as the narrow channel may require

Chapter 15 — The Florida Panhandle

Choctawhatchee Bay, FL

LA GRANGE BAYOU		Largest Vessel	VHF	Total Slips	Approach/ Dockside Depth	Floating Docks	Gas/ Diesel	Repairs/ Haulout	Min/Max Amps	Pump-Out Station
1. Freeport Marina and Yacht Club WIFI GIWW 249.0 mi. EHL	(850) 835-2035	55	9	50	11.0 / 4.0	F	G		30	P

WIFI Wireless Internet Access
Visit www.waterwayguide.com for current rates, fuel prices, website addresses and other up-to-the-minute information. (Information in the table is provided by the facilities.)

Scan here for more details:

Source: Aqua Map and NOAA data

coordinated meeting or passing. Barges, especially empty ones, are exceptionally difficult to handle for towboat operators in heavy wind and current.

While the cut is frequently dredged to 10.5-foot MLW depths, shoaling is chronic so hold to the center except when passing and realize that if you hug the shore too closely while passing you will likely run aground in soft mud. Also use particular caution when transiting after strong winds or heavy rain when large pine trees can break away from the nearly vertical banks and float downstream.

As you travel into Choctawhatchee Bay from the east the water deepens from about 9 to 38 feet MLW but is generally shallow along its southern shore. Be cautious passing Tucker Bayou (Mile 254 EHL) at the entrance (or, as in this case, exit) of the Grand Canyon as it sometimes shoals to 3-foot MLW depths or less at its mouth.

The route is closely pegged with markers for the first 5 to 6 mile but as the bay broadens and deepens, buoys thin out. Markers are used mainly to indicate shallows to the south and these should be given a wide berth due to the possibility of shoaling. There is room to roam in this large, open bay (about 30 miles long and 3 to 5 miles wide) but be aware that it can get rough in hard easterly or westerly blows due to the east-west fetch. The approach to the 64-foot fixed vertical clearance **Mid-Bay (SR 293) Bridge** (Mile 234.2 EHL) is well marked from both east and west.

Dockage: In La Grange Bayou off the north side of the Choctawhatchee Bay are a few marinas with limited services including Freeport Marina and Yacht Club with slip rentals, dry storage, RV storage and a Ship Store. Note that dockside depth is reported to be 4 feet MLW.

Near the center of the long Choctawhatchee Bay south of Mile 239 EHL in Horseshoe Bayou is the full-service Sandestin's Baytowne Marina, part of a large resort community that stretches from the bay to the beach. The gated community offers marina guests all resort amenities. The Village of Baytowne Wharf has many charming shops and boutiques, restaurants, nightclubs, art galleries and

Chapter 15

Choctawhatchee Bay, FL

HORSESHOE BAYOU		Largest Vessel	VHF	Total Slips	Approach/ Dockside Depth	Floating Docks	Gas/ Diesel	Repairs/ Haulout	Min/Max Amps	Pump-Out Station
1. Sandestin's Baytowne Marina WiFi GIWW 240.0 mi. EHL	(850) 267-7773	130	16	120	8.0/7.0		GD	R	30/100	P
WARD COVE										
2. Bluewater Bay Marina WiFi GIWW 232.0 mi. EHL	(850) 897-2821	110	16	120	8.0/8.0		GD	R	30/50	P

WiFi Wireless Internet Access
Visit www.waterwayguide.com for current rates, fuel prices, website addresses and other up-to-the-minute information. (Information in the table is provided by the facilities.)

Scan here for more details:

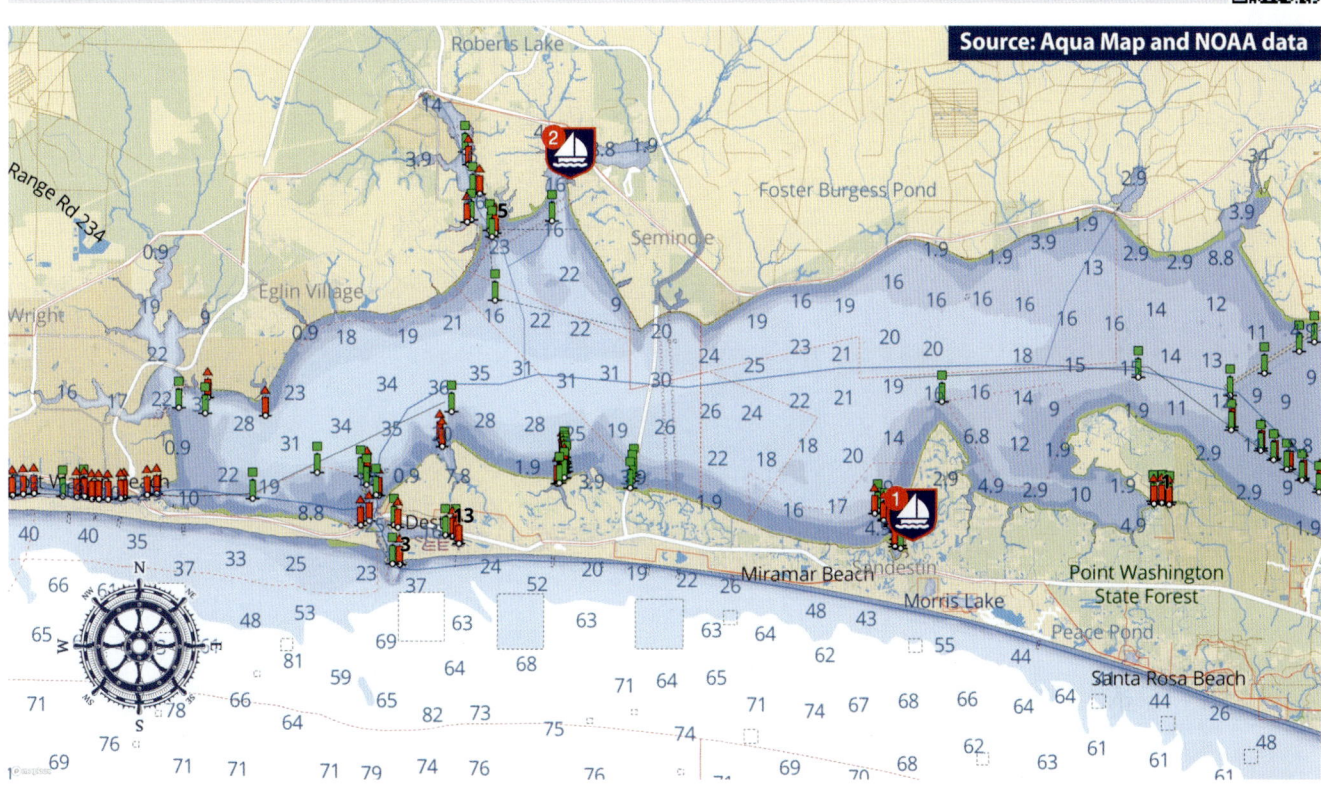

Source: Aqua Map and NOAA data

other facilities. To approach the marina, head south once you are clear of Four Mile Point and line up for flashing green "1" and flashing red "2" at the beginning of the entrance to the facility. Be careful to avoid the shoal depths when approaching shore to the east.

After passing under the Mid-Bay Bridge (Mile 234.3 EHL) and after flashing red "58" head northwest a little more than 3 miles along the northern shore to flashing green "1" and turn north for Rocky Bayou. Ward Cove is to the east as you approach Rocky Bayou on the north side of Choctawhatchee Bay. Green daybeacon "1" and flashing red "2" mark the entrance to Ward Cove and Bluewater Bay Marina. This is a full resort complex with slips (to 110 feet), repairs and an outstanding Ship Store. They also offer "high and dry" boat storage.

Anchorage: Burnt Mill Creek at Mile 277.7 EHL on the northern shore of West Bay has 7 to 9 feet MLW. If you need it you can find anchorage in 7 feet MLW over good holding ground in the lee of the causeway on either side of the Choctawhatchee Bay Bridge at Mile 250.3.

Rocky Bayou on the north shore provides a scenic anchorage. To enter Rocky Bayou follow the directions above for Bluewater Bay Marina but pass Ward Cove. The Nelson Point anchorage offers 12 to 14 feet MLW with protection from the south and only a small amount of fetch from the north before the charted 20-foot fixed vertical clearance bridge. A tighter but even more protected (except from the south) option is the northwest fork of Rocky Bayou in 7 to 10 feet MLW.

You can also anchor in Boggy Bayou to the west, either at Toms Bayou with 13-foot MLW depths or at Niceville in 11 to 12 feet MLW.

SOUTHERN EDITION   557

Chapter 15: The Florida Panhandle

Choctawhatchee Bay, FL

DESTIN		Largest Vessel	VHF	Total Slips	Approach/ Dockside Depth	Floating Docks	Gas/ Diesel	Repairs/ Haulout	Min/Max Amps	Pump-Out Station
1. Destin Marina	(850) 837-2470	30		10	6.0 / 6.0		G			
2. HarborWalk Marina GIWW 230.0 mi. EHL	(850) 650-2400	85	16	52	10.0 / 6.0	F	GD		30 / 50	P

WiFi Wireless Internet Access
Visit www.waterwayguide.com for current rates, fuel prices, website addresses and other up-to-the-minute information. (Information in the table is provided by the facilities.)

Scan here for more details:

For an anchorage on the south side of the bay, turn south at Mile 230 EHL for the marked entry to Joes Bayou, a 360° protected anchorage with a soft mud bottom and depths of 10 feet MLW or more.

Destin–GIWW Mile 227 EHL

Destin lies just north and east of the Choctawhatchee Bay Entrance from the Gulf on the barrier peninsula sheltering the bay on the south. Destin is renowned for its sparkling beaches, crystal-clear waters and seaside resort activities, which are accessible year-round, thanks to an average air temperature of 67.3° maximum with a minimum average of 52.2° from October through March. Full-service marinas, waterfront hotels and restaurants abound.

NOTE: This is sportfishing country and Destin sponsors numerous tournaments each year. The entire month of October is devoted to the more than 50-year-old Destin Fishing Rodeo. Big game fish ply the Loop Current that circulates clockwise in the Gulf of Mexico and that current comes relatively close to shore near Destin. The rodeo draws thousands of expectant anglers who search the offshore waters, inshore bays and bayous for prize-winning fish worth thousands of dollars.

NAVIGATION: Use NOAA Chart 11385. The main docking area in Destin is immediately south and east of the fixed bridge over the Choctawhatchee Bay entrance from the Gulf (south of the GIWW). The charted vertical bridge clearance at the **William T. Marler (US 98/SR 30) Bridge** (locally known as the Destin Bridge) is 49 feet but there have been reports that 48 feet is closer to reality so sailors should use caution if their vessel's mast height is more than that.

If entering East Pass from the Gulf, care should be taken when crossing the bar if there is a swell running. Also note that buoys are not charted

558 WATERWAY GUIDE 2024 www.waterwayguide.com

America's Waterway Guide Since 1947 **Chapter 15**

in the Choctawhatchee Bay entrance channel as constant shoaling necessitates frequent relocation. This is a pass that needs to be negotiated with local knowledge, in flat water, with good visibility and during reasonable tides.

To enter the main Destin Harbor (commonly called Old Pass Lagoon) turn sharply to east after passing under the bridges (or before if coming from the Gulf). The channel into the large harbor is narrow but well-marked with daybeacons. It runs between the mainland to the north and the protective sandbar to the south.

Marine facilities line the northern shore of the harbor. The pristine beaches and dunes of Santa Rosa Island are located across the peninsula on the Gulf side. Because of the substantial development along the beach, you will have to search for a public beach access.

Dockage: Along the north shore of the harbor Destin Marina located north of the William T. Marler (US 98/SR 30) Bridge has just eight slips and few amenities. It is, however, within walking distance of downtown. Transient dockage is available at HarborWalk Marina located southeast of the bridge and on the north side of Destin Harbor. This facility gets high marks from cruisers for the friendly and helpful staff. Provisions are within walking distance of the marina.

The entrance is a little tricky to Destin Harbor. Turn directly after passing under bridge and follow the (unlit) channel, staying closer to the north side of harbor. Destin Fisherman's Co-op is located on the north side of the harbor. Local fishermen established the co-op in 1989 to help them and other fishermen buy discounted fuel. They may sell you fuel but have no transient slips. Several locally popular eating establishments also offer dockage with everything from snacks to gourmet meals.

Anchorage: Destin Harbor provides excellent anchorage with no surge. You can anchor on the southwest side of the harbor or just off Harbor Docks Restaurant (850-837-2506) to the east. There are restaurants all around with dinghy docks. A municipal water taxi service is available during the summer months.

NOTE: The harbor is a No-Discharge Zone.

Side Trip: Crab Island

Although more of a submerged sandbar than an island, Crab Island attracts hundreds of boaters who wade in 1- to 4-foot-deep clear waters in search of sea life. Located on the north side of the Destin Bridge it is open to the inflow and outflow of the crystal clear water from the Gulf yet protected from the surf and waves. Crab Island is only accessible by boat (or kayak or stand-up paddleboard). There are several floating businesses where you can find food, drinks, live music and even a playground for kids. Although Crab Island is accessible year round, the

Chapter 15 — The Florida Panhandle

Crab Island

floating vendors are typically only open from March through October. By the way, you cannot buy alcoholic beverages here but you can bring your own (and many do).

Fort Walton Beach–GIWW Mile 224 EHL

Fort Walton Beach combines the many charms of a major seaside resort and is well worth a cruising layover. Besides the swimming and snorkeling in crystal-clear water, the area is an angler's delight.

Need a break from the water? This captivating town is a shopper's bonanza with antiques stores, novelty shops, boutiques, upscale dress shops and bookstores. Golf and tennis facilities abound and there is an eclectic variety of restaurants and nightclubs. This is also home to Eglin Air Force Base, a military facility that's larger than the entire state of Rhode Island.

NAVIGATION: Use NOAA Chart 11385. The channel at Fort Walton Beach is well marked on the approach from the east. Flashing green "1" and red nun "2" are almost 2 miles west of the entrance to North Channel.

The GIWW narrows considerably on the west side of **Brooks Memorial Bridge** (50 foot fixed vertical clearance) at Mile 223.1 EHL and you will come across a series of floating marks that will get that point across to you quite well.

Dockage: Although off the "main drag," transient space may be found on the eastern shore of the entrance to Garnier Bayou, approximately 2 miles northwest of GIWW Mile 225 EHL. A well-marked channel entrance with a tall, cylindrical water tower serves as a beacon to Two Georges Marina. The well-maintained marina is located on five landscaped acres with slips with full amenities and repair and maintenance services. While Cinco and Garnier Bayous offer a number of marine facilities, the 19-foot fixed vertical clearance **Elgin Parkway Bridge** limits access to both.

The dock at Little Marler Park on the east side of Brooks Memorial Bridge at Mile 223.3 EHL can fit two 50-footers. Tie-up is challenging as there are no cleats and the pilings are short. There are no amenities other than what is offered in the park. The friendly Adventure Marina is on the west side of Brooks Memorial Bridge with 130 slips and a complete service department. They also have an active boat brokerage on site. They may accommodate you if they have space. Call ahead.

Fort Walton Beach Yacht Basin at Mile 222 EHL is one of the region's oldest family-owned and -operated marinas offering competitive transient rates (to 50 feet) and fuel prices.

One-half mile west of Brooks Memorial Bridge, Fort Walton Beach City Dock offers a free pump-out station on the north side of the waterway. You are welcome to stay at overnight but there are no amenities. Depth at the dock's T-head is 6 feet MLW but it is considerably shallower near the shore. *NOTE: You must call the Fort Walden Beach Police Dept. to reserve a slip prior to arrival (850-833-9546).*

This is a busy waterway and there is not much room for anchoring except near the free dock so why not tie up?

The Narrows & Santa Rosa Sound–GIWW Mile 223 to Mile 189 EHL

From the southwestern terminus of Choctawhatchee Bay, west of Fort Walton Beach, the GIWW enters a

America's Waterway Guide Since 1947 — Chapter 15

Choctawhatchee Bay, FL

FORT WALTON BEACH		Largest Vessel	VHF	Total Slips	Approach/ Dockside Depth	Floating Docks	Gas/ Diesel	Repairs/ Haulout	Min/Max Amps	Pump-Out Station
1. Two Georges Marina WiFi GIWW 225.0 mi. EHL	(850) 651-0510	125	16	134	32.0 / 8.0		GD	RH	30 / 50	P
2. Adventure Marina WiFi GIWW 222.9 mi. EHL	(850) 581-2628	50	16	24	8.0 / 8.0		G	RH	30 / 50	
3. Fort Walton Beach Yacht Basin GIWW 222.0 mi. EHL	(850) 244-5725	50	16	94	9.0 / 7.0		G		30 / 50	P

WiFi Wireless Internet Access
Visit www.waterwayguide.com for current rates, fuel prices, website addresses and other up-to-the-minute information. (Information in the table is provided by the facilities.)

Scan here for more details:

section known as The Narrows. This waterway, which is actually the eastern end of Santa Rosa Sound, is appropriately named.

Although well marked, the channel twists back and forth through shallows for about 6 miles before it widens somewhat as it approaches Santa Rosa Sound proper. As the GIWW winds through Santa Rosa Sound to Pensacola Bay, you will see an abundance of attractive homes along the mainland side with beach communities dotting the barrier side.

Pensacola Bay, west of Deer and Fair Points, has always been considered one of Florida's largest and safest harbors. It has served as a heavy weather refuge for commercial and naval ships as well as smaller craft.

NAVIGATION: Use NOAA Charts 11378 and 11385. At Mile 206.7 EHL the **Navarre Beach Causeway (CR 399) Bridge** has a charted fixed vertical clearance of 50 feet but may have only a 48-foot fixed vertical clearance due to tide conditions. There are reportedly no clearance boards on this bridge at either end so extreme care should be taken when transiting.

While transiting The Narrows monitor VHF Channels 16 and 13 for barge traffic to avoid a "squeeze" when meeting with an oncoming barge.

- **"Passing one whistle"** means that you and the tow agree to alter course to starboard and pass port-to-port.

- **"Passing two whistles"** means that you are altering course to port and will pass starboard-to-starboard.

SOUTHERN EDITION 561

Chapter 15: The Florida Panhandle

If you ask the skipper of the tow what is best for him, you will likely get extreme cooperation. Remember that barges are not maneuverable like your pleasure craft so give the barge traffic the benefit of the doubt.

At Mile 205 EHL the GIWW emerges from shoal territory into Santa Rosa Sound. Although the GIWW does move through some shoal areas in Santa Rosa Sound (5- and 6-foot MLW depths), for the most part it carries respectable depths of 13 to 17 feet MLW all the way to the **Bob Sikes (Pensacola Beach/SR 399) Bridge** at Mile 189.1 EHL.

Anchorage: While there are no marine facilities here for cruising vessels, anchorages abound in The Narrows. Mary Esther at GIWW Mile 219.7 EHL has at least 4 feet MLW and good holding. On Santa Rosa Island there are four main anchorages:

- Mile 217.4 EHL: Spectre Island just west of green daybeacon "51"
- Mile 215 EHL: Santa Rosa Island by green daybeacon "69"
- Mile 213.9 EHL: Manatee Point on the south shore at red daybeacon "74A"
- Mile 208.6 EHL: Lower Pritchard on the north shore at Long Point by green daybeacon "85"

All of these anchorages have a sandy bottom with good holding. What they do not have is shore access.

You can also drop the hook on either side of the Navarre Beach Causeway Bridge at green daybeacon "89" at Navarre Park on the south shore just east of the bridge or at "93" on the west side of the bridge at Navarre Beach.

Juana's Pagodas & Sailors' Grill (850-939-1092) next to the boat ramp on the west side of the bridge has a great little beach (with chair and umbrella rentals) and serves breakfast, lunch and dinner daily. They also rent all types of watercraft from Waverunners to Hobie Cats.

Santa Rosa Sound, which is not much wider than The Narrows, has numerous coves and good anchorages along its shores. Be sure to check your depths and remember the effect of the wind on tides as the anchorages may be somewhat more shallow than charted.

Chapter 15

Pensacola Bay, FL

PENSACOLA BEACH AREA		Largest Vessel	VHF	Total Slips	Approach/Dockside Depth	Floating Docks	Gas/Diesel	Repairs/Haulout	Min/Max Amps	Pump-Out Station
1. Santa Rosa Yacht & Boat Club WiFi GIWW 189.0 mi. EHL	(850) 934-1005	70	16	40	8.0 / 8.0		GD		30 / 100	P
2. Pensacola Beach Marina WiFi GIWW 189.0 mi. EHL	(850) 932-0304	100	16	30	/		GD		30 / 50	P
3. Sabine Marina WiFi GIWW 189.0 mi. EHL	(850) 932-1904	57	16	64	9.0 / 8.0				30 / 50	P

WiFi Wireless Internet Access
Visit www.waterwayguide.com for current rates, fuel prices, website addresses and other up-to-the-minute information.
(Information in the table is provided by the facilities.)

Scan here for more details:

SOUTHERN EDITION 563

Chapter 15 — The Florida Panhandle

Pensacola Bay, FL

SAYVILLE HARBOR		Largest Vessel	VHF	Total Slips	Approach/Dockside Depth	Floating Docks	Gas/Diesel	Repairs/Haulout	Min/Max Amps	Pump-Out Station
1. Seville Harbour Marina 186 EHL	(850) 432-9620	50	16	43	7.0 / 7.0				30	
2. Palafox Pier Yacht Harbor WiFi GIWW 186.0 mi. EHL	(850) 432-9620	175	16	88	20.0 / 13.0	F	GD		30 / 50	P
3. Baylen Slips Marina WiFi	(850) 432-9620	55	16	24	20.0 / 13.0	F	GD		30 / 50	P

WiFi Wireless Internet Access
Visit www.waterwayguide.com for current rates, fuel prices, website addresses and other up-to-the-minute information. (Information in the table is provided by the facilities.)

Scan here for more details:

Source: Aqua Map and NOAA data

■ PENSACOLA & PERDIDO BAYS

The Pensacola Bay area blends the influences of the outstanding beach, extensive military history, active art scene and hikeable woodlands create a destination where there's something for everyone.

Pensacola Bay is relatively narrow (3 miles) and stretches in an east-west direction for about 22 miles. On its west side Escambia Bay and East Bay extend some 10 miles north. Pensacola Bay carries depths of 20 to 50 feet but the bays to the north run 9 to 12 feet (at MLW) with more extensive shoals as you go north. Many marine facilities are located in Sabine Bay, located just west of the Bob Sikes (Pensacola Beach/SR 399) Bridge (65-foot fixed vertical clearance) at GIWW Mile 189.1 EHL.

NAVIGATION: Use NOAA Charts 11378. Keep within all channel markers if you are entering Pensacola Bay from the Gulf of Mexico on the Caucus Channel. This good all-weather passage is subject to shoaling, which is almost always well marked.

A principal mark for the entrance is the 171-foot conical brick Pensacola Light. Currents can be significant in this channel, especially at the 90-degree turn into the Bay. The Pensacola Coast Guard Station is 1 mile east of Pensacola Light.

Chapter 15

Pensacola Bay, FL

PENSACOLA AREA		Largest Vessel	VHF	Total Slips	Approach/ Dockside Depth	Floating Docks	Gas/ Diesel	Repairs/ Haulout	Min/Max Amps	Pump-Out Station
1. Pensacola Yacht Club-PRIVATE GIWW 185.0 mi. EHL	(850) 433-8804	100	16	58	8.0 / 8.0		GD		30 / 50	P
2. Yacht Harbor Marina WiFi GIWW 185.0 mi. EHL	(850) 455-4552	65	16	52	9.0 / 6.5	F	D		30 / 50	P
3. Palm Harbor Marina - Pensacola WiFi GIWW 185.0 mi. EHL	(850) 455-4552	70		64	9.0 / 6.5	F			30 / 50	P
4. Pelican's Perch Marina & Boatyard WiFi GIWW 185.0 mi. EHL	(850) 453-3471	50			15.0 / 6.0	F		RH	30 / 50	P
5. Island Cove Marina WiFi GIWW 185.0 mi. EHL	(850) 455-4552	75		94	7.0 / 6.0				30 / 50	P
6. Pensacola Shipyard Marina & Boatyard WiFi GIWW 185.0 mi. EHL	(850) 439-1451	200		52	18.0 / 7.0	F	D	RH	30 / 100	P

WiFi Wireless Internet Access
Visit www.waterwayguide.com for current rates, fuel prices, website addresses and other up-to-the-minute information. (Information in the table is provided by the facilities.)

Scan here for more details:

Source: Aqua Map and NOAA data

CAUTION: For westbound skippers, as you enter Pensacola Bay note that after passing flashing green "145" (at about GIWW Mile 184.2 EHL) the buoys shift to that of the Pensacola Ship Channel (red-right-returning for vessels in-bound from the Gulf). Thus, if traveling the GIWW from this point across Pensacola Bay to the Pensacola Landcut and then re-entering the GIWW at about GIWW Mile 179.5 EHL, you should leave red markers to port and green to starboard. (These markers carry the appropriate small yellow triangles and squares indicating their dual role as GIWW route markers.)

Dockage: Immediately east of the Bob Sikes (Pensacola Beach/SR 399) Bridge at GIWW Mile 189.1 EHL on the north side of Santa Rosa Sound is the 40-slip Santa Rosa Yacht & Boat Club, which is private but offers transient dockage (if space is available). All transient arrivals should dock at the fuel pier and contact the dockmaster for slip assignment. Vessels arriving outside of regular business hours–including holidays–must make prior arrangements with the dockmaster. .

Just past the bridge, if you turn south and run parallel to it, you will see channel markers for Little Sabine Bay. Pensacola Beach Marina is the first marina on the port side after entering Little Sabine Bay. They maintain four transient slips plus offer fishing charters, dolphin cruises and boat rentals. Expect the docks to be busy in the summer months. Just to the south in Little Sabine Bay is Sabine Marina, which may also have transient space and is home to the Frisky Dolphin Sunset Oyster Bar & Grill (850-934-3141).

Quiet Water Beach Pier is a free dock (no services) to the east of the bridge. The local ferry docks where no mooring signs are posted. The north end of the dock

Chapter 15: The Florida Panhandle

carries about 10 foot MLW. There are no cleats on the pier so expect to tie to pilings.

Six miles northeast of the GIWW on the west side of the Commercial Port of Pensacola is Seville Harbour Marina with facilities just three blocks from downtown Pensacola. The slips at Palafox Pier Yacht Harbor are on floating piers with deep water. Other amenities include a small Ship Store. The 24-slip Baylen Slips Marina may also have transient space on their floating docks. Downtown Pensacola Public Dock is a free dock (no services) with a 60-foot bulkhead. There is no room for anchoring in the harbor.

Anchorage: You can anchor in Little Sabine Bay at Quiet Water Beach in 7 to 11 feet MLW or west of the bridge in 5 to 11 feet MLW. This is a tight area.

English Navy Cove on the north shore of Santa Rosa Sound carries 11 to 15 feet MLW. Expect wakes from large fishing vessels.

Bayou Chico

One mile southwest of the Port of Pensacola is a channel running northwest to Bayou Chico (GIWW Mile 185 EHL), which has full-service boatyards and marinas. The 65-foot fixed vertical clearance **Bayou Chico (SR 292) Bridge** crosses Bayou Chico.

Dockage: South of the bridge in Bayou Chico is the private Pensacola Yacht Club. They recognize reciprocal privileges from yacht clubs throughout Florida, all along the Gulf Coast and in many southeast cities with GYA lake-based yacht clubs.

Yacht Harbor Marina and Palm Harbor Marina to the south before the high-rise Bayou Chico (SR 292) Bridge and Island Cove Marina beyond the bridge are co-managed. All offer some transient space on floating docks with full amenities.

Also north of the bridge is Pelican's Perch Marina & Boatyard. This family-owned facility has floating docks and maintains a comprehensive listing of qualified local marine contractors. A little farther up Bayou Chico is the Pensacola Shipyard Marina & Boatyard, a full-service marina and boatyard facility with some transient slips and full amenities. The Oar House on Bayou Chico may have space for you if you dine with them. Call ahead (850-432-9620).

Anchorage: You can anchor north of the marinas in Bayou Chico in 9 to 11 feet MLW with good holding in mud and all-around protection. The public boat ramp before the bridge allows access to the main road. Shopping is a two-mile walk west or you can take the bus.

Bayou Grande at Jones Point to the southwest has 9-foot MLW depths and offers good protection from wind and wakes. Anchor in the basin before the **Murray Road Bridge** (14-foot fixed vertical clearance).

Big Lagoon–GIWW Mile 179 to Mile 172 EHL

Continue west from Pensacola Bay into the GIWW. The intersection is about 1 mile from the exit into the Gulf of Mexico. It is a run of about 8 to 10 miles from Fort McRee at Pensacola's Gulf entrance to the Alabama line at about Mile 170 EHL. Ahead on the GIWW are some fabulous anchorages, great waterfront restaurants and fine repair facilities.

NAVIGATION: Use NOAA Chart 11378. As previously mentioned, traffic here can get confusing because the markers change to red-right-returning for vessels inbound from the Gulf to Pensacola to the GIWW (red on the north or land side and green on the south or Gulf side).

After flashing green "15" in the middle of the Caucus Channel between Forts Pickens and Barrancus, head west-southwest to green can "1" and flashing red "2" to transit the short and narrow but well-marked passage known locally as the Pensacola Land Cut (about Mile 178 to Mile 179 EHL) leading to Big Lagoon.

Be careful not to confuse green can buoy "1" with green can buoy "13" just to its south, which is a marker for the Caucus Channel. You can also line up the range markers to get to the land cut, which leads into Big Lagoon. As you enter keep an eye out for shoaling caused by strong tidal currents through the Caucus Channel. The shallows are easily seen on sunny days but if it is overcast, they will be harder to make out so stay to the center except to pass. Wait if you see a barge entering the pass. There is not much room in there.

Anchorage: There is a great anchorage at Fort McRee in 10 to 13 feet MLW in Big Lagoon at GIWW Mile 178.4 EHL. This is adjacent to Fort McRee so expect to see planes flying overhead. Dinghy to the beaches on the Bay or Gulf side. This anchorage is somewhat exposed to the west.

Redfish Point is a good anchorage south of the GIWW that is well protected in most weather. Turn south before flashing red "10," which marks a very shallow shoal. You can anchor as close to shore as your draft permits in hard sand. You can also turn north at red "10" to access Trout Point with 11 feet MLW and good holding.

If you continue to flashing green "15" and double back toward the beach on Perdido Key, you will find 12-foot MLW depths with good holding. For a bit of shore side recreation swim or dinghy to the beach. The Gulf beach is a short walk across the dunes, which are part of the Gulf Coast Island National Seashore Park. This is a favorite weekend getaway for locals but there is a bothersome chop during a northerly.

You can anchor before the bridge at Siguenza Cove (Mile 172 EHL) in 5 to 7 feet MLW. This is somewhat exposed to the east and wakes.

Perdido Bay–GIWW Mile 172

From Big Lagoon it is a short trip to Perdido Bay, sliced down the middle by the state line separating Florida from Alabama. Perdido Bay offers a variety of enticements for the cruising yachtsman.

NAVIGATION: Use NOAA Chart 11378. Leaving either the anchorage or the marinas, as you approach the left turn at the west end of Big Lagoon be careful not to shortcut the channel as flashing red "12" is well up in the cove and hard to see.

The area southeast of green can buoy "11" is shallow (which will be evident by the pelicans walking on the bar) so favor the center of the channel to avoid joining the many who have run aground here. Follow the markers because this entire area is surrounded by shoal water. After a turn at flashing red "16" and green daybeacon "15" you will see the **Gulf Beach Highway (SR 292) Bridge** at Mile 171.8 EHL with a 73-foot fixed vertical clearance.

After flashing green "35" at Mile 170 EHL, enter the open but shoaled area between Perdido Key (FL) and Ono Island (AL). The GIWW is well marked as it extends along the northern side of Ono Island and Innerarity Peninsula. From flashing green "57" the GIWW swings north into Perdido Bay. The last of Florida, Innerarity Point, will be to the north and the first part of Alabama, Ono Island, is to the south. (Contrary to popular belief, not all of Alabama is west of Florida.)

Dockage: Immediately before the bridge on your left is the Perdido Key Oyster Bar Restaurant & Marina, LLC (at green daybeacon "31"). They offer slips and a face dock for larger vessels (to 150 feet). The restaurant serves lunch and dinner, has an outdoor bar and frequently host live music. Just after the bridge is the 24-slip A & M Perdido Resort and Marina, an RV resort with condos and a marina. Call ahead for slip availability.

Perdido Key

Chapter 15 — The Florida Panhandle

Perdido Bay, FL

PERDIDO KEY		Largest Vessel	VHF	Total Slips	Approach/ Dockside Depth	Floating Docks	Gas/ Diesel	Repairs/ Haulout	Min/Max Amps	Pump-Out Station
1. Perdido Key Oyster Bar Restaurant & Marina	GIWW 172.0 mi. EHL (850) 492-5600	150		50	10.0 / 12.0		GD		30 / 50	
2. A & M Perdido Resort and Marina	WiFi 171.8 EHL (850) 492-7304	40		24	/				30 / 50	P
3. Holiday Harbor Marina & Grill	GIWW 171.0 mi. EHL (850) 492-0555	125	16	48	7.0 / 7.0		GD	H	30 / 50	P

WiFi Wireless Internet Access
Visit www.waterwayguide.com for current rates, fuel prices, website addresses and other up-to-the-minute information. (Information in the table is provided by the facilities.)

Scan here for more details:

If you are in need of repairs or a break, just 0.5 mile west of the bridge and immediately past flashing green "35" you can turn south and follow the private markers a short distance to Holiday Harbor Marina & Grill. The marina offers transient dockage and a popular waterfront restaurant. Use lots of fenders to cushion wakes from the GIWW. They are either the last marina in Florida heading west or the first marina in Florida heading east, depending on your perspective.

Anchorage: Tarkiln Bay (Mile 166.3 EHL) on the east shore of Perdido Bay offers 7- to 9-foot MLW depths and protection from all but southwest winds. On the western side of Perdido Bay there are anchorages at Soldier Creek and Palmetto Creek, which offer protection from the north and good holding in mud.

Side Trip: Perdido Pass (Orange Beach)

Spanish explorer Carlos Sequenza was looking for a permanent base when he stumbled upon Perdido Bay, which means "lost" in Spanish. Presumably Perdido Bay was named "lost" because of its narrow entrance. Pirates reportedly once favored the bay and the many coves and bayous in the area because they made good hiding places. Citizens using picks and shovels opened the Perdido Pass inlet from the Gulf in Orange Beach proper in 1906.

NAVIGATION: Use NOAA Chart 11378. At Mile 170 EHL, heading west on the GIWW, the tip of private Ono Island appears to the south as you cruise the straight westward line of the GIWW to the entrance to Perdido Bay. At flashing green "57" turn north to explore Perdido Bay or southwest to explore Bayou St. John.

WATERWAY GUIDE
THE CRUISING AUTHORITY

savvy navvy

iNavX

SEA*iq* Pilot

AGLCA

Waterway Guide App

Aqua Map

Our Data.
Across Multiple Platforms.
From One Place.

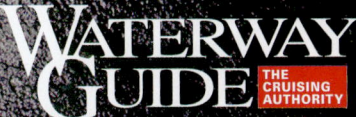

Providing verified information to the world's leading navigation platforms and boating organizations.

WWW.WATERWAYGUIDE.COM

Experience
ORANGE BEACH MARINA

Home of the Mobile Big Game Fishing Club

Haven or Heaven
Enjoy the experience.

Relax. Every need is met at our beautifully secluded, secure location with covered and open slips available. Enjoy on site waterfront dining and shopping as your yacht gets all the attention it needs with on site service and repair. Located just minutes from the Gulf of Mexico at Perdido Pass and the Intercoastal Waterway.

TENANT AMENITIES
Outstanding Marina Staff
2 Restaurants On Site
6 Bay Fuel Dock
Upscale Dock Store
Dockage to 130'
Private Showers & Restrooms

ON SITE SERVICES
Fisher's at Orange Beach Marina
    Upstairs & Dockside
Mobile Big Game Fishing Club
Saunders Marine Center
Bluewater Yacht Sales
Boat Washing & Detailing Service
Inshore & Offshore Charters

NEARBY
White Sand Beaches
Commercial & Private Airports
Walking, Biking & Nature Trails
Shopping & Outlet Centers
Grocery & Drug Stores
Golf Courses - 6 within 20 Minutes

27075 Marina Road • Orange Beach, AL • 251.981.4207 • OrangeBeachMarina.com

Chapter 15

Perdido Pass Area, FL

		Largest Vessel	VHF	Total Slips	Approach/Dockside Depth	Floating Docks	Gas/Diesel	Repairs/Haulout	Min/Max Amps	Pump-Out Station
COTTON BAYOU										
1. Reel Surprise Marina GIWW 167.0 mi. EHL	(251) 981-5423	68	16	53	5.0 / 5.0		GD			P
2. Zeke's Landing Marina GIWW 163.0 mi. EHL	(251) 981-4044	100	69	50	7.0 / 7.0		GD	H	50	P
TERRY COVE										
3. Orange Beach Marina WiFi GIWW 163.0 mi. EHL	(251) 981-4207	95	16	161	9.0 / 8.0		GD	RH	30 / 100	P
4. Safe Harbor Sportsman WiFi GIWW 163.0 mi. EHL	(251) 981-6247	140	19	100	12.0 / 8.0		GD	RH	30 / 100	P

WiFi Wireless Internet Access
Visit www.waterwayguide.com for current rates, fuel prices, website addresses and other up-to-the-minute information. (Information in the table is provided by the facilities.)

Scan here for more details:

Source: Aqua Map and NOAA data

SOUTHERN EDITION

Chapter 15: The Florida Panhandle

From flashing green "57" on the GIWW there is a marked channel extending from the GIWW through Bayou St. John to Perdido Pass to the Gulf of Mexico. The pass has a 9-foot MLW controlling depth and Perdido Pass (SR182) Bridge has a 54-foot fixed vertical clearance. This pass is a popular well-marked gateway to and from the Gulf of Mexico.

A number of restaurants and marinas are located in the bays and bayous on the way to Perdido Pass. To visit Perdido Pass turn southwest off the GIWW at flashing green "57" then head for green daybeacon "17," which is the last buoy of the Perdido Pass Inlet channel. Pass between green daybeacon "17" (which will be to the west) and quick flashing red "18" (to the east) and then continue that orientation toward Perdido Pass as you come around to the west. Note that at the beginning of this channel there are several private markers to a small cut into Ono Island to the south, which you should not follow.

If you want to explore marinas and facilities in Cotton Bayou, Terry Cove or Johnson Cove, make a soft turn further west at green can buoy "1" making sure not to cut the shallows between that and red nun buoy "8" for the Perdido Pass Channel. Parallel the Perdido Pass (SR182) Bridge by running west on its north side. At the western end of the bridge there are two channels—one that goes farther west into Cotton Bayou and the other going north from red nun buoy "8" and green can buoy "9." This will take you into both Terry Cove and Johnson Cove.

If you choose to enter Cotton Bayou, be careful of shoal water. Downtown Orange Beach amenities can be reached from the bayou. There is a moderate current here as you pass the inlet so be careful. Boaters with deep-draft vessels should use caution in Cotton Bayou; keep an eye on your depth sounder. Six-foot MLW depths have been observed here even though the chart shows differently.

Reversing course toward the GIWW, as you leave Bayou St. John you can safely cut across from green daybeacon "17" (which will be to the west) to GIWW flashing red "58" (leave to the east as you are back on the GIWW westbound) at Mile 166 EHL.

Dockage: Reel Surprise Marina on the south side of Cotton Bayou offers a wide assortment of activities from boat rentals and diving to fishing charters, and Zeke's Landing Marina to the south boasts the largest charter fishing fleet on the Gulf Coast. Both maintain a few transient slips.

If you are heading up to Terry Cove from either Cotton Bayou or Perdido Pass, you will pass a boat ramp on the west headland and just past this boat ramp, flashing red "12." For Orange Beach Marina look due west (about 150 to 200 yards) for green daybeacon "1" and red daybeacon "2." This privately marked channel curves southward and then westward along private docks and residences. Follow it keeping red to starboard and at the very end you will see the marina's private channel, running due south. The full-service marina has plenty of transient dockage in a secluded and fully protected harbor with all the usual amenities plus a popular restaurant. This location does not monitor VHF channels. Reach them by phone or stop at the fuel dock. The full-service Saunders Marine Center–Orange Beach is on site.

Safe Harbor Sportsman on the north shore of Johnson Cove or eastern end of Terry Cove is easy to reach. At flashing red "12" in Johnson Cove carefully proceed north by northeast but give flashing red "12" a wide berth to avoid shoals lying east of the marker. The marina offers marine services, has an on-site tiki bar and restaurant and maintains 25 transient slips.

Anchorage: There is an anchorage at Bayou St. John with 7 to 8 feet at MLW and excellent holding in sand. (Somewhat exposed to the west.)

■ NEXT STOP

From here you will be entering the waters of Alabama's Gulf Coast and the vast delta of Mobile Bay, where those traveling the Great Loop will exit the inland river system.

Mobile Bay Area to Bay St. Louis, MS — Chapter 16

Chapter 16: Mobile Bay Area to Bay St. Louis, MS

■ NAVIGATION NOTES

The protected Gulf Intracoastal Waterway (GIWW) route arcs 870 miles from Pensacola to the Rio Grande. Expect to encounter a variety of conditions, ranging from open water on Mississippi Sound to narrow, sometimes cramped, canals and waterways. Lagoons and bayous often alternate with long and sometimes tedious land cuts. The route runs past historic southern cities rich in antebellum history, such as New Orleans, to coastal towns that cater specifically to boaters like Kemah (Clear Lake).

Weather

Summers are hot but tolerable in the Gulf states; otherwise, this is an exceptional area from April through November. The area is semi-tropical and influenced heavily by the Gulf of Mexico, which creates warm, moist air flowing generally northward from spring to fall, bringing relatively high temperatures and rain. New Orleans can be soggy and humid, while coastal waters in Texas often experience strong gales.

> **CAUTION:** Hurricane season is May to November. Since 2017, six major storms of either Category 4 or 5 strength have made landfall along the Gulf Coast. We recommend you call ahead to any facility you plan to visit in this area.

Fog is an occasional problem in the Mississippi Delta region westward to the mid-Texas coast in springtime but seldom drops visibility below 2 miles. In these cases, be especially cautious of the commercial traffic that is more frequent in this area than in other parts of the Gulf Coast.

Dockage & Anchorage

In many areas of the western Gulf Coast, marinas and fuel stops are scarce and often hold irregular hours. Keep a sizable reserve in your tanks and call ahead to fuel docks as soon as you are in range. Because the GIWW was once strictly a commercial waterway, many facilities remain geared to commercial vessels. In Louisiana and Texas a cell phone is a necessity as many facilities geared to pleasure craft no longer monitor the VHF.

Commercial Traffic

Many commercial ships run offshore in the Gulf of Mexico heading from port to port or serving offshore oil rigs. Gulf Coast waters are also worked intensively by large fishing and shrimping fleets as well as by the ever-present sportfishing vessels running in and out of the many passes. Once inside, the GIWW is often crowded with tugs and barges.

Barge rigs can be enormous, exceeding 1,000 feet in length in some cases. Vessels of this size must swing wide in turns and need up to a quarter mile to stop. Moreover, they usually travel together. Commercial craft expect yachts to stay clear and give way under all circumstances.

Most of the professional captains working these waters are valuable sources of information and normally happy to help visiting boaters. It is hard to overestimate the importance of VHF radio. Call captains to find out when it is safe to pass, what traffic lies ahead and the best way to pass. Know the whistle signals; you will be told to pass on one whistle, two whistles or not at all. Call towboats on VHF Channels 13 or 16. In areas with heavy commercial traffic, you may want to leave your VHF on Channel 13.

An Automatic Identification System (AIS) is also useful along this coast. When linked to a chart-plotter or tablet navigation system, AIS accurately pinpoints the location of all transmitting vessels and greatly improves safety when navigating the inland waterways. Most commercial vessels utilize AIS while running the rivers and when docked at their destinations. In addition to locating tows, AIS will generally report other pertinent information: the vessel's name, length, draft, heading, speed and current status. We recommend AIS that both transmits and receives, thus enabling other vessels to see you as well.

Locking Through

- When locking through, the lockmaster may direct you to hold position "at the dolphins." Do not attempt to tie to the dolphins or any structure near the lock. Engines must be in idle and ready to make a move at any moment to maneuver through traffic.

- Place fenders on both sides of the boat. A dock pole or boat hook is handy for keeping the boat away from the concrete sidewalls of the chamber. Boats less than 40 feet usually use one breast (forward) line, while larger vessels use fore and aft lines.

- Once inside, the lockmaster may ask one crewmember to stand ready on the bow with a line. The line should be about 30 feet in length with a loop tied in one end. You may be asked to pass the looped end to an attendant on top of the wall. Make one turn with the other end around a mid-ship cleat, pull it taut and secure by hand.

- The boat will be moving up or down, so tend the line at all times. *Do not pull the line taught and secure it to a cleat!* You must be able to tighten or loosen the line when the elevation changes.

- You may be asked to "float the chamber," which means hold your boat (by power) in the middle of the lock. You may be instructed to tie side-by-side with another vessel.

- Tie-up procedures vary and many times securing to the hip of a tug or barge is better than the normal wall position. The most unlikely and untenable position is to line up in any fashion behind a large tow vessel. If lined up behind a tow vessel, use a bow and stern line. Then after you have changed elevation, consider taking two turns on a cleat so you can handle the prop wash from the tow ahead.

- "Red Flag" tows carrying hazardous cargo fly red flags on their barges and display a blue light at night. Regulations prohibit passenger and pleasure craft from sharing the lock with a "Red Flag" tow.

Chapter 16: Mobile Bay Area to Bay St. Louis, MS

 GIWW Mile 170 EHL-Mile 54 EHL

■ MOBILE BAY AREA

West of the Pensacola Inlet you will enter the GIWW, pass Sherman Cove to the north and enter Big Lagoon. As you approach Mobile Bay, you are entering a vast delta basin fed by many rivers. These rivers feed into the bay and spread across the area to comprise the second largest drainage basin in the U.S. with the largest being the Mississippi River Delta. The GIWW to the west promises adventures with a rich history, scenic beauty and endless opportunities to entice the cruising boater.

Along this stretch of the GIWW you will cross into Alabama waters. The waterway route from the Alabama border at Mile 170 EHL through Mile 160 EHL is a wonderland of excellent protected anchorages including Roberts Bayou, Ingram Bayou and Graham Bayou. Check your charts and pick any one of these for a pleasant, protected overnight stop.

There are also plenty of marinas in the area, along with repair facilities, restaurants and other amenities. Until you get to Mobile Bay the only water-accessible town is Orange Beach, AL, named for the orange groves that once were plentiful there.

No Wake Zones, Idle Speed Zones and various Speed Limit restrictions are in effect throughout the waterways included in this chapter. Exercise diligence in knowing the regulations by observing signs and other markers. Enforcement is always present. As always, be courteous to other vessels and avoid manatees and other marine life.

Perdido Bay to Bon Secour Bay– GIWW Mile 151 EHL

There are many "must-see" spots off the GIWW, particularly for gunkholers. Many cruisers have a problem when they visit this bountiful area in that they do not want to leave. Some who plan to stay for a week or so stay several weeks or even permanently.

NAVIGATION: Use NOAA Chart 11378. From flashing green "57" the GIWW swings north into Perdido Bay.

The last of Florida, Innerarity Point, will be to the north and the first part of Alabama, Ono Island, is to the south. (Contrary to popular belief, not all of Alabama is west of Florida.)

The channel around Mill Point is well marked but is narrow and shallow on the edges. A sharp watch is required. Once in Arnica Bay the channel opens up–particularly to the north–before it closes down again off Hatchett Point at flashing red "68." From flashing red "68" to red daybeacon "90" the GIWW is relatively open through Bay La Launch, past Sapling Point and through the straight shot across Wolf Bay to red daybeacon "90" at the entrance to Portage Creek.

From here (Mile 160 EHL) the GIWW is bordered by land all the way to Oyster Bay at Mile 152.5 EHL. Along this route you will pass under **Foley Beach Expressway Bridge** at Mile 158.7 EHL, which has a fixed vertical clearance of 73 feet. The next and last bridges along this route are the **Gulf Shores Parkway (SR 59) Twin Bridges** at Mile 154.9 EHL with fixed vertical clearances of 73 feet.

A tugboat crew change station and supply store is east of the twin bridges. There is an Idle-Speed/No-Wake Zone along this stretch. Shrimp boats and barges sometimes tie up to both banks east of the bridge to wait out inclement weather.

Dockage: Most of the marinas here welcome transients (and there are several small ones not listed here). These and the facilities at Gulf Shores, AL, are the last recreational boat marinas located on or near the GIWW east of New Orleans. Full-service marinas at Mobile and Fairhope, AL; Biloxi and Gulfport, MS; and Slidell, LA, all require side trips of up to 20 miles from the GIWW proper.

After curving around the green buoys off Bear Point into Arnica Bay you will encounter the 83-slip Bear Point Harbor, located south of green daybeacon "65" at Mile 165 EHL. This has traditionally been a favorite stopover for cruising boats. In addition to slips, they also have a well-stocked Ship's Store and a restaurant on site.

At Mile 165 EHL Pirates Cove Marina & Restaurant has 16 reserved transient slips. You will see the entrance to the marina docks and boatyard off to the west as you approach the narrow cut into Roberts Bayou. Barber Marina is located north off the GIWW at Mile 163 EHL (at red daybeacon "74") in Bay La Launch. This marina can accommodate boats on floating docks,

America's Waterway Guide Since 1947 Chapter 16

Perdido Bay, FL

ORANGE BEACH AREA		Largest Vessel	VHF	Total Slips	Approach/ Dockside Depth	Floating Docks	Gas/ Diesel	Repairs/ Haulout	Min/Max Amps	Pump-Out Station
1. Bear Point Harbor WiFi GIWW 165.0 mi. EHL	(251) 981-2327	47	16	83	12.0 / 6.0		GD		30 / 50	P
2. Barber Marina WiFi GIWW 163.0 mi. EHL	(251) 987-2628	125		155	12.0 / 12.0	F	GD	RH	30 / 200+	P
3. Pirates Cove Marina & Restaurant GIWW 165.0 mi. EHL	(251) 987-1224	65		16	10.0 / 10.0				30	P

WiFi Wireless Internet Access
Visit www.waterwayguide.com for current rates, fuel prices, website addresses and other up-to-the-minute information.
(Information in the table is provided by the facilities.)

Scan here for more details:

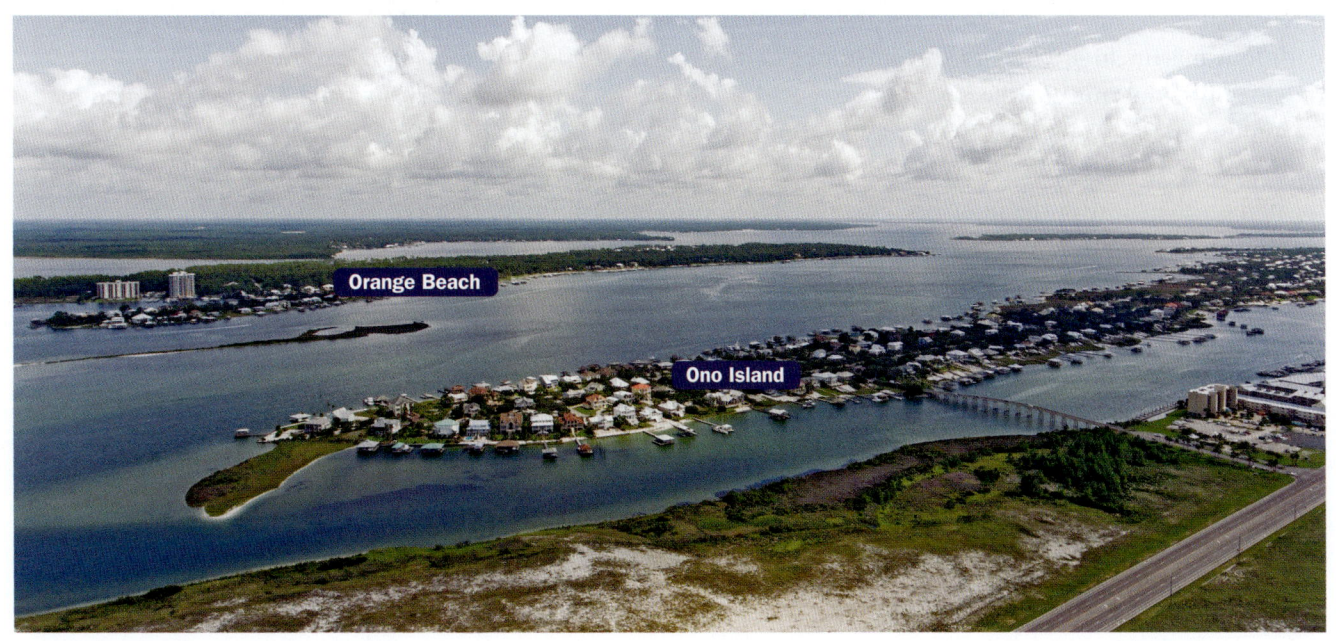

SOUTHERN EDITION 577

Chapter 16 — Mobile Bay Area to Bay St. Louis, MS

Gulf Shores Area, AL

GULF SHORES		Largest Vessel	VHF	Total Slips	Approach/ Dockside Depth	Floating Docks	Gas/ Diesel	Repairs/ Haulout	Min/Max Amps	Pump-Out Station
1. The Wharf Marina WiFi 158.8 mi. EHL	(251) 224-1900	150	16	210	10.0 / 10.0	F	GD		30 / 100	P
2. Homeport Marina WiFi GIWW 155.0 mi. EHL	(251) 968-4528	115	16	77	10.0 / 8.0	F	GD		30 / 100	P

WiFi Wireless Internet Access
Visit www.waterwayguide.com for current rates, fuel prices, website addresses and other up-to-the-minute information. (Information in the table is provided by the facilities.)

Scan here for more details:

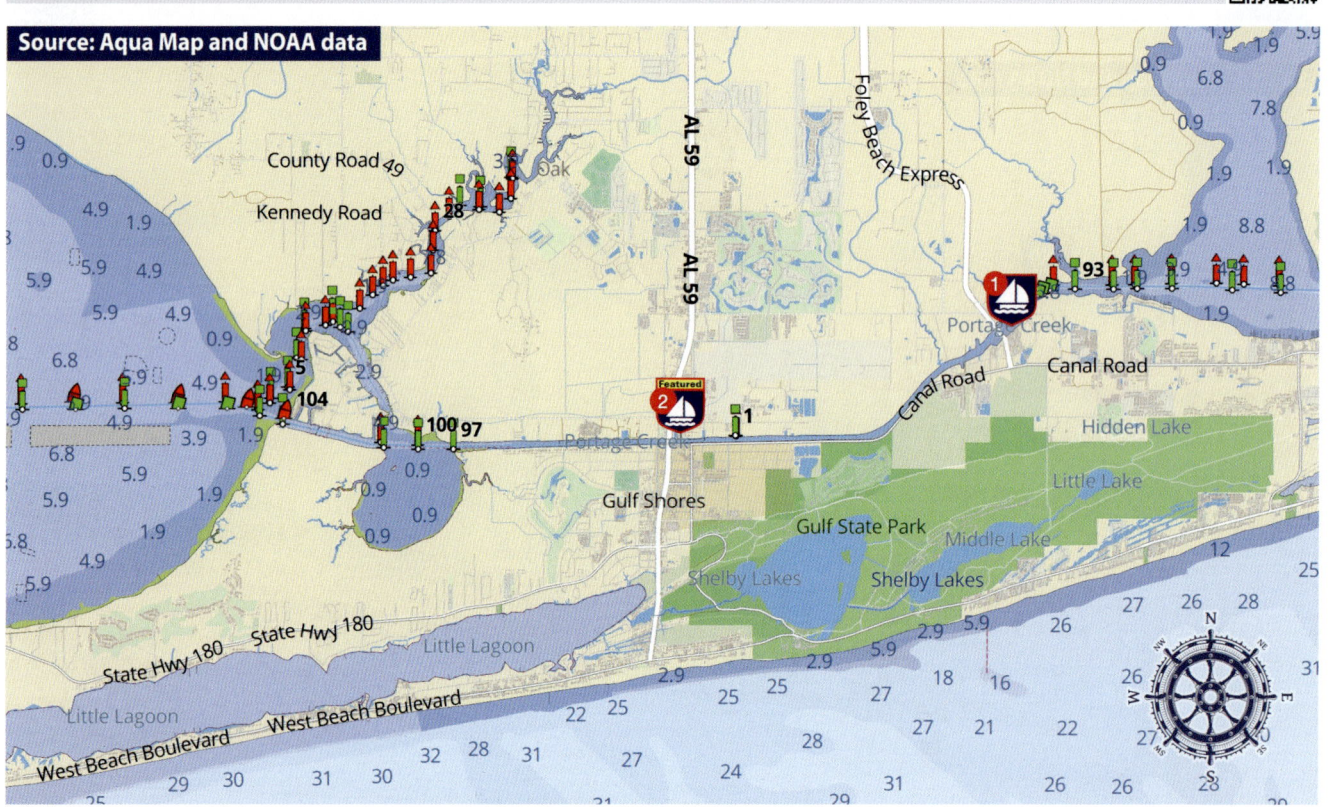

Source: Aqua Map and NOAA data

offers boat sales, dry storage, services and a boatyard with four marine lifts. There are no amenities here outside of the marine complex.

Activity increases on the GIWW as you approach Gulf Shores. The 210-slip The Wharf Marina is located on the shore at the high-rise Foley Beach Expressway Bridge at Mile 158.8 EHL. This marina offers resort amenities including shopping, golf, dining and entertainment in addition to slips on floating docks.

The full-service Saunders Yachtworks–Gulf Shores is located at GIWW Mile 155.5 EHL. They can handle most any service, repair or refit. Call ahead for slip availability.

Homeport Marina is located at Mile 155.0 EHL, just east of the Gulf Shores Parkway (SR 59) Twin Bridges with room for transients on floating docks. They offer all the usual amenities plus the on-site LuLu's, the original restaurant of three operated by Lucy Buffett (Jimmy's sister). There is a 120-foot-long dock with a minimum of 6-foot MLW depths in front of the restaurant where you can tie up if you are stopping to eat. The daily "count-down to sunset" is not to be missed.

Fort Morgan Marina is southwest of Bon Secour Bay with dock store, dry storage, transient slips and private charters. The fun Tacky Jacks 2 is located here.

Anchorage: You can anchor just to the west of Bear Point Harbor at Bear Point Marina Cove and dinghy in. This is open and exposed to the north and west as well as wakes. Almost due north on the

America's Waterway Guide Since 1947 — Chapter 16

HOMEPORT MARINA

Transient Slips Available with Member Discounts:

- BoatUS Cooperating Marina
- Waterway Guide — The Cruising Authority
- marinalife
- America's Great Loop Cruisers' Association

America's Great Loop — Gulf of Mexico

VALVTECT Ethanol-Free Gasoline & Diesel

AMENITIES AVAILABLE

- 24-Hour Restrooms, Showers & Laundry
- Bellingham Marine Concrete Floating Dock System
- Cable & Wifi
- Close to Beach
- Ethanol-Free Valvtect Gasoline & Valvtect Diesel
- Marine Store
- Next to Jack Edwards Airport in Gulf Shores
- Pump Out
- Safety from Storms
- Security
- Saunders Yachtworks Located 1/2 Mile to the East

Lucy Buffett's LuLu's — FUN • FOOD • MUSIC

LuLu's Restaurant on Premises
GREAT FOOD • LIVE MUSIC
BOAT DOCKAGE (Gulf Shores Location)
Gulf Shores • Destin • www.lulubuffett.com

Gulf Shores, AL ■ MM•155•ICW ■ 251-968-4528 ■ www.homeportmarina.net

---

WE ARE SAUNDERS.
COMMITTED *to the* CRAFT

251.981.3700 | *saundersyacht.com* | GULF SHORES, AL

SOUTHERN EDITION

Chapter 16: Mobile Bay Area to Bay St. Louis, MS

Gulf Shores Area, AL

BON SECOUR BAY	Largest Vessel	VHF	Total Slips	Approach/ Dockside Depth	Floating Docks	Gas/ Diesel	Repairs/ Haulout	Min/Max Amps	Pump-Out Station
1. Fort Morgan Marina GIWW 135.0 mi. EHL (251) 540-2628	70	16	70	4.0 / 4.0		GD	H		P

📶 Wireless Internet Access

Visit www.waterwayguide.com for current rates, fuel prices, website addresses and other up-to-the-minute information. (Information in the table is provided by the facilities.)

Scan here for more details:

Source: Aqua Map and NOAA data

opposite side of Arnica Bay (GIWW Mile 165 EHL) is Roberts Bayou, commonly known both to cruisers and locals as "Pirates Cove." There is a narrow entrance with private markers leading to the bayou. While the narrow entrance may seem intimidating, there is plenty of depth. There is a spot at the mouth of the bayou and the end of the entrance channel that narrows to one boat width so plan ahead. Roberts Bayou is a popular anchorage for cruisers and locals. As in any anchorage that is already or might become crowded, it is a good idea to buoy your anchor with a trip line, not only so someone will not drop their hook over your rode, but to prevent snarling and tangling in tight quarters.

Larger boats can find 8-foot MLW depths just past the sharp bend to the left at the head of Ingram Bayou in Bay La Launch (GIWW Mile 162.5 EHL). Turn right at red daybeacon "72" and then proceed straight into Ingram Bayou, right down the center of the channel. There is shoaling on either side of this excellent, all-weather anchorage but 9-foot MLW depths hold most of the way in. Once inside you will be surrounded by total greenery and quiet (except on a busy weekend) and there is usually a breeze to keep the bugs away. Keep an eye out for visiting dolphins.

There are also plenty of places to anchor in 5- to 8-foot MLW depths at Wolf Bay including in Graham Bayou and at Wolf Bay Lodge.

You can anchor up the Bon Secour River off Bon Secour Bay by red daybeacon "38" in 4 to 7 feet MLW with good holding in mud. Note that local boats may buzz by you here throwing wakes.

A better anchorage is located south of the GIWW near Edith Hammock in Bon Secour Bay. There is a cut through the spoil area at flashing green "123" to reach the anchorage. Watch your chart and take care to avoid the fish haven and submerged pilings as you head toward the water tower. Anchor in sand in 7 to 9 feet MLW. You are protected from the southwest through southeast and exposed to northerly winds. Holding is good.

Mobile Bay

Mobile Bay sits on the northern Gulf Coast, 40 miles west of Pensacola and 90 miles northeast of South Pass at the Mississippi River. It is the approach to the City of Mobile and to the Alabama and Tombigbee Rivers. The Bay has depths of 7 to 12 feet MLW outside the dredged channels.

NOTE: Mobile Bay is shallow and with its long fetch running south to north, it can build substantial waves. It will be rough in 15-knot winds and dangerous in winds at greater speeds.

The best way to cover cruising in Mobile Bay is through a literary "tale of two shores." The eastern shore is anchored by the quintessential southern City of Fairhope and the western shore by the bustling Port of Mobile.

NAVIGATION: Use NOAA Charts 11376 and 11378. Bon Secour Bay lies at the southeasterly reaches of Mobile Bay. Continuing west on the GIWW enter Bon Secour Bay from the Bon Secour River at the 17-foot flashing green "103" and red nun buoy "104."

You can cruise north into Mobile Bay by leaving the GIWW and navigating through the open waters of the Bay, or continue east and turn north when you enter the Main Ship Channel. The GIWW tracks west across lower Mobile Bay, takes a turn to northwest at flashing green "157" and crosses the Main Ship Channel at flashing red "26" on the channel (Mile 133.75 EHL).

The ship channel provides a well-defined, well-marked route to follow north. You can leave the channel almost anywhere. It is bordered by spoils but local boaters say the depth over the spoils is about 10 feet MLW.

The alternative route is to leave the GIWW at green "129" (Mile 145 EHL) on a course of 337° magnetic. Continue for 8 nm to the 30-foot flashing red "2" at Mullet Point. Continue on a course of 341° magnetic for another 4.8 nm to the 37-foot flashing red "4" at Great Point Clear. Leave the charted shoals to the east.

Chapter 16: Mobile Bay Area to Bay St. Louis, MS

> NOTE: The northern entrance into Mobile Bay marks the end of the inland river system portion of the Great Loop. The Loop trail turns east and follows the Florida Panhandle but do not overlook the intrigue of continuing westward.

Mobile Bay–Gulf Approach

The Gulf approach to the Bay is 3 miles wide and is bordered by Mobile Point on the east and Pelican Point on the west. Stay in the dredged channel to avoid shoals that extend 4 miles south (into the Gulf) on both sides. The Port of Mobile is 25 miles to the north. Expect heavy traffic.

High-rise condominiums are prominent along the shoreline and can be seen on approach. West of the entrance is a chain of low, wooded islands for 50 nm. The black conical tower that is Sand Island Light is the most prominent landmark near the entrance at 131 feet. On the east side of the entrance the pentagon-shaped walls of Fort Morgan at Mobile Point are clearly visible. To the west of the entrance a spherical, elevated tank 2 miles west of Fort Gains on the east end of Dauphin Island at Pelican Point is clearly visible.

Mobile Bay–Eastern Shore

The allure of the east is its attractive, character-filled communities including beautiful Fairhope. If you are continuing north, turn to starboard on a course of 142° magnetic. The Town of Fairhope is 4 miles farther on this course then 1 mile to the east.

To reach the marinas at Fly Creek continue a course of 142° magnetic for 1 mile then turn east for 1 mile. If you want to continue a northerly trek in the Bay, it is best to go west to the ship channel.

Dockage: Stay to the south side of channel as you enter Fly Creek to avoid the 3-foot shoal. Fairport Yacht Club is the first facility to starboard (south). They welcome visiting boats from reciprocal clubs to their facility. The municipal Fairhope Docks Marina is on the north side of the channel with covered and open slips and the usual amenities. Approach depths are 8 feet MLW. The family-owned and -operated Fly Creek Marina is located

Downtown Mobile

further up the creek. This marina–like many others on the eastern shore–is heavily populated by sailboats. It is a tidy, clean marina in a lovely wooded area and the only dry storage facility on the eastern shore.

Port of Mobile

The City of Mobile has a busy commercial waterfront. There is heavy barge traffic from the Tennessee-Tombigbee Waterway, on the northern end of Mobile Bay near the mouth of the Mobile River. There is also a cruise ship terminal, which adds to waterfront traffic.

Mobile is a cultural center with numerous festivals, museums and historical sites. One attraction worth mentioning is GulfQuest National Maritime Museum of the Gulf of Mexico, which is dedicated to the rich traditions, history and culture of the Gulf. The museum has 90 interactive exhibits, simulators and theaters covering an array of maritime topics including early settlements and trade routes, marine archeology and shipwrecks, marine life, weather and hurricanes, marine and coastal environments, maritime commerce and shipbuilding, ship navigation and communication, offshore oil/gas platforms and much more. The museum is located at 155 S. Water St. (251-436-8901).

Dockage: The Mobile Convention Center wall is free for 12 hours. A floating dock just above the wall belongs to the city as well. This is a fantastic stop because of the close proximity to the old town.

Anchorage: There are several anchorages north of Mobile on the Mobile River. These are covered in more detail in the Great Lakes Vol. 2 edition of *Waterway Guide*.

> NOTE: We do not recommend that you or your pet swim here. There seem to be more and more alligators every year, and there's no need to feed the wildlife!

Mobile Bay–Western Shore

On the western shore of Mobile Bay boaters will find work-a-day marinas with good basic services but few amenities. Some, however, are within convenient reach to downtown Mobile, either by rental car or marina courtesy car.

NAVIGATION: Use NOAA Chart 11376. All cruising boats visiting the western shore will want to move north in the large ship channel. Boats heading west across Bon Secour Bay can leave the GIWW at the 17-foot flashing green "147." Set a course of 301° magnetic for 5.5 nm to a cut through the spoil into the ship channel. Follow the same course through the cut for 1.2 nm and enter the ship channel at the 17-foot flashing red "34."

Boats coming from the west through Pass Aux Heron can leave the GIWW at red nun "10" and green can "9" after passing under the **Dauphin Island Causeway Bridge**. Set a course of 61° magnetic for 5 miles to the cut entering the ship channel. Follow the same course for 1.5 miles and enter the ship channel at the 17-foot flashing green "33."

Moving north in the ship channel for 6.5 nm you will come to a cut in the spoil just before 17-foot flashing green "49." To access the facilities on the western shore at Fowl River, exit the ship channel before green "49" on a course of 275° magnetic for 3.5 nm to the channel entry at green daybeacon "1" and flashing red "2."

Farther north (2.2 nm) in the ship channel you will pass the Hollingers Island and Theodore Ship Channel, opposite the 17-foot flashing red "54." The channel leads to an industrial complex with no facilities for cruising boats.

Continuing north past the 17-foot flashing green "63" and flashing red "64" for 4 nm where you will intersect the channel to Dog River to the west. Enter the channel between green daybeacon "1" and red daybeacon "2." Stay in the channel on a heading of about 307° magnetic for 2 nm to green daybeacon "5." Channel depths are charted at 6.5 feet at MLW. Turn west at green "5" and follow the channel for 1.7 nm to the **Dog River (SR 163) Bridge** (73-foot fixed vertical clearance). Several marinas are located just past the bridge.

Dockage: Working clockwise around Mobile Bay from the southwest corner, the channel into Fowl River is well marked. Fowl River Marina is located 0.5 miles upriver on the north side at red daybeacon "16," before the 45-foot fixed vertical clearance **East Fowl River (SR 193) Bridge**. The Pelican Reef seafood restaurant is on site (251-973-2670).

There is a cluster of marinas on Dog River to the north on the western shore of Mobile Bay, roughly two-thirds of the way up the ship channel from the pass entering Mobile Bay. Marinas are on each side of the river within 100 yards of the Dog River Bridge.

Beachcomber Marina is the first marina on the south side of the bridge. They have transient slips, a dry dock and a restaurant. Grand Mariner Marina & Mariner

Chapter 16: Mobile Bay Area to Bay St. Louis, MS

Goin' Ashore
FAIRHOPE, AL

There is much to intrigue and delight visiting cruisers to Mobile Bay's eastern shore. The people who began the initial experimental community were a freethinking, intellectual group. Fairhope continues to attract artists, philosophers, musicians, and writers. The town boasts independent bookstores and hardware stores in the thriving downtown district. Unique art galleries, shops and restaurants abound. An Art Walk featuring art exhibits and musical entertainment is held the first Friday of every month in downtown Fairhope. Between 20 and 30 venues are open between 6:00 p.m. and 8:00 p.m. for the Art Walk.

This is a great place to embark on the scenic Eastern Shore Trail, a bike trail that stretches for over 30 miles along Mobile Bay. Or check out Weeks Bay Reserve with hiking trails, kayaking tours and educational programs. (Transportation required.)

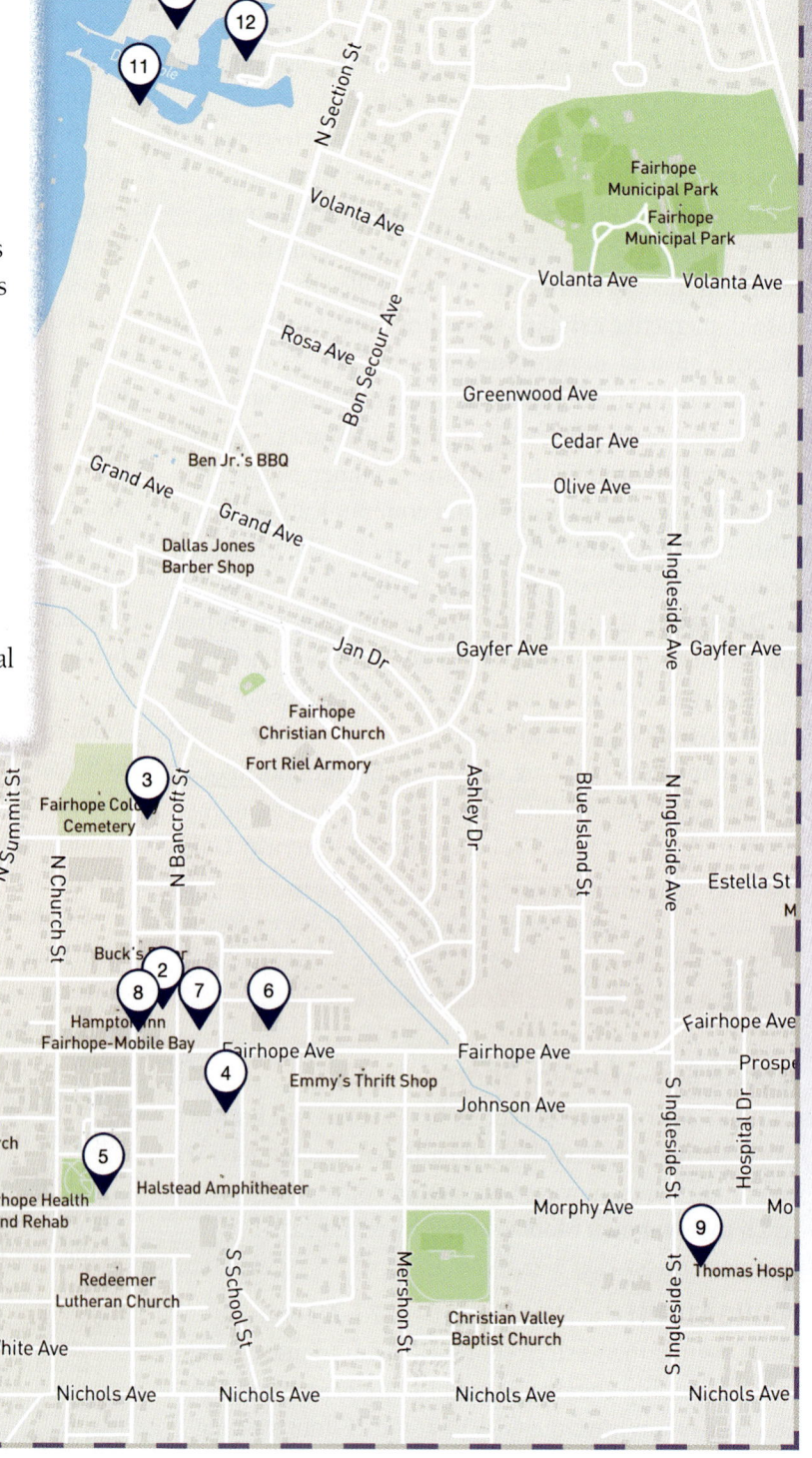

584 WATERWAY GUIDE 2024 www.waterwayguide.com

America's Waterway Guide Since 1947 — Chapter 16

ATTRACTIONS

1. **Fairhope Municipal Pier**
   Well-known fishing pier offering scenic views, lots of pelicans and a seafood restaurant at 1 N. Beach Rd.

2. **Fairhope Museum of History**
   Highlights the unique history of Fairhope in a Spanish Mission Revival structure originally built in 1928 (24 N. Section St., 251-929-1471).

3. **Eastern Shore Art Center**
   Center that showcases the work of local artists. Free to the public. Open 10:00 to 2:00 most days at 401 Oak Ave. (251-928-2228).

4. **Marietta Johnson Museum**
   Tells the story of Marietta Johnson who founded Fairhope's first school, the School for Organic Education, in 1907. Visionary educator and author boasted "no tests, no grades, no shoes" at 10 S. School St. (251-990-8601).

SERVICES

5. **Colony Animal Clinic**
   359 Morphy Ave. (251-928-7728)

6. **Fairhope Post Office**
   509 Fairhope Ave. (251-990-3623)

7. **Fairhope Public Library**
   501 Fairhope Ave. (251-928-7483)

8. **Fairhope Welcome Center**
   20 N. Section St. (251-928-5095)

9. **Thomas Hospital**
   750 Morphy Ave. (251-928-2375)

MARINAS

10. **Fairhope Docks Marina**
    848 Sea Cliff Dr. (251-929-0365)

11. **Fairhope Yacht Club**
    101 Volanta Ave. (252-928-3276)

12. **Fly Creek Marina**
    831 N. Section St. (251-928-4868)

SOUTHERN EDITION

Chapter 16 — Mobile Bay Area to Bay St. Louis, MS

Mobile Bay, AL

FAIRHOPE AREA		Largest Vessel	VHF	Total Slips	Approach/Dockside Depth	Floating Docks	Gas/Diesel	Repairs/Haulout	Min/Max Amps	Pump-Out Station
1. Fairhope Yacht Club—PRIVATE	(251) 928-3276	40		134	/			H		P
2. Fairhope Docks Marina WiFi GIWW 134.0 mi. EHL	(251) 929-0365	90	79	81	8.0 / 6.0		GD		30 / 50	P
3. Fly Creek Marina WiFi	(251) 928-4868	100	16	50	9.0 / 5.5				30 / 50	P

WiFi Wireless Internet Access
Visit www.waterwayguide.com for current rates, fuel prices, website addresses and other up-to-the-minute information.
(Information in the table is provided by the facilities.)

Scan here for more details:

Source: Aqua Map and NOAA data

Restaurant is the second facility south of the bridge when heading upriver. This full-service marina has ample dockage and a well-respected restaurant.

The full-service Turner Marine Supply Inc. is about 150 yards past the bridge on the north shore with yacht sales, slips and repairs. The full-service Dog River Marina and Boat Works Inc. is on the same side a little farther north around the curve. This is a working boatyard offering a comprehensive range of services. The complex hosts all manner of services and a West Marine.

To the north is Dockside Marina Dog River in a quiet, protected harbor. This marina is usually fully booked and has a waiting list so call ahead. The inviting stretch of beach and easy access for larger boats in a family-friendly environment are the main draws.

Three miles upriver from the bridge is River Yacht Basin Marina, which may have space for you. This is a quiet marina with mostly covered docks.

Anchorage: There is room to anchor up the East Fowl River in 6 to 8 feet MLW if you can fit under the 45-foot fixed East Fowl River (SR 193) Bridge. Dog River offers a good anchorage near River Yacht Basin Marina. Anchor in 6 to 7 feet MLW according to wind direction.

■ TO BAY ST. LOUIS

Navigation Notes

West of Mobile Bay the GIWW opens up to the Mississippi Sound, a bay-like expanse of water between the mainland and a string of barrier islands known as the Gulf Islands National Seashore. This open stretch of waterway extends from east to west for 85 miles.

The width of the sound is 10 to 12 miles. This long stretch and significant width when combined with a 15-knot wind will result in considerable chop. When the winds blow over 15 knots consider staying in a safe harbor or looking for shelter if you find yourself underway in these conditions. Wait for fair weather and this can be a very enjoyable and rewarding cruising area worth exploring in detail. Sunrise over the beaches of Horn Island has been heralded as truly spectacular.

Shoreside facilities are limited. The number and quality of destinations is growing, however, due to both the popularity of the area as well as the ongoing rebuilding effort from past hurricanes. Pleasure boaters should keep in mind that traveling west from this point will increase the frequency of encounters with commercial vessels,

View Across Mobile Bay From Fairhope, AL

Chapter 16: Mobile Bay Area to Bay St. Louis, MS

Mobile Bay, AL

FOWL RIVER		Largest Vessel	VHF	Total Slips	Approach/ Dockside Depth	Floating Docks	Gas/ Diesel	Repairs/ Haulout	Min/Max Amps	Pump-Out Station
1. Fowl River Marina	(251) 973-2670	50	16	60	5.0 / 5.0	F	GD		50	P

WiFi Wireless Internet Access
Visit www.waterwayguide.com for current rates, fuel prices, website addresses and other up-to-the-minute information. (Information in the table is provided by the facilities.)

Scan here for more details:

Source: Aqua Map and NOAA data

most often towboats. Give these vessels a wide berth, particularly in shallower waters and narrow channels. As suggested earlier it is advisable to monitor both VHF Channels 13 and 16. Additionally Automatic Identification System (AIS) is used extensively on the GIWW.

Gulf inlets (referred to in these waters as "passes") are not all trustworthy. Only the three inlets at Pascagoula, Biloxi and Gulfport provide reliable access to the Gulf of Mexico. Throughout Mississippi Sound there are constant dredging operations. Stay alert.

Dauphin Island– GIWW Mile 130 EHL

On the west side of the entrance to Mobile Bay, Dauphin Island with its long sandy spit to the west is the first of the barrier islands running from Mobile Bay to New Orleans. Of the many recreational and boating centers in the Mobile area Dauphin Island is the closest to the GIWW. The island is a pleasant and interesting stopover with a sizable marina, anchorages along the entire length of the island and excellent beaches.

On Dauphin Island, less is more. The little island is well known and much loved for being less congested than other Gulf Coast resorts. It's also noted for its breathtaking sunsets, pristine beaches, walking and biking trails, bird sanctuaries, charter fishing boats, ferry across Mobile Bay, outdoor recreation and historic sites. Truth is, Dauphin Island is awash in history.

Dauphin Island is home to Fort Gaines (251-861-3607), once a Confederate stronghold used to defend the east entrance to Mobile Bay. The fort is located at the east end of the island and is now a historic site and museum. Nearby is Dauphin Island Sea Lab, Alabama's marine

America's Waterway Guide Since 1947

Chapter 16

Mobile Bay, AL

DOG RIVER AREA		Largest Vessel	VHF	Total Slips	Approach/Dockside Depth	Floating Docks	Gas/Diesel	Repairs/Haulout	Min/Max Amps	Pump-Out Station
1. Beachcomber Marina	(251) 443-8000	65		96	9.0 / 16.0			RH	30	
2. Turner Marine Supply Inc. WiFi	(251) 476-1444	60	16	135	8.0 / 6.0			RH	30 / 50	
3. Dog River Marina and Boat Works Inc. WiFi GIWW 134.0 mi. EHL	(251) 471-5449	200	16	100	8.0 / 10.0		GD	RH	30 / 100	P
4. Grand Mariner Marina & Restaurant WiFi GIWW 134.0 mi. EHL	(251) 443-7160	100	16	75	15.0 / 12.0		GD	RH	30 / 50	
5. Dockside Marina Dog River	(251) 479-2772	70			/				30 / 50	P
6. River Yacht Basin Marina WiFi	(251) 776-4435	70		75	6.0 / 6.0				30 / 50	

WiFi Wireless Internet Access
Visit www.waterwayguide.com for current rates, fuel prices, website addresses and other up-to-the-minute information.
(Information in the table is provided by the facilities.)

Scan here for more details:

SOUTHERN EDITION 589

Chapter 16: Mobile Bay Area to Bay St. Louis, MS

education and research center (251-861-2141). The lab operates the Estuarium, an extensive public aquarium, displaying features of coastal Alabama's ecosystems: the Delta, Mobile Bay and the Gulf of Mexico.

NAVIGATION: Use NOAA Chart 11378. It is possible to enter Dauphin Island Bay via two channels. Middle Ground is the first channel for boats heading west across Mobile Bay. Middle Ground is on the east side of the island by Fort Gains at Pelican Point. (This entrance is referred to locally as "Billy Goat Hole.") Move west through the channel in the spoil areas at flashing green "25" and flashing red "26." Local knowledge suggests that depth over the spoils is about 10 feet MLW. Turn south to the well-marked channel through Billy Goat Hole. You will pass a Coast Guard Station and ferry dock just inside the entry. Depths are charted at 4.5 feet MLW. (Check the latest chart.)

> **CAUTION:** Significant post-hurricane shoaling has been reported in the vicinity of the entrance to Pelican Bay and the Pelican Bay Fish Haven. Charted depths are reportedly no longer accurate. Mariners transiting the area are advised to use extreme caution.

The second channel is Aux Heron's Channel, 1.6 miles west of the **Dauphin Island Causeway Bridge** (fixed 83-foot vertical clearance) at Mile 127.8 EHL. Entrance via this second channel is limited by the **Dauphin Island Bridge** with 25-foot fixed vertical clearance.

At red "22" in the Aux Heron's Channel leave the GIWW on a southeast course and pick up flashing green "Bayou Aloe Junction Light" marking the entrance to a channel to Bayou Aloe. Proceed on a southeast course past green daybeacon "1" followed by the 17-foot flashing red "2" and green daybeacon "3." After a slight turn to the east, the next marker should be green daybeacon "1" leading into a privately marked channel to Chugae Point and the clearly visible Dauphin Island Causeway Bridge. Depths are charted at 4.5 feet at MLW.

Dockage: The only marina here is Dauphin Island Marina, a full-service facility welcoming transients. It would be prudent to call ahead for reservations and the latest information on markers and water depths. Many charters and tours leave from here. Motels, restaurants and groceries are a short walk from the marina.

Anchorage: Dauphin Island has many fine anchorages protected from southerly winds but not from the north. Hurricane Rita broke through the middle of Dauphin Island, leaving a breach in the island. Keep this in mind when deciding where to anchor.

On the south side of the island you can find a quiet anchorage in Pelican Bay. Leave the main ship channel at green "15" and navigate past the shoals at Pelican Island, which has become more of a peninsula, then into the smaller bay/lagoon where you should find good holding. As previously noted, significant post-hurricane shoaling has been reported at the entrance to Pelican Bay and in the bay. Charted depths are reportedly no longer accurate. Proceed with caution.

Dauphin Island

America's Waterway Guide Since 1947 — Chapter 16

Mississippi Sound, MS

DAUPHIN ISLAND		Largest Vessel	VHF	Total Slips	Approach/Dockside Depth	Floating Docks	Gas/Diesel	Repairs/Haulout	Min/Max Amps	Pump-Out Station
1. Dauphin Island Marina WiFi GIWW 127.8 mi. EHL	(251) 861-2201	55	16	90	6.0 / 8.0		GD	RH	30 / 50	P

WiFi Wireless Internet Access
Visit www.waterwayguide.com for current rates, fuel prices, website addresses and other up-to-the-minute information.
(Information in the table is provided by the facilities.)

Scan here for more details:

Source: Aqua Map and NOAA data

If you need someplace close to the channel entrance on the east side of the island, you can also anchor in Billy Goat Hole. Move west through the channel in the spoil areas at flashing green "25" and flashing red "26." Local knowledge suggests that depth over the spoils is about 10 feet MLW. Turn south to the well-marked channel through Billy Goat Hole. You will pass a Coast Guard Station and ferry dock just inside the entry. Put your bow on the beach and carry an anchor to shore to make sure you stay away from service boats and the ferry.

A deeper anchorage (6 to 9 feet MLW) is Confederate Pass, also on the eastern end. This is well protected and marked and is within dinghy distance of a restaurant; however, it is usually occupied by commercial boats. Other options are Bayou Aloe with good holding in sand (very shallow) and near green daybeacon "27" to the west in 7 to 9 feet MLW.

Pass Aux Heron to Pascagoula Bay– GIWW Mile 125 EHL to 104 EHL

Pascagoula is primarily a commercial shipping port. The harbor is located about 9 miles north of Horn Island Pass and is one of the important deep water ports on the Gulf Coast. The city, which is located at the mouth of the Pascagoula River, is home to many large industries, which contribute to commercial ship traffic.

NAVIGATION: Use NOAA Charts 11367, 11372, 11373, 11374 and 11375. From Mobile Bay the GIWW passes through Pass Aux Herons Channel at Dauphin Island Causeway Bridge and then enters Mississippi Sound. When leaving the channel at Mile 124 EHL most markers are lighted and elevated, although some are up to 4 miles apart. Pay close attention to compass headings and position fixes on the long run between markers.

SOUTHERN EDITION   591

Chapter 16: Mobile Bay Area to Bay St. Louis, MS

Mississippi Sound, MS

		Largest Vessel	VHF	Total Slips	Approach/ Dockside Depth	Floating Docks	Gas/ Diesel	Repairs/ Haulout	Min/Max Amps	Pump-Out Station
PASCAGOULA										
1. Singing River Yacht Club - PRIVATE	(228) 769-1876				/ 6.0					
2. Pascagoula Inner Harbor Marina	(228) 938-6694	40		60	7.0 / 3.0				30 / 50	P
GAUTIER										
3. Mary Walker Marina WiFi GIWW 96.0 mi. EHL	(228) 497-3141	50		150	6.0 / 5.0		GD		30 / 50	P

WiFi Wireless Internet Access
Visit www.waterwayguide.com for current rates, fuel prices, website addresses and other up-to-the-minute information. (Information in the table is provided by the facilities.)

Scan here for more details:

Source: Aqua Map and NOAA data

The next 70 or more miles are a long and only partially protected passageway. Natural depths of 12 to 18 feet MLW are found throughout the sound and a channel from Mobile Bay to New Orleans is regularly dredged. Stay in the channel to GIWW Mile 118.5 EHL at 17-foot flashing red "40" and green "41." The next channel marker is 17-foot flashing green "5" at GIWW Mile 114 EHL at a distance of 4.5 miles on a course of about 264° magnetic. Chart your course to stay in or close to the GIWW channel through the rest of the sound.

It is 10.2 nm from the large ship channel at Horn Island Pass to Pascagoula. North in the Pascagoula Channel you will encounter a Y at flashing red "36." To port is the route to Pascagoula; to starboard is Bayou Casotte.

Dockage: Singing River Yacht Club is private but accepts transients (space provided) and recognizes reciprocity from other clubs. Pascagoula Inner Harbor Marina is at Lake Yazoo and has limited space. They report 3-foot MLW dockside depths so call ahead. Also off of the Pascagoula River to the north and west is the Mary Walker Marina, catering mostly to sportfishing vessels (reporting 5-foot MLW dockside depths) but welcoming to transients of all kinds. There is a restaurant next door plus more conveniences nearby.

Anchorage: It is possible to anchor in Lake Yazoo in 5 feet MLW with all-around protection. Another option is north of the **CSX Transportation Railroad Bridge** (8-foot vertical clearance, usually open) and the **US 90 Bridge** (80-foot fixed vertical clearance), where you will find 8 to 15 feet of depth on the Pascagoula River. This is easy to reach with a wide, sparsely occupied river.

Pascagoula Bay to Biloxi Bay– GIWW Mile 104 EHL to Mile 87.5 EHL

Biloxi is a city on a peninsula jutting east into Mississippi Sound. The port is accessible from the Gulf through Dog Keys Pass and Little Dog Keys Pass and from the GIWW, which passes through Mississippi Sound about 6 miles south of the city. It is an important sportfishing and resort area with a large commercial seafood industry. Keesler Air Force Base and a large veteran's hospital are at the west end of the city. The waterfront on the sound is protected by Deer Island and the harbor in Back Bay of Biloxi is landlocked.

NAVIGATION: Use NOAA Charts 11372, 11373 and 11374. Cross the Pascagoula Channel at flashing green "29" and flashing red "30." Continue west in the Mississippi Sound and the next GIWW mark will be flashing green "1" in 4.4 miles. From here, continue for 2 miles to 17-foot flashing red "2" and 17-foot flashing green "3." Turn to star-board (north) on a course of about 320° magnetic for 2.5 miles to 17-foot flashing green "5A." The GIWW makes this turn to the north to avoid the shoals at Middle Ground and will shoal slightly (8 to 12 feet MLW) until you reach flashing green "5." Continue west for 8.5 miles to Biloxi Bay Channel.

At Mile 87.5 EHL follow the Biloxi Ship Channel into Biloxi Bay and turn to port at green daybeacon "35" and red daybeacon "26." Do not drift outside the channel as the water depth is as low as 2 to 4 feet MLW on the edges with an oyster shell bottom. Deer Island is south of the channel. Heading west-southwest the channel opens up to the Biloxi waterfront and many marine facilities at red daybeacon "26."

Eastbound cruisers can return to the GIWW along the Biloxi Ship Channel, as described above. Westbound cruisers can save some time by continuing along the Biloxi Channel extending east to west along the city and then changing direction to the south toward the GIWW.

From the Biloxi waterfront travel west to flashing red "12" and then turn south to green daybeacon "5" and flashing red "6." This section of the channel is 150 feet wide and 6 feet deep with a soft mud bottom. The Biloxi Ship Channel continues north into Back Bay of Biloxi. Three bridges cross the channel. The first is the **Biloxi Bay (US 90) Bridge** with a fixed 95-foot vertical clearance; the second is an abandoned bridge (now used as a fishing pier) with channel sections removed, and the third is a **CSX Transportation Railroad Bridge** with a 14-foot closed vertical clearance (opens on signal).

Dockage: The municipal Point Cadet Marina at the eastern tip of Biloxi offers transient berths. The Biloxi Schooner Pier Complex, 0.5 mile west of Point Cadet, includes some transient slips at the Maritime & Seafood Industry Museum facility. This complex is walking distance to several casinos. It is also the home base of the two historic Biloxi Schooners, replicas of turn-of-the-century oyster ships that make daily sails around Mississippi Sound.

Beyond the bridges in Back Bay is Biloxi Dock and Ice offering hi-speed fueling (120 gallons/minute), restrooms and FREE ice. They mostly cater to tugs and barges

Chapter 16: Mobile Bay Area to Bay St. Louis, MS

Mississippi Sound, MS

BILOXI		Largest Vessel	VHF	Total Slips	Approach/Dockside Depth	Floating Docks	Gas/Diesel	Repairs/Haulout	Min/Max Amps	Pump-Out Station
1. Point Cadet Marina GIWW 88.0 mi. EHL	(228) 436-9312	100	16	246	12.0 / 10.0	F	GD		30 / 50	P
2. Biloxi Schooner Pier Complex WiFi GIWW 88.0 mi. EHL	(228) 435-6320	90		27	10.0 /	F			30 / 50	
3. Biloxi Small Craft Harbor	(228) 374-6600	50	16	124	/		GD		30 / 50	P

WiFi Wireless Internet Access
Visit www.waterwayguide.com for current rates, fuel prices, website addresses and other up-to-the-minute information.
(Information in the table is provided by the facilities.)

Scan here for more details:

Source: Aqua Map and NOAA data

but welcome larger cruising vessels as well. They have expansion plans so stay tuned at Waterway Explorer (www.waterwayguide.com).

Anchorage: You can drop the hook anywhere in Back Bay. For northeast protection, anchor in deep water (at least 14 feet) at Big Lake west of the **Popps Ferry Road Bridge**. The 25-foot closed vertical clearance bridge will open on signal except from 7:30 a.m. to 9:00 a.m. and from 4:30 p.m. to 6:00 p.m., Monday through Friday (except federal holidays), when the draw need not open for the passage of vessels.

Biloxi Bay to Gulfport–GIWW Mile 87.5 to Mile 69 EHL

Gulfport is one of Mississippi's most successful commercial ports and a major center for tourism. For the cruising boater Gulfport features casinos, restaurants, museums and the ferry to Ship Island, all near the marinas.

NAVIGATION: NOAA Chart 11372. Cross the Biloxi Bay Channel in Mississippi Sound south of green daybeacon "1" and flashing red "2." Set a course to the west for 15 miles to Gulfport Sound Channel. The first marker you will see is the flashing red Ship Island Light ("2") in 5.5 miles.

Continue west 5.5 miles to flashing red "4" then 4 miles to the well-marked Gulfport Sound Channel. Pass between flashing green "43" and flashing red "44" and then travel along Gulfport Shipping Channel to flashing red "62." From here follow the channel markers. There is only one tidal cycle per day here with a very small tidal range of just over 1 foot.

Dockage: The friendly Gulfport Municipal Marina is a deep-water marina that can accommodate vessels up to 140 feet. This modern facility offers easy access (no bridges to negotiate) and all the usual amenities plus security, wide fairways and full-length finger piers. They offer a 24-hour fuel dock and a beautiful white sand beach right on the Gulf. Casinos and downtown restaurants are within walking distance.

Long Beach Harbor, about 3 miles to the west of Gulfport, has suffered substantial hurricane damage and remained closed in 2023 to all but trailered vessels. (The fuel docks remain open and operational.) Verify current status with the harbormaster prior to arrival.

Chapter 16: Mobile Bay Area to Bay St. Louis, MS

Mississippi Sound, MS

GULFPORT		Largest Vessel	VHF	Total Slips	Approach/Dockside Depth	Floating Docks	Gas/Diesel	Repairs/Haulout	Min/Max Amps	Pump-Out Station
1. Gulfport Municipal Marina-MS WiFi	(228) 867-8721	140	16	327	12.0 / 11.0		GD		30 / 100	P
2. Long Beach Harbor - Closed Until Further Notice. Fuel Dock Open WiFi	(228) 863-4795	65	16	213	8.0 / 8.0		GD		30 / 100	P

WiFi Wireless Internet Access
Visit www.waterwayguide.com for current rates, fuel prices, website addresses and other up-to-the-minute information.
(Information in the table is provided by the facilities.)

Scan here for more details:

Source: Aqua Map and NOAA data

Anchorage: Drop the hook north of Long Beach Harbor in 8 to 9 feet MLW with excellent holding in soft mud. Keep in mind that this is exposed to the south.

Gulfport to Bay St. Louis–GIWW Mile 69 to Mile 54 EHL

At the western entrance to St. Louis Bay the town of Bay St. Louis is the last of the Mississippi coastal resorts. Visiting shallow-draft vessels will find many suitable anchorages and fine fishing here.

NAVIGATION: Use NOAA Chart 11372. From GIWW Mile 54 EHL at the junction of Marianne Channel and the Grand Island Channel travel 5.2 nm north to flashing red "2" (west side of Square Handkerchief Shoal) and then 2.6 nm to the **Bay St. Louis Railroad Bridge** (13-foot closed vertical clearance), which opens on signal. This is followed by the **Bay St. Louis (US 90) Bridge** (85-foot vertical clearance).

Bayou Caddy, located along the shoreline just a few miles west of Bay St. Louis, is mostly a commercial fishing port. Carefully follow the 50-foot-wide channel (5.5-foot MLW depths) into the bayou, which itself has 6-foot MLW depths. The atmosphere is very friendly toward visiting pleasure boaters. Many interesting hours can be spent watching the commercial and private fishermen as they come and go.

Heron Bay just northwest of Lighthouse Point and north of flashing green "3" may look like a good anchorage or fishing hole but note its shallow depths. The many fishing boats you see are of the Lafitte skiff type, which draw less than 2 feet.

Dockage: There are two marked channels leading to the pleasant and well-protected Pass Christian Harbor, located about 4 miles east of Bay St. Louis. The eastern channel reportedly has better depths. Both Pass Christian Harbor and the Pass Christian East Harbor Expansion have slips. Water and pump-out service are available at each slip but the restrooms are public at these municipal marinas.

Chapter 16: Mobile Bay Area to Bay St. Louis, MS

Mississippi Sound, MS

BAY ST. LOUIS		Largest Vessel	VHF	Total Slips	Approach/Dockside Depth	Floating Docks	Gas/Diesel	Repairs/Haulout	Min/Max Amps	Pump-Out Station
1. Bay St. Louis Municipal Harbor WiFi	(228) 467-4226	110	16	214	8.0 / 8.0		GD	R	30 / 100	P
2. Bay Marina & R.V. Park WiFi 55 EHL	(228) 466-4970	50	16	75	5.0 / 5.0		GD	R	30 / 50	P
3. The Marina at Diamondhead WiFi 16	(228) 216-9059	40		53	6.0 / 6.0	F	G		50	

WiFi Wireless Internet Access
Visit www.waterwayguide.com for current rates, fuel prices, website addresses and other up-to-the-minute information.
(Information in the table is provided by the facilities.)

Scan here for more details:

Source: Aqua Map and NOAA data

Mississippi Sound, MS

PASS CHRISTIAN		Largest Vessel	VHF	Total Slips	Approach/ Dockside Depth	Floating Docks	Gas/ Diesel	Repairs/ Haulout	Min/Max Amps	Pump-Out Station
1. Pass Christian East Harbor Expansion	(228) 452-5128	70	16	164	10.0 / 10.0		GD		30 / 50	P
2. Pass Christian Harbor GIWW 60.0 mi. EHL	(228) 452-5128	100		164	10.0 / 10.0				30 / 50	P

WiFi Wireless Internet Access
Visit www.waterwayguide.com for current rates, fuel prices, website addresses and other up-to-the-minute information.
(Information in the table is provided by the facilities.)

Scan here for more details:

SOUTHERN EDITION

Chapter 16: Mobile Bay Area to Bay St. Louis, MS

Less than 5 nm to the west Bay St. Louis Municipal Harbor is conveniently located between the bridges and offers transient slips for vessels up to 110 feet with full amenities. The new Pier 5, which will house 43 new slips for larger boats, will be at the east end of the harbor. (Construction in progress at press time.) Shopping and restaurants are nearby as is beach access. The Bay Marina & R.V. Park has slips to 50 feet. Facilities include an outdoor bar overlooking the Edwards Bayou. The Marina at Diamondhead has 4 transient slips to 40 feet for a flat rate. Dockage is free to diners at the on-site Camphouse Restaurant.

■ NEXT STOP

You have reached the end of our Waterway Guide Southern edition coverage but not necessarily the end of your voyage. From here you can continue westward to New Orleans, the Louisiana low country and the windswept Texas coast all the way to Mexico. This area is detailed in our Gulf Coast edition.

Mississippi Sound

Marina/Sponsor Index

Sponsors are listed in **BOLD** and are highlighted in yellow in marina tables.

A

Abaco Beach Resort, 15

A & B Marina, 419, 420, 422

A & M Perdido Resort and Marina, 567, 568

Admirals Cove Marina, 282, 283

Adventure Marina, 560, 561

America's Great Loop Cruisers' Association (AGLCA), 11

Anchorage Resort & Yacht Club, 373, 374

Anchorage Yacht Basin, 208, 212

Anclote Harbors Marina, 517, 518

Anclote Isles Marina, 517, 518

Anclote Village Marina, 516, 517

Apalachicola Marina, Inc., 547, 548, 549

Apollo Beach Marina, 497, 498

Arlington Marina, Inc., 138

B

Bahamas Ministry of Tourism, 10

Bahia Honda State Park & Marina, 410, 412, 413

Bahia Mar Yachting Center, 307, 308, 310

Bal Harbour Yacht Club-PRIVATE, 329, 330

Banana Bay Resort & Marina, 401, 402, 404

Barber Marina, 576, 577

Battery Park Marina, 27, 547, 548, 549

Bay Marina & R.V. Park, 598, 600

Bay Pines Marina, 509, 510

Bay St. Louis Municipal Harbor, 598, 600

Bayfront Yacht Works & Marina, 479, 481

Baylen Slips Marina, 564, 566

Bayshore Landing, 353, 355, 356

Beachcomber Marina, 583, 589

Bear Point Harbor, 576, 577, 578

Belle Harbour Marina, 517, 518

Bentley Bay Marina, 337, 338

Big River Marina and Lodge, 153, 154

Bill Bird Marina at Haulover Park, 329, 330

Billfish Marina, 319

Biloxi Schooner Pier Complex, 593, 594

Biloxi Small Craft Harbor, 594

Bird Key Yacht Club, 482, 483

Black Point Park & Marina, 357

Blackfin Resort and Marina, 401, 402, 404

Blind Pass Marina, 509, 510

Blowing Rocks Marina, 280

Blue Pelican Marina, 526

Bluewater Bay Marina, 557

Boathouse Marina, 146, 148

Boca Chita Key - Biscayne National Park, 370

Boca Grande Marina, 470-472

Boca Raton Resort & Club, 88, 299, 300

Boot Key Harbor City Marina, 401-405, 409

Boynton Harbor Marina, 295

Bradenton Beach Marina, 491, 492

Bradenton Yacht Club-PRIVATE, 494, 495

Bristol Harbor, 553, 554

B's Marina & Campground, 529, 530

Buccaneer Marina, 286, 288

Bud'n Mary's Fishing Marina, 394, 395

Burdines Waterfront Marina, 401, 402, 404

C

C-10 Caloosa Marina, 266, 267

Cabbage Key Inn, 463, 464

Caladesi Island State Park Marina, 514, 515

Caloosa Cove Marina & Resort, 395, 396

Cannonsport Marina, 285, 286, 288

Cape Crossing Marina, 198, 199

Cape Haze Marina, 474, 475

Cape Marina, Port Canaveral, 200, 202

Capt. Hiram's Sebastian Marina, 216, 217, 218

Captain's Cove Marina, 551, 552

Causeway Cove Marina & RV Park, 227, 230

Cayo Costa State Park, 463, 464

Cedar Point Marina, 141

Charlotte Harbor Yacht Club, 468, 469

Chart House Marina, 512, 513

City Marina at Garrison Bight, 419, 421, 422, 425

SOUTHERN EDITION 601

Marina/Sponsor Index

Sponsors are listed in **BOLD** and are highlighted in yellow in marina tables.

City of Fort Myers Yacht Basin, 267, 268, 271

City of Tarpon Springs Municipal Marina, 517, 518

Clearwater Beach Marina, 512, 513

Clearwater Municipal Marinas (Clearwater Beach Marina), 512, 513

Clearwater Municipal Marinas (Clearwater Harbor Marina), 512, 513

Clearwater Yacht Club-PRIVATE, 512, 513, 515

Cocoa Village Marina, 204, 205, 206

Cocohatchee River Park Marina, 450, 451

Conch Harbor Marina, 419, 421, 422

Conch House Marina, 168, 169, 173

Cooley's Landing Marina, 315-318

Coquina Marina, 177, 178, 180

Coral Bay Marina, 379, 382, 383

Coral Reef Yacht Club-PRIVATE, 353, 355, 356

Coral Ridge Yacht Club-PRIVATE, 307, 309

C-Quarters Marina, 540, 541

Crandon Park Marina, 349, 351

Crow's Nest Marina & Restaurant, 478, 480

Crystal Cove Marina & RV Resort, 146, 148

D

Dania Beach Marina, 323, 324

Dauphin Island Marina, 590, 591

Davis Island Yacht Club-PRIVATE, 499, 500

Daytona Marina & Boat Works, 177, 178, 180

Delray Beach City Marina, 296, 297

Delray Harbor Club Marina, 296, 297

Deltaville, VA, 20, 21

Destin Marina, 558, 559

Dinner Key Marina, 352, 353, 355, 356

Dockside Marina & Resort, 227, 230

Dockside Marina Dog River, 587, 589

Doctors Lake Marina, 142, 143

Dog River Marina and Boat Works Inc., 587, 589

Downtown Sanford Marina, 157, 158

Dunedin Municipal Marina, 514, 515

E

Eau Gallie Yacht Basin, 208, 209, 210

Emerald Harbor Marina, 553, 554

English Landing Marina, 170, 172

Epic Marina, 343, 346, 344

Equity Lifestyle Properties, Outside Front Flap

Escape at Casey Key Resort & Marina, 478, 480

Esplanade Marina, 444, 445

Everglades Isle Marina, 439, 440

Everglades Rod & Gun Club, 439, 440

Explorer Chartbooks, 226

F

Fairhope Docks Marina, 582, 585, 586

Fairhope Yacht Club-PRIVATE, 585, 586

Faro Blanco Marina, 401, 402, 404, 407

5th Street Marina, 343, 346

Fins Marina, 216, 217

First Mate Yacht Services, 168

Fisherman's Wharf Marina of Venice, 478, 480

Fishermen's Village Marina, 468, 469

Flamingo Marina, 435, 436

Florida Yacht Club-PRIVATE, 141, 142

Fly Creek Marina, 582, 585, 586

Fort George Island Marina, 129, 130

Fort Marine, 224, 230

Fort Morgan Marina, 578, 580

Fort Pierce City Marina, 224, 227, 228, 230, 231

Fort Pierce Inlet Marina, 227, 230

Fort Walton Beach Yacht Basin, 560, 561

Four Fish Inn & Marina, 232, 235

Four Winds Marina, 466

Fowl River Marina, 583, 588

Franklin County, FL, 26, 27

Freeport Marina and Yacht Club, 556

G

Galati Yacht Basin, 492, 493

Galleon Marina, 419, 420, 422, 423

Garden Cove Marina, 390, 391

Garrison Bight Marina, 419, 421, 422

Gateway Marina, 533, 534

Gator Harbor West Marina-PRIVATE, 334

Georgetown Marina, Lodge & RV Park, 150, 151

Gilbert's Resort and Marina, 373, 374

Good Times Motel & Marina, 535, 536

Grand Mariner Marina & Restaurant, 583, 589

Grandview Palace Yacht Club-PRIVATE, 334

Greater Beaufort – Port Royal CVB, 24, 25

Green Cove Springs City Pier, 144, 145

Green Cove Springs Marina, 144, 145

Grills Riverside, 201, 205, 208

Grove Harbour Marina, 353, 355, 356

Gulfport Municipal Marina, 508, 509, 511

Gulfport Municipal Marina-MS, 595-597

H

Halifax Harbor Marina, 177, 178, 180

Halifax River Yacht Club-PRIVATE, 177, 178, 180

Hall of Fame Marina, 307, 310

Hallandale Beach City Marina, 325

Hamilton Harbor Yacht Club-PRIVATE, 448

Hammock Beach Marina, 175

Hampton, VA, 22, 23

Harbortown Marina - Canaveral, 198, 199

HarborWalk Marina, 558, 559

Harbour Isle Marina, 227, 230

Harbour Towne Marina, 323

Harbourside Marina, 511, 512

Hawks Cay Resort Marina, 403, 407, 408

Herbert Hoover Marina at Homestead Bayfront Park, 357

Heritage Boat Yard & Marina, 224, 228, 230

Hernando Beach Marina, 525, 526

Hinckley Yacht Services Stuart, 237, 240

HMY at Waterway Marina, 245, 246

Holiday Harbor Marina & Grill, 568

Hollywood Marina, 324, 325

Home Port Marina, 514, 515

Homeport Marina, 578, 579

Hontoon Island State Park, 155, 156

Hontoon Landing Resort & Marina, 155, 156

Huckins Yacht Corp., 139, 141

Hurricane Cove Marina & Boatyard, 343, 346

Hutchinson Island Marriott Beach Resort & Marina, 233, 235, 237

I

Indian Springs Marina, 511, 512

Indiantown Marina, 252-254, 256

Isla Del Sol Yacht & Country Club-PRIVATE, 507, 508

IslaMarina, 380, 382

Islamorada Yacht Basin, 379, 383, 384

Island Cove Marina, 565, 566

Island Time Marina, 203

J

Jensen Beach Mooring Field, 232, 235

Jensen's Twin Palm Cottages and Marina, 461, 462

JIB Yacht Club Marina, 280, 281

John Pennekamp Coral Reef State Park, 390, 391, 392

John's Pass Marina, 509, 510

Julington Creek Pier 3 Marina, 142, 143

Jupiter Yacht Club & Marina-PRIVATE, 282, 283

K

Kennedy Point Yacht Club & Marina, 196, 197

Key Biscayne Yacht Club-PRIVATE, 349, 351

Key Colony Beach Marina, 403, 406

Key Largo Harbor Marina, 391, 393

Key West Bight Marina, 419, 421, 422, 425

Key West Yacht Club-PRIVATE, 419, 421, 422

Keys Fisheries Marina, 402, 404

Keystone Point Marina, 329, 330

Marina/Sponsor Index

Sponsors are listed in **BOLD** and are highlighted in yellow in marina tables.

L

La Siesta Resort & Marina, 394, 395

LaBelle City Dock, 263, 265

Laishley Park Municipal Marina, 468, 469

Lake Park Harbor Marina, 286, 287

Lamb's Yacht Center, 141

Lauderdale Marina/15th Street Fisheries, 310, 311

Lauderdale Yacht Club-PRIVATE, 310, 311

Legacy Harbour Marina, 268, 269, 271

Lighthouse Marina, 553, 555

Lighthouse Point Yacht Club, 302, 303

Little Harbor Marinas, 496, 498

Loblolly Marina, 277-279

Loggerhead Marina - Aventura Marina, 328, 329

Loggerhead Marina - Cortez Village Marina, 491, 492

Loggerhead Marina - Daytona Beach Marina, 177, 178, 180

Loggerhead Marina - Fish-Tale Marina, 452, 454

Loggerhead Marina - Hollywood Marina, 325

Loggerhead Marina - Inlet Harbor Marina, 182, 184

Loggerhead Marina - Jupiter Marina, 282, 283

Loggerhead Marina - Lantana Marina, 293, 294

Loggerhead Marina - Marker 1, 514, 515

Loggerhead Marina - Palm Beach Gardens, 282, 283

Loggerhead Marina - Palm Harbour Marina, 474, 475

Loggerhead Marina - Riverwatch Marina, 245, 246

Loggerhead Marina - Riviera Beach Marina, 286, 287

Loggerhead Marina - South Lantana, 293, 294

Loggerhead Marina - St. Petersburg Marina, 505, 506

Loggerhead Marina - Vero Beach Marina, 218, 219

Long Beach Harbor, 595, 596, 597

Longboat Key Club Moorings, 483, 486

M

MacRae's of Homosassa, 526, 527

Madeira Beach Moorings Yacht Harbor & Resort, 509, 510

Madeira Beach Municipal Marina, 509, 510

Manatee Marina, 237, 238, 240

Mandarin Holiday Marina, 142, 143

Mangrove Marina, 376, 380

Marathon Boat Yard, 401, 402, 404

Marco Island Marina, 445, 446

Marina at Naples Bay Resort, 449

Marina Bay Yachting Center, 318, 319

Marina Boathouse of Fort Lauderdale, 310, 311

Marina Del Mar Resort and Marina, 391, 393

Marina Jack Yacht Basin, 482-484

Marina Mile Yachting Center, 318, 319

Marina Palms Yacht Club, 328, 329

Marinatown Yacht Harbour, 267, 268

Marine Stadium Marina, 349, 350

Marineland Marina, 174, 175

Mariner Cay Marina, 236, 237, 240

Marjorie Park Yacht Basin, 499, 500

Marker 24 Marina, 203

Marker 8 Hotel & Marina, 168, 169

Marlin Bay Resort & Marina, 401, 402, 404, 405

Marriott Tampa Water Street Hotel & Marina, 499, 501

Marsh Harbor Marina of Shell Point, 538, 539

Mary Walker Marina, 592, 593

Matanzas Inn Bayside Resort and Marina, 453, 454

Matheson Hammock Marina, 356, 357

Maximo Marina (IGY), 508

Melbourne Harbor Marina, 212, 213, 214

Meridian Marina & Yacht Club, 245, 246

Miamarina at Bayside, 338, 341

Miami Beach Marina, 334, 337-339

Miami Beach Resort & Spa, 335, 336

Miami Yacht Club-PRIVATE, 338, 341

Moore Haven City Docks, 261, 262

Morningstar Marinas Mayport, 129, 130

Moss Marina, 453, 454

MS Dockside Marina & Boatyard, 540, 541

Multihull Company, 16

Murrelle Marine, 293, 294

N

Naples Boat Club Marina, 449

Naples City Dock, 449

Naples Sailing & Yacht Club-PRIVATE, 449

Naples Yacht Club-PRIVATE, 448, 449

Nettles Island Marina, 231, 235

New River Downtown Docks, 315-318

New Smyrna Beach City Marina, 185, 186, 188

New Smyrna Marina dba The Fishing Store, 185

Night Swan Bed & Breakfast, 185, 186, 188

Norseman Shipbuilding Corp., 343, 346

North Causeway Marine, 185, 188

O

Oasis Boatyard & Marina, 170, 172

Oasis Marinas at Fernandina Harbor, 121, 122, 124, 125

Oasis Marinas at Westshore Yacht Club, 500, 501

Ocean Club Marina at Port Canaveral, 200

Oceans Edge Key West Resort & Marina, 414, 415

Old Bridge Marina, 267, 268

Olde Fish House Marina, 466

Onancock, VA, 18, 19

Opal Key Resort and Marina, 420, 422

Orange Beach Marina, 570-572

Owl Creek Boat Works, 267

Ozona Fish Camp, 514, 515

P

Palafox Pier Yacht Harbor, 564, 566

Palm Beach Yacht Center, 295

Palm Beach Yacht Club & Marina-PRIVATE, 291

Palm Cay Marina, Inside Front Flap

Palm Coast Marina, 174, 175

Palm Cove Marina, 160, 161, 162

Palm Harbor Marina - Pensacola, 565, 566

Palm Harbor Marina, 291, 292, 566

Pancho's Marina and Fuel Dock, 402, 404

Pasadena Marina, 508, 509

Pasadena Yacht & Country Club-PRIVATE, 508, 509

Pascagoula Inner Harbor Marina, 592, 593

Pass Christian East Harbor Expansion, 597, 599

Pass Christian Harbor, 597, 599

Pelican Bend Restaurant & Marina, 444, 445

Pelican Harbor Marina, 334

Pelican Isle Yacht Club-PRIVATE, 450, 451

Pelican Pier Marina, 445

Pelican Yacht Club, 227, 230

Pelican's Perch Marina & Boatyard, 565, 566

Pensacola Beach Marina, 563, 565

Pensacola Shipyard Marina & Boatyard, 565, 566

Pensacola Yacht Club-PRIVATE, 565, 566

Perdido Key Oyster Bar Restaurant & Marina, 567, 568

Pete's Pier Inc., 528, 529

Pier Sixty-Six Marina, 310, 311

Pier Sixty-Six South, 310, 311

Pilot House Marina & Restaurant, 391, 393

Pink Shell Beach Resort and Marina, 453, 454

Pirates Cove Marina & Restaurant, 576, 577

Pirates Cove Marina, 553, 555, 576

Pirate's Cove Resort & Marina, 236, 237, 240

Plantation Yacht Harbor Marina, 380-382

Playboy Marine Center, 324

Point Cadet Marina, 593, 594

Point South Marina Bay Point, 553, 555

Point South Port St. Joe Marina, 551, 552

Port 32 Fort Lauderdale, 318, 319

PORT 32 Jacksonville, 141

Port 32 Lighthouse Point, 302, 303

Port 32 Palm Beach Gardens, 283, 284

Port 32 Tampa, 500, 501

Marina/Sponsor Index

Sponsors are listed in **BOLD** and are highlighted in yellow in marina tables.

Port 32 Tierra Verde, 506, 507
Port Canaveral Yacht Club-PRIVATE, 200
Port Consolidated - Fernandina Beach, 121, 124
Port LaBelle Marina, 263, 265
Port of the Islands Marina, 441
Port Tarpon Marina, 517, 518
Postcard Inn Marina at Holiday Isle, 394, 395

Q

Quality Inn & Suites Riverfront, 146, 148

R

Ramada by Wyndham Sarasota, 487
Reel Surprise Marina, 571, 572
Reynolds Park Yacht Center, 144, 145
Rickenbacker Marina Inc., 349, 350
River Cove Marina, 346, 348
River Forest Yachting Center - LaBelle, 255, 263, 264
River Forest Yachting Center - Stuart, 254, 255, 264
River House Marina, 261, 262
River Yacht Basin Marina, 587, 589
Rivers Edge Marina, 170, 172
Riverside Marina & Cottages, 529, 530
Riverside Marina at Marco Island Yacht Club, 445, 446
Riviera Beach City Marina, 286-288
Riviera Dunes Marina, 495
RMK Merrill-Stevens, 343, 346
Roland and Mary Ann Martins Marina & Resort, 260, 261
Rose Marina, 445, 446
Royal Palm Marina, 475, 476
Royal Shell Port Sanibel Marina, 459, 460
Royale Palm Yacht Basin, 323, 324

S

Sabine Marina, 563, 565
Safe Harbor Burnt Store, 467
Safe Harbor Calusa Island, 442, 443
Safe Harbor Cape Harbour, 272, 274
Safe Harbor Harborage Yacht Club, 245, 246
Safe Harbor Harbortown, 225, 228, 230
Safe Harbor Islamorada, 382, 383
Safe Harbor Lauderdale Marine Center, 318, 319
Safe Harbor Marathon, 401, 402, 404
Safe Harbor New Port Cove, 286, 288
Safe Harbor North Palm Beach, 284, 285
Safe Harbor Old Port Cove, 283, 284, 285
Safe Harbor Pier 77, 492, 493
Safe Harbor Pineland, 465, 466
Safe Harbor Regatta Pointe, 495
Safe Harbor Rybovich, 291
Safe Harbor Siesta Key, 479, 481
Safe Harbor Sportsman, 571, 572
Sailfish Marina of Stuart, 236, 240, 241
Sailfish Marina Resort, 286, 288
Salty Sam's Marina, 453, 454
Sandestin's Baytowne Marina, 556, 557
Sandpiper Bay Marina, 245, 246
Sands Harbor Resort & Marina, 303
Sanford Boat Works & Marina, Inc., 157, 158
Sanibel Harbour Yacht Club-PRIVATE, 459, 460
Sanibel Marina, 458, 459, 460
Santa Rosa Yacht & Boat Club, 563, 565
Sara Bay Marina, 487
Sarasota Sailing Squadron, 482, 483
Sarasota Yacht Club, 470, 482, 483
Saunders Yachtworks, 578, 579
Scipio Creek Marina, 547, 548, 549
Sea Hag Marina, 535, 536
Sea Love Boat Works Inc., 182, 184
Seafarer's Marina, 135, 138
Seafood Shack Marina, Bar & Grill, 491, 492
Seahaven Superyacht Marina, 323, 324
Sebastian River Marina & Boatyard, 216, 217
Sebastian Saltwater Marina Restaurant, 216, 217
Seven Seas Cruising Association (SSCA), 15

Seven Seas Marina & Boatyard, 182, 183

17th Street Yacht Basin at the Hilton Marina Hotel, 310, 311

Seville Harbour Marina, 564, 566

Shell Point Marina, 496, 498

Shelter Cove Marina, 9

Shields Marina, 536, 537

Singing River Yacht Club - PRIVATE, 592, 593

Skipjack Resort Suites and Marina, 403, 404

Smyrna Yacht Club-PRIVATE, 185, 186, 188

Snook Bight Marina, 452, 454

Snook Inn, 444, 445

Sombrero Marina Dockside, 401, 403, 404

South Pointe Yacht Club and Marina-PRIVATE, 448

South Seas Marina, 461

Soverel Harbour Marina, 283, 284

Spongeorama, 517, 518

St. Andrews Marina, 553, 554

St. Augustine Marine Center, 171

St. Augustine Municipal Marina, 166, 168, 169, 172

St. Charles Yacht Club, 272, 273

St. Johns Boat Company, 130

St. Johns Marina North, 154, 155

St. Johns Marina South, 154, 155

St. Lucie South Campground & Marina, 253, 254

St. Marks Yacht Club-PRIVATE, 537

St. Petersburg Municipal Marina, 501, 503, 504, 505

St. Petersburg Yacht Club-PRIVATE, 501, 503-505

Steinhatchee Marina at Deadman Bay, 535, 536

Steinhatchee River Inn and Marina, 536

Stock Island Yacht Club and Marina, 414, 415

Stuart Corinthian Yacht Club-PRIVATE, 237, 238, 240

Sun Dance Marine Jensen Beach/Stuart, 232, 235

Sunrise Harbor Marina, 307, 309

Sunrise Marina, 200, 201

Sunset Bay Marina & Anchorage, 242, 245, 246, 247

Sunset Harbour Yacht Club-PRIVATE, 337, 338

Sunset Marina Key West, 421, 422

Suntex Marinas, Inside Back Cover and Flap

Sweetwater Landing Marina, 266, 267

T

Tampa Convention Center Transient Marina, 499, 500

Tarpon Landing Marina, 517, 518

Tarpon Point Marina, 272-274

Tarpon Springs Yacht Club-PRIVATE, 517, 518

Tavernier Creek Marina, 376, 380

Telemar Bay Marina, 208, 212

The Cove Waterfront Restaurant & Tiki Bar and Marina, 299, 300

The Dock on the Bay, 486, 487

The Gasparilla Inn & Club, 470, 471

The Glades Marina, 263, 264

The Harborage at Waterview Marinas, 504, 505

The Marina at Diamondhead, 598, 600

The Marina at Edison Ford, 268, 269

The Marina at Factory Bay, 444, 445

The Moorings of Carrabelle, 541, 542

The Pass-A-Grille Marina, 506, 507

The Perry Hotel and Marina, 414-416

The Seagate Yacht Club, 296, 297

The Suwannee Marina, 533, 534

The Tarpon Club Marina, 444, 445

The Wharf Marina, 578

Tierra Verde Marina, 505, 506

Tiger Point Marina, 121, 124

Titusville Marina, 193, 194, 196, 197

Town of Palm Beach Marina, 291, 292

Transmission Marine Inc., 320

Treasure Island Marina, 553, 555

Tropic Isles Marina, 494, 495

Trout Creek Marina, 144, 145

Turner Marine Supply Inc., 587, 589

Turtle Cove Marina, 517, 518

'Tween Waters Island Resort & Spa, 461, 462

Twin Dolphin Marina, 495

Twin Rivers Marina, 528, 529

Two Georges Marina, 560, 561

Marina/Sponsor Index

Sponsors are listed in **BOLD** and are highlighted in yellow in marina tables.

U

Uncle Henry's Marina, 470, 471

V

Venetian Marina & Yacht Club, 338, 341

Venice Yacht Club, 478, 480

Vero Beach City Marina, 219, 220, 222

Vice City Marina, 343, 344, 346

Vinoy Resort Marina, 501, 503, 504

W

W.P. Franklin Campground-Boat-In Docks, 265, 266

Walker's Cay Development, Outside Back Flap

Walker's Coon Key Marina, 442, 443

Water Street Hotel and Marina, 548, 549

Waterline Marina, 208, 209, 210, 492

Westland Marina, 193, 196

White Marlin Marina-FL, 403, 406

Williams Island Marina, 304, 327-329

Windward at Adventure Yacht Harbor, 182, 183

Windward at Alligator Point Marina, 539, 540

Windward at Amelia Island Marina, 120, 121, 124

Windward at Camachee Cove Yacht Harbor, 165, 168, 169, 171

Windward at Sadler Point Marina, 140, 141

Windward at Sebastian Inlet Marina, 217

Windward at St. Augustine Shipyard, 170, 172

Windward at Stump Pass Marina, 473, 475

Windward Marina Group, 3

Windward Jax Beach Marine, 161, 163

World Wide Sportsman / Bayside Marina, 382, 383, 384

Y

Yacht Harbor Marina, 565, 566, 382

Yacht Haven Grande Miami, 338, 341

Yacht Haven Marina, 403, 404

Yacht Haven Park & Marina, 319

Yankeetown Marina, 529, 530

Z

Zeke's Landing Marina, 571, 572

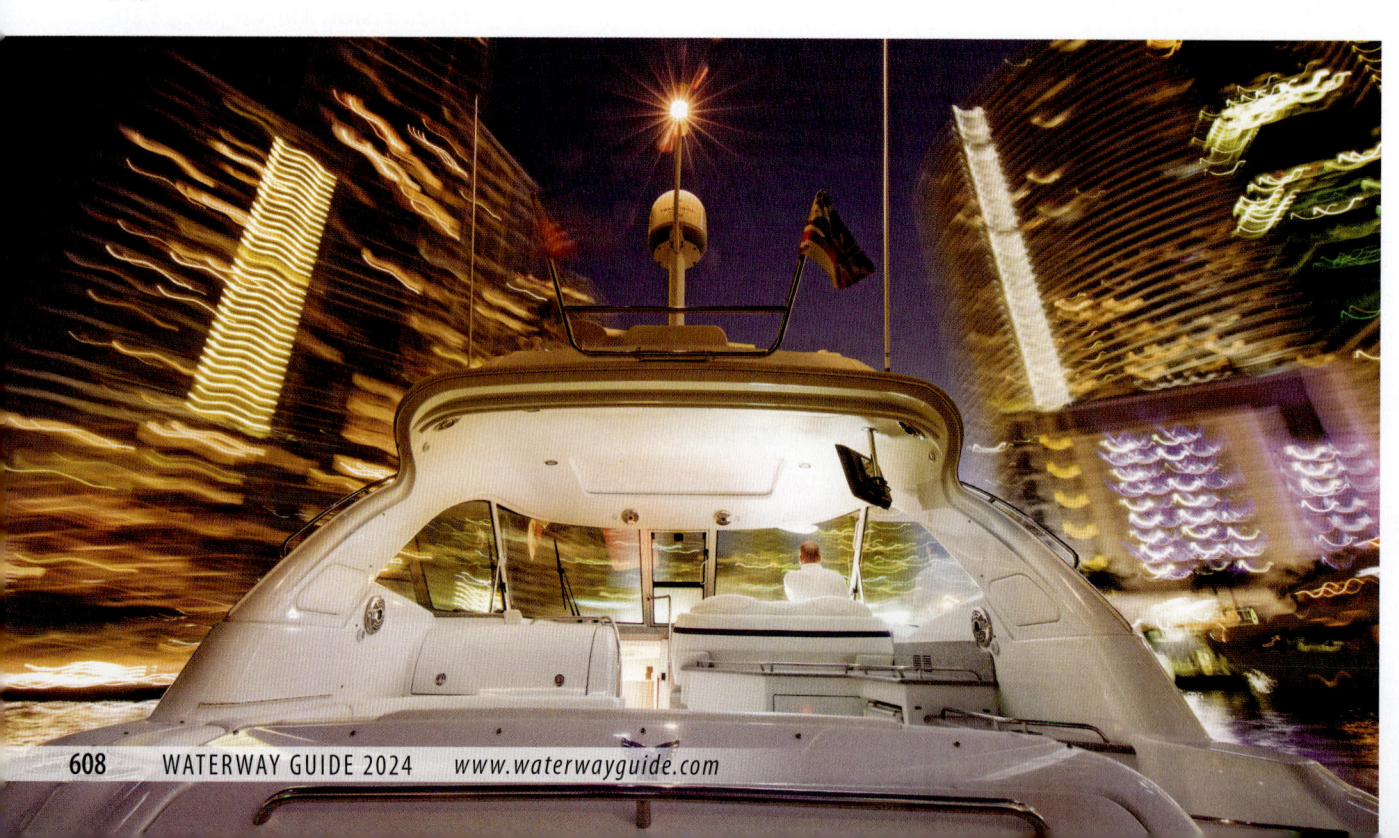

Subject Index

Most relevant pages are listed in **BOLD**

A

Alligator Harbor, 539
Amelia Island, 120-126
Anclote Key, 507, **515-516**, **518**, 523-525, 530
Angelfish Creek, 366, 372, **388-390**, 392, 428-429
Anna Maria Island, 490-493
Apalachicola, 540, 544, **545-549**, 550
Apalachicola River, 549-550
Apollo Beach, 496-498

B

Bahia Honda, 397, **409-411**, 412-413, 429-430
Bakers Haulover (North Miami Beach) Inlet, 326-329, 332
Banana River, 190, **197-199**, 201, 203, 205, **209**, **212**
Barnes Sound, 372-373, 428
Bay St. Louis, 587, 597-600
Bayou Chico, 565-566
Big Carlos Pass, 450-451, 453
Big Lagoon, 566-567, 576
Biloxi Bay, 593-595
Biscayne National Park, 332, 348, 357, 368-370
Boca Chita Key, 369-371
Boca Ciega Bay, 498, 501, **505-507**, 509, 511, 513
Boca Grande, 458, 460, 462, 464, 467, 469, **470-471**
Boca Grande Pass, 460, 462, 464, 469-470
Boca Raton, 295-296, **297**, **299-300**, 301
Bon Secour Bay, 576, 578, **580-581**, 583
Boot Key, 368, 385-387, 397, **399-409**, 412, 429-430
Boynton Beach, 293-295
Boynton Inlet, 294, 296
Bradenton, 490-492, 494-496

C

Cabbage Key, 462-464
Caladesi Island State Park, 515-516,
Caloosahatchee Canal, 259, 261-262, 263-264
Caloosahatchee River, 250-251, **265-269**, 433, 458
Canaveral Barge Canal, 184, 193, **197-199**, 209, 212
Cape Canaveral Lock, 197-201, 209
Cape Coral, 250, 265, 267, **269**, **272-274**, 433, 457
Cape Florida, 341-342, 348, 350-351, 366, **387-389**
Cape Sable, 433-437
Card Sound, 366, 369, 372, 428
Carrabelle, 457, 515-516, 518, 523-525, 530, 532, **540-542**, 544-545, 549
Cayo Costa, 250, 263, 433, 458, 462, **463-465**, 470
Cedar Key, 515, 523-526, **530-531**, 536
Channel Five, 366, 369, **384**, 385, 387-388, **393-397**, 429, 434
Charlotte Harbor, **458-469**, 470
Choctawhatchee Bay, **555-538**, 559-560
Clearwater, 488, 507, 511, **512-515**, 524-525
Clewiston, 250, 252, 254, 257-259, **260-261**
Cocoa Beach, 199, 201, 203, 212
Cocoa Village, 204-208
Coconut Grove, 330, 348, **352-356**, 387

Coral Gables, 330, 356-357
Cowpens Cut, 376, 380-381
Crab Island, 559-560
Cross-Florida Canal, 151
Crossroads, The, 224, 231, **234**, 236, 277
Crystal River, 523-525, **526-529**, 530-533, 535

D

Dames Point, 127, 134-135
Dania Cut-Off Canal, 306, 318, 320, **321**, **323-324**
Dauphin Island, 582, 583, 587, 588, 590-591
Daytona Beach, 160, 174, 176, **177-181**
Delray Beach, 296-297
Destin, 544, 558-559
Doctors Lake, 142-143
Dog Island, 539, 542
Dry Tortugas, 364, 425-427
Dunedin, 514-515

E

East Cape, 434-437
East Pass, 523, 525, 532, 540, **544-545**, 549, 558-559
Eau Gallie, 205, 208-210
Egmont Key, 492
Elliot Key, 351, 369-371
Everglades City, 433, 435, 438-441

F

Faka Union River, 441
Fernandina Beach, 120-125, 160
Fishermans Channel, 334, 338-341

SOUTHERN EDITION   609

Subject Index

Most relevant pages are listed in **BOLD**

Flamingo, 433-436, 438, 503

Fort George River, 127

Fort Lauderdale, 273, 290, 295-296, 304, **306-319**, 320-324, 333

Fort Myers, 234, 251, 260, **265-271**, 436

Fort Myers Beach, 450-454, 458

Fort Pierce, 222, 224-225, 227, 228, 231-233, 289

Fort Pierce Inlet, 224, **225-227, 228, 230**, 232-233, 289

Fort Walton Beach, 560

Franklin Lock, 253, 265-267

G

Goodland, 442-443

Gordon Pass, 446-447, 449-450

Government Cut, 158, 296, 320, 322, 326, **332-335**, 336-337, **340-342**, 350, 357, 388

Grand Lagoon, 553, 555

Green Cove Springs, 132-133, 142, **143-145**, 146

Gulfport, 509, 511, 576, 588, 595-597

H

Hallandale, 324-326

Haulover Canal, 190-192

Hawk Channel, 341-342, 348, 366, 369-372, 382, 384, **387-399**, 403, 410, 412, 416-417, 429

Hillsboro Inlet, 300-304

Hobe Sound, 277-281

Hollywood, 324-326, 336

Homestead, 356-357

Homosassa, 524-527

Hontoon Landing, 152, 154-156

Hutchinson Island, 225, 227, 231, 233, 235

I

Indian Creek, 335-336

Indian River, 158, 183, 185, 186, 188, **190-193**, 194, 197, 203-205, 209-210, 213, 218, 224-225, 231, 233

Islamorada, 368-369, **377-384**, 388

J

Jacksonville, 127-128, 130, 132, **133-139**, 140-141, 151, 160, 212

Jacksonville Beach, 127, 130, 160-161, 212

Jewfish Creek, 348, 369, 372-374

J.N. "Ding" Darling National Wildlife Refuge, 460

John Pennekamp Coral Reef State Park, 390-392

Julington Creek, 142-143

Jupiter Inlet, 279-281

K

Key Biscayne, 330, 348, **349**, 350, **351-352**, 387-388

Key Largo, 366, 372-373, 389, **390-392**, 393

Key West, 364, 368-369, 377, 386-388, 395, 397, 409, 411-414, 416, **417-425**, 426, 430, 434, 446, 513

L

La Belle, 254, 264-265

Lake George, 133, 150-152, 154

Lake Monroe, 133, 149, 152, 154, 156, **157-158**

Lake Okeechobee, 151, 234, 244, 250-254, **257-262**, 265

Lake Worth Creek, 280-283

Lake Worth (Palm Beach) Inlet, 287-288, **289**, 290, 296, 320, 359-360

Lantana, 292-295

Largo Sound, 389-392, 429

Lemon Bay, 475-476

Lignumvitae Basin, 382, 384

Lignumvitae Key, 379, 384-384, 429

Little Manatee River, 496, 498

Little Sarasota Bay, 477, 481-482

Little Shark River, 436, 438-439, 442

Long Key, 385, 392, 393, **397**, **399**, 426, 429-430, 434

M

Manatee Pocket, 234, 236-240

Manatee River, 491, **492**, **494**, 495-496, 498

Marathon, 364, 366, 368-369, 384, 386, 393, 397, **399-409**, 412, 433-434

Marco Island, 340, 433-434, 437, **441-446**, 447, 449

Marquesas Keys, The, 425-426

Matanzas River, 162, 165, 172-173, 174-175

Melbourne, 203-205, 209, **212-215**

Miami Beach, 296, 297, 322, 326, 329-330, 332, **335-336**, 340-342, 357

Miami River, 330, 334, 340, **342-346**

Mobile Bay, 572, 576, **581-588**, 590-591, 593

Moore Haven, 257-258, 261-263

Moser Channel, 364-366, 369, 385-386, 388, 397, 399, 410, **411-412**, 429, 434

610 WATERWAY GUIDE 2024 www.waterwayguide.com

N

Naples, 434, 437-438, 442, **446-450**, 453, 470
Nassau Sound, 125-127
New River, 306, 310, **312-319**
New Smyrna Beach, 181, 184-188
North Biscayne Bay, 332-335, 337, 342
North Captiva Island, 460-462
North Palm Beach, 283-285
Northwest Channel, 364, 369, 411-412, 434, 531

O

Ormond Beach, 175-177
Ortona Lock, 263-264

P

Pablo Creek, 127, 133, 158, 160-161
Palatka, 133, 139, 142, 145-149
Palm Beach, 234, 251, 277, 279, 283, 285, 287-291, **292-293**, 295-297, 320, 359-360
Palm Coast, 174-175
Palm Valley Cut, 161-164
Panama City, 545, 550, 552-555
Pascagoula Bay, 591-593, 595
Pass Aux Heron, 583, 591-593
Peanut Island, 283, 285, 287-288, 289, 290
Pensacola Bay, 544-545, 561, 564-566
Perdido Bay, 567-568, 576
Perdido Pass (Orange Beach), 568, 571-572
Pine Island, 458, 460-464, **465-466**
Pompano Beach, 274, 295, 301, 303-304, 306
Ponce de Leon Cut, 181, 183-184
Ponce de Leon (New Smyrna) Inlet, 175, 177, 182-183, 184
Port Canaveral Inlet, 128, 184, 197, 201
Port Everglades, 289, 290, 304, **309-311**, 318-323, 357
Port Everglades (Fort Lauderdale) Inlet, 290, 319-320, 322-323
Port Mayaca, 251-253, **254, 256**, 257-258, 260
Port Salerno, 236-240

R

Riviera Beach, 285-288

S

Sand Key, 417, 428
Sanford, 130, 152, 154, 157-158
Sanibel Island, 451, 458-461
Santa Rosa Sound, 555, **560-563**, 565-566
Sarasota Bay, 469, 477, **481-488**, 491
Seahorse Reef, 530-532
Sebastian, 172, 213, 217-218, 225
Sombrero Key Reef, 385
St. Augustine, 144, 158-164, **165-168**, 172-174, 177, 187
St. Augustine Inlet, 161-162, 164-165, 168
St. George Island, 525, 549
St. Johns River Entrance, 125, 128-130, 133
St. Lucie Inlet Preserve State Park, 278-279
St. Lucie Lock, 250, 253, 254, 261
St. Lucie River, 192, **234-245**, 250-251, 277
St. Marks, 532, 536-539, 540, 550
St. Martins Outer Shoal, 525-528
St. Petersburg, 490, 498, **501-505**, 507, 554
Steinhatchee River, 535-537
Stock Island, 364, 412, **414-416**, 417, 420-421
Stuart, 232, 236, **237**, 238, **241-245**, 252, 254, 260, 264
Suwannee River, 523, 528, 532-534

T

Tampa Bay, 427, 433, 466, **490-507**
Tarpon Springs, 433, 457, 490, 498, 507, **516-518**
Ten Thousand Islands, 433, 436, 441-442
Titusville, 190, 192-197
Trout River, 134-135

V

Vaca Key, 397, 400, 407, 434
Venice, 273, 306, 309, 458, **476-478**, 480-481
Vero Beach, 213, **218-222**, 224-225
Virginia Key, 342, 348-350, 351, 369, 387

W

Welaka, 149-151
West Palm Beach, 251, 290-293, 296
White City, 549-550, 552
Withlacoochee River, 523, 528-530

Y

Yacht Channel, 434
Yankeetown, 523, 528-530

Goin' Ashore & Inlets Index

Goin' Ashore Index

Cocoa Village, FL, 206
Coconut Grove, FL, 354
Daytona Beach, FL, 178
Eau Gallie, FL, 210
Fairhope, AL, 584
Fernandina Beach, FL, 122
Fort Lauderdale (New River), FL, 314
Fort Myers, FL, 270
Fort Pierce, FL, 228
Islamorada, FL, 378
Jacksonville, FL, 136
Key West, FL, 418
Marathon, FL, 400
Melbourne, FL, 214
Miami (Downtown), FL, 344
New Smyrna Beach, FL, 186
Port Salerno, FL, 238
Sarasota, FL, 484
St. Augustine, FL, 166
St. Petersburg, FL, 502
Stuart, FL, 242
Titusville, FL, 194
Vero Beach, FL, 220

Inlets Index

East Coast

Bakers Haulover (North Miami Beach) Inlet, 92
Boca Raton Inlet, 88
Cape Florida (Biscayne Bay) Inlet, 96
Fort Pierce Inlet, 80
Government Cut (Miami) Inlet, 94
Hillsboro Inlet, 89
Jupiter Inlet, 84
Lake Worth (Palm Beach) Inlet, 86
Ponce de Leon (New Smyrna) Inlet, 76
Port Canaveral Inlet, 78
Port Everglades (Fort Lauderdale) Inlet, 90
St. Augustine Inlet, 74
St. Johns River Entrance, 72
St. Lucie Inlet ("The Crossroads"), 82

Gulf Coast

Boca Grande Pass (Charlotte Harbor), 102
Capri Pass (Marco Island), 98
Egmont Channel Inlet (Tampa Bay), 108
Gordon Pass (Naples Bay), 100
Indian Key Pass, 97
Longboat Pass (Sarasota Bay North), 107
Mobile Bay Entrance, 114
New Pass (Sarasota Bay South), 106
Pensacola Bay Entrance, 112
Saint Andrew Bay Entrance (Panama City), 110
San Carlos Bay Entrance/Matanzas Pass, 101
Venice Inlet, 104